# THE DYNAMICS OF POLITICAL COMMUNICATION

D1297107

The third edition of *The Dynamics of Political Communication* continues its comprehensive coverage of communication and politics, focusing on problematic issues that bear on the functioning of democracy in an age of partisanship, social media, and political leadership that questions media's legitimacy.

The book covers the intersections between politics and communication, calling on related social science disciplines as well as normative political philosophy. This new edition is thoroughly updated and includes a survey of the contemporary political communication environment, unpacking fake news, presidential communication, hostile media bias, concerns about the waning of democracy, partisan polarization, political advertising and marketing, the relationship between social media and the news media, and the 2020 election, all the while drawing on leading new scholarship in these areas.

It's ideally suited for upper-level undergraduate and graduate political communication courses in communication, journalism, and political science programs.

This edition again features online resources with links to examples of political communication in action, such as videos, news articles, tweets, and press releases. For instructors, an instructor's manual, lecture slides, and test questions are also provided. Access the support material at www.routledge.com/9780367279417

**Richard M. Perloff**, Professor of Communication, Political Science, and Psychology at Cleveland State University, is well-known for his scholarship on the third-person effect, hostile media biases, and persuasion, including a seventh edition of *The Dynamics of Persuasion*. Perloff also is the author of *The Dynamics of News*, as well as articles in *Communication Research*, *Communication Theory*, and *Mass Communication and Society*. He has published many essays in *The* (Cleveland) *Plain Dealer* on topics such as news and political history, along with an essay on the 50th anniversary of the Kent State shootings in *The New York Times*. A dedicated teacher, Perloff has received awards for his teaching at Cleveland State.

# THE DYNAMICS OF POLITICAL COMMUNICATION

## Media and Politics in a Digital Age

**Third Edition**

**Richard M. Perloff**

Routledge
Taylor & Francis Group

NEW YORK AND LONDON

Third edition published 2022
by Routledge
605 Third Avenue, New York, NY 10158

and by Routledge
2 Park Square, Milton Park, Abingdon, Oxon, OX14 4RN

*Routledge is an imprint of the Taylor & Francis Group, an informa business*

© 2022 Taylor & Francis

First edition published by Routledge 2013
Second edition published by Routledge 2018

*Library of Congress Cataloging-in-Publication Data*
A catalog record for this book has been requested

ISBN: 978-0-367-25282-3 (hbk)
ISBN: 978-0-367-27941-7 (pbk)
ISBN: 978-0-429-29885-1 (ebk)

Typeset in Times New Roman
by Apex CoVantage, LLC

Access the support material: www.routledge.com/9780367279417

# Contents

# Preface

All we're missing is the asteroid landing with flesh-eating zombies, and our year will be complete.

—Paul Lux, supervisor of elections in Okaloosa County, Fla. (Bosman et al., 2020)

Mr. Lux could have added that the flesh-eating zombies were tweeting, then eating their blue and red victims, and we would have a fitting completion to the political communication year as well.

The 2020 election year was devastating, shattering, and illuminating. The third edition of *The Dynamics of Political Communication* covers the election, but also the politics of the previous four years, focusing the book around issues, events, and ideas. It was a challenge to write this book, as events changed by the day, and I sought to combine the here-and-now with the venerable concepts that underpin our field.

Once again, the book is organized around the core importance of democracy, flawed but indispensable as it is, and the possibilities—and limits—of political communication. It emphasizes anew the importance of appreciating multiple concepts, different disciplinary ideas, and contrasting political viewpoints. You won't find one party line in the book, but rather lots of perspectives and constant devil's advocate questioning, a hallmark of the intellectual mission. I tried to be fair to all sides and was particularly mindful of this as I discussed Donald J. Trump, his rhetoric and coverage in the news. In particular, I wanted to be fair to those millions of voters who supported him in 2016 and 2020, trying to understand their grievances. However, I could not ignore empirical evidence or jarring examples of Trump's democracy-eroding activities. To do so would also display prejudice. My goal was to be tolerant, except when communication became anti-democratic, racist, or otherwise prejudiced. In those cases, as an author of a book on political communication and democracy, I expressed a point of view. The book underscores the importance of democratic norms; a free, robust press; political tolerance; institutions that glue democracy together; and transformative political communication. These are old verities, adapted to the present age, and if we are to sustain democratic government and the fond hopes of democratic theorists, then we need to respect and apply them.

It is my hope that the book entertains, as well as communicates the complexities of political communication. It integrates the events of 2020—politics of the pandemic, the George Floyd protests, and the election—with theory and research. It reflects a thorough review of current research in the field—scholarly examination of articles in the latest major journals and books—as well as consideration of the becalming continuities offered by political history. Every edition has to bend to reflect changing times, or an author isn't doing his or her job. So, I made some changes—many actually.

- **Chapter 1** goes right to the elephant in the room, discussing fake news, misinformation, the politics of the pandemic, and systemic flaws that ail American politics and communication. The focus of the chapter and book is the United States, but examples and research cover other countries as well.

- **Chapter 2** defines politics and political communication, focusing on symbols, technology, and the decline of gatekeepers.

- **Chapter 3** expands the discussion of normative democratic issues, examining the many problems that roil contemporary democracy, as well as its virtues.

- **Chapter 4**, introducing the second part of the book, showcases the field of political communication, explaining changes and continuities.

- **Chapters 5 and 6** focus on citizenship, with Chapter 5 examining media effects on knowledge (as well as misinformation) and Chapter 6 delving into political socialization.

- **Chapter 7** covers the venerable agenda-setting concept, along with priming, agenda-building, and policy issues, with new research and examples from the 2020 election and the George Floyd protests figuring prominently.

- **Chapter 8** discusses framing, with new sections on frame-building.

- **Chapter 9** is a new chapter that takes some material from Chapter 12 in the second edition, cuts some, and adds lots of new content. It appropriately offers a discussion of the political psychology of partisanship, examining new research on selective perception, confirmatory biases, the hostile media effect, selective exposure, and polarization, along with questions about the pervasiveness of polarization.

- **Chapter 10** begins the third section on communication and the election. It offers a critical look at presidential rhetoric, with a historical review of 20th-century presidential communication strategies from JFK through Clinton, and 21st-century exemplars, notably Obama and Trump's rhetoric of tweets.

- **Chapter 11** tackles news bias, defining bias, debunking the liberal bias notion, and examining contemporary partisan wrinkles.

- **Chapter 12** focuses entirely on gender bias and news.

- **Chapter 13** covers the horse race and other press campaign biases, along with polling.

- **Chapter 14** focuses on political communication in the nomination campaign, along with conventions.

- **Chapter 15** examines political advertising in depth, beginning with contemporary advertising strategies, from microtargeting to digital developments, as well as advertising effects, normative issues, and fact-checking.

- **Chapter 16** unpacks presidential debates, their effects, drawbacks, and strengths. This final section takes stock of the election, describes democratic conundrums, and offers a smattering of suggestions to improve the quality of politics and political communication.

A glossary follows, with a definition of main terms.

I wrote the book so it would be an interesting read, but also thorough in its scholarly sweep. I hope that readers question their own views of politics, look at democracy differently, appreciate the important insights research offers, and come away with a more critical, but efficacious, perspective of political communication. And I hope scholars and colleagues find this to be a helpful contribution to the field, an enjoyable-to-read, integrative sourcebook that embraces the importance of political communication, pulls different areas together, and shows how concepts illuminate understanding of storied conundrums of politics and media.

## REFERENCE

Bosman, J., Mervosh, S., Ember, S., Fortin, J., & Gebeloff, R. (2020, October 28). How the surging virus has crashed into campaigning in every imaginable way. *The New York Times*. Online: www.nytimes.com/2020/10/28/us/covid-election.html. (Accessed: October 29, 2020).

# Acknowledgments

I want to first thank Felisa Salvago-Keyes for her support of this project and for working flexibly with me, tempering realism with positive feedback and good tidings about what the book can offer. Thank you, once again, Grant Schatzman for working so steadfastly, kindly, and efficiently. An additional thanks goes to Autumn Spalding for her buoyant, enjoyable emails that injected some spirit into the meticulous proofreading task.

Sharon Muskin, you did it again, with your amazing knowledge, technical expertise, and eternal patience. Thanks for everything you did—on a daily basis!

I also thank colleagues to whom I sent chapters out of the blue, and who commented, acknowledged, or otherwise gave a solipsistic book writer buoyant support. A special thanks to Bruce Newman for reinforcing and insightful comments and to Danna Young for thoughtful, resonating notes. I appreciate the comments and encouragement of so many other outstanding political communication colleagues: David J. Atkin, Jessica Baldwin-Philippi, Matthew Barnidge, Geoffrey Baym, Erik Bucy, Michael X. Delli Carpini, Stephanie Edgerly, Lauren Feldman, Alexandra Filindra, Carroll Glynn, Kate Kenski, Silvia Knobloch-Westerwick, Daniel Kreiss, Yanna Krupnikov, Shannon McGregor, Douglas M. McLeod, Miriam J. Metzger, Mehnaaz Momem, Sarah Ann Oates, Andrew Rojecki, John Barry Ryan, Lisa Sanchez, Dhavan Shah, Hillary Shulman, Sarah Sobieraj, Elizabeth Stoycheff, Jennifer Stromer-Galley, Talia Stroud, Yariv Tsfati, Nikki Usher, Chris Vargo, Emily Vraga, Karin Wahl-Jorgensen, Brian Weeks, Silvio Waisbord, Nathan Walter, Lars Willnat, Magdalena Wojcieszak, and Weiwu Zhang.

Thanks to my political communication classes, including Fall 2020 political communication students, who stayed a half-hour after class on Zoom on a couple of occasions, for such stimulating discussion. Thanks in particular to Elliot Jarrous, Jenny Fraley, Frank Mecham, Rayan Nasser, Tino Perez, and Andrea Strong for your vigorous debating of ideas.

And, also, on the local front, thank you to Anup Kumar for his bracingly critical views of news media; Rob Kraftowitz for relentlessly highlighting *New York Times* bias, proving you only critique the medium you love; Howard Abramoff for satirizing what everyone assumes to be true; and Ron and Joan Arnson for wit, as well as insights, on Trump and politics writ large and small. Thank you also Roknedin Safavi for your perspectives on humanity and politics.

And to Michael, with your substantial accomplishments in legally righting the state's excesses, doing so much to bolster civil liberties, and to Cathy, boasting a prodigious record in financial journalism, never compromising on truth, I thank you both for challenging me in the fabled, if all-too-familiar, John Stuart Mill tradition, as we discussed liberalism and news objectivity. Thank you, Julie, for your support and sitting at dinner talking about big issues.

# PART ONE

# Foundations of Political Communication

# CHAPTER

# 1

# **Prologue**

One of the verities of political communication—a centerpiece of democracy in the best of times, a symptom of its roiling polarities in the worst of times—is change. By the time you read this book charting the dynamics of political communication, the world will have changed since I described its contours, working at my laptop, viewing news of the endless devastation wrought by the pandemic, bruising presidential campaign ads, and the tumultuous finale of the 2020 election, marked by a mob of pro-Trump rioters ransacking the Capitol to disrupt the certification of the Electoral College vote. The events of the past 4 years are a testament to change, with one unbelievable series of events replaced by another and then another, in a reverberation of head-spinning chaotic gyrations.

It began back in 2016 with the astonishing electoral victory of Donald Trump, followed by allegations, then proof of Russian interference in the election; repeated denunciations of fake news disseminated by Trump that conveniently exempted Fox News from the list; his firing of an FBI director who challenged him; Robert Mueller's investigation into possible linkages between the Trump campaign and Russian electoral interference, the ways that was spun and framed by different partisan groups; Trump's vitriolic tweets; the much-discussed tax cuts Congress passed that improved the economy, some parts more than others; domestic terrorism at a Pittsburgh synagogue primed by extremist, conspiracy theory social media commentaries; a Ukraine scandal that led to Trump's impeachment by the House, his subsequent acquittal by the Senate, all covered carefully by the news, sometimes with a partisan spin; followed not long after by the coronavirus pandemic, with its beginning in China, a source of controversy along with Trump's rhetoric, then the multitude of deaths during a spring of sadness, culminating in national protests over a police killing, public opinion shifts, and symbolic changes; a national campaign waged with vigor and venom, and the contentious outcome of a presidential election. It continued into 2021, with the violent insurrection of the Capitol by hundreds of violent extremists, delusional in their belief the election was unfair, willing to interrupt the official congressional certification of a fair, democratic presidential election. With about a week left in Trump's presidency, the House of Representatives, furious that Trump had incited the rioters' siege of a democratic ritual, proceeded with an unprecedented second impeachment proceedings, leading to Trump's impeachment, followed again by Senate acquittal.

It was the old Billy Joel history song ("We Didn't Start the Fire") on steroids, played at warp speed. But as you read this, new tumult has overtaken the turmoil of yore, raising questions about whether the once-vibrant American experiment can maintain its vitality or is creaking toward dissolution. For all the strengths of American democracy—its capacity to renew itself, checks and balances, an unbridled free press—dysfunctions are apparent everywhere. For example: politics gamed by the rich, majority sentiments ignored or silenced due to structural flaws, social media awash in misinformation.

This is the backdrop for the issues discussed in this book. It's certainly not an inviting beginning—no metaphorical promise of chocolate or basks in the sun. And it noticeably minimizes the positive influences that political communication can achieve, as well as the passion many young people felt as they protested racial injustice in the spring of 2020. But the negative attracts outsize attention psychologically, has become the dominant way most people view the political world, and therefore commands attention. Let's begin then with the catalogue of complaints that frequently greet political communication, as this provides a familiar way to enter the political communication territory, while offering a pathway to critiquing these very shortcomings, in this manner opening up the discussion to broader, cross-disciplinary, and socially significant issues.

## THE DISTURBING POLITICAL COMMUNICATION ENVIRONMENT

Table 1.1 lists seven problems that characterize our once-promising, now disruptive political media ecology. The problems go beyond communication to

**Table 1.1  Contemporary conundrums in American politics and political communication.**

1. Racial injustice and civil unrest continue to roil America.
2. Fake news has proliferated, even as questions remain about its effects.
3. Ideological media sites have multiplied, politicizing the truth.
4. The American political environment is more divisive and partisan than in recent years.
5. Populism and distrust have become woven into the texture of contemporary political communication.
6. Politics is mean and uncivil.
7. Systemic problems illuminated by the coronavirus pandemic demand political solutions.

encompass structural aspects of American society. But political communication always exists in a broader social fabric, so it's important to examine these factors, including those that examine systemic issues involving American society.

## 1. Racial Injustice and Civil Unrest Continue to Roil American Politics

It was a jarring split-screen tableau. A day after Georgia—long a bastion of red-state conservatism—turned blue, electing two Democrats, including a young Jewish filmmaker and Georgia's first Black senator, a mob of pro-Trump, paramilitary violent vigilantes stormed the U.S. Capitol, brandishing Confederate flags and wearing anti-Semitic T-shirts. The parade of falsehoods and conspiracy theory dogma that dominated their online outlets contrasted sharply with the outpouring of criticism that flooded conventional news channels, consumed by concerns about the anti-democratic insurgency that gripped the Capitol on January 6, 2021. It illustrated the continuity of national civic unrest, but also "the nation's original paradox: a commitment to democracy in a country with a legacy of racial exclusion" (Herndon, 2021).

Just 6 months earlier, racial issues had jumped to center stage, with images of police violence against African Americans; massive protests against police shootings; looting, vandalism, and property damage wrought by angry mobs; and counter-demonstrators vowing to protect a city from protesters. Such was the situation that unfolded in America during the throes of a pandemic and the 2020 presidential election.

In 1903, W.E.B. Du Bois, the distinguished American academic, famously said that "the problem of the twentieth century is the problem of the color line." His prophetic statement remains true more than a century after he penned it. As a result of institutional racism and systematic political indifference to the problems plaguing Black communities, scalding racial disparities remain. The net worth of a White family is about 10 times greater than that of a typical Black family, a gap that has significantly widened over the years, abetted by continuing subtle discrimination in employer hiring practices (McIntosh et al., 2020; Luo, 2009). Blacks attend less economically resourced schools than Whites and Asian Americans, contributing to economic discrepancies that perpetuate disparities in wealth and home ownership (Kristof, 2016; Bouie, 2020). African American college graduates have fewer financial assets than Whites who did not complete high school (Hannah-Jones, 2020). Health disparities are particularly grievous as diabetes, cardiovascular disease, and chronic lung illnesses are more common among African Americans, contributing to a lower life expectancy among Blacks (Villarosa, 2020).

These problems aren't new, but they took on particular resonance in 2020 when the political communication environment changed in the blink of a viral moment. A nation reeling from a pandemic, rankled by partisan divisions, and beset by Depression-level unemployment found itself in the throes of violent civil unrest. Within days after a White Minneapolis police officer killed George Floyd, an African American man in police custody, by pressing his knee to the back of Floyd's neck for nearly nine minutes, protests broke out from coast to coast.

The video of the incident went viral, outraging Americans of different racial and ethnic backgrounds, stirring tens of millions to protest to express their anger that yet another unarmed Black person had been killed by a White police officer (Williams, 2016; Chan, 2020; see Figure 1.1). Other videos of police aggression sparked anger, but the Floyd video was more impactful because the violence was spectacularly graphic, and it coincided with the recent deaths of other innocent Black Americans, also under police custody, including Ahmaud Arbery and Rayshard Brooks of Georgia, Elijah McClain of Colorado, and Breonna Taylor of Kentucky. In addition, the video reached a wider audience, in view of high unemployment and the number of people isolated in their homes. It

**Figure 1.1  Racial problems continue to beset America, and with unpredictable results. When more than 4,500 protests erupted in thousands of small towns and cities across America in the wake of the murder of George Floyd in 2020, Americans' attitudes toward race began to change, with large majorities of Whites acknowledging that racism, and systemic problems in law enforcement, were major issues facing the country and its criminal justice system. Stark racial disparities in income, education, and health care remain, reflections of fundamental problems in the country's politics.**

*Source*: www.gettyimages.com/detail/news-photo/protesters-march-in-manhattan-over-the-death-on-may-25-of-news-photo/1247899621?adppopup=true also stirred the passions of African Americans and young people from different racial groups, sympathetic with the positions articulated by Black Lives Matter, fuming about the striking racial disparities in deaths from the coronavirus, and hungering for an opportunity to translate frustrations into tangible action. Over the course of the spring, the nation experienced one of the largest protest movements in American history, as some 23 million people took part in demonstrations (Chan, 2020).

The impact of the video and impassioned conversations on social media, complemented by days of ceaseless news coverage, serves as a testament to the power of political communication. It also showcases the intersection between political media and the social circumstances in which media effects occur.

News covered the racial issue, framing it in different ways, depending on the news outlet's journalistic and political perspective. Social media was on fire, as videos and tweets circulated, people shared passionate positions about racial issues, and extremist groups widely shared falsehoods. It wasn't a simple picture. Many protesters wore masks and were peaceful, but a handful of demonstrators destroyed property and set fires. Some police visibly supported Black Lives Matter, whereas many others kicked and brutalized protesters.

Surprisingly, polls—a key aspect of the political communication nexus—showed there was more unanimity than usual. A majority of Americans strongly disapproved of the Minneapolis police officers' actions and said the police were more likely to use excessive force against Blacks (Skelley, 2020). Seventy-one percent of Whites acknowledged that racism and discrimination were big problems facing the country. About 70 percent of people believed the killing was part of a more substantial problem with law enforcement, and more than three-fourths of the public said the protesters' anger was justified (Edmondson & Fandos, 2020; Russonello, 2020). Even attitudes toward the controversial activist group Black Lives Matter changed. For the first time ever, a majority of the public supported Black Lives Matter (up to 52 percent from 42 percent a month-and-a-half earlier; Edsall, 2020a).

When you probed deeper, you found the usual fissures. More than eight in ten Democrats were more concerned about policing that caused Floyd's death than the protests, while about five in ten Republicans held the opposite view (Lerer & Umhoefer, 2020). Many Americans disapproved of the violent protests, and support for Black Lives Matter dropped dramatically over the summer months, although a majority still endorsed the movement (Thomas & Horowitz, 2020). Yet by March 2021, trust in Black Lives Matter had declined among both Blacks and Whites, triggered by animus toward the proposal to defund the police (Blow, 2021). Evaluations of the movement varied, undoubtedly as a function of partisan sentiments, old-fashioned racial prejudice, and the particular media outlets where people obtained their information (e.g., Stamps & Mastro, 2020).

Yet to many African Americans, the problems of systemic disparities—in both Blacks' deaths from police violence and long-festering health conditions—remained. The color line continued to roil America more than a century after Du Bois uttered his prophecy.

Unfortunately, there is more: more problems on different levels that raise concerns about politics, democracy, and political communication.

## 2. Fake News Has Snowballed

Like everything else in politics and journalism, fake news has roots in the past. It dates at least as far back as 1835, when *The New York Sun* ran stories that described spectacular revelations of an ingenious race of strange, winged creatures who looked like human beings, averaging just four feet in height, and lived on the moon in temples they created. New Yorkers could not get the moon hoax stories fast enough; it was the only topic they talked about. But the stories were false, the facts were fake, and the only thing that was true was the stories sold newspapers, plenty of them.

In the political arena, fake news—false information dressed up as news in an effort to spread disinformation—has been a favorite government propaganda technique for decades. Governments—Nazi Germany and Russia, among many—have spread fake news for years; the U.S. too has circulated faux information to prop up regimes abroad. But the quantity of disinformation does mark a new normal in contemporary political communication, as online platforms spread falsehoods, partisan extremists share fabricated facts, and bots magnify these effects (Southwell, Thorson, & Sheble, 2018; Freelon & Wells, 2020; Li, 2020). We even have a more exact definition of **fake news**: "news articles that are intentionally and verifiably false, and could mislead readers," dressed up, as they are, as real news (Allcott & Gentzkow, 2017, p. 213; Bradshaw et al., 2020).

The issue of fake news specifically, and deliberately diffused disinformation more generally, became a cause célèbre in 2016 when Russian agents, hoping to discredit Hillary Clinton's 2016 presidential election campaign, posted more than 130,000 inflammatory Twitter messages and 80,000 divisive messages on Facebook that were shared by other users, reaching as many as a whopping 126 million on Facebook (Isaac & Wakabayshi, 2017).

In U.S. electoral politics, fake reports have become common, even expected, exemplified by a doctored videotape that showed 2020 Democratic presidential contender Joe Biden uttering racist remarks, and one spread by pro-Democratic operatives, taking a chapter from Russia's 2016 cyber-tactics, that smeared an Alabama Republican senator by linking his reelection campaign with Russian accounts that followed the candidate on Twitter (Shane & Blinder, 2018).

During the white-hot 2020 presidential campaign, the viral load metastasized: A right-wing radio commentator claimed the Democrats were preparing a coup against President Trump on Election Day; an extreme left-wing site falsely contended that Trump was behind a bizarre plot to kidnap Michigan's Democratic governor; and during the election's turbulent aftermath, false claims that Biden was stealing the election from Trump spread like wildfire (e.g., Alba, 2020). These messages can diffuse widely, in some cases disseminated through trolls, amplifying their anti-democratic effects.

Fake news knows no borders, as became evident during the coronavirus outbreak. In an attempt to divert attention from its initial cover-up of the spread of the virus in Wuhan, China, Chinese government cyber-operatives circulated conspiracy theory rumors throughout social media in China that the virus was created by a biochemical laboratory in the U.S. (Bernstein, 2020). Other fake news stories that circulated on social media involved supposed government plots, miracle cures, rumors that Bill Gates was responsible for the virus outbreak, and a widely circulated video, "Plandemic," that claimed a secret group of powerful people, including Dr. Anthony Fauci, had seized on the virus and a vaccine to gain riches, acquire power, or aid patent holders of harmful vaccines (Frenkel, Alba, & Zhong, 2020).

Political leaders on both sides of the aisle have fanned the viral flames. President Donald Trump, of course, made fake news famous, tweeting the term more than 600 times, using it to disparage press reports he didn't like or that criticized his policies. He called journalists "fraudulent" and maligned reporters as "the enemy of the American people." His charge was disturbing. It is a time-honored function of the press—or news media—to hold leaders' feet to the fire, revealing information citizens need to know to make informed choices, facts that leaders would sometimes rather silence than reveal. Trump's attacks on the news media, with the fake news mantra, encouraged leaders of more than 40 foreign governments to summon the fake news specter to besmirch journalists, part of a wide-ranging, contemporary assault on the truth (Editorial Board, 2019).

Important as this is, it's useful to offer a caveat. There is scholarly debate about the scope and effects of fake news. Some researchers are concerned, noting fake news' prevalence, capacity to deceive voters, and ability to gain credence by becoming part of legitimate news stories (Avram et al., 2020; Guo & Vargo, 2020; Lukito et al., 2020; Pennycook, Cannon, & Rand, 2018; Ridout & Fowler, 2018). Others cite evidence that political ads placed by Russian cyber-operatives on social media in 2016, especially those with inflammatory, threatening language, stimulated significant user engagement via clicks (see Vargo & Hopp, 2020 for a fascinating study). Yet other scholars question how attentive people are to online political fakeries, whether they even process them, and whether they are as powerfully influenced as fake news proponents charge (Krafft &

Donovan, 2020; Keller et al., 2020). And, of course, engagement with faux messages doesn't tell us how much impact falsehoods exert. We don't have as much evidence as we would like about the *effects* of political falsehoods on the body politic. What we can say is that fake news and political disinformation are out there in increasing, disturbing numbers, making it difficult for citizens to know what to believe, and contaminating the climate of factual discourse.

### 3. The Growth of Ideological Media Has Led to the Diffusion of Slanted Views of Truth, Along With Lies and Politicized Conspiracy Theories

In the old days, it was simple and centralized. The main **gatekeepers**—those who controlled society's information, the organizations that decided which information passed through society's "informational gates" to reach citizens and leaders—were three broadcast networks, national newsmagazines, and leading newspapers. These informational sources were imperfect, to be sure, with biases that favored the status quo and a preference for homogenized news (Gitlin, 1980; Hallin, 1986). But they generally excluded information that did not fulfill consensual rules for journalistic evidence or played to conspiracy theories. Information frequently flowed from government leaders through the mainstream news media to the broader reaches of the public. Then it all changed, as mainstream gatekeepers lost power in the new digital era.

Over the past several decades, newspapers have been in free fall. Hundreds of daily newspapers closed shop, in the wake of readers drifting to online informational sites for news, as well as dramatic reductions in advertising. Television ratings sagged, and TV news' once-preeminent role as the most trusted medium in America, along with its decades-long reputation as the main source for Americans' news, plummeted. Power abhors a vacuum, and the air in the informational field has been sucked up by online news and social media. The overwhelming majority of Americans get at least some of their news online, often via Facebook, and frequently perused through apps on mobile devices (Digital News Fact Sheet, 2019).

In some cases, this information is false and falls under the category of misinformation. **Misinformation** is information deemed inaccurate, based on the foremost evidence available from relevant experts on the issue (Vraga & Bode, 2020). (Misinformation and disinformation are used interchangeably in discussions that follow.)

Although left-wing outlets have spread misinformation, right-wing sites have been more successful in conveying fake information to their base and, then, to the public via mainstream media (Schradie, 2019). For example, during the tumultuous spring of 2020, a study challenged the consensus, propounded by public health experts, that coronavirus deaths were mounting, arguing instead that the mortality rate was much lower in comparison to the number of people infected. The researchers maintained (incorrectly, as it turned out) that effects of the virus were less severe than epidemiologists had projected, about as dangerous as an ordinary flu (see Bajak & Howe, 2020). Although there were methodological problems with the study, the conclusions were a matter of complex statistical debate. What happened in the politically polarized environment in which even health is weaponized was that the study became a political football, with condemnations hurled by liberal opinion sites and praise provided by conservative sites. The findings offended liberals, who, contending that fatality rates were continuing to rise, favored strict shelter-at-home policies that delayed reopening. They delighted conservatives, who distrusted the heavy-handed consensus of public health authorities, as well as government control over individuals' private activity, and pressed for government to lift stringent lockdown policies.

In a manner befitting the "no-holds-barred" media environment, conservative sites leapt into action, no less convinced the study was correct than liberals were that it was procedurally flawed. Conservatives shared and tweeted about the study one Friday morning, leading to thousands of retweets and, within hours, its publication on prominent right-leaning sites (Bajak & Howe, 2020; see Figure 1.2). Those on the extremes of both sides of the political spectrum took their cues from the spin on the study that their side applied, bereft of the more fair-minded analysis conventional media gatekeepers could offer. In this case the content, while interesting, was open to statistical question, but the science got lost in the emotional firestorm, as conservatives (it could be liberals in other cases) viewed the study in partisan terms, sharing and disseminating information that fit their point of view.

In other instances, the truthfulness of content that appears on ideological media is more tenuous, in some cases flat-out false. Social media sites have blurred the boundary between news and journalism, disseminating information that has the patina of news, does not constitute journalism, but can algorithmically and psychologically animate like-minded users.

One of the most disturbing sites is QAnon, the broad term for right-wing conspiracy theories that bizarrely maintain the world is run by a cadre of Satan-worshipping pedophiles, which supposedly includes leading Democrats, who operate a worldwide sex-trafficking cabal and plotted against President Trump (Roose, 2020). QAnon has attracted millions of online followers, including older Americans, Republican politicians, and even a community college professor, who promote its baseless bizarre claims, including the belief that because Q is the 17th letter in the alphabet, a Trump mention of 17 offered potential support for their cause. Egged on by Trump, who refused to denounce the movement, it became an established, if small, force in the Republican Party.

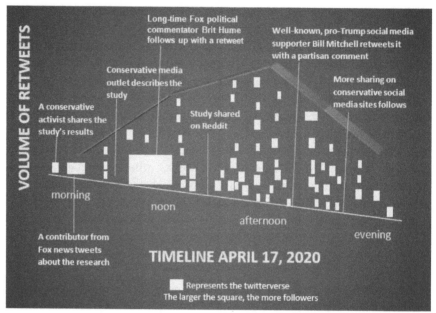

**Figure 1.2  This graph traces the path of a controversy about a credible scientific study suggesting the effects of the coronavirus were less dire than projected, a conclusion consistent with conservative perspectives. As is the norm in such cases, the information spread and increased in perceived importance as more prominent conservative commentators retweeted it. A giant echo chamber accentuating the volume and significance of a supportive viewpoint built, despite serious problems with the research and the absence of views from the other side. Within hours, an interesting, but suspect, finding took on the patina of fact in the one-sided information environment of partisan social media.**

**RETWEETING DISTORTIONS IN THE ONLINE ECHO CHAMBER**

*Source*: Adapted from Bajak and Howe (2020)

Some have even resorted to violence in support of their beliefs, and this was before mobs, incited by Trump's tweets, ransacked the Capitol on January 6, 2021 (Barry & Frenkel, 2021). In 2018, an Arizona man was arrested following his occupation of a cement plant tower that he maintained was hiding a child sex-trafficking ring, recalling a 2016 election online falsehood that a Washington, D.C. pizza restaurant, Comet Ping Pong, surreptitiously operated as a child abuse ring led by Hillary Clinton. And that falsehood, like a bad penny or its viral equivalent in Bitcoin, never failed to disappear, circulating several years later in the form of the fiction that Justin Bieber had been a victim of the child sex ring, another chapter in the conspiracy theory dubbed PizzaGate. As of June 2020, TikTok posts, affiliated with the #PizzaGate hashtag, had been viewed 82 million times over the course of several months (Kang & Frenkel, 2020). In a similar fashion, wildly false, visually rich misinformation about

COVID-19 (and later coronavirus vaccines), fueled by global conspiracy theories, flew across the world (Brennen, Simon, & Nielsen, 2021). Conspiracy theories, while hardly new in American politics, have swelled in popularity today, in light of rising feelings of disenfranchisement that are salved by simplistic theories of blame and amplified by the global Internet.

Political leaders can make things worse, fanning the flames of false information by communicating directly with extremist followers or retweeting faux reports. To be sure, presidents, legislators, and other elected officials who convey information directly to followers online can propel activists in their party to be more engaged in politics, which is a good thing. Donald Trump, who transformed Twitter into a political communication tool, has done this effectively and positively at many times during his presidency, bringing many voters formerly alienated from politics into the electoral fold. The rub occurs when leaders link or retweet in ways that diffuse false, incendiary, or prejudiced reports, spreading false information across partisan pipelines, with uncertain, possibly untoward effects. Trump did this frequently. A systematic investigation showed that Trump's Twitter feed was awash in pro-Russian accounts, QAnon posts, conspiracy theories, racists, and White nationalist tweets that tagged his Twitter handle (McIntire, Yourish, & Buchanan, 2019).

The danger is that when information spreads in this way, it legitimizes falsehoods, muddles facts, and brings "conspiracy talk out of the fringes into mainstream discourse," fueling animus and mistrust (Waisbord, Tucker, & Lichtenheld, 2018, p. 28). Making matters more difficult for the dissemination of truth, Facebook's reluctance to police incendiary speech has allowed falsehoods to propagate (Isaac, 2020). It all reached a feverish pitch shortly after the 2020 election when social media was inundated with false allegations of voter fraud, stoked by President Trump's tweets, prompting the creation of a Stop the Steal Facebook group. Even as Twitter and Facebook took steps to flag false statements or remove hateful speech, the challenge to limit misinformation on global social networks remains daunting.

Of course, it remains an empirical question. Just what *are* the effects of fake news, false statements, and conspiracy theory reports, frequently laced with prejudice? The content is pervasive, and technological manipulations, such as those that permit video and audio deepfake manipulations, can be effective (Dobber et al., 2021). But, in general, in diverse real-life contexts, what are the influences of misinformation? Are fears of its influences real or exaggerated? Social scientists cannot assume content has effects just because it's out there, as noted earlier. As Chapter 9 notes, the effects of this incendiary information is likely to be greatest on extremist partisans, who subscribe to political dogma and distrust mainstream media (Hopp, Ferrucci, & Vargo, 2020). They then share the falsehoods, magnifying their perceived impact, and what started as a brushfire spreads, fueling serious issues for democracy.

## 4. Our Political Communication Environment Is More Divided, With Strong Partisans Feeding on Information That Supports Their Side

The explosion of one-sided inflammatory tweets occurs in an already partisan, polarized, "my way or the highway" political communication environment. Congress is riven by political divisions, as shown by the Senate's impeachment trial of President Trump in 2020. Unlike President Bill Clinton's impeachment in 1998, where both sides worked together on processes that could help resolve the conflict, and Nixon's case, where Republican House Judiciary Committee members voted in favor of impeachment, in 2019 Republicans and Democrats could not even agree on the ground rules, or on whether the Senate trial was fundamentally legitimate (Baker, 2019). The Democrats said it unquestionably was constitutionally appropriate, given President Trump's abuse of his office; the Republicans viewed it as a sham, designed to throw out an elected president on partisan grounds. Ultimately, of course, Congress divided on strictly party lines on impeachment. The Democrat-controlled House of Representatives impeached Trump, while the Republican-dominated Senate refused to remove him from office.

There is also political polarity in the public at large (though primarily on national issues). The typical Democrat has moved further to the left, and the average Republican gravitated more to the right over the past three decades (Young, 2020). Voters with strong positions sort themselves into social environments that mirror their politics, viewing media outlets that conform to their positions and distrusting those from the other side. Staunch partisans view political issues in strikingly different ways, as seen with climate change, where more than three times as many Democrats as Republicans view climate change as a top policy priority (Popovich, 2020). Democrats trust most national news outlets, but Republicans don't, with the exception of a few, like Fox News and Sean Hannity's radio show (Jurkowitz et al., 2020). As Abramowitz and Webster note, "large majorities of Democrats and Republicans truly despised the opposing party's nominee" (Edsall, 2018).

Partisan differences emerged with striking regularity in the calamitous spring of 2020. You saw it in masks, where staunch liberals viewed masks as essential to preserve public health, while strong conservatives felt they infringed on personal liberty. Similarly, more than eight in ten Democrats were concerned that state governments would lift restrictions on public activity too quickly, while nearly five in ten Republicans feared that restrictions would not be lifted quickly enough (see Most Americans Say, 2020; Daniller, 2020). Intriguingly, even among people who knew someone who had gotten infected with the virus or lived in a community with many infections, Republicans were less likely than Democrats to social distance (Fleming-Wood, Margalit, & Schaffner, 2020; Clinton et al., 2020). There are many reasons for these differences, including the different values Republicans and Democrats hold toward liberty and government regulations. However, some of this results from the use of different political media. Conservative media downplayed the virus; outlets with a Democratic focus emphasized deaths and infections.

Partisanship can even extend to friendships—and marriage! Americans, especially those with strong positions, are 17 percentage points less likely to be close friends with an individual from the opposing political party and 36 percentage points more willing to marry a political ally than a partisan opponent (Mason, 2018).

American liberals and conservatives even differ in the types of political entertainment they prefer. Liberals like ironic satire, such as that dished out by Stephen Colbert; conservatives prefer in-your-face, outrage-laced political opinion programs, as purveyed by Fox's Sean Hannity and Laura Ingraham. Their different tastes in political humor are rooted in the different personality characteristics and psychological make-up of conservatives and liberals. That's the conclusion of political communication scholar Dannagal G. Young (2020), who incidentally practices what she rhetorically preaches, doing improvisational comedy at a Philadelphia comedy club.

With the proliferation of multiple online platforms for information, voters with strong political positions gravitate to outlets that reinforce what they think, derogating disagreeable information they encounter. After reading even ambivalent evidence, they end up feeling even stronger that they are right, in this way hardening attitudes and bolstering resistance to new ideas (see Chapter 9).

## 5. On a Broader Level, Instability, Populism, and Distrust Have Become Woven Into the Texture of Contemporary Political Communication

Political communication takes place in a broader cultural context, and events of the past decades vividly demonstrate the import of larger, macro factors. President Trump's surprising election victory in 2016 and his transformation of the communicative landscape were an outgrowth of volcanic shifts in the economic and social landscape.

Globalization, automation, massive corporate outsourcing of American jobs to Asian countries, and the U.S. government's indifference to the plight of displaced workers hemorrhaged manufacturing jobs in the United States. Across the country, and particularly in the industrial Midwest, blue-collar employment plummeted in the late 20th century and early in this century. The wealthiest got richer on the backs of the working class through stock buybacks that benefitted rich stockholders, not workers. The typical American worker is making less money today than in 1973, adjusting for inflation, while the rich are raking it in with stock buybacks (Schumer & Sanders, 2019). In 1982 the average meatpacker made $24 an hour, taking into account inflation, but today the same worker, processing substantially more meat, makes less than $14 an hour (Editorial Board, 2020a). America's home health care aides, frequently women and minorities, can work so hard they have difficulty finding time to attend to their own families. Over the past four decades, the incomes of U.S. families with a college-educated head of household has tripled, but the income levels of families with a non-college-educated head of household has scarcely grown (Bartscher, Kuhn, & Schularick, 2019).

At the same time as inequality soared, social transformations took hold. The women's rights movement, which produced more egalitarian norms and took millions of women from housewife tedium to meaningful, well-paying jobs, inexorably changed the gender role dynamics of American families, precipitating divorces and causing dramatic increases in the number of single-parent families. These economic and family stressors, noticeably occurring in working-class households, had major impacts on quality of parenting and belief in traditional moral values, leading to less participation in organized religion, frequently a ballast against the tumultuous effects of social change. The deteriorating economic environment and diminished spirituality, occurring concomitantly with structural impediments to lower-class children's ability to climb the educational ladder, had crushing effects on many working-class families, experienced most dramatically in addiction to drugs and opioids (Putnam, 2015; Kristof & WuDunn, 2020).

These gaping inequalities in opportunities for social and educational advancement, exacerbated by feelings that elites look down on rural Americans, have produced seething anger at the leadership classes (Markovits, 2019). The political consequences, while complex, have helped fuel a return to the on-again, off-again political philosophy, or narrow worldview, popularly known as **populism** (see Müller, 2016).

Populism, scholars Pippa Norris and Ronald Inglehart (2019) explain, is a rhetorical style that claims the authentic power in a democracy rests with "the people" rather than with specialized elites. It can be viewed as a communication phenomenon with three core elements: (1) emphasis on the hard-working, honest working people; (2) a battle against a corrupt establishment led by unresponsive leaders; and (3) a focus on how "they," the out-group, oppose "us," the people (de Vreese et al., 2018; Kaltwasser et al., 2017). Who could disagree with a philosophy that venerates "the people," one might ask? A closer look at populism reveals the problems beneath the appealing veneer.

Dating back to widespread anger against moneyed interests in the 1880s, populism frequently reflects working-class Whites' hostility toward **elites**—a general term that popularly encompasses rich capitalists who have greedily exploited workers, government bureaucrats, political leaders viewed as out of touch with working-class folks, and, nowadays, prominent news organizations, who are seen as part of the cultural "they think they're better than us" class. Frequent targets of populism include political parties, viewed as dysfunctional; lobbyists, seen as corrupt; the news media, filled with fake news; the Constitution, regarded as a rigged political document; and cultural minorities, viewed as a threat to the people (Norris & Inglehart, 2019; Fawzi, 2019). Some of populism's anger at democracy is well-taken: frustration with lobbyists and entrenched political parties; resentment that other groups unfairly obtain resources at the expense of the working class (Hameleers, Bos, & de Vreese, 2018). However, other elements, notably rejection of constitutional norms, hard-working elected officials, and a free press, can lead to widespread rejection of time-honored norms of democracy.

Populists tend to be hostile to illegal immigrants, whom they resent, sometimes understandably, for posing a (perceived or real) threat to their jobs. In many other instances, given evidence that immigrants, illegal or otherwise, don't imperil Americans' jobs, the hostility is rooted in prejudice. Populism has a long-standing authoritarian quality that values security against risks posed by foreigners supposedly stealing "American jobs"; broad group conformity to maintain valued traditions that safeguard Americans' cultural heritage; and loyalty to "our" national leaders who promise to protect the country from looming external threats (Norris & Inglehart, 2019).

Trump famously tapped into these class concerns, with his intense language, notably arguments that blamed workers' problems on global trade deals, illegal immigration, and the "somebody is taking everything you are used to and you had" storyline, with a strong racial subtext (Cohen, 2016, p. 6; see Chapter 8).

Populism has also resonated outside of the U.S. In a 2016 referendum in the United Kingdom, a bare majority (52 percent) of voters opted to leave the European Union (EU), the union of some 27 European countries that imposes economic and political policies on all member states. The outcome was popularly known as Brexit, for British exit from the EU. The narrow vote, endlessly debated and negotiated in Britain over the next 3 years and vindicated in a general election victory for the country's pro-Brexit prime minister in 2019, was, at one level, a "stick it in their faces" pro-nationalist, populist rejection of European globalism, a cultural backlash partly rooted in nostalgia for the good old days of White Anglo-Saxon preeminence and economic security for British workers. It also was shaped by a series of dishonest and false promises by Britain's pro-Brexit leaders that unleashed economic tremors for the once-mighty UK (Perloff, 2019). Populist, anti-elite sentiments have also been on the rise in France, where masses of citizens violently protested against gas hikes and government proposals to overhaul the bewilderingly complex French pension system.

To be sure, the picture is muddied by other elections across the continent, in which anti-populist candidates wrested control. In the U.S., despite Trump's followers' strong support for his anti-immigration policies, most Americans opposed his plan to construct a wall along the U.S.–Mexico border. Still, populism remains a vital force in western democracies, a rising tide in response to leaders' indifference to the economic consequences of globalization and transparent increases in inequality (Saez & Zucman, 2019). For those who feel on the social margins, victimized by globalization, disrespected by society's elites, populism—from Donald Trump to Brexit—offers a nod of recognition and a measure of self-respect (Edsall, 2020b).

Populism has positive and negative implications for political communication and democratic government, more generally. It can encourage disaffected, economically marginalized citizens to channel their frustrations into participating in campaign communication rather than withdrawing or resorting to violence. But it has negative components as well, as when it incites prejudice against minorities, reduces support for a free press, and (in its worst manifestations) favors authoritarian leaders at the expense of democratic norms, tendencies that have all increased in recent years (Plattner, 2020; Eatwell & Goodwin, 2018; Hanitzsch, Van Dalen, & Steindl, 2018; Ladd & Podkul, 2019). Populism becomes fundamentally anti-democratic when significant proportions of a population support authoritarian positions.

In fascinating, disturbing research, Alexandra Filindra (2018) found that more than one-third of White Americans support having a strong leader "even if the leader bends the rules to get things done"; nearly half believe "our country would be great" if they "get rid of the 'rotten apples' who are ruining everything," and more than half agree that the country needs a strong leader who will "crush evil" and take us back to our "true path." These prejudices implicitly denigrate minority sentiments and, abetted by right-wing leaders, can push people away from democratic values. This broad-based populism made Trump's rise possible, while Trump sensed, accessed, and exploited some of its worst elements. It was a two-way street.

It all came to a crashing, infamous climax on January 6, 2021, 2 weeks before Trump yielded the office to his successor, Joseph R. Biden, Jr. Hundreds of rioters—domestic terrorists, really—stormed the Capitol effusively, gleefully, ransacking offices, destroying precious property, even smoking marijuana, intent on deliberately disrupting Congress's certification of Biden's Electoral College victory. Some had firearms and bombs, and one threatened to kill Speaker of the House Nancy Pelosi. The rioters, part of a larger crowd that numbered into the tens of thousands, had gathered, at Trump's behest, to "be strong" and "fight like hell," to protest an election he had falsely told them for weeks was rigged and stolen. Encouraged, inspired, and incited by Trump's rhetoric, the group, a motley part of his most extremist populist base—White supremacists, conspiracy theorists, virulent anti-Semites—swarmed and stormed the Capitol in a melee that led to the deaths of five people, including a police officer, as well as the evacuation of Congressional representatives until they could safely reconvene later in what was popularly called the People's House to resume the electoral certification (Tavernise & Rosenberg, 2020). It was an intersection of the worst of populist fervor and Trump's vitriolic rhetoric, the two forces reflecting and reinforcing each other in a moment that symbolized the depths of the problems wracking American democracy.

## 6. Our Politics Is Mean, Peevish, and Uncivil

As if this was not enough, other enduring problems plague American politics, focused on its verbal incivility. This is the characteristic of our politics that unnerves many people. Jeffrey M. Berry and Sarah Sobieraj (2014) describe contemporary political communication as "the outrage industry." Diana C. Mutz (2015) refers to it as "in your face" media politics.

Incivility is ubiquitous, spanning Trump's more than 5,000 attacks on individuals, particularly minorities (see Chapter 10), to zealous supporters of Democratic Senator Bernie Sanders, who placed snakes—emojis and doctored pictures—on social media feeds of his 2020 Democratic rival, Senator Elizabeth Warren, as well as directing death threats against well-known feminist authors who declined to endorse Sanders (Flegenheimer, Ruiz, & Bowles, 2020).

How far this departs from the ideal! The great moral philosopher John Rawls exclaimed that public civility is "among the cooperative virtues of political life" (2001, p. 117). He emphasized that "the ideal of citizenship imposes a moral, not a legal, duty—the duty of civility . . . a willingness to listen to others and a fair-mindedness in deciding when accommodations to their views should reasonably be made" (Rawls, 1996, p. 217). How unusual this spirit is in contemporary politics, where elected officials excoriate the opposition, and 42 percent of partisans in both parties view their opponents as "downright evil," with 20 percent saying they "lack the traits to be considered fully human—they behave like animals" (Brooks, 2019, p. A27).

What is incivility exactly? Kevin Coe, Kate Kenski, and Stephen A. Rains (2014) define it as "features of discussion that convey an unnecessarily disrespectful tone toward the discussion forum, its participants, or its topics" (p. 660). Coe and his colleagues classified more than 20 percent of comments in online discussions as disrespectful—and that was back in 2014! Name-calling and vulgarity are perceived as particularly uncivil (Kenski, Coe, & Rains, 2020), which is troubling given the frequency of name-calling in online Twitter rants (Darcy, 2020).

Incivility can leave an imprint. Uncivil political content and news stories reduce engagement with news, trust, and intent to participate in politics, while increasing closed-mindedness (Mutz, 2015; Young, Hoffman, & Roth, 2019; Otto, Lecheler, & Schuck, 2020; Goovaerts & Marien, 2020; Muddiman, Pond-Cobb, & Matson, 2020; Hwang, Kim, & Kim, 2018). Violent rhetoric can increase partisan polarization, even causing an increase in hate crimes, perhaps encouraging (we can't know for sure) an anti-government group to plot to kidnap Michigan's governor, who imposed tough restrictions in the wake of a surge of infections in her state (Kalmoe, Gubler, & Wood, 2018; Edwards & Rushin, 2018). Months of Trump's virulently false claims that the 2020 election was stolen from him, followed by his encouraging right-wing fringe groups to be "wild" as they protested the certification of the electoral vote, inexorably led to mobs swarming the Capitol, ransacking offices in early January 2021 (Barry & Frenkel, 2021).

Will civility return, as President Joseph R. Biden Jr. has promised? Time will tell, but the strains of incivility have been hammered into place, and incivility has become an accepted norm among extremist groups. It will not be easy to restore political decency to national politics.

### 7. Systemic Problems Illuminated by the Coronavirus Cry for Political Solutions

In spring 2020, as deaths from the coronavirus devastated families, shutdowns emptied the cultural landscape, and the economy cratered, crevices and fissures in American society could not be ignored. More than 25 million economic claims were filed by mid-April 2020, lines for food distribution stretched for blocks, and businesses closed due to mounting debts. The country's economic health plummeted. But problems had been building for years. The inequalities of capitalism, with its gleaming opportunities but mixed record in delivering the mythical American dream, became excruciatingly clear (Saez & Zucman, 2019).

Throughout much of Trump's term, the stock market soared and aggregate economic indicators punched upward; at the same time, unemployment fell to the lowest rate in half a century, and African American unemployment hit rock-bottom levels. However, darker realities loomed not far from the surface. Over the past decades, the income of the lower half of American wage earners increased by just 20 percent, after-tax incomes of middle-class workers rose by 50 percent, but for the wealthiest Americans, the gains have been astronomical, a rise of 420 percent since 1980, outpacing the rise in the gross domestic product and blazing far ahead of the incomes of most American adults (Leonhardt & Serkez, 2020). With blinding, morally brutal clarity, the pandemic illuminated the systemic foundational problems at the core of the American project. (To be sure, other countries suffered gravely too, casting a mirror on their own systemic conundrums, including a failure to efficiently vaccinate citizens. However, the tragedies that afflicted the U.S., as a political and economic model for the world, were particularly salient.)

By summer 2020, the U.S., long envied by other nations for the quality of its medicine, was a public health scourge, weighing in with the highest growth of new infections in the world (Barry, 2020). Put more starkly, at this juncture the United States had 4 percent of the world's population but about one-fourth of the total coronavirus cases, and more deaths than any other country (Andrew, 2020; see Figure 1.3). In just one of many indicators of the alarming statistics, during the span of 1 month, nearly two million Americans tested positive for the virus, more than five times as many as in Canada, Europe, and three other countries combined (Leonhardt, 2020). Reflecting inequality's cracked mirror, deaths fell disproportionately on Blacks and Latinos. There were many reasons for these calamities.

Historically, Americans tend to prize the individual over the larger collective. Individuality is an admirable value, enshrining psychological growth, fulfillment, and a limitless existential "becoming." A 2011 Pew poll found that nearly six in ten Americans said "freedom to pursue life's goals without interference

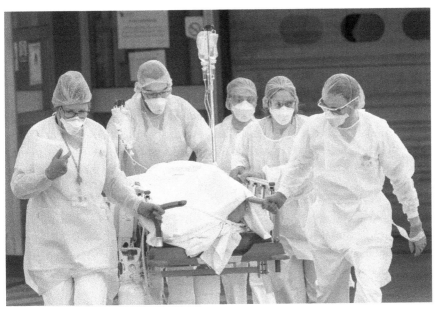

**Figure 1.3  The coronavirus pandemic brutally pierced the sheen of American political ideals, illuminating fundamental problems. With more cases than the rest of the world, and afflicted by the highest growth rate in the summer of 2020, the U.S. stood out. The nation's failure to take appropriate public health measures were rooted in a variety of structural problems.**

*Source*: www.gettyimages.com/detail/news-photo/medical-staff-push-a-patient-on-a-gurney-to-a-waiting-news-photo/1207510948?adppopup=true from the state" was more important to them than the state guaranteeing "nobody is in need" (Fitzpatrick & Wolfson, 2020, p. 46).

Psychologically, American values dating back to the Revolution celebrate individual liberty, taking umbrage at government regulations, some of which are onerous, others necessary during a pandemic. With society fragmented, amplified by divisive social media platforms, America lacked shared cultural norms that, in earlier times such as the Depression and World War II, brought people together around the need to fight a common enemy. The nation's storied emphasis on individual liberty blinded us to social responsibilities we share to each other and society.

The capitalist economic system has many virtues, in terms of efficiency and opportunities it offers people to rise from rags to riches. But, with its resistance to public sector intervention, it eschewed common-sense solutions to economic distress, such as those employed by European countries, which covered as much as 90 percent of workers' wages during the early months of the pandemic (Goodman, 2020). The political economy of American capitalism has enabled the wealthiest Americans and their lobbies to exert an outsized impact on public policy (Page & Gilens, 2017). Thus, the fine print of a federal stimulus package gave breaks to retailers, big hotels, and the multinational company Boeing, but the nation's schools, which desperately needed money to make improvements protecting students and teachers, received no special provision, imperiling students and teachers as the fall semester approached (Lipton & Vogel, 2020). Congress, beset by polarization, could not find ways to pass compromise legislation to fund a cohesive plan to expand badly needed testing (Bourdeaux, Cameron, & Zittrain, 2020). The initial federal aid package gave households and businesses a needed economic boost, but partisan deadlock impeded legislative efforts to maintain the financial lifeline in unemployment benefits, putting millions of Americans in economic jeopardy, unable to pay their mortgage or their rent.

The federalist system of power sharing in the U.S., for good historical reasons, gave considerable leeway to the states, but in the case of the coronavirus the absence of a national digitized public health reporting system led to bottlenecks in contact tracing and transmitting test results (Kliff & Sanger-Katz, 2020).

Communication factors also played a pivotal role, also reflecting a failure of collective leadership. Leaders' messaging was inconsistent. Trump downplayed the severity of the crisis and claimed it would disappear; some states' governors agreed, whereas others disagreed, resulting in a confusing pastiche of information (Leonhardt, 2020; Lipton et al., 2020). In contrast, in countries where the death toll was less staggering, leaders offered more unified, scientifically informed messages. One reason for this difference is that, for all of the perils of a strong federal government, in a public health crisis it can cut through the muck, providing a unified strategy to cope with the problems. (But it was not a panacea, as critics identified a host of problems with European governments' responses to the pandemic, a topic that goes beyond the scope of this book.)

In the U.S., the feisty, no-holds-barred vibrant media system exacerbated problems by allowing Americans of strong political persuasions to receive news that fit their viewpoints, helping some to conveniently ignore warnings about excessive partying in public. In the face of the Surgeon General's pleas to wear masks, Fox News prime-time anchors Tucker Carlson and Laura Ingraham offered up misleading information that pooh-poohed masks' importance (Gertz, 2020).

The outbreak also illuminated racial inequities that are never far from the surface, but frequently presumed to have been eradicated by affirmative action and boosts in African Americans' incomes. In 2020 the virus killed a disproportionately high number of Blacks, whose poorer economic fortunes placed them in closer proximity to others and at greater health risk due to long-standing racial inequities in the quality of health care, one of many ugly fissures in an economic system that America's political leaders have allowed to fester (Bouie, 2020; Oppel et al., 2020; see also Sanchez, 2020). Other inequities became apparent as time wore on; people with lower incomes experienced greater health risks because their jobs required that they work outside their homes, and less educated individuals were more affected by the economic slowdown (Fernandez et al., 2020). While the American economy rebounded more quickly than experts predicted, lower-income Americans, and those of color, experienced the greatest financial hardships.

The issues are not liberal or conservative, but national dilemmas that cut into the national fabric, raising questions about the sustainability of can-do American optimism. Political, economic, and cultural fault lines have emerged, illuminated by the virus. Even after the presidential election, the same inequities roiled the country. In apparent recognition of all this, more Americans said the country was headed on the wrong rather than the right track (Leonhardt & Serkez, 2020). Beset by economic problems, concerned about racial turmoil, exhausted by political vitriol, they feared the nation had careened off its rails (Lerer & Umhoefer, 2020). It's hard to disagree.

## On the Other Hand . . .

Well, maybe you can contest the critics, even if you share the unhappy prognosis discussed here. And perhaps there are positive features of political communication, so roundly criticized in the previous sections of the chapter.

One of the themes of this book is that we benefit intellectually from viewing issues not from one perspective, but many. As the philosopher Blaise Pascal noted, people do not show their "greatness by being at one extremity, but rather by touching both at once." Thus, racial animus that poisoned the country showed signs of abating, as White Americans at last recognized systemic problems with discrimination and policing. Kamala Harris, the daughter of Jamaican and Indian immigrants, became the first woman and woman of color to be elected vice president of the United States, a source of pride to millions.

The online media that have spread fake news and partisan prejudices also enabled millions of citizens to register immediate objection to politicians or policies they dislike; allowed dissident groups, such as the Tea Party on the right and Black Lives Matter on the left, to organize online; helped political candidates, from Trump to Sanders to Obama, challenge the status quo and recruit money outside the corporate funding apparatus; and provided citizens worldwide with a cornucopia of digital sources of information, which have richly expanded their knowledge and offered alternatives to mainstream news. While social media fuels animus, it also is an outlet for free expression, offering new avenues for political engagement, forums to challenge mainstream media, and ways to challenge the status quo (Barnidge et al., 2018).

Political campaigns can engage voters, as occurred with the surge in voter turnout in the 2020 campaign. For all the back-biting candidate comments, there were many cognitive virtues in the 2020 Democratic primaries. Bernie Sanders raised a host of issues, from health care to the ills of capitalism. Biden and Trump offered different worldviews from which voters could choose, presenting their differences through the realm of persuasive communication rather than coercive appeals or, as in the old days, gun duels. Climate change and racial prejudice were major topics of discussion in the presidential debates. And, despite the problems, accurate information about the coronavirus, relayed by dedicated reporters, was widely available to help people make rational choices about their health.

What's more, the foundation of democracy—voting—showed its resilience in 2020, as some 160 million people voted, nearly two-thirds of the electorate, casting more votes than in any election in U.S. history. A nonpartisan project, VoteEarly2020, marshalled volunteers to encourage people to vote before the election. Inspired by trucks with the words "Democracy is Delicious" emblazoned on the side, volunteers for a nonpartisan election project delivered some 50,000 pizzas, as well as milkshakes and hamburgers, to polling stations in 48 states (Editorial Board, 2020b). For days after the election, ballot counters, the foot soldiers of democracy, rigorously tallied votes, even in the face of anti-democratic protests to stop counting ballots. After the election, Georgia's officials defied a president, standing by their vote tabulations that showed Biden had won the state. Congress, in the face of violent ransacking of the Capitol, returned to business that same night to ratify the results of the 2020 election, certifying that Biden would be the 46th president of the U.S.

It is important to remember that negative forces have always tugged at American politics. Except for rare periods of relative political consensus, such as those that followed the Depression and World War II, partisan divisions have been a constant (Tomasky, 2019). For all the liberal-conservative polarization, partisan prejudice hasn't increased as much as some critics feared (Westwood, Peterson, & Lelkes, 2019). What's more, increases in partisanship have occurred primarily among strong party supporters, who drive the attention of members of Congress. The media focus on partisanship at the elite level creates the impression there are more disagreements among Americans than there actually are (Barberá et al., 2019; Levendusky & Malhotra, 2016).

Partisanship also has its positive features. It has encouraged those with strong political positions—those who supported the conservative Tea Party on the right and Occupy Wall Street on the left—to actively participate in political issues. Incivility is not all bad (Kenski, Coe, & Rains, 2019), as we see when politicians call out their opponents for making racist, sexist, or anti-religious statements.

Populism (until it turned ugly) provided a wake-up call to politicians of both parties, whose messages frequently ignored the grievances of working-class Whites. A host of other political movements have also gained footing among people of color in the U.S., attesting to the vibrancy of American democracy.

Today's incivility might be viewed more tolerantly when compared with the slanderous slurs—invectives and epithets—hurled at politicians and media over the years, to say nothing of physical violence, assassinations, and torching of newspapers that occurred during the 19th century. As problematic as the structural problems illuminated by the coronavirus are, beneficial things have happened too, such as incredible sacrifices made by health care professionals, gratitude paid to them by members of the public, and a perceptual focus outward to the problems the pandemic posed for society-as-a-whole, rather than an exclusive emphasis on personal dilemmas (Cappelen et al., 2020).

So, there is good, as well as bad, and this book will delve into the textured aspects of the issues described earlier, as well as touching on just what those terms "good" and "bad" mean in political communication. It does not seek to whitewash the serious problems ripping the fabric of American democracy, but aims to offer a broader, deeper examination of political issues. Besides explaining the dynamics of political communication and what ails it, the book is committed to the proposition that many perspectives—a pluralism of viewpoints—shed light on complex, contentious ideas. Yet it is important to emphasize that pluralism doesn't mean every perspective receives the same acclaim. Normative philosophies emphasize that political communication must advance democratic aims, affirm democracy's norms, and treat minority views with respect. When political leaders, media, or citizens act with prejudice or denigrate democratic norms, they fall outside the domain of ethical discourse, and must be condemned. When mobs storm the U.S. Capitol to protest a fair, democratic election, they fall far outside the realms of tolerance and respect.

## THE FOCUS OF THIS BOOK

The chapters that follow examine the complex, volatile intersection between politics and media and how it plays out in contemporary democracy. The foundation for the book is academic research in the interdisciplinary field of political communication, with its roots in communication, political science, sociology, social psychology, and political marketing. You can't cover everything in a book, and because the universe of political communication is so immense—news, political marketing, global misinformation, ads, polls, and the voluminous academic literature on these topics—I concentrate on political communication in America. The U.S. is not the only country in which political communication occurs—far from it—and it is important to conduct comparative research in other national contexts (Esser, 2019; Boulianne, 2019; Rojas & Valenzuela, 2019). Indeed, I discuss global aspects of political communication in the next chapter and call on research from across the world in many discussions. However, to provide depth and avoid superficial discussions of issues in different nations, the U.S. is the focus of the book, with attention to theories and ideas that offer broad communicative and philosophical insights.

Here is a roadmap of what you can expect. The first section, launched by this chapter, offers a foundational perspective on political communication. Chapter 2 introduces the political terrain, defining politics and political communication. Chapter 3 offers a philosophical perspective, laying out ideals of what democracy should do and how it falls short.

The second portion of the book introduces you to core political communication concepts and issues in the field. Chapter 4 describes the colorful intellectual history of the academic field of political communication. Chapters 5 and 6, focusing on citizenship, examine how well news serves democracy and processes of political socialization. Chapters 7 and 8 examine the central ideas of agenda-setting, priming, and framing, the heart of the study of political media effects. Chapter 9 delves deeply into the biased perceptions we all hold about politics and how they intersect with communication.

The third section examines communication and the electoral campaign. Chapter 10 examines presidential rhetoric and its uses in a tweet-filled, social media era. Chapters 11–13 look at the content of political news, focusing on news biases. Chapter 11 unpacks the controversial area of news bias, defines bias, and debunks a prominent myth, while highlighting the importance of political news. Chapter 12 returns to the bias issue, this time delving into the thicket of coverage of women presidential candidates on the campaign trail. Chapter 13 discusses the issue of journalistic biases in presidential election news, as well as the role polling plays in the campaign. Chapter 14 explains the crazy-quilt presidential nomination process in a media age. Chapter 15 explores the effects of political advertising, and Chapter 16 describes the effects and normative features of presidential debates. It concludes with a postscript, evaluating our politics and offering suggestions to improve politics and political communication in America.

## CONCLUSIONS

Political communication is vital and vibrant, but also vituperative, its teeming animus raising significant questions for the conduct of politics in an online age. The chapter began by describing seven problems that characterize the contemporary political media milieu: roiling racial animus and civic unrest; proliferation of fake news; growth of ideological media that offer a distorted, slanted view of truth and, at their worst, disseminate lies to extremist followers; partisan divisions that fragment the populace; broad economic and social insecurities that have produced populism with authoritarian streaks; uncivil politics; and systemic problems thrown into sharp relief by the pandemic.

Not a great way to begin a book, but alas, those are the realities.

These are serious problems, put into a broader perspective by the writer Andrew Marantz:

> Creepy surveillance, dissolution of civic norms, widening unease, infectious rage, a tilt toward autocracy in several formerly placid liberal democracies— these are starting to seem like inherent features, not bugs. The real scandal is not that the system can be breached; the real scandal is the system itself.
> (Marantz, 2020, p. 55)

Now, there are silver linings and good points. The same forces that have produced partisan animus have led to political change. Despite convulsive forces, electoral guardrails protected a national election in 2020. Politics has always been dirty. Nonetheless, there is little doubt that our political communication system performs well below the ideals that are hauled out on national holidays and in civics books. There is no doubt anti-democratic forces are loose in the country, threatening the fabric of the nation's storied ideals.

Is it any wonder that, on the eve of a recent Independence Day in America, just 17 percent of Americans said they felt proud when thinking about the state of the nation? (Brooks, 2020). Is it any surprise that less than half of the citizenry felt extremely proud to be Americans, and more than eight in ten were dissatisfied with the way things are going in the U.S.? (Perloff, 2020; Baker et al., 2020). Where does this come from? How can we understand the state of American politics and political communication in the U.S.? What ails the country? Where are wellsprings of hope? These questions will occupy us as we begin our journey.

## REFERENCES

Alba, D. (2020, October 29). Riled up: Misinformation stokes calls for violence on Election Day. *The New York Times*. Online: www.nytimes.com/2020/10/13/technology/viral-misinformation-violence-election.html. (Accessed: November 11, 2020).

Allcott, H., & Gentzkow, M. (2017). Social media and fake news in the 2016 election. *Journal of Economic Perspectives*, *31*, 211–236.

Andrew, S. (2020, June 30). The US has 4% of the world's population but 25% of its coronavirus cases. *CNN Health*. Online: www.cnn.com/2020/06/30/health/us-coronavirus-toll-in-numbers-june-trnd/index.html. (Accessed: November 11, 2020).

Avram, M., Micallef, N., Pati, S., & Menczer, F. (2020). Exposure to social engagement metrics increases vulnerability to misinformation. *The Harvard Kennedy School Misinformation Review*. Online: https://misinforeview.hks.harvard.edu/wp-content/uploads/2020/07/FORMATTED_Avram_July28.pdf. (Accessed: August 14.2020).

Bajak, A., & Howe, J. (2020, May 14). A study said Covid wasn't that deadly. The right seized it. *The New York Times*. Online: www.nytimes.com/2020/05/14/opinion/coronavirus-research-misinformation.html. (Accessed: June 19, 2020).

Baker, P. (2019, November 12). Two impeachments, but two radically different accusations. *The New York Times*. Online: www.nytimes.com/2019/11/12/us/politics/impeachment-clinton-trump.html. (Accessed: November 11, 2020).

Baker, P., Branch, J., Eligon, J., Epstein, R.J., Levin, D., & Stein, M. (2020, August 30). Stories of 2020: Five lives caught in a year of upheaval and pain. *The New York Times*. Online: www.nytimes.com/2020/08/30/us/politics/2020-year.html. (Accessed: September 28, 2020).

Barberá, P., Casas, A., Nagler, J., Egan, P.J., Bonneau, R., Jost, J.T., & Tucker, J.A. (2019). Who leads? Who follows? Measuring issue attention and agenda setting by legislators and the mass public using social media data. *American Political Science Review*, *113*, 883–901.

Barnidge, M., Huber, B., Gil de Zúñiga, H., & Liu, J.H. (2018). Social media as a sphere for "risky" political expression: A twenty-county multilevel comparative analysis. *The International Journal of Press/Politics*, *23*, 161–182.

Barry, D., & Frenkel, S. (2021, January 7). "Be there. Will be wild": Trump all but circled the date. *The New York Times*. Online: www.nytimes.com/2021/01/06/us/politics/capitol-mob-trump-supporters.html. (Accessed: January 7, 2021).

Barry, J.M. (2020). Politics won't stop the pandemic. *The New York Times*. Online: www.nytimes.com/2020/07/14/opinion/coronavirus-shutdown.html. (Accessed: July 14.2020).

Bartscher, A.K., Kuhn, M., & Schularick, M. (2019, July 23). The college wealth divide: Education and inequality in America, 1956–2016. *CESifo Working Paper No. 7726*. Online: https://papers.ssrn.com/sol3/papers.cfm?abstract_id=3421153. (Accessed: July 30, 2020).

Bernstein, R. (2020, April 3). Investigating China's coronavirus propaganda wildfire. *The Daily Signal*. Online: www.dailysignal.com/2020/04/03/investigating-chinas-coronavirus-propaganda-wildfire/#dear_reader. (Accessed: April 4, 2020).

Berry, J.M., & Sobieraj, S. (2014). *The outrage industry: Political opinion media and the new incivility*. New York: Oxford University Press.

Blow, C.M. (2021, March 7). The allies' betrayal of George Floyd. *The New York Times*. Online: https://www.nytimes.com/2021/03/07/opinion/george-floyd-protests.html. (Accessed: March 16, 2021).

Bouie, J. (2020, April 14). Why coronavirus is killing African Americans more than others. *The New York Times*. Online: www.nytimes.com/2020/04/14/opinion/sunday/coronavirus-racism-african-americans.html. (Accessed: April 19, 2020).

Boulianne, S. (2019). US dominance of research on political communication: A meta-view. *Political Communication, 36*, 660–665.

Bourdeaux, M., Cameron, B., & Zittrain, J. (2020, July 16). Testing is on the brink of paralysis. That's very bad news. *The New York Times*. Online: www.nytimes.com/2020/07/16/opinion/coronavirus-testing-us.html. (Accessed: November 11, 2020).

Bradshaw, S., Howard, P.N., Kollanyi, B., & Neudert, L-M. (2020). Sowing and automation of political news and information over social media in the United States, 2016–2018. *Political Communication, 37*, 173–193.

Brennen, J.S., Simon, F.M., & Nielsen, R.K. (2021). Beyond (mis)representation: Visuals in COVID-19 misinformation. *The International Journal of Press/Politics, 26*, 277–299.

Brooks, D. (2019, March 19). Cory Booker finds his moment. *The New York Times*, A27.

Brooks, D. (2020, July 2). The national humiliation we need. *The New York Times*. Online: www.nytimes.com/2020/07/02/opinion/coronavirus-july-4.html. (Accessed: July 3, 2020).

Cappelen, A.W., Falch, R., Sorensen, E.O., Tungodden, B., & Wezerek, G. (2020, April 16). What do you owe your neighbor? The pandemic might change your answer. *The New York Times*. Online: www.nytimes.com/interactive/2020/04/16/opinion/coronavirus-inequality-solidarity-poll.html. (Accessed: April 19, 2020).

Chan, M. (2020, September 21, 28). The price of protest. *Time*, 56–61.

Clinton, J., Cohen, J., Lapinski, J.S., & Trussler, M. (2020, June 22). *Partisan pandemic: How partisanship and public health concerns affect individuals' social distancing during COVID-19*. Online: https://papers.ssrn.com/sol3/papers.cfm?abstract_id=3633934. (Accessed: July 8, 2020).

Coe, K., Kenski, K., & Rains, S.A. (2014). Online and uncivil? Patterns and determinants of incivility in newspaper website comments. *Journal of Communication, 64*, 658–679.

Cohen, R. (2016, September 11). We need "somebody spectacular". *The New York Times* (Sunday Review), 1, 6–7.

Daniller, A. (2020, May 7). *Americans remain concerned that states will lift restrictions too quickly, but partisan differences widen*. Pew Research Center (FactTank: News in the Numbers). Online: www.pewresearch.org/fact-tank/2020/05/07/americans-remain-concerned-that-states-will-lift-restrictions-too-quickly-but-partisan-differences-widen/ (Accessed: May 20, 2020).

Darcy, O. (2020, July 14). Controversial opinion writer Bari Weiss resigns from *The New York Times*, blasting paper for "illiberal" environment. *CNN Business*. Online:

www.cnn.com/2020/07/14/media/bari-weiss-resigns-new-york-times/index.html. (Accessed: July 14.2020).

de Vreese, C.H., Esser, F., Aalberg, T., Reinemann, C., & Stanyer, J. (2018). Populism as an expression of political communication content and style: A new perspective. *The International Journal of Press/Politics, 23*, 423–438.

Digital News Fact Sheet (2019, July 23). *Pew Research Center: Journalism & Media.* Online: https://www.journalism.org/fact-sheet/digital-news/ (Accessed: March 16, 2021).

Dobber, T., Metoui, N., Trilling, D., Helberger, N., & de Vreese, C.H. (2021). Do (microtargeted) deepfakes have real effects on political attitudes? *The International Journal of Press/Politics, 26*, 69–91.

Eatwell, R., & Goodwin, M. (2018). *National populism: The revolt against liberal democracy.* New Orleans: Pelican.

Editorial Board (2019, November 30). Editorial: Fake news. *The New York Times.* Online: www.nytimes.com/interactive/2019/11/30/opinion/editorials/fake-news. html. (Accessed: September 29, 2020).

Editorial Board (2020a, June 24). The jobs we need. *The New York Times* (Sunday Review). Online: www.nytimes.com/2020/06/24/opinion/sunday/income-wealth-inequali ty-america.html. (Accessed: July 5, 2020).

Editorial Board (2020b, November 3). Feel inspired, America. *The New York Times.* Online: www.nytimes.com/2020/11/03/opinion/volunteers-election-2020.html. (Accessed: November 4, 2020).

Edmondson, C., & Fandos, N. (2020, June 9). G.O.P. scrambles to respond to public demands for police overhaul. *The New York Times.* Online: www.nytimes.com/2020/06/09/us/ politics/republicans-police-reform.html. (Accessed: June 10, 2020).

Edsall, T.B. (2018, March 1). What motivates voters more than loyalty? Loathing. *The New York Times.* Online: www.nytimes.com/2018/03/01/opinion/negative-parti sanship-democrats-republicans.html. (Accessed: May 19, 2020).

Edsall, T.B. (2020a, June 10). How much is America changing? *The New York Times.* Online: www.nytimes.com/2020/06/10/opinion/george-floyd-protests-trump.html. (Accessed: June 10, 2020).

Edsall, T.B. (2020b, July 29). Trump is trying to bend reality to his will. *The New York Times.* Online: www.nytimes.com/2020/07/29/opinion/trump-2020-populism. html. (Accessed: July 30, 2020).

Edwards, G.S., & Rushin, S. (2018, January 14). The effect of President Trump's elec- tion on hate crimes. *SSRN.* Online: https://papers.ssrn.com/sol3/papers.cfm?ab stract_id=3102652. (Accessed: October 9, 2020).

Esser, F. (2019). Advances in comparative political communication research through contextualization and cumulation of evidence. *Political Communication, 36*, 680–686.

Fawzi, N. (2019). Untrustworthy news and the media as "enemy of the people"? How a populist worldview shapes recipients' attitudes toward the media. *The Interna- tional Journal of Press/Politics, 24*, 146–164.

Fernandez, M., Bosman, J., Harmon, A., Ivory, D., & Smith, M. (2020, December 5). The virus is devastating the U.S., and leaving an uneven toll. *The New York Times.* Online: www.nytimes.com/2020/12/04/us/covid-united-states-surge.html. (Accessed: December 5, 2020).

Filindra, A. (2018). *Of regimes and rhinoceroses: Immigration, outgroup prejudice, and the micro-foundations of democratic decline.* Paper presented to the annual convention of the Midwest Association for Public Opinion Research, November, Chicago.

Fitzpatrick, A., & Wolfson, E. (2020, September 21, 28). COVID-19 has killed nearly 200,000 Americans. How many more lives will be lost before the U.S. gets it right? *Time*, 42–47.

Flegenheimer, M., Ruiz, R.R., & Bowles, N. (2020, January 27). Bernie Sanders and his internet army. *The New York Times*. Online: www.nytimes.com/2020/01/27/us/politics/bernie-sanders-internet-supporters-2020.html. (Accessed: November 11, 2020).

Fleming-Wood, B., Margalit, Y., & Schaffner, B. (2020, June 21). The emergent partisan gap in social distancing. *Data for Progress*. Online: www.dataforprogress.org/blog/2020/6/21/the-emergent-partisan-gap-in-social-distancing. (Accessed: June 27, 2020).

Freelon, D., & Wells, C. (2020). Disinformation as political communication. *Political Communication, 37*, 145–156.

Frenkel, S., Alba, D., & Zhong, R. (2020, June 1). Surge of virus misinformation stumps Facebook and Twitter. *The New York Times*. Online: www.nytimes.com/2020/03/08/technology/coronavirus-misinformation-social-media.html. (Accessed: July 14, 2020).

Gertz, M. (2020, August 20). Fox's ongoing attacks on masks are a public health menace. *Media Matters for America*. Online: www.mediamatters.org/fox-news/foxs-ongoing-attacks-masks-are-public-health-menace. (Accessed: August 7, 2020).

Gitlin, T. (1980). *The whole world is watching: Mass media in the making & unmaking of the new left*. Berkeley, CA: University of California Press.

Goodman, P.S. (2020, April 2). The Nordic way to economic rescue. *The New York Times*. Online: www.nytimes.com/2020/03/28/business/nordic-way-economic-rescue-virus.html. (Accessed: July 31, 2020).

Goovaerts, I., & Marien, S. (2020). Uncivil communication and simplistic argumentation: Decreasing political trust, increasing persuasive power? *Political Communication, 37*, 768–788.

Guo, L., & Vargo, C. (2020). "Fake news" and emerging online media ecosystem: An integrated intermedia agenda-setting analysis of the 2016 U.S. presidential election. *Communication Research, 47*, 178–200.

Hallin, D. (1986). *The "uncensored war": Media and Vietnam*. New York: Oxford University Press.

Hameleers, M., Bos, L., & de Vreese, C.H. (2018). Selective exposure to populist communication: How attitudinal congruence drives the effects of populist attributions of blame. *Journal of Communication, 68*, 51–74.

Hanitzsch, T., Van Dalen, A., & Steindl, N. (2018). Caught in the nexus: A comparative and longitudinal analysis of public trust in the press. *The International Journal of Press/Politics, 23*, 3–23.

Hannah-Jones, N. (2020, June 26). It is time for reparations. *The New York Times Magazine*. Online: www.nytimes.com/interactive/2020/06/24/magazine/reparations-slavery.html. (Accessed: June 28, 2020).

Herndon, A.W. (2021, January 8). America in 2021: Racial progress in the south, a White mob in the Capitol. *The New York Times*. Online: www.nytimes.com/2021/01/08/us/politics/trump-georgia-capitol-racism.html. (Accessed: January 9, 2021).

Hopp, T., Ferrucci, P., & Vargo, C.J. (2020). Why do people share ideologically extreme, false, and misleading content on social media? A self-report and trace data-based analysis of countermedia content dissemination on Facebook and Twitter. *Human Communication Research, 46,* 357–384.

Hwang, H., Kim, Y., & Kim, Y. (2018). Influence of discussion incivility on deliberation: An examination of the mediating role of moral indignation. *Communication Research, 45,* 213–240.

Isaac, M. (2020, July 8). Facebook's decisions were "setbacks for civil rights," audit finds. *The New York Times.* Online: www.nytimes.com/2020/07/08/technology/facebook-civil-rights- audit.html/ (Accessed: July 9, 2020).

Isaac, M., & Wakabayashi, D. (2017, October 31). Broad reach of campaign by Russians is disclosed. *The New York Times,* B1, B3.

Jurkowitz, M., Mitchell, A., Shearer, E., & Walker, M. (2020, January 24). *U.S. media polarization and the 2020 election: A nation divided.* Pew Research Center (Journalism & Media). Online: www.journalism.org/2020/01/24/u-s-media-polarization-and-the-2020-election-a-nation-divided/?utm_source=newsletter&utm_medium=email&utm_campaign=newsletter_axiosam&stream=top. (Accessed: March 21, 2020).

Kalmoe, N.P., Gubler, J.R., & Wood, D.A. (2018). Toward conflict or compromise? How violent metaphors polarize partisan issue attitudes. *Political Communication, 35,* 333–352.

Kaltwasser, C.R., Taggart, P.A., Espejo, P.O., & Ostiguy, P. (Eds.). (2017). *The Oxford handbook of populism.* Oxford, UK: Oxford University Press.

Kang, C., & Frenkel, S. (2020, June 27). "PizzaGate" conspiracy theory thrives anew in the TikTok era. *The New York Times.* Online: www.nytimes.com/2020/06/27/technology/pizzagate-justin-bieber-qanon-tiktok.html. (Accessed: June 28, 2020).

Keller, F.B., Schoch, D., Stier, S., & Yang, J. (2020). Political astroturfing on Twitter: How to coordinate a disinformation campaign. *Political Communication, 37,* 256–280.

Kenski, K., Coe, K., & Rains, S.A. (2019). Perceptions of incivility in public discourse. In R.G. Boatright, T.J. Shaffer, S. Sobieraj, & D. Goldthwaite Young (Eds.), *A crisis of civility? Political discourse and its discontents* (pp. 45–60). New York: Routledge.

Kenski, K., Coe, K., & Rains, S.A. (2020). Perceptions of uncivil discourse online: An examination of types and predictors. *Communication Research, 47,* 795–814.

Kliff, S., & Sanger-Katz, M. (2020, July 13). Bottleneck for U.S. coronavirus response: The fax machine. *The New York Times.* Online: www.nytimes.com/2020/07/13/upshot/coronavirus-response-fax-machines.html?rref=collection%2Fissuecollection%2Ftodays-new-york-times&action=click&contentCollection=todayspaper&region=rank&module=package&version=highlights&contentPlacement=1&pgtype=collection. (Accessed: July 14, 2020).

Krafft, P.N., & Donovan, J.N. (2020). Disinformation by design: The use of evidence collages and platform filtering in a media manipulation campaign. *Political Communication, 37,* 194–214.

Kristof, N. (2016, April 2). When Whites don't just get it, Part 6. *The New York Times.* Online: www.nytimes.com/2016/04/03/opinion/sunday/when-whites-just-dont-get-it-part-6.html. (Accessed: June 6, 2020).

Kristof, N., & WuDunn, S. (2020, January 9). Who killed the Knapp family? *The New York Times* (Sunday Review). Online: www.nytimes.com/2020/01/09/opinion/sunday/deaths-despair-poverty.html. (Accessed: May 16, 2020).

Ladd, J.M., & Podkul, A.R. (2019). Distrust of the news media as a symptom and a further cause of partisan polarization. In T.N. Ridout (Ed.), *New directions in media and politics* (2nd ed., pp. 54–79). New York: Routledge.

Leonhardt, D. (2020, August 6). The unique U.S. failure to control the virus. *The New York Times*. Online: www.nytimes.com/2020/08/06/us/coronavirus-us.html. (Accessed: August 7, 2020).

Leonhardt, D., & Serkez, Y. (2020, April 10). America will struggle after coronavirus. These charts show why. *The New York Times*. Online: www.nytimes.com/interactive/2020/04/10/opinion/coronavirus-us-economy-inequality.html. (Accessed: April 20, 2020).

Lerer, L., & Umhoefer, D. (2020, June 12). On the future, Americans can agree: It doesn't look good. *The New York Times*. Online: www.nytimes.com/2020/06/12/us/politics/election-coronavirus-protests-unemployment.html. (Accessed: June 13, 2020).

Levendusky, M., & Malhotra, N. (2016). Does media coverage of partisan polarization affect political attitudes? *Political Communication, 33*, 283–301.

Li, J. (2020). Toward a research agenda on political misinformation and corrective information. *Political Communication, 37*, 125–135.

Lipton, E., Sanger, D.E., Haberman, M., Shear, M.D., Mazzetti, M., & Barnes, J.E. (2020, April 11). He could have seen what was coming: Behind Trump's failure on the virus. *The New York Times*. Online: www.nytimes.com/2020/04/11/us/politics/coronavirus-trump-response.html. (Accessed: April 12, 2020).

Lipton, E., & Vogel, K.P. (2020, May 5). Fine print of stimulus bill contains special deals for industries. *The New York Times*. Online: www.nytimes.com/2020/03/25/us/politics/virus-fineprint-stimulus-bill.html. (Accessed: July 14.2020).

Lukito, J., Suk, J., Zhang, Y., Doroshenko, L., Kim, S.J., Su, M-H., Xia, Y., Freelon, D., & Wells, C. (2020). The wolves in sheep's clothing: How Russia's Internet Research Agency tweets appeared in U.S. news as vox populi. *The International Journal of Press/Politics, 25*, 196–216.

Luo, M. (2009, November 30). In job hunt, college degree can't close racial gap. *The New York Times*. Online: www.nytimes.com/2009/12/01/us/01race.html. (Accessed: June 6, 2020).

Marantz, A. (2020, March 9). #Winning. *The New Yorker*, 44–55.

Mason, L. (2018). *Uncivil agreement: How politics became our identity*. Chicago, IL: University of Chicago Press.

McIntire, M., Yourish, K., & Buchanan, L. (2019, November 2). In Trump's Twitter feed: Conspiracy-mongers, racists and spies. *The New York Times*. Online: www.nytimes.com/interactive/2019/11/02/us/politics/trump-twitter-disinformation.html. (Accessed: August 14, 2020.)

McIntosh, K., Moss, E., Nunn, R., & Shambaugh, J. (2020, February 27). Explaining the Black-White wealth gap. *Brookings*. Online: www.brookings.edu/blog/up-front/2020/02/27/examining-the-black-white-wealth-gap/. (Accessed: June 6, 2020).

*Most Americans say Trump was too slow in initial response to coronavirus threat.* Pew Research Center: U.S. Politics & Policy. Online: www.people-press.org/2020/04/16/most-americans-say-trump-was-too-slow-in-initial-response-to-coronavirus-threat. (Accessed: April 21, 2020).

Muddiman, A., Pond-Cobb, J., & Matson, J.E. (2020). Negativity bias or backlash: Interaction with civil and uncivil online political news content. *Communication Research, 47*, 815–837.

Müller, J-W. (2016). *What is populism?* Philadelphia: University of Pennsylvania Press.

Mutz, D. (2015). *In-your-face politics: The consequences of uncivil media*. Princeton, NJ: Princeton University Press.

Norris, P., & Inglehart, R.F. (2019). *Cultural backlash: Trump, Brexit and authoritarian populism*. Cambridge, UK: Cambridge University Press.

Oppel, R.A., Jr., Gebeloff, R., Lai, K.K.R., Wright, W., & Smith, M. (2020, July 5). The fullest look yet at the racial inequity of coronavirus. *The New York Times*. Online: www.nytimes.com/interactive/2020/07/05/us/coronavirus-latinos-african-ameri cans-cdc-data.html. (Accessed: July 6, 2020).

Otto, L.P., Lecheler, S., & Schuck, A.R.T. (2020). Is context the key? The (non-)differential effects of mediated incivility in three European countries. *Political Communication, 37*, 88–107.

Page, B.I., & Gilens, M. (2017). *Democracy in America? What has gone wrong and what can we do about it?* Chicago, IL: University of Chicago Press.

Pennycook, G., Cannon, T.D., & Rand, D.G. (2018). Prior exposure increases perceived accuracy of fake news. *Journal of Experimental Psychology General, 147*, 1865–1880.

Perloff, R.M. (2019, February 15). Border wall is nothing compared to Brexit crisis, and what it reveals. *The Plain Dealer*, E2.

Perloff, R.M. (2020, July 3). Do our partisan animosities portend another 1876 debacle? *The Plain Dealer*, E2.

Plattner, M.E. (2020). Democracy embattled. *Journal of Democracy, 31*, 5–10.

Popovich, N. (2020, February 21). Rise in concern on climate, but not for everyone. *The New York Times*, A15.

Putnam, R.D. (2015). *Our kids: The American dream in crisis*. New York: Simon & Schuster.

Rawls, J. (1996). *Political liberalism* (Paperback edition). New York: Columbia University Press.

Rawls, J. (2001). *Justice as fairness: A restatement* (E. Kelly, Ed.). Cambridge, MA: Harvard University Press.

Ridout, T.N., & Fowler, E.F. (2018). Fake news: What is the influence of fabricated stories and efforts to undermine media credibility? In T.N. Ridout (Ed.), *New directions in media and politics* (2nd ed.). New York: Routledge.

Rojas, H., & Valenzuela, S. (2019). A call to contextualize public opinion-based research in political communication. *Political Communication, 36*, 652–659.

Roose, K. (2020, August 20). What is QAnon, the viral pro-Trump conspiracy theory? *The New York Times*. Online: www.nytimes.com/article/what-is-qanon.html. (Accessed: August 20, 2020).

Russonello, G. (2020, June 5). Why most Americans support the protests. *The New York Times*. Online: www.nytimes.com/2020/06/05/us/politics/polling-george-floyd-protests-racism.html. (Accessed: June 9, 2020).

Saez, E., & Zucman, G. (2019, October 13). Taxing our way to justice. *The New York Times* (Sunday Review), 6.

Sanchez, L. (2020). The sleeping giant awakens: Latinos in the 2020 election. In D. Jackson, D.S. Coombs, F. Trevisan, D. Lilleker, & E. Thorsen (Eds.), *U.S. election analysis 2020: Media, voters and the campaign*. Online: www.electionanalysis. ws/us/president2020/section-2-voters/the-sleeping-giant-awakens-latinos-in-the-2020-election/. (Accessed: November 18, 2020).

Schradie, J. (2019). *The revolution that wasn't: How digital activism favors conservatives*. Cambridge: Harvard University Press.

Schumer, C., & Sanders, B. (2019, February 3). Schumer and Sanders: Limit corporate stock buybacks. *The New York Times*. Online: www.nytimes.com/2019/02/03/opin ion/chuck-schumer-bernie-sanders.html. (Accessed: July 5, 2020).

Skelley, G. (2020, June 2). How Americans feel about George Floyd's death and the protests. *FiveThirtyEight*. Online: https://fivethirtyeight.com/features/how-ameri cans-feel-about-george-floyds-death-and-the-protests/. (Accessed: June 6, 2020).

Southwell, B.G., Thorson, E.A., & Sheble, L. (Eds.). (2018). *Misinformation and mass audiences*. Austin, TX: University of Texas Press.

Stamps, D., & Mastro, D. (2020). The problem with protests: Emotional effects of race-related news media. *Journalism & Mass Communication Quarterly, 97*, 617–643.

Tavernise, S., & Rosenberg, M. (2021, January 8). These are the rioters who stormed the nation's Capitol. *The New York Times*. Online: www.nytimes.com/2021/01/07/us/ names-of-rioters-capitol.html/ (Accessed: January 8, 2020).

Thomas, D., & Horowitz, J.M. (2020, September 16). *Support for Black lives matter has decreased since June but remains strong among Black Americans*. Pew Research Center (FactTank: News in the Numbers). Online: www.pewresearch.org/fact-tank/2020/09/16/support-for-black-lives-matter-has-decreased-since-june-but-re mains-strong-among-black-americans/. (Accessed: September 25, 2020).

Tomasky, M. (2019). *If we can keep it: How the republic collapsed and how it might be saved*. New York: Liveright Publishing Co.

Vargo, C.J., & Hopp, T. (2020). Fear, anger, and political advertisement engagement: A computational case study of Russian-linked Facebook and Instagram content. *Journalism & Mass Communication Quarterly, 97*, 743–761.

Villarosa, L. (2020, April 29). "A terrible price": The deadly racial disparities of Covid-19 in America. *The New York Times*. Online: www.nytimes.com/2020/04/29/maga zine/racial-disparities-covid-19.html. (Accessed: June 6, 2020).

Vraga, E.K., & Bode, L. (2020). Defining misinformation and understanding its bounded nature: Using expertise and evidence for describing misinformation. *Political Communication, 37*, 136–144.

Waisbord, S., Tucker, T., & Lichtenheld, Z. (2018). Trump and the great disruption in public communication. In P. Boczkowski & Z. Papacharissi (Eds.), *Trump and the media* (pp. 25–32). Cambridge: MIT Press.

Westwood, S.J., Peterson, E., & Lelkes, Y. (2019). Are there still limits on partisan prej udice? *Public Opinion Quarterly, 83*, 584–597.

Williams, T. (2016, July 7). Study supports suspicion that police are more likely to use force on blacks. *The New York Times*. Online: www.nytimes.com/2016/07/08/us/ study-supports-suspicion-that-police-use-of-force-is-more-likely-for-blacks.html. (Accessed: June 3, 2020).

Young, D.G. (2020). *Irony and outrage: The polarized landscape of rage, fear, and laughter in the United States*. New York: Oxford University Press.

Young, D.G., Hoffman, L.H., & Roth, D. (2019). "Showdowns," "duels," and "nail-biters": How aggressive strategic game frames in campaign coverage fuel public percep tions of incivility. In R.G. Boatright, T.J. Shaffer, S. Sobieraj, & D.G. Young (Eds.), *A crisis of civility? Political discourse and its discontents* (pp. 83–94). New York: Routledge.

# CHAPTER

# 2

# Introduction to Political Communication

It comes down to this: We cannot talk about politics without invoking media, and we cannot understand contemporary media without appreciating the role they play in the political system. If you doubt this, consider how you learned about the 2020 presidential debates, political aspects of the coronavirus, the George Floyd protests in 2020, and the January 6, 2021, attack on the nation's Capitol. Your learning was primarily indirect, mediated, whether by Facebook, Twitter, a partisan website, a link, posted video, social media announcement of a speech, or through mainstream news, received on a phone, PC, or television.

A candidate can't mount a credible campaign for office without crafting an image, and an image is conveyed, disseminated, and constructed through the multiplicity of media. Images, alas, can be deceptive and superficial, designed to brand candidates as smart, likable, and with just enough anti-Washington, D.C. bluster to win over voters who profess to be sick and tired of—the cliché is apt and time-honored—"politics as usual." But political communication isn't just the realm of politicians. It is the domain of journalists, activists, and passionate citizens who tweet, link, and send vibrant messages all day long. It's all politics, or media-politics, or mediated political realities, terms that seem so interwoven one can't effectively disentangle them.

A recent president launched his career as the poster child of New York tabloids, which, long before the emergence of the anti-liberal-elite Fox News brand, uniquely appealed to disaffected working-class Americans. The tabloids helped create the media marriage between the billionaire Trump and working-class readers, planting a seed of populism before it fully blossomed in 2016. "Tabloid media played a central role in building the foundations of Trump's political identity," Geoffrey Baym (2019) observed, in a perceptive analysis of the 45th president, who, as far back as the 1990s, proclaimed that "the show is *Trump*" (pp. 396, 406). Trump's image as a self-made, devil-may-care celebrity real estate builder, who refused to let effete liberal institutions stand in the way of his unrestrained libido, resonated with the mythic values of many blue-collar Americans. Far from serving as Trump's detractor, the media he castigated as president co-created his brazen brand in a symbiotic relationship that helped the media cultivate audiences, enabled Trump to create a fictive image, and allowed disaffected working-class Americans to believe they found a hero who would champion their cause.

After the tabloids and Trump co-constructed his image, Trump was ready for the screen. He appeared in a movie and a TV sitcom before launching a big-time reality show, *The Apprentice*. The show gave him a telegenic presence that was more exciting than the real estate deals he negotiated in his non-TV life: a tinsel brand, famous image ("coming down a gleaming escalator, an image he cribbed for his campaign kickoff"), and a platform he used to build an audience, filled with razzmatazz, messages of hope for voter-viewers, and increasingly incendiary statements, offered to a celebrity-hungry press (Poniewozik, 2019a, p. A16). Other presidents have exploited TV entertainment for political gain: Richard Nixon appeared on the '60s variety show *Laugh-In*, and Bill Clinton belted out his saxophone on *The Arsenio Hall Show* (Parkin, 2015). However, Trump was unique in that his political brand (also a media-age phrase) was inseparable from television—his creation of a TV celebrity profile, tough-guy hosting of *The Apprentice*, and symbiotic relationship with Fox News. "TV was his soul mate," observed media critic James Poniewozik (2019b). "Everything he achieved, he achieved by using TV as a magnifying glass, to make himself appear bigger than he was." He did the same with social media, cultivating a powerful, distinctive political communication style that thrilled supporters and repulsed adversaries, even as it falsely suggested he was a thriving billionaire when, in reality, he was beset by millions of dollars in financial losses (Buettner, Craig, & McIntire, 2020). Just as television saw an opportunity to monetize Trump's celebrity status, Twitter did as well, thrilled that it could capitalize on Trump at a time when it needed highly visible media stars to grow its nascent brand (Roose, 2021).

This panoply of American media-politics is viewed every day through the window of pop culture, an area with which it is seamlessly linked. This includes late-night talk shows, constant chatter on Twitter, wickedly funny conservative lampooning of political correctness, creepy, doctored Joe Biden pictures on Pinterest, T-shirts making fun of Biden's telling the president to shut up at the first presidential debate, and satirical songs—like a remake of Don McLean's "American Pie" that featured an anti-Trump refrain, "No, don't let democracy die," sung to the music of McLean's 1971 ballad (Founders Sing, 2020).

Political communication, the focus of this book, is a realm frequently lampooned (for good reason, given some of the cartoonish characters who parade across the mediated stage). People view the political communication environment as foolish, mean-spirited, prejudiced, and corrupt. There is much truth to this view, as discussed in the previous chapter. Yet, at the same time, communication is a centerpiece of democracy, a critical arena for the diffusion of democratic discourse. In this chapter and those that follow, I will help you appreciate what may seem like a distant realm: how media construct our high-adrenaline, ego-driven, and ideologically polarized world of contemporary politics. Our aim is to understand the processes of political communication, mediated communication effects on citizens and elections, and broader philosophical issues, such as whether the media landscape advances democratic aims. We want to criticize political communication when it fails to achieve democratic ideals and celebrate it when it spurs citizens to work collectively to change the status quo.

But let's get something straight at the get-go. When you talk about politics, many people's eyes glaze over. They don't think about their own lives, but about gridlock in Washington and how Congress can't accomplish anything. Or maybe they think about Stephen Colbert, Seth MacFarlane's *Family Guy*, or an uproarious YouTube political video, and crack a smile. But—you know what?—they're wrong. Politics and political communication affect us all, whether we like it or not.

If you're a college student working full-time who lost her job due to the coronavirus, you were relieved to have received a $1,200 check from the government as part of a $2 trillion stimulus package that Democrats and Republicans contentiously debated, but finally passed to cushion some of the hardship workers faced. But with a couple of years left before you claimed your degree, you may have been devastated that your parents had trouble getting federal assistance for their business, such as a children's clothing store, while mega-corporations like Boeing and wealthy real estate investors reaped huge benefits. You may have been furious when you discovered that a friend who was nervous she got the virus had to wait 2 weeks to get her test results, but wealthy people in New York City, who had the money to sign up for medical concierge practices, got their results in 24 hours (Goodman, 2020). Politics—the lack of government-coordinated streamlined testing for all—contributed to the disparity.

If you are nearly done with college and breathe a sigh of relief because you will still be covered on your parents' health insurance until you are 26, politics provided a benediction. Obama's health care legislation let you stay on your parents' plan; the health care law was bitterly contested (and still is)—nothing if not political.

Or perhaps concerned about the senseless death of unarmed African Americans at the hands of police, you marched through the streets to protest George Floyd's death in 2020, feeling you had a moral obligation to show your disgust at centuries-long oppression of African American citizens.

Or, on the other end of the political spectrum, you may be angry that liberal critics focused endlessly on bad things they claim Donald Trump did as president rather than crediting him for his many accomplishments: record-shattering economic gains (prior to the coronavirus) and standing up to Chinese stealing of American technology companies' intellectual property. Perhaps you posted comments on topics such as these. Or maybe you feel strongly about abortion and have participated in pro-life demonstrations to display your moral commitment to the preservation of human life.

Maybe, just maybe, you are someone who has strong political interests or attitudes on issues such as these, channeling your passions to volunteer in election campaigns, or helping create the social media arm of a mayor's community outreach efforts. Or perhaps you are on the other end of the spectrum— cynical, convinced that our politics is full of vitriol and news is hopelessly biased. You find politics as it is practiced in America conniving, cunning, and at times corrupt. In either case, far from being indifferent, you have attitudes toward politics, ideas about current political issues, feelings about candidates running for office, and perhaps a commitment to exercise your right to vote in local and national elections. Politics may not be as foreign as you may have assumed.

With these issues as a backdrop, this chapter introduces political communication, beginning with definitions of basic terms—*politics* and *political communication*—and moving to a description of the key features of contemporary political communication.

## POLITICS

What thoughts cross your mind when someone mentions "politics"? Gridlock? Corrupt wheeling and dealing? Bloviating politicians? Endless one-sided diatribes on Fox News, CNN, and MSNBC marked by condemnation of the other side? Nonstop acrimonious posts from dogmatic Democrats and rabid Republicans?

Does that cover it?

Notice I didn't say anything positive. That's because for most people, the word "politics" evokes sighs, recriminations, and even disgust. It has been this way for years in America. Distrusting politicians—"them bums"—goes back to the late 19th century, if not before, when Mark Twain called politicians "dust-licking pimps," and cartoonists such as Thomas Nast depicted politicians as "vultures and rats" (Grinspan, 2014, p. A19). Although democracy involves a popularly elected government accountable to the public, Americans have historically derided elected officials and even the concept of government (Schutz,

1977). Long before television shows like *Veep* viewed politicians with derision, *Scandal* focused on their venality, and *House of Cards* dramatically conveyed the lengths to which politicians will go to maintain power, humorists and writers looked disdainfully at America's politicians and the messages they deliver.

And so it is today. "It's just words," voters tell pollsters, when asked to describe their views of politics. One voter lamented that politics involves "such a control of government by the wealthy that whatever happens, it's not working for all the people; it's working for a few of the people" (Greenberg, 2011, p. 6). We say "it's just politics" when we want to deride the actions of elected representatives. But political scientist Samuel Popkin offers a different view, noting that the phrase "it's just politics" is "the saddest phrase in America, as if 'just politics' means that there was no stake" (Morin, 1996, pp. 7–8).

Consider this: One of the greatest presidents of the United States was "one of the most astute professional politicians the country has produced" (Blumenthal, 2012, p. 34). Abraham Lincoln cut deals, gave political favors, and applied canny strategic skills to persuade Congressmen to approve the Thirteenth Amendment, which abolished slavery from the U.S. Constitution. When one Congressional representative indicated he would support the amendment, the president rewarded him by appointing him as minister to Denmark. Lincoln recognized that "great change required a thousand small political acts" (Blumenthal, p. 35). The Steven Spielberg movie *Lincoln* celebrates Lincoln's moral and political achievements in persuading Congress to pass the Thirteenth Amendment (see Figure 2.1).

Politics calls up negative associations, but it can be harnessed for good, as well as pernicious, outcomes. Without politics, landmark legislation on civil rights, Medicare, the minimum wage, tax reform, health care, and the $1.9 trillion COVID-19 relief bill would never have been enacted. Absent political achievements, the U.S. (during George W. Bush's administration) would not have invested in a global AIDS program that gave millions of African AIDS patients

**Figure 2.1 Abraham Lincoln showcased the ways politics could be harnessed for morally positive ends. He used the tools of political persuasion to convince Congress to pass the Thirteenth Amendment that abolished slavery.**

*Source*: www.istockphoto.com/vector/abraham-lincoln-gm482763363-16114717

life-saving drugs. Without politics, the American public would not have elected Barack Obama the first African American president, viewed by diverse generations of Americans as one of the most consequential political events of their lifetimes (Deane, Duggan, & Morin, 2016). Kamala Harris wouldn't have served as the first Black female vice president, inspiring millions of young women. Absent politics and the power of protest, Americans would not have changed their attitudes toward racial issues in policing after George Floyd's death, and NASCAR would still allow Confederate flags at its racetracks.

During the throes of civil unrest that followed the death of George Floyd at the hands of a Minneapolis police officer in 2020, Stacey Abrams (2020), a prominent Black politician, acknowledged that "voting feels inadequate in our darkest moments." She then emphasized the importance of political action—voting, coalition-building, and protest. "Voting will not save us from harm, but silence will surely damn us all," she wrote (see Figure 2.2). So too will silence from other political activities, from campaigning to organizing social movements. The same theme was championed by former President Barack Obama in a speech to the 2020 Democratic National Convention. He warned that if people gave up on politics, then "democracy withers, until it's no democracy at all."

**Figure 2.2 Stacey Abrams, a prominent Democratic politician, has emphasized that politics can be a force for change. Acknowledging that voting can feel inadequate in times of despair, she stressed that the political action may not "save us from harm, but silence will surely damn us all."**

*Source*: www.gettyimages.com/detail/news-photo/democratic-politician-stacey-abrams-speaks-to-the-media-news-photo/1188999034?adppopup=true

Politics can be a force for change, as well as an impediment to progress. It has accomplished great things, but has stifled innovation. It can inspire pride as well as disgust.

What is politics, more broadly and formally? Pulling together different definitions (Lasswell, 1936; Offe, 1984; Wolin, 1996), focusing on their commonalities and the foundational aspects, I define **politics** as: the public clash and debate among groups (who have different degrees of power) regarding resources, visions, and policies, with the goal of reaching broad-based decisions that are binding on, and may benefit, the larger collective.

People sometimes lament why there has to be so much arguing in the political domain. One reason frequently overlooked is that issues are complicated, leaders have different ideas on how to solve problems, and easy answers elude us. Do you allow abortions, even if they involve cruel, sometimes inhumane procedures, or ones that offend many people? How do you interpret the Second Amendment? Does the use of the term "well-regulated militia" mean that, more than 200 years after the clause was written, individuals are free to own and carry guns, even if they're not part of a militia per se? Should colleges be tuition free, even if that would give an unfair benefit to wealthier universities? Was Facebook's policy of giving employees 10 weeks of paid time off to take care of a child whose school closed due to the coronavirus fair to other employees without kids, who now had to shoulder some of the responsibility? People diverge sharply on these issues, displaying a range of values and emotions.

Politics is rife with passion and controversy. It is a unique domain in which power, compromise, and strong values—racial justice, women's rights, and free speech—make uneasy alliance. Because politics has a multitude of components—quest for power; harnessing storied symbols such as the flag; advocating strong, sometimes unpopular positions in the face of public opposition; and brokering agreement among diverse constituents—it can be conflicted and full of sound and fury. Politics is the domain where people express their opinions, exercise their will, and try to change society. It can be ineffectual, is rarely pretty, but perhaps wasn't meant to be. It is the arena in which democracy's citizens and representatives clash in public, argue, organize into partisan groups, and try to develop policies that can improve the lives of hundreds of millions of people, who place their trust, frequently reluctantly, in political leaders. Politics, flawed and impactful, is endemic to democracy. Unfortunately, politics has devolved. The spirit of compromise and focus on coalition-building that have produced political change look to be a relic of the past. Rabid partisanship and public display of resentments—tweeted each day by the left and the right— have paralyzed politics, making it a performance art of indignation (Brooks, 2020). But it need not be this way.

A couple of centuries ago, you could explain American politics without talking much about the media. In the 19th century, political party bosses ran the show. A coercive quid pro quo frequently operated: Bosses gave jobs to immigrant voters, and in exchange immigrants gratefully voted the party line. Chomping cigars and spewing smoke into the political air, party leaders played a key role in selecting party nominees. This has changed. The road to the White House winds through CNN, Fox, and *The New York Times*, while snaking through Twitter, Facebook, and countless blogs.

"Political life in any mass society is impossible without established methods of political communication," Pye (1993) observed (p. 443). As Esser (2013) noted, the major aspects of the political system—socialization of citizens, candidate selection, elections, and governing—are performed to a considerable degree via mediated communication. At the most basic level, citizens learn about political events from the media, increasingly on their smartphones. Citizens' preferences are widely diffused through media-communicated or media-constructed opinion polls. Candidates must persuade and leaders must govern by harnessing the media to productive ends. The media offer a common forum by which all this comes together, sometimes helping society move forward, but in other cases polarizing and dividing society into camps.

## DEFINING POLITICAL COMMUNICATION

Political communication. It's an abstract phrase, an ambiguous, fraught two words that, once you start thinking, call to mind so many ideas—electoral shenanigans, the storied ideals of democracy, and the ubiquitous, in-your-face media—that it's hard to know what to think when someone utters the words or you contemplate taking a course in this area. Yet the term "political communication" is important because it cuts to the core of contemporary democratic government. So just what does it mean?

Scholars have defined political communication in a variety of ways (Pye, 1993; Blumler, 2014; Jamieson & Kenski, 2014; Denton & Kuypers, 2008; McNair, 1995; Powell & Cowart, 2003). The definitions emphasize that political communication cuts a large swath across the public landscape, encompassing citizens, the media, campaigns, government, and even social movements. They stress the flow of messages between two different institutions—political and media—that are disseminated to, and processed by, a nation's citizenry.

Although politics and media overlap, they are fundamentally different institutions. Politics is about the allocation of resources and decision-making by representatives elected to serve constituents' needs. Media are organizations powered by technologies that intercede between the communicator and message recipients, diffusing opinions through public space, dramatizing political debate, interpreting public issues, and enabling people to participate, frequently acrimoniously, in political discourse (e.g., Marcinkowski & Steiner, 2014). Building on these definitions and scholarship in the field, I define **political communication** as: a complex, communicative activity in which language and symbols, employed by leaders, media, citizens, and citizen groups, exert a multitude of effects on individuals and society, as well as on outcomes that bear on the public policy of a nation, state, or community.

It's a general, all-purpose definition without any of the anger and exhilaration that propel political communication. Those of you with strong political attitudes may find the definition almost antiseptic. Fair enough. But, to a considerable extent, this is what we want in social scientific definitions of concepts—a comprehensive, multifaceted view of a phenomenon that can be bent, viewed, and examined from different philosophical viewpoints, one that sets the stage for understanding political communication. More broadly, we want a clear, erudite definition that, with normative yardsticks, can help us determine whether political communication fulfills democratic objectives or is a dismal failure.

## COMPONENTS OF POLITICAL COMMUNICATION

There are seven core dimensions of political communication (see Table 2.1). The next sections review each of them in detail.

### 1. Complex Bridge Between Political and Media Institutions

Political communication is distinctive in that it does not focus solely on media, or on political institutions, but on both. It involves the intersection of two different social institutions, with different philosophical frameworks, organizational imperatives, and societal roles. The American news media are, in the main,

**Table 2.1 Core features of political communication.**

1. Complex communicative activity bridging political and media institutions
2. Emphasizes symbols, language, and the different meanings symbols call up
3. Is fundamentally a mediated experience
4. Centered on technology, with changing online technologies influencing delivery and reception of messages
5. Revolves around diverse, multifaceted media, marked by a decline in journalistic gatekeepers
6. Involves interplay among three key players: leaders, media, and citizens
7. Operates on a worldwide basis, with commonalities across borders, and differences as a function of a country's economic and political structures

private, for-profit businesses, with journalistic traditions, that have grown up with strong norms of openness, distrust of politicians, and First Amendment freedom. Social media companies are also huge capitalist entities that make money by (controversially) monetizing people's private information, distributing news and information through algorithmic rules, with little regard for the values that animate journalism.

Campaign organizations and government institutions are concerned with political issues—winning elections and administering public programs. Campaigns want to win; candidates aspire to power. Government serves a multitude of purposes, balancing the public's needs with the interests of influential actors from the private and public sectors, working within bureaucratic constraints that can stifle change. The two institutions—political and media—differ in the aims, cultures, and roles they play in a democratic system.

Some scholars argue that the media, with its focus on finding stories that emphasize sometimes trivial conflicts between candidates, is particularly unsuited to playing a core role in an electoral system that should emphasize broader issues of interest to the bulk of citizens (Patterson, 1993). Others believe that the out-in-the-open theater of contemporary media politics cultivates a more transparent, democratic political discourse than the Whites-only, closed-door, smoke-filled rooms of yore. Nowadays, on social media there is continued debate about where to draw the line between tolerance of freewheeling expression of opinions, on the one hand, and barring speech that offends, disrespects, symbolically threatens, or is out-and-out false on the other hand.

Political communication effects can occur on the **micro level**, affecting individuals' thoughts, candidate assessments, feelings, attitudes, and behavior. Political advertisements and presidential debates work on this level, trying to change attitudes in pursuit of persuasion. News also bolsters strong attitudes, primes emotions, and can influence how people interpret complex issues.

Political communication also works on the **macro level**, exerting broad-based effects on public opinion, institutional change, political activism, and public policy. *The Washington Post*'s groundbreaking coverage of President Nixon's unethical actions during the Watergate scandal of the early 1970s led to macro-level institutional changes, such as the appointment of a special prosecutor, a series of Senate hearings, which ultimately paved the way for Nixon's resignation, and campaign finance regulations to stave off political corruption. The nonstop 24/7 lewd news coverage of President Clinton's affair with Monica Lewinsky created the groundwork for Clinton's impeachment in 1998. The slew of tweets, online news, and mobile phone alerts about Trump's attempts to press a Ukrainian leader to investigate his political rivals gave gravitas to Democrats' drive to impeach him in 2019.

In all of these cases, as Schudson (1995) notes,

> the news constructs a symbolic world that has a kind of priority, a certification of legitimate importance. . . . When the media offer the public an item of news, they confer upon it public legitimacy. They bring it into a common public forum where it can be discussed by a general audience.
>
> (pp. 19, 33)

And although this is complicated today by the large number of partisan news sites, when it comes to consequential political events (such as presidential elections and impeachments), the media are the electronic stage which broadly display, legitimize, and sometimes undercut the processes by which leaders are deemed suitable or unfit for public office. By repeatedly and carefully explaining that Joe Biden had amassed the electoral votes needed to win the 2020 election, the news media legitimized his victory, symbolically drowning out, at least for most Americans, false accounts spreading across social media that the electoral results were riddled with fraud. And when the news covered the January 6 rampage at the Capitol, reporters conveyed the horror of what happened, underscoring the importance of a peaceful transfer of presidential power.

A core focus of political communication is power. Politics revolves centrally around the pursuit and exercise of power, with its Machiavellian, strategic, and inequitable aspects. Political communication involves messaging designed to influence diverse components of a complex political universe.

Thus, as Jay G. Blumler (2015) observed, political communication is a multilevel phenomenon, with effects on individuals and social systems, as well as connections among media organizations, political institutions, and the electorate. It represents a unique confluence of politics and media, "a volatile politics-media axis" (p. 426). Yet increasingly, as discontent with democracies broadens and false information continues to circulate, disruptive political communication is becoming the new normal (Bennett & Pfetsch, 2018; Bennett & Livingston, 2018),

Disruptions can bring about helpful change or they can unleash chaos and feelings of hopelessness. It is important to remember, when discussing these diverse disruptions, that political communication takes place in a larger political, economic, and social system. It reflects the system and can produce changes, but is enmeshed in a larger structure. Political communication can be frustrating when it showcases incivility, institutional intransigence, and established leaders' refusal to make radical policy changes, as on issues such as climate change. Yet there is a limit to what political communication can do. It can't by itself foment revolutions or structural reforms. It can, however, in concert with reform-minded leaders and groups, set an agenda for change, galvanize groups, and frame issues in ways that mobilize social movements. It can also clarify issues and offer forums for discussion of ideas. The extent to which it propels—or retards—political change is a complex, important issue, discussed at various points in this book.

## 2. Symbols and Language

Political communication involves a seemingly endless number of messages from different actors. Messages are simultaneously sent, interpreted, tweeted, comprehended, miscomprehended, and received differently, depending on individual biases, institutional objectives, and political goals.

Political communication is the domain of words and symbols, with leaders using "language to move people to think and act in ways that they might not otherwise think and act" (Ball, 2011, p. 42). Presidents, including Franklin Delano Roosevelt, Ronald Reagan, and Barack Obama, harnessed language to arouse the imagination of Americans, using speech to captivate, symbols to mobilize, and metaphors to galvanize support for their policies (Hart, 1984). FDR's "the only thing we have to fear is fear itself"—heard as families huddled together listening to radio sets during the cold, despairing days of the 1930s Depression—emotionally moved listeners, offering up hope and optimism, activating the collective confidence of a country (Euchner, 1990). Reagan's rhetoric about America as a "shining city on a hill" evoked patriotism, while Obama's eulogies after incidents of gun violence offered a sense of unity and hope, albeit short-lived. Trump's famous slogan, MAGA (Make America Great Again), instilled pride in many Americans, who were frustrated by the economic and social effects of a global economy.

Presidents can also use words deceptively to maintain power or disguise risky decisions, like President Richard Nixon did with his description of the U.S. military "incursion," rather than "invasion," of Cambodia in 1970. Nixon also used the slogan "law and order" as a racial dog whistle to appeal to Whites' fear of Black crime (Nunberg, 2016). Words are often weapons that maintain elite control. Scholar Murray Edelman (1964, 1971), viewing politics through the lens of symbolic construction, described ways that leaders construct political action by applying symbols that reify power. He argued that campaigns are essentially political spectacles by which politicians cleverly exploit patriotic symbols and cherished group meanings to promote the interests of the few rather than the many.

The language of political communication is laden with symbols. A **symbol** is a form of language in which one entity represents an idea or concept, conveying rich psychological and cultural meaning. There also can be powerful visual elements, as when a tattoo is an emblem of White supremacist hate or forming a V by holding up the index and middle finger is the world-famous peace sign (Bucy & Joo, 2021).

Symbols commonly include words such as *justice*, *freedom*, and *equality*, as well as the flag, a patriotic object so redolent with symbolism that candidate Barack Obama was patently asked why he chose not to wear a flag pin on his lapel during a 2008 Democratic debate in Philadelphia. (After the dust-up, he decided to wear the pin.) Flags, in different countries and regions of a country, are powerful symbols. In southern states such as Mississippi, the Confederate flag was long viewed as an emblem of the state's centuries-old heritage, until years of protest against this view culminated, after the George Floyd protests, in a new understanding of the racist underpinning of the flag. In June 2020, Mississippi did what was long thought politically impossible: It removed the Confederate battle emblem from the state flag.

In America, elected officials frequently invoke the Founding Fathers, Lincoln, Jefferson, freedom, and equality. The founders of the conservative political group, the Tea Party, harnessed the symbolism of the colonial-inspired political protest, associating their group with the cause of liberty and freedom from government control. During the all-encompassing coronavirus pandemic of 2020, Trump enlisted the imagery of war, saying "we are fighting an invisible enemy." It was a worthy metaphor, but it fell short in that we weren't battling a human adversary with a poisonous ideology. Instead, we were in the throes of a global health crisis; there were no soldiers drafted by their nation to combat an enemy force, but private citizens, doctors, and nurses trying to save lives (Blow, 2020).

Symbols can be apt or inept, but they are conferred to convey meaning to foreboding events. Words convey different meanings to different groups. Symbols are increasingly objects of fractious debate. To conservatives, particularly rural Americans, guns symbolize liberty, freedom from meddlesome government encroachment, and even preservation of a way of life in an increasingly alien culture (Hayes, 2016). For liberals, guns represent violence tearing at the fabric of America and senseless devastation of innocents and loved ones.

The term "socialism" conjures different symbolic associations, linked with communism and government seizing of private property, in the view of some conservatives. To many young people, particularly supporters of Bernie Sanders, the self-described democratic socialist who ran for president in 2020, socialism does not have these negative connotations and is linked with good things, such as providing government health care to all Americans. In fact, socialism is a complex philosophical term, with different attributes and roots in some government control of market functions. Although Sanders was not, by economic criteria, a radical socialist who sought to nationalize private markets or employ central planning to run the economy, he was frequently branded one by political opponents, who wielded the "socialism" label as a political cudgel, given its negative connotations in American politics (Krugman, 2020). It was therefore ironic that Republicans, who emphasized their antipathy to big government and cast the Democrats as socialists, had to grudgingly acknowledge that the $2 trillion coronavirus economic stimulus package that included billions in loans for businesses and $1,200 payments to ordinary Americans (reminiscent of Democratic primary contender Andrew Yang's proposal) had socialist overtones. It was truly "politics through the looking glass," as the virus muddied traditional right versus left positions, a testament to the complexity of political issues, which symbols obfuscated (Rutenberg, 2020).

In a world of ethnic frustrations and entrenched group loyalties, it is fanciful to presume that symbols can be decoupled from perceptions and the emotions they evoke in individuals from different political sectors. Thus, the term Brexit—the moniker for the United Kingdom's withdrawal from the European Union in 2016 (British exit)—is powerful, precisely because it elicits images of a proud England slavishly controlled by European bureaucrats to its supporters and a Britain dangerously unmoored from global realities to its opponents. In a similar fashion, Trump's tweets to "Build the Wall" and his "Make America Great Again" mantra appealed to working-class Whites frustrated by inequalities exacerbated by globalization, as well as the sense that the Norman Rockwell-esque culture in which they grew up had been thrown under the bus by educated, multicultural elites. Trump's populist symbols elicited scorn and loathing from opponents when he used them as cudgels to attack minority groups (Shear et al., 2019). Increasingly, political symbols, once badges of unity, are wedges that divide more than they bring us together.

Symbols are part and parcel of politics, the objects inseparable from the meanings they convey. Just think about how a piece of cloth designed to protect one's health during the coronavirus outbreak took on outsize proportions. Masks symbolized government interference in people's lives to conservatives, a necessary instrument for public health to liberals, and an object to shame people who weren't strictly following health rules to social justice warriors. In Asian countries, mask wearing has long symbolized good hygiene and consideration for others, but in the U.S. it became an object of partisan rift, a political, rather than public health, symbol.

## 3. Mediation and Mediatization

By definition, political media *mediate* between citizens and institutions of government (Iyengar, 2004; Strömbäck & Kaid, 2008), but the media are far from neutral, bland go-betweens. They apply their own judgments and rules, in this way transforming politics (Mazzoleni & Schulz, 1999). If there is one concept that captures the media's role in transforming contemporary politics, it is **mediatization**. Mediatization emphasizes not simply that media come between politicians and citizens, but how media have transformed the structural relations of politics in society. As Jesper Strömbäck and Frank Esser (2014) helpfully observe, the mediatization of politics is "a long-term process through which the importance of the media and their spill-over effects on political processes, institutions, organizations and actors have increased" (p. 6).

Mediatization can be viewed as the process by which the media have come to play a central role in politics, influencing institutions, performing strategic functions for political elites (Van Aelst & Walgrave, 2016), imparting information (and misinformation), socializing young citizens into civic society, creating the public spectacle we call politics, and serving as the playing field on which politics occurs (Jones, 2010). People do not experience politics directly, unless they are among the small minority of individuals who canvass for candidates door-to-door, do volunteer work for political advocacy groups, or participate in political protests. As Strömbäck (2008) notes, "The mediated reality becomes more important than the actual reality, in the sense that it is the mediated reality that people have access to and react to" (p. 238).

When we talk about mediatization, we emphasize the ways media have influenced the practice of politics and set basic ground rules. Because of social media's emphasis on memorable memes and emotional tweets, candidates must demonstrate immediacy and authenticity, even if they squeeze complexity out of the issue. Candidates must communicate in the argot of the media—short, encapsulated soundbites and brief, clever tweets. Candidates must adapt to "media logic" for covering campaigns, adjusting to the news media's focus on conflict, novelty, big personalities, and dramatic made-for-TV moments (e.g., Altheide & Snow, 1979).

As scholars have long emphasized, the presidential nominating process, in particular, revolves around the news media. Publicity advances a candidacy, poor primary debate performance or post-debate coverage can impair it, and cable networks sponsor pre-primary debates, sometimes deciding who participates based on media-circulated polls, the debates taking on a "Hunger Games aura," raising "the question of whether unaccountable media institutions should determine the roles of accountable politicians" (Blumler, 2014, p. 37). Even non-electoral campaigns, such as for the nomination of a Supreme Court justice, are waged via media, comporting with the logic of diverse media platforms and harnessing the vast armamentarium of contemporary political marketing (Manheim, 2011). Partisan groups spend millions on Facebook ads with dark images and intense language to influence public opinion.

The relationship between media and politics cuts both ways. The political system, guided by an overall political logic, influences media, just as media influence politics. The nomination system has a set of rules that candidates must follow. Their media strategies reflect the timing of the primaries, and number of convention delegates at stake, and the hegemony of two-party politics in America. When national crises ensue, government can impose limits on news-gathering, and government institutions manipulate the news that citizens receive.

The notion that political media are governed by an overarching, homogenous media logic may oversimplify issues today (Esser & Strömbäck, 2014). There may no longer be a singular media logic, but different logics that vary as a function of the interplay of mass and social media, electoral context, and the country in which the campaign occurs (Kunelius & Reunanen, 2016; Schulz, 2014).

## 4. Media Technology

Media technology effects on politics occurred long before the advent of network news, Facebook, and Twitter. The popularity of newspapers among elites in early America helped build political parties, paving the way for blistering attacks on candidates from Hamilton to Jackson that makes today's negative campaigning look tame by comparison. The introduction of photojournalism in the mid-19th century gave voters the chance to view the visage of candidates for elective office, foreshadowing the rise of image politics. Magazines, from *McClure's* in the early 20th century, which revealed corporate abuses, to *Ramparts* in the 1960s, with its no-holds-barred, left-wing exposés of Vietnam-era deceptions that anticipated websites of today (Grimes, 2016), offered platforms for investigative journalism. Radio gave citizens the first aural exposure to distant events, offering a personal connection to world affairs. Television transformed politics by providing graphic, live exposure to tragedies, such as assassinations and wars, as well as presidential debates, highlighting the role of visual images, suddenly a major player in political campaigns (Flew & Swift, 2015). TV also elevated the importance of news in society, as television became a fixture in American homes, and viewing the half-hour newscast became an accepted family dinner ritual. Journalists, who for years were longer on scruff than flash, became celebrities and their version of news was viewed, for a time, as veridical, objective, and of preeminent importance.

Political communication is now a multimedia game. It is not just 24/7 news on a small television screen, but second-by-second updates and posts on very small cell phone screens, with editors curating content at social media platforms such as Snap, Twitter, and Facebook. Digital technologies now comprise a "fifth estate," complementing traditional news media (the fourth estate, which historically built on the clergy, nobility, and common people—the first, second, and third estates, respectively; see Dutton & Dubois, 2015).

Long before Twitter's blue bird became part of its branded logo, political leaders used the media to communicate about politics. Ronald Reagan, appreciating the visual format of the television medium, harnessed props, visual devices, and pictures, such as TV cameras panning on magnificent monuments, to access patriotic themes (Jamieson, 1988). Reagan was so consumed by visual media that on at least two occasions he called on words eliciting military bravery, suggesting they had come from the Defense Department when they actually were excerpts from old movies. The Reagan White House was consumed by image management, scripting Reagan's remarks, and coming up with "the line of the day" that would provide a way to market and organize his communications with the press.

Reagan, a consummate political media performer, was an actor, who had to take into account the personal depth of the people he was portraying. However, former president Donald Trump, as a reality TV star, brought a different understanding of media genres to his political role. "Playing a character on reality TV means being yourself, but bigger and louder," Poniewozik (2019b) notes, adding that:

> Being real is not the same thing as being honest. To be real is to be the most entertaining, provocative form of yourself. It is to say what you want, without caring whether your words are kind or responsible—or true—but only whether you want to say them.

For Trump, who told his staffers "to think of each presidential day as an episode in a television show in which he vanquishes rivals," the outrageous, unrestrained world of reality television and presidential politics were inseparable, for better or worse, depending on your view (Haberman, Thrush, & Baker, 2017, p. 1). Even when he was sick, the show went on; hospitalized with the virus, Trump left the hospital for a short motorcade ride around the hospital's perimeters to project an image of strength, even though he put others who rode with him in the vehicle at risk (Poniewozik, 2020; Baker & Haberman, 2020).

Trump was consumed by news coverage, beginning his day by watching cable news coverage, especially Fox, which he put on a pedestal, and even MSNBC, allowed in "for rage viewing" (Rogers & Karni, 2020, p. A1). During the virus outbreak, his consummate focus was on how his performance—his management of the virus crisis—was assessed in the news media and how he could exploit media to his advantage. Throughout his administration, he used social media, notably Twitter, so frequently and vociferously that he flooded the zone, commandeering the news cycle. As soon as one of his tweets or comments provoked outrage, he sent out another, supplanting the latest outrage with yet another controversy.

Trump's craving for public attention—and his need, like other presidents, to manipulate appearances to bolster an image—reached a low during protests outside the White House in the wake of the death of George Floyd. Seeking to demonstrate strength as "your president of law and order," Trump decided to walk across Lafayette Square to a nearby church, where he could hold a Bible, a symbol that would resonate with Americans. But to do this, police had to forcibly remove protesters with tear gas and violence, injuring demonstrators and infringing on their First Amendment rights. His supporters enjoyed the show of strength against a group of disrespectful demonstrators who maliciously taunted the president. But his critics, including some Republicans, called it "a ham-handed photo opportunity" that interfered with the right to dissent (Baker et al., 2020).

**Twitter.** Online messaging plays a critical role in the presidential election. It is no longer the mass media election, as Thomas Patterson (1980) dubbed it, but the interactive media election, tweeted election, or "all media all the time" election. Twitter has become a weapon of power in the new hybrid media system, which political communicators—presidents, protest leaders, and political campaigns—strategically use to achieve their goals and undermine the objectives of their adversaries (Chadwick, 2017).

Campaigns deploy a digital cocktail of media technologies to influence voters, harnessing messages that are exquisitely targeted to particular voters' social media profiles (Stromer-Galley, 2014). They also circumvent journalistic mediation, reaching the public directly by distributing live videos of convention speeches to followers across the nation (Shear & Corasaniti, 2016). The game is still power, but the techniques are refined and more personalized, harnessed by politicians, remarked upon by journalists on the ubiquitous Twitter, and discussed by politically minded citizens in their social networks (Jungherr, 2014). Social media has transformed political campaigns, reducing the power of traditional gatekeepers, such as mainstream journalists, while increasing the ability of insurgent candidates (think Trump in 2016) to develop a following on Twitter, enabling challengers to build a base of support around issues and personality characteristics. When it comes to protests on the right and the left, social media are indispensable, recruiting demonstrators to events and relaying graphic videos that highlight interpretations that are favored by protesters.

If, in a macro fashion, print cultivates cognitive analysis and television encourages a focus on the visually compelling, Twitter favors affective immediacy and partisan emotions—what one writer called "140-character bursts of id" (Manjoo, 2016, p. B1). Twitter, columnist Bret Stephens (2020) notes, "is speech designed for provocations and put-downs; for making supporters feel smug; for making opponents seethe; for reducing national discourse to the level of grunts and counter-grunts."

Political leaders—Trump on the right and New York City Congresswoman Alexandria Ocasio-Cortez on the left—tweet short, simple, seemingly authentic messages that turbocharge their electoral base. Twitter helps elites control the political universe, and sometimes the agenda. Tweets do this by corralling followers to leaders' political space, capturing news media attention, dominating discussion, and directing the public to these corners of the online world.

Like all media technologies, Twitter is harnessed for positive and negative political purposes. Trump—who viewed Twitter as "his Excalibur," the modern equivalent of King Arthur's magical sword—transformed Twitter into a political weapon during his 2016 campaign with his thousands of presidential tweets (Haberman, Thrush, & Baker, 2017, p. 1; Shear et al., 2019). To his credit, he mobilized voters who might be otherwise alienated from the political process. At the same time, his tweets were frequently factually incorrect—filled with false statements, sometimes promoting conspiracy theories. Trump's tweets regularly attacked groups (particularly news organizations, with the exception of Fox News, which usually received praise), and they frequently excoriated racial minorities and immigrants, as when he called a majority-Black district in Baltimore a "disgusting, rat and rodent infested mess" and told four Congresswomen of color to "go back" to the countries they came from, branding Ocasio-Cortez, one of the four House members, a "wack job" (Shear et al., 2019).

Ocasio-Cortez, or AOC as she is popularly known, responded by calling Trump "a criminal who betrays our country," pleasing her liberal supporters but frustrating those who regard it as inappropriate to tweet back to a president in this manner. (People differed on the appropriateness of her responses, with some finding them offensive, and others elated that a woman House member refused to take guff from the male chief executive.) Yet she too could be drawn into aggressive excess, as when she blocked a former New York City elected official from her Twitter account merely because he criticized her, a decision that violated constitutional protection of free speech (Gold, 2020). Unquestionably, Ocasio-Cortez creatively branded herself with her tweets, exciting supporters and encouraging young people to participate in politics (see Figure 2.3).

Twitter's effects are complex. Leaders' tweets, at their best, can inspire citizens to become involved in politics; at their worst, they can incite mobs to violence. (Citing concerns that his tweets could inspire violence like the January 6, 2021 riot, Twitter banned Trump permanently from its site two days after the melee.) But Twitter is not all-powerful. The mobilizing impacts that Trump's tweets exerted on his base were offset by the negative coverage his more outrageous tweets received in mainstream media. This in turn led some voters who supported him in 2016 to oppose him in 2020. Political technologies do not speak in one voice, but in many.

**All Politics Is Public Now.** Another effect of technology on political communication concerns the ways so much information is out in public now. Online media have pushed into public view content that would have been hushed up years ago, a function of both digital technologies and the notion that the public has a right to know intimate details about politics (Schudson, 2015), a norm that would have shocked the privacy-obsessed Founding Fathers. It is now out there—public, porous, for citizens to peruse—and the content is frequently salacious.

During the vitriolic 2016 campaign, the release of a lewd 2005 video revealed Trump boasting, in tawdry terms, of how he could grope women and get away with

**Figure 2.3  If, as Shakespeare said, brevity is the soul of wit, it is also the soul of Twitter, one of the most influential political communication platforms. New York City Congresswoman Alexandria Ocasio-Cortez used Twitter to build an army of loyal followers who admire her politics, style, and forthright tweets, though she has been drawn into aggressive excess.**

*Source*: Stock Image ID: 10595655a

www.shutterstock.com/editorial/image-editorial/two-trillion-dollar-coronavirus-covid19-stimulus-package-reached-at-us-house-washington-usa-27-mar-2020–10595655a

"anything" because he is a celebrity. Unlike previous eras, when there was no video or digital recording of lascivious, offensive comments, the information here— Trump's remarks, the voice that spoke them, and the face shown in the video—were indisputably Trump's, giving the revelations instant credibility and political combustibility (Barbaro & Healy, 2016; Burns, Haberman, & Martin, 2016).

This was hardly the last time sex abuse became enmeshed with issues of political power. In September 2018, a professional psychologist, Christine Blasey Ford, told a packed Senate Judiciary Committee and national television audience that Supreme Court nominee Brett Kavanaugh had sexually assaulted her in high school, an allegation that would never have been revealed publicly a generation ago. Ford's allegation tapped into very different partisan reactions. It resonated with liberals, who were outraged that a man who had committed sexual assault was being considered for the Supreme Court, and infuriated conservatives, who doubted the veracity of her account, angry that a possibly distorted memory would bring down a capable Supreme Court justice. (Kavanaugh was narrowly confirmed in a strict party-line vote.) The public nature of the dispute tarnished the reputation of the Court and the credibility of a number of senators from both parties. But it also put sexual assault at the political foreground and served notice that the most powerful men in society would be held to account for what they had done, or rather, for acts they allegedly committed. Liberals were gratified that sexual abuse was at last the focus of discussion in the corridors of public power, but conservatives lamented that an act of questionable veracity clouded the judicial issues at stake in the nomination.

In all of these cases, online, digital media have made possible revelations that would have been kept behind closed doors in years past, a testament to the eviscerated boundaries between private and public, and the ways that contemporary technologies have put virtually everything out in the open, for better and sometimes worse. The sordid, sometimes salutary blending of private and public in contemporary life raises questions about whether we are better off when information that would have been hushed up and kept private is now squarely in the public domain, or whether intrusions on political leaders' private lives are inappropriate, coarsening our public discourse and exposing children to socially inappropriate information that diminishes their faith in politics (Meyrowitz, 1986).

## 5. Diverse, Multifaceted Media and the Decline of Gatekeeping

Pundits typically refer to the media as an all-powerful singular term, invoking the powerful aura of other monolithic entities such as the Vatican or the Establishment. They utter the phrase, as one word, in a dry, stentorian tone, or they speak it derisively, as when critics talk about The Liberal (or Capitalist) Media. In fact, there are many media and diverse media platforms: newspapers with their online websites, local TV news, talk radio, 24/7 cable TV news programs, blogs, ideologically partisan political websites, and the complex array of citizen-journalist posts (Baker & Blaagaard, 2016).

It is misleading to lump all of these platforms together under the moniker "media." There are differences among media in terms of their functions, aims, structure, and economic foundations. For many years in political communication, the term "media" was synonymous with "news media," or conventional journalism.

As noted in the last chapter, for much of the 20th century, the news media were the centerpieces, the key nodes, *the* "gatekeepers" in the flow of information from the powers-that-be to the people. Typically, government officials would relay facts, proposals, and policy announcements through the main news outlets of the time—newspapers, radio, and broadcast news. News organizations—transforming the information into news so it was more dramatic, up-to-date, and had the patina of sober importance—transmitted it dutifully to the public. "That's the way it is," as the news anchor Walter Cronkite intoned, at the end of each weekday's evening newscast. Of course, news did not offer a perfect rendition of the political world. Journalists projected a host of pro-status-quo biases, as well as perspectives guided by the economics and professional routines of news.

And yet how quaint, how simple, how linear, unidirectional, and centered on the once-powerful conventional news the process once was. Nowadays, it is very different.

**Who Let the Dogs In? How Gatekeeping Has Been Transformed.** "Anyone who influences your physical or mental space, anyone who has the ability to place news or content in those spaces—or take it out—that's real power," a technology writer said (Warzel, 2020). These content controllers are the keepers of our informational gates, society's gatekeepers. **Gatekeeping** is the process of crafting the seemingly infinite amounts of information that permeates society into "the limited number of messages that reach people each day" (Shoemaker & Vos, 2009, p. 1). From a democratic perspective, the concept is important because it determines the flow of political information, the fundamental bricks and mortar needed for communication in a democratic society. Citizens, after all, cannot effectively participate in democracy, activists cannot push for change, and leaders cannot competently govern in the absence of reliable information about political issues.

News gathered by reporters now sits side-by-side stories produced by a host of other groups, which vary greatly in their integrity and commitment to tried-and-true journalist values. Conventional mainstream news organizations—national newspapers, magazines, and television—are still important, particularly when the news concerns health epidemics, foreign crises, and national elections, where people are particularly likely to tune into news and journalists can persuasively frame the issues of the day. In the 2020 election, mainstream journalists reclaimed their role as responsible gatekeepers by repeatedly calling out Trump on his anti-democratic actions (Kreiss, 2020). Recognizing that Trump had exploited the classic media model to his advantage, they decried Trump's false statements, such as that the election was fraudulent and that he had won, resolving "to stop the flow of disinformation for the good of democracy," as Sarah Oates (2020) observed.

But danger signs remain. The advent of a host of online news platforms—Breitbart News on the right and The Intercept on the left—have cut into mainstream news's audience, with their predictable right- and left-wing takes on politics. Some of the large cable news sites, such as Fox News and MSNBC, provide a reliably partisan spin on news that appeals to, and pleasantly reinforces, the biases of their audience. News is now a fraught term that encompasses more than journalism, involves information whose provenance is unknown or unclear, can be hard to verify, and gyrates across the Internet via outlets that did not gather the information, posts that are shared by like-minded others or, at their worst, through extremist sites that harvest false, conspiracy theory–laced speculations gaining increased credibility through the heuristic that if they are posted by multitudes, they must therefore be true.

Communication scholars used to lament how the media inculcated a pro-System set of facts that told only one very limited side of the story. If only there were more choices, critics said, then people could develop a more thoughtful, skeptical perspective on politics. Well, the flow of political messages is less top-down, we have more diverse media fare, and people don't all tune into the same homogenized content, but there are drawbacks aplenty. Be careful what you wish for! As Dhavan V. Shah and his colleagues (2017) note, contrasting today's news environment from that of the past:

> As the media choices and content exposure of audience members have withdrawn into more ideologically homogenous niches, divergent realties have emerged. . . . This communication ecology contributes to acceptance of ideologically consistent facts, and rejection of those facts that do not comport with a skewed social reality.
>
> (pp. 494–496)

Gatekeeping occurs in a network more of people's own liking, part of what Sharon Meraz and Zizi Papacharissi (2013) call "networked gatekeeping." Information is disseminated online, sometimes via biased sites, and through social media, which uses algorithms favoring posts that create buzzy controversy and partisan videos (Edgerly, 2020). In some cases, these sites allow extremist, prejudicial ideas to become part of public discourse, making matters worse by failing to consistently apply their own monitoring policies (Beam, 2020). It's all part of a variegated, hybrid, cacophonous news ecosystem (Chadwick, 2013)—one that prizes diversity but also poses predicaments for a democracy that requires common frameworks, as well as shared yardsticks, for determining what is true and deserving of public attention.

## 6. Interplay Among Leaders, Media, and Citizens

Political communication is dynamic, chaotic, cacophonous, hardly linear, never going in just one direction rather than the other, but active, intersectional, and interactional. Scholars like to simplify the process by breaking it down into its constituent parts.

Political communication involves the flow of messages among leaders (politicians and candidates), media, and citizens. (In the political science literature, leaders are called elites, which strikes some observers as a holier-than-thou way of describing these actors in the political process.) Political candidates can initiate the process with a statement, policy pronouncement, or tweeted criticism of an opponent. The president can dominate political communication, as President George W. Bush did after the tragedy of September 11, beginning with a moving speech to the nation on September 20, 2001, in which he articulated the threats the nation faced from terrorist groups, while taking pains to show respect for Muslims in America and throughout the world. Through his rhetoric and actions, Bush rallied the country around a new and unsettling war on terror, influencing the media agenda and citizenry.

Political leaders do not always dominate political communication. Media can instigate the process, as when news about an upstart Democratic candidate named Barack Obama—with his charisma and cri de coeur, "Yes, we can"— provided a favorable picture of the young Illinois senator, helping propel Obama to victory in the primaries (Falk, 2010). More recently, it occurred with the iconic video of George Floyd's death, which changed public attitudes toward policing within weeks of its diffusion across multiple media, a function of the particular context in which the video emerged.

The public can also launch or catalyze political communication. Typically, the public makes its presence known through a disembodied, but statistically accurate, instrument: opinion polls. This occurred back in 1992 and 2008, when polls showed that voters were primarily concerned with the economy after a recession and financial crisis adversely affected financial markets. Public concern fed back to influence media coverage and candidate messaging, which in turn affected voting, so much so that it was an important reason why the party that occupied the White House was defeated in both of these elections. In the case of the 2020 coronavirus pandemic, the public's concern about safety, spurred by health experts' warnings, influenced candidate communications and news coverage, although its influences were filtered through more partisan media voices than during previous eras.

A fourth group of players in political communication—besides political leaders, news, and the mass citizenry—are the active members of the public, the sometimes opinion leaders, staunch partisan activists from the left and the right on issues spanning abortion, immigration, and health care. Online media have given partisan activists on the left and right new megaphones to influence the process.

Figure 2.4 shows how the three key political communication agents—political actors, media organizations, and the public—partake in a dynamic flow of influence, with different arrows of causal influence. It can get very complicated. There are different theories as to which player—political leaders, media, or public—is more influential and when.

Some scholars emphasize elite institutions' capacity to build the agenda in ways that reinforce the powers-that-be (Herman & Chomsky, 2002). Other scholars

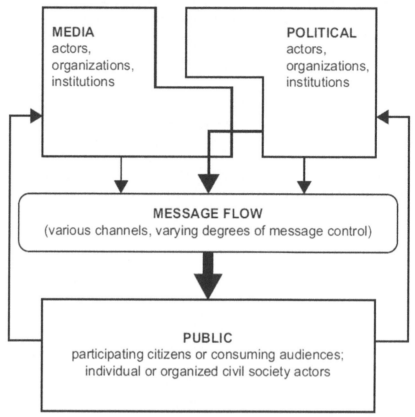

Long-term formal and informal interactions, creating "patterned" types of relationships over time

MEDIA actors, organizations, institutions

POLITICAL actors, organizations, institutions

**MESSAGE FLOW**
(various channels, varying degrees of message control)

**PUBLIC**
participating citizens or consuming audiences; individual or organized civil society actors

**Figure 2.4  A model of the flow of political communication. Political leaders, media, and the public exert a dynamic effect on political communication. Different models put the onus on different actors.**

*Source:* From Pfetsch & Esser (2012)

emphasize media power, arguing that media set the agenda and frame issues, influencing the dynamics of strategic battles for public opinion. Still others place an onus on citizens, particularly during close elections when voter concerns about hot-button issues or economic distress push candidates to be responsive.

Political communication is increasingly polycentric, or characterized by several centers, not just one monolithic voice that dominates discourse (Chadwick, 2013; Chadwick, Dennis, & Smith, 2016). And, of course, much messaging is multidirectional and filtered through partisan voices (Entman & Usher, 2018; see Chapter 8 for different models of the process).

Scholars emphasize that political communication involves a high-stakes battle among groups with varying degrees of power to influence public opinion and increasingly highly partisan bases of support. The media—both mainstream journalistic and social networking sites—are the field of battle, where competing agendas, political frameworks, and cascading opinions vie for attention and constitute the symbolic weaponry of political combat. Sometimes the interplay among the forces produces meaningful political change; far too often, anger, vitriol, polarization, and paralysis ensue.

## 7. A Global Phenomenon: Differences and Similarities Across Nations

Political communication—its warts and occasional wonders—transcends America. Political marketing takes place in electoral campaigns across the world, with political advertising and candidate branding a factor in elections in European countries, Israel, and even Russia (Lees-Marshment, 2010; Rose, 2010; Scammell, 2014).

When it comes to elections, mediatization has become coin of the realm, the common currency of elections across the world. Scholars point to four similarities in the roles played by media in election campaigns in democracies across the world: (1) Candidates adapt their strategies to fit news and interactive media technologies; (2) journalists play an important part in defining and framing political issues; (3) political marketing, opinion polling, and increasingly misinformation are campaign constants; and (4) politics is personalized, with media conveying personality attributes (frequently leaders' colossal egos), rather than focusing solely on policy issues (Esser & Strömbäck, 2012; Swanson & Mancini, 1996).

At the same time, there are substantial differences in political media among different countries, as a function of cultural, structural, and economic parameters. As Hallin and Mancini (2004) explain, a political communication system consists of smaller media and political systems, each with a series of defining characteristics. Components of the media system include the development of an autonomous, professional ethos among journalists, and formal connections between the press and political parties. Aspects of the political system include whether electoral politics are dominated by two political parties (as in the U.S) or a number of parties, such as in European countries; the degree of power-sharing among diverse political party coalitions; and whether the government intervenes in, or takes a hand-off posture toward, the news media (Pfetsch & Esser, 2012; Jungherr, Posegga, & An, 2019). Media and political system differences can influence political advertising, candidate debates, and news, such as the average length of soundbites (e.g., Esser, 2008). They also affect polarization and trust. In several European democracies, such as Germany, people trust different media outlets, regardless of their partisan attitudes. In the U.S., trust in news media outlets can follow partisan lines, intensifying partisanship and polarization (Van Aelst & Walgrave, 2019).

The overlap and differences in political media systems, along with their implications for media content and effects, form the foundation of the study of **comparative political communication** (Hallin & Mancini, 2004; Pfetsch & Esser, 2012; Esser, 2019; Esser & Strömbäck, 2012). While a detailed discussion of comparative issues is beyond the scope of this book, it is worth noting that there is no perfect political/media culture; all have strengths and shortcomings. A comparative approach to political communication is important. It reminds us that the American model is one of many, and political communication does not operate in a vacuum. Instead, media must be understood by taking into account such broader contours as the nature of the electoral system, types of media markets, how journalists define professionalism, and the extent of government intervention in media issues.

Yet for all this nuance, there are complex, sometimes disturbing, commonalities in global political communication. As noted earlier, populism has become a potent political force in the United States and across Europe. Trust in democratic institutions has declined. Disinformation via fake news occurs in a host of nations, abetted by trolls and bots. Political parties, government leaders, and rogue political activists in countries spanning Honduras, India, Azerbaijan, and Brazil have spread fake news on Facebook in an effort to undermine elections (Silverman, Mac, & Dixit, 2020). There are also increasing disruptions in the political sphere, with viscerally uncivil political discourse and mounting concerns about the integrity of elections, in light of the susceptibility of voting machines to malicious hacks (Bennett & Livingston, 2018).

Over the past several years, leaders of more than three dozen countries followed former President Trump's strategic playbook, vilifying the press, tweeting about "fake news," a moniker Trump popularized, in these ways sowing confusion and perhaps diminishing faith in democratic processes (Editorial Board, 2019). Populist leaders—Trump, India's Narendra Modi, and Hungary's Viktor Orbán—have harnessed personality-based brands of leadership, while revising democratic norms, as they primed nationalist sentiments and bypassed conventional media by speaking directly to their supporters through Twitter (Gettleman, 2019; see Figure 2.5).

New informational technologies, once hailed as a "digital utopia" that could empower citizens to circumvent oppressive government structures, have become enmeshed in these very governments, as seen in systematic disinformation campaigns waged by countries such as Russia to disrupt democratic elections (Miller & Vaccari, 2020). The Russian scheme to diffuse disinformation on social media, launched during the 2016 U.S. presidential election, is now the playbook for unscrupulous political groups worldwide (Frenkel, Conger, & Roose, 2019). An Iranian campaign, seeking to influence opinions across the Middle East and Asia, used Facebook to suggest that the U.S. government

**Figure 2.5** Political communication is a global phenomenon with features unique to particular countries and similarities that cut across national borders. Exemplifying the commonalities are populist leaders—India's Narendra Modi (top) and Hungary's Viktor Orbán (bottom)—who have been wildly popular with the public, displaying personalized brands of leadership. However, they have stoked anti-democratic sentiments by scapegoating the media and threatening to quash dissent.

*Source*: www.gettyimages.com/detail/news-photo/hungarian-prime-minister-viktor-orban-addresses-during-the-news-photo/466387860?adppopup=true
www.gettyimages.com/detail/news-photo/indian-prime-minister-narendra-modi-speaks-at-the-public-news-photo/1134962604?adppopup=true

executed the September 11 terrorist attacks. In the run-up to a 2018 Brazilian presidential election campaign, candidates' supporters diffused digital dirt on their opponents, doctoring photographs and using WhatsApp to spread misleading election information (Frenkel, Conger, & Roose, 2019). In the United Kingdom, even the elite, white-shoe Conservative Party spread a video that was deliberately edited to make it appear that the opposition candidate could not answer a question about Brexit. Misinformation has become a counterfeit coin of the political realm across the world.

## CONCLUSIONS

Politics, this chapter has emphasized, is typically inseparable from media. Yet the two arenas—media and politics—are very different institutions, with different cultures, histories, and governing philosophies. Politics, frequently disparaged, has many direct and indirect effects on our lives, reminding us that it is better to understand its effects than retreat into our personal cocoons. Politics, emphasizing the public clash among groups regarding resources and policy visions, aims to reach broad-based consensus on decisions that can benefit the larger community. Politics has produced great achievements, while also boosting the power of the few at the expense of the many.

While you could understand politics a century or more ago without considering media, today that is impossible. Political life in mass society is not possible without the intervention of media, which conveys and constructs the political spectacle. Scholars have defined political communication in different ways, and calling on these definitions, the chapter emphasized that political communication is: (1) a *complex activity* bridging political and media institutions; (2) conveyed by controversial *symbols* that can unify, but frequently divide and fractionate; (3) a *mediated experience*, with conventional and social media defining the terms in which politics is contested; (4) critically influenced by *technology* that has allowed leaders to communicate directly with citizens in an atmosphere where everything is public; (5) *multifaceted* and increasingly unmoored in an era of *declining news gatekeepers*; (6) defined by a *dynamic interplay* among leaders, media, activists, and citizens; and (7) a *global phenomenon*, with structural differences, but also commonalities, as seen in the rise in political marketing, populism, and toxic Twitter messages that some national leaders have stoked to light populist fires.

Amidst this all are the basic questions: Is politics advancing democratic aims? Does political communication enhance the public good? What unnerves the populace and ails contemporary media democracies? To grapple with these questions, we need to explore classic normative approaches, the focus of the next chapter, one that offers historic and philosophical grounding.

## REFERENCES

Abrams, S. (2020, June 4). Stacey Abrams: I know voting feels inadequate right now. *The New York Times*. Online: www.nytimes.com/2020/06/04/opinion/stacey-abrams-voting-floyd-protests.html. (Accessed: June 5, 2020).

Altheide, D.L., & Snow, R.P. (1979). *Media logic*. Beverly Hills, CA: Sage.

Baker, M., & Blaagaard, B.B. (2016). Reconceptualizing citizen media: A preliminary charting of a complex domain. In M. Baker & B.B. Blaagaard (Eds.), *Citizen media and public spaces: Diverse expressions of citizenship and dissent* (pp. 1–22). New York: Routledge.

Baker, P., & Haberman, M. (2020, October 5). As Trump seeks to project strength, doctors disclose alarming episodes. *The New York Times*. Online: www.nytimes.com/2020/10/04/us/politics/trump-virus.html. (Accessed: October 5, 2020).

Baker, P., Haberman, M., Rogers, K., Kanno-Youngs, Z., & Benner, K. (2020, June 2). How Trump's idea for a photo op led to havoc in a park. *The New York Times*. Online: www.nytimes.com/2020/06/02/us/politics/trump-walk-lafayette-square.html. (Accessed: June 3, 2020).

Ball, T. (2011). Manipulation: As old as democracy itself (and sometimes dangerous). In W. Le Cheminant & J.M. Parrish (Eds.), *Manipulating democracy: Democratic theory, political psychology, and mass media* (pp. 41–58). New York: Routledge.

Barbaro, M., & Healy, P. (2016, October 9). Why Republicans broke out in sudden revolt this time. *The New York Times*, 1, 27.

Baym, G. (2019). "Think of him as the President": Tabloid Trump and the political imaginary, 1980–1999. *Journal of Communication, 69*, 396–417.

Beam, M.A. (2020). Partisan media ecosystems and polarization in the 2020 U.S. election. In D. Jackson, D.S. Coombs, F. Trevisan, D. Lilleker, & E. Thorsen (Eds.), *U.S. election analysis 2020: Media, voters and the campaign*. Online: www.electionanalysis.ws/us/president2020/section-4-news-and-journalism/partisan-media-ecosystems-and-polarization-in-the-2020-u-s-election/. (Accessed: November 16, 2020).

Bennett, W.L., & Livingston, S. (2018). The disinformation order: Disruptive communication and the decline of democratic institutions. *European Journal of Communication, 33*, 122–139.

Bennett, W.L., & Pfetsch, B. (2018). Rethinking political communication in a time of disrupted public spheres. *Journal of Communication, 68*, 243–253.

Blow, C. (2020, March 30). The politics of a pandemic. *The New York Times*, A21.

Blumenthal, S. (2012, October 22). Lincoln plays to win. *Newsweek*, 32–38.

Blumler, J.G. (2014). Mediatization and democracy. In F. Esser & J. Strömbäck (Eds.), *Mediatization of politics: Understanding the transformation of western democracies* (pp. 31–41). London: Palgrave Macmillan.

Blumler, J.G. (2015). Core theories of political communication: Foundational and freshly minted. *Communication Theory, 25*, 426–438.

Brooks, D. (2020, June 25). America is facing 5 epic crises all at once. *The New York Times*. Online: www.nytimes.com/2020/06/25/opinion/us-coronavirus-protests.html. (Accessed: June 26, 2020).

Bucy, E.P., & Joo, J. (2021). Editors' introduction: Visual politics, grand collaborative programs, and the opportunity to think big. *The International Journal of Press/Politics, 26*, 5–21.

Buettner, R., Craig, S., & McIntire, M. (2020, September 27). Long-concealed records show Trump's chronic losses and years of tax avoidance. *The New York Times*. Online: www.nytimes.com/interactive/2020/09/27/us/donald-trump-taxes.html. (Accessed: September 30, 2020).

Burns, A., Haberman, M., & Martin, J. (2016, October 8). Tape reveals Trump boast about groping women. *The New York Times*, A1, A12.

Chadwick, A. (2013). *The hybrid media system: Politics and power*. New York: Oxford University Press.

Chadwick, A. (2017). *The hybrid media system: Politics and power* (2nd ed.). New York: Oxford University Press.

Chadwick, A., Dennis, J., & Smith, A.P. (2016). Politics in the age of hybrid media. In A. Bruns, G. Enli, E. Skogerbø, A.O. Larsson, & C. Christensen (Eds.), *The Routledge companion to social media and politics*. New York: Routledge.

Deane, C., Duggan, M., & Morin, R. (2016, December 15). *Americans name the 10 most significant historic events of their lifetimes*. Pew Research Center: U.S. Politics & Policy. Online: www.people-press.org/2016/12/15/americans-name-the-10-most-significant-historic-events-of-their-lifetimes/. (Accessed: January 7, 2017).

Denton, R.E., Jr., & Kuypers, J.A. (2008). *Politics and communication in America: Campaigns, media, and governing in the 21st century*. Long Grove, IL: Waveland Press.

Dutton, W.H., & Dubois, E. (2015). The fifth estate: A rising force of pluralistic accountability. In *Handbook of digital politics* (pp. 51–66). Cheltenham: Edward Elgar.

Edelman, M. (1964). *The symbolic uses of politics*. Urbana, IL: University of Illinois Press.

Edelman, M. (1971). *Politics as symbolic action: Mass arousal and quiescence*. New York: Academic Press.

Edgerly, S. (2020). YouTube as a space for news. In D. Jackson, D.S. Coombs, F. Trevisan, D. Lilleker, & E. Thorsen (Eds.), *U.S. election analysis 2020: Media, voters and the campaign*. Online: www.electionanalysis.ws/us/president2020/section-4-news-and-journalism/youtube-as-a-space-for-news/. (Accessed: November 16, 2020).

Editorial Board (2019, December 1). Who will tell the truth about the press? (Editorial). *The New York Times* (Sunday Review), 8.

Entman, R.M., & Usher, N. (2018). Framing in a fractured democracy: Impacts of digital technology on ideology, power and cascading network activation. *Journal of Communication, 68*, 298–308.

Esser, F. (2008). Dimensions of political news cultures: Sound bite and image bite news in France, Germany, Great Britain, and the United States. *Press/Politics, 13*, 401–428.

Esser, F. (2013). Mediatization as a challenge: Media logic versus political logic. In H. Kriesi, S. Lavenex, F. Esser, J. Matthes, M. Bühlmann, & D. Bochsler (Eds.), *Democracy in the age of globalization and mediatization* (pp. 155–176). London: Palgrave Macmillan.

Esser, F. (2019). Advances in comparative political communication research through contextualization and cumulation of evidence. *Political Communication, 36*, 680–686.

Esser, F., & Strömbäck, J. (2012). Comparing election campaign communication. In F. Esser & T. Hanitzsch (Eds.), *Handbook of comparative communication research* (pp. 308–326). New York: Routledge.

Esser, F., & Strömbäck, J. (2014). A paradigm in the making: Lessons for the future of mediatization research. In F. Esser & J. Strömbäck (Eds.), *Mediatization of politics: Understanding the transformation of western democracies* (pp. 223–242). London: Palgrave Macmillan.

Euchner, C.C. (1990). Presidential appearances. In *The presidents and the public* (pp. 109–129). Washington, DC: Congressional Quarterly Inc.

Falk, E. (2010). *Women for president: Media bias in nine campaigns* (2nd ed.). Urbana, IL: University of Illinois Press.

Flew, T., & Swift, A. (2015). Engaging, persuading, and entertaining citizens: Mediatization and the Australian political public sphere. *Press/Politics, 20,* 108–128.

*For local news, Americans embrace digital, but still want strong community connection* (2019, March 26). Pew Research Center (Journalism & Media). Online: www.journalism.org/2019/03/26/for-local-news-americans-embrace-digital-but-still-want-strong-community-connection/. (Accessed: February 19, 2020).

Founders Sing (2020, February 6). *The day democracy died.* Online: www.youtube.com/watch?v=-Ue5F57dZMU. (Accessed: June 22, 2020).

Frenkel, S., Conger, K., & Roose, K. (2019, February 1). After Russia, false posts on Twitter going global. *The New York Times,* B1, B7.

Gettleman, J. (2019, May 21). India's voters seem poised to reward Modi's populist approach. *The New York Times,* A1, A7.

Gold, M. (2020, November 2). Ocasio-Cortez apologizes for blocking critic on Twitter. *The New York Times.* Online: www.nytimes.com/2019/11/04/nyregion/alexandria-ocasio-cortez-twitter-dov-hikind.html. (Accessed: March 18, 2021).

Goodman, J.D. (2020, August 31). A quick virus test? Sure, if you can afford it. *The New York Times.* Online: www.nytimes.com/2020/08/31/nyregion/rapid-coronavirus-test.html. (Accessed: September 2, 2020).

Greenberg, S.B. (2011, July 31). Why voters tune out Democrats. *The New York Times* (Sunday Review), 1, 6.

Grimes, W. (2016, August 26). Warren Hinckle, editor of *Ramparts* and voice for radical left, dies at 77. *The New York Times,* B14.

Grinspan, J. (2014, September 13). Don't throw the bums out. *The New York Times,* A19.

Haberman, M., Thrush, G., & Baker, P. (2017, December 10). The president versus the presidency. *The New York Times,* 1, 22–23.

Hallin, D.C. (1986). *The "uncensored war": The media and Vietnam.* New York: Oxford University Press.

Hallin, D.C., & Mancini, P. (2004). *Comparing media systems: Three models of media and politics.* New York: Cambridge University Press.

Hart, R.P. (1984). *Verbal style and the presidency: A computer-based analysis.* Orlando: Academic Press.

Hayes, D. (2016, August 21). Donald Trump takes aim. *The New York Times* (Sunday Review), 1, 7.

Healy, J., Robertson, C., & Tavernise, S. (2020, March 2). How response to virus is already being seen through partisan lens. *The New York Times,* A21.

Herman, E.S., & Chomsky, N. (2002). *Manufacturing consent: The political economy of the mass media.* New York: Pantheon.

Iyengar, S. (2004). Engineering consent: The renaissance of mass communications research in politics. In J.T. Jost, M.R. Banaji, & D.A. Prentice (Eds.), *Perspectivism in social psychology: The yin and yang of scientific progress* (pp. 247–257). Washington, DC: American Psychological Association.

Jamieson, K.H. (1988). *Eloquence in an electronic age: The transformation of political speechmaking*. New York: Oxford University Press.

Jamieson, K.H., & Kenski, K. (2014). Political communication: Then, now, and beyond. In K. Kenski & K.H. Jamieson (Eds.), *The Oxford handbook of political communication*. Online: www.oxford.handbooks.com. (Accessed: July 17, 2016).

Jones, J.P. (2010). *Entertaining politics: Satiric television and political engagement* (2nd ed.). Lanham, MD: Rowman & Littlefield.

Jungherr, A. (2014). The logic of political coverage on Twitter: Temporal dynamics and content. *Journal of Communication, 64*, 239–259.

Jungherr, A., Posegga, O., & An, J. (2019). Discursive power in contemporary media systems: A comparative framework. *The International Journal of Press/Politics, 24*, 404–425.

Kreiss, D. (2020). Media and social media platforms finally begin to embrace their roles as democratic gatekeepers. In D. Jackson, D.S. Coombs, F. Trevisan, D. Lilleker, & E. Thorsen (Eds.), *U.S. election analysis 2020: Media, voters and the campaign*. Online: www.electionanalysis.ws/us/president2020/section-5-social-media/media-and-social-media-platforms-finally-begin-to-embrace-their-roles-as-democratic-gatekeepers/. (Accessed: November 16, 2020).

Krugman, P. (2020, February 13). Bernie Sanders isn't a socialist. *The New York Times*. Online: www.nytimes.com/2020/02/13/opinion/bernie-sanders-socialism.html. (Accessed: February 29, 2020).

Kunelius, R., & Reunanen, E. (2016). Changing power of journalism: The two phases of mediatization. *Communication Theory, 26*, 369–388.

Lasswell, H. (1936). *Politics: Who gets what, when, how*. New York: McGraw-Hill.

Lees-Marshment, J. (2010). Global political marketing. In J. Lees-Marshment, J. Strömbäck, & C. Rudd (Eds.), *Global political marketing* (pp. 1–15). New York: Routledge.

Manheim, J.B. (2011). *Strategy in information and influence campaigns: How policy advocates, social movements, insurgent groups, corporations, governments, and others get what they want*. New York: Routledge.

Manjoo, F. (2016, November 17). Social media's globe-shaking power. *The New York Times*, B1, B7.

Marcinkowski, F., & Steiner, A. (2014). Mediatization and political autonomy: A systems approach. In F. Esser & J. Strömbäck (Eds.), *Mediatization of politics: Understanding the transformation of western democracies* (pp. 74–89). London: Palgrave Macmillan.

Markovits, D. (2019). *The meritocracy trap: How America's foundational myth feeds inequality, dismantles the middle class, and devours the elite*. New York: Penguin Press.

Mazzoleni, G., & Schulz, W. (1999). "Mediatization" of politics: A challenge for democracy? *Political Communication, 16*, 247–262.

McNair, B. (1995). *An introduction to political communication*. London: Routledge.

Meraz, S., & Papacharissi, Z. (2013). Networked gatekeeping and networked framing on #Egypt. *The International Journal of Press/Politics, 18*, 138–166.

Meyrowitz, J. (1986). *No sense of place: The impact of electronic media on social behavior*. New York: Oxford University Press.

Miller, M.L., & Vaccari, C. (2020). Digital threats to democracy: Comparative lessons and possible remedies. *The International Journal of Press/Politics, 25*, 333–356.

Morin, R. (1996, February 5–11). Tuned out, turned off. *The Washington Post National Weekly Edition*, 6–8.

Müller, P., Schemer, C., Wettstein, M., Schulz, A., Wirz, D.S., Engesser, S., & Wirth, W. (2017). The polarizing impact of news coverage on populist attitudes in the public: Evidence from a panel study in four European democracies. *Journal of Communication, 67*, 968–992.

Norris, P., & Inglehart, R.F. (2019). *Cultural backlash: Trump, Brexit and authoritarian populism*. Cambridge, UK: Cambridge University Press.

Nunberg, G. (2016, July 28). Is Trump's call for "law and order" a coded racial message? *NPR*. Online: www.npr.org/2016/07/28/487560886/is-trumps-call-for-law-and-order-a-coded-racial-message. (Accessed: June 22, 2020).

Oates, S. (2020). The day the music died: Turning off the cameras on President Trump. In D. Jackson, D.S. Coombs, F. Trevisan, D. Lilleker, & E. Thorsen (Eds.), *U.S. election analysis 2020: Media, voters and the campaign*. Online: www.electionanalysis.ws/us/president2020/section-4-news-and-journalism/the-day-the-music-died-turning-off-the-cameras-on-president-trump/. (Accessed: November 18, 2020).

Offe, C. (1984). *Contradictions of the welfare state*. Cambridge, MA: MIT Press.

Parkin, M. (2015). *Talk show campaigns: Presidential candidates on daytime and late night television*. New York: Routledge.

Patterson, T.E. (1980). *The mass media election: How Americans choose their president*. New York: Praeger.

Patterson, T.E. (1993). *Out of order*. New York: Knopf.

Pfetsch, B., & Esser, F. (2012). Comparing political communication. In F. Esser &T. Hanitzsch (Eds.), *Handbook of comparative communication research* (pp. 25–47). New York: Routledge.

Poniewozik, J. (2019a, May 9). A titan of business (at least that's who he played on TV). *The New York Times*, A16.

Poniewozik, J. (2019b, September 6). The real Donald Trump is a character on TV. *The New York Times*. Online: www.nytimes.com/2019/09/06/opinion/sunday/trump-reality-tv.html. (Accessed: January 17, 2020).

Poniewozik, J. (2020, October 4). Sick with Covid, Trump tries to paint the picture of health on TV. *The New York Times*. Online: www.nytimes.com/2020/10/04/arts/television/trump-covid-19.html. (Accessed: October 5, 2020).

Powell, L., & Cowart, J. (2003). *Political campaign communication: Inside and out*. Boston: Allyn and Bacon.

Pye, L.W. (1993). Political communication. In V. Bogdanor (Ed.), *The Blackwell encyclopedia of political science* (2nd ed., pp. 442–445). Cambridge, MA: Blackwell.

Riccardi, N., & Fingerhut, H. (2019, November 14). AP-NORC/USA Facts poll: Americans struggle to ID true facts. *AP News*. Online: https://apnews.com/c762f01370ee4bbe8bbd20f5ddf2adbe. (Accessed: January 11, 2020).

Rogers, K., & Karni, A. (2020, April 24). No rallies and no golf, just the TV to rankle him. *The New York Times*, A1, A5.

Rojas, H., & Valenzuela, S. (2019). A call to contextualize public opinion-based research in political communication. *Political Communication, 36*, 652–659.

Rojecki, A., & Meraz, S. (2016). Rumors and factitious informational blends: The role of the web in speculative politics. *New Media & Society, 18*, 25–43.

Roose, K. (2021, January 9). In pulling Trump's megaphone, Twitter shows where power now lies. *The New York Times*. Online: www.nytimes.com/2021/01/09/technology/trump-twitter-ban.html. (Accessed: January 10, 2021).

Rose, J. (2010). The branding of states: The uneasy marriage of marketing to politics. *Journal of Political Marketing, 9*, 254–275.

Rosenberg, M., Perlroth, N., & Sanger, D.E. (2019, January 10). Voting security evolves. So do Russian trolls. *The New York Times*, A1, A16-A17.

Rutenberg, J. (2020, April 5). Politics through the looking glass: Virus scrambles the left-right lines. *The New York Times*. Online: www.nytimes.com/2020/04/05/us/politics/coronavirus-democrats-republicans-trump.html. (Accessed: April 6, 2020).

Salam, M. (2018, August 24). The persistence of Stormy Daniels. *The New York Times*. Online: www.nytimes.com/2018/08/24/us/politics/stormy-daniels-cohen-donald-trump.html. (Accessed: January 19, 2020).

Scammell, M. (2014). *Consumer democracy: The marketing of politics*. New York: Cambridge University Press.

Schudson, M. (1995). *The power of news*. Cambridge, MA: Harvard University Press.

Schudson, M. (2015). *The rise of the right to know: Politics and the culture of transparency, 1945–1975*. Cambridge, MA: Belknap Press of Harvard University Press.

Schulz, W. (2014). Mediatization and new media. In In F. Esser & J. Strömbäck (Eds.), *Mediatization of politics: Understanding the transformation of western democracies* (pp. 57–73). London: Palgrave Macmillan.

Schutz, C.E. (1977). *Political humor: From Aristophanes to Sam Ervin*. Rutherford, NJ: Fairleigh Dickinson University Press.

Shah, D.V., McLeod, D.M., Rojas, H., Cho, J., Wagner, M.W., & Friedland, L.A. (2017). Revising the communication mediation model for a new political ecology. *Human Communication Research, 43*, 491–504.

Shane, S., & Blinder, A. (2018, December 19). Secret experiment in Alabama Senate race imitated Russian tactics. *The New York Times*. Online: www.nytimes.com/2018/12/19/us/alabama-senate-roy-jones-russia.html. (Accessed: January 8, 2020).

Shear, M.D., & Corasaniti, N. (2016, July 25). Live videos, small screens: Campaigns hope voters like what they see. *The New York Times*, A12.

Shear, M.D., Haberman, M., Confessore, N., Yourish, K., Buchanan, L., & Collins, K. (2019, November 2). How Trump reshaped the presidency in over 11,000 tweets. *The New York Times*. Online: www.nytimes.com/interactive/2019/11/02/us/politics/trump-twitter- presidency.html. (Accessed: January 19, 2020).

Shoemaker, P.J., & Vos, T.P. (2009). *Gatekeeping theory*. New York: Routledge.

Silverman, C., Mac, R., & Dixit, P. (2020, September 14). "I have blood on my hands": A whistleblower says Facebook ignored global political manipulation. *BuzzFeed News*. Online: www.buzzfeednews.com/article/craigsilverman/facebook-ignore-political-manipulation-whistleblower-memo. (Accessed: September 21, 2020).

Stephens, B. (2020, June 5). Donald Trump is our national catastrophe. *The New York Times*. Online: www.nytimes.com/2020/06/05/opinion/donald-trump.html. (Accessed: June 6, 2020).

Stout, D. (2019, May 28). Edmund Morris, presidential biographer, dies at 78. *The New York Times*, A25.

Strömbäck, J. (2008). Four phases of mediatization: An analysis of the mediatization of politics. *International Journal of Press/Politics, 13*, 228–246.

Strömbäck, J., & Esser, F. (2014). Mediatization of politics: Towards a theoretical framework. In F. Esser & J. Strömbäck (Eds.), *Mediatization of politics: Understanding the transformation of western democracies* (pp. 3–28). London: Palgrave Macmillan.

Strömbäck, J., & Kaid, L.L. (2008). A framework for comparing election news coverage around the world. In J. Stromback & L.L. Kaid (Eds.), *The handbook of election news coverage around the world* (pp. 1–18). New York: Routledge.

Stromer-Galley, J. (2014). *Presidential campaigning in the Internet age.* New York: Oxford University Press.

Swanson, D.L., & Mancini, P. (1996). Patterns of modern electoral campaigning and their consequences. In D.L. Swanson & P. Mancini (Eds.), *Politics, media, and modern democracy: An international study of innovations in electoral campaigning and their consequences* (pp. 247–276). Westport, CT: Praeger.

Van Aelst, P., & Walgrave, S. (2016). Information and arena: The dual function of the news media for political elites. *Journal of Communication, 66,* 496–518.

Van Aelst, P., & Walgrave, S. (2019). The Information and Arena Model: Its value and limitations. *Political Communication, 36,* 203–207.

Waisbord, S., Tucker, T., & Lichtenheld, Z. (2018). Trump and the great disruption in public communication. In P.J. Boczkowski & Z. Papacharissi (Eds.), *Trump and the media* (pp. 25–32). Cambridge, MA: MIT Press.

Warzel, C. (2020, September 22). America's tech billionaires could help protect the election. If they wanted to. *The New York Times.* Online: www.nytimes.com/2020/09/22/opinion/sunday/2020-election-security-tech.html/. (Accessed: September 28, 2020).

Wolin, S.S. (1996). Fugitive democracy. In S. Benhabib (Ed.), *Democracy and difference: Contesting the boundaries of the political* (pp. 31–45). Princeton, NJ: Princeton University Press.

# 3 Philosophy, Democracy, and Political Communication

Do you know that famous Churchill quote about democracy? You may have come across it and never knew it had been uttered by the great British prime minister and wordsmith. It's a classic, pithy, substantive statement about democratic government.

Democracy, opined Winston Churchill—the British prime minister who led his country through the dark days of World War II only to face domestic troubles as prime minister after the war—is the worst form of government, except for all the others. It sounds good, until you ask yourself what all the others really are, and if they're so bad—like fascism, for example—then democracy's philosophical victory is not all that impressive.

Churchill's quote is regularly bandied about in political philosophy circles (see Figure 3.1). One reason is its choice of words. It sets up an expectation, with the use of the superlative adjective "worst," that an unfavorable picture is to be drawn of democracy only to upend it with a surprising turn of phrase. The phrase is disarmingly clever. But it's also disarmingly glib and, by the darkened lights in democratic societies today, seems like a sleight of hand that allows us to forgive democracy for all its sins.

What is democracy? Does it serve noble philosophical ends, or is it tainted beyond repair, sullied by economic, political, and communicative shortcomings? How do we reconcile democracy's deficits (Norris, 2011) with its deliverables? These are important questions for a political communication book to ponder, as thoughtful political communication is a component of democracy at its finest, while dismal political communication is cause and effect of democracy on the ropes.

This chapter takes a **normative** approach to democracy, focusing on the ethical or philosophical frameworks that provide prescriptive guidelines for a phenomenon. Taking a normative approach, I will examine perspectives on what democracy *should* do, discussing ways that it departs from these ideals, and offering a balance sheet on the state of democracy and democratic political communication, particularly in the U.S., where it has faced persistent pressures. You probably have opinions about politics—perhaps that it's too angry, or not angry enough, or is controlled by the rich and powerful. Opinions are the oxygen of democracy, and they are to be celebrated and appreciated. But—there is always a "but" when we talk about politics!—we need a yardstick against which we can evaluate these criticisms, a broader vantage point with which to examine the state of politics today. We need to know just what democracy means, its core components, and where it has fallen short of crowning philosophical ideals.

**Figure 3.1 Winston Churchill, the great British prime minister and wordsmith, penned the most famous paradoxical aphorism about democracy.**

*Source*: https://en.wikipedia.org/wiki/File:Sir_Winston_Churchill_-_19086236948.jpg

This chapter begins by introducing three normative perspectives on democracy. The second section defines democracy and looks at its checkered history in the U.S. The third portion of the chapter discusses the many shortcomings in U.S. democracy. The final section offers reflections on democracy, with its implications for political communication.

## CLASSICAL PHILOSOPHICAL PERSPECTIVES

### Greek Democracy

Current views of democracy flow from the strengths and flaws of previous philosophical perspectives and the voluminous scholarly literature on democracy. They build on classical direct democracy in Athens, Greece, where a quorum of 6,000 Athenians met more than 40 times each year, discussing, debating, and making policy on taxes, foreign alliances, and declaration of war. For the

**Figure 3.2 The Greek philosopher Aristotle championed political communication, arguing that the good life involves active participation with others on common political tasks.**

Greeks, the centerpiece of democracy was the demos, the populace of the ancient city-state. The Greek model presumed that individuals directly participated in everyday legislative and judicial activities. In the Greeks' direct democratic model, citizens were expected to participate in politics. The statesman Pericles put it bluntly: "We do not say that a man who takes no interest in politics is a man who minds his own business; we say that he has no business here at all" (Held, 2006, p. 14).

Imagine a politician who uttered those words today. She or he would be called an elitist (as well as a sexist) and would be parodied on YouTube. But, for the ancient Greeks, political participation was endemic to citizenship. It was a view embraced by the great philosopher, Aristotle (see Figure 3.2).

Although civics books traditionally sing the praises of Greek democracy, it had shortcomings. The Athenian model enshrined equality, but only allowed male citizens over the age of 20 to participate in politics. Slaves outnumbered free male citizens, but they were precluded from participating in politics. Women had few civic rights and no political rights whatsoever. To paraphrase Orwell (1946), all Athenians were (in theory) equal, but free male Athenians were much more equal than others.

## Liberal Democracy

There is not one model of liberal democracy, but many. The models have been articulated by some of the most celebrated theorists of democracy, including John Locke, John Stuart Mill, and James Madison. Liberal democratic concepts, which emphasize individual rights and representative government, are popularly associated with democracy. However, liberal democracy theorists do not use the term "liberal" in the sense that we use it today, as when we refer to liberal Democrats. Theoretically, the term corresponds more closely to "libertarian," emphasizing a system of democracy that preserves individual liberties and disdains government intervention.

Liberal perspectives on democracy emphasize *the natural rights of individuals*—their right to life, liberty, property, and pursuit of happiness, to combine the writings of Locke and Thomas Jefferson. This was exciting and important stuff, the notion that individuals had inalienable rights that government could not sever. Liberal democratic approaches have emphasized that an individual should be allowed to follow his (much later, her) own drummer in matters of speech, press, religion, and economics. People needed a sphere of life where despotic monarchs could not intervene. Thus, liberal theories embraced the *private sphere*: for example, private enterprise and private property.

Appreciating that society's size discouraged participation by everyone, liberal theorists recognized that the Athenian notion of direct democracy was impractical for mass society. They advocated **representative government**, in which citizens elected others to stand in for them and represent their viewpoints on matters of policy. Elections provided a way to ensure that individuals determined government policy, making "public officials the servants rather than the masters of the citizenry" (Katz, 1997, p. 63). It was a good concept in theory, but, like all democracies, American democracy had to articulate rules for voting—specifically which citizens got to vote. As we now know, the rules were prejudiced from the get-go. Voting was cruelly limited to Whites and those who owned property. Even now, there remain exclusionary problems, laws that restrict voting in ways that punish minorities.

In its 19th-century formulation, liberal democracy accorded an important role to the communication of politics. With its emphasis on the private market, liberal democracy theorists viewed politics as a marketplace of ideas, in which a variety of media products—good and bad, accurate and inaccurate—competed for audience attention. Just as different products compete in the economic market, political ideas collide in the intellectual marketplace. In the end, some philosophers argued, truth will win out. Noting that "people are able and willing to put aside their social biases," liberal theorists emphasized that "the best way to guarantee truth in the public sphere is free, open, and unchecked debate in which both error and truth have equal access" (Christians et al., 2009, p. 49). The press was the instrument by which this happened.

In a freewheeling, acrimonious social media age, these ideas meet with resistance. If people are algorithmically tuned into their own media outlets that spit back only what they already believe, how can they ever come across a correction to an incorrect belief? How can truth collide with error if people refuse to accept the error of their ideological ways? When fictitious reports spread with warp speed across social media, reaching hundreds of millions, sometimes overwhelming truthful information, how can one maintain that truth can overwhelm falsehood? Or should we trust people's ability to ferret out falsehoods, resist government intervention, and maintain an unchecked political debate, where fakery and truths battle it out? Complicating matters still, are there times when an all-encompassing defense of free speech blinds one to instances when posts are so racist and sexist that they do not deserve to be aired in a public forum?

## Deliberative Democracy

Deliberative democracy theorists, the newest intellectual kids on the democracy block, take issue with liberal democratic theory. Deliberative democracy advocates look at liberal democracy through a different set of lenses, noting that liberalism's elevation of the individual encourages the pursuit of untrammeled self-interest, furthering a system in which personal selfishness trumps community values. They argue that the marketplace metaphor diminishes the deeper role that politics ought to play in the lives of its citizens. Voters are not mere *consumers* choosing among different political brands, but *citizens* whose thoughtful participation in politics serves as the foundation for democratic government. Politics, they emphasize, should not focus simply on protecting the *rights* of individuals, but on discovering ways to enhance the collective *good of* society. They urge "an imaginative rethinking of democracy offering a new kind of participation, one that not only gives citizens more power, but also allows them more opportunities to exercise this power thoughtfully" (Held, p. 235).

The cornerstone is the concept of deliberation. Unlike conversations or dialogue, deliberation focuses on tackling a shared social or political problem with the goal of coming up with solutions. It involves civil disagreements among people, assessments of the merits of different arguments, willingness to revise opinions in light of ideas put forth by other discussants, and participation in the hard work of devising a solution that is workable and pleasing to all or most parties (Chambers, 2003; Stromer-Galley, 2007).

Based on these distinctions, Stromer-Galley (2007) defines **deliberation** as "a process whereby groups of people, often ordinary citizens, engage in reasoned opinion expression on a social or political issue in an attempt to identify solutions to a common problem and to evaluate those solutions" (p. 3). On a broader level, deliberation helps citizens view the public sphere as a vital arena in which they can contribute (Jacobs, Cook, & Delli Carpini, 2009; Habermas, 1996). Deliberation also prizes civility and respect for different political views, sorely lacking in today's politics.

Deliberative democracy has its share of drawbacks. It sadly underestimates the difficulty of partisans reaching agreement when they disagree on the pivotal assumptions underlying core issues. It is also hard to implement, with so few opportunities to bring people of different perspectives together. But it does suggest a strategy for improving the quality of democratic discourse.

## DEFINING DEMOCRACY

Each of the three perspectives celebrates democracy, focusing on different elements. Classical Greek democracy prizes citizen participation, liberal democracy emphasizes individual rights, while deliberative democracy highlights the importance of thoughtful discussion of public issues.

By braiding the different strands of these approaches, we can appreciate the core characteristics of democratic government. The term *democracy* is a prosaic idea, an everyday platitude, a term advocates throw into a conversation when they want to bolster their side, like a child who says that a popular classmate supports her idea. Yet it is also a noble idea, and "its core idea is disarmingly simple: as members of a community, we should have an equal say in how we conduct our life together" (Bradatan, 2019, A19). But therein complications lurk, for there are many conceptions of what is meant by an equal say and how it should be harnessed to help members of a community conduct their lives together. Democracy, as we have seen, is a multifaceted term, defined differently over the years and subject to much scholarly discussion. By integrating the work of scholars, one gains insights into underlying aspects of the concept.

**Democracy** has eight core characteristics, some focused on the centerpiece of demos, the populace which participates in elections, others on individual and civil liberties, derived from classic liberal democracy, and other aspects concerned with the public good, based on deliberative democracy and related normative ideas. Thus, democracy is a form of government that:

1. presupposes the right of all adult citizens to vote and run for office;
2. holds free, fair elections that involve competition between more than one political party;
3. guarantees the legitimacy of free, fair elections by insisting that winning and losing candidates graciously accept the electoral outcome;
4. grants citizens individual liberties and freedom of expression, including those who oppose the party in power;
5. ensures protection of human rights, notably those of minorities, or others out of step with the majority;
6. grants the news media freedom to cover events and challenge the powers-that-be;
7. presupposes a civil society characterized by the right to form associations, such as parties and interest groups, that attempt to shape the agenda and influence public policy; and
8. provides opportunities for reasoned public deliberation.
   (Coleman & Blumler, 2009; Dahl, 1989; Kriesi, 2013; *The Economist*, 2013)

Nations clearly differ on these characteristics, and democracy can be viewed as lying along a continuum on different categories, from elections to individual rights to civility of the public sector.

While the majority of the people in the world choose their governments freely, there is variability in the degree to which these countries can be viewed as full democracies (Kriesi, 2013). Some countries, as much as 30 percent of the world's nations, have virtually no democratic characteristics; they are authoritarian regimes. Russian elections are more charade than truly democratic, and Chinese repression of ethnic minorities reveals its anti-democratic values. Other countries, such as those in Latin America and Eastern Europe, are defective democracies, lacking some of the core democratic characteristics, such as free and fair elections. Countries whose leaders impose controls over opposition parties, imprison anti-government activists, or threaten journalists—such as Hungary, Nicaragua, and Serbia—are case studies of imperiled democracies. Freedom House, an organization that supports and monitors democracies, has found that in recent decades democracies have declined in their protection of political rights and civil liberties for a number of reasons, notably the increase in national leaders with autocratic tendencies and their supporters' willingness to trample on democratic norms (Freedom House, 2019).

## The Checkered Story of Democracy, American-Style

The United States has its own spotty history of democratic governance. Using the prior eight attributes as a democratic yardstick, it is patently clear that the United States—for all the rhetoric and textbook socialization—did not qualify as a democratic society throughout much of the 19th and 20th centuries. We like to think of the American Revolution as blazing new paths for democratic government, and the revolution did achieve important social and political goals (Wood, 1991). But during the 19th century, when slavery deprived Blacks of their freedom and dignity, forcing them to endure unimaginable physical and emotional cruelty, the U.S. was not a democratic society. Southern political leaders feared Black suffrage, claiming it would grant political power to "ignorant, stupid, demi-savage paupers" (Blight, 2020). For years African Americans could not vote or run for office. When barriers were lifted, but Jim Crow laws restricted voting and barred Blacks from elective office (among other monstrous restrictions), elections remained neither free nor fair (see Figure 3.3). Literacy tests were rigged so Blacks could not vote. Lynching was countenanced by authorities. When other minorities were also treated with prejudice and could not contest the party in power, liberty and individual freedom hardly reigned.

Thanks to civil rights protests and sweeping legal, as well as institutional, changes over the past 50 years, the situation changed. The U.S. has traditionally been among the approximately 15 percent of the countries in the world that are regarded as a full democracy (*The Economist*, 2013). Yet in the wake of

**Figure 3.3  During the 19th and 20th centuries, Jim Crow laws sanctioned brutal racial segregation in the U.S., notably separate accommodations for Blacks and Whites, and widespread suffrage restrictions that disenfranchised Black people from voting and participating in politics. The U.S. was certainly not a functioning democracy during this period.**

*Source*: www.gettyimages.com/detail/news-photo/view-of-a-passengers-under-a-sign-that-reads-colored-news-photo/515058721?adppopup=true

declining trust of government and elected public officials, a prominent study downgraded the U.S. slightly, but to a sufficient degree that it dropped to the second tier category of a "flawed democracy" (*The Economist*, 2017). It continues to be a vital democracy, getting a B, 86 out of 100, lower than France, Germany, and the United Kingdom, faring well on freedom of assembly and tolerance of public protests. The U.S. slid downward in equal treatment of groups under the law, due to its harsh treatment of illegal immigrants (Freedom House, 2019).

Discussion of U.S. democratic deficits has become a cottage industry among political scientists—a worthy one, to be sure—and a multitude of books and articles have catalogued democracy's weaknesses in the U.S. In one incisive account, Benjamin Page and Martin Gilens (2017) focused on these issues, first laying out the ideals democracy should achieve, and then offering a brief indictment:

> To ensure democratic outcomes, it is . . . important that *all citizens*—or at least a truly representative group of citizens—*actually vote*. Voters need to have *attractive choices* to vote for, not be forced to pick the lesser evil. *Good*

**Table 3.1  Problems plaguing American democracy, politics, and political communication.**

1. Outsize role money plays in politics
2. Will of the people is thwarted through:
   a) Influence of the rich
   b) Gerrymandering and the Electoral College
   c) Polarization
   d) Voting regulations and technological shortcomings
3. Playing field of democracy, underpinned by democratic norms, has become frayed
4. Facts are under fire, eroding the foundations of democratic decision-making

*information* should be available concerning what the candidates would be likely to do if they took office. *Only voters*, not financial donors or party activists, should affect the outcomes of elections. After elections, *only citizens' preferences*, not pressure from lobbyists (or anticipation of lucrative job opportunities after leaving office), should affect what officials do. *Political institutions* should give an *equal voice* to all citizens, and should be *able to act* on their wishes. The realities of American politics do not live up to these conditions.

(pp. 54–55)

With this sober warning in mind, let's examine some of the major shortcomings in democracy, American-style, in the early decades of the 21st century (see Table 3.1).

## DEMOCRACY'S DEFICITS IN THE U.S.

### 1. Politics Is Awash in Greenbacks

An estimated $7 billion was spent on election advertising in 2020, and that didn't even include other campaign marketing costs, such as hosting fundraisers and paying political strategists (Adgate, 2020). A hefty amount of the cash was doled out by the uber-rich, not ordinary Americans.

Contrary to democratic ideals, all citizens do not have equal access to the political process. Those with more money—millionaires and billionaires—have an enormous impact on politics. Partly as a result of a controversial 2010 Supreme Court decision, spending by independent political groups has grown exponentially over the past decade. Major donations are frequently kept secret, and donations are slipped through tax-exempt groups that can hide the names of donors who doled out the cash. Organizations with patriotic-sounding names such as Alliance for a Free Society spend millions of dollars promoting issue positions, disguising the fact that they are front organizations for groups that stand to benefit financially from the positions they embrace (Confessore & Willis, 2014). This system is deceptive and runs counter to democratic norms of transparency.

The name of the game is lobbying, paying to play—advocacy for companies large and small. Those who have more money have greater access to power. As Baumgartner and his colleagues (2009) concluded, "defenders of the status quo usually win in Washington" (p. 239). "Of the billions of dollars spent annually on lobbying in Washington, 72 percent comes from organizations representing business interests, and no more than 2 percent from organizations representing the vast majority below the very top," Schlozman, Verba, and Brady noted (2012, p. 2). The influence of lobbies and the super-rich in campaigns has grown markedly over the past decades. In 1980, 15 percent of campaign contributes came from the top .01 percent of Americans. In 2016 (and it is undoubtedly worse today), about 40 percent of campaign contributions came from some 25,000 donors, the upper .01 percent of the population (Editorial Board, 2017).

This skews the playing field to the rich, allowing them to have greater access to powerful political figures than do the overwhelming majority of citizens. The White House has long catered to the wealthy. President Clinton gave perks to top Democratic Party donors, rewarding them with jogs alongside the president, golf excursions, and overnight stays in the fabled Lincoln Bedroom. President Trump went further. Pledging to drain the corrupt Washington swamp, he infested the waters with more mega-rich political crocodiles. More than 200 advocacy groups (for example, the Food Marketing Institute), businesses (the Morgan Stanley financial services company), and religious organizations (the Christian Broadcasting Network) patronized Trump resorts and hotels, receiving lavish benefits in return. Unlike other presidents, Trump profited personally, pocketing some $12 million, in the process raising ethical questions of conflict of interest and showing how the wealthy can exploit their access to reap rewards not available to ordinary citizens (Confessore et al., 2020).

Empirical data offer bear this out. "When the preferences of economic elites and the stands of organized interest groups are controlled for," Gilens and Page (2014) concluded, "the preferences of the average American appear to have only a miniscule, near-zero, statistically non-significant impact upon public policy, . . . In the United States, the majority does *not* rule" (pp. 575–576). For example, despite public pleas for government assistance to help tens of millions of people who lost their jobs during the coronavirus, Congress, in a fine-print provision, gave a windfall to the rich. Millionaires could reap a jackpot of $1.6 million a year, compared to the paltry $1,200 ordinary Americans received (Kristof, 2020).

It's inequality in action, disenfranchising the overwhelming majority of citizens and advantaging those with property, resources, and greenbacks to pay off politicians. Americans see this situation, and they have registered their discontent. During the Eisenhower years, in 1958, three in four Americans said they trusted the federal government to do the right thing; by 2019, less than one in five Americans felt this way (Tavernise, 2020).

## 2. The Will of the People Is Often Ignored

Democratic theory presupposes that government does what the people want, that policies reflect public sentiments. On one level, this is very complicated and hinges on the particular institutional mechanism to translate public opinion into policy and the nature of the feedback loops between the public and its leaders. Nonetheless, the basic premise of democracy is that the people are sovereign.

Consider that three-fourths of Americans, including solid majorities of Republicans and Democrats, support federal government policies that would give people jobs working on infrastructure repairs. Most Americans support immigration reform that couples strict enforcement of border security with a pathway to U.S. citizenship for undocumented immigrants who already live here. On the fractious gun issue, more than 80 percent support background checks for individuals buying guns at private sales and gun shows (Page & Gilens, 2017). But Congress has never translated these overwhelming policy preferences into laws. When it came to the coronavirus, although 61 percent of Americans believed it was mainly the federal responsibility to coordinate testing, in 2020, Congress shied away from adopting this policy, preferring to leave it to the states (see Stolberg, 2020). Even more dramatically, in the fall of 2020, eight in ten Americans supported a new coronavirus relief package, which could aid workers and businesses in desperate need of help after the spring stimulus expired (see Tankersley & Cochrane, 2020), but Congress refused to act until late December. (In an apparent exception, President Biden's $1.9 trillion economic rescue plan that provided stimulus payments and wide-ranging relief from the financial pain imposed by the pandemic enjoyed support from 70 percent of the population.)

Exceptions notwithstanding, there are, in general, many reasons for the gap between public opinion and policy action. One explanation is that the wealthy have greater access to legislators than do ordinary Americans in the corrupt "pay to play" political playbook. The rich have little interest in common-sense proposals that would not benefit them, such as economic aid for Americans affected by the economics of the pandemic. In addition, activists and donors underwriting campaigns have become increasingly extreme, situated at the poles of the two parties. This means they support like-minded extremist candidates for their party's nomination and push these candidates in the general election. As a result, the political gravity moves toward the extreme ends of the political distribution, away from the bulk of voters in the electorate. The forces of political gravity have been even more potent for the Republican Party, which has become more ideologically homogenous than Democrats (Klein, 2020). But, given the Democrats too have shied away from a policy a majority of Americans favored, raising taxes on the rich when Obama was in the White House, it is hard not to agree that the U.S. "is less of a democracy and more of an oligarchy then we like to think" (Krugman, 2020).

A second factor that undercuts the will of the majority is gerrymandering, the legal, but questionable, way of drawing up voting districts. This gimmick was named after Elbridge Gerry, the early 19th-century governor of Massachusetts, who allowed his party to wind and coil a political district in so obviously partisan a way that it resembled a *salamander* (hence Gerry-*mandering*). **Gerrymandering** is a way the dominant political party bends the political map in its direction, drawing voting districts so they dilute the strength of the opposing party, ensuring that opponents will go down to defeat. "An efficiently gerrymandered map has a maximum number of districts that each contain just enough governing-party supporters to let the party's candidate win," a reporter explains (Wines, 2019, p. A14; see Figure 3.4).

**Figure 3.4  The political will of the majority is deliberately diluted through political gimmicks such as gerrymandering, named after Elbridge Gerry, the early 19th-century governor of Massachusetts, that effectively allows parties to draws the lines of political districts to their benefit, but arguably to the detriment of democracy.**

*Source*: www.gettyimages.com/detail/news-photo/principals-and-protestors-in-front-of-the-supreme-court-news-photo/1208197452?adppopup=true

Gerrymandering, with its different strategies, including computational models that map out partisan districts, can guarantee that candidates from the dominant party in a state are elected, even if they do not represent the majority of the electorate. For example, although about the same number of Democrats as Republicans reside in Wisconsin, the Republicans held 65 percent of the seats some years back (Ellenberg, 2017). Although they garnered less than 45 percent of the vote in 2018, Republicans maintained control of the Wisconsin State Assembly (Bazelon, 2020). Democrats pulled a similar ploy in New Jersey. To the extent that gerrymandered districts on the state and federal levels don't accurately represent the overall distribution of voters, voters' preferences are ignored, shunted aside in favor of the political bases that return candidates to office. When districts are gerrymandered, legislators have no incentive to compromise with the opposition to win election, contributing to polarization, discussed later. Gerrymandering, as one expert noted, lets experts rig "the system for their own benefit," allows them "to manipulate the playing field to entrench themselves," and is without a doubt "antithetical to democracy" (see Edsall, 2020).

A third, related problem—so complexly discussed over the years as to be beyond the scope of this book, but actually spectacularly simple—is the Electoral College. Designed to protect the smaller, less populous states hundreds of years ago, the Electoral College is viewed as a barrier to democracy by many Americans and scholars of different political persuasions (Astor, 2020). In five national elections, including 2000 and 2016, the popular vote winner lost the election, effectively disenfranchising the majority of the public and creating byzantine situations, as occurred in 2020, where the ballots of a handful of voters in battleground states exerted a greater impact than the votes of millions across the country. The Electoral College defaces the principle of majority rule that treats all voters as equals (Wegman, 2020). The rank, undemocratic nature of the Electoral College, reduces confidence in democracy.

A fourth factor tilting politics in an anti-democratic direction has been spurred by gerrymandering and the rise of extremist factions in political parties. It is **polarization**, the sharp division between two stridently opposed groups, with the two groups moving into ever-more-separated poles along the political axis. Political partisanship, at least on national issues, drives a wedge through Americans' political attitudes; partisan animus is higher nowadays than in previous decades (Pew Research Center, 2014, 2019). Polarization has increased in Congress, as party representatives forcefully disagree about a host of policy issues. And while partisan differences are more intense than they were years ago, the partisanship driving this change is among strong party supporters, who get more media coverage and push their representatives to take more extreme stands.

It was not always this way. During the 1960s and throughout the '70s, members of different parties worked together, sometimes compromising so that important bills could pass. Many legislators who served during these years had experienced the ravages of the Depression and World War II, providing them with a shared sense of patriotism and national unity that allowed them to forge bipartisan compromises (Tomasky, 2019). They weren't free of prejudices, but they could work together for the common good.

This changed over the 1980s and 1990s with cultural schisms on gender and racial issues, such as abortion and affirmative action, conservative backlashes on immigration and property taxes, divisive effects of careening inequality, and the growth of a conservative movement with foundations in grassroots disdain for liberal political correctness, but also deeper roots in right-wing-leaning ideology. These changes have made for a more polarized electoral politics, particularly at the national level.

The number of "swing districts" that are up for grabs has plummeted over the years. Only about one in five Congressional seats are actually competitive. The majority of elections are taken-for-granted victories by the party that has majority control of the Congressional district. The number of moderates in the House of Representatives—House members who broker compromises between the two parties—has declined dramatically over the past four decades.

In short, gridlock, not consensus-building, has become the byword in Congress. While Congress has passed major legislation on tax cuts and trade in recent years, policies that advance proposals favored by the majority of Americans frequently are stymied. A sad effect of a fragmented public agenda is that the connection between government and the citizens it represents is impaired (Edy & Meirick, 2019). We'll see if bridges can be built over the course of the Biden administration, with Biden's lofty unifying rhetoric and the possibility that bipartisan moderates can band together to forge compromises. But history suggests bridges will be difficult to construct.

A fifth factor pushing politics in an anti-democratic direction involves voting itself: who votes, and structural factors that have kept turnout down. While most Americans acknowledge that voting is important, around 55 percent of the voting-age population casts ballots in presidential elections, and fewer than 30 percent vote in primary elections, a lower percentage than in most developed countries (DeSilver, 2018). The 2020 election was a prominent exception, though even here many working-class Americans stayed home on Election Day, citing disillusionment and distrust of politics, a reflection of contemporary political animus and alienation from social institutions (Tavernise & Gebeloff, 2020).

Thus, in general elections (and it's worse in primaries), more than four in ten American voters aren't casting votes. This means that, due to choice or structural impediments, electoral outcomes don't reflect the sentiments of the majority of the electorate. What's more, people who vote are White, richer, more educated, and older than those who don't, adding another layer of non-representativeness.

Structural factors have also reduced voter turnout. Some laws require voters to show they have photo identification before they can receive a ballot. Others have eliminated the opportunity to register and vote on the same day, set up roadblocks to registration, or closed down early-voting sites (Berman, 2018; Wines & Hakim, 2018). The laws are controversial, with defenders (including a majority of the Supreme Court) as well as detractors. Importantly, these laws disproportionately affect lower-income and minority citizens, the most vulnerable members of society. By preventing people from registering and voting on the same day, a virtual necessity for poorer Americans who move a lot and don't always update their voting information, the laws in some states can reduce turnout among lower-income citizens. By accepting some types of photo IDs at the polls, such as gun permits (held primarily by Whites), but not others (employee or state school IDs), Texas may be inadvertently or deliberately preventing minorities from voting, continuing an ugly legacy that dates back to Jim Crow (Rutenberg, 2015). Several states, including Kansas, passed confining voter identification laws demanding proof of citizenship, which imposed undue burdens on non-White voters, who were less likely to have the needed paperwork (Rutenberg, 2020).

A number of states have curtailed voting access, purging people from voter rolls, ostensibly to eliminate voter fraud. In Ohio, voters who miss an election, fail to respond to a card indicating they have been marked inactive, and do not vote in two subsequent elections are removed from the voting records. "It's shocking," one expert said. "We don't ask gun owners to fire their weapons every two years and revoke their licenses four years later if they don't" (Wines & Hakim, p. A22). However, after Biden's election, Republican leaders in more than 24 states mounted aggressive attacks on the right to vote, introducing legislation in state after state that would significantly curtail voting, particularly for racial minorities. In Georgia, where Republicans were determined to exploit the law to prevent electoral losses such as those that occurred in 2020, a new law placed restrictions on voting, limited drop boxes and even prohibited giving water to voters waiting in line to vote (Corasaniti & Epstein, 2021). The GOP effort represented a cynical attack on voting, the bedrock of democracy.

As if this were not enough, technological shortcomings have thwarted democracy. Many localities use electronic voting equipment that cannot be adequately audited. They lack a paper trail that can be examined if the system breaks down or files are hacked (Sanger, Epstein, & Wines, 2019). It's a real problem. Several years back, the candidate for judge in a small city in Pennsylvania actually garnered 26,142 votes, but the voting machines said he had just 164. The touchscreens were beset by a bug in the software; had there been no paper ballot to verify the results, he might have lost (Corasaniti, 2019). In other cases, the equipment is aging, possibly in danger of breaking down, and elected officials have done little to allocate funds to replace the equipment with modern backup systems (Editorial Board, 2019).

In still other cases, the technology can be so novel, untested, and complicated to use in the high-stress, chaotic electoral environment that it causes a vote-reporting meltdown. This occurred when the perfect electoral (though happily not electric) storm occurred during the 2020 Iowa Democratic caucuses. A flawed, inadequately tested smartphone app used by political party volunteers unfamiliar with its technical features in a complex election with multiple candidates broke down, leading to crushing delays in vote reporting and new questions about the reliability of election returns in a digital age (Leatherby, Gamio, & Collins, 2020). It happened again several months later during Georgia's primary elections with missing or malfunctioning new voting machines and long lines at polling sites resulting, in part, from poor advance planning by election officials (see Figure 3.5).

These prospects have psychological repercussions. Increasingly cognizant of the shortcomings, nearly half of Americans have confessed that they didn't think their votes would be counted in a fair manner, and about one-third believed it

**Figure 3.5  Voters wait in long lines in Georgia's 2020 primary election, as a result of malfunctioning voting machines and poor advance planning. More generally, aging voting machines, flawed software, and potential electronic tampering by foreign agents have raised questions about the integrity of the foundation of democracy: the ballot box.**

is likely a foreign nation will meddle with electoral results (Tufekci, 2018). As one writer thoughtfully observed:

> The ballot box is the foundation of any democracy. It's not too grand to say that if there's a failure in the ballot box, then democracy fails. If the people don't have confidence in the outcome of an election, then it becomes difficult for them to accept the policies and actions that pour forth from it.
>
> (Zetter, 2018)

### 3. The Playing Field of Democracy Has Become Frayed

Democracy, like sports, has a set of rules that govern the way the game is played. While the rulebook has always been manipulated, sometimes cruelly, democracy does operate by norms that are designed to ensure its survival. As political scientists Steven Levitsky and Daniel Ziblatt (2018) explained, if democracies are to function effectively, they must enforce an unwritten rule emphasizing basic tolerance. When politicians and their supporters engage in mutual tolerance, they respect the legitimacy of their adversaries, acknowledging that, while they disagree, their opponents love the country in the same way they do. One force that can tear at the foundations of tolerance is polarization. While some polarization is acceptable, vicious polarization is toxic. As Levitsky and Ziblatt point out:

> When societies divide into partisan camps with profoundly different worldviews, and when those differences are viewed as existential and irreconcilable, political rivalry can devolve into partisan hatred. Parties come to view each other not as legitimate rivals but as dangerous enemies. Losing ceases to be an accepted part of the political process and instead becomes a catastrophe. When that happens, politicians are tempted to abandon forbearance and win at any cost. If we believe our opponents are dangerous, should we not use any means necessary to stop them?
>
> (p. 6)

This has happened in other countries, such as Chile in the 1970s and Turkey today. The Turkish government had arrested scores of journalists, fired many government workers, and eliminated core democratic safeguards. In a similar fashion, Poland subverted an independent judiciary and undermined the state media to such a degree that the opposition has had difficulty challenging the government (Mounk, 2018).

Politicians have long disparaged their opponents. In the early 19th century, John Adams and Thomas Jefferson's supporters hurled insults freely. However, condemnations have diffused more widely and publicly in an era of partisanship and social media that allows politicians and their supporters to belittle their adversaries from behind the protective blanket of an electronic device. Consider that Senator Chuck Schumer, a New York Democrat, said, on the steps of the Supreme Court, that Republicans "won't know what hit you if you go forward with these awful decisions," referring to their striking down women's abortion rights (Hulse, 2020, p. A14). While Schumer said he regretted his words, his comments could have been construed as subtly threatening Republican Supreme Court justices.

Modern presidents and their minions have long attacked their opponents, as Richard Nixon and Bill Clinton famously did. But Trump went further, with vitriolic Twitter attacks, comprising more than half of his posts for much of his term (Shear et al., 2019; see Chapter 10).

Threatening to lock up his 2016 election opponent if he were elected (which inspired widespread imitation among followers), denouncing legitimate government investigations, such as his 2019 impeachment inquiry, and retaliating against his opponents by firing two witnesses who testified against him in the House impeachment hearings, his actions eroded modern democratic norms. Even more brazen Trumpian statements, unprecedented in recent American political history, such as his call to indict 2020 opponent Joe Biden, undermined the underpinnings of democracy. Free elections are predicated on the winner recognizing the legitimacy of the opposition, and democratic government requires that the chief executive must not derail lawful investigations of presidential actions.

What's more, he refused to commit to a peaceful transfer of power after the presidential election (Crowley, 2020). Doubling down on this statement the morning after the election, Trump maintained he had won the election, even though votes were still being counted in battleground states, and he declared that vote counting should be halted (Burns & Martin, 2020). Over the ensuing weeks, he did everything he could to overturn the results of a democratic election that officials concluded had run remarkably smoothly, unquestionably free of fraud. Trump tweeted false accusations, ran ads on YouTube that made baseless claims, enlisted support from Republicans all too ready to curry favor, and filed lawsuits that made outrageous allegations that courts uniformly rejected as lacking evidence, all part of a brazen scheme without precedent, even considering the sordid history of presidential electioneering.

Freedom House, the organization that advocates for democracy, concluded that Trump had eroded the values of the American constitutional system. "No president in living memory has shown less respect for its tenets, norms, and principles," an author wrote, noting that, through his statements and actions, Trump had assaulted basic democratic institutions, such as a free press, an independent judiciary, protections against corruption, and the basic legitimacy of elections (Abramowitz, 2019).

And this was even before the world learned that Trump pressured and threatened Georgia's secretary of state to overturn the November election results, demanding that he recalculate the votes so that Trump would emerge victorious, winning the state's 16 electoral votes.

But Trump wasn't the only one willing to challenge the results of a fair election. One hundred and twenty-six House Republicans supported his efforts to overturn the electoral results; so distasteful did they find the possibility that Democrats could take office that they were willing to nullify an election. Even in the wake of a violent insurrection designed to interrupt the ratification, more than 120 members of Congress voted against the certification of the results of a fair American presidential election. The mob of rioters, fed a diet of falsehoods that stoked extremist prejudices, showcased their rejection of democratic procedures.

The events indicated how frayed the democratic playing field had become. As one political theorist averred, "For democracies to work, politicians need to respect the difference between an enemy and an adversary. An adversary is someone you want to defeat. An enemy is someone you have to destroy" (see Mounk, 2018, p. 113).

### 4. Facts Are Under Fire, Eroding the Foundations of Democratic Decision-Making

"Fact" has become a four-letter word.

A centerpiece of the Enlightenment and democratic society is now one of the many concepts up for grabs, questioned and contested by both sides, weaponized in the partisan wars. For years, facts relayed by government, reported by journalists, and discovered by scientists were accepted, perceived as credible, and considered by the public in their social and political decision-making. Then it got messy.

During the 1960s, the public learned that the government glibly lied about facts, hiding key information about the Vietnam War from American citizens. The press, which slanted its coverage to favor the White House during the years of the war (Hallin, 1986), paraded government falsehoods as facts. Even scientists could inquire more about facts that put the majority culture's health at risk than those that imperiled the health of minorities. Over the latter decades of the 20th century, correctives were made, but they went too far. Postmodern thinkers wrote books noting that facts necessarily favored the powers-that-be, and social scientists emphasized that facts are socially constructed and therefore relative. Some of this debate was healthy, but it became problematic when all facts, even those gathered by estimable scientific analysis or representing the consensus of credible accounts, were viewed as suspect, as has been the case with evolution or the myth that vaccines cause autism (Kinch, 2018).

Extremist, factually specious accounts gain added credence in a social media age, when anti-vaccination zealots can gain an online microphone and, through algorithms that favor views congenial to their audience, transmit a diet of supportive information to their followers. In the political sphere, with the decline of major journalistic gatekeepers, a host of ideological outlets have filled the void left by the once-dominant broadcast networks and newspapers, as they reach millions of like-minded left-wing and right-wing online readers.

MSNBC presented a limited, one-sided view of the Trump administration's decision to kill a top Iranian general. On Fox News, star host Sean Hannity, an ardent supporter of President Trump, advanced a false conspiracy theory, claiming the coronavirus was a "fraud" perpetrated by government bureaucrats who opposed Trump (Peters & Grynbaum, 2020).

A lot of solid political journalism can still be found in mainstream news outlets, such as *The Washington Post*, *Politico*, and CBS. Yet the confusing architecture of contemporary news, where an activist's rant or ideological news site's opinion-laced story adjoins a thorough CNN report or an impeccable *New York Times* exposé, can confuse and bewilder ordinary citizens.

The proliferation of partisan websites, misleading combination of opinion and facts on social media, presence of promotional content that is deceptively designed to resemble news but actually promotes a commercial product, as well as endless remonstrations about fake news, have produced "a strange new normal" for many Americans, causing people to feel "numb and disoriented, struggling to discern what is real in a sea of slant, fake and fact" (Tavernise & Gardiner, 2019; see also Vraga et al., 2011). An Associated Press/National Opinion Research Center poll found that 47 percent of Americans believe it is difficult to know whether the information they come across is true (Tavernise & Gardiner, 2019). As one political adviser observed:

> We're in a dangerous moment. The danger is people come to believe that nobody is giving them the facts and reality, and everybody can make up their own script and their own narrative.
>
> (see Baker, 2019)

Accompanying this issue has been precipitous declines in the health of the press over the years, particularly in the U.S. (Hanitzsch, Van Dalen, & Steindl, 2018). As a result of the growth of unbridled online media, with their intermingling of facts and opinions, faith in news has declined. "If people do not trust the institutions that deliver the news," Hanitzsch and his colleagues ask, "how could they make informed decisions in the political domain?" (p. 18).

Leaders' repeated dismissal of press reports as "fake news" adds to the confusion, causing even citizens not strongly allied with one or the other political party to wonder about the credibility of what they read. This encourages them to simplistically reject media reports because they're "biased" (a loaded, actually complex, term), and throw up their hands, concluding that nothing is true. If everything is possible—and all views including the most bizarre are equally credible—then nothing, including the most factually accurate of reports, is true, to paraphrase the philosopher Hannah Arendt (1951). Politics comes to resemble an Alice in Wonderland rabbit hole.

And if—though we're not there yet—truth, or, more precisely, factual assessments reached by scientists and journalists, becomes imperiled, then a foundation of democratic discourse is endangered. Facts, as Michael X. Delli Carpini (2018) observes, "prevent debates from being disconnected from the material conditions they attempt to address." He insightfully notes that:

> (Facts) allow individuals and groups with widely varied experiences and philosophies to have some common basis of comparison—some common language with which to clarify differences, identify points of agreement, and establish criteria for evaluation. They tether public discourse to objective conditions while allowing for debates over what objectivity means.
>
> (p. 23)

From a broader perspective, widely diffused false claims about everything from vaccines to fraudulent rigging of the 2020 election (Corasaniti, Epstein, & Rutenberg, 2020) have contributed to an erosion of faith in facts and perhaps diminution of respect for democratic institutions.

Of course, disrespect for political traditions and chicanery are not new in politics. You can find hundreds of examples of vitriolic criticisms of adversaries, even brawls, as well as vote-stealing in nefarious 19th-century elections (Freeman, 2018; Grinspan, 2020; see also Carnell, 2020). Appreciating how bad American politics was in the past, with gun duels and political score-setting, does offer repose, signifying that there has always been something dirty about politics. But this doesn't negate the problems we face today; if anything, the past offers a cautionary tale, suggesting we should be even more vigilant about protecting the sacred traditions of democracy.

Erosion of the larger soil of democratic norms can, little by little, threaten the broader environment required for democracy to thrive. When erosion—of facts, civic respect, and the legitimacy of the playing field—has reached the point that people believe the political leadership "does not appear to govern on its behalf" or "is favoring new social groups over established groups," they become resentful, convinced the system has no legitimacy; aggrieved and entitled, they may be willing to take their symbolic protest to the point of favoring candidates who they know are "lying demagogues," to assert a voice they believe has been stifled (Hahl, Kim, & Sivan, 2018, p. 3). When this condition occurs, the fundamental trust and decency that underpins democratic government has been lost.

As political communication researcher Elizabeth Stoycheff (2020) perceptively notes, "Today's democratic reversal is not a grandiose political upheaval, but rather a quiet and persistent chipping away at its core norms and values" (p. 401).

## PERSPECTIVES

Of course, democracy is always relative. There has never been a country that has even approached the goal posts of democracy. Democracy is a "moving target" (Kriesi, 2013), a work in progress, in theory the best of all political systems, but in reality, a far-from-perfect form of government—an ideal toward which governments strive. The Electoral College has problems, but other democratic systems also have drawbacks in the way they select their leaders. Britain's parliamentary system has flaws. Some years back during a British election, the 160,000 members of the Conservative Party chose Britain's prime minister because the system mandates that the prime minister is selected directly by the country's governing party. This meant that less than 1 percent of registered UK voters decided who their leader was, which was especially grating as it came during the height of the Brexit crisis (Yeginsu, 2019). In Israel, when neither political party's candidate has enough electoral support to form a majority coalition, the choice of prime minister is up to Israel's ceremonial president, who must decide which candidate is most likely to be able to develop a workable coalition government (Halbfinger & Kershner, 2019). One person made a choice for millions.

Democratic government cannot prevent people—voters who constitute the electorate—from electing a dictator, demagogue, or leader who tramples on human rights. And during the coronavirus pandemic, governments took expansive powers that extended beyond the legitimate need to protect citizens from the virus, steps that infringed on basic rights, such as closing down courts, stifling dissent, and holding citizens indefinitely (Gebrekidan, 2020).

Viewing the issue broadly, the Czech human rights activist and philosopher Václav Havel eloquently stated in an address to the U.S. Congress:

> As long as people are people, democracy, in the full sense of the word, will always be no more than an ideal. One may approach it as one would the horizon in ways that may be better or worse, but it can never be fully attained. In this sense, you, too, are merely approaching democracy.
>
> (Dionne, 1991, epigram; see Figure 3.6)

**Figure 3.6 Václav Havel, the courageous Czech dissident, political philosopher, and Czechoslovakian president, wrote eloquently about democracy.**

*Source*: https://ku.m.wikipedia.org/wiki/W%C3%AAne: V%C3%A1clav_Havel_na_V%C3%A1clavsk%C3%A9m_ n%C3%A1m%C4%9Bst%C3%AD_17._listopadu_2009b.jpg

A writer, Costica Bradatan, described the quandary eloquently, even romantically:

Democracy is so hard to find in the human world that most of the time when we speak of it, we refer to a remote ideal rather than a fact. That's what democracy is ultimately about: an ideal that people attempt to put into practice from time to time. Never adequately and never for long—always clumsily, timidly, as though for a trial period. Yet democracy is one of those elusive things—happiness is another—whose promise, even if perpetually deferred, is more important than its actual existence. We may never get it, but we cannot afford to stop dreaming of it.

(2019, p. 19)

## CONCLUSIONS

People have a multitude of opinions about politics. In a democracy, we would not have it any other way. But opinions can differ in quality and substance. In order to assess the quality of these opinions—to separate out the philosophical wheat from the chaff—it is instructive to review normative philosophies of democracy. Truth be told, there is not one theory of democracy, but many, with each offering different perspectives on the proper role of citizens, government, and communication.

The classical Greek model emphasizes direct citizen participation in politics and citizens' obligation to contribute to the common good of the community. Liberal democratic theories stress individual liberty, politics as a marketplace of ideas, in which truth emerges in its collision with falsehood, and a feisty no-holds-barred press that challenges government. The deliberative democracy model, arguing that the liberal marketplace metaphor diminishes the deeper role politics ought to play in public life, highlights the importance of thoughtful communication that seeks to encourage collective deliberation on community problems.

Building off these and other perspectives, theorists have articulated core aspects of democracy, including the right of all citizens to vote, free and fair elections, individual liberty, a press that challenges government, and a civil society, with opportunities to form associations and interest groups that enrich and challenge the status quo. Thriving, open political communication is a cornerstone of a vibrant democracy. Even as it has emerged as a relatively democratic society (after years of exclusion of minority groups), American democracy remains awash in conundrums and shortcomings.

Money plays an outsize role in politics, showcasing the ways the rich and influential can use money to wield power. The will of the public is ignored in a multitude of ways, through (1) gerrymandering political districts, which sanctions the election of legislators who do not represent the majority of voters; (2) increased political party polarization, an impediment to Congress passing legislation favored by the majority of citizens; (3) structural factors that have reduced minority citizens' access to the ballot; and (4) technological shortcomings in voting machines which, along with electronic tampering by foreign governments, can rock the material and psychological foundation of democracy: the ballot box. Disturbing violations of norms of political tolerance, as well as undermining of factual discourse, also plague contemporary democracies.

Of course, there are counterarguments to some of these objections. For example, you can argue that campaign money is a type of protected speech under the First Amendment of the Bill of Rights, but this doesn't negate the greater access the wealthy have to power or lack of transparency in political advertisements that allows powerful organizations to sponsor ads without disclosing their donors, along with a diminution of democratic norms. As two noted political scientists put it, "at the moment, America is a democracy, but it is not very democratic" (Achen & Bartels, 2016, p. 327).

Alas, democracy is always elusive, for it is, in the end, never fully achievable by flawed human political actors. It is a goal to aspire to, an ideal glimmering in the distance. As the human rights activist Václav Havel said of democracy: "One may approach it as one would the horizon in ways that may be better or worse, but it can never be fully attained" (Dionne, 1991, epigram).

Like Gatsby's green light, we keep striving to reach it.

## REFERENCES

Abramowitz, M. (2019). The struggle comes home: Attacks on democracy in the United States. *Democracy in retreat: Freedom in the world 2019*. Freedom House. Online: https://freedomhouse.org/sites/default/files/Feb2019_FH_FITW_2019_Report_ForWeb-compressed.pdf. (Accessed: September 4, 2020).

Achen, C.H., & Bartels, L.M. (2016). *Democracy for realists: Why elections do not produce responsive government*. Princeton, NJ: Princeton University Press.

Adgate, B. (2020, August 11). Kantar estimates 2020 election ads will cost $7 billion. *Forbes*. Online: www.forbes.com/sites/bradadgate/2020/08/11/2020-an-election-year-like-no-other/#7502299638d1. (Accessed: September 8, 2020).

Arendt, H. (1951). *The origins of totalitarianism*. New York: Harcourt, Brace and Co.

Astor, M. (2020, November 6). The Electoral College is close. The popular vote isn't. *The New York Times*. Online: www.nytimes.com/article/popular-vote-electoral-college.html. (Accessed: November 7, 2020).

Baker, P. (2019, December 9). Lies, damned lies and Washington. *The New York Times*. Online: www.nytimes.com/2019/12/09/us/politics/lies-damned-lies-and-washington.html. (Accessed: February 5, 2020).

Baumgartner, F.R., Berry, J.M., Hojnacki, M., Kimball, D.C., & Leech, B.L. (2009). *Lobbying and policy change: Who win, who loses, and why?* Chicago, IL: University of Chicago Press.

Bazelon, E. (2020, May 5). Will Americans lose their right to vote in the pandemic? *The New York Times Magazine*. Online: www.nytimes.com/2020/05/05/magazine/voting-by-mail-2020-covid.html. (Accessed: May 10, 2020).

Berman, A. (2018, October 28). Blocking the ballot box. *The New York Times* (Sunday Review), 1, 4.

Blight, D.W. (2020, April 11). Trump reveals the truth about voter suppression. *The New York Times* (Sunday Review). Online: www.nytimes.com/2020/04/11/opinion/sunday/republicans-voter-suppression.html. (Accessed: April 11, 2020).

Bradatan, C. (2019, July 6). Democracy is for the gods. *The New York Times*, A19.

Burns, A., & Martin, J. (2020, November 4). As America awaits a winner, Trump falsely claims he prevailed. *The New York Times*. Online: www.nytimes.com/2020/11/04/us/politics/election-trump-biden-recap.html. (Accessed: November 4, 2020).

Carnell, R. (2020, November 15). A divisive 1710 election reveals the value of political pragmatism. *Cleveland.com*. Online: www.cleveland.com/opinion/2020/11/a-divisive-1710-election-reveals-the-value-of-political-pragmatism-rachel-carnell.html. (Accessed: November 17, 2020).

Chambers, S. (2003). Deliberative democratic theory. *Annual Review of Political Science*, 6, 307–326.

Christians, C.G., Glasser, T.L., McQuail, D., Nordenstreng, K., & White, R.A. (2009). *Normative theories of the media: Journalism in democratic societies*. Urbana, IL: University of Illinois Press.

Coleman, S., & Blumler, J.G. (2009). *The Internet and democratic citizenship: Theory, practice and policy*. New York: Cambridge University Press.

Confessore, N., & Willis, D. (2014, November 3). Hidden donors spend heavily on attack ads. *The New York Times*, A1, A16.

Confessore, N., Yourish, K., Eder, S., Protess, B., Haberman, M., Ashford, G., LaForgia, M., Vogel, K.P., Rothfeld, M., & Buchanan, L. (2020, October 10). The swamp that Trump; built. *The New York Times*. Online: www.nytimes.com/interactive/2020/10/10/us/trump-properties-swamp.html. (Accessed: October 11, 2020).

Corasaniti, N. (2019, December 1). A Pennsylvania candidate had 26,142 votes. The machines counted 164. *The New York Times*, 20.

Corasaniti, N., & Epstein, R.J. (2021, March 26). Georgia law kicks off partisan battle over Accessed: March 27, 2021).

Corasaniti, N., Epstein, R.J., & Rutenberg, J. (2020, November 10). The Times called officials in every state: No evidence of voter fraud. *The New York Times*. Online: www.nytimes.com/2020/11/10/us/politics/voting-fraud.html/ (Accessed: November 15, 2020).

Crowley, M. (2020, September 23). Trump won't commit to "peaceful" post-election transfer of power. *The New York Times*. Online: www.nytimes.com/2020/09/23/us/politics/trump-power-transfer-2020-election.html. (Accessed: September 24, 2020).

Dahl, R.A. (1989). *Democracy and its critics*. New Haven: Yale University Press.

Delli Carpini, M.X. (2018). Alternative facts: Donald Trump and the emergence of a new U.S. media regime. In P.J. Boczkowski & Z. Papacharissi (Eds.), *Trump and the media* (pp. 17–23). Cambridge, MA: MIT Press.

DeSilver, D. (2018, May 18). *U.S. trails most developed countries in voter turnout*. Pew Research Center (FactTank: News in the Numbers). Online: www.pewresearch.org/fact-tank/2018/05/21/u-s-voter-turnout-trails-most-developed-countries/. (Accessed: January 31, 2020).

Dionne, E.J., Jr. (1991). *Why Americans hate politics*. New York: Simon & Schuster.

Editorial Board (2017, December 16). The tax bill that inequality created. *The New York Times*. Online: www.nytimes.com/2017/12/16/opinion/sunday/tax-bill-inequality-created.html. (Accessed: January 29, 2020).

Editorial Board (2019, July 28). Mr. Mueller is right to be worried. *The New York Times* (Sunday Review), 10.

Edsall, T.B. (2020, August 12). The politics we don't see matter as much as those we do. *The New York Times*. Online: www.nytimes.com/2020/08/12/opinion/census-politics-gerrymandering-redistricting.html. (Accessed: August 12, 2020).

Edy, J.A., & Meirick, P.C. (2019). *A nation fragmented: The public agenda in the information age*. Philadelphia: Temple University Press.

Ellenberg, J. (2017, October 6). How computers turned gerrymandering into a science. *The New York Times*. Online: www.nytimes.com/2017/10/06/opinion/sunday/computers-gerrymandering-wisconsin.html. (Accessed: January 30, 2020).

Freedom House (2019). *Democracy in retreat. Freedom in the world 2019*. Online: https://freedomhouse.org/report/freedom-world/freedom-world-2019/democracy-in-retreat. (Accessed: January 29, 2020).

Freeman, J.B. (2018, September 9). The violence at the heart of our politics. *The New York Times* (Sunday Review), 4.

Gebrekidan, S. (2020, March 30). For autocrats, and others, coronavirus is a chance to grab even more power. *The New York Times*. Online: www.nytimes.com/2020/03/30/world/europe/coronavirus-governments-power.html. (Accessed: March 31, 2020).

Gilens, M., & Page, B.I. (2014). Testing theories of American politics: Elites, interest groups, and average citizens. *Perspectives on Politics*, *12*, 564–581.

Grinspan, J. (2020, October 24). How to steal an election. *The New York Times*. Online: www.nytimes.com/2020/10/24/opinion/sunday/stealing-elections.html. (Accessed: October 25, 2020).

Haberman, M., Cochrane, E., & Tankersley, J. (2020, August 3). With jobless aid expired, Trump sidelines himself in stimulus talks. *The New York Times*. Online: www.nytimes.com/2020/08/03/us/politics/congress-jobless-aid-talks-trump.html. (Accessed: August 4, 2020).

Habermas, J. (1996). *Between facts and norms: Contributions to a discourse theory of law and democracy*. Cambridge, MA: MIT Press.

Hahl, O., Kim, M., & Sivan, E.W.Z. (2018). The authentic appeal of the lying demagogue: Proclaiming the deeper truth about political illegitimacy. *American Sociological Review*, *83*, 1–33.

Halbfinger, D.M., & Kershner, I. (2019, September 18). Voters in Israel keep an election too close to call. *The New York Times*, A1, A13.

Hallin, D.C. (1986). *The "uncensored war": The media and Vietnam*. New York: Oxford University Press.

Hanitzsch, T., Van Dalen, A., & Steindl, N. (2018). Caught in the nexus: A comparative and longitudinal analysis of public trust in the press. *The International Journal of Press/Politics*, *23*, 3–23.

Held, D. (2006). *Models of democracy* (3rd ed.). Stanford, CA: Stanford University Press.

Hulse, C. (2020, March 6). Schumer regrets content, but not spirit, of warning. *The New York Times*, A14.

Jacobs, L.R., Cook, F.L., & Delli Carpini, M.X. (2009). *Talking together: Public deliberation and political participation in America*. Chicago, IL: University of Chicago Press.

Katz, R.S. (1997). *Democracy and elections*. New York: Oxford University Press.

Kinch, M. (2018). *Between hope and fear: A history of vaccines and human immunity*. New York: Pegasus Books.

Klein, E. (2020, January 26). Polarization and the parties. *The New York Times* (Sunday Review), 2.

Kriesi, H. (2013). Democracy as a moving target. In H. Kriesi, S. Lavenex, F. Esser, J. Matthes, M. Buhlmann (two dots over u), & D. Bochsler (Eds.), *Democracy in the age of globalization and mediatization* (pp. 19–43). New York: Palgrave Macmillan.

Kristof, N. (2020, May 23). Crumbs for the hungry but windfalls for the rich. *The New York Times*. Online: www.nytimes.com/2020/05/23/opinion/sunday/coronavirus-economic-response.html. (Accessed: May 24, 2020).

Krugman, P. (2020, July 1). Why do the rich have so much power? *The New York Times*. (Sunday Review). Online: www.nytimes.com/2020/07/01/opinion/sunday/inequality-america-paul-krugman.html. (Accessed: July 5, 2020).

Leatherby, L., Gamio, L., & Collins, K. (2020, February 5). Everything that went wrong. *The New York Times*, A18.

Levitsky, S., & Ziblatt, D. (2018, January 28). Is our democracy wobbly? *The New York Times* (Sunday Review), 6.

Mounk, Y. (2018). *The people vs. democracy: Why our freedom is in danger and how to save it*. Cambridge, MA: Harvard University Press.

Norris, P. (2011). *Democratic deficit: Critical citizens revisited*. New York: Cambridge University Press.

Orwell, G. (1946). *Animal farm*. New York: Harcourt, Brace.

Page, B.I., & Gilens, M. (2017). *Democracy in America? What has gone wrong and what can we do about it?* Chicago, IL: University of Chicago Press.

Peters, J.W., & Grynbaum, M.M. (2020, March 12). To doctors, it's a crisis. To Hannity, it's a "hoax". *The New York Times*, A12.

Pew Research Center (2014, June 12). *Political polarization in the American public*. Pew Research Center (U.S. Politics & Policy). Online: www.people-press.org/2014/06/12/political-polarization-in-the-american-public/. (Accessed: February 3, 2020).

Pew Research Center (2019, December 17). *In a politically polarized era, sharp divides in both partisan coalitions*. Pew Research Center (U.S. Politics & Policy). Online: www.people-press.org/2019/12/17/in-a-politically-polarized-era-sharp-divides-in-both-partisan-coalitions/. (Accessed: February 3, 2020).

Rutenberg, J. (2015, December 20). Block the vote. *The New York Times Magazine*, 30–37, 57.

Rutenberg, J. (2020, September 30). The attack on voting. *The New York Times Magazine*. Online: www.nytimes.com/2020/09/30/magazine/trump-voter-fraud.html. (Accessed: October 4, 2020).

Sanger, D.E., Epstein, R.J., & Wines, M. (2019, July 27). States rush to make voting systems secure as new threats emerge. *The New York Times*, A15.

Schlozman, K.L., Verba, S., & Brady, H.E. (2012, November 11). Sunday dialogue: Giving all citizens a voice. *The New York Times* (Sunday Review), 2.

Shear, M.D., Haberman, M., Confessore, N., Yourish, K., Buchanan, L., & Collins, K. (2019, November 2). How Trump reshaped the presidency in over 11,000 tweets. *The New York Times*. Online: www.nytimes.com/interactive/2019/11/02/us/politics/trump-twitter-presidency.html. (Accessed: January 19, 2020).

Stolberg, S.G. (2020, May 28). Biden's testing strategy sets up a clear contrast with Trump on the coronavirus. *The New York Times*. Online: www.nytimes.com/2020/05/28/us/politics/biden-trump-coronavirus- testing.html. (Accessed: May 29, 2020).

Stoycheff, E. (2020). Relatively democratic: How perceived Internet interference shapes attitudes about democracy. *The International Journal of Press/Politics*, *25*, 390–406.

Stromer-Galley, J. (2007). Measuring deliberation's content: A coding scheme. *Journal of Public Deliberation*, *3*, 1–35.

Tankersley, J., & Cochrane, E. (2020, October 7). In scuttling stimulus talks, Trump invites political risk for himself and Republicans. *The New York Times*. Online: www.nytimes.com/2020/10/07/business/economy/trump-stimulus-bill-republicans.html. (Accessed: October 8, 2020).

Tavernise, S. (2020, May 23). Will the coronavirus kill what's left of Americans' faith in Washington? *The New York Times*. Online: www.nytimes.com/2020/05/23/us/coronavirus-government-trust.html. (Accessed: May 24, 2020).

Tavernise, S., & Gardiner, A. (2019, November 18). "No one believes anything": Voters worn out by a fog of political news. *The New York Times*. Online: https://www.nytimes.com/2019/11/18/us/polls-media-fake-news.html. (Accessed: November 17, 2020).

Tavernise, S., & Gebeloff, R. (2020, October 26). They did not vote in 2016. Why they plan to skip the election again. *The New York Times*. Online: www.nytimes.com/2020/10/26/us/election-nonvoters.html. (Accessed: October 27, 2020).

*The Economist* (2017, January 25). Declining trust in government is denting democracy. Online: www.economist.com/blogs/graphicdetail/2017/01/daily- chart-20. (Accessed: February 9, 2017).

Tomasky, M. (2019). *If we can keep it: How the republic collapsed and how it might be saved*. New York: Liveright Publishing Co.

Tufekci, Z. (2018, November 5). The election has already been hacked. *The New York Times*, A27.

Vraga, E.K., Edgerly, S., Wang, B.M., & Shah, D.V. (2011). Who taught me that? Repurposed news, blog structure, and source identification. *Journal of Communication*, *61*, 795–815.

Wegman, J. (2020, December 13). Joe Biden won the most votes. It doesn't matter. *The New York Times*. Online: www.nytimes.com/2020/12/13/opinion/electoral-college-trump-election.html. (Accessed: December 18, 2020).

Wines, M. (2019, June 28). Rigged maps, partisan legislatures and the legacy of Elbridge Gerry. *The New York Times*, A14.

Wines, M., & Hakim, D. (2018, November 4). "This definitely interferes": Four fights over voting rights. *The New York Times*, A22.

Wood, G.S. (1991). *The radicalism of the American revolution.* New York: Vintage Books.

Yeginsu, C. (2019, July 21). 1% of voters will pick Britain's prime minister. The rest are fuming. *The New York Times*, 10. See Taub, A. (2019, December 17).

Zetter, K. (2018, September 26). The crisis of election security. *The New York Times Magazine.* Online: https://www.nytimes.com/2018/09/26/magazine/election-security-crisis-midterms.html. (Accessed: March 20, 2021).

# PART TWO

# Political Communication Concepts and Effects

# 4 The Study of Political Communication

For nearly a century, the debate has raged. Does political communication have massive, even "propagandizing" effects on the public? Are its effects more limited, circumscribed by psychological and sociological factors? Do political media effects (especially in an era of partisan social media posts) simply reinforce what people already believe, or do they exert more substantial influences on individuals and the political system? How strong are political media effects, what approaches should we harness to study them, and what methods reign supreme?

Although the study of political communication is popularly believed to have begun with television, it actually dates back a century. Walter Lippmann, the American journalist writing in the 1920s, insightfully appreciated the power of media to shape perceptions of places and events people had never experienced directly. He eloquently described the media's ability to mold the images people carried in their heads about a distant world that was "out of reach, out of sight, out of mind" (see Figure 4.1). This chapter describes the journey Lippmann helped launch, describing the history of political communication research, focusing on continuities and changes in academic thinking about political communication over the past century.

The history of political communication research is not a placid story of academic scholars gathering facts and dutifully placing each droplet of information into the vessel of knowledge. On the contrary, it is more like a maritime expedition, with competing explorers, armed with different maps and diving equipment. One group amasses findings, only to have these notions questioned by another group of explorers, who, guided by their own maps, probe a different portion of the ocean's depths, uncovering new facts and theories of what constitutes the underlying structure of the sea. All too often we think of the history of an academic discipline as a monotonous description of how naïve thinkers developed ideas that were overturned by their more intelligent, savvy,

**Figure 4.1 Walter Lippmann, the journalist and scholar who helped pioneer scholarship on political communication. Lippmann argued that in a political world few experienced directly, media symbols and interpretations influenced public attitudes and opinions. His writings spotlighted the impact of media, but were vulnerable to criticism that they privileged elites at the expense of a vital, deliberative public.**

and contemporary disciples. But this understates the excitement of intellectual discovery. By reviewing the key twists and turns in the history of political communication research, I hope to engage readers, helping them appreciate the intellectually vigorous issues that animate scholars.

The first part of the chapter reviews pioneering perspectives in political communication research. To offer a thumbnail sketch of the early scholarship in the field, I summarize four seminal political communication projects, beginning with Walter Lippmann, in Table 4.1. Subsequent sections describe the classic limited effects model, along with criticisms, continuities and changes in political communication scholarship, and the current zeitgeist or perspective on politics and media.

## THE LIMITED EFFECTS APPROACH

Joseph Klapper posed a question: What are the effects of mass media and political communication? Guided by Lazarsfeld, his dissertation adviser, Klapper thought it was high time that someone wrote up a summary statement about this new field of communication research. Now that there had been many studies of mass media effects and a new decade—the 1960s—was poised to begin, it seemed a propitious moment to put together a book that summarized knowledge of media effects.

Following the tradition blazed by Katz and Lazarsfeld, Klapper (1960) concluded that media influences on society were small to modest. People had acquired strong preexisting attitudes before they came to media. They were members of reference groups, like the family, religious organizations, and labor unions. These groups generally exerted a stronger impact on attitudes than did mass media. The media were not the sole or primary agent that influenced political attitudes and behavior. Instead, Klapper emphasized, media worked together with social environmental factors, contributing to or

**Table 4.1  Milestones in political communication scholarship.**

| Year | Event | Significance | Continuing Issues |
|------|-------|-------------|-------------------|
| **1922** | Walter Lippmann's *Public Opinion* is published. | The book articulated an extraordinarily prescient thesis, arguing that the new mass media shaped public opinion through subtle manipulation of symbols. | Critics argued his approach to rectifying democracy's problems was elitist, placing faith in political experts rather than emphasizing citizens' ability to participate in democratic dialogue. But it was a landmark publication, stimulating new thinking about media effects and a continuing dialogue on how the public should participate in democracy. |
| **1937** | Institute for Propaganda Analysis is formed. | The group assembled a list of the "ABCs of propaganda," including bandwagon, testimonials, and glittering generalities, illuminating government exploitation of messages, as propagated by Nazi Germany. | It helped diffuse the fraught term "propaganda" with its powerful, negative, pejorative connotations, a term that resurfaced with the 2016 Russian disinformation campaign and spread of extremist social media falsehoods. |
| **1944** | *The People's Choice*, the first major, now seminal, study of political media effects in Erie County, Ohio, is published (Lazarsfeld, Berelson, & Gaudet, 1944). | The study represented the first social scientific investigation of the impact of the growing political media on voting behavior, ushering in concepts like the two-step flow and opinion leadership. The authors argued that certain individuals serve as **opinion leaders** for others, influencing followers' political views. Ideas seemed to flow from radio and newspapers to these influential leaders; opinion leaders then scooped them up, distilled them, and conveyed them to the less active members of the electorate. This was called the **two-step flow**. | The study surprised experts by concluding that media effects are modest, playing second fiddle to influential interpersonal agents and political groups. Its findings would be dissected and debated, provoking revisionist interpretations of stronger political media effects. |

*Continued*

**Table 4.1  (Continued)**

| Year | Event | Significance | Continuing Issues |
|------|-------|--------------|-------------------|
| **1955** | Katz and Lazarsfeld's *Personal Influence* is published. | Elaborating on *The People's Choice*, Katz and Lazarsfeld explicated the notion of personal influence and opinion leadership in different contexts. | The study was later criticized for treating political opinion as a commercial marketing construct, reflecting a pro-system bias. At the same time, the book helped generate interest in the role communication plays in the leadership of opinions about products and ideas in interpersonal and, much later, social media contexts. |

**Figure 4.2  He doesn't seem so bad!**

Joseph Klapper is the legendary bête noire of the field of political (and mass) communication because he downplayed media effects during a time when media had outsize impacts, seeming to minimize the significance of communication scholars' work. But contemporary revisionist views have resurrected his contributions, to some degree, viewing his classic, controversial notion of limited effects in a more complex, positive light.

*Source*: www.gettyimages.com/detail/news-photo/portrait-of-dr-joseph-klapper-director-of-social-research-news-photo/862361916?adppopup=true

reinforcing the effects these other agents exerted. This became known as the **limited effects model**.

Klapper acknowledged that mass media could strengthen attitudes. But, to Klapper, they did not have the immense effects that many observers attributed to them. People were not a "tabula rasa" on which media could imprint their message. They brought preexisting group identifications (such as religion) and attitudes (such as liberalism or conservatism) to their encounters with media. Their well-learned beliefs and preexisting biases helped determine how individuals reacted to political media fare, as well as the effects media exerted.

In the years that followed the publication of his book, as the field of political communication emerged, Klapper's work became a focus of controversy. For many years scholars criticized his conclusions, partly because they seemed so out of whack with the transformative effects media were exerting and partly because his pooh-poohing of media seemed to minimize the importance of their own work as communication researchers. But when he published his book in 1960, it looked as if he had captured a large kernel of truth about the effects of mass media (see Figure 4.2).

## A NEW PERSPECTIVE

Suddenly, things changed.

During the decade when Klapper published a book describing minimal media effects, something very different was occurring in the supposedly minimally significant mass media. The very different phenomenon was television news. It swept the country by storm, expanding to a half-hour, capturing viewers, and captivating audiences with vivid, sometimes visceral images. Televised pictures and sounds bombarded Americans in the 1960s. There was a handsome John F. Kennedy challenging the jowl-faced, sweaty Richard Nixon in the first 1960 presidential debate; Southern police clubbing impassioned Black protesters; gut-wrenching scenes of American soldiers battling enemy troops in the rice paddies of Vietnam; angry, long-haired, but impassioned college students holding signs, circling around campus buildings, protesting, denouncing a president, or strumming guitars, singing blissfully of a nonviolent future. These images, TV's ubiquity, and the media's presumptive effects clashed with Klapper's thesis that the media were of little consequence. Intuitively, it seemed, broadcast news exerted a strong impact on Americans' political attitudes, even if no one had yet documented the effects empirically (Lang & Lang, 2006).

There was also this quandary, frequently bandied about: If media were so ineffective, why did advertisers spend so much on commercials for cars such as the hot new Mustang? Why were they spending money to promote candidates such as Richard Nixon in 1968, whose blatant marketing spawned a book called *The Selling of the President*? (McGinniss, 1969). True, the paradox of advertisers spending lavishly on a supposedly ineffective media did not scientifically prove that media advertising had effects, but the question could not be ignored.

### A New Set of Questions

"There has to be a problem, this just can't be right, the media obviously have an impact, the limited effects view must be wrong." Ruminations like these no doubt settled in a growing number of researchers' minds as the stormy '60s ended. Political communication researchers began to take another look at the research that purported to show minimal effects. Carefully reexamining Lazarsfeld and his colleagues' 1940s research, with an eye toward media effects, scholars discovered that his study had underestimated press influences on both Democrats and Republicans. Other scholars, noting that media could influence factors other than voting, such as political cognitions (Chaffee & Hochheimer, 1985; McCombs & Shaw, 1972; McLeod, Becker, & Byrnes, 1974, Becker, McCombs, & McLeod, 1975), highlighted the embarrassingly obvious fact that Klapper had based his conclusions on studies that had been conducted before television had become the preeminent medium of political communication. Other research demonstrated that media could also influence the dynamics of the larger political system, as when the news media's ubiquitous presence during Watergate—and the very public impeachment hearings shown on television—encouraged political leaders to hold Nixon accountable for crimes he committed (Lang & Lang, 1983).

The effects of media—once questioned, frequently misunderstood, and always changing as a function of the times—became increasingly salient over the ensuring decades, as candidates harnessed negative advertising and adapted political rhetoric to television, in simplified, but visually appealing ways, as Reagan masterfully did during the 1980s. Media increasingly played an important part in strategic battles over policy reforms, displayed in the insurance industry's televised ads that helped derail Bill Clinton's health care reform plans, and George H.W. Bush's political public relations campaign to persuade the public to support the 1990 Kuwait war. With these developments on the forefront and research overwhelmingly demonstrating media effects, it was no longer plausible to argue the media had small, limited effects that played second fiddle to interpersonal influences. But this conclusion too would be shaped, sculpted, and modified.

## PUTTING IT ALL TOGETHER

Let's bring past and present together. What can we conclude from this historical review of political communication research? What do the twists and turns in the intellectual history of American political communication research tell us? What general themes emerge? Threading together Lippmann, Lazarsfeld, Klapper, and the voluminous research since then, we can identify six important themes.

**1. Lippmann was right: Media shape our images of the world.** Lippmann famously suggested that the media form the "pictures in our heads" of the world that lies outside our immediate experiences. His insight was prescient and continues to be true today. We do not experience politics directly. Instead, citizens necessarily rely on mainstream and social media to learn what is happening in Washington, D.C., China, and Iran. The media supply us with images that we use to construct beliefs about the political world. This is one reason why they are powerful. Media-instigated perceptions—and how they are constructed is complex—exert a multitude of effects on beliefs and behaviors, from voting to protests.

**2. Social networks matter.** Opinion leaders are important. Katz and Lazarsfeld called attention to this in their book *Personal Influence* (see Table 4.1), and it remains true today, ever more so in the era of social media. In our social media-dominated environment, national companies such as American Eagle and Hewlett-Packard hire opinion-leading student ambassadors, who promote the brand on Facebook, exploiting their social connections to market the product (Singer, 2011). Political conversations about politics occur frequently on social media (Southwell, 2014), often tendentiously, with conversations frequently reinforcing people's views of the political world. In electoral contexts, interpersonal influence and frequency of discussion complexly affect political decisions and participation in politics (Huckfeldt & Sprague, 1995; Eveland & Hively, 2009). But opinion leadership online is alive, as endorsements from family and friends influence the political content people seek on Facebook (Anspach, 2017).

In a similar fashion, other research documents that individuals' political networks can moderate media effects. For example, voters who spend time in politically consonant networks, characterized by political agreement among members, feel more strongly about their voting preferences when exposed to candidate ads (Neiheisel & Niebler, 2015). When a real-life Facebook friend posts a news story on Facebook and is perceived to be an opinion leader, social media recommendations amplify media trust, inducing people to want to read more news from the particular media platform in the future (Turcotte et al., 2015). Intriguingly, over the course of a presidential election campaign, strong Republican and Democrat partisans, by retweeting messages that are favorable to their side, act as opinion leaders, diffusing a biased, pro "our side" message to their followers (Shin & Thorson, 2018). What's more, opinion leaders aren't all high-status individuals who use elite media, as sometimes assumed, but include lower-status people who use tabloids and social media, befitting a populist era (Mangold & Bachl, 2018).

In these ways, a concept advanced in 1955—interpersonal influence—continues to plays a vital role in political communication today, as controversies persist about whether opinion leader–recommended content reinforces preexisting biases or offers more salutary electoral effects.

**3. A review of the early research shows that it was right about some things, wrong about others, but got people thinking.** The two-step flow—whereby media influence opinion leaders, who in turn affect others—was an innovative, heuristic concept when it was proposed in 1944. It still operates today, as when a health campaign about Juul influences older siblings, who in turn shape the beliefs of younger brothers, sisters, or friends. There is also evidence suggesting a two-step flow operates in online political marketing. For example, campaigns ask activists—for example, union supporters in Ohio who visited a Big Labor website—to contact less politically involved union members from work who might be susceptible to an appeal from a trustworthy, politically similar source (see Duhigg, 2012).

Researchers have studied diffusion over the past decades, assembling a variety of conclusions about the channels from which people learn about events of national consequence, when news diffuses first from media, when it spreads primarily through interpersonal communication channels, and when followers spread information to leaders (Weimann, 1994; Kaye & Johnson, 2011). These lines of inquiry were generated by the original research on the two-step flow.

In the main, research on **news diffusion**, the idea that mass-communicated news spreads political information through society, helped establish the importance of media in society when broadcast news was coming into its own in the 1950s and 1960s. Nowadays, the diffusion concept is, to some degree, out of date and less novel than in the old days, because people quickly and obviously obtain information instantly from Twitter and a host of online platforms. Many people learned about the George Floyd killing by watching the horrifying video on social media. But this wasn't true of everybody. Friends shared the video with friends (with the former serving as opinion leaders of sorts). Young people who were outraged at police brutality likely shared information about protests with friends on social media. But older Americans probably found out by watching television. In a similar fashion, images of the violent paramilitary insurrection of the Capitol cascaded across social media, as well as television, illustrating the continued importance of diffusion and the jarring power of visual images in politics (Bucy & Joo, 2021).

It may be a truism that hundreds of millions of people learn about events through social media, but that doesn't tell us the source of the information. Was it a liberal outlet that praised racial justice protests or a conservative outlet that denounced them? Diffusion can also be experienced very differently. It can feel impersonal, when you are watching TV by yourself in a lonely dorm room, or more personal, as when relayed through a two-step flow by opinion-leader colleagues or shared simultaneously and enthusiastically with friends. Unlike the old days, when diffusion went one-way, from media source to receiver, on social media receivers can post and retweet, influencing the ways politics is experienced.

Nowadays, diffusion questions, while less salient, revolve around the dynamics, content, accuracy, and degree of bias that occurs when people acquire information instantaneously from online media. They also have morphed from looking at how information relayed by TV spreads across society to more au courant issues, such as how misinformation spreads or even the dissemination via social media of visual protest images. Protest strategies diffuse like memes across social media, as when umbrellas, famously used in Hong Kong protests to erect barricades, were employed protectively by Portland protesters in 2020 (Bromwich, 2020). In these ways, an old concept expands in form and content, offering new applications to understanding political communication effects (see Figure 4.3).

**4. Two different political communication perspectives can be simultaneously true.** The media profoundly influence politics. The early work (pre-Lazarsfeld) got that right. At the same time, voters harbor strong attitudes. What people bring to media can strongly influence how they use and process media content, and can limit the impact of media on attitudes. As Klapper emphasized, people filter campaign messages through their attitudes, rejecting communications that

Figure 4.3 Diffusion is a classic concept in political communication research, an example of a term that, like fine wine, gets better, or at least stays relevant, with age. Originally invoked to explain the role of mass media in disseminating innovations and news, it has morphed to help us understand how memes and objects of protest spread globally via social media, as when umbrellas, the symbol of pro-democracy protests in Hong Kong (top) in 2014 and 2019, were employed in racial justice protests in Portland (bottom) in 2020.

*Source*: https://commons.wikimedia.org/wiki/File:Hong_Kong_protests_-_Kwong_Tong_March_20190824_-_P1066237.jpg
www.gettyimages.com/detail/news-photo/protestors-carry-umbrellas-as-they-gather-at-the-mark-o-news-photo/1227797313?adppopup=true

conflict with their political attitudes and accepting those that comport with what they believe. Klapper was correct that preexisting biases dampen media effects, but his work underplayed the subtle ways political media influence cognitions (Tessler & Zaller, 2014), as well as their macro effects on institutions, such as the presidential nominations and the larger political system, as when 2020 news coverage about Biden's victory helped symbolically certify the outcome. What's more, the concepts of strong media effects and powerful preexisting psychological attitudes can interact, as when committed partisans tune into politically congruent social media posts and the content leads them to feel even more strongly about their preferred candidate.

**5. Perceptions of powerful media effects are a consistent theme in political communication.** Scholars have detected an interesting continuity in communication research. During the 1930s, critics worried about pernicious influences wielded by radio programs. When comic books came around, fears centered on them. Not to be outdone, television, particularly violence, then video games, next the Internet, and now social media are the repository of concerns about—typically—harmful media effects. As Ellen A. Wartella and her colleagues noted, both academics and the public-at-large typically *assume* that the new media will exert powerful effects (Wartella, 1996; Wartella & Reeves, 1985). Over time, as the technology diffuses and becomes part of everyday life, a more modest and complex theory takes hold. Scholars change their tune, recognizing that the medium is not as powerful as they once feared, and they qualify their conjectures (Wartella, 1996).

This has stimulated an interesting "meta-debate" among communication researchers. For many years it was widely assumed that early propaganda researchers believed in a simplistic model of media effects that likened the media to a hypodermic needle that injected a message into audiences. But when scholars tried to find the term in the early research of the 20th century, they could find little evidence that the phrase *hypodermic needle* was invoked to describe mass media effects (Chaffee & Hochheimer, 1985; see also Bineham, 1988). Adding another layer to the discussion, Wartella and Stout (2002) reported that some research conducted during the 1930s adopted a more complex and nuanced view of media effects, hardly what one would expect if all the researchers thought of media in simple terms. Other scholars (Lubken, 2008) have even argued that the hypodermic needle notion served the function of a "straw man" for contemporary researchers. It allowed them to pat themselves on the back for coming up with a more sophisticated perspective on media, when in fact few scholars actually held a simplistic view in the 1930s and 1940s.

Academics aside, there is no question that across different eras, many people have *assumed* the media exert powerful effects. In 1922, Lippmann worried that the powers-that-be could instill pictures in our heads and manufacture consent. In 2011, a *New York Times* critic, describing video art, remarked on "the degree to which our world, what we take for reality, is formed by recording and image-making machinery." He noted that "our minds organize incoming information into images and narratives that may or may not be true to the facts," adding "we live in a world of scary, reality-determining technologies" (Johnson, 2011, p. C22).

The critic may be correct, but the point is you could have found a similar paragraph in articles writers penned in the 1920s, except they would have worried that movies or radio or propaganda controlled us. This represents a common thread in American political history. "The central paradox of America's constitutional tradition," Hogan (2013) observes, "lies in a persistent tension between our commitment to popular sovereignty and fears that 'the people' might be too easily distracted or manipulated to govern themselves" (p. 10). A conundrum of democracy is that government needs an institutional mechanism to inform and persuade the citizenry. However, the presence of both institutionalized public relations and mass media generate fears of abuse, some based in fantasy, others in fact. When is the public justified in fearing manipulation? When are fears about propaganda and massive media effects out of whack with reality? When should critics worry about White House news management? When do these worries reflect a cynical projection of sinister motives to well-intentioned policies developed by the nation's leaders? Do partisans' perceptions of hostile media effects exacerbate polarization? (see Chapter 9). These important questions thread their way through American political communication.

**6. Continued debate and dialogue characterize current political communication scholarship.** There is not a party line, but continuing questions, the mark of a healthy discipline. Do social media facilitate or impede democracy? Is the social media glass half empty, in view of the spread of misinformation, or is it half full, in light of social media's ability to convey and organize social justice protests? Do campaigns inform or mislead the electorate? Some scholars are more optimistic about the Internet and social media effects, arguing they can strengthen civic engagement (Boulianne, 2009). Others see a more negative picture, arguing that they merely reinforce existing prejudices (Sunstein, 2001). Some researchers point to the deceptive, manipulative aspects of campaigns, emphasizing their singular ability to cultivate beliefs that align with the powers-that-be (Le Cheminant & Parrish, 2011). Newer approaches emphasize the multitude of diverse platforms, as well as the ways that social media reaffirm what people believe via the online architecture of social networking sites, characterized by strong personalized connections to a narrow range of (frequently congenial) partisan views (Seaton, 2016). This too has stimulated debate between critics who believe social media promotes new forms of participation and others who fear it divides and polarizes. Dialogue among proponents of different scholarly frameworks is healthy. It generates vigorous discussion and helps researchers develop more sophisticated models of political communication.

## WHERE WE ARE NOW

Amid all the debate, a new scholarly consensus has emerged. As social media have proliferated, people no longer simultaneously receive the same mass message delivered by television; individuals are more likely to receive news customized to their own political tastes on Facebook, and boundaries between opinion and fact have blurred. The long-held consensus that political media exert simultaneous, homogenizing effects on the mass public is a matter of debate, at the very least.

The dominant model in the past emphasized that political media had top-down influences, with government and leading political elites exploiting media to promote particular political perspectives. It was never that simple, of course, as there has long been a pluralism of elite viewpoints on most issues in America. However, the media-to-public model, with news as a centerpiece, had considerable support. In contemporary scholarship, the mass-mediated model has been supplemented with a "networked public sphere" (Friedland, Hove, & Rojas, 2006). Mainstream media exist online alongside competing platforms and a multitude of online posts. Citizens are no longer exclusively receivers of political messages, but now initiate political conversations with friends, journalists, and leaders, frequently seeking out information that confirms what they already believe (Bennett & Iyengar, 2008). What's more, with individuals increasingly living in communication enclaves peopled by those who share their perspective, there are questions about whether citizens gain exposure to a common set of consensually agreed-on facts (like on climate change), when they even come into contact with facts that call their biases into question, and if they are open to viewpoints other than their own.

And so it has come to this: After decades of critiquing the notion of limited effects, proclaiming and demonstrating that political media had strong influences, it's back. Limited effects is back, at least sort of.

When people were part of a mass audience that received the same news, advertisements, and commentaries, in isolation from one another, it was eminently reasonable to argue that media had uniformly large influences. Nowadays, in an age when people can create congenial messages, as often as they receive impersonal, mass-mediated ones, in an era of networked gatekeeping, that thesis is under fire, taking us back to Klapper's once-controversial notion that media have limited effects.

What goes around comes around. During a time when individuals, particularly strong partisans, tune into media outlets that reinforce their existing viewpoints, the psychology of the selective audience is a central issue in research. Scholars have documented that when people have strong political attitudes, they gravitate, almost reflexively it sometimes seems, to media that parrot what they already believe. For example, in a well-conducted study, Matthew Barnidge and his colleagues (2020) found that conservatives prefer conservative to liberal news outlets, liberals prefer liberal to conservative outlets, and the stronger individuals' political opinions, the more likely they are to turn to media fare that supports what they already believe.

The idea of the selective, biased political media audience (or group of receivers, since "audience" implies passivity) is in vogue. Many researchers are focusing on this issue, training their empirically trained eyes on different, subtle aspects of the ways political biases determine uses of media (see Chapter 9). Are people gaining (algorithmically determined) exposure to like-minded content, or do people have more contact with information contesting their viewpoints than is frequently assumed? What factors determine whether you are more likely to be exposed to messages that offer a refreshingly different point of view? How does this link up to media effects? The debate about campaign effects continues apace today, with some scholars arguing that campaigns exert the minimal effects emphasized by Lazarsfeld and his associates (Kalla & Broockman, 2018), and others emphasizing that media frames push people toward media-centric ways of looking at problems. There is continued debate about this classic issue in the field, and there probably always will be.

On the stronger effects side of the spectrum, Lance Holbert and his colleagues (2010) argued that media messages, including those on Facebook and Twitter, continue to influence political attitudes. A persistent finding in the field is that media are particularly impactful under key conditions. This conclusion need not reflect disillusionment with media effects, but rather, a more mature understanding of their complexity (Neuman, 2018). For example, political media can be particularly influential during presidential primaries, as well as when campaigns successfully identify the core of persuadable voters torn by conflicting loyalties (Kalla & Broockman, 2018). This is a tension in political communication research today, reflecting consideration of both ends of the media effects continuum, the pole that suggests media effects only reinforce existing attitudes of minds already made up, and the pole emphasizing that effects can be larger and substantial. Yet there is consensus that even if media reinforce, rather than change, attitudes, these effects can be important in certain contexts, and media can both reinforce on the individual level and exert transformative effects on a macro level, as seen in the ways social media have altered campaigns.

The George Floyd video exemplified this effect. It was one of the most consequential media—actually social media—stimuli in the history of mass communication research. Exerting an arguably greater effect than the fictional Orson Welles "War of the Worlds" radio drama of 1938, the video lit a fire under the American consciousness, triggering mass protests and producing more sympathetic public attitudes toward racial justice (see Chapter 1). But it was not a simple effect that hypodermically and instantly changed attitudes. Like all political media influences, it cannot be understood outside of the social context: years of political seed-planting by Black Lives Matter; staccato repetition of unarmed Blacks recently killed by police; and masses of young people frustrated by a pandemic, yearning to do something outside their isolated homes, scrutinizing a video they might have ignored had they been working full-time.

Beyond the Floyd example, there is a great deal of vitality in current research on political communication. There are pressing normative concerns about whether and how online media may be undercutting democratic norms (Shah et al., 2017), fascination with the sinister ways fake news and "stealth media" insinuate themselves into citizens' political media uses (Kim et al., 2018), interest in the complicating possibility that such claims of media impact are exaggerated and driven by biased perceptions, and concern about the overall health of a political media system gatekept by social media companies with little commitment to journalistic or democratic norms. Like much academic research these days, the scholarship reflects a skeptical attitude toward democracy, lacking the wild (and unrealistic) optimism of years past, harnessing empirical theories and methods to shed light on democracy's limits and potential (see Box 4.1).

---

### BOX 4.1 CONTEMPORARY POLITICAL COMMUNICATION METHODOLOGIES

Nearly 50 years ago, when the modern field of political communication was launched (Chaffee, 1975), the discipline was dominated by traditional tools of social science research. These included **content analyses**, systematic examinations of media messages; **surveys**, real-world, questionnaire studies that document relationships between variables but don't convincingly show causation; and **experiments**, with their scientific demonstration of cause and effect, but shortcomings in external or real-world validity. Over the past decades, the intellectual horizons of the field have expanded, and with this have come improvements in these methods, as well as a proliferation of new and improved strategies for research (Arceneaux, 2010; Kosicki, McLeod, & McLeod, 2011; Hoffman & Young, 2011; Krupnikov & Searles, 2019). These include the following:

- **Secondary analysis**, a technique that allows researchers to reanalyze national data sets with a particular focus or innovative twist (Holbert & Hmielowski, 2011).
- **Focus groups**, in which a trained leader coordinates a group interview that can yield rich insights on a variety of topics, such as how people talk about politics in everyday life, why many young people do not vote, and reactions to political ads (Jarvis, 2011).

*Continued*

- **Multiple discourse strategies** to explore communication that occurs in deliberative meetings. This includes systematic analysis of discussion at a school board meeting or town hall forum, as well as post-meeting follow-up interviews with participants (Black et al., 2011).
- **Psychophysiological measures** of heart rate, facial muscle activation, brain imaging, and other bodily arousal that occurs while watching candidate speeches and negative (rather than positive) political ads (Bucy & Bradley, 2011; Soroka et al., 2019).
- **Big data and online analytics:** This is a major methodological development, one of the most exciting in the field today. Researchers are focusing on the voluminous amounts of big data available online by examining tweets, web pages, and blogs that can set a different agenda of important issues than conventional news can (Neuman et al., 2014). Other researchers have used digital data and methods unavailable in previous eras. Colleoni, Rozza, and Arvidsson (2014) examined the degree to which Twitter serves as an echo chamber for what Democrats and Republicans already think by content-analyzing more than 200,000 tweets. Guo and colleagues (2020) documented the ways au courant crowdcoding could efficiently annotate election tweets. Song, Cho, and Benefield (2020) explored real-world message selection in an online discussion forum, using a causally focused time-series approach, to determine if people seek out information confirming their viewpoints. Still other research has harnessed top-of-the-line digital methodologies, as in Young Mie Kim and her colleagues' (2018) use of a digital advertising tracking instrument that identified groups that sponsored 2016 stealth Facebook advertising campaigns.

Intriguing as these studies are, they face the usual questions of validity and cause and effect, but the methods are exciting because they can tap into the volatile world of online political messaging and effects.

## CONCLUSIONS

This chapter traced the trajectory of political communication research, describing milestones, critical junctures, the current zeitgeist (or consensus about scholarly effects), and research methods used to test hypotheses. Emphasizing that the history of a field of study is not a boring, straight-line summation of facts, the discussion tracked political communication's zigzag path of historical development. Based on research of the 1940s and 1950s, researchers concluded that political media had minimal effects. This perspective, epitomized by Klapper's (1960) conclusions, proved controversial, rankling scholars who believed media exerted a preeminent role in politics. With the diffusion of television and growing scientific evidence of strong political communication influences,

Klapper's limited effects model fell by the wayside, supplanted by models that emphasized the direct, indirect, micro, and macro ways media influence politics.

Reviewing the history of political communication scholarship, one glimpses twists and turns, as well as continuities. As will be discussed throughout this book, political media decidedly influence our pictures of the world, molding ideas and helping us construct beliefs about politics. Interpersonal influence, an old concept that became passé in the 1970s and '80s as television exerted significant effects (and the field sought to define itself in terms of primordial media impact), has become important again. We live in an era of both conventional media and online social networks, where communication that occurs online has accoutrements of old-style interpersonal communication. Socially mediated opinion leadership, coupled with online media use, can influence political participation, while also reinforcing selective exposure to politically congruent information. Political media exert a wealth of effects, but—packaging old political communication wine in new online bottles—refinements of Klapper's view have some support.

Yet for all the contemporary revisionism, Klapper's mid-20th-century limited effects view reflected the scholarly zeitgeist of his era, and it does minimize both the exciting and democratically deleterious effects of media-by-context interactions. Since the time Klapper wrote his book, the field has taken off in ways that were unimaginable then, expanding to ask questions about the macro, rhetorical, and ideological climates in which political communication occurs.

Over the many decades, researchers have documented a multitude of political communication effects, such as agenda-setting, priming, and framing, that result from cognitive processing of electoral messages. They have explored these and other influences in a variety of arenas, testing theoretical hypotheses with a host of new research methods. There continue to be lively debates about whether political media exert strong or modest impacts, the nature of the processes that mediate communication effects, the extent to which messages inform or obfuscate issues, and the degree to which new media are unraveling democratic processes or contributing to their revitalization.

## REFERENCES

Anspach, N.M. (2017). The new personal influence: How our Facebook friends influence the news we read. *Political Communication, 34*, 590–606.

Arceneaux, K. (2010). The benefits of experimental methods for the study of campaign effects. *Political Communication, 27*, 199–215.

Barnidge, M., Gunther, A.C., Kim, J., Hong, Y., Perryman, M., Tay, S.K., & Knisely, S. (2020). Politically motivated selective exposure and perceived media bias. *Communication Research, 47*, 82–103.

Becker, L.B., McCombs, M.E., & McLeod, J.M. (1975). The development of political cognitions. In S.H. Chaffee (Ed.), *Political communication: Strategies for research* (pp. 21–63). Newbury Park, CA: Sage.

Bennett, W.L., & Iyengar, S. (2008). A new era of minimal effects? The changing foundations of political communication. *Journal of Communication, 58*, 707–731.

Bineham, J.L. (1988). A historical account of the hypodermic model in mass communication. *Communication Monographs, 55*, 230–246.

Black, L.W., Burkhalter, S., Gastil, J., & Stromer-Galley, J. (2011). Methods for analyzing and measuring group deliberation. In E.P. Bucy & R.L. Holbert (Eds.), *The sourcebook for political communication research: Methods, measures, and analytical techniques* (pp. 323–345). New York: Routledge.

Boulianne, S. (2009). Does Internet use affect engagement? A meta-analysis of research. *Political Communication, 26*, 193–211.

Bromwich, J.E. (2020, July 31). Why protest tactics spread like memes. *The New York Times*. Online: www.nytimes.com/2020/07/31/style/viral-protest-videos.html. (Accessed: August 2, 2020).

Bucy, E.P., & Bradley, S.D. (2011). What the body can tell us about politics: The use of psychophysiological measures in political communication research. In E.P. Bucy & R.L. Holbert (Eds.), *The sourcebook for political communication research: Methods, measures, and analytical techniques* (pp. 525–540). New York: Routledge.

Bucy, E.P., & Joo, J. (2021). Editors' introduction: Visual politics, grand collaborative programs, and the opportunity to think big. *The International Journal of Press/Politics, 26*, 5–21.

Chaffee, S.H. (Ed.). (1975). *Political communication: Issues and strategies for research.* Beverly Hills, CA: Sage.

Chaffee, S.H., & Hochheimer, J.L. (1985). The beginnings of political communication research in the United States: Origins of the "limited effects" model. In M. Gurevitch & M.R. Levy (Eds.), *Mass communication review yearbook* (Vol. 5, pp. 75–104). Newbury Park, CA: Sage.

Colleoni, E., Rozza, A., & Arvidsson, A. (2014). Echo chamber or public sphere? Predicting political orientation and measuring political homophily in Twitter using Big Data. *Journal of Communication, 64*, 317–332.

Duhigg, C. (2012, October 14). Campaigns mine personal lives to get out vote. *The New York Times*, 1, 14.

Eveland, W.P., Jr., & Hively, M.H. (2009). Political discussion frequency, network size, and "heterogeneity" of discussion as predictors of political knowledge and participation. *Journal of Communication, 59*, 205–224.

Friedland, L.A., Hove, T., & Rojas, H. (2006). The networked public sphere. *Javnost—The Public, 13*(4), 5–26.

Guo, L., Mays, K., Lai, S., Jalal, M., Ishwar, P., & Betke, M. (2020). Accurate, fast, but not always cheap: Evaluating "crowdcoding" as an alternative approach to analyze social media data. *Journalism & Mass Communication Quarterly, 97*, 811–834.

Hoffman, L.H., & Young, D.G. (2011). Political communication survey research: Challenges, trends, and opportunities. In E.P. Bucy & R.L. Holbert (Eds.), *The sourcebook for political communication research: Methods, measures, and analytical techniques* (pp. 55–77). New York: Routledge.

Hogan, J.M. (2013). Persuasion in the rhetorical tradition. In J.P. Dillard (Ed.), *The persuasion handbook: New directions in theory and research.* Thousand Oaks, CA: Sage.

Holbert, R.L., Garrett, R.K., & Gleason, L.S. (2010). A new era of minimal effects? A response to Bennett and Iyengar. *Journal of Communication, 60*, 15–34.

Holbert, R.L, & Hmielowski, J.D. (2011). Secondary analysis in political communication viewed as a creative act. In E.P. Bucy & R.L. Holbert (Eds.), *The sourcebook for political communication research: Methods, measures, and analytical techniques* (pp. 81–95). New York: Routledge.

Huckfeldt, R., & Sprague, J. (1995). *Citizens, politics, and social communication: Information and influence in an election campaign.* New York: Cambridge University Press.

Jarvis, S.E. (2011). The use of focus groups in political communication research. In E.P. Bucy & R.L. Holbert (Eds.), *The sourcebook for political communication research: Methods, measures, and analytical techniques* (pp. 283–299). New York: Routledge.

Johnson, K. (2011, August 26). Unfiltered images, turning perceptions upside down. *The New York Times*, C22.

Kalla, J.L., & Broockman, D.E. (2018). The minimal persuasive effects of campaign contact in general elections: Evidence from 49 field experiments. *American Political Science Review, 112,* 148–166.

Katz, E., & Lazarsfeld, P.F. (1955). *Personal influence: The part played by people in the flow of mass communications.* Glencoe, IL: Free Press.

Kaye, B.K., & Johnson, T.J. (2011). *The shot heard around the World Wide Web: Who heard what where about Osama bin Laden's death.* Paper presented to annual convention of Midwest Association for Public Opinion Research, Chicago.

Kim, Y.M., Hsu, J., Neiman, D., Kou, C., Bankston, L., Kim, S.Y., Heinrich, R., Baragwanath, R., & Raskutti, G. (2018). The stealth media? Groups and targets behind divisive issue campaigns on Facebook. *Political Communication, 35,* 515–541.

Klapper, J.T. (1960). *The effects of mass communication.* New York: Free Press.

Kosicki, G.M., McLeod, D.M., & McLeod, J.M. (2011). Looking back and looking forward: Observations on the role of research methods in the rapidly evolving field of political communication. In E.P. Bucy & R.L. Holbert (Eds.), *The sourcebook for political communication research: Methods, measures, and analytical techniques* (pp. 543–569). New York: Routledge.

Krupnikov, Y., & Searles, K. (2019). New approaches to method and measurement in the study of political communication effects. *Political Communication, 36,* 209–213.

Lang, G.E., & Lang, K. (1983). *The battle for public opinion: The president, the press, and the polls during Watergate.* New York: Columbia University Press.

Lang, K., & Lang, G.E. (2006). *Personal Influence* and the new paradigm: Some inadvertent consequences. *Annals of the American Association of Political and Social Science, 608,* 157–178.

Lazarsfeld, P.F., Berelson, B., & Gaudet, H. (1944). *The people's choice: How the voter makes up his mind in a presidential campaign.* New York: Columbia University Press.

Le Cheminant, W., & Parrish, J.M. (2011). Introduction: Manipulating democracy: A reappraisal. In W. Le Cheminant & J.M. Parrish (Eds.), *Manipulating democracy: Democratic theory, political psychology, and mass media* (pp. 1–24). New York: Routledge.

Lippmann, W. (1922). *Public opinion.* New York: Free Press.

Lubken, D. (2008). Remembering the straw man: The travels and adventures of *hypodermic.* In D.W. Park & J. Pooley (Eds.), *The history of media and communication research: Contested memories* (pp. 19–42). New York: Peter Lang.

Mangold, F., & Bachl, M. (2018). New news media, new opinion leaders? How political opinion leaders navigate the modern high-choice media environment. *Journal of Communication, 68,* 896–919.

McCombs, M.E., & Shaw, D.L. (1972). The agenda-setting function of mass media. *Public Opinion Quarterly, 36,* 176–187.

McGinniss, J. (1969). *The selling of the president*. New York: Penguin.

McLeod, J.M., Becker, L.B., & Byrnes, J.E. (1974). Another look at the agenda- setting function of the press. *Communication Research, 1*, 131–165.

Neiheisel, J.R., & Niebler, S. (2015). On the limits of persuasion: Campaign ads and the structure of voters' interpersonal discussion networks. *Political Communication, 32*, 434–452.

Neuman, W.R. (2018). The paradox of the paradigm: An important gap in media effects research. *Journal of Communication, 68*, 369–379.

Neuman, W.R., Guggenheim, L., Jang, S.M., & Bae, S.Y. (2014). The dynamics of public attention: Agenda-setting theory meets big data. *Journal of Communication, 64*, 193–214.

Seaton, J. (2016). The new architecture of communications. *Journalism Studies, 17*, 808–816.

Shah, D.V., McLeod, D.M., Rojas, H., Cho, J., Wagner, M.W., & Friedland, L.A. (2017). Revising the communication mediation model for a new political communication ecology. *Human Communication Research, 43*, 491–504.

Shin, J., & Thorson, K. (2018). Partisan selective sharing: The biased diffusion of fact-checking messages on social media. *Journal of Communication, 67*, 233–255.

Singer, N. (2011, September 11.) On campus, it's one big commercial. *The New York Times* (Sunday Business), 1, 4.

Song, H., Cho, J., & Benefield, G.A. (2020). The dynamics of message selection in online political discussion forums: Self-segregation or diverse exposure? *Communication Research, 47*, 125–152.

Soroka, S., Fournier, P., Nir, L., & Hibbing, J. (2019). Psychophysiology in the study of political communication: An expository study of individual-level variation in negativity biases. *Political Communication, 36*, 288–302.

Southwell, B.G. (2014). Two-step flow, diffusion, and the role of social networks in political communication. In K. Kenski & K.H. Jamieson (Eds.), *The Oxford handbook of political communication*. New York: Oxford University Press. Online: www.oxfordhandbooks.com/view/10.1093/oxfordhb/9780199793471.001.0001/oxfordhb-9780199793471-e-024. (Accessed: November 20, 2020).

Sunstein, C. (2001). *Republic.com*. Princeton, NJ: Princeton University Press.

Tessler, M., & Zaller, J. (2014). The power of political communication. In K. Kenski & K.H. Jamieson (Eds.), *The Oxford handbook of political communication*. Online: www.oxfordhandbooks.com. (Accessed: June 7, 2014).

Turcotte, J., York, C., Irving, J., Scholl, R.M., & Pingree, R.J. (2015). News recommendations from social media opinion leaders: Effects on media trust and information seeking. *Journal of Computer-Mediated Communication, 20*, 520–535.

Wartella, E. (1996). The history reconsidered. In E.E. Dennis & E. Wartella (Eds.), *American communication research—The remembered history* (pp. 169–180). Mahwah, NJ: Lawrence Erlbaum Associates.

Wartella, E.A., & Reeves, B. (1985). Historical trends in research on children and the media: 1900–1960. *Journal of Communication, 35*, 118–135.

Wartella, E.A., & Stout, P.A. (2002). The evolution of mass media and health persuasion models. In W.D. Crano & M. Burgoon (Eds.), *Mass media and drug prevention: Classic and contemporary theories and research* (pp. 19–34). Mahwah, NJ: Lawrence Erlbaum Associates.

Weimann, G. (1994). *The influential: People who influence people*. Albany: State University of New York Press.

# CHAPTER

# 5 Media and Political Knowledge

Let's begin with Madison.

James Madison, the brilliant architect of the Constitution, firmly believed in the power of knowledge. As he famously said,

> a popular government, without popular information, or the means of acquiring it, is but a prologue to a farce or a tragedy; or perhaps both. And a people who mean to be their own governors, must arm themselves with the power which knowledge gives.

It's an eloquent statement. Madison recognized that you cannot have a functioning democratic society if citizens are ignorant of basic facts of government and cannot grasp the array of problems facing society (see Figure 5.1).

Normative democratic theories place a premium on citizen knowledge and competence. As political scientists Niemi and Junn (1998) noted, "for democratic decision making to be meaningful and legitimate, citizens must be capable of understanding what is at stake in politics, what their alternatives are, and what their own positions are" (p. 9). There are a variety of ways for people to acquire knowledge, but the onus rests with media—the instruments by which information is transmitted, constructed, and built into nuggets of knowledge brought to bear on policy decisions by politicians, activists, and everyone else.

So, what do people know about politics? Are they adequately informed? How well are different media—online news outlets and social media—doing in informing the public? Are the media performing their storied civic function?

This chapter and the one that follows offer an in-depth examination of citizenship in an age of mediated politics. The present chapter focuses on knowledge, and Chapter 6 examines the socialization of political beliefs and attitudes. This chapter is divided into four sections. The first section explores what Americans know about politics, what they don't know, and the reasons why knowledge levels are not as high as they could or should be. The second portion examines the media's impact on knowledge acquisition, guided by different disciplinary perspectives. The third section discusses the ups and downs of political learning in a digital age. The fourth and final section focuses directly on misinformation in an online partisan age.

## WHAT DO AMERICANS KNOW ABOUT POLITICS?

First, the good news.

In a classic book, Michael Delli Carpini and Scott Keeter (1996) concluded that Americans are modestly informed about politics and have basic knowledge of a number of aspects of government. But when you look at basic civics, or what people know about government, ignorance and disparities in knowledge, are well . . . nothing short of breathtaking:

● Just over one-fourth of the public can name all three branches of government (executive, legislative, and judicial, in case you forgot); almost three in four did not know the Constitution is the highest law in the nation; and one in ten college graduates thought TV's Judge Judy was a member of the Supreme Court, while two-thirds could name a

**Figure 5.1 The erudite James Madison emphasized the important role that knowledge plays in democracy, famously recognizing that one cannot have a functioning democratic society if citizens lack basic political knowledge. Given Madison's role in promoting the infamous constitutional compromise that counted each slave as three-fifths of a person, his emphasis on citizen knowledge was restricted to Whites; Blacks did not become citizens of the U.S. until the passage of the Fourteenth Amendment. Still, his philosophical argument about the importance of knowledge in a democracy continues to resonate.**

*Source*: https://en.wikipedia.org/wiki/File:James_Madison_Portrait2.jpg

TV judge on *American Idol* (Wegman, 2018; Annenberg Public Policy Center, 2016; Breyer, 2010).

● Just 35 percent could name both senators from their state. Three-quarters of all Americans do not appreciate the difference between a legislator and a judge (Breyer, 2010).

● About 25 percent of Americans can identify *more than one* of the five freedoms ensured by the First Amendment (freedom of speech, press, religion, assembly, and petition for redress of grievance). But more than half had no trouble naming two members of *The Simpsons* (Shenkman, 2008).

● Forty-four percent of Americans without health insurance believed Obama's health care law would exert no impact on the quality of health care they receive, even though the law improves the overall quality of health care (Goodnough & Kopicki, 2013).

● There are widespread inequalities in political knowledge. Educated and wealthier Americans are considerably more knowledgeable than their less educated and poorer counterparts.

It's complicated. When the stakes are high, as during Watergate, the 1998 Clinton impeachment scandal, Trump's 2019 impeachment, and the turbulent events of 2020, polls show the majority of the public was familiar with the basic issues. A large majority of Americans closely followed the 1973 Watergate hearings and believed Nixon had engaged in wrongdoing. A sizable number knew Clinton committed perjury, and that impeachment involved consequences of his sexual affair with a White House intern. The public was broadly familiar with the 2019 impeachment process to acquit or remove President Trump from office. During the 2020 coronavirus outbreak, nearly nine in ten Americans closely followed news of the pandemic (Jurkowitz, 2020). A substantial majority was also familiar with the federal aid package adopted in March (Mitchell, Oliphant, & Shearer, 2020). In a similar fashion, more than eight in ten Americans said they were closely following news of the George Floyd protests (Mitchell et al., 2020).

There is a paradox here. Never before has society had so much political information, and never before has it been easier to locate political facts. Technology has provided unprecedented access to information about a wealth of topics, putting knowledge literally at people's fingertips. Yet citizens can be uninformed about political issues and the Internet is awash in falsehoods, as the very technology that has provided unparalleled access to truths has allowed for the development of divisive outlets that traffic in misinformation, perhaps helping to propagate anti-democratic attitudes (Filindra, 2018). Democracy requires political knowledge and an appreciation of democratic norms, but citizens' knowledge does not come close to approximating the levels deemed appropriate by political philosophers and can include beliefs that are dangerously undemocratic in character.

## Why Don't People Know More About Political Issues?

Delli Carpini and Keeter's book, a classic in the field, is old, but current research confirms a number of its basic contours. Based on a collection of studies, many scholars find Americans' ignorance of basic facts about government disturbing. Americans know significantly less about political issues, particularly international problems, than do citizens from a host of European countries (Aalberg & Curran, 2012). What accounts for knowledge deficits? Four explanations have been advanced.

One reason is lack of incentive. A key way people make their voices known in democracy is through voting. Yet one person's vote makes virtually no difference in the outcome of an election. From a purely rational perspective, it is not in an individual's self-interest to expend much time soaking up political information when his or her input is of such little consequence.

A second explanation emphasizes the way news is presented. Its focus on facts, figures, and jargon can overwhelm people. News about the economic crisis can contain mind-numbing discussion of *mortgage-backed securities, over-leveraging,* or *liquidity shortfall,* concepts that most people do not understand and are explained poorly, if at all, by journalists. In addition, American television networks devote less time to news during peak hours (7 to 10 p.m.) than do European broadcasts (Aalberg, van Aelst, & Curran, 2012). Despite the growth of CNN and Fox, there is actually less news provided during prime time in the U.S. than in six European nations. This helps explain why Americans know less about politics than their European counterparts do, although, in fairness, many British citizens had distorted views about the number of UK immigrants prior to the 2016 Brexit vote, as a result of campaign prevarications (Perloff, 2019).

A third explanation lies in the expansion in media choices. With a multitude of entertaining cable channels, YouTube, and social media sites, news may be swamped by other channels, lost in the mix. "Those who prefer nonpolitical content can more easily escape the news and therefore pick up less political information than they used to," one scholar observes (Prior, 2005, p. 577). On digital platforms, news is frequently swamped by other content, such as entertainment stories, and it can be hard to get past the clutter to focus on a key local story. On social media, stories can be summarized in snippets that don't provide important details about an issue. Or stories may simply be fabricated (Jurkowitz & Mitchell, 2020a).

Fourth, leaders deliberately dissemble information, intentionally conveying misleading political facts. Back in the 1990s, some political leaders described Social Security in doomsday terms, talking about the "impending bankruptcy" of the financial program. Policymakers claimed that the program would run out of cash by the 2030s, even though there would actually be enough funds available to pay retirees for another two decades to come. Some politicians may have resorted to hyperbole in an effort to push Congress into acting sooner rather than later. Others may have had more opportunistic motives. Whatever the reason, the political rhetoric did not match the facts, yet it had demonstrable effects on public knowledge. During the debate about Social Security in 1998 and 1999, as many as one-third of Americans incorrectly believed that Social Security would completely run out of money (Jerit & Barabas, 2006). In a similar fashion, President Trump falsely claimed on a number of occasions that a vaccine would be available before Election Day 2020, played down the importance of masks, and touted the effectiveness of hydroxychloroquine in treating the virus, despite lack of medical evidence. Republicans who relied on Trump for their news about the coronavirus were less likely to believe that health professionals got their facts right, probably causing them to harbor incorrect beliefs on the effectiveness of masks and other preventive measures (Jurkowitz & Mitchell, 2020b).

## An Optimistic View and Reflections on Citizenship

Maybe it's not so bad. Perhaps the criticisms of citizens are misplaced, placing unreasonable expectations on contemporary voters. Perhaps people are doing just fine, when all is said and done. Cogent arguments have been advanced for this position.

Scholars acknowledge that in an ideal world, people would closely follow politics and formulate thoughtful perspectives on every issue. But this is unrealistic, given the demands on citizens' time and the difficulty of comprehending torturously complex issues. Consequently, people develop cognitive shortcuts or **heuristics** to help them make political decisions. Voters evaluate candidates based on whether short descriptions of candidates' positions are roughly congenial with their own values. They use political party labels as guides, casting a vote for nominees of their preferred party. Voters loosely follow presidential debates, checking to see if their candidate is knowledgeable about the issues and can competently defend their positions. They may rely on the views of respected opinion leaders, as expressed in newspaper editorials, on cable TV, or in blogs. People may fall short in their knowledge of basic civics or international issues, but nonetheless remain capable of making reasonable decisions in elections (Sniderman, Brody, & Tetlock, 1991).

Some researchers point out that tests of political knowledge are flawed, requiring people to supply trivial facts that are peripheral to the actual task of citizenship. Questions asking the names of politicians in the news are efficient for researchers, enabling them to score tests quickly, but may unfairly penalize citizens (Graber, 2012). Lupia (2016) notes that there has never been any demonstration that the recall questions on these tests constitute "necessary or sufficient conditions for the broader competences or important kinds of knowledge" that citizenship requires (p. 229). He also points out that recall questions can use confusing jargon, pose issues vaguely, and offer little motivation for respondents to answer questions correctly.

Others note that good citizenship does not require expert knowledge of every issue covered in the news. Citizens can scan the political environment, looking out for dangers to their personal well-being and the public welfare. They can fulfill their civic duty by broadly monitoring the political environment, using shortcuts, and gathering information about the broad contours of politics (Schudson, 1998; Ytre-Arne & Moe, 2018; see also Zaller, 2003). With access to the Internet instantly accessible through mobile phones, people may not need a storehouse of political knowledge, so long as they know where to find the information (Kleinberg & Lau, 2019).

Some scholars go further, noting that the system can function adequately so long as a healthy minority of individuals closely follow political issues, remain knowledgeable about politics, and partake in activist causes. Everyone does not have to boast top-flight knowledge, so long as some do. According to this view, emphasizing the virtues of elite democracy, politics in industrialized democracies has become so complicated and time-consuming that it requires a class of experts to make high-level political decisions. These experts are elected officials, who are accountable to the people through free and fair elections. Political theorist Joseph Schumpeter (1976) bluntly noted that "democracy means only that the people have the opportunity of accepting or refusing the (people) who are to rule them. . . . Now one aspect of this may be expressed by saying that democracy is the rule of the politician" (pp. 284–285).

As you might expect, this elite view of democracy has generated considerable criticism. Leave democracy to the politicians? That's precisely the problem with modern politics, critics charge. Professional politicians are not responsive to the people, but rather to lobbyists and moneyed interests who finance their campaigns. Advocates of deliberative democracy argue that even in our mediated age, democracy must be based on the active engagement of citizens in decisions that affect their lives. Fair enough. But how much should people know about politics? What does the good citizen need to know to fulfill civic duty? What facts can the dutiful voter reasonably ignore? There are not hard-and-fast answers to these questions.

Still others take a more jaundiced view of the entire scholarly area. Why, critics ask, should we even insist on good citizens when American democracy is broken, rigged for the powerful, and too often treats its minority citizens with prejudice? If leaders have failed the citizenry, why should we be bothered if people don't know specific aspects of a democracy that doesn't work for them anyway? The criticisms are worthy, but they do not negate the importance of knowledge, even from a more radical perspective. Citizens must know the workings of a system they want to change, if they are to mount successful reform efforts.

The late Doris Graber (2006) offered an integrative view on these different perspectives. She suggested that if people understand the main impact that problems exert on their lives, are aware of their values and priorities, familiar with the major options, and talk about issues with others, they are adequately informed as citizens. On some issues, such as policing, people may be very informed, acutely aware of the problems, particularly in their neighborhoods, even if they can't remember every aspect of the Bill of Rights. On other topics, such as health care, people may appreciate the problem but harbor misconceptions due to the intricacy of the information, shortcomings in how news conveys it, or their own biased political communication network.

And yet if people fall prey to their biases, they aren't fulfilling the venerated canons of citizenship, a sacred centerpiece of a democracy. We want citizens—as opposed to mere voters—to deliberate on the issues, questioning their biases so they can grow politically and improve the state of democracy.

## MEDIA AND POLITICAL KNOWLEDGE

How do people acquire information about government and public affairs? What are the sources of their knowledge? Obviously, the media play an important role, providing the raw materials from which citizens construct beliefs about politics. We gain insight on the impact media exert on political knowledge by exploring different perspectives on the issue. The approaches discussed in the following sections emphasize concepts from the fields of mass communication, psychology, and sociology.

### The Media-Focused Perspective

A classic mass media perspective examined the distinctive effects that a particular communication medium exerted on knowledge. Older research suggested that reading newspapers should facilitate cognitive information-holding, while watching TV should impart emotional information, particularly (though not exclusively) among those of lower educational levels. The picture is now complicated by the fact that newspaper websites blend traditional long-form articles with visuals and TV-style interviews, while television network sites offer articles that can be read online, as well as graphic visuals. Thus, in the online age it is harder to make a simple distinction between print and television or to argue they are qualitatively different platforms that exert different influences on knowledge.

Indeed, as Kruikemeier, Lecheler, and Boyer (2018) note, digital platforms can be characterized by the degree to which they are highly linear (like the old newspapers) or less linear and more interactive (as in some of the best news websites). Linearity can be good in that it helps train readers' focus rather than sidetracking it, but interactivity has positive aspects, too. It encourages cognitive absorption and deeper learning when people click on related sites. What's the verdict? Old-fashioned reading of print news, with its more concentrated linear focus, produces more overall knowledge gain. When it comes to specific stories in which readers are interested, websites fare better. It seems as if those interactive bells and whistles facilitate learning, but only on issues that engage readers' interest (Kruikemeier, Lecheler, & Boyer, 2018). For regular online news readers, knowledge may be deeper today than in previous eras, but probably just on issues that connect with people's values.

A more specific, still-relevant mass communication approach is **constructionism**, pioneered by W. Russell Neuman, Marion R. Just, and Ann N. Crigler (Neuman, Just, & Crigler, 1992; Armoudian & Crigler, 2010). Constructionism examines how people construct meaning from media messages. Like the limited effects perspective discussed in Chapter 4, constructionism emphasizes that media rarely have simple, uniform effects on everyone. Unlike the limited effects view, it stipulates that political media can strongly influence cognitions. Constructionism says that effects depend on the interaction among demographic categories, the psychology of the audience member, content of a particular medium, and the nature of the media environment (Just & Crigler, 2020).

## Psychological Approach

A psychological viewpoint focuses more directly on the many cognitive and emotional attributes individuals bring to political media. Like constructionism, the psychological view emphasizes that you cannot appreciate the effects of news media on knowledge without understanding how people process or think about news.

A key psychological factor is a **schema**, defined as "a cognitive structure consisting of organized knowledge about situations and individuals that has been abstracted from prior experiences" (Graber, 1988, p. 28). Graber extensively studied the types of political schemas citizens employ in processing the news. She shook up the political communication field by showing that viewers do not just soak up whatever happens to be shown on the nightly news. Instead, processing of news is active, not passive. People don't start with a blank slate. The act of remembering news invariably involves relating the news to what people already know or believe. You might have a schema for politicians, or for issues like gun rights, immigration, or tax cuts; these cognitive structures would serve as filters or information storehouses that influence how you process political information.

## Sociological Approach

A sociological view emphasizes the impact of broad demographic and social structural factors on knowledge levels. Education is a time-honored predictor of knowledge. With more education comes significantly greater knowledge about politics (Delli Carpini & Keeter, 1996; Fraile, 2011). Social class also exerts a major impact on knowledge. Wealthier individuals know more than their less affluent counterparts about politics. This is not to say that those with little education or income lack knowledge about issues that bear directly on their well-being, or they lack political opinions. However, at least as judged by standard tests of political knowledge, lower-education and lower-income individuals do not fare as well as those with more money and education. Social class enhances knowledge for a couple of reasons. First, people with a college degree are better able to understand and process the news. Second, middle- and upper-middle-class individuals are freed from the strains of poverty, which affords them more time (one might say the luxury) to reflect on political issues.

Research has combined sociological and mass communication perspectives, focusing on intersections between the disciplines. One of the persistent findings in political communication research is that there are **knowledge gaps**, where media exacerbate differences produced by two sociological factors: income and education, called socioeconomic status, or SES (see Figure 5.2). According to the knowledge gap hypothesis, people higher in socioeconomic status are, at the outset, more knowledgeable about politics than their lower-socio-economic counterparts. Ideally, publicity, media messages, or an Internet campaign should provide the "have-nots" with more information, leveling the gap. But the knowledge gap hypothesis asserts that the opposite occurs: High-status, well-informed citizens acquire more information and at a faster clip than do their low-status, poorly informed counterparts. They benefit from skills in encoding, storing, and retrieving news information (Grabe, Kamhawi, & Yegiyan, 2009). Thus, the knowledge gap widens, rather than closes (Gaziano, 1997; Nadeau et al., 2008; Tichenor, Donohue, & Olien, 1970; Grabe, Yegiyan, & Kamhawi, 2008; Bas & Grabe, 2015). The knowledge-rich (particularly the better-educated) get richer, and the less-informed fall farther behind (e.g., Brundidge & Rice, 2009; Lind & Boomgaarden, 2019; Leeper, 2020). This is unfair and does not comport with the value that democratic theorists—philosophers, scholars, all of us really—place on equality.

When higher-socioeconomic groups benefit more from mediated information on topics spanning climate change, automobile company safety cover-ups, and health care, they can take preventive steps more efficiently and efficaciously than can lower-SES citizens. When media accentuate knowledge gaps, the system fails the poor, less educated, and marginalized, contributing to their greater disenfranchisement. For example, despite the wide diffusion of the Affordable Care Act, a law that significantly expands health care for the poor, many uninsured Americans had no knowledge of the law, impeding their efforts to get insurance for their families (MacGillis, 2015). Some scholars have suggested that moderately arousing and visual formats might be most conducive to increasing information gain among less-educated citizens (Grabe, Yegiyan, & Kamhawi, 2008; Grabe, Kamhawi, & Yegiyan, 2009). And yet, the democratizing potential of the Internet (and social media) to reduce knowledge gaps remains in doubt, not least because tens of millions of Americans lack access to high-speed, broadband transmission technologies (Von Drehle, 2017).

It is possible that the instantaneity of information—transmitted on Facebook Live, Twitter's Periscope, or on cell phone apps—may provide such

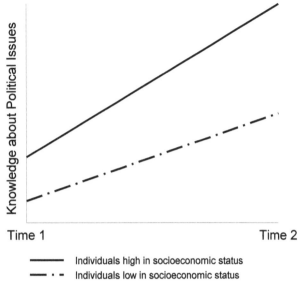

Individuals high in socioeconomic status
Individuals low in socioeconomic status

**Figure 5.2  Diagram of the knowledge gap in political communication. Knowledge is measured at Time 1, before media publicity of a political issue, and again at Time 2, after the issue has been publicized in the media.**

wide, pervasive access to cutting-edge information that we will see a diminution in gaps in factual knowledge rooted in SES differences. To be sure, political content on social media reaches those who are least engaged in politics (Bode, 2016). But research shows that, overall, online media use increases knowledge inequities (Lind & Boomgaarden, 2019), perhaps because the more knowledgeable individuals process information more deeply, access more links, or read more articles thoroughly. This dampens a totally optimistic thesis about the ability of news to bridge class-based information gaps.

## Putting It Together

What do we take from all this? News media have a variety of effects, some positive, others less so, helpfully explained by social structural and psychological factors. Research offers five broad conclusions about media and knowledge levels.

1. *The media play an instrumental role in informing Americans, but they are imperfect informational vessels.* For all their faults, the media provide information that is indispensable to informed citizenship. "Those who follow the news in any medium are more knowledgeable than their peers who do not," observed political communication scholar Steven H. Chaffee (Chaffee & Yang, 1990 p. 138; see also Barabas & Jerit, 2009; Pasek, Sood, & Krosnick, 2015).

The downside is that the informational diet that citizens consume can be low in analytical content, offering limited context and depth. As a long-time journalist noted,

> people are turning more frequently to skeletal updates they consume quickly on the small screens of their phones and tablets. During many hours of the day, even the news channels are devoting prime-time hours to opinion shows and infotainment about travel, food and sports, (offering) the news equivalents of those 100-calorie bags of chips and cookies.
>
> (Begleiter, 2015)

The information is out there, and news consumers acquire knowledge from attending to news, but the quality of what they learn is a subject of concern and debate.

Social media evokes affect well, with its ability to arouse emotion in a nanosecond (anger from outrageous tweets; grief from heart-rending videos). However, it doesn't provide context or offer interpretation, two of the canons of journalism. A video of a terrorist bombing is obviously newsworthy, but it is important to understand the degree of damage, whether it was domestic or foreign terrorism, how authorities reacted, and the grievances that propelled the group to take this violent action, Some social media reports are snippets taken out of context, or polarizing posts, probably from the political side people agree with. And with young adults "snacking" on news, ingesting information in small quantities from many platforms, there remains a question about the depth of knowledge that Millennial and Gen Z users are acquiring (Diehl, Barnidge, & Gil de Zúñiga, 2019).

2. *There are issues and conditions that facilitate knowledge acquisition.* When information is clearly presented and personally relevant, people are motivated to process information systematically. Presidential elections tend to involve people because they concern material economic issues, raise highly charged symbolic concerns, and are covered incessantly. As noted earlier, the public closely followed other critical national events, such as Trump's 2019 impeachment, the coronavirus outbreak, and the Floyd protests, but when information is complex, elites disagree among themselves, or leaders dissemble, offering misleading, cleverly packaged snippets, political learning is compromised.

3. *We should be suspicious about simple statements about the "powers of media."* Media are plural, they have different content, and the particular content can determine what people learn. Effects depend on the specific medium, content of the information, the style the program uses to depict an issue, the age and cognitive skills of the news consumer, and gratifications sought from political media. Statements about learning from social media can be misleading

because it is not clear if people are getting information from mainstream news outlets relayed through social media platforms, snippets from graphic videos, or politically polarized posts.

4. *Individuals bring a great deal to the news media equation.* You cannot talk about media effects in the abstract. What people know—or think they know—influences what they learn from media. People who know a lot about politics and have strong cognitive abilities get more out of the news and process it more thoughtfully than those who know less and have not yet developed strong political cognitive skills. What's more, a voter does not soak up political information like a sponge. Instead, as constructionist scholars emphasize, "people learn through the development of a composite framework, not by remembering disparate facts. Through the 'barrage' of campaign messages, voters extract and compile information to 'construct' candidates" (Armoudian & Crigler, 2010, p. 310). The news influences what people know, but what people already know affects how they integrate information into their worldviews. Individuals with less knowledge or cognitive skills gain information from assorted news media, but they are more likely to learn if the format is moderately arousing and favors visuals over turgid presentations of facts.

5. *Media effects on knowledge are indirect and complex. Sociological factors, working via communication and psychological processes, influence political knowledge.* Figure 5.3 shows how broad demographic factors (box 1) set psychological and communication forces in motion. Cognitive skills, schemas, and biased beliefs (box 2) are a function of social structural factors. Differential political media use (box 3) results from these factors as well, which in turn leads to surveillance, attention, and elaboration of news (box 4), with elaboration differing as a function of prior levels of information (Eveland, Shah, & Kwak, 2003). Thus, news gives people new facts, ideas, as well as schemas, which help them better understand political issues. News also leads to discussion, which helps people connect different arenas of the political world, expanding schemas and facilitating knowledge (box 5). Of course, knowledge levels can vary, with knowledge of civics and certain foreign affairs and domestic issues low; knowledge of national crises such as impeachment and the coronavirus is frequently higher, though as we will see, it is filtered through political biases.

Of course, we need to be careful not to be elitist. Poorer individuals can know a great deal about political issues that impinge directly on their well-being, such as how people cheat the welfare system (Vance, 2016), or the ways poverty and race conspire to lead to unjust incarceration of African Americans. And in a social media age, access to information is instantaneous and more readily available to citizens of all economic stripes than it was in previous times. However, gaps in understanding political issues, abetted by SES, ideology, and selective exposure to information on social media, continue apace.

**Figure 5.3  Political knowledge determinants and processes.**

## POLITICAL KNOWLEDGE IN THE AGE OF THE INTERNET AND SOCIAL MEDIA

So, you may be thinking, what does all this have to say about the current communication environment, with its multifaceted features: constant updates on news feeds; ceaseless political coverage on cable television, with plenty of opinionated talk; a plethora of detailed analyses of politics from top newspapers and websites; YouTube videos; and apps on Facebook, Twitter, and all the rest?

Let's briefly review a little history. In the mid-20th century, television supplanted print as the main source for news. In the early 21st century, Internet and websites began to replace television, and in today's era, social media is eclipsing print and perhaps TV for young adults. As Figure 5.4 shows, more than four in ten Americans get their political news online (18 percent from social media, 25 percent from websites or apps). Interestingly, 45 percent get news from television (cable, broadcast networks, or local news), showing that, for all the online migration, TV is still a major source of information. The remainder of the public gets news from print and radio. Showcasing the decline of print newspapers, once the dominant force in the news business, more Americans get their news from social media than from print (Geiger, 2019).

Social media is particularly important for Generation Zers, young people born between 1997 and 2012. Nearly 60 percent of Gen Zers get information from social media, such as Snap, YouTube, and Instagram, one poll reports (Taylor, 2019. (Surprisingly, TV is not far behind at 50 percent.)

There are complexities. When research finds that social media or the Internet is a primary source of news and political information, it may appear as if conventional news channels are no longer seen or read, but this is not so. Many people searching for news on the Internet turn to newspaper and television news sites, as well as news assemblers such as Google and Yahoo!, which also obtain information from conventional news organizations. Social media users open apps for *The New York Times*, *The Wall Street Journal*, *Time* magazine, CNN, Fox, and other mainstream media news. At the same time, people, typically strong partisans, are increasingly exposed to ideological sites that do not subscribe to

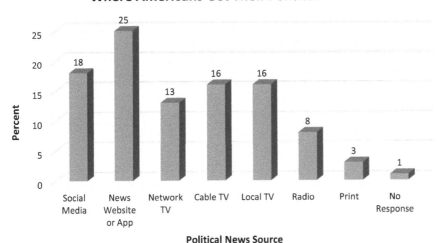

**Where Americans Get Their Political News**

Figure 5.4  **Percentage of American adults who say that this is the most common way they get their political and election news.**

*Source*: From Jurkowitz & Mitchell (2020a)

journalistic norms of relative fairness and will publish information skewed by a right-wing or left-wing perspective that can be of questionable factual accuracy.

There is good news here, seen in evidence that the Internet and social media exert salutary effects on information-holding, perhaps because it is easy to access news online. Interactivity also encourages cognitive absorption of political content. Online use of news can theoretically bolster political efficacy, or the belief that "people like me" can influence government, because it is much easier to get in touch with elected officials—and hear back—online than through the slower transmission channels of yore. Consistent with this view, there is evidence that online exposure to political information is associated with greater political knowledge, interest, efficacy, and political engagement, expanding the universe of political participation (Boulianne, 2009; Dimitrova et al., 2014; Kenski & Stroud, 2006). Engagement with, or active use of, online media predicts political participation, both offline, such as signing a petition or attending a rally, and online, as in sending an email political message or making an online candidate contribution (Boulianne, 2020; Kwak et al., 2018; Bakker & de Vreese, 2011; Bode et al., 2014; Brundidge et al., 2014; Gil de Zúñiga et al., 2019; Gil de Zúñiga, Jung, & Valenzuela, 2012; Gil de Zúñiga, Molyneux, & Zheng, 2014; Shehata, Ekström, & Olsson, 2016; Xenos, Vromen, & Loader, 2014; Zhang, Seltzer, & Bichard, 2013; Kahne & Bowyer, 2018).

This is complicated stuff. There are undoubtedly individual-level, motivational, and contextual factors that facilitate knowledge and political engagement. For example, much depends on how users engage with the site; using Facebook for news sharing doesn't seem to promote cognitive processing. In fact, it impedes political learning (Cacciatore et al., 2018). Absent a theory of online news and political involvement, it is hard to gain deeper insights into what is going on. We don't want to lump all online media together, as digital platforms differ in their features, uses, and effects (Bode & Vraga, 2018).

The direction of causation can also work in different ways. First, media can increase political knowledge, interest, and efficacy. Or, people who are already knowledgeable, interested, and politically efficacious may gravitate to online news and related apps to reinforce their civic engagement. More complexly, it could work both ways, with the politically knowledgeable gravitating to online media, and media enhancing their participation in online and offline causes (Shehata, Ekström, & Olsson, 2016). But the evidence paints a generally positive picture: Online news use exerts positive effects on knowledge and political participation. Unfortunately, there is also a darker side.

## FACTS IN A PARTISAN, ONLINE AGE

Facts are an essential component of political discourse because they provide shared yardsticks for comparison, offering common metrics to crystallize differences and understand policy disputes. While there will always be differences in determining what constitutes a fact and how high the bar should be set before it is regarded as accurate, there is consensus on what constitutes reasonable evidence for a claim, whether scientific or policy-based.

Yet increased polarization and segregation of political groups into universes that reinforce their own political habits undermines core norms of political discourse. "When beliefs become shortcuts for knowledge, all that political elites and media pundits need to communicate to audiences fragmented along partisan lines," notes Douglas B. Hindman (2009), "is what the reference group believes about the issue, regardless of inconsistencies with traditional ideological principles or contrary facts" (p. 793). It's a dark possibility, with some support and complicating evidence, yet another indication of a contemporary political communication paradox: There is more information available and more ways to check information's empirical basis, yet continued, troubling examples of ignorance or tenacious adherence to beliefs founded on falsehoods (Hochschild & Einstein, 2015).

This tendency—fidelity to falsehoods—is more common than you might think (or maybe you don't need any convincing of this point). Sociologist Arlie Russell Hochschild demonstrated this in a 2016 book, based on in-depth, deeply empathic interviews with working-class White supporters of the conservative Tea Party. The residents of the Louisiana bayou area had considerable—understandable, in many cases—anger at the ways elites were "cutting in line," unfairly imperiling their chances of achieving the American Dream. But some of their beliefs were based in factual inaccuracies. Consider these examples:

| Incorrect Beliefs of Louisiana Working-Class White Respondents | Facts Based on Data |
|---|---|
| 1. "The government spends a lot of money on welfare." | About 8 percent of the U.S. budget goes to welfare benefits that are based on income needs. |
| 2. "People on welfare depend entirely on money from us taxpayers to live." | For the poorest one-fifth of Americans, only about 37 percent of their income was from government; the rest came from income from work. |
| 3. "A lot of people—maybe 40 percent—work for the federal and state government." | In one standard year, government statistics showed that fewer than 17 percent of Americans were employed by government. |
| 4. "Public sector workers are way overpaid." | Private sector workers actually earn 12 percent more than those from the government public sector (Hochschild, pp. 255–257; see also Cramer, 2016). |

Partly as a result of their inaccurate beliefs, these bayou residents felt alienated and angry—"strangers in their own land," as Hochschild aptly put it. Their anger had political consequences—quite probably, animus toward fellow citizens they perceived as much different from themselves, distrust of the political establishment they felt had others' interests at heart, and a desire to throw out political leaders, some of whom actually were quite sympathetic to their socioeconomic plight, but were rejected as part of the elite.

This illustrates a disturbing psychological reality that researcher Brian E. Weeks has documented: When people are angry about political issues, they process information defensively, in line with their biases, and in ways that make them more inclined to believe misinformation about their political adversaries (Weeks, 2015, 2020). Egged on by partisan media outlets that put an emotional spin on partisan information, they may be more likely to believe false narratives about political issues. The alchemy of exposure to partisan information, while in an angry, embittered state, makes people susceptible to falsehoods that derogate their opponents, contaminating the political space of democratic society. We can glean real-world implications of the impact of exposure to partisan information sources in the white-hot 2019 Trump impeachment.

## An Impeachment Example

In 2019, Americans' factual knowledge of Trump's impeachment depended heavily on where they got their facts. The House impeached Trump in

December 2019 for abuse of power and obstruction of Congress stemming from his use of the power of his office to interfere with democratic processes. In July 2019, Trump pressured Ukraine's president to investigate leading Democratic rivals and then withheld $391 million in military assistance in an effort to coerce Ukraine to dig up political dirt on his adversaries. By arguably using his office for personal gain, he abused his power as president and refused to provide Congress with important subpoenaed documents relevant to its investigation. Trump's supporters did not think his actions warranted impeachment or removal from office.

President Joe Biden, then a leading contender for the 2020 Democratic nomination at the time, figured centrally in Trump's actions. Trump argued that as vice president from 2009 to 2017, Biden had improperly used his influence to remove Ukraine's prosecuting general because—it gets a little hairy here—Biden allegedly wanted to block the prosecutor from investigating a natural gas company linked to his son, Hunter. (Hunter sat on the board of the company.) Although Biden undoubtedly exercised poor judgment in allowing his son to serve on the board (because it created, if nothing else, the appearance of conflict of interest), there was no factual evidence supporting Trump's claim. In fact, there was no evidence whatsoever that Biden used his personal influence to fire the top prosecutor; instead, the facts suggested that he intervened to fire Ukraine's prosecutor for honorable reasons, because the prosecuting general had averted his eyes to corruption and was a corrupt official unworthy of U.S. support (Alba, 2019).

Now let's look at the role played by the intersection of partisanship and news channel. Republicans who received political news only from outlets with right-leaning viewers (such as Fox) differed from Democrats who only got news from media sites with left-leaning viewers (such as MSNBC) in an important respect: their beliefs about why Trump withheld aid to the Ukraine. More than eight in ten of these Republican media users said they thought Biden had sought to remove the Ukrainian prosecutor to protect his son (which was untrue) rather than to root out Ukrainian corruption (Jurkowitz & Mitchell, 2020c). Partisan media reinforced this incorrect narrative, persuading their viewers to buy into falsehoods.

## Misinformation Galore

The world was awash in falsehoods during the frightening early days of the virus pandemic. A patient in New York went to the doctor after vomiting from drinking a bleach concoction falsely billed as a virus cure on YouTube. A British paramedic assisted an ill patient who refused to go to the hospital after he came across misleading information on social media about poor medical treatment (Satariano, 2020). Empirically affirming anecdotes like these, a UK study found that, even as the virus ravaged the globe, 1 in 20 individuals thought there was no strong evidence the virus exists, and 30 percent falsely believed the virus was probably cooked up in a lab. People who subscribed to conspiracy theories, like believing there is no strong evidence the virus existed, were three times as likely as non-believers to break the country's lockdown rules (Duffy & Allington, 2020). Now we don't know if the false information about the virus caused conspiracy theory advocates to break lockdown rules. However, the widespread dissemination of false information can sow doubt among many members of the public, once again undermining the credibility of facts.

There may be a small silver lining, coming from a conventional place: mainstream media. First, the bad news: In a study conducted before the pandemic regarding beliefs about vaccines, people who were most misinformed about vaccines were those who distrusted experts and had greater exposure to vaccine information on social media. But the good news is that people who got their information from traditional media held more accurate beliefs about vaccines (Stecula, Kuru, & Jamieson, 2020). Once again, it is hard to parcel out cause from effect, as it is quite possible that those who held more inaccurate beliefs gravitated to social media, and those with more informed beliefs got their news from conventional sources. But media probably contributed to knowledge, and the study suggests that professional journalistic media can help educate the populace about important health issues.

## CONCLUSIONS

"A democracy can't be strong if its citizenship is weak," observed political scientist William A. Galston (2011). Others have echoed this sentiment, emphasizing that democracy depends in important ways on the political character of its citizenry and the quality of citizens' opinions and beliefs (see Roberts, 2015). Meaningful democratic decision-making requires that citizens understand the basic facts of government and issues that are at stake in elections. National surveys show that most Americans know key aspects of the U.S. Constitution and civil liberties. Happily, they also know the number of senators from their state! But people are woefully ignorant of basic civics and can lack knowledge of candidates' stands on key political issues. This underscores a time-honored paradox of political communication: There is more information available than ever before, yet citizens' knowledge levels do not approach normative ideals (e.g., Neuman, 1986).

Do low knowledge levels offer a compelling indictment of the state of political citizenship? There are different views here. Some scholars, with an eye on normative democratic ideals, answer in the affirmative, but a number of theorists make a compelling case that effective citizenship does not require knowledge of arcane government facts. Citizens can fulfill their democratic duties by relying on shortcuts to make political decisions, as well as by scanning the political environment to detect dangers to their personal well-being and the public welfare. Indeed, when it comes to important issues facing the country—impeachment, the pandemic, and police violence—most people follow issues closely, exhibiting more-than-adequate knowledge of the problems. But the psychology of partisan attitudes (see Chapter 9) and exposure to like-minded news outlets can skew knowledge among strong partisans. Critics with a systemic bent argue that if the nation's political system served citizens better, people would be motivated to process information more conscientiously. The problem, they suggest, is with our leaders and democracy, not its citizenry.

What are the sources of political knowledge? The mass media, Internet, and social media impart voluminous amounts of information, providing the raw materials from which people construct political beliefs. There is abundant evidence that individuals who follow the news are more knowledgeable about politics than their counterparts who do not turn to the news media for political information. At the same time, there are striking inequalities in political knowledge, even in a society such as the United States, where media are inescapable.

Media do not exert uniform effects on knowledge. What people know influences what they learn from media. The ways that individuals process information and construct events influence what they acquire from political news. The implication is that if you want to devise strategies to increase learning from news, you need to appreciate how people think about news at the get-go. You tailor your strategies so they are in sync with individuals' styles of processing political information.

Citizens are increasingly getting news online and from social media, although (contrary to popular opinion) much of the information has been gathered and packaged by conventional media outlets, as well as by ideological sites. There are different perspectives on how online news influences knowledge. Some scholars are skeptical, arguing that because individuals are no longer perched before their television sets for the evening news, they are less likely to gain incidental information from the evening news. However, there is considerable evidence for a more optimistic view, indicating that online media and new informational platforms are keeping individuals informed, enhancing political participation, and expanding the nature of participation beyond that possible in the analog era. These findings "should ease the concerns of cyber-pessimists who feared that Internet would have a negative effect on the efficacy, knowledge, and participation," observed political communication scholars Kate Kenski & Natalie Stroud (2006, p. 189). It remains a mixed bag. Social media is good at evoking emotion, showing graphic pictures, and providing up-to-the-minute news. Many users don't get context and, sometimes, factual accuracy from what they see and read.

Low knowledge levels can have important effects. Virulently negative attitudes toward government can have their roots in mistaken beliefs, such as grossly exaggerated views of how much money the government spends on foreign aid, or incorrect notions, fueled by stereotypes, that people on welfare are robbing the taxpayers blind (Krugman, 2017). Skepticism toward big government is reasonable and rooted in classic conservative values, but rejection of government that is steeped in lack of knowledge, even ignorance, can undermine democratic government, leading to support for draconian cutbacks in government programs that violate even conservative precepts. And when more than three-fourths of the supporters of a candidate who lost a presidential election—Trump in 2020—profess, in the wake of abundant facts to the contrary, that his opponent won through fraud or the election was stolen from him (Tavernise, 2020), then misinformation has begun to bite at the foundations of American democracy.

Increased polarization and diffusion of partisan media outlets can exacerbate these problems, spreading false information among certain politically susceptible members of the population. Madison's warning that "a popular government, without popular information . . . is but a prologue to a farce or a tragedy" becomes prescient. As the critic Michiko Kakutani (2018) reminds us:

> Without commonly agreed-upon facts—not Republican facts and Democratic facts; not the alternative facts of today's silo-world—there can be no rational debate over policies, no substantive means of evaluating candidates for political office, and no way to hold elected officials accountable to the people. Without truth, democracy is hobbled.
>
> (pp. 172–173)

For this reason, some reformers believe that the nation needs to launch a systematic program to reduce partisanship and educate citizens about democratic institutions (Perloff, 2017). They argue that America should institute national service that puts people from different political, demographic, and social backgrounds together to promote tolerance. Broader ideas are also afoot. In the dizzying new political media environment, where young adults are simultaneously confronted online with both society's inequities and opportunities to challenge these wrongs, alternative forms of citizenship are increasingly possible. These include critical, engaged, and participatory citizens, who don't passively accept status quo values, but find ways of confronting and remedying political wrongs (Kligler-Vilenchik, 2017). If communication can facilitate these vital forms of citizenship, then there is renewed hope for democracy.

## REFERENCES

Aalberg, T., & Curran, J. (Eds.). (2012). *How media inform democracy: A comparative approach*. New York: Routledge.

Aalberg, T., van Aelst, P., & Curran, J. (2012). Media systems and the political information environment: A cross-national comparison. In T. Aalberg & J. Curran (Eds.), *How media inform democracy: A comparative approach* (pp. 33–49). New York: Routledge.

Alba, D. (2019, October 29). Debunking 4 viral rumors about the Bidens and Ukraine. *The New York Times*. Online: www.nytimes.com/2019/10/29/business/media/fact-check-biden-ukraine-burisma-china-hunter.html. (Accessed: February 26, 2020).

Annenberg Public Policy Center (2016, September 13). *Americans' knowledge of the branches of government is declining*. The Annenberg Public Policy Center of the University of Pennsylvania. Online:www.annenbergfpublicpolicycenter.org/americans-knowledge-of-the-branches-of-government-is-declining/. (Accessed: March 28, 2017).

Armoudian, M., & Crigler, A.N. (2010). Constructing the vote: Media effects in a constructionist model. In J.E. Leighley (Ed.), *The Oxford handbook of American elections and political behavior* (pp. 300–325). New York: Oxford University Press.

Bakker, T.P., & de Vreese, C.H. (2011). Good news for the future? Young people, Internet use, and political participation. *Communication Research, 38*, 451–470.

Barabas, J., & Jerit, J. (2009). Estimating the causal effects of media coverage on policy-specific knowledge. *American Journal of Political Science, 53*, 73–89.

Bas, O., & Grabe, M.E. (2015). Emotion-provoking personalization of news: Informing citizens and closing the knowledge gap. *Communication Research, 42*, 159–185.

Begleiter, R. (2015, October 24). Sunday dialogue: The media gap. *The New York Times*. Online: www.nytimes.com/2015/10/25/opinion/sunday-dialogue-the-media-gap.html. (Accessed: November 21, 2020).

Bode, L. (2016, July–September). Pruning the news feed: Unfriending and unfollowing political content on social media. *Research & Politics*, 1–8. Online: https://journals.sagepub.com/doi/pdf/10.1177/2053168016661873. (Accessed: July 11, 2020).

Bode, L., & Vraga, E.K. (2018). Studying politics across media. *Political Communication, 35*, 1–7.

Bode, L., Vraga, E.K., Borah, P., & Shah, D.V. (2014). A new space for political behavior: Political social networking and its democratic consequences. *Journal of Computer-Mediated Communication, 19, 414–429.*

Boulianne, S. (2009). Does Internet use affect engagement? A meta-analysis of research. *Political Communication, 26*, 193–211.

Boulianne, S. (2020). Twenty years of digital media effects on civic and political participation. *Communication Research, 47*, 947–966.

Breyer, S. (2010). *Making our democracy work: A judge's view*. New York: Knopf.

Brundidge, J., Garrett, R.K., Rojas, H., & Gil de Zúñiga, H. (2014). Political participation and ideological news online: "Differential gains" and "differential losses" in a presidential election cycle. *Mass Communication and Society, 17*, 464–486.

Brundidge, J., & Rice, R.E. (2009). Political engagement online: Do the information rich get richer and the like-minded more similar? In A. Chadwick & P.N. Howard (Eds.), *Routledge handbook of Internet politics* (pp. 144–156). New York: Routledge.

Cacciatore, M.A., Yeo, S.K., Scheufele, D.A., Xenos, M.A., Brossard, D., & Corley, E.A. (2018). Is Facebook making us dumber? Exploring social media use as a predictor of political knowledge. *Journalism & Mass Communication Quarterly, 95*, 404–424.

Chaffee, S.H., & Yang, S-M. (1990). Communication and political socialization. In O. Ichilov (Ed.), *Political socialization, citizenship education, and democracy* (pp. 137–157). New York: Teachers College Press.

Cramer, K.J. (2016). *The politics of resentment: Rural consciousness in Wisconsin and the rise of Scott Walker*. Chicago, IL: University of Chicago Press.

Delli Carpini, M.X., & Keeter, S. (1996). *What Americans know about politics and why it matters.* New Haven: Yale University Press.

Diehl, T., Barnidge, M., & Gil de Zúñiga, H. (2019). Multi-platform news use and political participation across age groups: Toward a valid metric of platform diversity and its effects. *Journalism & Mass Communication Quarterly, 96,* 428–451.

Dimitrova, D.V., Shehata, A., Strömbäck, J., & Nord, L.W. (2014). The effects of digital media on political knowledge and participation in election campaigns: Evidence from panel data. *Communication Research, 41,* 95–118.

Duffy, B., & Allington, D. (2020, June 18). Covid conspiracies and confusions: The impact of compliance with the UK's lockdown rules and the link with social media use. *The Policy Institute.* Online: www.kcl.ac.uk/policy-institute/assets/covid-conspiracies-and-confusions.pdf. (Accessed: August 18, 2020).

Eveland, W.P. Jr., Shah, D.V., & Kwak, N. (2003). Assessing causality: A panel study of motivations, information processing and learning during campaign 2000. *Communication Research, 30,* 359–386.

Filindra, A. (2018). *Of regimes and rhinoceroses: Immigration, outgroup prejudice, and the micro-foundations of democratic decline.* Paper presented to the annual convention of the Midwest Association for Public Opinion Research, November, Chicago.

Fraile, M. (2011). Widening or reducing the knowledge gap? Testing the media effects on political knowledge in Spain (2004–2006). *International Journal of Press/Politics, 16,* 163–184.

Galston, W.A. (2011, November 6). Telling Americans to vote, or else. *The New York Times* (Week in Review), 9.

Gaziano, C. (1997). Forecast 2000: Widening knowledge gaps. *Journalism & Mass Communication Quarterly, 74,* 237–264.

Geiger, A.W. (2019, September 11). *Key findings about the online news landscape in America.* Pew Research Center (FactTank: News in the Numbers). Online: www. pewresearch.org/fact-tank/2019/09/11/key-findings-about-the-online-news-landscape-in-america/. (Accessed: February 27, 2020).

Gil de Zúñiga, H., Diehl, T., Huber, B., & Liu, J.H. (2019). The citizen communication mediation model: A multilevel mediation model of news use and discussion on political participation. *Journal of Communication, 69,* 144–167.

Gil de Zúñiga, H., Jung, N., & Valenzuela, S. (2012). Social media use for news and individuals' social capital, civic engagement and political participation. *Journal of Computer-Mediated Communication, 17,* 319–336.

Gil de Zúñiga, H., Molyneux, L., & Zheng, P. (2014). Social media, political expression, and political participation: Panel analysis of lagged and concurrent relationships. *Journal of Communication, 64,* 612–634.

Goodnough, A., & Kopicki, A. (2013, December 19). Uninsured skeptical of health care low in poll. *The New York Times,* A1, A27.

Grabe, M.E., Kamhawi, R., & Yegiyan, N. (2009). Informing citizens: How people with different levels of education process television, newspaper, and Web news. *Journal of Broadcasting & Electronic Media, 53,* 90–111.

Grabe, M.E., Yegiyan, N., & Kamhawi, R. (2008). Experimental evidence of the knowledge gap: Message arousal, motivation, and time delay. *Human Communication Research, 34,* 550–571.

Graber, D.A. (1988). *Processing the news: How people tame the information tide* (2nd ed.). New York: Longman.

Graber, D.A. (2006). Government by the people, for the people—Twenty-first century style. *Critical Review*, *18*, 167–178.

Graber, D.A. (2012). Government by the people, for the people—Twenty-first century style. In J. Friedman & S. Friedman (Eds.), *The nature of belief systems reconsidered* (pp. 207–218). New York: Routledge.

Hindman, D.B. (2009). Mass media flow and differential distribution of politically disputed beliefs: The belief gap hypothesis. *Journalism & Mass Communication Quarterly*, *86*, 790–808.

Hochschild, A.R. (2016). *Strangers in their own land: Anger and mourning on the American right*. New York: New Press.

Hochschild, J.L., & Einstein, K.L. (2015). *Do facts matter? Information and misinformation in American politics*. Norman, OK: University of Oklahoma Press.

Jerit, J., & Barabas, J. (2006). Bankrupt rhetoric: How misleading information affects knowledge about Social Security. *Public Opinion Quarterly*, *70*, 278–303.

Jurkowitz, M. (2020, May 22). *Americans are following news about presidential candidates much less closely than COVID-19 news*. Pew Research Center (FactTank: News in the Numbers). Online: www.pewresearch.org/fact-tank/2020/05/22/americans-are-following-news-about-presidential-candidates-much-less-closely-than-covid-19-news/. (Accessed: November 21, 2020).

Jurkowitz, M., & Mitchell, A. (2020a, March 25). *American who primarily get news through social media are least likely to follow COVID-19 coverage, most likely to report seeing made-up news*. Pew Research Center (Journalism & Media). Online: www.journalism.org/2020/03/25/americans-who-primarily-get-news-through-social-media-are-least-likely-to-follow-covid-19-coverage-most-likely-to-report-seeing-made-up-news/. (Accessed: November 21, 2020).

Jurkowitz, M., & Mitchell, A. (2020b, October 12). *Republicans who rely most on Trump for COVID-19 news see the outbreak differently from those who don't*. Pew Research Center (FactTank: News in the Numbers). Online: www.pewresearch.org/fact-tank/2020/10/12/republicans-who-rely-most-on-trump-for-covid-19-news-see-the-outbreak-differently-from-those-who-dont/. (Accessed: November 20, 2020).

Jurkowitz, M., & Mitchell, A. (2020c, January 24). *Views about Ukraine-impeachment story connect closely with where Americans get their news*. Pew Research Center (Journalism & Media). Online: www.journalism.org/2020/01/24/views-about-ukraine-impeachment-story-connect-closely-with-where-americans-get-their-news/. (Accessed: February 26, 2020).

Just, M.R., & Crigler, A.N. (2020). Learning from the news in a time of highly polarized media. In D. Jackson, D.S. Coombs, F. Trevisan, D. Lilleker, & E. Thorsen (Eds.), *U.S. election analysis 2020: Media, voters and the campaign*. Online: www.electionanalysis.ws/us/president2020/section-4-news-and-journalism/learning-from-the-news-in-a-time-of-highly-polarized-media/. (Accessed: November 16, 2020).

Kahne, J., & Bowyer, B. (2018). The political significance of social media activity and social networks. *Political Communication*, *35*, 470–493.

Kakutani, M. (2018). *The death of truth: Notes on falsehood in the age of Trump*. New York: Tim Duggan Books.

Kenski, K., & Stroud, N.J. (2006). Connections between Internet use and political efficacy, knowledge, and participation. *Journal of Broadcasting & Electronic Media*, *50*, 173–192.

Kleinberg, M.S., & Lau, R.R. (2019). The importance of political knowledge for effective citizenship: Differences between the broadcast and Internet generations. *Public Opinion Quarterly, 83*, 338–362.

Kligler-Vilenchik, N. (2017). Alternative citizenship models: Contextualizing new media and the new "good citizen". *New Media & Society, 19*, 1887–1903.

Krugman, P. (2017, March 17). Conservative fantasies run into reality. *The New York Times*, A25.

Kruikemeier, S., Lecheler, S., & Boyer, M.M. (2018). Learning from news on different media platforms: An eye-tracking experiment. *Political Communication, 35*, 75–96.

Kwak, N., Lane, D.S., Weeks, B.E., Kim, D.H., Lee, S.S., & Bachleda, S. (2018). Perceptions of social media for politics: Testing the slacktivism hypothesis. *Human Communication Research, 44*, 197–221.

Leeper, T.J. (2020). Raising the floor or closing the gap? How media choice and media content impact political knowledge. *Political Communication, 37*, 719–740.

Lind, F., & Boomgaarden, H.G. (2019). What we do and don't know: A meta-analysis of the knowledge gap hypothesis. *Annals of the International Communication Association, 43*, 210–224.

Lupia, A. (2016). *Uninformed: Why people know so little about politics and what we can do about it*. New York: Oxford University Press.

MacGillis, A. (2015). Who turned my blue state red? *The New York Times* (Sunday Review), 1, 4.

Mitchell, A., Jurkowitz, M., Oliphant, J.B., & Shearer, E. (2020, June 12). *Majorities of Americans say news coverage of George Floyd protests has been good, Trump's public message wrong*. Pew Research Center (Journalism & Media). Online: www.journalism.org/2020/06/12/majorities-of-americans-say-news-coverage-of-george-floyd-protests-has-been-good-trumps-public-message-wrong/. (Accessed: March 21, 2021).

Mitchell, A., Oliphant, J.B., & Shearer, E. (2020, April 29). *About 7-in-10 U.S. adults say they need to take breaks from COVID-19 news*. Pew Research Center (Journalism & Media). Online: www.journalism.org/2020/04/29/about-seven-in-ten-u-s-adults-say-they-need-to-take-breaks-from-covid-19-news/. (Accessed: May 10, 2020).

Nadeau, R., Nevitte, N., Gidengil, E., & Blais, A. (2008). Elections campaigns as information campaigns: Who learns what and does it matter? *Political Communication, 25*, 229–248.

Neuman, W.R. (1986). *The paradox of mass politics: Knowledge and opinion in the American electorate*. Cambridge: Harvard University Press.

Neuman, W.R., Just, M.R., & Crigler, A.N. (1992). *Common knowledge: News and the construction of political meaning*. Chicago, IL: University of Chicago Press.

Niemi, R.G., & Junn, J. (1998). *Civic education: What makes students learn*. New Haven: Yale University Press.

Pasek, J., Sood, G., & Krosnick, J.A. (2015). Misinformed about the Affordable Care Act? Leveraging certainty to assess the prevalence of misperceptions. *Journal of Communication, 65*, 660–673.

Perloff, R.M. (2017, April 5). A national civics exam. *The New York Times* (Letter to the Editor), A22.

Perloff, R.M. (2019, February 15). Border wall is nothing compared to Brexit crisis, and what it reveals. *The Plain Dealer*, E2.

Prior, M. (2005). News vs. entertainment: How increasing media choice widens gaps in political knowledge and turnout. *American Journal of Political Science*, *49*, 577–592.

Roberts, S. (2015, January 15). Walter Berns, whose ideals fueled neoconservative movement, dies at 95. *The New York Times*, A20.

Satariano, A. (2020, August 17). Coronavirus doctors battle another scourge: Misinformation. *The New York Times*. Online: www.nytimes.com/2020/08/17/technology/coronavirus-disinformation-doctors.html. (Accessed: August 18, 2020).

Schudson, M. (1998). *The good citizen: A history of American civic life*. New York: Martin Kessler Books.

Schumpeter, J. (1976). *Capitalism, socialism and democracy*. London: Allen and Unwin.

Shehata, A., Ekström, M., & Olsson, T. (2016). Developing self-actualizing and dutiful citizens: Testing the AC-DC model using panel data among adolescents. *Communication Research*, *43*, 1141–1169.

Shenkman, R. (2008). *Just how stupid are we? Facing the truth about the American voter*. New York: Basic Books.

Sniderman, P.M., Brody, R.A., & Tetlock, P.E. (1991). *Reasoning and choice: Explorations in political psychology*. New York: Cambridge University Press.

Stecula, D.A., Kuru, O., & Jamieson, K.H (2020). How trust in experts and media use affect acceptance of common anti-vaccination claims. *The Harvard Kennedy School Misinformation Review, 1*. Online: https://misinforeview.hks.harvard.edu/wp-content/uploads/2020/01/v2_vaccinessocialmedia_jan29-1.pdf. (Accessed: November 23, 2090).

Tavernise, S. (2020, December 14). What's next for Trump voters who believe the election was stolen? *The New York Times*. Online: www.nytimes.com/2020/12/14/us/trump-voters-stolen-election.html. (Accessed: December 15, 2020).

Taylor, K. (2019, July). The state of Gen Z. *Business Insider*. Online: www.businessinsider.com/gen-z-changes-political-divides-2019-7. (Accessed: June 23, 2020).

Tichenor, P.J., Donohue, G.A., & Olien, C.N. (1970). Mass media flow and differential growth in knowledge. *Public Opinion Quarterly*, *34*, 159–170.

Vance, J.D. (2016). *Hillbilly elegy: A memoir of a family and culture in crisis*. New York: HarperCollins.

Von Drehle, D. (2017, April 10). What it will take to rebuild America. *Time*, 23–27.

Weeks, B.E. (2015). Emotions, partisanship, and misperceptions: How anger and anxiety moderate the effect of partisan bias on susceptibility to political misinformation. *Journal of Communication*, *65*, 699–719.

Weeks, B.E. (2020). Angry voters are (often) misinformed voters. In D. Jackson, D.S. Coombs, F. Trevisan, D. Lilleker, & E. Thorsen (Eds.), *U.S. election analysis 2020: Media, voters and the campaign*. Online: www.electionanalysis.ws/us/president2020/section-2-voters/angry-voters-are-often-misinformed-voters/. (Accessed: November 15, 2020).

Wegman, J. (2018, November 24). City high schoolers get their day in court. *The New York Times*, A24.

Xenos, M., Vromen, A., & Loader, B.D. (2014). The great equalizer? Patterns of social media use and youth political engagement in three advanced democracies. *Information, Communication and Society*. DOI: 10.1080/1369118X.2013.871318.

Ytre-Arne, B., & Moe, H. (2018). Appropriately informed, occasionally monitorial? Reconsidering normative citizen ideals. *The International Journal of Press/Politics, 23*, 227–246.

Zaller, J. (2003). A new standard of news quality: Burglar alarms for the monitorial citizen. *Political Communication, 20*, 109–130.

Zhang, W., Seltzer, T., & Bichard, S.L. (2013). Two sides of the coin: Assessing the influence of social network site use during the 2012 U.S. presidential campaign. *Social Science Computer Review, 31*, 542–551.

# 6 Contemporary Political Socialization

Brian Michelz is still haunted by his debts, poor credit score, and his stomach-churning financial insecurity. When he was 18, more than a decade ago, he struggled to pay for two stays at the hospital. Then he grappled with college loans, and when he finished college, he learned his credit score was so bad he couldn't quality for a credit card.

Brian grew up in a small town in the eastern part of Michigan, living near his grandparents, cleaning up weeds during the summer. When he was about 18, the economic devastation wrought by the 2008 global financial crisis hit home. His mother lost her house she had worked so hard to pay for after Brian's father died. Hoping to make his way up by attending college, Brian attended a small religious college in Minnesota, and his curiosity took him online, as he began following the Occupy Wall Street protesters' argument about the stark differential between the income of the top 1 percent of Americans and everyone else.

One day around this time, watching television at his grandparents' house, he heard Bernie Sanders discussing the social injustice of American health care. His mind turned to his own medical debt and the injustice of his going to school to learn about teaching, only to find he could make more money working at a local tire store.

"Mr. Sanders seemed to be telling him why his life looked and felt the way it did," the perceptive reporter Sabrina Tavernise explained. "His financial instability was not some individual failure, but a function of a broader economic system that had become so unequal that fixing it was a moral calling" (Tavernise, 2020, p. 20). In 2016, Brian drove with his grandfather to the local polling station to vote in the primary election. His granddad voted for Trump, and he voted for Sanders.

Four years later, married, still struggling with debt, unable to get a loan to buy a car, and desperate to buy a nice car for his wife, Sarah, he felt he had gotten wiser, no longer buying into the American Dream that everyone can get richer through their own hard work. "That's a big lie that benefits the rich and keeps the system the same," he said, echoing the mantra of Sanders, the candidate he intended to vote for in the 2020 primary. "Even if it doesn't work, I'm going to throw my vote that way," he said. "I have nothing to lose" (p. 20).

Brian Michelz's melancholy story—his tale of how family circumstances, economic woes common to many in his generation, and an a-ha! moment pushed him toward the insurgent candidate Bernie Sanders—is a case study in the ways people form political attitudes. It showcases the processes underlying political socialization, though the particular direction it took—from economic deprivation to voting for a democratic socialist—is not preordained. Indeed, economic woes, experienced in different family and cultural contexts, can lead to the formation of conservative Republican values or indifference toward national politics. There are a multitude of ways that people form political attitudes that can last years, even a lifetime. Parents, peers, and media—television news, satire, film, and music, from folk to hip-hop—shape political attitudes that vary in their intensity and direction.

Political socialization is the focus of this chapter. How *do* we acquire political attitudes and beliefs? What role do historical events play in the development of political values? Why do some people participate in politics, yet others shy away? What role do the endless variety of media play in the acquisition of political attitudes? The first section of the chapter explores a prominent theme in political socialization research: continuity and change in the development of political attitudes. The second portion describes interpersonal and family influences. The third section summarizes the impact of schools, while the fourth portion, guided by theory and research, pinpoints the different ways media influence the development of political attitudes.

## THEMES IN POLITICAL SOCIALIZATION

Citizenship is not passed through the genes. It is learned. Indeed, as one scholar observed, "democracy's vitality and continuity greatly depend upon transmitting to each young generation the visions of the democratic way of life and the commitment to it" (Ichilov, 1990, p. 1). This is the central premise in the study of **political socialization**, "the way in which a society transmits political orientations—knowledge, attitudes or norms, and values—from generation to generation" (Easton & Dennis, 1973, p. 59). Democratic societies in particular seek to nurture four virtues in citizens: (1) *knowledge of the political system*; (2) *loyalty to democratic principles*; (3) *adherence to traditions like voting*; and (4) *identification with citizenship* (Dahlgren, 2000). Of course, as discussed in Chapter 3, nations do not always practice what they preach: Democratic principles such as voting can be breached or denied to particular citizens. The

U.S. boasts a history of grand noble ideas, a patchwork of democracy attained, violated with impunity, and constantly evolving. Like other aspects of politics and political communication, political socialization reflects biases, as well as beatific aims. Two themes weave their way through the socialization of political attitudes: continuity and change.

Continuity refers to the fact that political predispositions that we acquire at a young age tend to persist throughout our lives. Attitudes are formed through early macro- and micro-level experiences. On the broader, macro level, national events that people experience during their youth shape political attitudes. Events—wars, assassinations, political protests, technological changes, and economic catastrophes—that occur during a "critical period" of late childhood, adolescence, and early adulthood can leave a lasting imprint on memories, feelings, and political behavior (Schuman & Corning, 2012). World War II loomed as a defining political event for "Greatest Generation" Americans born in the early 1900s, particularly 1920s, while Vietnam, civil rights, and gender roles were important issues for Baby Boomers. For Americans born over the course of the succeeding decades, events such as the Reagan presidency, Clinton's impeachment, 9/11, the 2008 financial crisis, and the infusion of social media shaped attitudes and interpretations of subsequent political events. A national online survey of the American public offers specifics.

Survey participants were asked to indicate the ten historic events that occurred in their lifetimes they believed had the greatest impact on the country. Respondents were divided into four groups: (1) the Millennial generation (born from 1981 to 1998, though 1996 is a better cutoff); (2) Generation X (born 1965 to 1980); (3) the Baby Boom generation (born 1946 to 1964), and (4) the Silent Generation (called this because of their so-called silence, lack of protest, and generalized trust in the wake of tumultuous change, born 1928 to 1945). Across several generations, September 11 and the Obama election were seen as among the events that exerted the greatest impact on the country. It is noteworthy that, despite growing up in different eras, Americans were unified in their horror about 9/11 and pride in the election of the first Black president. There were differences among groups, reflecting the ways that critical events of a particular era influence the mindsets of young people growing up during these political epochs (Deane, Duggan, & Morin, 2016).

Generational socialization has continued since the study was conducted. We also want to consider the experiences of post-Millennials or those from Generation Z, as they are known, born from 1997 to 2012 (Fry & Parker, 2018; Dimock, 2019). For Gen Zers, a host of different historic events shaped their political socialization. Key events likely include the advent of social media (its diffusion, role in everyday life, and privacy violations); consciousness of social issues (climate change and legalization of marijuana); the Trump presidency; diversity of racial and gender roles (acceptance of racial diversity, along with alternative gender identities, as well as awareness of sexual abuse, punctuated by the symbolic #metoo movement), and calamitous events (the coronavirus pandemic and racial protests after George Floyd's death). (See Table 6.1.)

We need to be cautious here. Although there are probably some differences among members of generations, the experiences of a particular generation are complex, as not all members of a particular generation fit the same social metric. Generational cutoffs are also somewhat arbitrary. In addition, there can be conservative, as well as liberal, Baby Boomers, and variation in the degree to which post-Millennials are comfortable with gender-bending norms. We also lack solid empirical evidence about how these events shaped generational norms. Nonetheless, macro events can imprint themselves on the socialization of different generational cohorts.

**Table 6.1  Americans' perceptions of most significant historic events by generational cohort.**

| Post-Millennials (Generation Z)* | Millennials | Generation X | Baby Boomers | Silent Generation |
|---|---|---|---|---|
| Diffusion of social media | September 11 | September 11 | September 11 | September 11 |
| Social issues (climate change and marijuana legalization) | Obama election | Obama election | JFK assassination | World War II |
| Trump presidency | Iraq/ Afghanistan wars | Fall of the Berlin Wall/End of the Cold War | Vietnam War | JFK assassination |
| Racial and gender diversity | Gay marriage | The tech revolution | Obama election | Vietnam War |
| Calamitous events (coronavirus pandemic and protests after death of George Floyd) | The tech revolution | Iraq/ Afghanistan wars | Moon landing | Moon landing |

Respondents were asked to name the ten historic events that occurred in their lifetimes that they thought had the greatest impact on the country. The top five are reprinted here; notice the similarities and differences that emerge as a function of political socialization. (Adapted from Deane, Duggan, & Morin, 2016).

*These events represent educated guesses, as this group was not studied by Deane et al. (2016).

The coronavirus is likely to exert transformative effects on post-Millennials or Generation Zers (and perhaps more so for the generation that follows). The pandemic stripped young adults of their "existential security," robbing them of their "sense of safety," the feeling of confidence that the future is theirs to mold and that society's institutions can protect them (Brooks, 2020). It exacerbated loneliness and estrangement from others, producing a "Doomer" malaise (Warzel, 2020).

A number of young Generation Zers (perhaps you, older siblings, or friends) lost their jobs or took a financial hit during the virus outbreak. During the 2020 coronavirus crisis, unemployment dropped by about one-fifth for people in their twenties. To the extent that these financial declines persist, they could spiral out to the political sphere, influencing post-Millennials' political attitudes. Research suggests that people who come of age during recessions move to the left politically, deciding, based on their experiences and those of others, that government should do more to reduce inequality. But they also can tilt rightward in other ways, distrusting government institutions that they believe have let them down (Porter & Yaffe-Bellany, 2020). Much depends on how political media and politicians frame these issues, as well as young adults' own ideology and demographic group. Lower-socioeconomic individuals were struck much harder by the coronavirus, making them perhaps more susceptible to political aftershocks.

In addition, the cascading wave of protests that followed George Floyd's death undoubtedly affected many young people, who were part of a generation that is sensitive to racial problems. For their part, nearly half of Generation Zers are ethnic or racial minorities (Fry & Parker, 2018). Many of the George Floyd protesters were young, who grew up cognizant of micro-aggression and Black Lives Matter; their long exposure to racial diversity could have enhanced the salience of racial issues (DeJesus, 2020). The protests primed these concerns, and, occurring as they did during the apex of their student years, they may constitute significant historical events in their political socialization. Or they may recede over time, depending on how the nation deals with racial injustice.

Yet while the Floyd protesters were a cultural touchstone, they were viewed differently by people with different political affiliations. This points to within-generation socialization influences, the next focus of discussion.

Political socialization also occurs on the micro or individual level. On this more molecular level, children form political attachments and develop political attitudes based on the views of their parents or influential socialization agents (Shulman & DeAndrea, 2014; Shehata & Amnå, 2019). Few individuals change party affiliations once they enter middle age. Attitudes toward race and the two political parties remain stable and influential across the life cycle (Sears & Funk, 1999; Sears & Brown, 2013).

The continuity perspective emphasizes the powerful impact that early socialization experiences exert on subsequent attitudes. Growing up in a household that rewards certain viewpoints, or associates these views with strongly held values, can bolster these attitudes and increase the likelihood they will be translated into action. "It was once said that the Jesuits could control people's thinking for life if they controlled their education up to the age of five," noted David O. Sears (1990), a proponent of the continuity view.

Social scientific concepts help explain why political attitudes formed at an early age persist over time. First, people acquire considerable information simply through **observational learning**, or modeling respected parental, peer, and media opinion leaders (Bandura, 1971). Children whose parents display a particular political identification are likely to exhibit the same political identification as their parents (Jennings & Niemi, 1968). If your parents are staunch Republicans, particularly if they are active politically, you are likely to be a strong Republican (Clawson & Oxley, 2013).

A second reason why attitudes persist across the life cycle is, as persuasion theories suggest, attitudes developed based on systematic thinking and reflection can stick with people over the course of many years. The more we think about an issue, the stronger and more elaborated are our cognitive beliefs. Third, political attitude stability is facilitated through repetition. Repeated exposure to political information leads to positive attitudes (Grush, McKeough, & Ahlering, 1978). The more people see and hear fellow citizens talking favorably about a candidate, political party, or ethnic group perspective, the more they come to develop a positive attitude toward this issue. Repetition breeds liking and facilitates the development of heuristics favoring the in-group. Fourth, children acquire emotion-packed attitudes via associations. Watching adults sing the national anthem at sports events powerfully links positive feelings to one's country of origin, helping bolster patriotism, though sometimes to the exclusion of tolerance for those, like Colin Kaepernick, who refused to stand to protest American treatment of ethnic minorities. By the same token, disturbing as it may be, children who grow up with White supremacist parents hear prejudiced epithets and conspiracy theories of QAnon discussed repeatedly and favorably, making it likely they will absorb their attitudes.

There is also evidence that some political attitudes have a genetic basis (Banaji & Heiphetz, 2010; Fazekas & Littvay, 2015). Beliefs about politics, ideologically based attitudes, and a tendency to engage in political discussion may, to some degree, be inherited genetically (Alford, Funk, & Hibbing, 2005; Fowler et al., 2011; Hatemi & McDermott, 2011; Hibbing, Smith, & Alford, 2014; York, 2019). However, few would suggest that genes are a primary determinant of political attitudes. Biological traits may perhaps predispose people in certain political directions, but how they do so and the degree to which attitudes form depends on culture. In any case, nature does not operate in isolation of nurture. Whatever influences genes exert on attitudes intersect with the environment, and interactions are critical. For example, research on twins indicates that heredity affects how strongly individuals feel about partisan politics, but not whether they *choose* to be liberal or conservative (Settle, Dawes, & Fowler, 2009). Your parents and other socialization agents influence your choice of a political party (or anti-Establishment cause), and partisan attitudes remain relatively stable over the course of the life cycle. The peer, family, and media environment in which you grow up has persistent influences on political attitudes and behavior.

Complicating matters, change is also part of the political socialization equation. Americans have dramatically changed their views of race, gender roles, and gay marriage over the past half-century (e.g., Leonhardt & Parlapiano, 2015). Media portrayals of prejudice, as well as interpersonal communication among members of different cultural groups, have shaken up individuals' assumptions, leading them to reconsider long-held stereotypes. Case in point: Michelle Moran—a young White woman from Manhattan, whose conservative political comments on race while in high school caused a Black classmate to cringe—participated in a protest after George Floyd's death. When her Black schoolmate learned Michelle was one of those injured in the protest, she was surprised. But Michelle, who said she "slowly but surely opened my eyes to the horrors of the criminal justice system" after following the news, was one of many White Americans who shifted their attitudes based on what they saw and read (Stewart, 2020).

Interpersonal experiences can also influence attitudes. When Shelley Taylor was 17 years old, growing up in a rural Ohio town, she became angry that her high school teachers were on a picket line when they should have been teaching her classes she needed to graduate. The teachers' supporters then boycotted her parents' hardware store, she recalled, perhaps in revenge. This seems to have pushed her to become more politically conservative (Gabriel, 2020). One suspects that Shelley's parents were more conservative than liberal to begin with; otherwise, perhaps, she would have supported the teachers' picket line. Still, experiences we have growing up, acquired through media and interpersonal communication, can change political attitudes, sometimes in unexpected ways.

A variety of political attitudes can be in flux, in the wake of increasing skepticism about elected leaders, perhaps even representative democracy itself (Norris, 2011). A life-span development view emphasizes that political socialization does not stop in childhood. Instead, it continues over the course of the life cycle, as people adjust to the procession of new developments on the political stage. In addition, as Zukin and his colleagues note:

> People also change as they grow older because of age-specific experiences. Different stages of the life-cycle bring different politically relevant events,

for example, paying income taxes for the first time, choosing a school for a child, or helping an elderly parent deal with Medicare and other health care choices.

(Zukin et al., 2006, p. 11)

Continuity and change are the yin and yang of political socialization.

## INTERPERSONAL AND FAMILY INFLUENCES ON POLITICAL SOCIALIZATION

In 1965 the Los Angeles Dodgers defeated the Minnesota Twins to win the World Series. If you were driving to the game, a gallon of gas would cost 31 cents. You could buy a car for $2,650. Skateboards were big that year. In academia during the same year, a landmark study was published that probed elementary and middle school children's attitudes toward government. The researchers found that children evaluated government very favorably, viewing government as benevolent, protective, and helpful (Easton & Dennis, 1965). Children's positive evaluations of government reflected the insular nature of the times. They showcased a faith in the system to do good things, displaying an admirable, if idealized, view of the country.

You would not find as many children who harbored such uniformly positive attitudes today. On television and social media, kids are exposed to sordid problems of society, the lascivious acts of politicians, and bitter denunciations of politics, politicians, and the opposing party by leaders and partisans alike. This may not be all bad. Mid-20th-century Americans had a naïve, pro-system view of their country that ignored or whitewashed the country's problems and its leaders' misdeeds. Children today probably have a more realistic view of the deep problems that beset the nation. Evidence indicates they no longer evaluate the president favorably, although, interestingly, they continue to hold positive attitudes toward the institution of the presidency (Oxley et al., 2020).

From an academic perspective, the 1965 study of children's attitudes toward government represented a pioneering investigation of political socialization. Scholars began exploring the topic, curious about the political psychology of the '60s protesters, cultural variations in socialization practices, and the role mass communication played in knowledge generation. They also examined interpersonal communication dynamics.

### Interpersonal Communication Processes

Communication researcher Michael McDevitt has articulated a dynamic approach, emphasizing that adolescents can play an active role in family communication about politics. The traditional view is that parents impart their attitudes to children in a top-down manner. McDevitt noted that the direction of influence can go the other way, trickling up from children to parents (McDevitt, 2006; McDevitt & Chaffee, 2002). Teens may bring up a perspective gleaned from movies, music, or social media that goads parents to defend, then rethink their position on the issue. They confront parents by describing their outrage over injustices, as could have happened in parent-adolescent conversations about gay or gender issues. The passion their children evinced could have led some parents to reconsider their own positions on the issues, leading to testy, but productive, reciprocal parent-child discussions that transform the family political communication dynamic. Of course, that's the ideal.

Dhavan V. Shah and his colleagues have examined the ways political socialization plays out in today's era, focusing on the notion of communication competence (Shah, McLeod, & Lee, 2009; Shah et al., 2005; McLeod & Shah, 2009). Communication competence involves an ability to thoughtfully deliberate about political issues, formulate cogent arguments, reflect on information presented in the media, and arrive at a complex understanding of public issues. Children and adolescents ideally develop these deliberative skills through communication with parents and peers, in school civics classes, and through exposure to media educational programs. The skills become the engine that propels participation in civic and political activities.

This is interesting because it shows that communication plays a key role, via the impact that thoughtful issue-oriented discussions in schools (as well as in families and peer groups) exert on democratic deliberation. The results optimistically indicate that, even in a society as fragmented and niche media-focused as ours, institutions can encourage the development of democratic norms. But there is a caveat: Schools and families that don't have the luxury to engage in these activities—either because they are economically impoverished or weighted down by other barriers, such as ethnic prejudice or parental dysfunction—cannot even come close to contemplating these tasks. When poverty, prejudice, or family stressors are operative, a thoughtful focus on democracy and civic engagement is unlikely to occur. Social class leads not only to gaps in knowledge, but also in democratic deliberation.

With these optimistic (and realistic) perspectives in mind, let's now review the effects of other major agents of political socialization, beginning with families and family communication.

## Family Communication

What was your dinner-table conversation like growing up? Was there much conversation about politics? Did your parents trash certain politicians? Did they encourage you to say what you thought, even if you disagreed with what they espoused? Were certain topics—entire categories of politics—off-limits? Did you even have conversations with a parent or parents over dinner?

These questions are the centerpiece of a time-honored factor that influences political socialization: family communication patterns. There are two core dimensions of parent-child communication: **socio-oriented and concept-oriented communication**. In socio-oriented families, parents emphasize harmony and deference to adults. These parents may have strong, heart-felt views on social issues they want to impart to their children. They may believe that the best way to raise socially adjusted children is to teach them to defer to their elders. However, socio-oriented parents tend to be intolerant of dissent. Concept-oriented families, by contrast, encourage open exploration of contemporary issues, facilitating an environment in which there is exposure to diverse perspectives. The child or adolescent is encouraged to challenge others' viewpoints (Chaffee, McLeod, & Wackman, 1973), though they may, in some cases, long for the structure socio-oriented parents provide.

Children who grow up in homes where parent-child communication is highly concept-oriented, but low in socio- or harmony orientation, are distinctive in a number of ways. They tend to be the most knowledgeable about politics and display the strongest preference for public affairs programs (Chaffee, McLeod, & Wackman, 1973). They are more likely to value exposure to opposing political information and to talk with others with whom they disagree (Borah, Edgerly, & Vraga, 2013).

Children reared in homes that encouraged discussion, but did not place a premium on harmony, are especially likely to participate in political discussions (Hively & Eveland, 2009). Children who grew up in families with considerable political discussion are more likely to participate in civic or political activities as adults than do kids who grew up in homes with no political talk. More than one-third of young adults who were frequently exposed to political discussions while growing up volunteer regularly, compared to 13 percent of those reared in homes with no political discussion (Zukin et al., 2006).

Presumably, when parents encourage children to openly explore ideas and challenge others' beliefs, their kids feel motivated to do the same on a larger level. Turned on to ideas and information, they may explore issues in the media, discuss political topics with others, and become active in civic causes. Conversely, children who grow up in homes where politics is not discussed—because parents are overwhelmed with financial woes or are distrustful of the system—may not follow political issues and frequently don't vote at all (Tavernise & Gebeloff, 2020).

Research on family communication and politics can miss these voters because research is usually conducted in affluent or middle-class contexts, particularly focusing on White families. The absence of research on political socialization among parents of color is a blind spot in the scholarly literature. Race and ethnicity play an incredibly important role in politics, and there is wide variation in family communication styles as a function of race, parents' experience of prejudice, and their attitudes toward racial bias in American society. African American and Hispanic parents undoubtedly have different discussions about racial issues than do White parents, as when two affluent Black parents sat down with their seventh-grade son and had "the talk." They "told him that he will be treated differently based upon the color of his skin for the rest of his life." They added that: "No matter what we say or do, no matter how good your grades, no matter where you go to school, this is the America we live in" (Washington, 2020). Their son was totally blown away, shell-shocked, but the parents felt they had to level with their son to help him, in this way influencing his political socialization.

While family communication differs as a function of race, ethnicity, and a host of other demographic factors, this does not negate the important role family communication plays in the socialization of politics. Depending on family dynamics and the nature of the communication, family political communication can enrich or depress political attitude development.

## SCHOOLS

Political philosophers have long argued that education is of central importance in teaching the values of democratic citizenship. If schools do not provide instruction on civics, focusing on issues such as civil liberties, the importance of dissent, and governmental checks and balances, who will? By the time or slightly before students graduate from high school, they will be able to vote and can be conscripted into military service. Clearly, it is important that young people have a functioning knowledge of democratic principles.

Key inputs come from high school civics and history courses. What impact does civics instruction exert on students' political knowledge? Although research results vary, the findings from an extensive national study offers convincing support for the notion that exposure to a high school civics curriculum significantly increases students' knowledge of American politics and government (Niemi & Junn, 1998). Knowledge is far from perfect, as we have seen, but it is substantially greater than it would be in the absence of civics books and coursework.

This does not mean that everyone is happy with the content of the curriculum. High school civics and history courses have become a battleground in the cultural wars between liberals and conservatives (see Figure 6.1). For much of the 20th century, history textbooks offered a puffed-up view of the American past, celebrating conquest of the American West and industrial

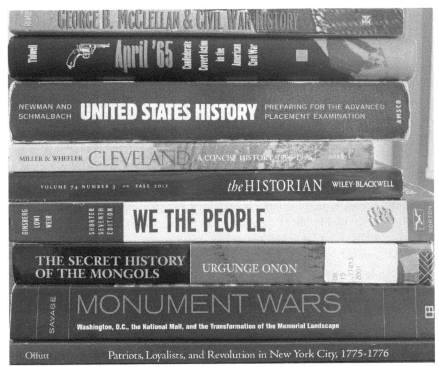

**Figure 6.1  History textbooks in the U.S. (and other countries) necessarily offer a perspective on the past. In the old days, when there was national consensus, textbooks provoked few controversies. However, they also offered a puffed-up, prejudiced view of the American past. In the wake of new evidence of racial, religious, and gender-based shortcomings in national leadership, textbooks have become battlegrounds in cultural wars. Ideally, textbooks should reflect the best historical evidence of a complex past, along with recognition of the limits in historians' knowledge.**

*Source*: Photograph by Temima Muskin

growth, despite injustices perpetrated on White blue-collar workers, Native Americans, and Blacks. In order to correct these errors, textbooks written over the past several decades articulated a different narrative, discussing prejudice and celebrating accomplishments of minorities and women. These books have rankled conservatives, who regard the books as politically correct and an attempt by Baby Boomer historians to rewrite history. Of course, history is always rewritten. There is no objective recitation of past events, for the past is necessarily subject to interpretation, reinterpretation, and revision in light of the present. Still, you do want a pluralistic version of American history, provided that it is steeped in democratic values and based on a consensual view of the facts.

In the U.S., there is no national, federal government–mandated curriculum that designates what students should know about American history. Instead, to a considerable degree, each state comes up with its own educational standards. As a result, history is taught differently, depending on the politics of a particular state. In liberal California, textbooks emphasize rampant housing discrimination against Blacks, but not in Texas, a more conservative state. When it comes to gender identities, California requires that schools teach contributions made by lesbian, gay, bisexual, and transgender Americans, but this is demeaned as politically correct in Texas, where textbook mentions of LGBTQ topics are centered on AIDS and marriage rights debates (Goldstein, 2020). In this way, political differences in the interpretation and teaching of history are not settled, but managed or massaged. Yet convulsing events can also force changes. As protests following the killing of George Floyd led to a national reckoning on race, historical accounts demolished storied myths, revealing, for example, racist brutality committed by the Texas Rangers centuries ago (Mervosh, Romero, & Tomkins, 2020). History is always a work in progress.

Controversies over the historical content of textbooks are a way that societies come to grip with different interpretations of the past and try to negotiate a common narrative. Indeed, the United States is far from the only country in which controversies over textbooks play out. This issue crosses national boundaries, as can be seen in controversies that have swirled over Israeli, Arab, German, and Japanese textbooks. For example, some Israeli textbooks have celebrated its history, described previous wars as justified acts of defense, and frequently portrayed Arabs as violent and treacherous. Palestinian textbooks, for their part, have suggested that the state of Israel should not exist. While many Israeli and Palestinian textbooks may no longer describe the other side in cruel, dehumanizing terms, they still present the out-group as the enemy and offer glowing descriptions of their side. Research suggests that 87 percent of maps in Israeli texts do not refer to the Palestinian Authority, while 96 percent of maps in Palestinian texts do not mention Israel (Wexler, Adwan, & Bar-Tal, 2013). Teenagers growing up in the Gaza Strip, controlled by the extremist Hamas movement, read texts that falsely claim that the Jewish Torah is "fabricated" and Zionism is a racist social movement that seeks to drive out Arabs (Akram & Rudoren, 2013).

It is not just the Middle East. For many years, German history books did not mention the Holocaust and barely described the horrific extermination of Jews that occurred in concentration camps. This has changed, as contemporary German textbooks devote considerable coverage to the Holocaust, describing it as one of the darkest periods in human history. In a similar fashion, textbooks used in Japanese high schools have offered a condensed, distorted version of World War II and Japanese war crimes. This aroused the ire of Japanese historians seeking a more truthful version of Japanese history. Thus, controversies over the role American history textbooks play in political socialization should be placed in a larger international context.

## MEDIA IMPACT ON POLITICAL SOCIALIZATION

Unlike parents and schools, mass media and the Internet typically do not deliberately seek to shape attitudes and beliefs. Yet they most assuredly exert these effects. Think about it: When you were a child, what was your first exposure to the president? Where did you first hear the words "politician," "candidate," "negative advertising," as well as Medicare for All, abortion on demand, and anchor babies? Where did you find out about candidates' sexual infidelities, impassioned protests, social justice, and alternatively, political correctness and cancel culture? Didn't TV news, online posts, offbeat websites, rancorous social media discussions, and even popular songs paint some of the political pictures in your head? And where if not from satirical media programs or YouTube snippets did you learn to laugh at politicians' missteps? The next portions of the chapter explore the dynamics of these issues, extending early research that explored the effects of news on political socialization by examining ways entertainment media can subtly influence political attitudes (Chaffee, Ward, & Tipton, 1970; Conway et al., 1981). Discussions focus on two broad concepts: cultivation and the time-honored arena of political satire.

### Cultivation of Politics

**Cultivation theory**, a classic mass communication perspective, emphasizes that media weave stories and construct narratives that convey a culture's values, ideologies, and underlying sociopolitical perspectives (Morgan, Shanahan, & Signorielli, 2009, 2012). A society's media system conveys information about society's "winners and losers. . . (and) who gets away with what, when, why, how and against whom" (Gerbner & Gross, 1976, p. 176). By creating a symbolic environment that promotes particular political views of the world, media communicate the political values of society, transmitting and inculcating these viewpoints.

Generations of television programs offered a simple, glorified view of police, depicting them as "the good guys," while "the bad guys are overwhelmingly Black" (Poniewozik, 2020). Famous shows such as *Dragnet*, *NYPD Blue*, *Law and Order*, *CSI*, and *Cops* could convey simple tropes (though *The Wire* offered a more complex portrait). TV programs cultivated a distorted worldview, inculcating beliefs that the criminal justice system is fair and effective, excessive police force is justified, and brutal police misconduct of Blacks "is inherently 'right' and 'good' by virtue of it being done by a 'beloved main character'" (Evelyn, 2020). For decades, viewers internalized these values.

Cultivation theory has traditionally argued that television, in particular, exerts a **mainstreaming** influence, bringing viewers from different social and political perspectives into a common fold, socializing young people to accept the preeminent, mainstream cultural viewpoints in a particular country. Is this still true today?

On the one hand, conventional television entertainment has presented a mainstream view of the political world that cultivates a moderate, conventional, pro-Americana political worldview (see Hardy, 2012, for a helpful review). But it's not clear that's true nowadays when popular shows elicit red-blue divides. For example, the once-popular show, *Duck Dynasty*, about an Evangelical Christian family that makes products for duck hunters, appealed to conservatives, whereas programs such as *Black-ish*, which focuses on a wealthy Black family trying to stay true to their ethnic roots, appeals more to liberals. The larger question is whether cultivation theory, with its emphasis on the dominance of *televised* storytelling, is still relevant in an era of fragmented, anything-goes, and personalized social media—a time when TV no longer reaches a mass audience with the same ubiquity and simultaneity of impact as it did in days gone by. Yet if cultivation's focus on television stories is passé, the concept remains relevant. Given the important role political stories continue to play in culture, transporting and immersing individuals, offering themes consonant with particular societal worldviews, it seems likely we will continue to observe media cultivation effects, but focused around the multitude of niche media offerings.

Increasingly, media can cultivate traditional political worldviews, while also exposing young people to oppositional perspectives through diverse social networking sites that take up alternative positions on gender roles and cultural diversity, or mock mainstream culture. Exposure to alternative viewpoints that are critical of conventional social values, from assimilation to political correctness, can override the dominant norms conveyed by conventional media. Thus, answers to the questions of political cultivation are more complicated than in years past. Do media still cultivate political attitudes, helping socialize young people into society? Undoubtedly, yes. Do media mainstream or promote primarily conventional political worldviews? Not necessarily. Do media impacts depend on the particular media platform viewers tune into, with effects less uniform than in years past? Increasingly, yes. Finally, do media content stifle or encourage needed political change? That's a difficult question.

As we know, young adults are connected to vast, richly diverse social networks, conveying political stories in traditional news formats and alternative venues, such as music. Sometimes cultivation favors change by diffusing stories that question the status quo; in other cases it reinforces the powers-that-be. It's all very complicated because of the many different media outlets everyone is tuned into. The broader normative question is how media *should* transmit cultural values in an American society where the old prejudiced platitudes no longer hold, society is divided into diverse social groups with their own political perspectives, and media are variegated, diversified socializing agents. How should the media cultivate political values so as to respect broad—if often unrealized—egalitarian ideals, while appreciating the rich, fractious diversity of the contemporary milieu?

To some, the country needs a new guiding myth that harnesses the best of the past's ideals so they are relevant today. As the poet Jericho Brown exhorted, perhaps considering the broad question of political socialization, the U.S. needs "to rethink/What it is to be a nation" (Perloff, 2020, p. E2).

That's a daunting, but important question. It deserves thoughtful consideration.

Let's move now from this serious topic to a more pleasant political socializing arena, one with more layers than you may have thought.

## POLITICAL SATIRE

If satire was in trouble, Donald Trump saved it from oblivion. Well, satire, given the many political characters asking for the comedic cut, probably was never in jeopardy. It certainly has been alive and comically well during the Trump years, with Trump receiving more jokes from top late-night talk show hosts during his first 100 days in office than other presidents received during their entire first year in the White House (Deb, 2017). And the jokes have kept coming, from Trevor Noah, Jimmy Fallon, Stephen Colbert, Samantha Bee, Dave Chappelle, and Alec Baldwin, who impersonated Trump for years on *Saturday Night Live*, or SNL (see Figure 6.2). It got personal between Baldwin and Trump, with Trump tweeting that Baldwin was "totally biased, not funny," and Baldwin replying: "Release your tax returns and I'll stop. Ha." Although Baldwin quit parodying Trump on SNL in 2019, other jokes kept coming, including some funny ones from humorist Andy Borowitz and *The Onion*, offering welcome humor from the coronavirus stress ("Trump Plans to Destroy Coronavirus With an Incredibly Mean Tweet"; "C.D.C. Director Says Coronavirus Effort Could Be Helped by Quarantining Pence"; "Trump Says Nation Will Have Vaccine Before It Sees His Taxes"; see Political Satire, 2020).

Over the years, Comedy Central produced a number of political satires, chief among them *The Daily Show* (originally with Jon Stewart, subsequently with Trevor Noah). Other televised satirical programs have included the ethnically focused *Key & Peele* and *Master of None*, and the televised political humor of Samantha Bee, Larry Wilmore, Bill Maher, John Oliver, and D.L. Hughley.

These comedians were out in force, isolated as they were, during the coronavirus pandemic, offering their monologues by iPhones or other seemingly low-tech equipment, with their families serving as substitute crews. Colbert, wearing a suit, delivered his monologue from a bubbly bathtub. Samantha Bee performed

**Figure 6.2 What would politics be without political humor and satire? In savaging opportunistic politicians, satire reveals a truthful underbelly of American politics, teaching, ridiculing, and offering an ever-revisionist perspective on political issues. Above: comedians Samantha Bee and Dave Chappelle.**

*Source*: https://commons.wikimedia.org/wiki/File:Samantha_Bee_(24112486327).jpg
https://commons.wikimedia.org/wiki/File:Dave_Chappelle_(cropped).jpg

her monologue from a forest, cracking jokes about panic shoppers, lamenting that she was down to her last roll of novelty toilet paper, which, the camera revealed, showed a mean-looking picture of Trump. Trevor Noah, casually dressed, offered up his quarantine tip of the day on what now was billed *The Daily Social Distancing Show with Trevor Noah*. Jimmy Kimmel, bearded and scruffy, didn't miss a beat, as he deadpanned:

> Yesterday our president, Donald Trump, gave himself a 10 out of 10 for the way he's handled this situation. He gave himself a 10, which incidentally is the same amount of testing kits that are currently available in the United States right now. This is an especially tough day to stay home, obviously because it's St. Patrick's Day, and I do want to say Happy St. Patrick's Day not just to our Irish friends and the Irish Americans watching, but to all alcoholics everywhere—and Happy Return of the potato famine, too.
>
> (*Jimmy Kimmel Live*, 2020)

In October, after the acrimonious first presidential debate, *Saturday Night Live* offered some refreshing satire. Toward the beginning of the mock encounter moderated by Chris Wallace (played by actor Beck Bennett), Trump (depicted by the hilariously snarling Alec Baldwin) and Biden (impersonated by the non-verbally fluid Jim Carrey) tangled. Here is a verbal excerpt that makes fun of Trump's anger and Biden's attempt at anger management:

(Trump runs through a series of false charges and allegations against Biden, charging Obama was spying on him)

*Wallace:* Mr. Vice President, please answer.
*Biden:* Now look, here's the deal.
*Trump*: Can I respond to that, Chris? (laughter)
*Biden:* Will you just *shut up*? (applause). Sorry. I'm sorry. I misspoke. What I meant to say was I'd appreciate it very much if you could just allow me to finish my responses as opposed to sabotaging every waking moment with a toxic geyser of verbal diarrhea. . . . (leans back, then grits teeth and berates himself) Losing control. . . (angry at himself and puts bag over his mouth and blows into it to calm down) . . . (After another Trump insult about Biden wearing a mask, Biden gets very mad, then catches himself.) Stop it, Joe, stop it. God, you can't lose your cool just 'cause this joker's raising a little monkey dust. The country's countin' on you. Just stand here and look lucid.
(First Debate Cold Open—SNL, 2020).

So, what is satire? **Satire**, as you probably know, is a form of humor that employs ridicule to expose human foibles, with its humorous hooks typically directed at the powers-that-be (Parker, 2015). It is complex, calling on a variety of humorous techniques to parody, frequently to deconstruct power (Bakhtin, 1981). These include slapstick imitations of presidents, buffoonery, fake news shows, and irony. **Irony** is a classic comedic device that uses language to suggest an incongruity between the surface and deeper meanings of an event. Satire and irony are also vibrantly alive and well outside the U.S, including in Britain, France, Russia, and Nigeria (Onishi, 2015).

## Processes and Effects of Satire

We know young people are exposed to televised satire. A national survey of some years back reported that young adults were more likely than older individuals to obtain campaign information from late-night comedy shows, and other research reports consistent exposure to the classic *Daily Show*, as well as SNL, among young adults (Young & Tisinger, 2006; Baumgartner & Morris, 2006; Chadwick, 2013). Indeed, younger adult viewers tend to feel more absorbed in satire than in conventional news, compared with older viewers (Boukes et al., 2015). And the plethora of online satire, from JibJab parodies of presidential candidates to YouTube's *Bad Lip Reading*, can become viral hits. Just watching satire does not translate to media influence. People bring attitudes acquired from other socialization agents, such as parents, to viewing political satire (LaMarre, Landreville, & Beam, 2009; Mohammed, 2014).

Satire, like much political humor, operates via incongruity, as people recognize there are two incongruous frameworks—the conventional one on the surface and the frame lurking at a deeper level. The sheer incompatibility of the two can provoke laughter, but the more serious effort occurs when people must reconcile the conflicting perspectives and bring a new, deeper perspective to bear on what they have seen or heard (Young, 2014). Satire doesn't just implant effects on audiences; they have to help create its meaning, as Young (2014) notes. Sometimes the political humor goes right over their heads. Other times, they get it, like a bullseye, and reach a new political understanding.

Consider, as an example, this somewhat bawdy joke: "People look at the Statue of Liberty and they see a proud symbol of our history as a nation of immigrants, a beacon of hope for people around the world. Donald (Trump) looks at the Statue of Liberty and sees a 'four' (Young, 2020, p. 82). To appreciate the joke, listeners must access the Statute of Liberty as a symbol of freedom and call to mind Trump's previous history of denigration of women's looks. The incongruity between a majestic statue that literally showcases a woman but symbolizes much more and Trump's presumed viewing the statue in its sexually objectified form is so incongruous, deviating from our storied image of the statue, that it's amusing.

To appreciate satire's effects more deeply, we need to understand how viewers think about political satire. This requires an exploration of the cognitive mechanisms at work when people watch late-night humor, as Young (2008a) and Mark Boukes and his colleagues (2015) have emphasized. On the one hand, when young adults are absorbed in a political satire, they can feel psychologically immersed or transported. This absorption in the satirical skit can diminish their motivation or ability to formulate mental arguments with what the satirist has suggested (Boukes et al., 2015; Young, 2008a). Thus, at some level, they are open to persuasion. On the other hand, people can enjoy a satirical skit, finding it funny, yet recognize it's just a joke, thereby discounting the satire as irrelevant to the more serious political attitudes they hold (Nabi, Moyer-Gusé & Byrne, 2007). No longer absorbed by the humor, but instead scrutinizing the message, perhaps selectively perceiving humor in terms of their prior attitudes, they remain steadfast in their preexisting beliefs, despite the intent of the humorist. Thus, discounting and absorption can cancel each other out (Boukes et al., 2015).

Alternatively, amusing incongruities can lead to attitude change. On the one hand, people may not mentally contest the satirical argument because they choose not to; they simply lack the motivation to do so. As a result, they're persuaded. Or, they don't mentally challenge the political argument because they lack the cognitive resources available to do so. Having devoted their mental energies to getting the joke (and sometimes, in public, pretending to get it when they don't!), they're exhausted. They lack the cognitive wherewithal—the requisite mental acumen—to challenge the humorist's argument.

Satire does not always produce attitude change. Voters who liked Trump would probably contest the assumption the Statue of Liberty joke makes about Trump and derogate the joke-teller rather than Trump. In fact, the effect of a joke on political attitudes depends on the political predisposition of the listener.

Satire itself can have different features. It can be ambiguous, ironic, and difficult to decipher. Appreciating, let alone systematically processing, humor requires some cognitive ability, and in the case of political satire, it requires political knowledge (LaMarre & Walther, 2013). You can't get a joke about the budget debt or Washington, D.C. gridlock if you are not familiar with these issues. Satire can be dramaturgically complicated. Satirists combine an appearance of seriousness with deeper ironic disparagement of the status quo, and those unfamiliar with the genre or the satirist may fail to get beyond the superficial to appreciate the satirist's underlying intent (Mohammed, 2014). In a similar fashion, younger adolescents or those at a lower cognitive-developmental stage may not understand satire well enough for the jokes to sink in. More generally, because satire involves such active audience participation in cognitive interpretation and reconciliation of incongruities, it depends on the mental acuity of audience members in a particular situation.

Some scholars emphasize that satire's impact hinges on other variables or moderators. In an intriguing study, Hoon Lee and Nojin Kwak (2014) reasoned that political satire bolsters political participation by eliciting particular negative emotions, such as anger. Feeling angry can motivate individuals to participate in politics to throw the bums out of office. Lee and Kwak found that satire was more likely to produce participation by evoking negative emotions, but primarily among individuals higher in education. "Those with greater skills and resources are more likely to obtain benefits from political satire," Lee and Kwak noted, "because understanding humor itself requires a certain level of expertise" (p. 322). In order for satire to enhance faith in politics, one needs a basic level of political knowledge and expertise.

Contemporary political satire may also appeal more to liberals than to conservatives. What, you say, don't conservatives have a sense of humor? Of course they do, and some of it is aggressively drilled at liberals! For their part, liberals push back with puns, amusing disparagement, but especially satire. In a fascinating account, Young (2020) argues that conservatives and liberals have different ways of expressing their political grievances, outgrowths of the different ways conservatives and liberals think about political issues.

For one thing, liberals are more concerned with fairness and social justice, whereas conservatives place a higher premium on respect for authority and loyalty to the nation (Graham, Haidt, & Nosek, 2009). There are interesting cognitive differences too, with conservatives (in general, there are always exceptions) scoring higher in a need for order and decisiveness, and liberals scoring higher in enjoyment of thinking and tolerance of ambiguity. Thus, conservatives can favor more direct, straight-out funny insults (as in a short-lived Fox conservative comedy show called *The ½ Hour News Hour*), while liberals appreciate incongruity and irony more, key elements of satire, emblematic of John Oliver, the host of HBO's *Last Week Tonight* and Stephen Colbert, host of *The Late Show* on CBS.

More broadly, when it comes to political expression, contemporary conservatives may naturally gravitate to anger and outrage, seen and heard regularly on Fox News. These hard-hitting forms of expressing political sentiments jibe with conservatives' preference for direct, orderly, decisive expression and discomfort with equivocating ambiguity. Liberals, who famously expressed outrage at Donald Trump, seem more comfortable with satire as an entertainment device to work through their political angst. Its meandering, irony-filled content appeals to liberals because, as a group, they enjoy the cognitive work required to make sense of mentally titillating incongruities. However, increasingly, as left-wing critics regard even the vaguest humorous slight as an instance of racism or sexism, even long-time liberal comedians such as Bill Maher worry that politically correct social justice warriors may be imperiling political satire (Marchese, 2019).

Young has a broader view. While noting that satire can be too diffuse and abstract to serve as a force for tactical political action, she likes its freewheeling experimentation and the ways it encourages the audience to actively ruminate about the paradoxes and problems that plague our politics. And this raises a broader question.

## Does Satire Promote or Hinder Political Change?

Some scholars have wondered if satire, funny as it sometimes can be, is good or bad for politics and the broader system. Researchers have suggested that, far from always exerting positive effects, satire, with its biting attacks on politicians, can bolster cynical beliefs about politics.

There is some data indicating that viewing satirical programs of some years back—*The Daily Show* with Stewart and *The Colbert Report*—was associated with cynicism, mistrusting media, and believing the political system is corrupt (Balmas, 2014; Guggenheim, Kwak, & Campbell, 2011; Baumgartner & Morris, 2006; Morris & Baumgartner, 2008). But there is also evidence that political satire has more beneficial effects. Satire, after all, contains an implicit idealism, offering up the hope that by humorously identifying the flaws of individual leaders, satirists can help people appreciate the visionary goals of the democratic system that leaders have selfishly or stupidly failed to implement (Schutz, 1977). Thus, satire can enhance knowledge, set the agenda, and facilitate deeper thinking about politics (Hardy et al., 2014; Young & Tisinger, 2006; Landreville & LaMarre, 2013; Boukes, 2019). Research has documented that satire increased political efficacy or the belief that citizens can influence politics; efficacy in turn enhanced and predicted political participation (Hoffman & Young, 2011; Hoffman & Thomson, 2009; Chen, Gan, & Sun, 2017; see Becker, 2014).

So, does satire increase cynicism or enhance efficacy? Does it amplify skepticism or bolster political participation? Both views might be correct, given that one can be cynical about politicians, yet motivated to change the system. A little cynicism could be a good thing if it leads to more questioning of authority.

On a broader level, satire can exert normative benefits (Holbert, 2013), illuminating deeper meanings and offering a way for society to renew its political health (Momen, 2020; Young, Holbert, & Jamieson, 2014). Endemic to democracy, but not limited to societies with democratic governments, satire socializes the young by helping to unmask the powerful. It disrupts "the herd thinking (and) the herd mood" (Parker, 2015, p. 51) and celebrates the ways free speech reveals political wrongdoing beneath the surface. Despite the appearance of negativity, satire is optimistic. It "weeps, scolds, and ridicules, generally with one major end in view: to plead with man for a return to his moral senses" (Bloom & Bloom, 1979, p. 38; Young, 2008b, 2014).

In this way, satire opens up pathways for questioning the status quo, enables vicarious talking back to authorities, and by channeling negative emotions into positive energy, can lay the groundwork for political change (Baym & Jones, 2012; Gray, Jones, & Thompson, 2009). Of course, it's only one factor in the mix, and for change to occur, the democratic soil must be tilled with the hard work of political participation and activism.

## CONCLUSIONS

Societies with diverse electoral and political structures educate and socialize citizens, introducing them to their country's foundational political values and norms. Of course, as we know, nations never live up to their ideals, and socialization, at its worst, can be a sham. At the same time, democratic societies do change, and the attitudes people learn as children frequently must be adapted to fit new understandings of the political present. People vary in the degree to which they do this, with some changing and others rigidly adhering to psychological vestiges of the past.

Children, adolescents, and young adults are not born with an appreciation for democratic values, and society needs to cultivate these ideals. Political communication plays an important part in political socialization. Communication of traditions and norms of citizenship are diffused through family, peer, school, and diverse media portrayals of politics. Political predispositions acquired at a young age, and through identification with a particular generational cohort, tend to persist throughout the life cycle. Attitudes acquired during one's youth can remain influential during the adult years. Just as there is continuity in political socialization, there is also change. As a result of exposure to media and interpersonal communication, Americans have changed their attitudes toward race, gay marriage, abortion, and big government over the past several decades.

Communication scholars emphasize that contemporary socialization to politics is dynamic, characterized by interaction among different socialization agents and growth in communication competence, a generalized ability that ideally should spur civic engagement. Parents are a major influence on children's political views, with family communication patterns exerting a significant influence on children's interest in politics. Schools also socialize children, through textbooks and the increasing number of programs designed to promote voting, deliberative debate, and civic participation. Of course, there are plenty of criticisms of conventional socialization, ranging from the view that socialization reflects a pro-secular bias to the concern that it embraces a rigid status quo.

Contemporary media represent portals that introduce young people to a world of politics that is constructed electronically, cinematically, and digitally. News, television dramas, movies, and music, from heavy metal to rap (Jackson, 2002), introduce young people to the serious and sublime—along with the admirable and absurd—aspects of contemporary politics. Meyrowitz (1986) has persuasively argued that electronic media (and the Internet) have profoundly influenced political socialization. By showing the "back regions" of public life and revealing the imperfections, personal shortcomings, and sexual infidelities of political leaders, the media have made it difficult for young people to revere elected officials or believe in the electoral system. But this has had a positive effect by giving young adults a realistic, rather than sugarcoated, view of the contemporary political world.

Cultivation theory offers rich insights into the ways contemporary media inculcate beliefs about the political world, including mainstreaming individuals to adopt views told through stories on television. However, today's teenagers and young adults are exposed to a panoply of political portrayals across different media platforms that are more diverse than those their parents and grandparents received via television. Mainstreaming is more complex and multifaceted in today's society, not necessarily cultivating a pro-system political perspective.

Media also shape political attitudes through satire, a favorite technique of political humorists throughout the ages, a strategy that, through criticism of democracy's actors, can ironically celebrate tenets of democratic government. Satire works through different psychological pathways, sometimes increasing cynicism, but frequently amplifying political efficacy and participation, particularly among those with a more educated, sophisticated view of the political world. It remains a vital part of political communication, providing a mechanism for dissent to push through society's rigid communicative strictures.

Political socialization is a work in progress, with new media genres that socialize young people emerging in our digital culture. Activists have devised innovative websites in an effort to promote civic engagement and political participation. These sites have a mixed record of success (Bachen et al., 2008; Bennett, Wells, & Freelon, 2011; Xenos & Foot, 2008). Many fail to offer interactive learning opportunities to which young people are accustomed, but social media can help catalyze offline participation in political activities, as seen in the conservative Tea Party movement and the many grassroots groups that challenged the Trump administration. These developments suggest that socialization is hardly a unitary force, but a dynamic process that can promote political change across the life cycle, at its best a way for society to renew and rejuvenate its political values.

## REFERENCES

Akram, F., & Rudoren, J. (2013, November 4). To shape young Palestinians, Hamas creates its own textbooks. *The New York Times*, A1, A11.

Alford, J., Funk, C., & Hibbing, J. (2005). Are political orientations genetically transmitted? *American Political Science Review*, *99*, 153–167.

Bachen, C., Raphael, C., Lynn, K-M, McKee, K., & Philippi, J. (2008). Civic engagement, pedagogy, and information technology on web sites for youth. *Political Communication*, *25*, 290–310.

Bakhtin, M.M. (1981). *The dialogic imagination: Four essays* (C. Emerson & M. Holquist, Trans.). Austin, TX: University of Texas Press.

Balmas, M. (2014). When fake news becomes real: Combined exposure to multiple news sources and political attitudes of inefficacy, alienation, and cynicism. *Communication Research*, *41*, 430–454.

Banaji, M.R., & Heiphetz, L. (2010). Attitudes. In S.T. Fiske, D.T. Gilbert, & G. Lindzey (Eds.), *Handbook of social psychology* (Vol. 1, 5th ed., pp. 353–393). New York: Wiley.

Bandura, A. (1971). Analysis of modeling processes. In A. Bandura (Ed.), *Psycho-logical modeling: Conflicting theories* (pp. 1–62). Chicago, IL: Aldine-Atherton.

Baumgartner, J., & Morris, J.S. (2006). *The Daily Show* effect: Candidate evaluations, efficacy, and American youth. *American Politics Research*, *34*, 341–367.

Baym, G., & Jones, J.P. (2012). News parody in global perspective: Politics, power, and resistance. *Popular Communication: The International Journal of Media and Culture*, *10*, 2–13.

Becker, A.B. (2014). Humiliate my enemies or mock my friends? Applying disposition theory of humor to the study of political parody appreciation and attitudes toward candidates. *Human Communication Research*, *40*, 137–160.

Bennett, W.L., Wells, C., & Freelon, D. (2011). Communicating civic engagement: Contrasting models of citizenship in the youth web sphere. *Journal of Communication, 61*, 835–856.

Bloom, E.A., & Bloom, L.D. (1979). *Satire's persuasive voice.* Ithaca, NY: Cornell University Press.

Borah, P., Edgerly, S., & Vraga, E.K. (2013). Hearing and talking to the other side: Antecedents of cross-cutting exposure in adolescents. *Mass Communication & Society, 16*, 391–416.

Boukes, M. (2019). Agenda-setting with satire: How political satire increased TTIP's saliency on the public, media, and political agenda. *Political Communication, 36*, 426–451.

Boukes, M., Boomgaarden, H.G., Moorman, M., & de Vreese, C.H. (2015). At odds: Laughing and thinking? The appreciation, processing, and persuasiveness of political satire. *Journal of Communication, 65*, 721–744.

Brooks, D. (2020, May 21). The first invasion of America. *The New York Times.* Online. (Accessed: May 22, 2020).

Chadwick, A. (2013). *The hybrid media system: Politics and power.* New York: Oxford University Press.

Chaffee, S.H., McLeod, J.M., & Wackman, D. (1973). Family communication patterns and adolescent political participation. In J. Dennis (Ed.), *Socialization to politics: A reader* (pp. 349–364). New York: Wiley.

Chaffee, S.H., Ward, S., & Tipton, L.P. (1970). Mass communication and political socialization. *Journalism Quarterly, 47*, 647–659, 666.

Chen, H-T., Gan, C., & Sun, P. (2017). How does political satire influence political participation? Examining the role of counter- and proattitudinal exposure, anger, and personal issue importance. *International Journal of Communication, 11*, 3011–3029.

Clawson, R.A., & Oxley, Z.M. (2013). *Public opinion: Democratic ideals, democratic practice* (2nd ed.). Thousand Oaks, CA: Sage/CQ Press.

Conway, M.M., Wyckoff, M.L., Feldman, E., & Ahern, D. (1981). The news media in children's political socialization. *Public Opinion Quarterly, 45*, 164–178.

Dahlgren, P. (2000). The Internet and the democratization of civic culture. *Political Communication, 17*, 335–340.

Deane, C., Duggan, M., & Morin, R. (2016, December 15). *Americans name the 10 most significant historic events of their lifetimes.* Pew Research Center: U.S. Politics & Policy. Online: www.people-press.org/2016/12/15/americans-name-the-10-most-significant-historic-events-of-their-lifetimes/. (Accessed: January 7, 2017).

Deb, S. (2017, May 5). Trump jokes are at a record level on late night. *The New York Times.* Online: www.nytimes.com/2017/05/05/arts/television/trump-jokes-record-level-on-late-night-tv.html. (Accessed: March 1, 2020).

DeJesus, I. (2020, June 10). "What can I do to fix this?": Why young people are fueling the protest movement. *Penn Live Patriot-News.* Online: www.pennlive.com/news/2020/06/what-can-i-do-to-fix-this-why-young-people-are-fueling-the-protest-movement.html. (Accessed: June 10, 2020).

Dimock, M. (2019, January 17). *Defining generations: Where millennials end.* Online: www.pewresearch.org/fact-tank/2019/01/17/where-millennials-end-and-generation-z-begins/. (Accessed: June 23, 2020).

Easton, D., & Dennis, J. (1965). The child's image of government. *The Annals of The American Academy of Political and Social Science, 361*, 40–57.

Easton, D., & Dennis, J. (1973). The child's image of government. In J. Dennis (Ed.), *Socialization to politics: A reader* (pp. 59–81). New York: Wiley.

Evelyn, K. (2020, January 25). How TV crime shows erase racism and normalize police misconduct. *The Guardian.* Online: www.theguardian.com/media/2020/jan/25/law-and-disorder-how-shows-cloud-the-public-view-of-criminal-justice. (Accessed: June 12, 2020).

Fazekas, Z., & Littvay, L. (2015). The importance of context in the genetic transmission of U.S. party identification. *Political Psychology, 36,* 361–377.

First debate cold open—SNL (2020, October 4). Online: www.youtube.com/watch?v=Wsije1KetVw. (Accessed: October 7, 2020).

Fowler, J.H., Loewen, P.J., Settle, J., & Dawes, C.T. (2011). Genes, games, and political participation. In P.K. Hatemi & R. McDermott (Eds.), *Man is by nature a political animal: Evolution, biology, and politics* (pp. 207–223). Chicago, IL: University of Chicago Press.

Fry, R., & Parker, K. (2018, November 15). *Early benchmarks show "Post-Millennials" on track to be most diverse, best educated generation yet.* Pew Research Center: Social & Demographic Trends. Online: www.pewsocialtrends.org/2018/11/15/early-benchmarks-show-post-millennials-on-track-to-be-most-diverse-best-educated-generation-yet/. (Accessed: March 8, 2020).

Gabriel, T. (2020, August 25). Trumps' fights are their fights. They have his back unapologetically. *The New York Times.* Online: www.nytimes.com/2020/08/25/us/politics/trump-reelection-supporters.html. (Accessed: August 26, 2020).

Gerbner, G., & Gross, L. (1976). Living with television: The violence profile. *Journal of Communication, 26,* 173–199.

Goldstein, D. (2020, January 13). Two states. Eight textbooks. Two American stories. *The New York Times,* A1, A14–A15.

Graham, J., Haidt, J., & Nosek, B.A. (2009). Liberals and conservatives rely on different sets of moral foundations. *Journal of Personality and Social Psychology, 96,* 1029–1046.

Gray, J., Jones, J.P., & Thompson, E. (2009). The state of satire, the satire of state. In J. Gray, J.P. Jones, & E. Thompson (Eds.), *Satire TV: Politics and comedy in the postnetwork era* (pp. 3–36). New York: New York University Press.

Grush, J.E., McKeough, K.L., & Ahlering, R.F. (1978). Extrapolating laboratory exposure research to actual political elections. *Journal of Personality and Social Psychology, 36,* 257–270.

Guggenheim, L., Kwak, N., & Campbell, S.W. (2011). Nontraditional news negativity: The relationship of entertaining political news use to political cynicism and mistrust. *International Journal of Public Opinion Research, 23,* 287–314.

Hardy, B.W. (2012). Cultivation of political attitudes in the new media environment. In M. Morgan, J. Shanahan, & N. Signorielli (Eds.), *Living with television now: Advances in cultivation theory and research* (pp. 101–119). New York: Peter Lang.

Hardy, B.W., Gottfried, J.A., Winneg, K.M., & Jamieson, K.H. (2014). Stephen Colbert's civic lesson: How Colbert Super PAC taught viewers about campaign finance. *Mass Communication & Society, 17,* 329–353.

Hatemi, P.K., & McDermott, R. (Eds.). (2011). *Man is by nature a political animal: Evolution, biology, and politics.* Chicago, IL: University of Chicago Press.

Hibbing, J.R., Smith, K.B., & Alford, J.R. (2014). *Predisposed: Liberals, conservatives, and the biology of political differences.* New York: Routledge.

Hively, M.H., & Eveland, W.P., Jr. (2009). Contextual antecedents and political consequences of adolescent political discussion, discussion elaboration, and network diversity. *Political Communication, 26*, 30–47.

Hoffman, L.H., & Thomson, T.L. (2009). The effect of television viewing on adolescents' civic participation: Political efficacy as a mediating mechanism. *Journal of Broadcasting & Electronic Media, 53*, 3–21.

Hoffman, L.H., & Young, D.G. (2011). Satire, punch lines, and the nightly news: Untangling media effects on political participation. *Communication Research Reports, 28*, 159–168.

Holbert, R.L. (2013). Developing a normative approach to political satire: An empirical perspective. *International Journal of Communication, 7*, 305–323.

Ichilov, O. (1990). Introduction. In O. Ichilov (Ed.), *Political socialization, citizenship education, and democracy* (pp. 1–8). New York: Teachers College Press.

Jackson, D.J. (2002). *Entertainment & politics: The influence of pop culture on young adult political socialization*. New York: Peter Lang.

Jennings, M.K., & Niemi, R.G. (1968). The transmission of political values from parent to child. *American Political Science Review, 62*, 169–183.

*Jimmy Kimmel live* (2020, March 17). Online: www.youtube.com/watch?v=PmCoT wsZHew. (Accessed: April 3, 2020).

LaMarre, H.L., Landreville, K.D., & Beam, M.A. (2009). The irony of satire: Political ideology and the motivation to see what you want to see in *The Colbert Report*. *International Journal of Press/Politics, 14*, 212–231.

LaMarre, H.L., & Walther, W. (2013). Ability matters: Testing the differential effects of political news and late-night political comedy on cognitive responses and the role of ability in micro-level opinion formation. *International Journal of Public Opinion Research, 25*, 303–322.

Landreville, K.D., & LaMarre, H.L. (2013). Examining the intertextuality of fictional political comedy and real-world political news. *Media Psychology, 16*, 347–369.

Lee, H., & Kwak, N. (2014). The affect effect of political satire: Sarcastic humor, negative emotions, and political participation. *Mass Communication and Society, 17*, 307–328.

Leonhardt, D., & Parlapiano, A. (2015, June 30). A march toward acceptance when civil rights is the topic. *The New York Times*, A3.

Marchese, D. (2019, September 30). Bill Maher on the perils of political correctness. *The New York Times Magazine*. Online: www.nytimes.com/interactive/2019/09/30/magazine/bill-maher-interview.html. (Accessed: August 15, 2020).

McDevitt, M. (2006). The partisan child: Developmental provocation as a model of political socialization. *International Journal of Public Opinion Research, 18*, 67–88.

McDevitt, M., & Chaffee, S. (2002). From top-down to trickle-up influence: Revisiting assumptions about the family in political socialization. *Political Communication, 19*, 281–301.

McLeod, J.M., & Shah, D.V. (2009). Communication and political socialization: Challenges and opportunities for research. *Political Communication, 26*, 1–10.

Mervosh, S., Romero, S., & Tomkins, L. (2020, June 16). Reconsidering the past, one statue at a time. *The New York Times*. Online: www.nytimes.com/2020/06/16/us/protests-statues-reckoning.html. (Accessed: November 22, 2020).

Meyrowitz, J. (1986). *No sense of place: The impact of electronic media on social behavior*. New York: Oxford University Press.

Mohammed, S.N. (2014). "It-getting" in the Colbert nation online forum. *Mass Communication and Society, 17*, 173–194.

Momen, M. (2020). The presidential debates: The media frames it all wrong. In D. Jackson, D.S. Coombs, F. Trevisan, D. Lilleker, & E. Thorsen (Eds.), *U.S. election analysis 2020: Media, voters and the campaign*. Online: www.electionanalysis.ws/us/president2020/section-6-popular-culture-and-public-critique/the-presidential-debates-the-media-frames-it-all-wrong/. (Accessed: November 16, 2020).

Morgan, M., Shanahan, J., & Signorielli, N. (2009). Growing up with television: Cultivation processes. In J. Bryant & M.B. Oliver (Eds.), *Media effects: Advances in theory and research* (3rd ed., pp. 34–49). New York: Routledge.

Morgan, M., Shanahan, J., & Signorielli, N. (2012). The stories we tell: Cultivation theory and research. In M. Morgan, J. Shanahan, & N. Signorielli (Eds.), *Living with television now: Advances in cultivation theory and research* (pp. 1–14). New York: Peter Lang.

Morris, J.S., & Baumgartner, J.C. (2008). *The Daily Show* and attitudes toward the news media. In J.C. Baumgartner & J.S. Morris (Eds.), *Laughing matters: Humor and American politics in the media age* (pp. 315–331). New York: Routledge.

Nabi, R.L., Moyer-Gusé, E., & Byrne, S. (2007). All joking aside: A serious investigation into the persuasive effect of funny social issue messages. *Communication Monographs, 74*, 29–54.

Niemi, R.G., & Junn, J. (1998). *Civic education: What makes students learn*. New Haven: Yale University Press.

Norris, P. (2011). *Democratic deficit: Critical citizens revisited*. New York: Cambridge University Press.

Onishi, N. (2015, December 6). In a Nigeria in need of laughs, comedians have crowds roaring. *The New York Times*, 1, 16.

Oxley, Z.M., Holman, M.R., Greenlee, J.S., Bos, A.L., & Lay, J.C. (2020). Children's views of the American presidency. *Public Opinion Quarterly, 84*, 141–157.

Parker, J. (2015, November 8). Is legitimate satire necessarily directed at the powerful? *The New York Times* (Book Review), 51.

Perloff, R.M. (2020, July 3). Do our partisan animosities portend another 1876 debacle? *The Plain Dealer*, E2.

Political Satire (2020). *The New Yorker*. Online: www.newyorker.com/tag/political-satire/page/4. (Accessed: November 23, 2020).

Poniewozik, J. (2020, June 10). "Cops" is off the air. But will we ever get it out of our heads? *The New York Times*. Online: www.nytimes.com/2020/06/10/arts/television/cops-canceled.html. (Accessed: June 12, 2020).

Porter, E., & Yaffe-Bellany, D. (2020, May 19). Facing adulthood with an economic disaster's lasting scars. *The New York Times*. Online: www.nytimes.com/2020/05/19/business/economy/coronavirus-young-old.html. (Accessed: May 19, 2020).

Schuman, H., & Corning, A. (2012). Generational memory and the critical period: Evidence for national and world events. *Public Opinion Quarterly, 76*, 1–31.

Schutz, C.E. (1977). *Political humor: From Aristophanes to Sam Ervin*. Rutherford, NJ: Fairleigh Dickinson University Press.

Sears, D.O. (1990). Whither political socialization research? The question of persistence. In O. Ichilov (Ed.), *Political socialization, citizenship education, and democracy* (pp. 69–97). New York: Teachers College Press.

Sears, D.O., & Brown, C. (2013). Childhood and adult political development. In L. Huddy, D.O. Sears, & J.S. Levy (Eds.), *The Oxford handbook of political psychology* (2nd ed., pp. 59–95). New York: Oxford University Press.

Sears, D.O., & Funk, C.L. (1999). Evidence of the long-term persistence of adults' political predispositions. *Journal of Politics, 61*, 1–28.

Settle, J.E., Dawes, C.T., & Fowler, J.H. (2009). The heritability of partisan attachment. *Political Research Quarterly, 62*, 601–613.

Shah, D.V., Cho, J., Eveland, W.P., Jr., & Kwak, N. (2005). Information and expression in a digital age: Modeling Internet effects on civic participation. *Communication Research, 32*, 531–565.

Shah, D.V., McLeod, J.M., & Lee, N.-J. (2009). Communication competence as a foundation for civic competence: Processes of socialization into citizenship. *Political Communication*, 26, 102–117.

Shehata, A., & Amnå, E. (2019). The development of political interest among adolescents: A communication mediation approach using five waves of panel data. *Communication Research, 46*, 1055–1077.

Shulman, H.C., & DeAndrea, D.C. (2014). Predicting success: Revisiting assumptions about family political socialization. *Communication Monographs, 81*, 386–406.

Stewart, N. (2020, June 26). Black activists wonder: Is protesting just trendy for White people? *The New York Times*. Online: www.nytimes.com/2020/06/26/nyregion/black-lives-matter-white-people-protesters.html. (Accessed: June 27, 2020).

Tavernise, S. (2020, March 8). 29 years old, buried by debt and putting trust in Sanders. *The New York Times*, 1, 20.

Tavernise, S., & Gebeloff, R. (2020, October 26). They did not vote in 2016. Why they plan to skip the election again. *The New York Times*. Online: www.nytimes.com/2020/10/26/us/election-nonvoters.html. (Accessed: October 27, 2020).

Warzel, C. (2020, June 22). Gen Z will not save us. *The New York Times*. Online: www.nytimes.com/2020/06/22/opinion/trump-protest-gen-z.html. (Accessed: June 23, 2020).

Washington, L. (2020, June 12). After George Floyd's death, an African American mother has "the talk" with her son. *The Chicago Sun-Times*. Online: https://chicago.suntimes.com/columnists/2020/6/12/21289699/george-floyd-the-talk-african-american-parents-children-raci. (Accessed: June 23, 2020).

Wexler, B.E., Adwan, S., & Bar-Tal, D. (2013, March 7). Trying to bridge the Mideast divide. *The New York Times* (Letter to the Editor), A22.

Xenos, M., & Foot, K. (2008). Not your father's Internet: The generation gap in online politics. In W.L. Bennett (Ed.), *Civic life online: Learning how digital media can engage youth* (pp. 51–70). Cambridge, MA: MIT Press.

York, C. (2019). Genetic influence on political discussion: Results from two twin studies. *Communication Monographs, 86*, 438–456.

Young, D.G. (2008a). The privileged role of the late night-joke: Exploring humor's role in disrupting argument scrutiny. *Media Psychology, 11*, 119–142.

Young, D.G. (2008b). *The Daily Show* as the new journalism: In their own words. In J.C. Baumgartner (Ed.), *Laughing matters: Humor and American politics in the media age* (pp. 241–259). New York: Routledge.

Young, D.G. (2014). Theories and effects of political humor: Discounting cues, gateways, and the impact of incongruities. In K. Kenski & K.H. Jamieson (Eds.), *The Oxford handbook of political communication*. Online: www.oxfordhandbooks.com/view/10.1093/oxfordhb/9780199793471.001.0001/oxfordhb-9780199793471-e-29. (Accessed: March 2, 2020).

Young, D.G. (2020). *Irony and outrage: The polarized landscape of rage, fear, and laughter in the United States*. New York: Oxford University Press.

Young, D.G., Holbert, R.L, & Jamieson, K.H. (2014). Successful practices for the strategic use of political parody and satire: Lessons from the P6 Symposium and 2012 election campaign. *American Behavioral Scientist, 58*, 1111–1130.

Young, D.G., & Tisinger, R.M. (2006). Dispelling late-night myths: News consumption among late-night comedy viewers and the predictors of exposure to various late-night shows. *Press/Politics, 11*, 113–134.

Zukin, C., Keeter, S., Andolina, M., Jenkins, K., & Delli Carpini, M.X. (2006). *A new engagement? Political participation, civic life, and the changing American citizen.* New York: Oxford University Press.

# 7 Setting and Building the Agenda

It was the ultimate media effect—global, existential, terrifying. The coronavirus pandemic, with its rapid spread across the world and staggering death toll, transfixed the world, upending routines, devastating economies, and charting a new, frightening course for everyday life. The news media covered the issue nonstop, with constant phone alerts, harrowing accounts, along with social media posts from people across the world, an endless stream of stories of anxiety, sadness, heroism, and struggles to adjust to an unfathomably new normal (see Figure 7.1).

The media brought the story to us. Without media, we would not have known, until the virus hit home in our communities, anything about this new coronavirus, its path from Wuhan, China, across the globe, the Chinese government's deliberate suppression of information early on, which allowed it to spread inside China to many other countries, the devastation it wrought in Italy, rising infections and death in the U.S., along with the Trump administration's fitful response to what was then just an epidemic as it denied there was a problem, played down its severity until finally reality set in, and the White House helped muscle a $2 trillion economic stimulus package through Congress (Sanger, Kanno-Youngs, & Swanson, 2020). We wouldn't have known about 20-second handwashing, self-quarantines, or the phrase of the year, social distancing.

Although only a handful of Americans experienced the terror of the virus early on, by March they all recognized it was a national problem, then a crisis, as universities moved to remote learning, the NBA season was cancelled, stores closed, and restaurants shifted to pick-up and delivery service only, developments they heard about, in the main, through media. It is almost a truism that the media galvanized public attention to the problem, not just reflecting reality, but shaping the interpretation of events. Over the course of the year, as the virus overtook everyday life and infections surged, the pandemic dominated

**Figure 7.1  In what has to be the gravest, most global example of agenda-setting, the media relentlessly covered the coronavirus pandemic during the spring of 2020 across a multitude of platforms.**

*Source*: www.gettyimages.com/detail/news-photo/will-dedicate-a-special-hour-of-its-broadcast-from-8-00-to-news-photo/1206445895?adppopup=true

the news, climaxing with heavy coverage of Trump's contracting the virus in October (Agiesta, 2020a).

A similar phenomenon occurred during the tumultuous spring of 2020, when the brutal death of George Floyd prompted protests in thousands of communities, in some cases sparking violence, as racial inequality became the focus of media attention and public discussion. The Floyd protests overtook the pandemic in late May, garnering ten times as many mentions (25 percent to 2.5 percent) on cable news channels (Fischer, Rothschild, & Walsh, 2020). And in a demonstration of the jarring unpredictability of political events in America, the media tableau changed again, with the violent insurrection at the Capitol on January 6, 2021.

In political communication parlance, the media set the agenda in all of these cases. This means the news—and media more broadly today—led people to believe the issue was salient or important. Agenda-setting is the classic political media effect that has showcased the subtle but inescapable power of media from the time it was conceptualized in the 1970s to the very different media world of today.

We often think of the news in terms of bias or massive effects. This chapter offers a more nuanced perspective, introducing agenda-setting in its classic and contemporary detail. The chapter is divided into six sections, reflecting the voluminous research on this topic. The first and second sections define agenda-setting and discuss social scientific research that explores its impact. The third portion examines consequences of agenda-setting, viewed through the lens of an intriguing concept called priming. In the fourth section, I examine electoral implications of agenda-setting and priming. The fifth and sixth sections examine the building of policy agendas and implications for a social media age. As you read this, keep in mind that agenda-setting has traditionally referred to the press, the news media, or conventional journalism. Because this is the focus of research, and still a mainstay of the concept, discussions will revolve around news media effects. However, as examined later in the chapter, agendas are set and built online and by social media, intersecting with traditional media in a number of ways.

## WHAT WE KNOW ABOUT AGENDA-SETTING

A lynchpin of agenda-setting is the term *agenda*. An **agenda** is defined as an issue or event that is perceived at a particular point in time as high in social or political importance (Rogers & Dearing, 1988). Groups that control a nation's agenda own the keys to the corridors of power. As the political scientist E.E. Schattschneider (1960) famously said, "the definition of the alternatives is the supreme instrument of power" (p. 68). There are a multitude of problems that afflict individuals and social systems, and governments cannot work on them all at once. Democratic societies must decide which problems to shelve, which ones to tackle, and how to formulate policies to address the problems they have chosen. "Every social system must have an agenda if it is to prioritize the problems facing it, so that it can decide where to start work. Such prioritization is necessary for a community and for a society," James W. Dearing and Everett M. Rogers (1996) explained (p. 1).

This is where the media come into the picture, as Lippmann noted presciently in 1922. Lippmann was among the first to call attention to the power of the press to create pictures in people's minds. He recognized that the world had changed with the growth of cities, advent of mass media, and the ways mediated political symbols shaped public opinion. He emphasized that citizens could only deal with a second-hand political reality conveyed by media (redolent of Plato's allegory of the cave, where the shadows projected on a wall constituted prisoners' only reality). Lippmann argued that the burgeoning news media serve as our window on the distant political world, shaping political beliefs and creating stereotyped pictures of political issues.

Some years later, during the television news era, commentators offered even stronger pronouncements about media effects. Journalist Theodore White observed that "the power of the press in America is a primordial one. It sets the agenda of public discussion. . . . It determines what people will talk and think about" (White, 1973, p. 327). Political scientist Bernard Cohen (1963) noted that "the press is significantly more than a purveyor of information and opinion. It may not be successful much of the time in telling people *what to think*, but it is stunningly successful in telling its readers *what to think about*" (p. 13, italics added).

Cohen's pithy statement is the most famous description of agenda-setting in the academic literature. Just about every major article or book on the subject quotes it. His observation highlighted the subtle, but powerful, effects that media could exert on public opinion. It also directed attention away from the popular belief that political communication swayed attitudes and voting behavior. Instead, it emphasized that media exerted effects in another arena, one traditionally overlooked: the simple, but politically consequential perception of what constitutes society's most important problems. By simply emphasizing certain problems rather than others, the media can influence public opinion, and sometimes policy.

There is also an important dysfunction or drawback of agenda-setting. By focusing on one or several problems, to the exclusion of others, news necessarily neglects other consequential issues. By focusing endlessly on the coronavirus pandemic, other problems—such as a variety of serious health ailments, abortion and the rights of the unborn, and gun safety—got short shrift, pushing them down on the national priority list, resulting in less policy attention to these issues. At the same time, the sad drumbeat of case after case, reaching more than 500,000 by early 2021, left a numbing imprint on people who had lost a loved one, the news pounding in a pain they yearned, at least for a time, to escape.

From an academic perspective, **agenda-setting** has a specific definition. It is defined as "a process through which the mass media communicate the relative importance of various issues and events to the public" (Rogers & Dearing, 1988, p. 555). As David Weaver (1984) explained, "Concentration by the media over time on relatively few issues leads to the public perceiving these issues as more salient or more important than other issues" (p. 682). Historically, by shining the beam of their searchlight on social inequities, the press has done considerable good, exposing political corruption, spotlighting fraudulent business practices, and revealing abuses that caused physical harm, among many Pulitzer Prize–winning stories.

Not every political media effect is agenda-setting. News can impart information, increase knowledge, intensify opposition to candidates, and elicit positive affect without influencing the political agenda. Agenda-setting refers specifically to the tendency of mediated news to elevate the importance people attribute to a political issue. As we will see, agenda-setting sheds light on a host of intriguing events in the world of politics. It offers an explanation of upending electoral effects and shifts in public opinion. And, turning the concept on its head, it suggests why few Americans worried about terrorism until 9/11, or a worldwide pandemic until 2020, although experts had long warned that they could exert devastating effects.

But before we can say with certainty that these effects are attributable to agenda-setting, there must be evidence that the media actually set the agenda. You may say that it is obvious that the media set the agenda, based on these examples or your own intuitions. But how do you know the examples accurately represent the political universe or your intuitions are correct? We turn to social science to determine the truth of hunches and assumptions.

Before proceeding, it is important to emphasize that agenda-setting has generated hundreds of studies and has different facets. Over the years, scholars have studied the ways news media elevate the importance of particular attributes of issues (see Chapter 8), as well as large networks or associations of attributes and ideas (McCombs & Valenzuela, 2021). This chapter focuses on the pivotal first level of agenda-setting, media impact on the perceived importance of political issues.

## Do the Data Support Agenda-Setting?

To demonstrate that media set the agenda, researchers need to do three things. First, they must show that there is a relationship between the media agenda—news stories appearing prominently in the media—and the public agenda, the issues people perceive to be the most important in the their community or nation. Second, they must show that agenda operates for different issues and in different contexts. Third, researchers need to establish that the media *cause* changes in citizens' ranking of the most important problems. To make the case for agenda-setting, researchers conduct experiments and surveys, including the pioneering survey published by Maxwell E. McCombs and Donald L. Shaw (1972) and other early research by Winter and Eyal (1981).

Agenda-setting effects have emerged for numerous issues, including energy, drugs, crime, and foreign affairs. What is more, effects have been obtained across the world, in studies conducted in Argentina, Britain, Germany, and Spain (McCombs, 2014). More than 425 studies of agenda-setting have been conducted, with substantial relationships between the media and public agendas. The hypothesis holds up strongly in the bulk of the research, as documented by reviews and statistical analyses of numerous empirical studies, which have continued to update the concept (Wanta & Ghanem, 2007; Skogerbø et al., 2016; Luo et al., 2019; Edy & Meirick, 2018).

## Evidence for Causation

So far the evidence shows that a strong relationship exist between the media and public agendas, but it does not conclusively demonstrate that the media exert a *causal* impact on the public agenda. To demonstrate causation, researchers conduct experiments that hone in on one factor and compare its effect to a control condition. Iyengar and Kinder (1987, 2010) employed just this strategy, publishing a series of experiments that demonstrated the impact that television news exerted on perceptions of the most important problems facing the nation.

In one key study, the researchers asked participants to evaluate the importance of a series of national problems. Over the course of a week, individuals viewed television newscasts that had been edited so they focused heavily on one particular problem. One group watched a week's worth of news that emphasized nuclear arms control, another group viewed news focusing on civil rights, and a third saw news on unemployment. Participants subsequently indicated their beliefs about the importance of national problems.

As agenda-setting predicted, individuals perceived the targeted problem to be more important after viewing the newscasts than prior to viewing the news (see Table 7.1). The results made it abundantly clear that sustained exposure to the news can exert a causal impact on beliefs about the importance of national problems.

Does this mean that the media's choice of top items influences the priorities of every online news outlet reader, blog scrutinizer, or viewer of television news? No, it does not.

Consider evidence that physical exercise is associated with health and well-being. This indicates that the more you exercise, the better your overall health. However, this does not mean that physical exertion will have an identical effect on the heart rate of each person who exercises frequently each week. Circumstances matter. Amount and type of exercise, time spent exercising, the genetic

**Table 7.1  Experimental evidence for agenda-setting.**

**Importance Rating of Problem**

|  | Pre-experiment | Post-experimental Change |  |
|---|---|---|---|
| Arms control | 76 | 82 | 6 |
| Civil rights | 64 | 69 | 5 |
| Unemployment | 75 | 82 | 7 |

*Source:* From Iyengar & Kinder (2010)

make-up of the individual, the person's overall health, and the juncture in the individual's life when he or she began exercising influence the strength of the relationship. It is the same with agenda-setting. "Agenda-setting does not operate *everywhere*, on *everyone*, and *always*," Rogers and Dearing explain (1988, p. 569).

You can think of issues the media could cover until the cows come home that would fail to influence the public agenda. Even if the media provided round-the-clock coverage of prejudice against left-handed individuals, it is unlikely this would register as a problem with the public (though left-handed people would organize a Facebook group). News coverage during wartime that tried to convince the public that the nation faced no foreign threat would be doomed to failure. When the media direct attention to an "implausible problem," one that flies in the face of common sense, their efforts are not likely to bear fruit (Iyengar & Kinder, 2010). For example, media covered climate issues for years, but it did make a dent in public consciousness until national leaders and credible spokespeople got behind the cause, and the evidence of climate change became too strong for even casual observers to ignore.

In addition, when news describes a problem that seems unbelievable to the public, contradicting their political beliefs or long-held expectations, it will not influence perceptions. For example, despite scrupulous *Washington Post* stories on Watergate in 1972 (and coverage on network news), the issue did not resonate with voters during the 1972 Nixon-McGovern election. Disbelieving what turned out to be true—that high-level political operatives engaged in political sabotage against their opponents in a gambit linked to the White House—few voters regarded honesty in government as a major campaign issue (Lang & Lang, 1983; McLeod, Becker, & Byrnes, 1974).

In general, across many situations, there is convincing evidence that media set the agenda. But *how* does it work psychologically? How do media agenda penetrate and influence viewers' minds? A first explanation emphasizes accessibility of information. A great deal of media coverage of an issue (say, terrorism) can *access* the issue, or bring it quickly to mind. When people are considering problems facing the country, the ones media frequently cover spring initially to mind. In addition, media coverage can cue a *heuristic*, or decision-making rule (Pingree & Stoycheff, 2013; Pingree et al., 2013; Stoycheff et al., 2018). I may observe that news has focused a lot on the national debt, recognize that journalists know more about politics than I do, and reason that if they think it's an important problem, it probably is. Alternatively, if I am personally concerned about an issue, such as opioid dependence, I may begin to read a lot of the news stories on my news feed and conclude, based on processing facts in the stories, that this is a pretty serious problem facing the country as a whole (Bulkow, Urban, & Schweiger, 2013).

The first explanation of agenda-setting emphasizes top-of-the-head, or short-circuited processing, while the second focuses on systematic processing of the media agenda, with an emphasis on perceived issue importance (Takeshita, 2006). The first process is more likely to hold when we are not particularly concerned about an issue, whereas the second operates when the issue affects us personally or symbolically. This is all well and good, but if the cues people use are misleading or biased, they may reach ill-informed conclusions about the real problems that afflict the nation.

## Agenda-Setting Wrinkles: Power of Context

After reading about agenda-setting, you might assume the media just set the agenda and suggest what the most important issues are, period. It does not work this way. Scientific research emphasizes that the effects of media do not occur in a vacuum, but hinge on the nature of the individual and social forces. When media effects depend on other factors, we emphasize that these factors **moderate** or help determine when media are influential and when they are less important. This is actually quite interesting, because it pinpoints the conditions under which media are effective and when they are not, illuminating agenda-setting effects.

At least three contingent conditions moderate agenda-setting effects. They are diverse, interesting, and tell us lots about issues in the news today.

### News Play

Stories that lead off network newscasts have a stronger influence than more ordinary stories on public perceptions (Iyengar & Kinder, 2010). Lead stories are influential partly because viewers assume network news is credible, inducing them to accept journalists' judgments that the first or second story is the most important. Lead stories also appear early—before people leave the room to get something to eat or text a friend. Transplanting these findings to contemporary media, one presumes that the stories that top the list of trending stories on a social media page would exert stronger agenda-setting effects than less prominent stories.

### Nature of the Issue

Agenda-setting depends on the particular issue or event (Rogers & Dearing, 1988). A rapid-onset issue involves critical, cataclysmic events such as terrorism, which occur immediately. These leap instantly or quickly to the top of the nation's agenda, as occurred in the wake of the George Floyd protests and the terrorist attacks on Paris and San Bernardino, California, some years back. Slow-onset issues have a gradual, less immediate trajectory, and these topics, such as climate change, can take longer to reach the agenda, because the problem is harder to visualize, effects are not immediate, and coverage is spottier. This is interesting because, according to some climate change experts, it took far too long for the media to place global warming at the apex of the public agenda. This may have stemmed from foot-dragging by public officials or widely publicized (and politicized) doubts that climate change was real. It took a while, but by 2020 the issue was squarely on the public agenda, as indicated by its prominence in the presidential debates.

The coronavirus pandemic began as a slower-onset issue in the United States when the virus afflicted mostly residents of Wuhan, China. It quickly gathered steam, becoming a super-rapid-onset issue in March 2020 as infections mounted, schools moved to remote learning, and businesses closed.

A related issue is obtrusiveness, or the extent of direct experience people have with the issue, the degree to which it impinges directly on their personal lives. On the one hand, the less direct experience individuals have with an issue, the more they will depend on news and come to accept the media agenda (Zucker, 1978; Mutz, 1998). When the issue is far-off, does not impinge directly on us and is unobtrusive, the media are the ones that bring the matter to us and shape our thinking. On the other hand, when issues are obtrusive, influencing us directly, we do not need the media to tell us the topic is important. The media might have less agenda-setting impact for obtrusive issues such as unemployment, when you are out of a job. Unemployment would already be on your mind, and you aren't likely to be more convinced by reading about the plight of displaced workers from a different region of the country. However, people who are unemployed may tune into coverage of the jobless rate, think a lot about it, relate the coverage to their own lives, and end up feeling all the more strongly and deeply that the problem affects the country as well.

There are not simple answers to these questions. Some people might be more affected by issue obtrusiveness than others, as a function of their need for political orientation and uncertainty (Kim, 2014; Matthes, 2006; McCombs & Reynolds, 2009). Moderating effects of issue obtrusiveness also depend on the degree to which people see a similarity between their own obtrusive problem (say, unemployment) and the people shown struggling with joblessness in media portrayals.

In the case of the coronavirus, media magnified the impact of personal anxieties, showcasing the reach of the virus, its macroeconomic devastation, and the dire shortage of hospital space and ventilators. But once this became a highly obtrusive issue, with schools and businesses closed, people didn't need the media to tell them this was an important problem. News influences switched to how the problem was framed and interpreted (see Chapter 8).

### Partisan Media

Agenda-setting makes a quaint assumption. It assumes that the media act pretty much in unison and carry the same agenda. That agenda filters to Americans, who trust the media and accept their take on issues. Does that sound like today? Not exactly! This was true in the three-networks-bestrode-the-colossus era of the mid-20th century, but it's not true today when news outlets can contain partisan biases and people apply these biases (and their own) to interpretations of news.

But first, yes, all media treat some issues as consequential, leading citizens to share this view. The coronavirus and, interestingly enough, the divisive issue of impeachment fit that bill. With impeachment blanketing the news and engaging Republicans and Democrats during the fall of 2019, as the House weighed impeaching Trump, it was a slam-dunk. A national survey of more than 100,000 respondents found that Americans viewed impeachment as the most important issue facing the nation, regardless of whether they supported or opposed it (Vavreck, Sides, & Tausanovitch, 2019).

But these high-profile, all-consuming issues can be the exception, rather than the agenda-setting rule—a far cry from decades past when there was bipartisan agreement on the most important national problems. Democrats generally assign more importance to health care and education; Republicans are more concerned with terrorism and the economy (Jones, 2019). Even when Democrats and Republicans agree that an issue is important, partisan differences surface. Although both Republicans and Democrats assigned high importance to the coronavirus issue, Biden voters believed it was the most significant issue facing the country, while Trump voters prioritized the economy (Medina & Russonello, 2020).

Similarly, a majority of Americans believe climate change should be a top priority for the president and Congress, but three times more Democrats than Republicans feel this way (Popovich, 2020). Republicans and Democrats also assign importance to immigration, but they differ on which aspect should be prioritized; stopping the policy of separating children from parents has tended to be important to Democrats, whose values emphasize social justice, while constructing a border wall is a big priority for Republicans, who are more concerned with order and loyalty to country. And while partisans from both parties thought impeachment was the most important problem facing the country in late 2019, they saw the issue through very different prisms.

So, there can be agreement on the most important problem, but this pales in significance when people disagree on the aspect of the issue that they regard as most pressing (McCombs & Ghanem, 2001) or the way the issue is framed, the focus of Chapter 8.

Partisan media agenda-setting can be a good thing if it allows for a variety of different agendas to take hold, reducing the ability of a handful of media outlets to create a homogeneous agenda. Diverse viewpoints celebrate a pluralistic spirit of democracy. Where partisan agenda-setting becomes problematic is when it merely reinforces what people already believe, causing media to become an echo chamber mirroring and strengthening perceptions of important issues rather than exposing individuals to different political agendas. Ironically, the old-style broadcast media, so lamented by scholars as fostering a single-minded, even hegemonic, view had a salutary feature. It offered a common agenda on which citizens could draw, strengthening communal bonds and national linkages, which shored up commitment to a common heritage. But in an era of niche media, full of partisan websites, if "like-minded media use encourages Republicans and Democrats to perceive different issues as important, it may become difficult to bring citizens together to solve the nation's problems," Natalie Stroud points out (2013, p. 15).

## CONSEQUENCES OF AGENDA-SETTING: THE POWER OF PRIMING

What difference does it make if the media set the agenda? True, the effect is interesting because it demonstrates a subtle and pervasive media influence. However, agenda-setting takes on more importance if it can be shown that it affects other aspects of the political system, such as voting behavior and policy-making. In their theoretical account of news impact, Iyengar and Kinder (2010) articulated an explanation of how agenda-setting can influence voting behavior. It is a five-step process that begins with what people cannot do.

First, individuals can't pay close attention to all or even most of what happens in the political world. "To do so would breed paralysis," the scholars noted (Iyengar & Kinder, 2010, p. 64).

Second, rather than carefully analyzing all issues, people rely on the most accessible information, or stuff that comes immediately to mind (though see Takeshita, 2006, for an alternative view). According to the accessibility approach, when evaluating the president, Americans do not draw on everything they know about the chief executive's policies, ideological positions, personal traits, achievements, and political mishaps. Instead, people call on a small sample of their knowledge—a snapshot that comes immediately to mind, or is accessible, at the time they must decide how to cast their vote.

Third, *the* media powerfully determine which issues come to mind. Problems that receive a great deal of news coverage are the ones people invariably mention when asked to name the most important problems facing the country. This, of course, is agenda-setting. Fourth, once the media set the agenda, they can prime voters. "By calling attention to some matters while ignoring others," Iyengar and Kinder (2010) observe, "television news influences the standards by which governments, presidents, policies, and candidates for public office are judged" (p. 63). Fifth, priming can influence the way people cast their votes.

Political communication research calls on this concept, suggesting that the media agenda primes other realms of political thought. Priming specifically refers to the impact of the media agenda on the criteria voters employ to evaluate candidates for public office.

In theory, it works this way: The issues that news happens to be covering at a particular time are communicated to voters. Voters—some more than others—then decide these are the most important issues facing the country. With these issues at the top of their political mindsets, people call on these issues and decide to evaluate the president or presidential candidates based on their performance in handling these particular problems. Schematically, in its most basic form, the model looks like this:

Media agenda → Voters' agenda → Priming → Voting

Importantly, a variety of factors determine whether priming leads to voting in a particular election, including the individual's party affiliation. The model offers a pure, simple illustration of the hypothesized pathways.

Researchers have tested priming in a number of studies. In their research, Iyengar and Kinder (2010) randomly assigned research participants to one of three experimental treatments. Over a week's time, one group of individuals watched newscasts that focused on unemployment. A second group viewed news that emphasized arms control. In a third condition, individuals watched newscasts with a strong focus on civil rights. According to priming, participants who viewed stories on a particular issue should accord more weight to the president's performance on the targeted issue when assessing the chief executive's overall performance. This is indeed what happened. Individuals who viewed unemployment stories gave more weight to the president's performance on unemployment after watching the news than they did before. Similarly, participants who viewed news emphasizing arms control and civil rights placed more weight on these issues when assessing the president's performance.

These were exciting findings, suggesting that agenda-setting had consequences and priming was real. Iyengar and Kinder's studies spurred researchers to examine priming in other contexts, and their findings demonstrated the generality of priming effects, as seen from the litany of published research (e.g., Domke, 2001; Kim, 2005; Krosnick & Kinder, 1990; McGraw & Ling, 2003; Moy, Xenos, & Hess, 2005; Pan & Kosicki, 1997; Valentino, 1999). Like agenda-setting, media priming has emerged in contexts outside the U.S, for example in

Israel, Switzerland, and South Korea (Balmas & Sheafer, 2010; Sheafer, 2007; Kuhne et al., 2011; Kim, Han, & Scheufele, 2010). Clearly, the media can exert strong effects on political agendas and priming. Pointing to research evidence for priming, some scholars argue that the media have a tremendous capacity to influence political thought. Iyengar and Kinder speak of its "insidious" effect.

## Nationalistic Primes in the Trump Era

Media primes can work on a deeper, more insidious level. To appreciate these media effects, we need to look at priming more psychologically. As a psychological concept, priming involves the influence of a prior message on responses to a subsequent message. Priming is an automatic process, about which individuals may be relatively oblivious and may even operate below conscious awareness (Bargh & Williams, 2006). Priming emphasizes that information is encoded in memory by nodes that represent concepts or ideas; these ideas are related to other concepts by associative pathways in the mind. When a particular concept is activated, primed, or accessed through media, it spreads its political meaning like wildfire through a forest, to related nodes, leading to instantaneous affective reactions.

This is pretty abstract, but you're going to appreciate its practical political import pretty soon. A fascinating series of experiments by Magdalena Wojcieszak and R. Kelly Garrett (2018) applied the priming concept to the provocative topic of immigration, an issue that has roiled American populists, who perceive that illegal immigrants jeopardize their economic livelihood. They also see immigrants as threatening their cultural identity by engulfing the country with "foreigners" harboring values alien to those they grew up with. Noting that national identity is a strong part of our sense of self, evoking patriotism, storied national sentiments, and a sense of "our" country's heritage, the researchers suspected that priming national identity could have particularly pernicious effects among those who harbored negative attitudes toward "them," the undocumented or (to use the more unfavorable adjective) illegal immigrants.

Wojcieszak and Garrett primed immigration opponents by simply asking them to focus on "one essential quality that you share with other Americans, something that unites us as a people" (p. 252). They subsequently assessed their attitudes toward illegal immigrants, comfort level with immigrants as colleagues, neighbors, and close friends, and how favorably they felt toward their in-group identity as Americans. Immigration opponents (but not immigration supporters) who were primed to think favorably about Americans felt relatively more positively about the American in-group and displayed more negative attitudes toward immigrants, indicators of affective polarization. By calling to mind positive "us-feelings" about America, immigration opponents automatically activated sentiments that are not logically connected with feeling good about America, but are "psycho-logically" linked—unfavorable feelings about "them," those "non-American" immigrants (see also Wojcieszak, Azrout, & de Vreese, 2018). The results shed light on priming's real-world insidious influences—cases where leaders in the U.S. and across the world have primed nationalist sentiments, causing prejudiced people to activate negative images of immigrants that precipitated verbal or even physical aggression.

The findings also help explain how hundreds of rioters—primed by Trump's falsehoods that the election was rigged, his call to "show strength" at the Capitol, and years of support for White nationalist rhetoric—could storm the Capitol when Congress certified the 2020 votes, accessing their anger, translating a misplaced fervor about America into anti-democratic, riotous behavior.

## Priming During a Classic Election

Priming also has important implications for normal electoral contexts. In 2016, many American voters did not trust Hillary Clinton. There were many reasons for this, spanning gender bias, belief that Clinton disdained traditional gender roles, and incessant news media focus on negative tidbits from her political career. Her trustworthiness became a cause célèbre during the 2016 campaign when a newspaper exposé revealed that Clinton had employed her personal email account for government business, raising questions about whether she had emailed classified information in violation of U.S. secrecy laws. While the issue was complex, and some critics felt the news overplayed a trivial issue, it played into the narrative that Clinton harbored a penchant for secrecy.

By fall the issue had faded from many voters' minds, but it burst into public view in late October 2016, when FBI director James Comey announced that he planned to review a new trove of Clinton's emails to see if they contained classified information. While Comey said that the review had uncovered no evidence of wrongdoing, his announcement followed a week of unrelenting news coverage and Republican attacks on Clinton, a sharp decline in Clinton's poll ratings, enough to cost her the election, in the view of a major pollster (Silver, 2017). It is quite possible—though not proven—that the announcement primed concerns about Clinton's purported secrecy, causing undecided voters to elevate the importance of trustworthiness in their voting calculus, to the detriment of Clinton. It could have supplanted doubts about Trump produced by the release of an *Access Hollywood* TV show tape, where he bragged about groping women (Rhodes et al., 2020).

While some of Clinton's trust problem can be pinned on her own communication style, there are broader issues about the wisdom of an FBI director upending policy by intervening in the midst of a contentious campaign, and the news media's decision to elevate this story above all others. Indeed, by passively covering the email story (as well as WikiLeaks' unethical dumping of Russia's hacking of Clinton's emails), and framing it around Clinton's supposedly duplicitous style, the news may have pumped up their effects on the public (Lawrence, 2019).

There was a more underhanded priming possibility that could have undermined Clinton's candidacy among undecided voters: the efforts by Russian cyber warriors, hackers, and trolls to infiltrate social media, creating false websites that offered links to so-called news, including 130,000 inflammatory Twitter posts and 80,000 divisive messages on Facebook that reached as many as 126 million Facebook users (Isaac & Wakabayashi, 2017). Hoping to reach persuadable conservative voters, Russian operatives created incendiary posts, such as the picture of a heavy man wearing a T-shirt with the words "UNDOCUMENTED UNAFRAID UNAPOLOGETIC" questioning why "this veteran gets nothing" and "this illegal gets everything." Another graphically depicted Satan in an arm wrestle with Jesus, with the headline, "Satan: If I win, Clinton wins!" (see Mayer, 2018). Fanciful as these were, they could have primed undecided voters who were already disenchanted with Clinton, due to their dissatisfaction with her perceived secular approach. These, along with stories about hacked Clinton emails, circulated via WikiLeaks, could have pushed their doubts to the surface, pushing these voters to go with Trump.

It's not that these primes were effective with every voter or even most voters, but by accessing fears about Clinton and activating doubts among persuadable undecided voters, the Russian primes and WikiLeaks stories could have made a difference. Their impact could have been accentuated by mainstream media, with its focus on edgy trending topics. This is the broad argument, along with others, advanced by Kathleen Hall Jamieson in an evidence-packed 2018 book aptly titled *Cyberwar*. The arguments are provocative. However, as Jamieson acknowledges, they don't provide unequivocal evidence that the stealth Russian cyber-campaign swung the election. There is no data showing that the primes caused voters to change their voting behavior or attitude, and of course, after the fact, such data would be hard to come by. The evidence, as one critic notes, is "only circumstantial" (Rimmer, 2019, p. 160).

Moreover, it is doubtful that the fake posts, vivid as they were, were noticed or believed by most voters. In addition, the volume of online information out there is formidable, meaning that it could have swamped the Russian bot-generated cyber-posts, which, in the case of Twitter, accounted for just 1 percent of all election-oriented tweets (Nyhan, 2018). Jamieson doesn't prove her case unequivocally with data. It's possible more standard political media fare undid Clinton's candidacy in three battleground states, but Jamieson's arguments, particularly those emphasizing news media's doing WikiLeaks's bidding, are provocative, pointing to the potential power priming exerts and the dangers that lurk in our stealth media environment.

## Other Electoral Priming

During presidential elections, candidates prime voters' attitudes, arguing that issues they emphasize should be key ingredients in voters' decision-making calculus. When economic problems beset the country, candidates—Clinton in 1992 and Obama in 2008—primed voters by suggesting that their ability to improve the economy was the most important factor to consider when voting. In other years, different primes were salient. In 2004 George W. Bush primed 9/11 by accessing voters' recollections of the tragedy and linking it with his national leadership. Several ads showed images of the Twin Towers' destruction, with a flag flying atop the area and fireman working feverishly amid the debris. (Critics said the ads, with their tagline "President Bush: Steady Leadership in Times of Change," were manipulative, exploiting tender emotions that were aroused by the tragedy.) In 2016, Hillary Clinton sought to prime Trump's offensive behavior with women, while Trump primed Clinton's emails, aided by Comey's October surprise that he planned to review the new email trove.

In 2020, as the country struggled with the personal and economic devastation wrought by the coronavirus, Trump's handling of the pandemic—praised by him, condemned by Biden—played a role in voters' evaluations, influenced, as always, by media coverage, party affiliation, and the perceived credibility of each candidate on the issue. While Trump sought to emphasize his steady leadership, punctuated by a daily television press briefing, Biden condemned the president's failure to act quickly when many deaths could have been prevented. If Bill Clinton's agenda-setting catchphrase in 1992 was "it's the economy, stupid," in 2020, a preeminent focus was "it's the pandemic, everyone," with one in five Americans saying this was the nation's most important problem, a significant number given that non-economic problems rarely reach this level in polls (Enten, 2020).

Democrats argued that Trump's slow response to the coronavirus in the spring of 2020 was an important factor in evaluating his presidency, one that redounded to their advantage. Applying the one-two agenda-setting, then priming punch, they capitalized on the strong salience of the coronavirus, turning next to argue that the key attribute in 2020 was the chief executive's ability to tame the virus. Seventy-three percent of voters who said the pandemic was an important issue to them voted for Biden, and more than half of voters who said the federal government's response to the virus was an important factor in their voting decisions cast ballots for Biden (see Tavernise & Eligon, 2020). (From an academic perspective, media can prime both personal experiences with the virus and collective judgments about the pandemic; see Mutz, 1992.)

The Trump campaign primed issues as well. Noting that Republicans tended to prioritize the economy more than the virus, Trump claimed that Biden would shut down the economy and ship jobs to China. Trump's messages also sought to access fears of crime, seeking to convince voters that these fears should be important ingredients in their voting decisions, even as his ads may have played on subtle stereotypes (see Chapter 8). Importantly, the crime theme could be played up by the news, which showed violent images from the George Floyd riots. Some protests unquestionably turned violent, marked by vandalism and looting. However, news could overplay these elements, exemplifying a classic cultivation effect that exacerbated fears among voters who were already convinced that racial violence was out of control and, in some cases, probably associating the violence with racial minorities. Nearly half of the voters who said that protests over police violence were important factors in their voting decision cast ballots for Trump (see Tavernise & Eligon, 2020).

## AGENDA-BUILDING

Agenda-setting takes us only so far. Evidence that media set the agenda does not explain the ways news intersects with policy-making and whether news influences policy legislation to address problems that media highlight. To appreciate these issues, we need to focus on the broader, macro issue of agenda-building, or how media work within the corridors of power politics, where agendas are an instrument of power, influence, and intrigue. Several concepts underlie the subsequent discussion. **Agenda-building** is defined as "a process through which the policy agendas of political elites are influenced by a variety of factors, including media agendas and public agendas" (Rogers & Dearing, 1988, p. 555). The **public agenda** consists of the issues the general public views as most important at a particular time. The **policy agenda** refers to the issues that top the priority list of political leaders.

### The Big Picture

National leaders face a dizzying array of problems. They cannot focus their resources on all issues simultaneously. They must select among issues, concentrating energies on certain social problems and letting others fall by the wayside. Issues compete for attention, and their proponents—well-heeled lobbyists, activists, and passionate ideologues—must persuade policymakers to devote time and money to their issue rather than someone else's. But, given the volume of problems on policymakers' plates, it is difficult for a particular social issue to make it to the top of their policy agendas.

Deciding that something is a problem is itself an important—and political—act. If an issue is not defined as a problem by the media or political elites, it cannot move through the series of stages necessary for a problem to be considered, discussed, and acted on. There is not a one-to-one relationship between the importance or breadth of the problem and its emergence on the media agenda. Epic tragedies such as the extermination of Jews during World War II (Lipstadt, 1986), institutional racism during the early 20th century, and the spread of AIDS (Kinsella, 1988) were not covered because they raised uncomfortable truths that threatened elites' belief systems and did not mesh with conventional journalistic news-gathering routines.

When media—and increasingly we are talking about a rich mashup of conventional news, specialized websites, and activist social media—direct their searchlights on an issue, a policy agenda can diffuse throughout society, leading to policy change. News effects on public opinion and policy are complex (Dearing & Rogers, 1996; Gonzenbach, 1996).

For agenda-building to occur, the news must work in concert with other powerful social forces. News is a necessary, not a sufficient, condition for policy change. Students sometimes conflate media with power, assuming that just because an issue is covered in The Media (capital letters reflecting the media's supposed omnipotence), policies will be changed. But the media are one of a number of actors on the public stage, and they work with other institutions, sometimes producing change, in other cases informing the public but failing to make a dent in an entrenched political establishment.

## A Complicated Process

Agenda-building plays an important role in democracy because it provides a pathway by which media and political institutions can sow the seeds for social change. Scholars have explored how and when agendas are built, focusing on when certain issues become matters of policy concern, occupy policymakers' attention, and produce meaningful change. Political scientists have emphasized that there must be a suitable or "ripe" issue climate for an issue to rise to the top of the policy agenda and action to be taken. Policymakers and journalists must recognize that (1) *a problem exists*, (2) *have available a variety of solutions*, and (3)*find themselves in a ripe social or political climate to act on the problem* (Cook & Skogan, 1991; Protess et al., 1991; Kingdon, 2011).

First, the media play a role in first bringing a problem to public attention, as they have in the case of countless issues—environmental pollution, health care inequities, racial injustice, and abortion on demand—that were viewed as unchanging aspects of modern life until media coverage transformed them to *problems* in need of corrective action. But attention is not sufficient.

For media, public, and policy agendas to trigger change, a second hurdle must be crossed: Policymakers must have viable solutions and there must be more unity than divisiveness among policymakers. One reason why health care reform occurred under Obama, not Clinton, despite mighty efforts to change health care during the Clinton years, is because there was more policy consensus on how to ameliorate health care when Obama was president, greater agreement among health care interest groups on how to proceed, more effective consensus-based politicking by the Obama team, and less conflicted media coverage about health care in Obama's first term than when Clinton tackled the fractious issue in 1993 (Kingdon, 2011). Media coverage of deficiencies in American health care over decades probably helped set the agenda, a necessary condition for media agenda-building, but it took years of concerted efforts on the policy front for an issue to move from the stage of problem attention to legislative implementation.

**Ripe Climate and News Flashpoints.** The third condition necessary for policy action is a ripe political climate, an opinion climate built over time by activists, journalists, policymakers, and changing public attitudes. The political timing must be right for policy change. However, if opponents persuasively argue that the problem is less serious than assumed, policymakers fail to pursue the issue, and media attention declines, then the issue can fall off the policy agenda. For action to be taken, there must be a confluence of positive forces operating simultaneously, with active, policy deliberations and media attention. In an online media era, we can broaden this to include a coalescing of agendas in mainstream news, alternative media outlets, blogs, hashtags, and trending stories. When there is alignment of discussion across diverse media outlets on an issue of deep-seated social importance, a **news flashpoint** has emerged. News flashpoints go beyond legacy news coverage and **intermedia agenda-setting** (where key news outlets influence the agenda of other media platforms). Flashpoints highlight unusual points of convergence in the ordinarily chaotic digital ecosphere, as Silvio Waisbord and Adrienne Russell (2020) insightfully note.

In January 2021, just when the country hoped that the beginning of a new year marked the end of jarring flashpoints, violent insurrectionists stormed the Capitol, preempting regular television programs, blanketing the nation's media, and galvanizing attention on the president's symbolic complicity with the rioters. And that followed two flashpoints that emerged in rapid succession in ripe opinion climates during the tumultuous spring of 2020. As the coronavirus outbreak spread, there was consensus about its obvious importance in media, public opinion, and among national leaders. Congressional Republicans and Democrats, who ordinarily disagree about everything, approved a $2 trillion economic stimulus package that gave unemployment benefits to individuals, funding for cash-strapped states, and hundreds of billions of dollars to small businesses and companies hit hard by the crisis. As differences of opinion about the virus's severity and consequences diffused, different frames emerged that eviscerated the consensus and eliminated—or complicated—the flashpoint. The usual cacophony in the eco-sphere returned.

A more dramatic flashpoint occurred in the wake of social media outcry, media coverage, spontaneous Black Lives Matter protests from coast to coast, and public attitude shifts that followed the police killing of George Floyd in

Minneapolis (see Figure 7.2). With nonstop agenda-setting news about the protests, alignment of diverse media around the issue, and consensus about the urgency of action in the political, business, and entertainment communities, reformist ideas that had been percolating for years were implemented to address the problem. Within weeks of the protests, a new agenda was set, primed, and built, as Congressional Democrats moved ahead on a bill that made it easier to prosecute excessive use of forcible techniques used by police, setting in motion new policy proposals to reduce discrimination (Edmondson & Fandos, 2020). With a speed rarely seen in American politics, transformative changes occurred in many sectors of society.

A number of states and cities instituted police reforms, banning chokeholds and mandating body cameras; Minneapolis required police officers to take action when they witnessed excessive use of force by another officer (Perez, 2020). Other indicators of a racial reckoning unfolded quickly. Mississippi removed its Confederate flag, NASCAR banned the display of Confederate flags at its events, the National Football League admitted it was wrong not to have listened

**Figure 7.2  News of the brutal police killing of George Floyd, and the ensuing Black Lives Matter protests, careened across media—mainstream channels as well as social media—offering an unexpected news flashpoint that influenced opinions and policy.**

*Source:* **Photograph by Temima Muskin**

to players who took a knee to protest racism, and American companies marked Juneteenth, which historically commemorated the end of slavery, as a work holiday. On the corporate front, companies pledged to increase the number of Black employees. Confederate statues linked with racial injustice were toppled or removed in the U.S. and across the world. The Merriam-Webster Dictionary changed its definition of racism to emphasize its systemic nature.

It was an unusual, potent instance of agenda-building, stimulated by a news flashpoint. Of course, there can be debate about just what constitutes a flashpoint, as well as the factors—nature of the issue, degree of alignment among different media actors, and broader political trends—that determine whether a flashpoint produces or inhibits policy change. The issue was also unusual because grassroots protests usually don't become major media agenda items, at least not for a while. In this case, due to the intensity of the protests and social context, protests set the agenda, attesting to the power that democratic movements can sometimes exert on the agenda-building process.

It was a distinctive instance, a case where a salient event increased media coverage, in line with Hellmeier, Weidmann, and Rød (2018), one of many studies on media and the trajectory of political protest (e.g., Gitlin, 1980). Yet usually things are different, as McLeod and Hertog (1992) showed. Media typically downgrade protesters, subtly derogating them as falling outside the dominant culture. In their classic study of media, public opinion, and protest in Minneapolis, McLeod and Hertog (1992) found that mainstream media constructed public opinion and protests in ways that focused on the deviance of the demonstrators, how they departed from appropriate appearance norms, and their divergence from mainstream American public opinion, all in all not a favorable portrait of dissent against the status quo.

But, lo and behold, in the case of the 2020 racial protests, public opinion took on different hues, at least in the immediate aftermath of the protests. About 70 percent of the public believed the Floyd killing was part of a more substantial problem with law enforcement; 57 percent of Americans said the protesters' anger was fully justified; and more than three-fourths of Americans considered racism a big problem facing the country (e.g., Edmondson & Fandos, 2020; Edsall, 2020; Russonello, 2020). The media—and, of course, there were differences, depending on the partisan slant of a particular outlet—took their lead from the public, the novelty of the events, and scope of the protests—more than 4,500 demonstrations in 2,500 different communities involving as many as 20 million people, the largest protest movement in U.S. history (Buchanan, Bui, & Patel, 2020).

Douglas M. McLeod, who co-authored the classic protest study, which coincidentally took place in Minneapolis, noted that the nonstop repetition of brutal police killings of Black people on social media left an imprint on attitudes, in a way that previous killings had not. This worked together with the social conditions that facilitated media effects; gradual seeding of positive attitudes toward Black Lives Matter over time (e.g., McLeod, 2007); ways that the magnitude of protests held sway over individuals, locked into social media; likely appreciation of the disproportionate effect the coronavirus had taken on African Americans; greater exposure to, and processing of, the videos due to sheltering-in-place; and a general malaise and frustration many felt, producing a collective outpouring of efficacy and action. "When these things accumulate over time, and we start to see more and more of these images, the evidence starts to become more incontrovertible," McLeod noted (Russonello, 2020).

Although communities and organizations took many tangible and symbolic steps, reforms on the federal level languished, as Congress, influenced by lobbying from powerful police unions, resisted passing systemic police reforms, pushing back against legislation that would curb aggressive police tactics (Broadwater & Edmondson, 2020). The issue is complicated. Police had reasons to oppose measures that could thwart crime-fighting efforts, but it is noteworthy that many of the reform ideas died before even getting voted on in the nation's legislative body, divided as usual on partisan lines. In California, although the public overwhelmingly favored police reform, the legislature, cowed by police unions, shied away from making any substantive legal changes in police practices (Pawel, 2020). In many cities, deeply entrenched legal and political systems, erected by police unions, continue to protect abusive police officers, keeping them on the force, expunging the offense from their records, giving them only a tap on the wrist, even when they have been accused of killing a suspect (Barker, Keller, & Eder, 2020). Despite all the significant symbolic strides and state policy changes that occurred after the flashpoint emerged, few sweeping legislative changes occurred on the national level, reminding us that agenda-building takes place in a highly politicized context.

**The Big Picture.** Thus, the path to change is frequently daunting. On issues such as health care, climate change, and gun violence, there are sharp differences in interpretation of the problem, political schisms, and powerful interest groups that impede collective efforts to build a bipartisan agenda around reforms.

Partisan media play a part in this nowadays, sometimes working hand-in-hand with the White House to build a particular agenda. During Trump's first term, there was strong anecdotal evidence that Fox News was helping construct Trump's agenda. Following a Fox News segment about two Somali refugees who were reportedly arrested in Tucson, Arizona, for giving support to the terrorist group ISIS, an item that played to his anti-illegal-immigration agenda, Trump tweeted out the story (Rupar, 2019). But let's be fair. It will be interesting to see if the same White House–partisan media symbiosis emerges on the left side of the street during Biden's time in the White House.

## AGENDAS IN THE DIGITAL AGE

Let's switch gears to examine the ways agenda-setting and agenda-building have changed in the contemporary digital environment. McCombs and Shaw developed the agenda-setting model during a time when mass media had enormous impact. Reporters were the primary gatekeepers; they decided, based on journalistic conventions, whether and what information would reach the public. Back in the day, media could present a fairly consistent and uniform agenda at any particular time (Metzger, 2009), but these assumptions are no longer tenable. People no longer rely exclusively on the conventional media for information. They turn to online news and social media sites. The media's ability to convey a singular agenda to hundreds of millions of Americans has slipped.

Over the past decade, a variety of studies have explored agenda-setting in a world of interactive media and intermedia agenda-setting effects, which occur when particular media outlets set the agenda for other news platforms (Johnson, 2014; Meraz, 2014; Tran, 2014). To be sure, when it comes to issues of national importance, such as health care and national elections, mainstream news coverage influences public opinion and policy agendas (Shehata & Strömbäck, 2013; Vargo & Guo, 2017). In the case of quick-onset issues with immediate national importance, such as terrorist attacks or a virus outbreak, mainstream media are key agenda setters. Indeed, mainstream news outlets continue to set the agenda for many political issues (Djerf-Pierre & Shehata, 2017), but they aren't the only big dogs in agenda-setting town.

Talk shows, blogs, and partisan niche media can influence or reinforce partisan agendas, as seen when conservative sites pushed discussion of Trump's issues in the 2016 campaign and liberal outlets emphasized pro-Democratic views during the fractious Kavanaugh hearings regarding allegations of sexual abuse (see Rojecki & Meraz, 2016; Vargo & Guo, 2017; Vargo et al., 2014). Research finds that blogs can set the agenda for mainstream media, creating a buzz that journalists follow and report (Meraz, 2011; Messner & DiStaso, 2008; Schiffer, 2006; Sweetser, Golan, & Wanta, 2008).

It's complex. Blogs, websites, and Twitter can affect the news agenda; however, conventional media also set an agenda for the blogosphere and Twitter (Conway-Silva, Kenski, & Wang, 2015; Conway-Silva et al., 2018; Tran, 2014; Harder, Sevenans, & Van Aelst, 2017). Partisan media, particularly the more animated right-wing outlets, sought mightily to influence the mainstream media agenda over the course of the Trump administration.

Trump proved adept at channeling his tweets so they dominated the news, setting a series of mini-fires everywhere that mainstream news covered, partly because presidential statements are newsworthy and also because they generated ratings. His ability to dominate the news agenda, including during the presidential election campaign (Agiesta, 2020b), were of a piece with his success in dominating the news during his days as a New York City real estate magnate, attesting to his showmanship and the news media's willingness to grant him a stage, preferring to cover Trump's latest firestorm than other more substantive issues on the national agenda. However, Trump's coverage was not always positive.

In today's era, one must also broach the issue of fake news—not just slightly inaccurate reports, but deliberate attempts at misinformation that can be part of an extremist ideological outlet's agenda. Fake news sites can borrow and distort information from conventional news sites, and sometimes can even influence agendas of partisan outlets (Guo & Vargo, 2020; Vargo, Guo, & Amazeen, 2018). And while fake news doesn't penetrate the information space of the overwhelming majority of Americans (Nyhan, 2018), extreme partisans may share it, wittingly or unwittingly regarding it as true.

What is the balance sheet? As agenda control was wrested from East Coast media hegemons—elite newspapers, magazines, and television networks—to a panoply of online platforms, activist bloggers, and citizen journalists, social influence has been diffused across a broader spectrum of political groups and citizens. The expansion of voices enriches democracy. Citizens have more control; they no longer must take their cues exclusively from elites. The downside is agenda-building blogs and partisan media spread inaccurate, even false, information. And when people just get information from one social media outlet, with a plethora of posts on one side, partisan agenda-setting and fragmentation can intensify. Digital media have tamed the power that East Coast elites exerted in agenda-setting, but they have given us a mongrel more variegated and equally, if not more, problematic.

## CONCLUSIONS

*The media set the agenda.*

This is the most famous of all political media effects, one that is well known in political and journalistic circles. It is among the most well-documented political communication effects. Agenda-setting is sometimes believed to be synonymous with any and all media influence. It is not. Agenda-setting has a precise meaning. It is the process through which media communicate the importance of specific issues to the public. It occurs when sustained media coverage of a problem causes the public to believe this issue is more salient than others. By defining a problem as important, media can profoundly influence public opinion and, under some conditions, policy-making. This is the fundamental insight of agenda-setting theory.

There is abundant evidence that the media help set the agenda. Evidence comes from cross-sectional and longitudinal surveys, experiments, and a variety of studies conducted in different countries across the world. Agenda-setting also has consequences. One consequence is the obverse—when issues deserving of attention are ignored by the media, they can be forgotten or shunted aside. A second consequence is that when the media shine their searchlights ceaselessly on one problem, other issues that are of national importance do not receive public or policy attention. During the height of the coronavirus pandemic, many other health, environmental, and social problems cried out for attention, but were unable to gain press coverage due to the volume of coronavirus coverage.

A third implication is priming. This occurs when the media agenda primes or influences the standards voters use to judge a president or political leader. By calling attention to certain issues and not others, news can affect the criteria voters invoke to judge candidates for office.

Priming and agenda-setting have intriguing implications for the conduct of political campaigns. Candidates try to harness conventional and social media to emphasize an issue central to their campaigns, and use advertising (as well as other messages) to prime these topics. Thus, the media, broadly defined, are an instrument by which politicians hope to influence voters. Candidates do not always succeed. The news must pick up on their issues, and the topics must resonate with voters. Candidate agendas vie with conventional news media agendas, as well as those on blogs and partisan media sites, for influence on the richly symbolic political stage.

Priming also has more nefarious implications in a social media era. Underhanded cyber campaigns directed at social media users, such as, perhaps, Russia's 2016 campaign and subtle patriotic ploys, access prejudices that can influence attitudes and voting behavior.

And yet there is a positive side of priming, concerning, of all things, the coronavirus pandemic. When a representative group of American adults were primed to think about the coronavirus, their focus turned outward, from themselves to society's problems rather than their own personal afflictions. They said it was more important to prioritize society's problems than their own. Interestingly and optimistically, the findings held for Republicans, Democrats, men, women, and both older and younger people (Cappelen et al., 2020). People may have felt a greater sense of solidarity because media coverage highlighted the sacrifices health professionals made for the larger community, as well as the interdependence among different aspects of society.

The media do not exist in a vacuum. Media agenda-setting operates in the context of a larger culture, society, and political environment. Deciding that something is a problem is itself an important—and political—activity. If an issue is not identified as a problem by the media or political elites, it cannot move through the series of stages necessary for the problem to be contemplated and hopefully solved. These broader questions are the purview of agenda-building, which examines the intersection among media agendas, public agendas, and policy-making. There are complex relationships among the media, public, and policy agendas, with media influencing policymakers' agendas directly, and indirectly via public opinion, notably when news flashpoints occur.

There is no guarantee a particular agenda will produce change or the presence of a problem will produce policy action. Well-resourced organizations generally have more access to media (Binderkrantz, Halpin, & Pedersen, 2020); change is the exception, not the rule. Policy change does occur, but it requires recognition on the part of policymakers and journalists that a problem exists, plausible solutions are available, and there is a ripe social climate for change.

In a digital age rife with partisan media, conventional media have less impact on agenda-building than they did when elite media ruled the roost. When agendas have fragmented along partisan lines, leaders lack "even a basic consensus on what issues are most important or which controversies are most pressing; (thus) there is little chance for deliberation in the first place" (Gruszczynski, 2019, p. 765).

Ultimately, the struggle in agenda-building is to control the direction the country takes and shape a policy agenda. It is a high-stakes battle. While many lament that "political games" must be played, the fact is these are endemic to democracy. Democratic societies must determine which problems to prioritize, which to put on the back burner, and how to reach consensus on public policy questions. Change is hard. Interests collide. Entrenched forces try to block innovation. Thus, when change occurs, through media and political agenda-building, it is appropriate to recognize the efforts so many individuals and groups expended on a solution and the sweeping positive effects democratically produced change can exert.

And yet, a hard-edge caveat needs to be sounded. For all the changes in communication and politics, America and other western democracies still struggle (endlessly, it seems) with intractable political problems—economic malaise, inequality, and climate change. Solutions continue to elude us, and consensus on how to solve national problems is bogged down in legislative gridlock. Different agendas compete for policy attention over an increasing number of electronic and online platforms. Despite all we know and breathtaking advances in political communication technologies, democracies continue to struggle to find solutions to problems that ail their citizens. Progress is fitful, and solutions are the exception, not the rule.

## REFERENCES

Agiesta, J. (2020a, October 8). In news about the presidential race, coronavirus overtakes nearly all else. *CNN Politics*. Online: www.cnn.com/2020/10/08/politics/the-breakthrough-trump-biden-coronavirus-debate/index.html. (Accessed: November 25, 2020).

Agiesta, J. (2020b, August 16). Here are the words defining the 2020 presidential campaign. *CNN Politics*. Online: www.cnn.com/2020/08/16/politics/election-2020-polls-biden-trump-breakthrough/index.html. (Accessed: November 25, 2020).

Balmas, M., & Sheafer, T. (2010). Candidate image in election campaigns: Attribute agenda setting, affective priming, and voting intentions. *International Journal of Public Opinion Research*, *22*, 204–229.

Bargh, J.A., & Williams, E.L. (2006). The automaticity of social life. *Current Directions in Psychological Science*, *15*, 1–4.

Barker, K., Keller, M.H., & Eder, S. (2020, December 22). How cities lost control of police discipline. *The New York Times*. Online: www.nytimes.com/2020/12/22/us/police-misconduct-discipline.html. (Accessed: December 23, 2020).

Binderkrantz, A.S., Halpin, D.R., & Pedersen, H.H. (2020). From policy interest to media appearance: Interest group activity and media bias. *The International Journal of Press/Politics*, *25*, 712–731.

Broadwater, L., & Edmondson, C. (2020, June 25). Police groups wield strong influence in Congress, resisting the strictest reforms. *The New York Times*. Online: www.nytimes.com/2020/06/25/us/politics/police-reforms-congress.html. (Accessed: June 26, 2020).

Buchanan, L., Bui, Q., & Patel, J.K. (2020, July 3). Black Lives Matter may be the largest movement in U.S. history. *The New York Times*. Online: www.nytimes.com/interactive/2020/07/03/us/george-floyd- protests-crowd-size.html. (Accessed: July 9, 2020).

Bulkow, K., Urban, J., & Schweiger, W. (2013). The duality of agenda-setting: The role of information processing. *International Journal of Public Opinion Research*, *25*, 43–63.

Cappelen, A.W., Falch, R., Sorensen, E.O., Tungodden, B., & Wezerek, G. (2020, April 16). What do you owe your neighbor? The pandemic might change your answer. *The New York Times*. Online: www.nytimes.com/interactive/2020/04/16/opinion/coronavirus-inequality-solidarity-poll.html. (Accessed: April 19, 2020).

Cohen, B.C. (1963). *The press and foreign policy*. Princeton, NJ: Princeton University Press.

Conway-Silva, B.A., Filer, C.R., Kenski, K., & Tsetsi, E. (2018). Reassessing Twitter's agenda-building power: An analysis of intermedia agenda-setting effects during the 2016 presidential primary season. *Social Science Computer Review*, *36*, 469–483.

Conway-Silva, B.A., Kenski, K., & Wang, D. (2015). The rise of Twitter in the political campaign: Searching for intermedia agenda-setting effects in the presidential primary. *Journal of Computer-Mediated Communication*, *20*, 363–380.

Cook, F.L., & Skogan, W.G. (1991). Convergent and divergent voice models of the rise and fall of policy issues. In M.E. McCombs & D.L. Protess (Eds.), *Setting the agenda: Readings on media, public opinion, and policymaking* (pp. 189–206). Hillsdale, NJ: Erlbaum Associates.

Dearing, J.W., & Rogers, E.M. (1996). *Agenda-setting*. Thousand Oaks, CA: Sage.

Djerf-Pierre, M., & Shehata, A. (2017). Still an agenda-setter: Traditional news media and public opinion during the transition from low to high choice media environments. *Journal of Communication, 67*, 733–757

Domke, D. (2001). Racial cues and political ideology: An examination of associative priming. *Communication Research, 28*, 772–801.

Edmondson, C., & Fandos, N. (2020, June 9). G.O.P. scrambles to respond to public demands for police overhaul. *The New York Times*. Online: www.nytimes.com/2020/06/09/us/politics/republicans-police-reform.html. (Accessed: June 10, 2020).

Edsall, T.B. (2020, June 10). How much is America changing? *The New York Times*. Online: www.nytimes.com/2020/06/10/opinion/george- floyd-protests-trump.html. (Accessed: June 10, 2020).

Edy, J.A., & Meirick, P.C. (2018). The fragmenting public agenda: Capacity, diversity, and volatility in responses to the "most important problem" question. *Public Opinion Quarterly, 82*, 661–685.

Enten, H. (2020, July 9). Trump's handling of the coronavirus is the only election issue that matters. *CNN Politics*. Online: www.cnn.com/2020/07/09/politics/2020-election-issues-coronavirus-trump/index.html. (Accessed: July 10, 2020).

Fischer, S., Rothschild, N., & Walsh, B. (2020, June 2). Protest coverage dwarfs coronavirus. *Axios*. Online: www.axios.com/george-floyd-protests-coronavirus-media-coverage-08e7aa7c-1a31-4f1a-98b1-adf3229797ca.html. (Accessed: June 24, 2020).

Gitlin, T. (1980). *The whole world is watching: Mass media in the making & unmaking of the New Left*. Berkeley, CA: University of California Press.

Gonzenbach, W.J. (1996). *The media, the president, and public opinion: A longitudinal analysis of the drug issue, 1984–1991*. Mahwah, NJ: Erlbaum Associates.

Gruszczynski, M. (2019). Evidence of partisan agenda fragmentation in the American public, 1959–2015. *Public Opinion Quarterly, 83*, 749–781.

Guo, L., & Vargo, C. (2020). "Fake news" and emerging online media ecosystem: An integrated intermedia agenda-setting analysis of the 2016 U.S. presidential election. *Communication Research, 47*, 178–200.

Harder, R.A., Sevenans, J., & Van Aelst, P. (2017). Intermedia agenda setting in the social media age: How traditional players dominate the news agenda in election times. *The International Journal of Press/Politics, 22*, 275–293.

Hellmeier, S., Weidmann, N.B., & Rød, E.G. (2018). In the spotlight: Analyzing sequential attention effects in protest reporting. *Political Communication, 35*, 587–611.

Isaac, M., & Wakabayashi, D. (2017, October 31) Broad reach of campaign by Russians is disclosed. *The New York Times*, B1, B3.

Iyengar, S., & Kinder, D.R. (1987). *News that matters: Television and American opinion*. Chicago, IL: University of Chicago Press.

Iyengar, S., & Kinder, D.R. (2010). *News that matters: Television and American opinion* (Updated ed.). Chicago, IL: University of Chicago Press.

Jamieson, K.H. (2018). *Cyberwar: How Russian hackers and trolls helped elect a president: What we don't, can't, and do know*. New York: Oxford University Press.

Johnson, T.J. (2014). (Ed.), *Agenda setting in a 2.0 world: New agendas in communication, A tribute to Maxwell McCombs*. New York: Routledge.

Jones, B. (2019, February 5). *Republicans and Democrats have grown further apart on what the nation's top priorities should be*. Pew Research Center (FactTank: News in the Numbers). Online: www.pewresearch.org/fact-tank/2019/02/05/republicans-and-democrats-have-grown-further-apart-on-what-the-nations-top-priorities-should-be/. (Accessed: March 28, 2020).

Kim, S-H., Han, M., & Scheufele, D.A. (2010). Think about him this way: Priming, news media, and South Koreans' evaluation of the president. *International Journal of Public Opinion Research, 22*, 299–319.

Kim, Y.M. (2005). Use and disuse of contextual primes in dynamic news environments. *Journal of Communication, 55*, 737–755.

Kim, Y.M. (2014). Contingent factors of agenda-setting effects: How need for orientation, issue obtrusiveness, and message tone influence issue salience and attitude strength. In T.J. Johnson (Ed.), *Agenda setting in a 2.0 world: New agendas in communication, A tribute to Maxwell McCombs* (pp. 65–81). New York: Routledge.

Kingdon, J.W. (2011). *Agendas, alternatives, and public policies* (Updated 2nd ed.). Boston: Longman.

Kinsella, J. (1988). *Covering the plague: AIDS and the American media*. New Brunswick, NJ: Rutgers University Press.

Krosnick, J.A., & Kinder, D.R. (1990). Altering the foundations of support for the president through priming. *American Political Science Review, 84*, 497–512.

Kuhne, R., Schemer, C., Matthes, J., & Wirth, W. (2011). Affective priming in political campaigns: How campaign-induced emotions prime political opinions. *International Journal of Public Opinion Research, 23*, 485–507.

Lang, G.E., & Lang, K. (1983). *The battle for public opinion: The president, the press, and the polls during Watergate*. New York: Columbia University Press.

Lawrence, R.G. (2019). Book Review Symposium: A discussion of Kathleen Hall Jamieson's *Cyberwar: How Russian hackers and trolls helped elect a president: What we don't, can't, and do know. Public Opinion Quarterly, 83*, 163–166.

Lippmann, W. (1922). *Public opinion*. New York: Free Press.

Lipstadt, D.E. (1986). *Beyond belief: The American press and the coming of the Holocaust 1933–1945*. New York: Free Press.

Luo, Y., Burley, H., Moe, A., & Sui, M. (2019). A meta-analysis of news media's public agenda-setting effects, 1972–2015. *Journalism & Mass Communication Quarterly, 96*, 150–172.

Matthes, J. (2006). The need for orientation towards news media: Revising and validating a classic concept. *International Journal of Public Opinion Research, 18*, 422–444.

Mayer, J. (2018, October 1). How Russia helped swing the election for Trump. *The New Yorker*. Online: www.newyorker.com/magazine/2018/10/01/how-russia-helped-to-swing-the-election-for-trump?reload. (Accessed: March 31, 2020).

McCombs, M. (2014). *Setting the agenda: The mass media and public opinion* (2nd ed.). Cambridge: Polity Press.

McCombs, M., & Ghanem, S.I. (2001). The convergence of agenda setting and framing. In S.D. Reese, O.H. Gandy, Jr., & A.E. Grant (Eds.), *Framing public life: Perspectives on media and our understanding of the social world* (pp. 67–81). Mahwah, NJ: Erlbaum Associates.

McCombs, M., & Reynolds, A. (2009). How the news shapes our civic agenda. In J. Bryant & M.B. Oliver (Eds.), *Media effects: Advances in theory and research* (3rd ed., pp. 1–16). New York: Routledge.

McCombs, M., & Shaw, D.L. (1972). The agenda-setting function of mass media. *Public Opinion Quarterly, 36*, 176–187.

McCombs, M., & Valenzuela, S. (2021). *Setting the agenda: The news media and public opinion* (3rd ed.). Cambridge: Polity.

McGraw, K.M., & Ling, C. (2003). Media priming of presidential and group evaluations. *Political Communication, 20*, 23–40.

McLeod, D.M. (2007). News coverage and social protest: How the media's protect paradigm exacerbates social conflict. *Journal of Dispute Resolution, 1*, 185–194.

McLeod, D.M., Becker, L.B., & Byrnes, J.E. (1974). Another look at the agenda-setting function of the press. *Communication Research, 1*, 131–165.

McLeod, D.M., & Hertog, J.K. (1992). The manufacture of "public opinion" by reporters: Informal cues for public perceptions of protest groups. *Discourse & Society, 3*, 159–175.

Medina, J., & Russonello, G. (2020, November 3). Exit polls showed the vote came down to the pandemic versus the economy. *The New York Times*. Online: www.nytimes.com/2020/11/03/us/politics/exit-polls.html. (Accessed: November 4, 2020).

Meraz, S. (2011). Using time series analysis to measure intermedia agenda-setting influence in traditional media and political blog networks. *Journalism & Mass Communication Quarterly, 88*, 176–194.

Meraz, S. (2014). Media agenda setting in a competitive and hostile environment: The role of sources in setting versus supporting topical discussant agendas in the Tea Party Patriots' Facebook group. In T.J. Johnson (Ed.), *Agenda setting in a 2.0 world: New agendas in communication, A tribute to Maxwell McCombs* (pp. 1–27). New York: Routledge.

Messner, M., & DiStaso, M.W. (2008). The source cycle: How traditional media and weblogs use each other as sources. *Journalism Studies, 9*, 447–463.

Metzger, M.J. (2009). The study of media effects in the era of Internet communication. In R.L. Nabi & M.B. Oliver (Eds.), *The Sage handbook of media processes and effects* (pp. 561–576). Thousand Oaks, CA: Sage.

Moy, P., Xenos, M.A., & Hess, V.K. (2005). Priming effects of late-night comedy. *International Journal of Public Opinion Research, 18*, 198–210.

Mutz, D.C. (1992). Mass media and the depoliticization of personal experience. *American Journal of Political Science, 36*, 483–508.

Mutz, D.C. (1998). *Impersonal influence: How perceptions of mass collectives affect political attitudes*. New York: Cambridge University Press.

Nyhan, B. (2018, February 13). Fake news and bots may be worrisome, but their political power is overblown. *The New York Times*. Online: www.nytimes.com/2018/02/13/upshot/fake-news-and-bots-may-be-worrisome-but-their-political-power-is-overblown.html. (Accessed: March 31, 2020).

Pan, Z., & Kosicki, G.M. (1997). Priming and media impact on the evaluations of the president's performance. *Communication Research, 24*, 3–30.

Pawel, M. (2020, September 9). Reform the police? Guess who funds my state's officials. *The New York Times*. Online: www.nytimes.com/2020/09/09/opinion/sunday/police-reform-defund-politicians.html. (Accessed: September 13, 2020).

Perez, M. (2020, June 5). Minneapolis city council agrees to ban use of chokeholds by police. *Forbes*. Online: www.forbes.com/sites/mattperez/2020/06/05/minneapolis-city-council-agrees-to-ban-use-of-chokeholds-by-police/#6b94996837a2. (Accessed: June 10, 2020).

Pingree, R.J., Quenette, A.M., Tchernev, J.M., & Dickinson, T. (2013). Effects of media criticism on gatekeeping trust and implications for agenda setting. *Journal of Communication, 63*, 351–372.

Pingree, R.J., & Stoycheff, E. (2013). Differentiating cueing from reasoning in agenda-setting effects. *Journal of Communication, 63*, 852–872.

Popovich, N. (2020, February 21). Rise in concern on climate, but not for everyone. *The New York Times*, A15.

Protess, D.L., Cook, F.L., Doppelt, J.C., Ettema, J.S., Gordon, M.T., Leff, D.R., & Miller, P. (1991). *The journalism of outrage: Investigative reporting and agenda building in America*. New York: Guilford Press.

Rhodes, J.H., Sharrow, E.A., Greenlee, J.S., & Nteta, T.M. (2020). Just locker room talk? Explicit sexism and the impact of the Access Hollywood tape on electoral support for Donald Trump in 2016. *Political Communication, 37*, 741–767.

Rimmer, J. (2019). Book review symposium: A discussion of Kathleen Hall Jamieson's *Cyberwar: How Russian hackers and trolls helped elect a president: What we don't, can't, and do know. Public Opinion Quarterly, 83*, 159–163.

Rogers, E.M., & Dearing, J.W. (1988). Agenda-setting research: Where has it been? Where is it going? In J. Anderson (Ed.), *Communication yearbook 11* (pp. 555–594). Newbury Park, CA: Sage.

Rojecki, A., & Meraz, S. (2016). Rumors and factitious informational blends: The role of the web in speculative politics. *New Media & Society, 18*, 25–43.

Rupar, A. (2019, July 30). Trump's latest live-tweeting binge shows how Fox News sets his agenda. *Vox*. Online: www.vox.com/2019/7/30/20747141/trump-fox-news-presidency-elijah-cummings. (Accessed: April 1, 2020).

Russonello, G. (2020, June 5). Why most Americans support the protests. *The New York Times*. Online: www.nytimes.com/2020/06/05/us/politics/polling-george-floyd-protests-racism.html. (Accessed: June 9, 2020).

Sanger, D.E., Kanno-Youngs, D., & Swanson, A. (2020, March 24). Slow response to the coronavirus measured in lost opportunity. *The New York Times*. Online: www.nytimes.com/2020/03/24/us/politics/coronavirus- ventilators.html. (Accessed: March 28, 2020).

Schattschneider, E.E. (1960). *The semi-sovereign people: A realist's view of democracy in America*. New York: Holt, Rinehart & Winston.

Schiffer, A.J. (2006). Blogswarms and press norms: News coverage of the Downing Street memo controversy. *Journalism & Mass Communication Quarterly, 83*, 494–510.

Sheafer, T. (2007). How to evaluate it: The role of story-evaluative tone in agenda-setting and priming. *Journal of Communication, 57*, 21–39.

Shehata, A., & Strömbäck, J. (2013). Not (yet) a new era of minimal effects: A study of agenda setting at the aggregate and individual levels. *International Journal of Press/Politics, 18*, 234–255.

Silver, N. (2017, May 3). The Comey letter probably cost Clinton the election. *FiveThirtyEight,* Online: https://fivethirtyeight.com/features/the-comey-letter-probably-cost-clinton-the-election. (Accessed: March 22, 2021).

Skogerbø, E., Bruns, A., Quodling, A., & Ingebretsen, T. (2016). Agenda-setting revisited: Social media and sourcing in mainstream journalism. In A. Bruns, G. Enli, E. Skogerbø, A.O. Larsson, & C. Christensen (Eds.), *The Routledge companion to social media and politics* (pp. 104–120). New York: Routledge.

Stoycheff, E., Pingree, R.J., Peifer, J.T., & Mingxiao, S. (2018). Agenda cueing effects of news and social media. *Media Psychology, 21*, 182–201.

Stroud, N.J. (2013). The American media system today: Is the public fragmenting? In T.N. Ridout (Ed.), *New directions in media and politics* (pp. 6–23). New York: Routledge.

Sweetser, K.D., Golan, G.J., & Wanta, W. (2008). Intermedia agenda setting in television, advertising, and blogs during the 2004 election. *Mass Communication and Society, 11*, 197–216.

Takeshita, T. (2006). Current critical problems in agenda-setting research. *International Journal of Public Opinion Research, 18*, 275–296.

Tavernise, S., & Eligon, J. (2020, November 7). Voters say Black Lives Matter protests were important. They disagree on why. *The New York Times*. Online: www.nytimes.com/2020/11/07/us/black-lives-matter-protests.html. (Accessed: November 8, 2020).

Tran, H. (2014). Online agenda setting: A new frontier for theory development. In T.J. Johnson (Ed.), *Agenda setting in a 2.0 world: New agendas in communication, A tribute to Maxwell McCombs* (pp. 205–229). New York: Routledge.

Valentino, R.A. (1999). Crime news and the priming of racial attitudes during evaluations of the president. *Public Opinion Quarterly, 63*, 293–300.

Vargo, C.J., & Guo, L. (2017). Networks, big data, and intermedia agenda-setting: An analysis of traditional, partisan, and emerging online U.S. news. *Journalism & Mass Communication Quarterly, 94*, 1031–1055.

Vargo, C.J., Guo, L., & Amazeen, M.A. (2018). The agenda-setting power of fake news: A big data analysis of the online media landscape from 2014 to 2016. *New Media & Society*, 20, 2028–2049.

Vargo, C.J., Guo, L., McCombs, M., & Shaw, D.L. (2014). Network issue agendas on Twitter during the 2012 U.S. presidential election. *Journal of Communication, 64*, 296–316.

Vavreck, L., Sides, J., & Tausanovitch, C. (2019, December 6). What is high priority for voters? In both parties, it's impeachment. *The New York Times*, A14.

Waisbord, S., & Russell, A. (2020). News flashpoints: Networked journalism and waves of coverage of social problems. *Journalism & Mass Communication Quarterly, 97*, 376–392.

Wanta, W., & Ghanem, S. (2007). Effects of agenda-setting. In R.W. Preiss, B.M. Gayle, N. Burrell, M. Allen, & J. Bryant (Eds.), *Mass media effects research: Advances through meta-analysis* (pp. 37–51). Mahwah, NJ: Erlbaum.

Weaver, D.H. (1984). Media agenda-setting and public opinion: Is there a link? In R.N. Bostrom (Ed.), *Communication yearbook 8* (pp. 680–691). Beverly Hills, CA: Sage.

White, T. (1973). *The making of the president, 1972*. New York: Bantam.

Winter, J., & Eyal, C. (1981). Agenda-setting for the civil rights issue. *Public Opinion Quarterly, 45*, 376–383.

Wojcieszak, M., Azrout, R., & de Vreese, C. (2018). Waving the red cloth: Media coverage of a contentious issue triggers polarization. *Public Opinion Quarterly, 82*, 87–109.

Wojcieszak, M., & Garrett, R.K. (2018). Social identity, selective exposure, and affective polarization: How priming national identity shapes attitudes toward immigrants via news selection. *Human Communication Research, 44*, 247–273.

Zucker, H.G. (1978). The variable nature of news media influence. In B.D. Ruben (Ed.), *Communication yearbook 2* (pp. 225–240). New Brunswick, NJ: Transaction Books.

# 8 Framing

This is the story of how two contemporary issues were framed. Let's begin with a word that gained currency during the turbulent spring of 2020.

*Looting.*

The word gained resonance and became a source of controversy after protesters took to the streets in thousands of American cities to protest the brutal killing of George Floyd and long-time shortcomings in policing. Some protests were peaceful, whereas others escalated into riots. In Portland, Oregon, demonstrators set fire, threw rocks, and vandalized stores, including an African American business. In Chicago, protesters who were angry about a rumor that falsely claimed the victim of a police shooting was 15 years old and unarmed, smashed windows and looted shops in the city's classy downtown business district (Bosman, Hauser, & Diaz, 2020). Chicago's African American mayor minced no words, calling the actions "abject criminal behavior." Even some supporters of Black Lives Matter opposed the looting, regarding it as wanton destruction of innocent people's livelihoods and counterproductive, creating a backlash against protesters' laudable goals.

A less conventional view, controversial but intriguing, was to view looting in the larger contest of systemic White racism. "Our country was built on looting—the looting of Indigenous lands and African labor. African Americans, in fact, have much more experience being looted than looting," historian Robin D.G. Kelley (2020) observed, poignantly noting:

> Our bodies were loot. The forced extraction of our labor was loot. A system of governance that suppressed our wages, relieved us of property and excluded Black people from equal schools and public accommodations is a form of looting. We can speak of the looting of Black property through redlining, slum clearance and more recently predatory lending.

By transposing "looting" to "loot," Kelley's account gains resonance. In his telling, looting stores in 2020 needed to be understood in the larger, historical context of America's long scourge of racism (Figure 8.1). Kelley's arguments would have been perceived as falling outside the political mainstream not so long ago. However, in 2020, they appeared in a mainstream outlet, viewed as a reasonable view, in the context of the year's tumultuous events.

And now the phrase that elicits frames on the second issue:

*Build the wall.*

This was the cri de coeur, the impassioned outcry of ardent conservative supporters of former President Trump, as they echoed his mantra. To many conservatives, erecting a border wall between the U.S and Mexico, symbolized by the three-word phrase "Build the wall," was the embodiment of what was good and right about America: the need to respect borders, insist on rules, and ensure that people can't sneak illegally into America, but enter in the old-fashioned way like so many Eastern Europeans did more than a century ago, by applying for citizenship.

Ah, but that's not the way liberals view—or, more specifically—frame the issue. What to conservatives is a symbol of the need to stop immigrants in their tracks, to erect a physical impediment against breaking the law, is to liberals an offense against the stored notion that America opened its borders to the needy and the oppressed. It's a reminder of a cruel policy separating children from parents who illegally crossed the border—"an immorality," or "a manhood thing" for Trump, as the Democratic Speaker of the House Nancy Pelosi put it at the time (Davis & Baker, 2019, p. 15).

To Democrats, a wall is an affront to social justice; to Republicans, an affirmation of the need to protect borders. There are cultural and racial meanings packed in here, too; liberals view the wall as stoking racial prejudice against people of color; conservatives retort that this misses the threat illegal immigrants pose to the nation's security.

These are case studies in the power of the *frame*—the different ways civil unrest and a border wall can be interpreted. Broader battles for public opinion and policy change can be viewed as a competition among different political frameworks, a combative struggle to see which frame will capture the greatest popular support. Framing has generated considerable research over the past decades (D'Angelo & Kuypers, 2010), and for good reason. It cuts to the core of the meanings people attach to political communication, pinpoints the impact that symbols exert on political behavior, and sheds light on the roles language, messages, and psychological constructions play in the pursuit of power. This chapter takes a broad look at framing, its social scientific bases, macro applications, and implications for presidential campaigns.

**Figure 8.1** Framing offers insight into the dynamics of the looting that occurred in the wake of nationwide protests over the police killing of George Floyd. A reasonable, conventional frame emphasized the perpetration of criminal, immoral acts against innocent businesses (top). An intriguing, radical view positioned morality in the context of how America had long "looted" African American lives, suggesting that property-damaging looting should be viewed in this context and as a way for long-oppressed voices to be heard (bottom).

*Source*: https://commons.wikimedia.org/wiki/File:Cub_Foods_Damage_-_Minneapolis_Riots.jpg
https://commons.wikimedia.org/wiki/File:George_Floyd_protests_in_Philadelphia_5C2A6126R.jpg

The first section introduces core features of framing, beginning with a definition of the concept, an explanation of how it differs from related terms, and a boxed section on Trump's controversial populist frames (see Box 8.1 on page 216). The second section defines key frames and reviews what we know about framing effects—when and why they work. In the third section, I discuss different models of frame-building, and the fourth section applies framing analysis to the electoral context.

## DEFINING FRAMING

To appreciate framing, it is helpful to differentiate it from its predecessor in the study of political communication effects on cognition—the Big Dog of political communication, the concept discussed in Chapter 7: agenda-setting. Both concepts elide the classical psychological examination of media effects on attitudes, or how media change people's feelings and evaluations about political issues. Instead, their focus is more subtle, how political media influence cognitions about politics. However, framing differs from agenda-setting in several respects.

Agenda-setting examines the salience of issues—their brute importance in voters' minds. While agenda-setting extended previous research by illuminating how political media could exert significant effects without necessarily changing voters' attitudes, it neglected the rich ways that people construct the political world, as well as the many strategies that leaders employ to define a problem in a particular fashion (Takeshita, 2006). As Kosicki (1993) observed, agenda-setting research frequently "strips away almost everything worth knowing about how the media cover an issue and leaves only the shell of the *topic*" (p. 112).

When it comes to policy debates that dominate mainstream media or bounce around social media, there is no question that the political agenda matters. But more than agenda-setting is going on. What makes for a colorful and consequential political debate is how different political actors describe the debate, the metaphors they use, and the spin they put on the issues at stake. Agenda-setting examines "*whether* we think about an issue." Framing explores "*how* we think about it" (Scheufele & Tewskbury, 2007, p. 14). Framing also assigns more importance to causal reasoning and the very different ways people explain the same problem (Maher, 2001; Pan & Kosicki, 1993). What's more, agenda setting and priming work in part by accessing, as when the media call to mind certain political ideas. Framing works also through resonance—the degree to which news coverage resonates with individuals' preexisting beliefs about the problem.

Agenda-setting examines the particular issue the media selects, stipulating that more coverage of the issue bolsters perceptions of importance and priming of political standards. Framing is less concerned with the particular issues the media decide to cover than on "the particular ways those issues are presented" (Price & Tewksbury, 1997, p. 184). Framing suggests the *applicability* of certain ways of thinking about the problem, calling attention to certain values and not others (Hertog & McLeod, 2001; Scheufele & Tewksbury, 2007). This can be powerful stuff.

Poverty did not catch anyone's attention when it was framed as part of the natural order of things, an unfortunate byproduct of survival of the fittest. This is the way the issue was implicitly framed in the first decades of the 20th century. When activists framed poverty as a social problem with human consequences, one that warranted government action, the media, the public, and policymakers took notice. On the other side of the political ledger, in the 1970s and 1980s, conservatives, arguing that federal government programs reduced individual initiative, reframed government as part of the problem, rather than a solution, changing the discourse and policy parameters over the course of decades.

While most scholars view framing as distinct from agenda-setting, some prefer to think of framing, agenda-setting, and priming as spokes within a larger conceptual wheel. Some agenda-setting scholars view framing as an additional level of agenda-setting, one that extends the media's impact on political saliences to a consideration of the attributes of the particular political issue (Maher, 2001; McCombs & Ghanem, 2001). This raises a nitpicky (though interesting) academic issue—the precise specification of a concept. The drawback of viewing framing as part of agenda-setting is that it muddies the waters. It places two somewhat different concepts under the same roof, in the process obscuring their differences and understating the richness of framing (Maher, 2001; Scheufele, 2000; Scheufele & Iyengar, 2014). These scholars prefer a clean break between framing and agenda-setting. Other researchers think it is helpful to place these different ideas under a common conceptual umbrella because it offers a more integrative view. Whichever approach one prefers, there is little doubt that framing differs from agenda-setting in several ways. It focuses more on problem definition than problem importance; covers a broader class of cognitions, such as causal attributions, moral evaluations, and potential remedies; and is explained less by the accessibility of the issue than with its resonance with particular knowledge structures or mental belief systems (Weaver, 2007; Cacciatore, Scheufele, & Iyengar, 2016). Framing provides a cognitive breadth agenda-setting lacks, but it can be vague and imprecise. Of course, in everyday political communication, framing, agenda-setting, and priming overlap. Issues that set the agenda can be framed in different ways; the frames, as well as agendas, can be primed, influencing evaluations and sometimes deep-seated emotions.

So, what is meant by framing? Given the complexity of the term, it is best to start simply, with the English language. We can view a frame as a noun. A picture frame encloses the picture. The frame of a house is the foundation that provides essential support. Frame is also a verb. You can frame a response, frame a policy, or frame an innocent man. Framing is a present participle, too. A trendy California store promotes its business by noting that it does needle-work framing, antique photo framing, and even sports jersey framing.

What all of these different grammatical forms have in common is they denote the ways that an entity defines and structures subordinate physical or verbal objects. In the social sciences, where framing has been invoked to explain a variety of phenomena, a **frame** is defined as a primary organizing theme or narrative that gives meaning to, and connects, a series of events (Gamson & Modigliani, 1987; see also Nisbet, 2010; Reese, 2007; Schaffner & Sellers, 2010). Robert M. Ent-man offered a more precise definition, defining **framing** as

> selecting and highlighting some facets of events or issues, and making con-
> nections among them so as to promote a particular interpretation, evaluation,
> and/or solution.
>
> (Entman, 2004, p. 5)

Frames, like social beliefs, contain different attributes. According to Entman, fully developed frames are composed of different elements, with four core char-acteristics: (1) problem definition, (2) hypothesized cause, (3) moral evalua-tion, and (4) proposed remedy. We can see how this applied to the coronavirus pandemic, where the problem could be defined in terms of human devastation or economic consequences, and could be explained in terms of a religious reck-oning, China's irresponsibility, Beijing censorship (Zhong et al., 2020), inept European government policies, or Trump's indifference. Moral evaluations could include shaming those who didn't wear masks or blaming governors who infringed on the liberties of people not to mask up. Remedies spanned requir-ing masks, lockdowns, doing more testing, speedily developing a vaccine, and applying social pressure to convince people to get their shots.

Framing operates at different levels. Politicians harness frames in an effort to advance a particular definition of a problem, hoping this will coalesce sup-porters around a piece of legislation or appeal to voters during an election campaign. Journalists use frames when they employ broad themes to structure factual details. Citizens interpret political issues in terms of broad principles or diffuse symbols that help them structure and organize the political world. The relationships among elite, media, and citizens' frames are complex, just as the relationships among these actors' different agendas are complicated. But fram-ing is at the heart of political discourse, suggesting the ways issues should be considered and how policies should be changed.

If you are looking for a simple, cynical term to describe "frames," think "spin." But this doesn't do it justice. If you want a broader synonym, think "perspective."

Offering a more scholarly approach, communication researchers David Tewksbury and Dietram A. Scheufele (2009) point out that frames are the rhetorical devices that make linkages among concepts. Information provides the starting point, but frames connect the dots and build critical associations, inviting citizens to view the issue in particular ways (see also Nisbet, 2010; Borah, 2011).

---

### BOX 8.1 HOW TRUMP FRAMED AMERICA, OR ONE PART OF AMERICA

Populism reemerged in 2016 in the wake of gaping inequality between the rich and poor, hopes sundered by unemployment, and increasing resentment of the "haves." Populism provided the soil in which Trump's frames could grow, and Trump's frames in turn helped exacerbate populist grievances, showcasing the ways context and media frames feed off and amplify each other.

By framing his message in blunt, unparsed, poll-oblivious speech, Trump, the scion of a wealthy real-estate developer and billionaire member of New York's elite, became the unlikely champion of (primarily White) blue-collar Americans. When Trump lambasted political elites, framing criticisms around time-honored populist criticism of career politicians' indifference, he became a tribune for the Republican (long ago, Democrats') base of working-class Whites, who viewed immigration and trade as symbolic signature issues, felt party leaders were indifferent to their problems, looked on Washington as "a gilded city of lobbyists, contractors and lawmakers," and found it cathartic to blame others for a nexus of elite-inflicted and culturally reinforced decay (Confessore, 2016, p. A12).

In 2016 Trump harnessed a complementary "somebody is taking everything you are used to and you had" frame that packed symbols, beliefs, and time-honored resentments into a cohesive populist framework (Cohen, 2016, p. 6). It and his other frames served as condensational symbols (Edelman, 1964) that distilled into a simple symbolic framework a multitude of emotions, hopes, recollections of previous glories, and remembrances of perceived and real indignities. In a similar fashion, "Make America Great Again" called up patriotic emotions, while also evoking the perception that America wasn't particularly good or great, along with a host of humiliations, materially and vicariously experienced, some projections of anger at the seemingly ill-begotten gains of other ethnic groups. Trump, attuned to his base's economic anxieties, cognizant

*Continued*

of their prejudices, traded on their fears, harnessing a potent "politics of insecurity," in Andrew Rojecki's (2016) apt phrase.

As one Pennsylvania Trump voter put it, "Donald Trump makes me feel good about who I am. I only have a high school education, but I got a good union job. I go to work every day. Why am I a bad guy?" (Goldmacher, 2020). He wasn't a bad guy, but Democratic Party elitism made him feel this way.

There was also a racial component, subtexts of Trump's frames that either contained prejudiced appeals or subtly (and sometimes not so subtly) invited followers to access ethnic biases. These included his aggressive questioning of Obama's birth certificate, even after it had been proven that the first African American president had been born in the U.S., as well as calls to bar Muslims from entering the U.S. based on a linkage of Muslims with terrorism. Theorists argue that White anxiety—steeped in economic insecurities and resentment of erosion of familiar cultural norms—formed the foundation of populist support for Trump's electoral frames (Klein, 2016). A menacing fear that the American way of life was being threatened by minorities and Whites' dominant status was under siege underpinned populist support for Trump's 2016 frames (Mutz, 2018; Taub, 2016). His use of code words ("They're taking our jobs") primed nationalistic, them-versus-us American stereotypes, as well as latent prejudices.

We need to be careful here. First, a number of Trump supporters weren't struggling blue-collar workers, but were better off financially than most Americans (Silver, 2016). Moreover, when it came to Trump's working-class voters, many voted for Obama and Bill Clinton (Cohen, 2016), and these and other voters would deeply resent a prejudiced label. Others turned to Trump not because they were bigots, "but because they didn't know where to turn and Trump spoke to their fears" (Kristof, 2017, p. A23). There is a debate in the research literature about whether White working-class support for Trump in 2016 (and, to some degree, in 2020) was based on economic grievances, social malaise, or racial prejudice. It is hard to unravel these motivations, and they overlap and intersect. A complex alchemy of humiliations, real and perceived, resentments at the cultural leftists who turned their nose down on "us," and ethnic antagonism (Bartels, 2020) formed the psychological foundation of ardent Trump supporters' political moorings. Unfortunately, some of his rhetoric, awash in falsehoods and racialized dog whistles, primed the darkest recesses of his supporters' belief systems.

*Continued*

The issues Trump raised were not new, but the manner in which he coalesced them—pulling together dark economic and cultural forces in the vernacular of the ordinary working-class American (delivered with the panache of a celebrity media pitchman)—appealed to his fervently loyal base. Economic afflictions and social antagonisms created the opportunity for Trump to emerge, and his frames took on a life of their own, politicizing anxieties and building a political movement that viewed him as a savior.

## SOCIAL SCIENTIFIC UNDERPINNINGS

Frames are complex because they operate on so many different levels of analysis. Even when examined on the narrow individual, psychological level, they are multifaceted because they can call on broad thematic constructs ranging from language to ideology to rhetoric. The most basic frame is the **equivalence frame**, in which identical information is framed differently through adroit use of logically equivalent, but differently phrased, information. For example, highlighting 6 percent unemployment, rather than 94 percent employment, would call attention to the down, rather than up, side of the economy. However, in the complex world of politics, issues do not always neatly present themselves in terms of logically identical features.

**Emphasis frames** highlight different message features and are more common in political communication. These frames do not necessarily present identical information. Instead, some frames emphasize certain considerations, while other frames call attention to alternative aspects of the problem, using such devices as metaphors and irony (de Vreese, 2010; Druckman, 2001a; Burgers, Konijn, & Steen, 2016). As McLeod and Shah (2015) nicely showed, terrorism can be framed around the individual (e.g., an Arab-American who fears the effects of anti-terrorism legislation) or the collective (the Arab-American organization that is worried about legislative effects on the group), as well as by emphasizing one theme (civil liberties) rather than another (national security).

Emphasis frames can complicate matters, muddying the waters, by encompassing more than just the equivalence-based mode of verbal or linguistic presentation (Scheufele & Iyengar, 2014). They are rich in ecological validity, but pose a problem: If everything in political persuasion is a frame, then the term becomes unwieldy.

All of this makes framing research interesting, but sometimes abstruse and hard to unravel. The increasing number of conceptualizations and operational measures of frames (e.g., Coleman, 2010) have made framing an exciting area of cross-disciplinary research, but also an area fraught with ambiguities, an issue of concern to precision-focused social science research (Cacciatore, Scheufele, & Iyengar, 2016; see also D'Angelo et al., 2019 for a review of current issues). The framing concept captures a great deal, but is vague and amorphous.

Do frames influence political attitudes? We cannot know for sure until research examines framing effects. Frames have been studied in classic experiments, where research participants are randomly assigned to read different frames and indicate their opinions on the issue. These studies, which have focused on emphasis frames, have found that beliefs can be altered merely by varying the frame, or the way the story is told (Druckman, 2001b; Nelson & Oxley, 1999; Iyengar, 1991).

The findings from these older studies nicely establish cause and effect, but, as is the case with laboratory experiments, they do not take into account real-world complexities. Framing experiments may be conducted on college students, who do not reflect the population of citizens, with their preexisting attitudes, strongly held frames, and pressing economic needs. The experiments typically do not expose research participants to competing frames—as when people come into contact with dueling, opposing frames on issues such as immigration, or hear different frames in political debates. In an effort to increase the breadth and validity of framing research, scholars have embarked on more in-depth, exter-nally valid studies in recent years, offering more generalizable insights about the impact of political frames (Brewer & Gross, 2010).

## How and When Do Frames Work in Real-World Contexts?

How do frames influence political beliefs? Which cognitive processes medi-ate framing effects? Three interpretations have been advanced to answer these questions. The first process is accessibility, discussed in the previous chapter, the notion that frames access particular attributes, making certain ideas more accessible (Shulman & Sweitzer, 2018). A second view highlights belief impor-tance, whereby political frames make some considerations appear more rele-vant than others, giving them more weight in an individual's decision-making, perhaps also rendering these attributes more applicable (Nelson, Clawson, & Oxley, 1997; Price & Tewksbury, 1997). A third interpretation emphasizes belief change, suggesting that frames offer new arguments on behalf of a polit-ical viewpoint.

Researchers who emphasize accessibility view framing as akin to priming, sug-gesting that political opinions are superficial, tilting with the political wind, susceptible to manipulation by "top-of-the-head" cues. Those who advance the other interpretations, notably belief importance, emphasize that framing can be more mindful, rendering individuals less susceptible to media persuasion, and requiring the deployment of more thoughtful, or at least more compelling, political messages (see Powell et al., 2019).

Just as media cannot create agendas out of whole cloth, they also cannot implant frames in audience members' minds. Media framing effects intersect with the values individuals bring to the media, in some cases inducing complex thinking (McLeod & Shah, 2015; Shah et al., 2004). Framing effects are more likely when frames are consistent or resonate with individuals' core values, connecting psychologically with political cognitions (Boyle et al., 2006; Brewer, 2001; Edy & Meirick, 2007; Keum et al., 2005; Nisbet et al., 2013; Shen & Edwards, 2005; Shah et al., 2009; Wagner & Gruszczynski, 2016; Kaiser, 2020).

Thus, frames do not operate in a vacuum. While experiments have examined framing effects in isolation, in the real world frames operate in a volatile political environment characterized by competition among frames, with frames exerting a panoply of effects on attitudes, beliefs, and behavior (Chong & Druckman, 2007a).

## MODELS OF FRAME-BUILDING

Just as agenda-building occurs in the context of a larger society, where politics, media, and public opinion play important roles, so too are frames built, diffused, and changed through macro processes. In largely democratic societies, leaders or activists rarely use coercion to build frames. Instead, frames are constructed through persuasion or mediated social influence. There are three models of frame-building: (1) **top-down**; (2) **bidirectional and bottom-up**; and (3) **partisan media-centered**.

Top-down, leader-initiated frame-building, in its simplest form, occurs when national leaders adopt a particular way of thinking about a problem and disseminate this frame through mainstream media, where it comes to influence the population as a whole (see Figure 8.2). This is a somewhat antiquated view of frame-building, as it assumes the government exerts a primordial effect on the public, speaks with one voice, and that mainstream media are the main conduits by which frames are communicated. The model may have accounted for how government leaders pushed jingoistic frames of foreign wars, from Vietnam to the 1990 Gulf War, on the public (e.g., Hallin, 1986). It also helps explain how the Bush administration persuasively framed 9/11 as justifying a war on terrorism. It was an understandable frame, given the horrors of September 11, but it reflected a clichéd and unsophisticated metaphor (war) when other frames emphasizing peace, coalition-building, and long-term belief change were equally tenable. But leaders make mistakes, and the frame played well because it resonated with horrified, grieving, angry Americans, suggesting the role played by public opinion in the second model described below.

An updated variant on the top-down thesis is indexing, which emphasizes that news doesn't always parrot the frames of leaders, but instead, will offer up divergent frames when political leaders and interest groups are divided. In these cases, news indexes its coverages to match the range of alternative voices rising up in Washington, D.C., to complement, question, or oppose the White House framework (Bennett, Lawrence, & Livingston, 2007). This occurred when Congressional Democrats opposed President George W. Bush's war in Iraq, as evidence showed Iraq did not possess weapons of mass destruction. Indexing has also emerged in a multitude of other policy debates, where the party out of power challenged the White House frame, spanning Republican opposition to Barack Obama's health care reform to Democrats' opposition to Trump's tax cuts. In these cases, news didn't just parrot the dominant frame of the White House, but described the conflict among different political actors and their divergent ways of framing the situation, providing mechanisms for opposition groups to challenge the powers-that-be.

Yet both the original top-down and more adaptable indexing models understate the role played by public opinion, polls, and political activists, who question leaders' frames or offer their own distinctive frames on contemporary issues.

A second frame-building model assigns a more central role to media and public opinion. This bidirectional approach is based on Entman's (2004) work. He proposed a cascading activation perspective, suggesting that frames, like a surging waterfall, can first flow downward from leaders to the public, like the top-down, leader-initiated approach emphasizes. In the second model, the media are not a handmaiden to national elites, but instead are an independent power center, shaping the course of public debate through their own frames and via public opinion polls, which news covers prominently (see Figure 8.3).

Frames can go from top to bottom, but also bubble up from **bottom to top**, showing how citizens have an impact on politics. For example, during the 2016 presidential campaign, both Republican and Democratic voters evinced some anger at Washington politicians and the political system. This anger manifested itself in polls, which then reached journalists, who packaged this into the "angry voter" narrative, influencing presidential candidates' frames as they expressed sympathy for the grievances of White blue-collar voters. (Politicians may have been further induced to buy into this frame as they presumed that media coverage represented public opinion; see Dekker & Scholten, 2017.) All of this was democracy in action, but it also worked the other way, as Bernie Sanders and Donald Trump pitched frames that triggered media stories intensifying anger. Trump focused on unlawful immigration and terrorism, while Sanders emphasized inequality, but both suggested that elites were ripping off the working

**TOP-DOWN MODEL OF FRAME-BUILDING**

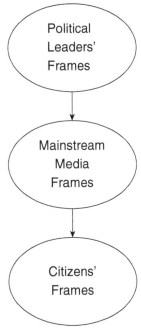

**Figure 8.2 Top-down model of frame-building.**

## BIDIRECTIONAL BOTTOM-UP MODEL OF FRAME BUILDING

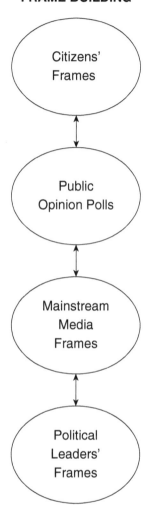

**Figure 8.3 Bidirectional bottom-up model of frame-building.**

class, a classic populist appeal that, as Figure 8.3 notes, evolved in top-down and bottom-up directions.

In other cases, change can bubble up from bottom to top, as grassroots activists reframe problems, complexly producing important reforms. Climate change offers a telling example. For decades, global warming was ignored, minimized, or not viewed as a product of human activity. But years of concerted grassroots activism by innovative citizens and activists, such as Al Gore and Bill McKibben on the public stage, began to shake things up. Slowly, but inexorably, media coverage began to pick up on their frames. Research shows that from 1988 to 2014, there was a decline in news frames focused on economic costs of taking steps to mitigate climate change. Instead, news frames increasingly emphasized the devastating harm climate change poses to the planet, and economic advantages of addressing the problem, with frames dramatizing the problem by using the present tense (Stecula & Merkley, 2019). These influenced elite leaders, who discussed the urgency of climate change, and arrows worked in a bidirectional way, going bottom-up from citizens and top-down from leaders.

Media frames in news, films, and social media posts influenced public attitudes, as more than three-fourths of Americans believe the Earth will get warmer and 82 percent attribute this to human activity (Krosnick & MacInnis, 2020). The framing process was complex. There was an added layer of activists shaping media, along with stunning economic growth in clean energy industries, which will soon account for 95 percent of all global power generation (Gore, 2020). There is no question that bidirectional framing was a critical force in changing attitudes, economics, and public reforms on the green energy front. However, the long time that it took for frames to popularly take hold showcases the power of capitalistic economic forces and institutional intransigence.

The third frame-building model is different and somewhat more negative in tone. Exquisitely geared to the partisan divide in national politics, it emphasizes the **power of partisan media outlets** (Entman & Usher, 2018; see Figure 8.4). It focuses on the ways elite leaders bypass mainstream media channels, diffusing frames on ideological news outlets, working in concert with partisan commentators to stoke anger toward the opposition and build political support. Conservative leaders have disseminated messages through Fox and right-wing sites such as Breitbart News; liberal leaders have done the same via MSNBC and left-wing sites, such as Daily Kos. Both leaders and media commentators drew on each other's narratives. Elites from both groups conveyed frames that accessed partisans' preexisting biases, producing a dynamic process whereby in-group political leaders, media opinion leaders, and their followers created a veritable echo chamber of mutually reinforcing frames.

During Trump's presidency, conservative media, in concert with Trump, promoted right-wing frames on immigration ("Build the wall") and other social issues. Some frames activated legitimate populist sentiments; others were based on falsehoods (Schmitt, Sanger, & Thrush, 2019). Consider QAnon, the ultra-right conspiracy theory–based movement that claims Satanic pedophiles, allegedly includ-

**PARTISAN-CENTERED MODEL OF FRAME-BUILDING**

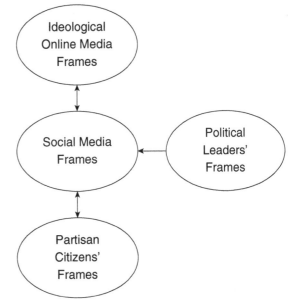

**Figure 8.4  Partisan-centered model of frame-building.**

ing leading Democrats and Hollywood entertainers, plotted against Trump, who ran for president to break up the child-abusing cabal. QAnon boasted thousands of accounts on Twitter and Facebook pages, claiming a following of millions. Trump praised QAnon followers, retweeted QAnon-focused hashtags and many others, so much so that his Twitter feed was awash in White nationalist posts and anti-Muslim videos (McIntire, Yourish, & Buchanan, 2019). In this way he spread and legitimized a deeply prejudiced frame, one that would never have spread into mainstream discourse without ideological outlets, social media, and a leader who stoked these sentiments for political gain.

The same thing happened in the aftermath of the 2020 election, when Trump made groundless claims that the electoral system was rigged by Democrats attempting to steal the election (Rosenberg, Rutenberg, & Corasaniti, 2020). His frames—including a totally false claim that Detroit had more voters than people—went viral on social media, eliciting retweets and shares, stimulating millions of views, and egging on social media supporters to form a Facebook group called "Stop the Steal" (later shut down by Facebook for provoking violence; see Qiu, 2020). In line with Figure 8.4, Trump's frames were widely shared on social media, then promulgated by right-wing sites, which intensified their impact, producing a firestorm of misinformation that spawned protests and undermined the legitimacy of a presidential election.

Partisan-centered framing can also occur on the left. One instance occurred in 2018 when left-wing media outlets, animated by Christine Blasey Ford's "it-has-to-be-true" Senate testimony that Supreme Court nominee Brett Kavanaugh had sexually assaulted her when they were teenagers, pushed the frame that Kavanaugh was, for this reason, unqualified to serve on the Supreme Court, while implicitly downplaying evidence that questioned Blasey Ford or pointed to the psychological gaps in people's memories of sexual abuse (Loftus & Ketcham, 1994). Both liberal and conservative partisans aggressively promoted their arguments in line with the partisan-framing model, probably exacerbating polarization (see Kalmoe, Gubler, & Wood, 2018).

An important feature of this model is the way that mainstream media is cut out of the picture. Partisan outlets spread their viewpoints to their followers, frequently egged on by political leaders, who retweet or post like-minded messages on social media, reinforcing the partisan feedback loop. Mainstream media can sometimes reinforce the message or deflect it, as they did by refuting Trump's claims of election fraud. Yet partisan-focused framing is truly a chamber of echoes. In theory, it has positive aspects, mobilizing activists to passionately participate in electoral politics. In practice, it intensifies partisanship untethered to facts.

## ELECTORAL IMPLICATIONS

Let's turn now to framing implications for the most familiar, fundamental part of politics: national elections.

"Campaigns," Kinder (2003) observed, "are not so much debates over a common set of issues as they are struggles to define what the election is about" (p. 365). Campaigns represent a battle among different value-based frames as they vie for public and elite attention (Bystrom & Banwart, 2014). The three actors in the political process—candidates, journalists (de Vreese, 2010), and citizens—can agree or diverge in the way they frame electoral issues, with plenty of framing variation within each group. These frameworks can be in sync, as in those rare instances during a national emergency when all three groups speak with roughly the same voice, but they are usually in conflict, increasingly bouncing off each other in the non-symmetrical domain of cyberspace, often in vituperative ways.

The 2020 election, like all elections involving incumbents, was fundamentally a referendum on Trump's term in office. In a well-received speech in Gettysburg that recalled Lincoln's ringing unifying rhetoric, Biden highlighted his recurrent theme that he would not build divisive walls, but unifying bridges. His empathic message of healing, framed around channeling of personal adversity and belief in American resilience, bespoke an optimism that has long been compelling in American elections (Zullow et al., 1988). More pragmatically, opposition to Trump was one of the few things that the Democrats, riven by ideological differences, could agree on.

Biden and Harris framed the election around Trump's mismanagement of the pandemic and moral failures to uphold basic American values (Glueck, Karni, & Burns, 2020). Trump sought to push the frame away from the pandemic to emphasize the economy, an issue that resonated with many voters reeling from the financial effects of the virus, particularly Republicans, who placed more emphasis on this issue. His base, which trusted Trump and was concerned about the economy, voted overwhelmingly for Trump in 2020, as it did in 2016 (Koliastasis & Lilleker, 2020). For other voters less enamored by Trump's style, but convinced by frames that Biden would raise their taxes or bring socialist plans to America, Trump could be a convincing messenger.

While Trump had little trouble framing Hillary Clinton in negative terms, because she was unpopular with many Americans, his brushstrokes were less successful with Biden, who was better liked. It was more difficult to frame Biden as elitist, out-of-touch with mainstream values in light of Biden's blue-collar roots and image as a friend of the working man and woman (even though he had long ties with the banking industry). As the campaign intensified, Trump caught his stride, framing Biden as advocating a far-left radical agenda. These frames resonated with Latino voters in Florida, who turned out for Trump in droves. Framing Biden as a socialist, priming fears of socialism among voters who had formerly lived in Cuba, Nicaragua, and Venezuela (countries voters negatively branded as socialist), Trump tweeted that the election was a choice between "the American dream and a socialist nightmare" (Boryga, Valdez, & Ariza, 2020). Of course, Biden, a long-time moderate who embraced a free-enterprise capitalist health care plan, was hardly a supporter of socialism, which advocates a system of government, community, or worker control of property. But the frame stuck among some voters.

Trump emphasized the deficits of Biden and the Democrats, adopting the time-honored law-and-order frame in the wake of racial justice protests and violence that occurred in response to police shootings of African Americans. It appealed to people nervous about their safety, while also priming a well-worn trope about the danger posed by African Americans. Trump tried to move the narrative away from the coronavirus pandemic to wedge issues that called up fears of a breakdown in order that would supposedly occur in a Biden presidency. In the wake of protests against racial injustice, he threatened to shoot or use violence against looters, called protesters "terrorists," and charged that Democrats would give "free rein" to "criminals who threaten our citizens." His law-and-order frames echoed the racially divisive soundtrack of segregationist George Wallace (Baker, 2020).

To be sure, people could be legitimately concerned about looting and vandalism, given their frequency and intensity in anti-police protests. Some voters were honestly concerned with the breakdown of order in their cities, and for reasons other than race, sought a leader who had "the stomach" to stand up to violent demonstrators (Glueck, 2020).

So, some of Trump's frames appealed to rational fears, but they can also be viewed as part of a longer Republican playbook that dates back to Nixon and Reagan. The script emphasized subtle appeals to law-and-order that functioned as dog whistles (sounds only prejudiced people could hear), calling up primitive fears of African Americans and rancid stereotypes (Lucks, 2020). The frames sought to prime—more in the psychological than agenda-setting sense—deep-seated attitudes, automatically, not necessarily consciously, activating prejudiced feelings that get linked to the object of fear (Mendelberg, 2001, 2008; Valentino, Hutchings, & White, 2002; Berinsky et al., 2020). Not all of Trump's law-and-order frames took this subterranean tack, and we don't know how many voters processed them in this way. However, politically coded racial stereotypes work best on voters who are high in prejudice, those who implicitly translate law-and-order into code words calling up primitive fears of violence against Whites (Skinner & Cheadle, 2016).

There was a bitter irony at work. Trump brandished law-and-order appeals against protesters demonstrating against racial injustice, appealing to supporters' biases. However, he refused to condemn—even embraced—the lawlessness of rioters who stormed the Capitol on January 6, 2021 (Plott, 2021). He used law-and-order selectively, strategically, and to elicit fears.

Fear was the frame du jour (Wahl-Jorgensen, 2020; Wahl-Jorgensen, 2018). For voters who were concerned about protests against police brutality, frames about lawlessness carried the day with Trump voters, while racism frames were persuasive for Biden voters (Tavernise & Eligon, 2020). It's hard to know, but protest-against-racism frames may have slightly redounded in Biden's direction. Sixty-three percent of Americans said they preferred a candidate who emphasized the cause of protests, even when they went too far, compared to 31 percent who favored a presidential candidate who took tough policies on demonstrations that went too far (Cohn, 2020).

But Trump's frames—identifying the Democrats as "them" to populist working-class Whites, appealing to fears that an elite socialist agenda would displace them or wreck the economy, and branding himself as a champion of a nostalgic American past—may have worked on an emotional level. They served psychological functions for his base and broad swaths of working-class voters who wanted to distance themselves from a virus that had, at that point, killed more than 200,000 Americans. If T.S. Eliot was correct in famously penning that "humankind cannot bear very much reality," then a veritable blue-collar billionaire who helped voters avert the glare of the painful 2020 reality (and steered them instead toward a storied way of life) could command allegiance, if not always liking.

In the end, Trump's frames failed to sway a majority of voters. Wearied by Trump's nonstop anger, in agreement with Biden's frame of the pandemic, and ready, as voters can be after 4 years of one president, to change the nation's thermostat to a different political temperature (Stimson, 2004), they voted Biden into office.

## CONCLUSIONS

Framing is a core concept in political communication because it illuminates the "how" of politics—how political leaders promote issues, media discuss national problems, and voters process political information. Framing focuses on how problems are defined, ways dots are connected to offer a thematic perspective, and the crux of a controversial political issue. Frames can approach problems in old-fashioned ways that prop up the powerful, or they can construct issues in innovative terms that suggest new ways to solve political conundrums. Issues spanning civil unrest, immigration, impeachment, health care, and terrorism can be framed very differently, reflecting different ideologies.

Agenda-setting overlaps with framing, and researchers have debated how best to differentiate the concepts. While agenda-setting examines whether we think about a particular issue, framing examines how we construct the problem—the metaphors, symbols, and perspectives we use when reflecting on it. Equivalence frames are the most basic, keeping the information equivalent, but using different words to overlay the facts. Emphasis frames are most common, focusing on different features of issues. For all of its intuitive appeal, framing lacks conceptual precision; the concept is vague and indelicately cuts across levels of analysis. The construct's amorphous content can frustrate the drive for academic precision, but also highlights its utility in a political world, where the ability to define the essence of problems is a key instrument of power (Schattschneider, 1960). Frames are spun by elites, promulgated by the news media, harnessed by activists, and harbored by citizens, who use them to make sense of the political world.

Research has documented framing effects, but of course, frames are not magic bullets. While they can change the language of public discourse, they are usually most likely to influence citizens when they resonate with core values and beliefs.

Scholars have advanced three models of frame-building. Theoretically, frames can be disseminated in a top-down, leader-initiated fashion, although this is pretty rare in democratic societies during a time when the power of leaders is constantly under siege by media and other influence agents. A second model emphasizes the ways that citizens—somewhat passively, through public opinion polls, and actively via innovative reformers—construct frames, in concert with media. This model show that frames can bubble up from the grassroots to produce significant reforms, as we've seen with climate change.

The third model emphasizes the ways partisan media, egged on by leaders, build frames, circumventing or minimizing the gatekeeping role of mainstream media. This model focuses on the ways that partisan outlets and social media operate as echo chambers that inject biased perspectives into the online sphere, eliding facts and exacerbating polarization. As these models indicate, framing can produce social change, but there's no guarantee, and sometimes it can have more corrosive effects.

In the end, democracy promises citizens "the freedom to choose." It does not "guarantee particular outcomes," nor that the outcomes will be framed in the most thoughtful or decorous ways (Chong & Druckman, 2007b, p. 652). As always, political communication presents us with a conflict between how candidates will frame issues to win elections, and what they—Democrat, Republican, or alternative party candidates—should do to promote a deliberative discussion of the issues. The conflict is endemic in politics, whether practiced in ancient Greece, 19th-century America, or today. But nowadays, with global problems spinning out of control, it is clear that the collectives of political communication—leaders, media, and citizens—must converge on frames that advance's humanity's dignity and health. Frames can be forces of change (Collyer, Melaku, & Perloff, 2020), rhetorical devices that move people to imagine the status quo in boldly innovative ways.

## REFERENCES

Baker, P. (2020, July 30). A half-century after Wallace, Trump echoes the politics of division. *The New York Times*. Online: www.nytimes.com/2020/07/30/us/politics/trump-wallace.html. (Accessed: July 31, 2020).

Bartels, L. (2020, August 31). Ethnic antagonism erodes Republicans' commitment to democracy. *PNAS: Proceedings of the National Academy of Sciences of the United States of America*. Online: www.pnas.org/content/early/2020/08/26/2007747117#sec-1. (Accessed: September 4, 2020).

Bennett, W.L., Lawrence, R.G., & Livingston, S. (2007). *When the press fails: Political power and the news media from Iraq to Katrina*. Chicago, IL: University of Chicago Press.

Berinsky, A.J., de Benedictis-Kessner, J., Goldberg, M.E., & Margolis, M.F. (2020). The effect of associative racial cues in elections. *Political Communication, 37*, 512–529.

Borah, P. (2011). Conceptual issues in framing theory: A systematic examination of a decade's literature. *Journal of Communication, 61*, 246–263.

Boryga, A., Valdez, Y.H.J., & Ariza, M. (2020, November 4) How Trump won big with Latinos in Florida—and then some. *The Sun Sentinel*. Online: www.sun-sentinel. com/news/politics/elections/fl-ne-latinos-miami-voting-20201104-eyydu3ltkb-fqrkklsg2jgtvy2i-story.html. (Accessed: November 4, 2020).

Bosman, J., Hauser, C., & Diaz, J. (2020, August 10). Chicago police arrest more than 100 people after looters batter downtown. *The New York Times*. Online: www.nytimes. com/2020/08/10/us/shooting-chicago-looting.html. (Accessed: August 11.2020).

Boyle, M.P., Schmierbach, M., Armstrong, C.L., Cho, J., McCluskey, M., McLeod, D.M., & Shah, D.V. (2006). Expressive responses to news stories about extremist groups: A framing experiment. *Journal of Communication*, *56*, 271–288.

Brewer, P.R. (2001). Value words and lizard brains: Do citizens deliberate about appeals to their core values? *Political Psychology*, *22*, 45–64.

Brewer, P.R., & Gross, K. (2010). Studying the effects of issue framing on public opinion about policy issues: Does what we see depend on how we look? In P. D'Angelo & J.A. Kuypers (Eds.), *Doing news framing analysis: Empirical and theoretical perspectives* (pp. 159–186). New York: Routledge.

Burgers, C., Konijn, E.A., & Steen, G.J. (2016). Figurative framing: Shaping public discourse through metaphor, hyperbole, and irony. *Communication Theory*, *26*, 410–430.

Bystrom, D.G., & Banwart, M.C. (2014). Reflections on the 2012 election: An agenda moving forward. In D.G. Bystrom, M.C. Banwart, & M.S. McKinney (Eds.), *alieNATION: The divide & conquer election of 2012* (pp. 328–336). New York: Peter Lang.

Cacciatore, M.A., Scheufele, D.A., & Iyengar, S. (2016). The end of framing as we know it . . . and the future of media effects. *Mass Communication and Society*, *19*, 7–23.

Chong, D., & Druckman, J.N. (2007a). A theory of framing and opinion formation in competitive elite environments. *Journal of Communication*, *57*, 99–118.

Chong, D., & Druckman, J.N. (2007b). Framing public opinion in competitive democracies. *American Political Science Review*, *101*, 637–655.

Cohen, R. (2016, September 11). We need "somebody spectacular". *The New York Times* (Sunday Review), 1, 6–7.

Cohn, N. (2020, June 25). In poll, Trump falls far behind Biden in six key battleground states. *The New York Times*. Online: www.nytimes.com/2020/06/25/upshot/poll-2020-biden-battlegrounds.html. (Accessed: June 26, 2020).

Coleman, R. (2010). Framing the pictures in our heads: Exploring the framing and agenda-setting effects of visual images. In P. D'Angelo & J.A. Kuypers (Eds.), *Doing news framing analysis: Empirical and theoretical perspectives* (pp. 233–261). New York: Routledge.

Collyer, R., Melaku, M., & Perloff, R.M. (2020, October 25). *Frank talk on the protest movement*. Community forum at the Unitarian Universalist Congregation of Cleveland (L.C. Imbornoni, Organizer). Shaker Heights, Ohio.

Confessore, N. (2016, March 28). How G.O.P. elites lost the party's base to Trump. *The New York Times*, A1, A12, A13.

D'Angelo, P., & Kuypers, J.A. (Eds.). (2010). *Doing news framing analysis: Empirical and theoretical perspectives*. New York: Routledge.

D'Angelo, P., Lule, J., Neuman, W.R., Rodriguez, L., Dimitrova, D.V., & Carragee, K.M. (2019). Beyond framing: A forum for framing researchers. *Journalism & Mass Communication Quarterly*, *96*, 12–30.

Davis, J.H., & Baker, P. (2019, January 6). How the wall has boxed in the president. *The New York Times*, 1, 15.

Dekker, R., & Scholten, P. (2017). Framing the immigration policy agenda: A qualitative comparative analysis of media effects on Dutch immigration policies. *The International Journal of Press/Politics, 22*, 202–222.

de Vreese, C.H. (2010). Framing the economy: Effects of journalistic news frames. In P. D'Angelo & J.A. Kuypers (Eds.), *Doing news framing analysis: Empirical and theoretical perspectives* (pp. 187–214). New York: Routledge.

Druckman, J.N. (2001a). The implications of framing effects for citizen competence. *Political Behavior, 23*, 225–256.

Druckman, J.N. (2001b). On the limits of framing effects: Who can frame? *Journal of Politics, 63*, 1041–1066.

Edelman, M. (1964). *The symbolic uses of politics*. Urbana, IL: University of Illinois Press.

Edy, J.A., & Meirick, P.C. (2007). Wanted, dead or alive: Media frames, frame adoption, and support for the war in Afghanistan. *Journal of Communication, 57*, 119–141.

Entman, R.M. (2004). *Projections of power: Framing news, public opinion, and U.S. foreign policy*. Chicago, IL: University of Chicago Press.

Entman, R.M., & Usher, N. (2018). Framing in a fractured democracy: Impacts of digital technology on ideology, power and cascading network activation. *Journal of Communication, 68*, 298–308.

Gamson, W.A., & Modigliani, A. (1987). The changing culture of affirmative action. In R.A. Braumgart (Ed.), *Research in political sociology* (Vol. 3, pp. 137–177). Greenwich, CT: JAI.

Glueck, K. (2020, September 1). Biden confronts Trump on safety: "He can't stop the violence." *The New York Times*. Online: www.nytimes.com/2020/08/31/us/politics/biden-speech-trump.html. (Accessed: September 1, 2020).

Glueck, K., Karni, A., & Burns, A. (2020, August 28). Rival themes emerge as race enters final weeks: Covid vs. law and order. *The New York Times*. Online: www.nytimes.com/2020/08/28/us/politics/joe-biden-trump-conventions.html. (Accessed: November 6, 2020).

Goldmacher, S. (2020, October 11). Can Trump squeeze more from his White base in Pennsylvania and beyond? *The New York Times*. Online: www.nytimes.com/2020/10/11/us/politics/trump-white-base-pennsylvania.html. (Accessed: October 12, 2020).

Gore, A. (2020, December 12). Where I find hope. *The New York Times*. Online: www.nytimes.com/2020/12/12/opinion/sunday/biden-climate-change-al-gore.html. (Accessed: December 16, 2020).

Hallin, D.C. (1986). *The "uncensored war": The media and Vietnam*. New York: Oxford University Press.

Hertog, J.K., & McLeod, D.M. (2001). A multiperspectival approach to framing analysis: A field guide. In S.D. Reese, O.H. Gandy, Jr., & A.E. Grant (Eds.), *Framing public life: Perspectives on media and our understanding of the social world* (pp. 139–161). Mahwah, NJ: Erlbaum Associates.

Iyengar, S. (1991). *Is anyone responsible? How television frames political issues*. Chicago, IL: University of Chicago Press.

Kaiser, J. (2020). Disentangling the effects of thematic information and emphasis frames and the suppression of issue-specific argument effects through value-resonant framing. *Political Communication, 37*, 1–19.

Kalmoe, N.P., Gubler, J.R., & Wood, D.A. (2018). Toward conflict or compromise? How violent metaphors polarize partisan issue attitudes. *Political Communication, 35*, 333–352.

Kelley, R.D.G. (2020, June 18). What kind of society values property over Black lives? *The New York Times*. Online: www.nytimes.com/2020/06/18/opinion/george-floyd-protests-looting.html. (Accessed: June 23, 2020).

Keum, H., Hillback, E.D., Rojas, H., Gil de Zuniga, H., Shah, D.V., & McLeod, D.M. (2005). Personifying the radical: How news framing polarizes security concerns and tolerance judgments. *Human Communication Research, 31*, 337–364.

Kinder, D.R. (2003). Communication and politics in the age of information. In D.O. Sears, L. Huddy, & R. Jervis (Eds.), *Oxford handbook of political psychology* (pp. 357–393). New York: Oxford University Press.

Klein, J. (2016, September 12–16). Don't believe the new myths about America's white working class. *Time, 34*.

Koliastasis, P., & Lilleker, D. (2020). A divided America guarantees the longevity of Trumpism? In D. Jackson, D.S. Coombs, F. Trevisan, D. Lilleker, & E. Thorsen (Eds.), *U.S. election analysis 2020: Media, voters and the campaign*. Online: www.electionanalysis.ws/us/president2020/section-2-voters/a-divided-america-guarantees-the-longevity-of-trumpism/. (Accessed: November 15, 2020).

Kosicki, G.M. (1993). Problems and opportunities in agenda-setting research. *Journal of Communication, 43*, 100–127.

Kristof, N. (2017, February 23). Fight Trump, not his voters. *The New York Times*, A23.

Krosnick, J.A., & MacInnis, B. (2020). *Climate insights 2020: Overall trends*. Washington, DC: Resources for the Future. Online: https://media.rff.org/documents/Climate_Insights_Overall_Trends_Final.pdf. (Accessed: December 15, 2020).

Loftus, E., & Ketcham, K. (1994). *The myth of repressed memory: False memories and allegations of sexual abuse*. New York: St. Martin's Press.

Lucks, D.S. (2020, July 19). Donald Trump, a true Reagan Republican. *Los Angeles Times*. Online: www.latimes.com/opinion/story/2020-07-19/ronald-reagans-racism-cleared-the-way-for-trump. (Accessed: August 29, 2020).

Maher, T.M. (2001). Framing: An emerging paradigm or a phase of agenda setting? In S.D. Reese, O.H. Gandy, Jr., & A.E. Grant (Eds.), *Framing public life: Perspectives on media and our understanding of the social world* (pp. 83–94). Mahwah, NJ: Erlbaum Associates.

McCombs, M., & Ghanem, S.I. (2001). The convergence of agenda setting and framing. In S.D. Reese, O.H. Gandy, Jr., & A.E. Grant (Eds.), *Framing public life: Perspectives on media and our understanding of the social world* (pp. 67–81). Mahwah, NJ: Erlbaum Associates.

McIntire, M., Yourish, K., & Buchanan, L. (2019, November 2). In Trump's Twitter feed: Conspiracy-mongers, racists and spies. *The New York Times*. Online: www.nytimes.com/interactive/2019/11/02/us/politics/trump-twitter-disinformation.html. (Accessed: August 14, 2020).

McLeod, D.M., & Shah, D.V. (2015). *News frames and national security: Covering Big Brother*. New York: Cambridge University Press.

Mendelberg, T. (2001). *The race card: Campaign strategy, implicit messages, and the norm of equality*. Princeton, NJ: Princeton University Press.

Mendelberg, T. (2008). Racial priming revived. *Perspectives on Politics, 6*, 109–123.

Mutz, D.C. (2018). Status threat, not economic hardship, explains the 2016 vote. *PNAS* (Proceedings of the National Academy of Sciences of the United States of America). Online: www.pnas.org/content/115/19/E4330 (Accessed: October 17, 2020).

Nelson, T.E., Clawson, R.A., & Oxley, Z.M. (1997). Media framing of a civil liberties conflict and its effect on tolerance. *American Political Science Review*, *91*, 567–583.

Nelson, T.E., & Oxley, Z.M. (1999). Issue framing effects on belief importance and opinion. *Journal of Politics*, *61*, 1040–1067.

Nisbet, E.C., Hart, P.S., Myers, T., & Ellithorpe, M. (2013). Attitude change in competitive framing environments? Open-/closed-mindedness, framing effects, and climate change. *Journal of Communication*, *63*, 766–785.

Nisbet, M.C. (2010). Knowledge into action: Framing the debates over climate change and poverty. In P. D'Angelo & J.A. Kuypers (Eds.), *Doing news framing analysis: Empirical and theoretical perspectives* (pp. 43–83). New York: Routledge.

Pan, Z., & Kosicki, G.M. (1993). Framing analysis: An approach to news discourse. *Political Communication*, *10*, 55–75.

Plott, E. (2021, January 16). Trump's "law and order": One more deceptive tactic is exposed. *The New York Times*. Online: https://www.nytimes.com/2021/01/16/us/politics/trump-law-order.html. (Accessed: January 17, 2021).

Powell, T.E., Boomgaarden, H.G., De Swert, K., & de Vreese, C.H. (2019). Framing fast and slow: A dual processing account of multimodal framing effects. *Media Psychology*, *22*, 572–600.

Price, V., & Tewksbury, D. (1997). News values and public opinion: A theoretical account of media priming and framing. In G.A. Barnett & F.J. Boster (Eds.), *Progress in communication sciences: Advances in persuasion* (Vol. 13, pp. 173–212). Greenwich, CT: Ablex.

Qiu, L. (2020, November 21). Superspreaders of false claims about the vote. *The New York Times*, A17.

Reese, S.D. (2007). The framing project: A bridging model for media research revisited. *Journal of Communication*, *57*, 148–154.

Rojecki, A. (2016). *America and the politics of insecurity*. Baltimore: Johns Hopkins University Press.

Rosenberg, M., Rutenberg, J., & Corasaniti, N. (2020, November 5). The disinformation is coming from inside the White House. *The New York Times*. Online: www.nytimes.com/2020/11/05/us/politics/trump-white-house-disinformation.html. (Accessed: November 8, 2020).

Schaffner, B.F., & Sellers, P.J. (2010). Introduction. In B.F. Schaffner & P.J. Sellers (Eds.), *Winning with words: The origins and impact of political framing* (pp. 1–7). New York: Routledge.

Schattschneider, E.E. (1960). *The semi-sovereign people: A realist's view of democracy in America*. New York: Holt, Rinehart & Winston.

Scheufele, D.A. (2000). Agenda-setting, priming, and framing revisited: Another look at cognitive effects of political communication. *Mass Communication & Society*, *3*, 297–316.

Scheufele, D.A., & Iyengar, S. (2014). The state of framing research: A call for new directions. In K. Kenski & K.H. Jamieson (Eds.), *The Oxford handbook of political communication theories*. New York: Oxford University Press. Online: www.oxford.handbooks.com.

Scheufele, D.A., & Tewskbury, D. (2007). Framing, agenda-setting, and priming: The evolution of three media effects models. *Journal of Communication*, *57*, 9–20.

Schmitt, E., Sanger, D.E., & Thrush, G. (2019, January 9). Experts reject claims by Trump that terrorists are menacing border. *The New York Times*, A13.

Shah, D.V., Kwak, N., Schmierbach, M., & Zubric, J. (2004). The interplay of news frames on cognitive complexity. *Human Communication Research, 30*, 102–120.

Shah, D.V., McLeod, D.M., Gotlieb, M.R., & Lee, N-J. (2009). Framing and agenda-setting. In R.L. Nabi & M.B. Oliver (Eds.), *The Sage handbook of media processes and effects* (pp. 83–98). Thousand Oaks, CA: Sage.

Shen, F., & Edwards, H.H. (2005). Economic individualism, humanitarianism, and welfare reform: A value-based account of framing effects. *Journal of Communication, 55*, 795–809.

Shulman, H.C., & Sweitzer, M.D. (2018). Advancing framing theory: Designing an equivalence frame to improve political information processing. *Human Communication Research, 44*, 155–175.

Silver, N. (2016, May 3). The mythology of Trump's "working class" support. *FiveThirtyEight*. Online: https://fivethirtyeight.com/features/the-mythology-of-trumps-working-class-support/. (Accessed: March 22, 2021).

Skinner, A.L., & Cheadle, J.E. (2016). The "Obama Effect"? Priming contemporary racial milestones increases implicit racial bias among Whites. *Social Cognition, 34*, 544–558.

Stecula, D.A., & Merkley, E. (2019). Framing climate change: Economics, ideology, and uncertainty in American news media content from 1988 to 2014. *Frontiers in Communication*. Online: www.frontiersin.org/articles/10.3389/fcomm.2019.00006/full. (Accessed: December 15, 2020).

Stimson, J.A. (2004). *Tides of consent: How public opinion shapes American politics*. New York: Cambridge University Press.

Takeshita, T. (2006). Current critical problems in agenda-setting research. *International Journal of Public Opinion Research, 18*, 275–296.

Taub, A. (2016, November 2). Behind the gathering turmoil, a crisis of white Identity. *The New York Times*, A6.

Tavernise, S., & Eligon, J. (2020, November 7). Voters say Black Lives Matter protests were important. They disagree on why. *The New York Times*. Online: www.nytimes.com/2020/11/07/us/black-lives-matter-protests.html. (Accessed: November 8, 2020).

Tewksbury, D., & Scheufele, D.A. (2009). News framing theory and research. In J. Bryant & M.B. Oliver (Eds.), *Media effects: Advances in theory and research* (3rd ed., pp. 17–33). New York: Routledge.

Valentino, N.A., Hutchings, V.L., & White, I.K. (2002). Cues that matter: How political ads prime racial attitudes during campaigns. *American Political Science Review, 96*, 75–90.

Wagner, M.W., & Gruszczynski, M. (2016). When framing matters: How partisan and journalistic frames affect individual opinions and party identification. *Journalism & Communication Monographs, 18*, 5–48.

Wahl-Jorgensen, K. (2018). Media coverage of shifting emotional regimes: Donald Trump's angry populism. *Media, Culture & Society, 40*(5), 766–778.

Wahl-Jorgensen, K. (2020). The emotional politics of 2020: Fear and loathing in the United States. In D. Jackson, D.S. Coombs, F. Trevisan, D. Lilleker, & E. Thorsen (Eds.), *U.S. election analysis 2020: Media, voters and the campaign*. Online: www.electionanalysis.ws/us/president2020/section-3-candidates-and-the-campaign/the-emotional-politics-of-2020-fear-and-loathing-in-the-united-states/. (Accessed: November 16, 2020).

Weaver, D.H. (2007). Thoughts on agenda-setting, framing, and priming. *Journal of Communication, 57*, 142–147.

Zhong, R., Mozur, P., Kao, J., & Krolik, A. (2020, December 19). No "negative" news: How China censored the coronavirus. *The New York Times*. Online: www.nytimes.com/2020/12/19/technology/china-coronavirus-censorship.html. (Accessed: December 20, 2020).

Zullow, H.M., Oettingen, G., Peterson, C., & Seligman, M.E. (1988). Pessimistic explanatory style in the historical record: CAVing LBJ, presidential candidates, and East versus West Berlin. *American Psychologist, 43*, 673–682.

# 9

# Biases, the Beholder, and Media Effects

## The Partisan Psychology of Political Communication

Pick an issue. It could be gun control, capital punishment, immigration, or wearing masks. On most issues, you will find a conspicuous disparity in perceptions that strikes at the heart of our political psychology today. The differences between those on the right and left are so pronounced you would think you are looking at two different political universes.

Consider Trump's first impeachment, which occurred back in 2019, but still provides a dramatic example of partisan perceptions. In interviews with 81 people from about 30 states in the U.S., reporters found that conservatives and liberals diverged sharply. Conservatives thought impeachment was a sham and Democrats' lame attempt to oust President Trump. For example:

> *"As a former law enforcement officer, there is no case there. Absolutely no case. The president did not do anything wrong. It's a shame that so many people hate the president to the point where they will try to make the case where there is none."*—Bill Marcy, 73, a Mississippi Republican

For Democrats, impeachment was part of a larger picture:

> *"This is bigger than this particular case—his mental ramblings, his strong support of strongmen in other countries, his completely flouting the democracy that we have. . . . There are so many reasons, but right now, I support that they are impeaching him for obstructing Congress and trying to do their job."* —Gina Fields, 54, a Democrat from Los Angeles

(Mervosh et al., 2020)

Partisan differences also emerged on Trump's role in the 2021 storming of the Capitol, which prompted a second impeachment. While 63 percent of Americans placed a good deal of blame on Trump, 96 percent of Democrats expressed that sentiment; yet 69 percent of Republicans didn't think Trump bore much blame for the insurrection. Similarly, in the immediate aftermath of the Capitol violence, 84 percent of Democrats thought steps should be taken to remove Trump from office, compared to only 15 percent of Republicans (Santhanam, 2021).

Partisan differences even emerge when the misconduct is apparent to the naked eye (and "naked" is the operative word here). Just 8 percent of Trump supporters believed that claims of sexual assault and sexual harassment against Trump were credible, even though he had famously bragged on an *Access Hollywood* television tape about groping women, and more than a dozen women made allegations of sexual misconduct (French, 2017). But the shoe was on the seducer's other foot when it came to Bill Clinton's impeachment. In this case, Republicans were aghast at Clinton's behavior, but Democrats were nonplussed. They pooh-poohed the seriousness of Clinton's sexual liaison with Monica Lewinsky and minimized its importance, a contention that seems all the more partisan in the light of Clinton's acknowledgment in a 2020 documentary that what he did was "awful."

When it came to the coronavirus, partisan differences were legendary. As noted in Chapter 1, liberal and conservative partisans differed on the severity of the virus and imposing legal restrictions on public activity. In mid-2020, Democrats were more likely than Republicans to don a mask and to refrain from watching movies in a theater (Casselman & Tankersley, 2020; Gebeloff, 2020). Republicans and 2020 Trump voters were less likely than Democrats and Biden voters to plan to get shots or even get vaccinated, even though vaccination represented the most effective way to end the pandemic and save their lives (Ivory, Leatherby, & Gebeloff, 2021). Partisans not only differ in their political opinions, but also in the facts that underlie their foundational beliefs (Delli Carpini, 2020).

The notion that political truth is in the eye of the biased beholder is the focus of this chapter, tailor-made for an age of partisan vitriol, in which selective media use increases the intensity of biased beliefs. The chapter, calling on both classic and contemporary research, examines the intersection between social psychology and political communication. The first section examines the rich literature on selective, biased perceptions of politics, including beliefs that media are hostile to partisans' side. A boxed section explains online implications of the classic spiral of silence effect. The next section looks at selective exposure to politically congruent information and the ways selective exposure can lead to confirmation of preexisting biases. The final portion of the chapter offers a counterpoint to this perspective, pointing to examples of political agreement. The conclusion pulls this together, ending on an optimistic note.

## SELECTIVE PERCEPTION

### Psychological Biases

Attitudes on political issues can be fiercely held. Strong attitudes are characterized by symbolic attachments, linkage to core social values, certainty (people are convinced their attitude is correct), and extremity (strong attitudes are on the extreme ends of the political distribution). Entrenched attitudes are likely to persist over time and prove impervious to influence (Krosnick & Petty, 1995).

Strong attitudes are a blessing and a curse: They embolden people to become involved in politics and work for change, but they also can blind individuals to alternative positions on the issue. When people have a strong position on an issue, they invariably see everything related to the topic through the lens of the attitude, a testament to the power of political socialization, the dynamics of social perception, and psychological resistance to accept new information that challenges a well-developed worldview. Armed with a strong attitude, people are hardly objective, but deeply subjective and frequently unwilling to consider alternative points of view, scorning opponents with a viral pen on social media (see Figure 9.1).

There aren't just a few studies that document the way strong attitudes skew our perceptions toward what we already believe. There are dozens, an entire literature in social and political psychology. The most famous is a study conducted more than 40 years ago by Lord, Ross, and Lepper (1979), which exposed people with strong attitudes in favor of and against the death penalty to objective evidence that, in some cases, showed that capital punishment deterred crime, but in other cases documented that it was an ineffective deterrent against crime, supposedly increasing crime rates. Now if people were fair, objective, and rational, they would acknowledge, even welcome, facts that suggested there was a different position on an issue they cared deeply about.

Of course, that's not what happened. Proponents of capital punishment found the pro-death-penalty evidence more convincing, while perceiving a study with exactly the same facts on the other side, which questioned the effectiveness of capital punishment, as full of flaws. The same held for opponents of capital punishment: Evidence that showed it was a poor policy choice was held up as solid evidence, while virtually the same facts that suggested the death penalty worked were discounted. What's more, proponents and opponents managed to feel even more strongly about their position at the conclusion of the study. Reviewing solid evidence that challenged their viewpoint didn't reduce biased perceptions; it caused partisans to become even *more* polarized, *more* convinced that they were right! Other, more recent research, has corroborated these findings (Kahan et al., 2017).

These studies illustrate **selective perception**, the psychological tendency to perceive messages through the lens of a strong preexisting viewpoint. Communications that seem to confirm a strong attitude are viewed as correct and valid, whereas messages that appear to disconfirm staunch beliefs are discounted, viewed as inaccurate or plainly wrong. This is also known as a **confirmation bias**.

Figure 9.1 Partisans view American politics through blue (Democratic) or red (Republican) colored glasses, selectively perceiving news so it fits their biases and selectively exposing themselves to information from their side. Such selectivity applies primarily to those with strong attitudes about politics.

Political messages—blogs, speeches, debate performances, and ads—run up against the blockage of psychological selectivity. Voters with strong partisan sentiments quickly reject positions that are at odds with their attitudes. They assimilate supportive, slightly ambiguous positions to their side, and contrast opposing views, assuming these are more different from their viewpoint than they actually are. Voters with strong partisan attitudes come to an election campaign with their minds made up, ready to pounce on weaknesses from the other candidate, affirm positions that support a preexisting viewpoint, and lambast a Facebook friend who dares to disagree, to the point of defriending or cancelling her (see Box 9.1 on the spiral of silence).

These selective psychological tendencies don't comport with deliberative democratic ideals. We want people to consider political information in an open-minded way so they can change their positions on issues when the facts warrant it.

## BOX 9.1 DO THE UNPOPULAR THING: YOU MAY TRIGGER AN ONLINE SPIRAL OF SILENCE

You wouldn't think it would have caused such a stir.

Back in spring 2020, a liberal Democrat who worked on President Obama's reelection campaign and was sympathetic with Black Lives Matter protests tweeted the summary of a political scientist's dry, but interesting, findings about the effects of social protest on voting behavior. The study showed that nonviolent protests during the 1960s pushed voters toward Democratic candidates, but violent protests caused White backlash, causing them to vote for Republicans, tipping the 1968 election to Richard Nixon.

The liberal Democrat, David Shor, tweeting on May 28, 2020, seemed to be trying to warn activists that if they did not do more to prevent George Floyd protests from turning violent, they could face an outcome antithetical to their goals: Trump's reelection. This might sound like a friend cautioning other friends to rethink their tactics, lest they have untoward effects. But for many radical-liberal social justice warriors, advocating a tempering of tactics amounts to pusillanimous, treasonous compromise, denying the legitimacy of whatever-it-takes protest to overcome years of racism. To them, there was no holding back on a response to Shor. The founder of a Democratic canvassing app viewed Shor's post as racist, tweeting back that "YOU need to stop using your anxiety and 'intellect' as a vehicle for anti-blackness." The head of the data analytics firm that employed Shor

*Continued*

also posted a disparaging remark. Other colleagues, who also worked at the company, said Shor's tweet threatened their safety. This was understandable, but hard to view as an entirely realistic fear given that it was directed to a liberal audience sympathetic with their point of view (Chait, 2020).

Attentive to the concerns of his colleagues, Shor actually apologized, promising to "be much more careful moving forward." It was too late. The company fired him. He couldn't talk about what happened because he signed a nondisclosure agreement, and no one at the firm would talk about it either.

The incident is an example of how many activist groups on the left (and right, too) brook no disagreement with their attitudes, feeling no compunction to tolerate views they feel are morally mistaken or endanger the group's political objectives. While one can appreciate the strength of activists' convictions, their willingness to tread on freedom of speech raises philosophical issues for political communication students. So do the striking absence of messages that support an individual, such as Shor, who had the temerity to challenge dominant political norms. In these situations, the online communication environment is notable not just for the number of posts that favor the group's perceived majority position but for the lack of messages that stake out an unpopular position or defend the minority who defy the norm.

Public opinion scholars have a name for this phenomenon, **the spiral of silence**. Originally and innovatively proposed by the German political scholar, Elisabeth Noelle-Neumann (1974), the spiral of silence argues that fear of social isolation can lead individuals to stifle unpopular sentiments. More specifically, individuals, fearing isolation, keep close tabs on the opinion environment in their social networks, whether online or off. They base judgments on whether to speak out on a host of variables, including their perceptions of majority sentiments. Spiral of silence has spawned a voluminous, complex literature on its processes and effects (e.g., Glynn, Hayes, & Shanahan, 1997; Scheufele & Moy, 2000). Current research shows that it remains a real and robust phenomenon. Spiral of silence effects are more likely for relevant social issues, among certain individuals, perhaps those who particularly fear isolation from others, and in discussions with family, friends, and neighbors (Matthes, Knoll, & von Sikorski, 2018). And, of course, they are endemic in largely totalitarian countries such as China and Russia, where governments reflexively stifle dissent. Their emergence in social networks in the U.S. is a source of interest and concern.

*Continued*

In the online world, opinion groups can enforce tight group norms, which proscribe speaking out or taking dissenting views, lest the messenger face the onslaught of attacks, social ostracism, or in unusual cases, cancellation. Individuals who perceive they are in the majority on a social network can be more likely to share their opinions than those who believe they're in the minority. Fearing isolation or online shunning if they share their views, those who think they're part of the minority on an issue can refrain from questioning the perceived majority, keeping their views to themselves. The majority opinion spirals out, as more people voice these views, and minority sentiments drop off the radar screen (see Gearhart & Zhang, 2015, for a particularly intriguing study). What's more, as Neubaum and Krämer (2018) reported, in a fascinating study, people are less likely to express a deviant, minority view online than in face-to-face environments. Given that online forums are likely to be larger, with a possibly unfriendly opinion climate, individuals are wary. "People perceive a greater fear of being personally attacked on the Internet than face-to-face," Neubaum and Krämer note (pp. 157–158).

And this is the way it can work in real life. In cases where people have tenaciously posted a minority sentiment, such as David Shor did, they are hit back with such verbal ferocity that they shy away in the future, and the fear of a similar backlash intimidates others from sharing a view.

This can occur on a host of topics: abortion, both sides of the gun issue, and climate change, where conservatives in the Trump administration and across the country have been loath to acknowledge scientific evidence on global warming (Davenport & Landler, 2019). After the 2020 election, Republican politicians who recognized the election had been conducted fairly were reluctant to admit this, for fear of alienating the majority of Republican leaders who falsely maintained the election was riddled with fraud. Spirals of silence have produced such chilling fears of self-censorship that nearly two-thirds of Americans agree that the political climate prevents them from saying things because of fear others might find them offensive (Ekins, 2020).

It has even gotten to the point that a student found his satirical mocking of campus norms, "Do the left thing," got him in trouble. The author, a cultural minority student at the University of Michigan (and a left-handed person), took humorous umbrage when "a white cis-gendered hetero upper-class man" offered his hand to help the student up when he slipped on the cold ground, telling the student, "I was just trying to do the right thing." The writer, tongue in check, penned that "this

*Continued*

was the microaggression that broke the gender-neutral camel's back."
Continuing, he said that

> the biggest obstacle to equality today is our barbaric attitude [toward
> left-handed people]. . . . It's a tragedy that I, a member of the left-handed
> community, had little to no idea of the atrocious persecution that we
> are dealt every day by institutions that are deeply embedded in society.
>
> (Mahmood, 2014)

His satire got under liberal students' skin. The college newspaper fired
him, and in his peer online environment that enforces similar values,
it might have been socially difficult for a student to have voiced the
minority position, embracing the value of satire. This is a humorous
example. Of course, it's not simple. Complex issues come to the fore
when groups that have faced oppression and are minorities in the larger
society receive criticism that seems to smack of the majority culture. In a
fractious democracy, there are important questions about which voices
get aired and are heard (Moy, 2020). Yet if online environments create
such interpersonal pressures that they stifle the expression of minority
opinions, dissent itself is threatened.

Classical traditions in political communication prize dissent. As John
Stuart Mill famously wrote, discussing problems with opinion censorship,

> if the opinion is right, (people) are deprived of the opportunity of
> exchanging error for truth: if wrong, they lose, what is almost as great
> a benefit, the clearer perception and livelier impression of truth, pro-
> duced by its collision with error.
>
> (Mill, 1859/2009, p. 20)

## Power of Political Group Membership

There is another aspect of selective perception that pushes people to value their
preferred group—the in-group—rather than "them," the other side, or the out-
group. As Leaf Van Boven and David Sherman (2018) explained:

> Among social psychology's fundamental lessons is that people are pro-
> foundly affected by what others think. In their desire to be upstanding mem-
> bers of their political tribe, people are pulled toward embracing the stances
> of their peers and loath to publicly disagree with them.
>
> (p. 2)

The desire to conform to one's political in-group leads people to selectively perceive messages in decidedly partisan ways. Two intriguing studies demonstrate
this point, the first on welfare policies, the second on climate change.

To appreciate the first study, we need to appreciate that liberals and conservatives have different attitudes about social welfare, attitudes that derive from their values. Liberals, emphasizing a value of compassion, favor government aid to the poor, whereas conservatives, stressing individual responsibility, support stricter government policies toward welfare. Cohen (2003) explored how these psychological biases played out in a study of liberals' and conservatives' attitudes toward welfare. Not surprisingly, Cohen found that liberal, pro-Democratic college students endorsed generous government welfare benefits for the poor, if they were told most Congressional Democrats favored the policy. Similarly, conservative, pro-Republican college students supported a more stringent government welfare policy when informed that most Congressional Republicans favored it. Here's the kicker, the intriguing finding: When liberal students were told that most Congressional Democrats favored a stricter, *conservative* welfare policy, they supported it; and when conservative students learned that most Congressional Republicans supported the *liberal* welfare policy, they favored it. That's right. Partisans altered their views to conform to what those on *their* side endorsed. When we hear that *our* side endorses a policy, even one we don't initially agree with, we may be willing to change our beliefs, because now it seems like it's the right policy, the one the good guys embrace.

Fifteen years later, with concerns mounting about the urgent need to address the reality of global warming, three researchers applied Cohen's logic to understanding the political psychological barriers to reaching bipartisan agreement on climate change policies. While acknowledging that Republicans and Democrats see climate change through partisan lenses, they suspected that, in view of the voluminous evidence, Republicans harbored some belief in climate change, but were unwilling to embrace change because their group opposed it. They also thought that Democrats could be pulled toward backing climate change policies of a more conservative vintage if they felt their Democratic peers endorsed them. This is exactly what Van Boven, Ehret, and Sherman (2018) found.

They chose a liberal, government-focused policy to address climate change, a cap-and-trade plan that, in general, caps total carbon emissions, taxes companies that produce more emissions than they are permitted, and permits companies that reduce their emissions to trade permits to other groups. They also selected a conservative policy that favored market incentives over government caps by reducing the payroll tax and shifting the tax to carbon dioxide in a revenue-neutral way. Pro-Democrat and pro-Republican partisans read descriptions of the policies emphasizing that Democratic or Republican members of Congress supported the cap-and-trade policy or the revenue-neutral carbon tax.

Respondents favored "party over policy," as the researchers put it, in a way that paralleled Cohen's results. Democratic respondents backed both conservative and liberal carbon policies when Democratic legislators proposed them, and Republican respondents supported liberal and conservative carbon policies more when Republican legislators proposed them. If ordinary people are influenced by these biases, consider how much more strongly politicians, who want to both serve their party's constituents and keep their jobs, are affected by the pull of partisan perceptions.

Van Boven and his colleagues illustrated his with two telling quotes, the first from a Democratic president, the second from a Republican legislator:

> If I proposed something that was literally word for word in the Republican Party platform, it would be immediately opposed by eighty to ninety percent of the Republican voters. And the reason is not that they've evaluated what I said. It's that I said it.
>
> —President Barack Obama

> In my first six years in Congress from 1993 to 1999, I had said that climate change was hooey. I hadn't looked into the science. All I knew was that (Democrat) Al Gore was for it, and therefore I was against it.
>
> —Republican Representative Robert Inglis

> (Van Boven, Ehret, & Sherman, 2018, p. 492)

You saw all this—party over policy—in action in the fall of 2020 when Democrats and Republicans sparred over the timing of a presidential nomination to replace the late Ruth Bader Ginsburg on the Supreme Court. Consider that in 2016 Republicans refused to consider President Obama's nominee to replace the late Justice Antonin Scalia, arguing that the Senate should not consider a replacement in an election year. Instead, it was more democratic, Republicans maintained, for the new president, duly elected by the voters, to pick a new Supreme Court nominee, who had life tenure on the Court. Democrats were outraged, noting that the Constitution stipulated that the president (who then was Obama) has the authority to nominate a justice, subject to the advice and consent of the Senate. Four years later, during a heated election campaign, it was a breathtakingly different story. The same Republicans now offered a torturous logic to argue that the president (Republican Donald Trump) had the right to nominate a replacement for Ginsburg rather than deferring to a new president. And the Democrats now cried foul, urging that a new justice should not be confirmed until after the election, placing their party over principles they had advocated 4 years earlier.

### Perceiving the Media Are Against Our Side

Liberals and conservatives not only believe their side is right and the other is wrong. They not only perceive that that when their party supports a position, it must be one worth embracing, even if it actually clashes with some of their beliefs. They also believe that the media is unfair and biased. The catch is they see the news as biased against their side and in favor of their opponents.

Bias is a complicated concept, one frequently studied in political communication (see Chapter 11). Of course the news is biased, but people have different ideas in mind when they say they distrust the news or claim it is full of biases (Jones & Ritter, 2018; Fenton, 2019; Lewis, 2019). By biased, people can mean the news is too sensational, covers the seamy, negative side of life too much, excessively criticizes public officials, or props up the status quo. Strong political partisans see a different bias, another example of selective perception, and one of the most visceral aspects of selective political beliefs.

Scholars have a name for this particular bias. It's called the hostile media effect. Except it's not an actual effect of news, or a bias the news actually harbors. Instead, the **hostile media effect** is a perception of bias, a belief on the part of partisans, or those with strong political attitudes, that media coverage is biased against their side and in favor of their antagonists (Vallone, Ross, & Lepper, 1985; Perloff, 2015; Tsfati, 2007). There are two parts to this effect: (1) the perception that the news slants coverage against one's favored in-group, and (2) a belief that because of the power of media, this coverage will lead the public to feel more antipathy toward one's side.

Ardent conservatives perceive that news harbors a liberal bias that, in their view, can push the audience in a more liberal direction. You hear this all the time when Fox News commentators bash what they presume to be a liberal news bias against their cause and derogate the mainstream media, calling it the "lamestream media," as Republican Sarah Palin famously did. However, research shows that the news does not show a predominately liberal Democratic bias, and can cover both parties negatively when events and candidate statements warrant such coverage (Schiffer, 2018; see Chapter 11). And conservatives don't consider the possibility the media could ever be critical of Democratic candidates; of course not, how could they?!

Strong liberals see an opposing reality, perceiving, for example, that news will push the public to dislike liberal, progressive perspectives. Liberals look at Fox News and proclaim, "See, they're bashing Joe Biden and still lauding Donald Trump, that shows how biased the media are." Yet while Fox News may have offered a pro-Trump perspective, this was not true of other news media outlets, which pointed to problems with Trump's leadership as president. And liberals never consider the possibility that news could also place conservatives in a bad light; of course not, how could they?!

Bias, alas, is in the eye of the partisan beholder. You can appreciate this, of course, but did you also notice that when people have strong partisan attitudes, they are predisposed to perceive that the news is *against* their political tribe? This exemplifies what psychologists call a contrast effect, where people contrast their views (say, pro-Biden) from what they "see" in the news (biased Fox reporters who dislike Democrats), frequently in the absence of evidence this is so (see Figure 9.2).

A hostile media effect occurs because partisans' strong attitude on the topic pushes them to see things primarily from the position of their favored in-group. They presume the media will apply different standards to their group than to their adversaries, fearing the media will hold their group to a higher standard.

**Figure 9.2 A fascinating aspect of partisan psychology is the tendency of people with strong views to perceive the media are biased—and against their side. Conservatives perceive the media are anti-conservative or anti-Republican. Liberal Democrats perceive the media as biased against liberals and anti-Democratic. Of course, just because people perceive news to be biased does not mean it actually is, or is biased in the way they perceive it.**

*Source*: https://commons.wikimedia.org/wiki/File:Anti-media_(48555557542).jpg

There is an insecurity here: People with strong views, sometimes acutely sensitive to the possibility the larger society will look askance at their viewpoint, project this onto media, presuming the Big Powerful Media will judge them negatively, while lauding their adversaries.

Nowadays, with increasing distrust of the news media, perceptions of hostile media biases have taken an interesting turn. People with more populist attitudes and those who tune into like-minded media outlets are particularly prone to believe the media are hostile to their side (Schulz, Wirth, & Müller, 2020; Barnidge et al., 2020; Tsfati, 2017).

Of course, people with strong attitudes look at media through thorn-covered glasses: They assume the "hostile media" excludes their preferred political groups. Conservatives condemn the media as hostile to their side, but they conveniently forget that Fox News, a super-popular conservative outlet, is part of the media. Liberals criticize the news as hostile to liberal viewpoints, but conveniently neglect to mention that one of those media outlets is the very liberal MSNBC. Both sides, relishing their own media outlets, can have tunnel vision when it comes to the media as a whole. They manage to perceive that their favorite self-selected media outlets are just fine—they report the facts!—but believe that the media system as a whole is biased against their group (see Barnidge et al., 2020, for intriguing results). This is the height of selective perception, presuming that media outlets that support your viewpoint are fair, but those that give credence to views other than your own are somehow biased.

Partisans' misperception that media are hostile to their side has another component. It frequently leads people to believe that this coverage will have large effects on the public, causing national public opinion to become negative to their side as well. News coverage may not actually have these effects, but partisans' beliefs that they will can further isolate and polarize them from equally patriotic citizens with different viewpoints. In today's media age, where many partisans get information from digital outlets that support their position, like-minded information can intensify the sense that the rest of society is not on their side, promoting defensiveness and resentment (Post, 2019; Kleinnijenhuis et al., 2020).

It's as if partisans think to themselves, "The mainstream media are hostile to what we think, we have to turn to our outlets to get the truth." Unfortunately, like-minded media channels (conservative outlets that attract primarily conservatives, liberal outlets that attract primarily liberals) can ignore or distort facts that contradict their side's viewpoint. This can make it difficult for people with strong views to fact-check their positions or even gain access to information that challenges their viewpoint. This fuels distrust and can lead extreme partisans to believe that the system is stacked against them ("The media keep saying this is true when our side knows it isn't. It's a conspiracy."). Yet, as political communication scholars Yariv Tsfati and Jonathan Cohen (2005) insightfully note: "Democracy requires institutional and social trust, and these are seriously challenged when one perceives a central democratic institution such as mass media as biased, imbalanced, and antagonistic" (2005, p. 44).

Hostile media biases, in concert with preferring party to principle, can have ominous implications for democracy. When a leader loses an election, persists in challenging the outcome, and gains the support of sycophantic legislators from his party, who dismiss news reports that provide evidence he legitimately lost as hostile media effects, the seeds are sown for the gradual erosion of democratic norms. And social media, by fueling anger, can make it worse, intensifying perceived media bias (Weeks et al., 2019) and magnifying polarization.

## SELECTIVE EXPOSURE

For Maggie Stoeffel, the day begins with Joe and Mika, sweetly squabbling about politics. (That's Joe Scarborough and Mika Brzezinski Scarborough, the married co-hosts of the MSNBC morning program, *Morning Joe*.) After dinner, Maggie loyally takes in the predictably progressive words of wisdom from Rachel (Maddow, of course). There's also the rest of the extended MSNBC family: the erudite Chris Hayes, Ari Melber, whose legal acumen and rap allusions viewers like, and—oh for sure—Nicolle Wallace, "a superstar," in Stoeffel's estimation, who gets added credibility points because she was George W. Bush's communications director before she saw the liberal light.

Such is the everyday life of "the MSNBC mom," as her daughter Kat Stoeffel, a Brooklyn writer, fondly calls her, one of a number of older liberal women who were deeply disenchanted with President Trump and sought "solace, companionship, and righteous indignation in cable news" (Stoeffel, 2018). For Maggie Stoeffel, MSNBC is the equivalent of Republicans' Fox News, a place where like-minded partisans gain affirmation and validation for their views of the political world. "You listen to someone say the things you feel in a more powerful, dramatic way," observed Sarah Sobieraj, who has studied media and political partisanship. Viewing liberal media programs from Rachel Maddow to the liberal podcast "Pod Save America" is like "going to a political church," Sobieraj said (Stoeffel, 2018).

Maggie Stoeffel and her dedicated compatriots on the left (and her counterparts on the right) exemplify a concept coined in the mid-20th century but that is alive and well today. It's selective exposure, a cousin of selective perception that focuses not on how people interpret like-minded content, but their preference for it. **Selective exposure** is the tendency of individuals to tune into and prefer information that supports their existing political beliefs. It occurs when liberals turn to *Morning Joe*, flip on MSNBC's Rachel Maddow's liberal evening program, or click onto the Daily Kos news site or Facebook posts that lambast Republicans. Selective exposure operates when conservatives gravitate to Fox News superstars Sean Hannity, Tucker Carlson, and Laura Ingraham, flip on Mark Levin's radio show, and click to conservative news sites like The Daily Caller.

It's typified by the divide around Fox News. Republicans have consistently placed more trust in Fox News than any other news outlet. Democrats distrust Fox more than any other news venue (Gramlich, 2020). In a dramatic illustration of selective exposure, Fox News claimed 45 percent of the television audience for the 2020 Republican National Convention, while the more liberal MSNBC accounted for 30 percent of the TV audience for the 2020 Democratic National Convention (Grynbaum, 2020). In our own lives, selective exposure occurs when we find ourselves reading more posts that agree with our positions on issues—immigration, animal research, abortion—than messages on the other side.

The concept dates back to the 1940s, when early political communication researchers found that political partisans were more likely to come across material that was consistent with their preexisting attitude than disputed their viewpoint (Lazarsfeld, Berelson, & Gaudet, 1944). According to classic social psychological ideas, people tune into politically congenial information because it is mentally comforting to read articles that confirm their attitudes. Reading articles on the opposite side of the issue provokes cognitive dissonance, an uncomfortable feeling that occurs when we come across information that conflicts with our attitudes. Dissonance is an unpleasant psychological state—it's not fun to hear someone disagree with a strong perspective we hold. One way to reduce dissonance that occurs when we learn others dispute our position is to locate articles and posts that affirm our preexisting viewpoint. Selective exposure offers the warm cocoon of social approval from others. Tuning into supportive material also is soothing because it is easier to process consistent than inconsistent information (Stroud, 2014).

Indeed, more is involved than cognitive dissonance, Miriam J. Metzger and her colleagues discovered. People may believe that communicators frequently quoted in news who share their political attitude are especially credible and reliable sources of information (Metzger, Hartsell, & Flanagin, 2020). Their trust of these like-minded sources may push them to follow what they say. It's a simpler, parsimonious twist on an old concept. And yet the perception that their side's sources are more credible than sources who are balanced or support the other side shows just how biased partisans can be.

Selective exposure is a feature of everyday life. We live in social worlds peopled by individuals who are like us. Americans tend to live near and talk to others who share their points of view (Bishop, 2008). Voters are more inclined to communicate with people who share their political attitudes than with their counterparts from the other side (Mutz, 2006). People are more apt to turn to blogs, talk radio, television news programs, and articles that support their political views than platforms that oppose their attitudes (Jamieson & Cappella, 2008; Feldman & Hart, 2018; Johnson, Bichard, & Zhang, 2009; Wicks, Wicks, & Morimoto, 2014; Skovsgaard, Shehata, & Strömbäck, 2016; Barfar, 2019).

Individuals share supportive content with others, spreading like-minded content across their networks of friends, and of course, following politically compatible commentators on Twitter (Aruguete & Calvo, 2018; Bou-Hamad & Yehya, 2020; Himelboim, Smith, & Shneiderman, 2013; Weeks et al., 2017). As Jurkowitz and Mitchell (2020a) note, partisans "get political news in a kind of media bubble"—and one that increasingly appeals not only to their politics, but also to their political and social identities (Lewis, Carlson, & Robinson, 2020).

## Complications

The collective evidence is pretty strong, but, scientifically, this does not definitively prove selective exposure. A correlation between partisan attitudes and seeking congenial information does not prove that your attitude causes you to seek out supportive political content. Perhaps Republicans listen to Sean Hannity's radio show because businesses that advertise on his program sell products that Republican entrepreneurs need to purchase. Maybe Democrats are drawn to NPR because NPR news stories furnish information about government that Democratic listeners, who may be public sector employees, need to perform their jobs effectively. Or maybe they both grew up with these networks as children and turn to them as a matter of habit. We need evidence from controlled experiments that show partisan political attitudes, rather than extraneous factors, cause people to prefer supportive information. And there is strong experimental evidence indicating partisans prefer like-minded political information.

Experiments show people gravitate to political content that supports their preexisting positions (Iyengar & Hahn, 2009; Knobloch-Westerwick & Meng, 2011; Westerwick, Johnson, & Knobloch-Westerwick, 2017). For example, in a controlled study with real-world overtones, Stroud (2011) gave research participants the opportunity to browse political magazines in a waiting room. To thank them for participation in the study, participants were told they could choose a free magazine subscription. True to selective exposure, conservatives and Republicans were more inclined to select subscriptions to politically conservative magazines, while liberals and Democrats were more likely to select subscriptions to liberal magazines. Living in echo chambers that reverberate with their political positions, partisans can feel even more strongly about their worldviews when they obtain information from congenial political media sources (Jamieson & Cappella, 2008; Stroud, 2010, 2011; Stroud & Muddiman, 2019). This in turn exacerbates polarization by inducing partisans to put more stock in news frames that spit back their view of the world, allowing them to feel more positively toward their political in-group and more negatively toward the out-group (Tsfati & Nir, 2017; Lu & Lee, 2019; Warner, 2018).

Of course, there are complications. Findings can depend on the particular method used in an experiment, for example, whether participants are required to view content they agree with or are permitted to choose between conge-nial or more disagreeable information (Arceneaux & Johnson, 2013; Stroud et al., 2019; Minchul & Yanqin, 2020). Individuals differ in how motivated they are to seek out news that sustains their worldview. People who enjoy think-ing and are skilled in cognitive reasoning are inclined to seek out supportive information that confirms their political viewpoint, because they are willing and able to engage in the mental effort needed to scrutinize different messages (Knobloch-Westerwick, Mothes, & Polavin, 2020). For individuals who enjoy thinking about issues, a credible communicator is particularly effective—not in getting them to change their views, but in reinforcing what they already think (Westerwick, Johnson, & Knobloch-Westerwick, 2017)! And although in the real world, people who have knee-jerk, simple views about issues also can grav-itate to media they like, Silvia Knobloch-Westerwick and her colleagues, who have done much intriguing work on selective exposure, offer a disconcerting caveat: "If advanced thinkers tend to fall victim to the confirmation bias when selecting political information, chances of balanced consideration and contem-plation on political issues in a democracy appear slim" (Knobloch-Westerwick et al., 2020, pp. 118–119).

## "Seek and You Will Find"

To make matters worse, a series of politically reinforcing spirals can ensue. People tune into like-minded political content, and the content propels them to feel even more strongly that their side is correct (Slater, 2015; Knobloch-West-erwick et al., 2015; Hutchens, Hmielowski, & Beam, 2019). Media exposure leads to strengthening of partisan beliefs, which leads to a preference for con-genial media, and renewed exposure in turn produces even stronger attitudes on the topic. It all resembles a spiraling curve that winds around the attitude, tight-ening the grip, producing a more polarized, less tolerant position on the issue.

Consider the contentious issue of global warming. Conservative news chan-nels such as Fox News tend to question evidence for global warming, while liberal news outlets such as MSNBC and CNN (along with most environmental scientists) treat it as a reality, caused by human beings. Lauren Feldman and her colleagues (2014) looked at media use and beliefs about global warming at two points in time: fall of 2008 and spring of 2011. In 2008, as selective exposure would predict, use of conservative media channels, such as Fox News and the late Rush Limbaugh's radio program, was associated with skepticism about global warming and lack of support for government policies to reduce global warming effects. Also, in line with selective exposure, use of more liberal media in 2008, such as MSNBC, CNN, and National Public Radio, was related to a belief in global warming and favoring government taking steps to reduce it. The researchers then re-interviewed survey respondents some 3 years later, asking them about their media use and global warming beliefs. Here is where the process gets interesting.

Use of conservative media in 2008 enhanced use of conservative media channels in 2011. Similarly, tuning into more liberal media in 2008 strengthened use of liberal media channels in 2011. Reliance on conservative and liberal media in turn contributed to stronger global warming beliefs in 2011, in line with partisan biases. Conservatives were more critical of global warming, liberals more convinced of its severity. It is a cyclical process: Use of like-minded media strengthens beliefs and causes you to gravitate to partisan media channels; consumption of the media then produces even stronger partisan beliefs. It is a closed system. A biblical "Ask and it will be given to you; seek and you will find" phenomenon seems to be occurring. But this creates a chamber of echoes, where people hear only their side and "may become more and more isolated on their own ideological islands in which certain facts are accepted while others are questioned and discarded." It therefore hampers "much-needed progress toward policy solutions to important problems such as global warming," Feldman and her colleagues observed (2014, p. 607).

It's not just global warming and not just the U.S. In a panel study conducted in Sweden, researchers Peter Dahlgren, Adam Shehata, and Jesper Strömbäck (2019) found evidence for these seek-and-you-shall-find reinforcing spirals. "People who seek-out left-wing news tend to develop a stronger left-wing ideological leaning over time, while the opposite occurs among those who seek-out right-wing news," they concluded (p. 170). And although users of one political side's news outlets did watch news from the other side (probably to criticize it), the findings were stronger in the online milieu than for good old-fashioned print (see also Pearson & Knobloch-Westerwick, 2019).

This has important implications for hot-button issues that political candidates prime online to rev up their base. Immigration opponents who focus on their identity as Americans are especially likely to seek out more anti-immigrant news stories, which increases their antipathy toward immigrants (Wojcieszak & Garrett, 2018). Pro-choice supporters tune into news sites that reinforce their beliefs, increasing their antipathy to the pro-life position. Watching news that supports preexisting attitudes also strengthens partisans' viewpoints by encouraging them to perceive that the public supports their view (Dvir-Gvirsman, Garrett, & Tsfati, 2018; Tsfati, Stroud, & Chotiner, 2014).

In a similar fashion, Republicans who were skeptical of dire warnings about the coronavirus that restricted their valued freedom of movement received supportive information from Fox. This probably made them more resistant to engaging in social distancing during the spring of 2020. Democrats, who tend to be more comfortable with social norms that recommended social distancing, gained their news from MSNBC and like-minded networks, which emphasized social distancing practices. This, in turn, reinforced their desire to practice social distancing. Partisan preferences drove people to friendly media, which strengthened their attitudes, magnifying Republican-Democrat differences in social distancing behavior (see Fleming-Wood, Margalit, & Schaffner, 2020; Heiss & Matthes, 2020; de Benedictis-Kessner et al., 2019).

Seek and ye shall find indeed.

## Selectivity in the Contemporary Media World: Tales of Complexity

How pervasive is selective exposure today? Are there conditions under which it is less likely to occur? These issues have sparked debate (Garrett, 2009a; Garrett et al., 2014; Holbert, Garrett, & Gleason, 2010). It's important to remember at the get-go that selective exposure is primarily a problem in democratic societies; in authoritarian countries, people have less freedom to be selective, though, even in Iran, selective exposure emerges (see Wojcieszak et al., 2019). With that caveat in mind, let's turn to the Western context.

First, it is important to note that while partisans can display preferences for opinion-congruent information (Stroud, 2014; Camaj, 2014), there is scant evidence that they *selectively avoid* opposing perspectives (Jang, 2014). In some instances, people seek out ideas from the other side (Garrett, 2009b; Garrett, Carnahan, & Lynch, 2013; Johnson & Kaye, 2013), particularly if they don't have strong political views (see Camaj, 2014; Edgerly, 2015). In many instances, people remain interested in a variety of perspectives, tuning into general-interest political media outlets for news and trusting balanced news sources (Weeks, Ksiazek, & Holbert, 2016; see also Metzger, Hartsell, & Flanagin, 2020).

When it comes to social media, the picture is more complicated. On the one hand, people come across plenty of non-supportive political ideas on their Facebook news feeds and social media environments (Manjoo, 2015; Barnidge et al., 2018; Messing & Westwood, 2014; Liang, 2014, 2018; Webster, 2014; Flaxman, Goel, & Rao, 2016). On the other hand, Facebook's algorithms are designed to determine content users liked in the past and offer up this information to them again and again. It's a profit-making model that helps build a big user base for social media advertisers. From a political viewpoint, the end result is feeding people back what they like, providing "a homogeneous information diet that lowers the chances of experiencing disagreement" (Krause et al., 2019, p. 67). Indeed, an intensive analysis of Facebook showed that selective exposure is the main determinant of information diffusion, promoting the development of politically homogeneous, polarized online communities (Del Vicario et al., 2016). For very partisan online reference groups, algorithms make it more likely that its members will like congenial items, even keeping this content at the top of the feed (Shmargad & Klar, 2020). So, selective exposure lives on social media and is even exacerbated by those emotionally charged comments that accompany news articles, polarizing people all the more (Asker & Dinas, 2019).

However, the bulk of the research suggests that selective exposure is most likely to emerge when people have strong political attitudes and are certain their attitudes are correct. Like political polarization, which is driven by partisans who increasingly dislike their counterparts from the other side (Lelkes, 2016), selective exposure to like-minded information is most frequently found among those with strong, passionate attitudes.

## A Fox News (and Partisan Media) Effect

Selectively tuning into platforms that reinforce their viewpoints, partisans can live in different "fact universes" (Fallows, 2016, p. 13), gaining access to social media that showcase "facts" they support and denigrating fact-checks that don't put their side in a positive light (Shin & Thorson, 2018; see also Garrett, Weeks, & Neo, 2016; Garrett, Long, & Jeong, 2019). A telling example is the way selective exposure to opinionated online sites undermines factually based political judgments.

We saw how this played out with the Trump impeachment back in 2019. It's old news now, but it was a white-hot political topic then, not only dividing Democrats and Republicans, but illustrating how selective exposure can offer a distorted view of the facts. A fascinating Pew Research Center study found that about two-thirds of Republican supporters who received their political news only from media outlets geared to primarily conservative audiences, such as Fox News, said Trump temporarily withheld U.S. aid to Ukraine to reduce corruption in the Ukraine (Jurkowitz & Mitchell, 2020b). This is what Trump claimed, as it offered a defensible reason why he held off on aid appropriated by Congress, in violation of the law. However, it isn't what the facts state.

Fact-checks show Trump did not raise corruption concerns in an all-important July 2019 phone call with the Ukrainian president, and instead, was consumed by digging up dirt on Joe Biden to help his reelection campaign (Qiu, 2019). Thus, by selectively tuning into Fox News that emphasized (sorry, Fox News viewers!) a misleading factual narrative, staunch Republicans bought into beliefs that conveniently fit what they wanted to believe about Trump.

This tendency has been dubbed the Fox News effect. It occurs when conservative viewers selectively tune into Fox News, can acquire information of questionable accuracy, and end up believing it. Intriguingly, 12 percent of Fox News viewers think that global warming is primarily caused by human activities compared with 62 percent of other Americans (Mahler & Rutenberg, 2019). During spring 2020, when the coronavirus outbreak reached pandemic proportions, substantially more Fox viewers than non-viewers thought the threat was generally exaggerated, a perception that flew in the face of medical evidence (Beauchamp & Animashaun, 2020).

At the same time, liberal viewers of MSNBC have selective exposure issues of their own. They could likely fall prey to an MSNBC News effect, just as liberal readers of a left-wing site such as Daily Kos could be susceptible to a Daily Kos effect. Exaggerations pushed by liberal online outlets, such as denying Trump any credit for improving the economy, could reinforce liberals' biased belief that Obama deserved all the credit for pre-coronavirus improvements in the economy. Liberally tilted Facebook posts also generated more incivility and anger in liberal partisans than conservatively slanted stories elicited from conservative partisans (Barfar, 2019). Strong liberals are especially likely to break off a friendship due to political differences (Mitchell et al., 2014). Liberals like to paint right-wing viewers as mad and outraged, but liberals get hot under the political collar too when opinions run counter to their views.

Egged on by social media algorithms and the blunt take-no-prisoners discourse on social networking sites, people are far more likely than would be ideal to disregard information they regard as factually untrue and to look askance at those with opposing views. And all this makes it more difficult to appreciate the demos in democracy, and the ways issues—immigration, climate change, and gun safety—have common, come-together implications for citizens and their leaders.

## IS POLARIZATION OVERBLOWN?

One of the themes of this book is Pascal's dictum that we need to appreciate multiple (even conflicting) perspectives to get a better handle on the truth. Here's the rub—actually, there are several. First, partisan polarization definitely occurs among the nation's leadership class—Democrats versus Republican legislators—but it is more complicated when it comes to the mass public. The virulent selective biases discussed in this chapter are found primarily among the staunchest partisans, those with ardent liberal or conservative attitudes.

This doesn't characterize the bulk of the American public, who actually show remarkable agreement on moderate reforms on issues ranging from immigration to gun safety (Fiorina, Abrams, & Pope, 2005; Page & Gilens, 2017). Political scientists point out that studies show that just between 15 to 20 percent of the American public is polarized.

"We are just not seeing the polarization among the masses that people imagine," said Sam Abrams, a public opinion scholar. "People who watch MSNBC and Fox are a loud but small minority. They are not representative of most Americans" (Tavernise & Cohn, 2019). More than one-third of the American public consider themselves moderate, and the number of Independents have increased in recent years (Wakin, 2019). While staunch, never-say-die Republicans and Democrats live in very different political universes, trusting sources their adversaries hate and distrusting sources their opponents love, the dichotomy is not as stark for moderates. While three-fourths of conservative Republicans trust Fox News, just over half of moderate Republicans do. Moderate and conservative Democrats are more than twice as likely as their liberal counterparts to trust Fox (Jurkowitz et al., 2020). In general, most people aren't political junkies and prefer entertainment to political media fare (Dvir-Gvirsman, Garrett, & Tsfati, 2018).

For all the evidence suggesting people cut off those who take a different viewpoint than their Facebook friends, other research points out this is limited to the staunchest partisans, whose loud, unrelenting voices "can ruin an otherwise enjoyable Thanksgiving celebration!" (Klar, Krupnikov, & Ryan, 2019). Samara Klar, Yanna Krupnikov, and John Barry Ryan acknowledge that weak partisans aren't overjoyed when an in-law from the opposing political party talks about political issues, but they're just as displeased when a son- or daughter-in-law from their *own* party persists in discussing politics! While about two in ten participants in a national survey said it was important for a married couple to be affiliated with the same political party, more than eight in ten said agreement in attitudes toward children was critical in a marriage (Klar, Krupnikov, & Ryan, 2019). The same percentage (over eight in ten respondents) said they're at least somewhat comfortable being neighbors or friends with individuals from the other party (Druckman & Levendusky, 2019). Moreover, selective avoidance is relatively unusual among weak partisans, or the majority of respondents to political surveys (Garrett, 2018; Song, Cho, & Benefield, 2020).

Now, don't get me wrong. Perceptual biases are real. Polarization has increased over the past decades, though its effects are probably most pronounced on the national level. We do perceive that media are hostilely biased against our side and assume others can be affected by this perceived bias. These biases are tenaciously held and can diminish democracy by reducing tolerance of facts that support the other side. But let's not project polarization and animus onto all voters, particularly those with a more mongrel, ambivalent, or indifferent outlook toward politics. Some of the widely held perception about problematic polarization stems from the fact that the polarized partisans receive the most coverage in media, which cultivates the belief that polarization is increasing, in turn pushing people to become more concerned about polarization in politics. The media love the polarization storyline because it feeds into conflict, juicy drama, and issues that can carve up loyal niches devoted to one tribe or another.

To some degree, polarization is a media effect, a belief cultivated by news stories that promote this narrative (Levendusky & Malhotra, 2016). Americans exaggerate the number of people who are strongly partisan, in part because they conjure up an unrepresentative picture of the angry Republican or Democrat featured in the news or on social media (Krupnikov & Ryan, 2020). And, as Shannon McGregor (2019) found, reporters can select highly partisan, angry posts trending on Facebook and Twitter to represent public opinion, offering up an inaccurate picture of a more nuanced American public. Unfortunately, if people perceive the country is more polarized than it actually is, they may become more cynical about democracy.

## CONCLUSIONS

Biases are frequently in the eye of the political beholder. People look at politics through the prisms of their political attitudes, leading to biased processing of candidate messages. When people have strong attitudes, they perceive messages selectively, not always fairly or even rationally. As examples like impeachment illustrate, and classic social psychological studies document, people reject credible evidence that is inconsistent with their worldviews, filter policy positions through their preferred political party, and mightily try to interpret messages so they confirm what they already think about politics. They are hardly open-minded, going along selectively, perhaps reflexively, with a policy endorsed by their favorite political party, even when the policy option is one they would ordinarily oppose.

We all have attitudes toward the media, but our biases become crystal-clear when news covers issues we feel passionate about. In these cases, individuals are psychologically constituted to presume the media are biased against their side, and to presume these perceived biases will cause the public to develop more antipathy toward their group. These hostile media biases are rooted in our political psychology, get egged on by like-minded online partisan media, and can propel us to conveniently ignore facts that don't fit our viewpoint, because THE MEDIA (not our favorite outlets, of course) have a distorted view of the issue.

There is considerable evidence that people are more likely to tune into information that supports their preexisting viewpoint, preferring ideologically congruent programs in mainstream and online media. But there are also complications. People don't necessarily go out of their way to avoid disconfirming information. There are personality differences in selective exposure, and strong attitudes play a particularly important role. People with the strongest partisan attitudes, a minority of the citizenry but influential in political discourse, are frequently most inclined to selectively tune into supportive information.

And, though it's rarely mentioned, partisanship can have beneficial features. Tuning into media outlets that reinforce your point of view energizes you, strengthens core beliefs, and propels you to get involved in political campaigns. In an engaging analysis, Natalie Jomini Stroud (2011) reported that "partisans using likeminded media are simply more active in politics. They seem to be motivated and energized by partisan media," she noted, adding that, "partisan media have a place in a democracy. They can unite likeminded individuals, help them to organize their political thinking and motivate them to participate" (pp. 176, 183; see also Wojcieszak et al., 2016; Hasell & Weeks, 2016; Arceneaux & Johnson, 2013).

If some degree of partisanship is healthy for politics, extreme doses are not. Fueled by digital algorithms that recommend supportive information, hostile media effects, and "seek-and-you-shall-find" politically reinforcing spirals, social media can promote ideological segregation, where people live in political worlds that reinforce what they already believe rather than challenging themselves with alternative viewpoints. Social media may not cause selective biases, but it enables and facilitates them (Settle, 2018).

Democracy, particularly the deliberative type, emphasizes an open-minded exploration of different perspectives through communication. Ideally, this involves a give-and-take persuasion, where citizens listen to different points of view. Unfortunately, political persuasion has become about talking points, preaching to the already converted. As Miller (2005) noted, "marshaling a cause to persuade those who start from a different perspective is a lost art. Honoring what's right in the other side's argument seems a superfluous thing that can only cause trouble, like an appendix." This kind of persuasion—which honors what is right in our adversary's arguments—sadly eludes us.

Of course, it doesn't have to. By encouraging a norm of open-mindedness, emphasizing that this is part of being a good citizen, the media can encourage people to attend more closely to both sides of the issue. But that is a tall order when people distrust their adversaries. A promising way to increase democratic tolerance is to harness the influence of the in-group, by having Democratic partisans encourage fellow Democrats to look at both sides of the issue, and Republicans to urge fellow Republicans to consider both viewpoints. There is actually some evidence this can reduce antipathy toward the other side, as well as polarization (Wojcieszak, Winter, & Yu, 2020). Another promising suggestion comes from a nifty 2017 study by Benjamin R. Warner and Astrid Villamil. They found that simply asking people to imagine conversing with a stranger from the opposing political party led partisans to feel less hostility toward adversaries from the other side, perhaps because they viewed them in more human, empathic terms rather than as "one of them." Another strategy is to encourage social media to algorithmically direct people to posts, ideally endorsed by members of their network, that offer cogent arguments for opposing political positions.

These suggestions would be difficult to put into practice though. And yet, as well-meaning partisans on both sides increasingly recognize, we need to band together to fight pressing problems that face us. In this light, these suggestions offer faint rays of hope. Here's one piece of evidence for that hope: During the height of the coronavirus crisis of spring 2020, as people experienced some of the same hardships, the proportion of Americans who felt they lived in a divided society dropped from 87 percent to 48 percent (Brooks, 2020). Let's hope, as vaccines become widespread and progress is made, that unity stands the test of time.

## REFERENCES

Arceneaux, K., & Johnson, M. (2013). *Changing minds or changing channels? Partisan news in an age of choice*. Chicago, IL: University of Chicago Press.

Aruguete, N., & Calvo, E. (2018). Time to #Protest: Selective exposure, cascading activation, and framing in social media. *Journal of Communication, 68*, 480–502.

Asker, D., & Dinas, E. (2019). Thinking fast and furious: Emotional intensity and opinion polarization in online media. *Public Opinion Quarterly, 83*, 487–509.

Barfar, A. (2019). Cognitive and affective responses to political disinformation in Facebook. *Computers in Human Behavior, 101*, 173–179.

Barnidge, M., Gunther, A.C., Kim, J., Hong, Y., Perryman, M., Tay, S.K., & Knisely, S. (2020). Politically motivated selective exposure and perceived media bias. *Communication Research, 47*, 82–103.

Barnidge, M., Huber, B., Gil de Zúñiga, H., & Liu, J.H. (2018). Social media as a sphere for "risky" political expression: A twenty-county multilevel comparative analysis. *The International Journal of Press/Politics, 23*, 161–182.

Beauchamp, Z., & Animashaun, C. (2020, March 27). New poll finds Fox News viewers think the coronavirus threat is exaggerated. *Vox*. Online: www.vox.com/policy-and-politics/2020/3/27/21195940/coronavirus-fox-news-poll-republicans-trump. (Accessed: May 15, 2020).

Bishop, B. (with R.G. Cushing). (2008). *The big sort: Why the clustering of like minded America is tearing us apart*. Boston: Houghton Mifflin.

Bou-Hamad, I., & Yehya, N.A. (2020). Partisan selective exposure in TV consumption patterns: A polarized developing country context. *Communication Research, 47*, 55–81.

Brooks, D. (2020, May 14). Ordinary people are leading the leaders. *The New York Times*. Online: www.nytimes.com/2020/05/14/opinion/coronavirus-us.html. (Accessed: May 15, 2020).

Camaj, L. (2014). Need for orientation, selective exposure, and attribute agenda-setting effects. *Mass Communication & Society, 17*, 689–712.

Casselman, B., & Tankersley, J. (2020, July 24). Would you go to a movie right now? Republicans say yes. Few others do. *The New York Times*. Online: www.nytimes.com/2020/07/24/business/economy/republicans-democrats-coronavirus-survey.html. (Accessed: November 28, 2020).

Chait, J. (2020, June 11). The still-vital case for liberalism in a radical age. *New York*. Online: https://nymag.com/intelligencer/2020/06/case-for-liberalism-tom-cotton-new-york-times-james-bennet.html. (Accessed: June 27, 2020).

Cohen, G.L. (2003). Party over policy: The dominating impact of group influence on political beliefs. *Journal of Personality and Social Psychology, 85*, 808–822.

Dahlgren, P.M., Shehata, A., & Strömbäck, J. (2019). Reinforcing spirals at work? Mutual influences between selective news exposure and ideological leaning. *European Journal of Communication, 34*, 159–174.

Davenport, C., & Landler, M. (2019, May 27). Trump administration hardens its attack on climate science. *The New York Times.* Online: www.nytimes.com/2019/05/27/us/politics/trump-climate-science.html. (Accessed: July 15, 2020).

de Benedictis-Kessner, J., Baum, M.A., Berinsky, A.J., & Yamamoto, T. (2019). Persuading the enemy: Estimating the persuasive effects of partisan media with the preference-incorporating choice and assignment design. *American Political Science Review, 113*, 902–916.

Del Vicario, M., Bessi, A., Zollo, F., Petroni, F., Scala, A., Caldarelli, G., Stanley, H.E., & Quattrociocchi, W. (2016). The spreading of misinformation online. *Proceedings of the National Academy of Sciences, 113*(3), 554–559.

Delli Carpini, M.X. (2020). When worlds collide: Contentious politics in a fragmented media regime. In D. Jackson, D.S. Coombs, F. Trevisan, D. Lilleker, & E. Thorsen (Eds.), *U.S. Election Analysis 2020: Media, voters and the campaign.* Online: www.electionanalysis.ws/us/president2020/section-4-news-and-journalism/when-worlds-collide-contentious-politics-in-a-fragmented-media-regime/. (Accessed: November 16, 2020).

Druckman, J.M., & Levendusky, M.S. (2019). What do we measure when we measure affective polarization? *Public Opinion Quarterly, 83*, 114–122.

Dvir-Gvirsman, S., Garrett, R.K., & Tsfati, Y. (2018). Why do partisan audiences participate? Perceived public opinion as the mediating mechanism. *Communication Research, 45*, 112–136.

Edgerly, S. (2015). Red media, blue media, and purple media: News repertoires in the colorful media landscape. *Journal of Broadcasting & Electronic Media, 59*, 1–21.

Ekins, E. (2020, July 22). Poll: 62% of Americans say they have political views they're afraid to share. *Cato Institute.* Online: www.cato.org/publications/survey-reports/poll-62-americans-say-they-have-political-views-theyre-afraid-share#_blank. (Accessed: July 24, 2020).

Fallows, J. (2016, September 11). Watch your rhetoric. *The New York Times* (Book Review), 13.

Feldman, L., & Hart, P.S. (2018). Broadening exposure to climate change news? How framing and political orientation interact to influence selective exposure. *Journal of Communication, 68*, 503–524.

Feldman, L., Myers, T.A., Hmielowski, J.D., & Leiserowitz, A. (2014). The mutual reinforcement of media selectivity and effects: Testing the reinforcing spirals framework in the context of global warming. *Journal of Communication, 64*, 590–611.

Fenton, N. (2019). (Dis)trust. *Journalism, 20*, 36–39.

Fiorina, M., Abrams, S.J., & Pope, J.C. (2005). *Culture war? The myth of a polarized America.* New York: Pearson, Longman.

Flaxman, S., Goel, S., & Rao, J.M. (2016). Filter bubbles, echo chambers, and online news consumption. *Public Opinion Quarterly, 80*, 298–320.

Fleming-Wood, B., Margalit, Y., & Schaffner, B. (2020, June 21). The emergent partisan gap in social distancing. *Data for Progress.* Online: www.dataforprogress.org/blog/2020/6/21/the-emergent-partisan-gap-in-social-distancing. (Accessed: June 27, 2020).

French, D. (2017, October 31). Mueller won't shake Trump's base. *The New York Times*, A23.

Garrett, R.K. (2009a). Politically motivated reinforcement seeking: Reframing the selective exposure debate. *Journal of Communication, 59*, 676–699.

Garrett, R.K. (2009b). Echo chambers online? Politically motivated selective exposure among Internet news users. *Journal of Computer-Mediated Communication, 14*, 265–285.

Garrett, R.K. (2018, March 6). Fake news is a symptom—not the cause—of Americans' growing reluctant to accept shared facts. *SSN Scholars Strategy Network: Key findings*. Online: https://scholars.org/sites/scholars/files/ssn_key_findings_garrett_on_misinformation-kg.pdf. (Accessed: March, 24, 2020).

Garrett, R.K., Carnahan, D., & Lynch, E.K. (2013). A turn toward avoidance? Selective exposure to online political information, 2004–2008. *Political Behavior, 35*, 113–134.

Garrett, R.K., Dvir-Gvirsman, S.D., Johnson, B.K., Tsfati, Y., Neo, R., & Dal, A. (2014). Implications of pro- and counterattitudinal information exposure for affective polarization. *Human Communication Research, 40*, 309–332.

Garrett, R.K., Long, J.A., & Jeong, M.S. (2019). New evidence on group polarization from partisan media to misperception: Affective polarization as mediator. *Journal of Communication, 69*, 490–512.

Garrett, R.K., Weeks, B.E., & Neo, R.L. (2016). Driving a wedge between evidence and beliefs: How online ideological news exposure promotes political misperceptions. *Journal of Computer-Mediated Communication, 21*, 331–348.

Gearhart, S., & Zhang, W. (2015). "Was it something I said?" "No, it was something you posted!" A study of the spiral of silence theory in social media contexts. *Cyberpsychology, Behavior, and Social Networking, 18*, 208–213.

Gebeloff, R. (2020, July 30). As Covid has become a red-state problem, too, have attitudes changed? *The New York Times*. Online: www.nytimes.com/2020/07/30/upshot/coronavirus-republican-voting.html. (Accessed: November 28, 2020).

Glynn, C.J., Hayes, A.F., & Shanahan, J. (1997). Perceived support for one's opinions and willingness to speak out: A meta-analysis of survey studies on the "spiral of silence". *Public Opinion Quarterly, 61*, 452–463.

Gramlich, J. (2020, April 8). *5 facts about Fox news*. Pew Research Center (FactTank: News in the Numbers). Online: www.pewresearch.org/fact-tank/2020/04/08/five-facts-about-fox-news/. (Accessed: May 15, 2020).

Grynbaum, M.M. (2020, August 28). TV ratings for Biden and Trump signal an increasingly polarized nation. *The New York Times*. Online: www.nytimes.com/2020/08/28/business/media/trump-biden-convention-ratings.html. (Accessed: August 30, 2020).

Hasell, A., & Weeks, B.E. (2016). Partisan provocation: The role of partisan news use and emotional responses in political information-sharing in social media. *Human Communication Research, 42*, 641–661.

Heiss, R., & Matthes, J. (2020). Stuck in a nativist spiral: Content, selection, and effects of right-wing populists' communication on Facebook. *Political Communication, 37*, 303–328.

Himelboim, I., Smith, M., & Shneiderman, B. (2013). Tweeting apart: Applying network analysis to detect selective exposure clusters in Twitter. *Communication Methods and Measures, 7*, 169–197.

Holbert, R.L., Garrett, R.K., & Gleason, L.S. (2010). A new era of minimal effects? A response to Bennett and Iyengar. *Journal of Communication, 60*, 15–34.

Hutchens, M.J., Hmielowski, J.D., & Beam, M.A. (2019). Reinforcing spirals of political discussion and affective polarization. *Communication Monographs, 86,* 357–376.

Ivory, D., Leatherby, L., & Gebeloff, R. (2021, April 17). Least vaccinated U.S. counties have something in common: Trump voters. *The New York Times.* Online: https://www.nytimes.com/interactive/2021/04/17/us/vaccine-hesitancy-politics.html. (Accessed: April 22, 2021).

Iyengar, S., & Hahn, K.S. (2009). Red media, blue media: Evidence of ideological sensitivity in media use. *Journal of Communication 59,* 19–39.

Jamieson, K.H., & Cappella, J.N. (2008). *Echo chamber: Rush Limbaugh and the conservative media establishment.* New York: Oxford University Press.

Jang, S.M. (2014). Challenges to selective exposure: Selective seeking and avoidance in multi-tasking media environment. *Mass Communication & Society, 17,* 665–688.

Johnson, T.J., Bichard, S.L., & Zhang, W. (2009). Communication communities or "cyberghettos"?: A path analysis model examining factors that explain selective exposure to blogs. *Journal of Computer-Mediated Communication, 15,* 60–82.

Johnson, T.J., & Kaye, B.K. (2013). The dark side of the boon? Credibility, selective exposure and the proliferation of online sources of political information. *Computers in Human Behavior, 29,* 1862–1871.

Jones, J.M., & Ritter, Z. (2018, January 17). *Americans see more news bias; most can't name neutral source.* Online: http://news.gallup.com/poll/225755/americans-news-bias-name-neutral-source. (Accessed: May 23, 2018).

Jurkowitz, M., & Mitchell, A. (2020a, March 4). *About one-fifth of Democrats and Republicans get political news in a kind of media bubble.* Pew Research Center (Journalism & Media). Online: www.journalism.org/2020/03/04/about-one-fifth-of-democrats-and-republicans-get-political-news-in-a-kind-of-media-bubble/. (Accessed: April 21, 2020).

Jurkowitz, M., & Mitchell, A. (2020b, January 24). *Views about Ukraine-impeachment story connect closely with where Americans get their news.* Pew Research Center (Journalism & Media). Online: www.journalism.org/2020/01/24/views-about-ukraine-impeachment-story-connect-closely-with-where-americans-get-their-news/. (Accessed: March 13, 2020).

Jurkowitz, M., Mitchell, A., Shearer, E., & Walker, M. (2020, January 24). *U.S. media polarization and the 2020 election: A nation divided.* Pew Research Center (Journalism & Media). Online: www.journalism.org/2020/01/24/u-s-media-polarization-and-the-2020-election-a-nation-divided/. (Accessed: April 22, 2020).

Kahan, D.M., Peters, E., Dawson, E.C., & Slovic, P. (2017). Motivated numeracy and enlightened self-government. *Behavioural Public Policy, 1,* 54–86.

Klar, S., Krupnikov, Y., & Ryan, J.B. (2019, April 12). Is America hopelessly polarized, or just allergic to politics? *The New York Times.* Online: www.nytimes.com/2019/04/12/opinion/polarization-politics-democrats-republicans.html. (Accessed: March 24, 2020).

Kleinnijenhuis, J.K., Hartmann, T., Tanis, M., & van Hoof, A.M.J. (2020). Hostile media perceptions of friendly media do reinforce partisanship. *Communication Research, 47,* 276–298.

Knobloch-Westerwick, S., & Meng, J. (2011). Reinforcement of the political self through selective exposure to political messages. *Journal of Communication, 61,* 349–368.

Knobloch-Westerwick, S., Mothes, C., Johnson, B.K., Westerwick, A., & Donsbach, W. (2015). Political online information searching in Germany and the United States: Confirmation bias, source credibility, and attitude impacts. *Journal of Communication, 65,* 489–511.

Knobloch-Westerwick, S., Mothes, C., & Polavin, N. (2020). Confirmation bias, ingroup bias, and negativity bias in selective exposure to political information. *Communication Research*, *47*, 104–124.

Krause, N.M., Wirz, C.D., Scheufele, D.A., & Xenos, M.A. (2019). Fake news: A news obsession with an old phenomenon? In J.E. Katz & K.K. Mays (Eds.), *Journalism & truth in an age of social media* (pp. 58–78). New York: Oxford University Press.

Krosnick, J.A., & Petty, R.E. (1995). Attitude strength: An overview. In R.E. Petty & J.A. Krosnick (Eds.), *Attitude strength: Antecedents and consequences* (pp. 1–24). Hillsdale, NJ: Lawrence Erlbaum Associates.

Krupnikov, Y., & Ryan, J.B. (2020, October 20). The real divide in America is between political junkies and everyone else. *The New York Times*. Online: www.nytimes.com/2020/10/20/opinion/polarization-politics-americans.html. (Accessed: October 27, 2020).

Lazarsfeld, P.F., Berelson, B., & Gaudet, H. (1944). *The people's choice: How the voter makes up his mind in a presidential campaign*. New York: Columbia University Press.

Lelkes, Y. (2016). Mass polarization: Manifestations and measurements. *Public Opinion Quarterly*, *80*, 392–410.

Levendusky, M.S., & Malhotra, N. (2016). (Mis)perceptions of partisan polarization in the American public. *Public Opinion Quarterly*, *80*, 378–391.

Lewis, S.C. (2019). Lack of trust in the news media, institutional weakness, and relational journalism as a potential way forward. *Journalism*, *20*, 44–47.

Lewis, S.C., Carlson, M., & Robinson, S. (2020). When journalism's relevance is also on the ballot. In D. Jackson, D.S. Coombs, F. Trevisan, D. Lilleker, & E. Thorsen (Eds.), *U.S. election analysis 2020: Media, voters and the campaign*. Online: www.electionanalysis.ws/us/president2020/section-4-news-and-journalism/when-journalisms-relevance-is-also-on-the-ballot/. (Accessed: November 18, 2020).

Liang, H. (2014). The organizational principles of online political discussion: A relational event stream model for analysis of Web Forum deliberation. *Human Communication Research*, *40*, 483–507.

Liang, H. (2018). Broadcast versus viral spreading: The structure of diffusion cascades and selective sharing on social media. *Journal of Communication*, *68*, 525–546.

Lord, C.G., Ross, L., & Lepper, M.R. (1979). Biased assimilation and attitude polarization: The effects of prior theories on subsequently considered evidence. *Journal of Personality and Social Psychology*, *37*, 2098–2109.

Lu, Y., & Lee, J.K. (2019). Partisan information sources and affective polarization: Panel analysis of the mediating role of anger and fear. *Journalism & Mass Communication Quarterly*, *96*, 767–783.

Mahler, J., & Rutenberg, J. (2019, April 3). Part 3: The new Fox weapon. *The New York Times Magazine*. Online: www.nytimes.com/interactive/2019/04/03/magazine/new-fox-corporation-disney-deal.html. (Accessed: May 15, 2020).

Mahmood, O. (2014, November 19). Do the left thing. *The Michigan Review*. Online: www.michiganreview.com/do-the-left-thing/. (Accessed: June 27, 2020).

Manjoo, F. (2015, May 8). Facebook finds opposing views trickle through. *The New York Times*, A1, B7.

Matthes, J., Knoll, J., & von Sikorski, C. (2018). The "spiral of silence" revisited: A meta-analysis on the relationship between perceptions of opinion support and political opinion expression. *Communication Research*, *45*, 3–33.

McGregor, S.C. (2019). Social media as public opinion: How journalists use social media to represent public opinion. *Journalism*, *20*, 1070–1086.

Mervosh, S., Bogel-Burroughs, N., Swales, V., Smith, M., Hassan, A., Rojas, R., Taylor, K., & Del Real, J.A. (2020, January 22). We asked 81 Americans about impeachment. Here's what they had to say. *The New York Times*. Online: www.nytimes.com/interactive/2020/01/22/us/impeachment-voters.html. (Accessed: March 9, 2020).

Messing, S., & Westwood, S.J. (2014). Selective exposure in the age of social media: Endorsements trump partisan source affiliation when selecting news online. *Communication Research, 41*, 1042–1063.

Metzger, M.J., Hartsell, E.H., & Flanagin, A.J. (2020). Cognitive dissonance or credibility? A comparison of two theoretical explanations for selective exposure to partisan news. *Communication Research, 47*, 3–28.

Mill, J.S. (1859/2009). *On liberty and other essays*. New York: Kaplan Publishing.

Miller, M. (2005. June 4). Is persuasion dead? *The New York Times*. Online: www.nytimes.com/2005/06/04/opinion/is-persuasion-dead.html. (Accessed: November 30, 2020).

Minchul, K., & Yanqin, L. (2020). Testing partisan selective exposure in a multidimensional choice context: Evidence from a conjoint experiment. *Mass Communication & Society, 23*, 107–127.

Mitchell, A., Gottfried, J., Kiley, J., & Matsa, K.E. (2014, October 21). *Political polarization and media habits*. Pew Research Center (Journalism & Media). Online: www.journalism.org/2014/10/21/political-polarization-media-habits/. (Accessed: November 30, 2020).

Moy, P. (2020). The promise and perils of voice. *Journal of Communication, 70*, 1–12.

Mutz, D.C. (2006). *Hearing the other side: Deliberative versus participatory democracy*. Cambridge, UK: Cambridge University Press.

Neubaum, G., & Krämer, N.C. (2018). What do we fear? Expected sanctions for expressing minority opinions in offline and online communication. *Communication Research, 45*, 139–164.

Noelle-Neumann, E. (1974). The spiral of silence a theory of public opinion. *Journal of Communication, 24*, 43–51.

Page, B.I., & Gilens, M. (2017). *Democracy in America? What has gone wrong and what we can do about it*. Chicago, IL: University of Chicago Press.

Pearson, G.D.H., & Knobloch-Westerwick, S. (2019). Is the confirmation bias bubble larger online? Pre-election confirmation bias in selective exposure to online versus print information. *Mass Communication & Society, 22*, 466–486.

Perloff, R.M. (2015). A three-decade retrospective on the hostile media effect. *Mass Communication and Society, 18*, 701–729.

Post, S. (2019). Polarizing communication as media effects on antagonists. Understanding communication in conflicts in digital media societies. *Communication Theory, 29*, 213–235.

Qiu, L. (2019, November 22). Trump's long list of inaccurate statements on "Fox & Friends". *The New York Times*. Online: www.nytimes.com/2019/11/22/us/politics/trump-fox-and-friends-fact-check.html. (Accessed: March 13, 2020).

Santhanam, L. (2021, January 8). Most Americans blame Trump for Capitol attack but are split on his removal. *PBS NewsHour*. Online: www.pbs.org/newshour/politics/most-americans-blame-trump-for-capitol-attack-but-are-split-on-his-removal. (Accessed: January 10, 2021).

Scheufele, D., & Moy, P. (2000). Twenty-five years of the spiral of silence: A conceptual review and empirical outlook. *International Journal of Public Opinion Research, 12*, 3–28.

Schiffer, A.J. (2018). *Evaluating media bias*. Lanham, MD: Rowman & Littlefield.

Schulz, A., Wirth, W., & Müller, P. (2020). We are the people and you are fake news: A social identify approach to populist citizens' false consensus and hostile media perceptions. *Communication Research, 47*, 201–226.

Settle, J.E. (2018). *Frenemies: How social media polarizes America*. Cambridge, UK: Cambridge University Press.

Shin, J., & Thorson, K. (2018). Partisan selective sharing: The biased diffusion of fact-checking messages on social media. *Journal of Communication, 67*, 233–255.

Shmargad, Y., & Klar, S. (2020). Sorting the news: How ranking by popularity polarizes our politics. *Political Communication, 37*, 423–446.

Skovsgaard, M., Shehata, A., & Strömbäck, J. (2016). Opportunity structures for selective exposure: Investigating selective exposure and learning in Swedish election campaigns using panel survey data. *The International Journal of Press/Politics, 21*, 527–546.

Slater, M.D. (2015). Reinforcing spirals model: Conceptualizing the relationship between media content exposure and the development and maintenance of attitudes. *Media Psychology, 18*, 370–395.

Song, H., Cho, J., & Benefield, G.A. (2020). The dynamics of message selection in online political discussion forums: Self-segregation or diverse exposure? *Communication Research, 47*, 125–152.

Stoeffel, K. (2018, June 8). The age of the MSNBC mom. *The New York Times* (Sunday Review). Online: www.nytimes.com/2018/06/08/opinion/sunday/msnbc-cable-news-viewers-moms.html. (Accessed: March 14, 2020).

Stroud, N.J. (2010). Polarization and partisan selective exposure. *Journal of Communication, 60*, 556–576.

Stroud, N.J. (2011). *Niche news: The politics of news choice*. New York: Oxford University Press.

Stroud, N.J. (2014). Selective exposure theories. In K. Kenski & K.H. Jamieson (Eds.), *The Oxford handbook of political communication*. New York: Oxford University Press. Online: www.oxfordhandbooks.com.

Stroud, N.J., Feldman, L., Wojcieszak, M., & Bimber, B. (2019). The consequences of forced versus selected political media exposure. *Human Communication Research, 45*, 27–51.

Stroud, N.J., & Muddiman, A. (2019). The American media system today: Is the public fragmenting? In T. RIdout (Ed.), *New directions in media and politics* (2nd ed., pp. 7–28). New York: Routledge.

Tavernise, S., & Cohn, N. (2019, September 24). The America that isn't polarized. *The New York Times*. Online: www.nytimes.com/2019/09/24/upshot/many-americans-not-polarized.html. (Accessed: March 24, 2020).

Tsfati, Y. (2007). Hostile media perceptions, presumed media influence, and minority alienation: The case of Arabs in Israel. *Journal of Communication, 57*, 632–651.

Tsfati, Y. (2017). Attitudes toward media, perceived media influence and changes in voting intentions in the 2015 Israeli elections. In M. Shamir & G. Rahat (Eds.), *The elections in Israel: 2015* (pp. 225–251). New Brunswick, NJ: Transaction Press.

Tsfati, Y., & Cohen, J. (2005). Democratic consequences of hostile media perceptions: The case of Gaza settlers. *The International Journal of Press/Politics, 10*, 28–51.

Tsfati, Y., & Nir, L. (2017). Frames and reasoning: Two pathways from selective exposure to affective polarization. *International Journal of Communication, 11*, 301–322.

Tsfati, Y., Stroud, N.J., & Chotiner, A. (2014). Exposure to ideological news and perceived opinion climate: Testing the media effects component of spiral-of-silence in a fragmented media landscape. *The International Journal of Press/Politics, 19*, 3–23.

Vallone, R.P., Ross, L., & Lepper, M.R. (1985). The hostile media phenomenon: Biased perception and perceptions of media bias in coverage of the Beirut massacre. *Journal of Personality and Social Psychology, 49*, 577–585.

Van Boven, L., Ehret, P.J, & Sherman, D.K. (2018). Psychological barriers to bipartisan public support for climate policy. *Perspectives on Psychological Science, 13*, 492–507.

Van Boven, L., & Sherman, D. (2018, July 29). Polarizing climate policy. *The New York Times* (Sunday Review), 2.

Wakin, E. (2019, January 6). Getting along. *The New York Times Book Review*, 10.

Warner, B.R. (2018). Modeling partisan media effects in the 2014 U.S. midterm elections. *Journalism & Mass Communication Quarterly, 95*, 647–669.

Warner, B.R., & Villamil, A. (2017). A test of imagined contact as means to improve cross-partisan feelings and reduce attribution of malevolence and acceptance of political violence. *Communication Monographs, 84*, 447–465.

Webster, J.G. (2014). *The marketplace of attention: How audiences take shape in a digital age*. Cambridge, MA: MIT Press.

Weeks, B.E., Kim, D.H., Hahn, L.B., Diehl, T.H., & Kwak, N. (2019). Hostile media perceptions in the age of social media: Following politicians, emotions, and perceptions of media bias. *Journal of Broadcasting & Electronic Media, 63*, 374–392.

Weeks, B.E., Ksiazek, T.B., & Holbert, R.L. (2016). Partisan enclaves or shared media experiences? A network approach to understanding citizens' political news environments. *Journal of Broadcasting & Electronic Media, 60*, 248–268.

Weeks, B.E., Lane, D.S., Kim, D.H., Lee, S.S., & Kwak, N. (2017). Incidental exposure, selective exposure, and political information sharing: Integrating online exposure patterns and expression on social media. *Journal of Computer-Mediated Communication 22*, 363–379.

Westerwick, A., Johnson, B.K., & Knobloch-Westerwick, S. (2017). Confirmation biases in selective exposure to political online information: Source bias vs. content bias. *Communication Monographs, 84*, 343–364.

Wicks, R.H., Wicks, J.L., & Morimoto, S.A. (2014). Partisan selective exposure during the 2012 presidential election. *American Behavioral Scientist, 58*, 1131–1143.

Wojcieszak, M., Bimber, B., Feldman, L., & Stroud, N.J. (2016). Partisan news and political participation: Exploring mediated relationships. *Political Communication, 33*, 241–260.

Wojcieszak, M., & Garrett, R.K. (2018). Social identity, selective exposure, and affective polarization: How priming national identity shapes attitudes toward immigrants via news selection. *Human Communication Research, 44*, 247–273.

Wojcieszak, M., Nisbet, E.C., Kremer, L., Behrouzian, G., & Glynn, C.J. (2019). What drives media use in authoritarian regimes? Extending selective exposure theory to Iran. *The International Journal of Press/Politics, 24*, 69–91.

Wojcieszak, M., Winter, S., & Yu, X. (2020). Social norms and selectivity: Effects of norms of open-mindedness on content selection and affective polarization. *Mass Communication and Society*. DOI: 10.1080/15205436.2020.1714663.

# PART THREE

# Communication and the Presidential Election Campaign

# 10 Presidential Rhetoric From Television to Tweeting

This much is obvious: Presidential election campaigns play a critical role in contemporary democracy. "Elections are arguably the single most important event in American democratic life," observed political scientist James A. Thurber. Elections, he explained, provide "an opportunity for Americans to both give their consent to be governed and to hold their representatives accountable for past performance" (Thurber, 2000, p. 1). In a similar fashion, Paolo Mancini and David Swanson (1996) noted that election campaigns

> select decision makers, shape policy, distribute power, and provide venues for debate and socially approved expressions of conflict. . . . Symbolically, campaigns legitimate democratic government and political leaders, uniting voters and candidates in displays of civic piety and rituals of national renewal.
>
> (p. 1)

These are also popular myths. In reality, elections are bruising, polarizing, and can increase cynicism about politics. Candidates try to manipulate the rules. Losers and their supporters can become embittered, and citizens feel frustrated by the lack of serious issue discussion. Presidential elections fail to engage millions of Americans: more than four in ten eligible voters typically choose not to vote in recent presidential elections. No surprise: They're vicious, no-holds-barred events that are dominated by two old-hat political parties, feature superficial debates, rarely spur meaningful change, and depend on cash infusions supplied by the very rich. And yet, they're all we have. Warts and all, elections remain the centerpiece of democracy, the best way for the demos—the populace—to select their government. And if we want to figure out ways to make elections more responsive to citizens, we have to understand what makes them tick.

Democracies, of course, cannot function without voters or, more broadly, citizens. But they certainly cannot operate without leaders—frequently maligned, impossibly human, and indispensable for democracy. Running for the presidency requires remarkable (perhaps abnormal) ambition, ego, vision, political acumen, willingness to sacrifice means to ends, and determination to make a difference in people's lives (Cramer, 1992; Stone, 2010). More complexly, politics requires a unique capacity to fuse extremities: selfish and selfless, practical and principled, sincere and strategic. To be a political candidate, observed Michael Ignatieff, a Canadian academic who entered politics, becoming leader of Canada's Liberal Party, is to be "worldly and sinful and yet faithful and fearless at the same time. You put your own immodest ambitions in the service of others. You hope that your ambitions will be redeemed by the good you do" (Brooks, 2014). But that good requires getting one's hands soiled and impure by running for election, "a noble struggle" (Ignatieff, 2013, p. 177).

From a communication perspective, it involves an ability to craft words in ways that elevate and inspire (Ellithorpe, Huang, & Oliver, 2019). It requires the ability to persuade and, calling on a term that dates back to antiquity, to harness rhetoric. Rhetoric is concerned with the symbols leaders use to persuade, the arguments in their political messages, and the verbal style in which talks and tweets are delivered. Scholars call the president "the symbolic embodiment of the nation" (Euchner, 1990, p. 120), emphasizing that presidential authority is meaningless unless presidents can convince the citizenry of the wisdom of their directives (Hart, 1984). Ours is a "rhetorical presidency" (Tulis, 1987), in which "deeds (are) done in words" (Campbell & Jamieson, 1990). It has also been a male presidency, as most members of Congress, state legislatures, and mayors of large U.S. cities are men (Lawless & Fox, 2012).

This chapter examines these and other communication underpinnings of what Ignatieff (idealistically perhaps) called the noble struggle of politics. It introduces the presidential election campaign, the focus of the next section of the book. Although we take campaigns for granted today, they were not part of the political landscape for the early years of the republic, a time when candidates eschewed public appearances. It was not until the late 19th century that campaigns began in earnest, and they took on the visual mass media trappings of today in the 1960 election, the starting point for our historical review. It is important to appreciate historical foundations of the present era. By apprehending the past, we more keenly understand that what seems new and disturbing is not so new (and therefore perhaps less disconcerting). We also gain keener insights into exactly which facets of contemporary election campaigns are unique. The first portion of the chapter discusses the rhetoric of major recent presidents, beginning with Kennedy and ending with Obama. The second part of the chapter, focusing on the contemporary presidential campaign, offers a critical review of Trump's presidential rhetoric. It includes a boxed section on political marketing. A final section offers perspectives on political rhetoric in a digital age.

## TELEVISION AND PRESIDENTIAL CAMPAIGNS: THE EMERGENCE OF IMAGE

### JFK

John F. Kennedy placed television on the political campaign map. He exploited its focus on images to strategic advantage, harnessing his physical attractiveness and visual acuity in the 1960 presidential debates. Kennedy also brought scientific opinion polling into the presidential campaign, using the polling expertise of Lou Harris to sculpt his image, soon to be a byword in presidential politics. Kennedy turned the press conference into a political art form, calling on a comedian's talent for using nonverbal expressions to make his point and a showman's ability to deflect a question to his tactical advantage, while cleverly avoiding reporters' questions (see Figure 10.1). The foreign policy demands facing Kennedy were intense, and he could spin information deceptively, as during the Bay of Pigs Cuban invasion fiasco, and thoughtfully, during his finest hour, averting nuclear war during the 1962 Cuban Missile Crisis.

During the 1960s, actually beginning in the late 1950s, concerns about elites' ability to manipulate symbols via television took on histrionic proportions. Critics speculated, in claims based more on Freudian fears than on empirical evidence,

**Figure 10.1  John F. Kennedy, who recognized the ability of television to project an image, used the small screen to project an impression many Americans found congenial.**

*Source*: www.gettyimages.com/detail/news-photo/view-of-a-television-screen-showing-the-nixon-kennedy-news-photo/451373957

that subliminal sexual images in advertising seduced the America public into buying products. Vance Packard (1957) worried, in *The Hidden Persuaders*, that "symbol manipulators" could sell politicians like soap. Daniel J. Boorstin (1964) warned of the ability of politicians to stage **pseudo-events**, or artificial events contrived to gain media coverage. Harking back to Plato's allegory of the cave, where prisoners believed that shadows projected on the wall of a cave were real, Boorstin challenged the widespread belief that political content on television was in some sense "real," arguing instead that political communications were frequently contrived, focused more on candidate make-up, lighting, and stagecraft, creating spectacles that an unsuspecting public perceived as authentic. Boorstin's book, aptly titled *The Image* and echoing Lippmann's (1922) concerns about the susceptibility of the mass public, had far-reaching effects on influential intellectuals (Greenberg, 2016). It presaged postmodern thinkers' concerns about a faux reality and comported with political communication scholarship, demonstrating that perceptions of media impact have strong effects, independent of any actual influences media exerted. And while Boorstin exaggerated the impact of pseudo-events on attitudes, he astutely highlighted the new reality of manipulating perceptions via the small television screen and the ways that political artifice had seamlessly become part of American political culture.

If Kennedy thrived on the image, Richard Nixon flailed with it, at first (in one sense admirably) opting to reject imagery by deciding not to wear makeup in the first 1960 presidential debate, yet reluctantly embracing image-making 8 years later, recognizing he needed to massage his own awkward visual appearances to persuade the American electorate that there was, as the expression went, a new Nixon. Fearing the press would disparage him as president, he felt his only recourse as president was to seize control, take matters into his own hands, and create the White House Office of Communications, which provided a centralized role for White House attempts at news management. Nixon made polling a centerpiece of his governing strategy, going so far as to manufacture supportive opinion poll findings and fabricate calls to news organizations, trying to make it appear like large numbers of ordinary citizens disapproved of what he saw as stridently negative media coverage of the presidency (Perloff, 1998). He harnessed the law-and-order slogan, positioning himself as the leader who would use the law to quell America's civic unrest. Law-and-order became a metaphorical dog whistle with racial overtones that suggested he would bring order to the "city jungle," a coded message that appealed to White voters and would be invoked by subsequent presidents, from George H.W. Bush to Donald Trump (Nunberg, 2016). Nixon, like the presidents who followed him, was preoccupied with his political popularity, perhaps to compensate for his indifference to appearances in the 1960 campaign.

Nixon's exploitation of image metastasized into the massive public cover-up of his aides' bugging the Democratic headquarters at the Watergate Hotel in 1972, in what he viewed as a mere public relations problem that could be solved with effective PR. "Craving positive news coverage was nothing new. But Nixon was unique in allowing that desire to spill over into rampant illegality," Greenberg observed (p. 400).

## Mastering the Art of Media Image-Making

The detritus of Nixon's presidency surely was cynicism about the truthfulness of presidential communication. With the public arguably frustrated with exploitation of media imagery for unethical ends, the pendulum turned. Images weren't out—they were necessary to govern—but the "anti-image image" became the byword during Jimmy Carter's presidency, as he wore cardigan sweaters rather than suits, and projected honesty, promising "I'll never tell a lie" in the fashion of John Boy Walton (the oh-so-genuine character in the eponymous 1970s drama). But, of course, presidents must massage the truth to some degree (the intent and degree to which they do this determining the ethics of their actions). Carter, beset by double-digit inflation, seizure of hostages in Iran, and a changing global scene, did not always level with the public to the degree he promised, and events, his management of them, and questions about his leadership led to his defeat in 1980 at the hands of the first presidential candidate who had honed his pre-presidential image as an actor and TV show host in the entertainment media.

Ronald Reagan was that president. If John F. Kennedy introduced television to the presidency, Ronald Reagan consummated the marriage. Dubbed the great communicator because he understood the grammar and syntax of the medium (conveying core emotions such as anger and reassurance convincingly on television with his nonverbal expressions), Reagan dismantled barriers of technology, speaking to Americans as if he was a close friend, creating "the illusion of eye contact with an unseen audience" (Jamieson, 1988, p. 132; Lanzetta et al., 1985; see Figure 10.2). Much as other presidents used the technology of their times to display leadership—Lincoln with the stump speech, FDR with radio—Reagan mastered the grammar of television, all while perpetrating the minor deception that the speechwriter's words he spoke were his own. He spoke plainly and optimistically, using words that would come off schmaltzy in other communicators, accessing the national heritage of proud patriotic experiences, and telling heroic stories about ordinary Americans. Consider the following speech excerpt, typical of Reagan:

> We have every right to dream heroic dreams. Those who say that we're in a time when there are no heroes, they just don't know where to look. You can see heroes every day going in and out of factory gates. . . . Their patriotism is deep. Their values sustain our national life.
>
> (Hart, 1984, p. 228)

**Figure 10.2 Ronald Reagan, with an actor's understanding of the grammar of television, conveyed compelling narratives that conjoined visuals with patriotic themes. He elevated visual image-making to an art, though the images were not always in sync with hard-fact economic realities America experienced during the 1980s (see Hertsgaard, 1988).**

Reagan's rhetoric, while rhetorically appealing and visually evocative, showcased his biases. Reagan perpetrated race-baited untruths about "a 'young buck' chiseling welfare and a wealthy Chicago 'welfare queen' tooling around in her Cadillac" (Baker, 2016, p. 7). Yet Reagan also used his rhetoric to unify Americans around common themes, build an optimistic ethos, and sow the seeds for the Soviet Union's demise.

Reagan's advisers honed the art of news management to a near-science, it sometimes seemed, bringing into the popular lexicon terms like photo op (a staged opportunity for a televised visual), soundbite (the ever-shorter summaries politicians spoke to conform to TV news constraints), and the line of the day (the major theme the White House would emphasize to the press on a given day to coalesce news coverage around one issue (Maltese, 1994). His communication strategies invited questions of whether lofty rhetoric invoked by presidents from Lincoln to Roosevelt had devolved in an age of simplified visual images—or whether the use of emotion-packed visuals exquisitely matched the communicative requirements of the times. Did Reagan deliver effective leadership, appropriately adapted to a television age, or had he substituted style for substance, offering simplified visual speechifying at the expense of thoughtful policy rhetoric?

By 1992, when Democrat Bill Clinton ran for office, it was a taken-for-granted precept that cable news had inaugurated a 24/7 news cycle and candidates needed a "war room" to craft strategy, prepare messages, and instantly respond to opposition attacks. Clinton masterfully—but dishonestly—navigated the storm of controversy emerging from charges of marital infidelity, appearing with his wife on *60 Minutes* to acknowledge, in the manner of the *Thirtysomething* TV show, that they did not have a perfect marriage, but cared deeply for one another, as he spun the story to suggest these were private, not public, matters.

In his 1992 presidential election campaign, Clinton marketed himself as a hipper, more compassionate alternative to President George H.W. Bush. Bush was, in Democrats' eyes, so out of touch he did not know what a supermarket scanner was and artlessly looked at his watch during a presidential debate. By contrast, Clinton played the saxophone on Arsenio Hall's late-night talk show, highlighting his familiarity with both contemporary music and media. During his first 2 years in office, Clinton conducted 82 talk radio interviews and invited radio talk show hosts to the White House in 1993 to promote his health care plan (Kurtz, 1996). But a multi-million-dollar advertising campaign financed by the Health Care Insurance Association of America successfully—if deceptively—reframed his health plan as federal government socialized health care. Lobbying groups, noting that Hillary Clinton was coordinating White House health reform, ridiculed her in spooky ads that mocked an old medical television show, *Dr. Kildare*. The narrator intoned, "She's a doctor with a prescription for disaster. She's Hillary Clinton and she's Doctor Hilldare" (Perloff, 1998, p. 251). Strategic political marketing, harnessed by wealthy groups, helped defeat a sensible, if complicated, health care plan. It would take the nation more than 15 years to achieve modest health care reform.

Clinton, like presidents who preceded and followed him, plainly stood for certain principles, notably harnessing smaller government and centrist leadership positions to help downtrodden Americans. He accomplished a number of his presidential goals. Yet, preoccupied with public image, he employed a variety of pollsters, who were skilled at quantifying presidential public opinion, relying on them to test-market ideas, roll out policy initiatives, and help craft messages on a variety of issues, including his notorious affair de la coeur with Monica Lewinsky, which cycled endlessly on television news, talk shows, and the new scandal-ridden Internet websites. He trifled with truth, saying he had not had "sexual relations with that woman, Miss Lewinsky," which was technically true since they had not engaged in intercourse, but in the moral universe, was an example of sexualized political spin.

Meanwhile, Republican legislators, outraged over Clinton's infidelity and lying under oath, sought his impeachment, keeping the story in the news, with journalists all too happy to cover the titillating tale, guaranteed to boost ratings. It was a battle of frames: Republicans hyping the sexual licentiousness of the president of the United States, Democrats emphasizing that the president's mistake was a private foible that did not bear on his public role as chief executive. Both sides spun the truth to their advantage. In the end, Congress acquitted Clinton narrowly, mirroring public opinion, which viewed Republican efforts as overreach. Public opinion, as measured by polls, constituted a democratic counterweight to the opposition party's efforts to excoriate Clinton, indicating, regardless of one's views of Clinton's behavior, that democratic processes informed policy decisions at the highest levels.

Three years later, the Clinton-Lewinsky saga, a national crisis at the time, was placed in larger perspective when the country was attacked on September 11, 2001. George W. Bush was president, having defeated Al Gore in a razor-thin electoral result ultimately decided by the Supreme Court. After some rhetorical success framing the war on terrorism in terms of good and evil, while being careful to separate Muslim Americans from terrorist acts committed in the name of Islam, Bush embarked on his controversial selling of a war against Iraq, arguing that Iraqi president Saddam Hussein possessed weapons of mass destruction. In a full-court press that called to mind Woodrow Wilson's propaganda-laced initiative launching American participation in World War I, the Bush administration engaged in a host of strategies, from leaking stories to public pronouncements, all spinning the false assertion that Saddam Hussein had weapons of mass destruction, necessitating, Bush claimed, an American invasion of Iraq (Rich, 2006). Saddam was ousted, but the human and international political costs were far greater than anticipated. In the 2004 election, Bush sought to access—his aides would say honorably, critics argued exploitatively—memories of the 9/11 attacks in a political ad that combined 9/11 images with the closing argument that Bush had made the country safer and stronger. It was a much darker "morning in America" than the one pleasantly invoked in a famous Reagan ad with that name, sadly illustrating the grimmer reality the nation faced.

If you thought adroit image manipulation ended in 2009 with the inauguration of Barack Obama, who earnestly promised to end bipartisan strife in his first presidential campaign, think again. Spontaneous as it seemed at the time, his message that the country needed to transcend poll-driven "politics as usual," abetted by the 2008 mantra "Yes We Can" (which went viral with a will.i.am hip-hop song), was pre-tested and pre-planned. Greenberg called it "the spin of no spin" (p. 441). As president, Obama employed some of the same techniques as his predecessors—polling, slogans, and use of current media, now the digitally based YouTube, email blasts, and Facebook—to promote his agenda and policy frames (see Figure 10.3). Obama recognized that political marketing does not end on Election Day, but continues throughout a president's term in office, in what is sometimes called the permanent campaign, a marketing effort steeped in persuasion, contemporary media, and that quintessential feature of modern politics: political spin (Greenberg, 2016; see Box 10.1). Obama found that even soaring rhetoric could not overcome diehard Republican opposition, the public's ambivalence, and the challenges of capturing a national audience in an era of myriad media and instantaneous platform shifting and phone screen swiping.

Unlike Clinton, and to some extent Bush, Obama faced a media environment in which television was no longer the main player. Faced with a blizzard of online media outlets, which framed his presidency in different ways, it was difficult for Obama to control the narrative on issues ranging from health care to Iran to the Supreme Court (Farnsworth, 2018). Yet he mightily tried, seeking, as the first African American president, to bring together Blacks and Whites, Republicans and Democrats, and people from different polarities around a message emphasizing common American values. He was remembered for that, as well as other accomplishments, such as sweeping health care legislation, significant economic growth, and the killing of Osama bin Laden, even as he found that launching post-partisan rhetoric was more difficult than he had hoped.

**Figure 10.3 Barack Obama harnessed the new interactive media to promote his programs, showcasing the importance of political marketing in "the permanent campaign" that extended well beyond the presidential election. His messages were frequently eloquent, but even Obama couldn't break the partisanship that gripped the nation during his administration.**

*Source*: www.gettyimages.com/detail/news-photo/president-barack-obama-speaks-at-a-town-hall-meeting-hosted-news-photo/126695005

## TRUMP AND THE TWEET-TRANSFORMED PRESIDENCY

Say what you want about Donald Trump. There can be no dispute that he transformed presidential communication style, taking it into the beating heart of the online media era by commandeering the tweet, exploiting it to set the agenda, frame issues, reinforce his base, and influence public opinion. Political marketing scholar Bruce Newman makes no bones about it: Trump, he says, metamorphosed political marketing (Newman, 2019). Now comes the controversy. Trump's supporters loved his feisty, take-no-prisoners style, finding it a long-overdue antidote to stifling political correctness. And yet. Over and over again—from immigration to post-election assaults on voting—he exploited Twitter to seize control of the narrative, goading his supporters to feel outrage at their adversaries, dividing more than unifying political groups. In the case of the coronavirus, critics argued, he failed to harness presidential messaging to provide all-important national leadership. Let's begin with his 2016 campaign, which first brought Twitter to the center of presidential politics.

---

### BOX 10.1 POLITICAL MARKETING

The contemporary presidential campaign is a dogged, brutish, and image-centric exercise in political marketing. Marketing is a broad concept that describes the processes by which a society communicates and distributes products and services of value to consumers. **Political marketing** involves the applications of marketing principles to political campaigns (both electoral and public opinion-focused), with the product a complex combination of the candidate, policy positions, and a cultivated image, communicated to voters and citizens through multiple media channels (Newman, 1994, 1999). Political marketing scholar Bruce I. Newman contributed the broad insight that campaigns quintessentially involve marketing principles, and campaigns can be broadly viewed not simply from the perch of political science analyses of political parties, but from a different vantage point: the careful application of marketing ideas to the political context. (See also Butler & Harris, 2009; Cwalina, Falkowski, & Newman, 2011; Winchester, Hall, & Binney, 2016.) Marketing now occurs in electoral campaigns across the world, in countries large and small, democratic and less democratic, attesting to the global reach of marketing communications (Rose, 2010).

Branding, an iconic term adapted from commercial marketing, plays a key role in this process. **Branding** is the process of creating a distinctive product image and identity, with "unique added values," in consumers' minds through the use of persuasion and marketing (de Chernatony, 1998, p. xvii; Fennis & Stroebe, 2010). Candidates strive to create a brand identity that is clear and distinguishes them from competitors. Candidates who are the best political communicators—Reagan, Clinton, until his sexual escapades tarnished his brand (in the language of political marketing), and Obama—have a clear, energizing brand identity.

*Continued*

Obama's brand emphasized that he was the thoughtful, cool-under-pressure communicator who could articulate problems and transcend petty partisanship. In its attempt to appeal to America's egalitarian ethos, it was an admirable branding message. Then reality set in, soiling Obama's brand when it was clear he could not tame the partisan tide of raucous Republican opposition to his programs, from gun control to climate change. Republicans were hell-bent on tarnishing Obama's administration from the get-go, but Obama made mistakes too: failing to respond in a muscular way to the humanitarian crisis in Syria and shying away from bare-knuckles LBJ politics that is anathema to academics, but gets legislation passed.

After Obama's "let us reason together" approach came Trump, who adopted a much different brand orientation. Trump's brand emphasized his brash, success-emblazoned, "tell it like it is no matter who it offends or mistreats" style. In 2016, Trump was unique in an important respect: Because of his world-famous hotels and casinos, real estate name, and television show, Trump was not just a candidate who used branded marketing. He was a brand—the first candidate in American history to ascend to the presidency with that distinction.

Trump was the unadulterated, unvarnished, there-for-all-to-see product, inextricably linked with the commercial marketplace where products are king. He revolutionized *place*, the geographic, interpersonal, or digital locale where products are distributed, circumventing the conventional news media, taking his campaign to a new platform, Twitter, where he built a base of supporters. Just as Uber deals directly with customers in the ride-sharing business, Trump did the same in the vote-snaring business, creating a new area of political place, the ideologically congenial environment of Twitter, for his supporters (Newman & Newman, 2017).

In these emotion-channeling ways, he amplified his brand, emphasizing a core component of commercial and political marketing: nurturing a relationship between the customer and company, in the case of commercial marketing, and between the voter and service provider or the candidate, in political marketing. Love him or hate him, there was no denying the abiding relationship between his base and his brand. As Bruce Newman and Todd Newman (2017) observed, "Donald Trump did to his brand what every person or organization has to do to successfully compete in any marketplace, and that is to create a narrative around their brand" (p. 75). From a normative perspective, the questions were

*Continued*

different: Was the narrative more divisive than unifying? How well did it serve the health and safety of the United States?

For his part, Trump's 2020 opponent, Joe Biden, defined his brand as the anti-Trump: the reliable, honest everyman who always had your back. If Trump could be the purveyor of snake oil drugs that, as with his recommendations during the coronavirus, didn't cure the patient's ailments, Biden was the honest pharmacist who kindly put his arm around you and offered you grandfatherly (bordering on senility, in the view of opponents) advice about which drug would help your aching back. Like all branded political marketing, his gentle healing personae papered over problematic complexities, such as a checkered record on racial justice and troubling relationships between key aides and the insider, corporate influence Washington establishment (Lipton & Vogel, 2020).

In the end, the core positive aspects of Biden's brand—his empathy and inclusiveness—more closely fit the political needs of the 2020 electoral moment than Trump's fiery communicative style (Bucy, 2020). Trump failed to adapt his brand to a market that had been drastically altered by the coronavirus and racial justice protests. Suddenly, "Trump didn't seem like the effective manager, strong leader and problem solver his brand promised and the crises COVID set into motion were hardly making America great again," Cosgrove (2020) observed. Over the next several years, we will see how Biden steps up to his own political marketing challenges that range from bargaining with Senate Republicans to navigating ideological differences between his party's progressives and moderates. Will his anti-Trump focus on "you the American people, not me" prove soothing or insufficiently muscular for an American president?

## Trump's Tweets in the 2016 Campaign

Twitter's brevity is a communicative virtue. Its original 140-character limit literally forced famously long-winded politicians "to quickly get to the point," circumvent the press, and build a following (Parmelee & Bichard, 2012, p. 206). It has allowed millions of people to participate more actively in politics and has helped social movements on the right and left mobilize supporters. Twitter has shortcomings as well. It encourages impulsivity, amplifies incivility, and diminishes respect; when used by journalists, it reinforces gender biases by granting more legitimacy to male than to female reporters (Ott, 2017; Jaidka, Zhou, & Lelkes, 2019; Usher, Holcomb, & Littman, 2018).

Trump brought Twitter into the political mainstream (see Box 10.2). He reached voters directly through Twitter, including disaffected Republicans, who tuned out conventional media, preferring instead his trending tweets that titillated their smartphones, bursting through the clutter of more normal political communication and helping him develop a deeply personal relationship with his supporters (Healy & Martin, 2016). And yet Twitter also contributed to his undoing, as many Americans who learned of his tweets from watching television news were turned off, finding his behavior unpresidential. From a media technology perspective, an older medium, television, undermined the effects of a newer one, a testament to the complexity and pluralism of the media system.

---

## BOX 10.2 POLITICAL RHETORIC IN A DIGITAL AGE

Twitter prizes authenticity. The very authenticity that Trump's followers saw and loved in him had a parallel in the endearment that New York City Congresswoman Alexandria Ocasio-Cortez elicited from her liberal Democratic followers. Beginning with a campaign video that rippled with youthful energy and idealism, she developed a strong social media presence, exemplified by a stunning growth in Twitter followers since she was elected in 2018; determination to challenge her opponents with upfront comments; and a personalized, self-disclosing narrative with dancing and cooking videos, even a picture of her campaign shoes so worn you could see the holes on the bottom, showcasing a visual and oral comfort in the online world. One supportive journalist said she was "extremely online," befitting "the digital native she is, meaning simply that she speaks the language of the Internet fluently" (Swisher, 2019, A19).

But she too could become a captive of the verbal viscera of the online world, blocking a former New York City politician from her Twitter account simply because he uttered a criticism of her, or focusing so much of her energies on social media messaging that she seemed not to appreciate the time-honored ways that legislation is politically crafted in the House.

On the campaign trail, social media is de rigueur. Senator Elizabeth Warren, trying to shed the perception she was a stodgy Harvard law professor, personalized her 2020 campaign with selfies. Her staff devised an impeccably organized procedure, where one staffer took the fan's bag, another her phone, another snapped the picture, and someone else thanked the individual for coming (Kaplan, Kalifa, & Weingart, 2019). Campaigns cultivate and track growth of their following on Twitter, Facebook, and Instagram, trying to devise catchy videos, like one of former

*Continued*

Texas Congressman Beto O'Rourke skateboarding through a Whataburger parking lot, or a kinetic Andrew Yang music video (Greenwood, 2018).

Contrary to the zeitgeist of the online world, social media do not mirror the political universe. Democrats who post political messages on social media are more likely to be liberal, have attended a political demonstration over the past year, and recently donated to a political cause. By contrast, Democrats who don't post political content are more inclined to be moderate or conservative, believe that political correctness is a problem, and steer clear of following the news (Cohn & Quealy, 2019). In a similar fashion, it's likely that Republicans who are politically active on Twitter and other social media are the activists with more extreme views on social issues.

Twitter does not exert a hypodermic impact. Instead, it provides a platform for candidates to mobilize like-minded voters, gain additional brand value via supportive comments from online opinion leaders, and capture positive media coverage. Direct messaging between candidates (or their aides) and followers adds an immediacy and real-time spontaneity that can be lacking in conventional news coverage or at large political rallies (Lee & Shin, 2014). Twitter can help candidates forge a relationship with supporters, a key aspect of branding, but it also carries risks; when online supporters dislike a candidate's tweets, they may respond with viral vitriol (Theocharis et al., 2016).

On a normative level, the politicization of digital media is a mixed bag. Some scholars praise digital technologies, noting they enhance civic engagement and provide a viable mechanism for outsider candidates to mobilize citizens; they also have expanded the parameters of political participation, offering more opportunities for activists to challenge elites (Campbell & Kwak, 2014; Chadwick & Stromer-Galley, 2016; Coleman, 2014; Dutton, 2014; (Edgerly et al., 2013).

Yet for all these benefits, social media, with their ability to arouse prejudices in a norm-shattering way that is not acceptable on mainstream channels, have made politics more combustible and unity more difficult, in some instances enabling strident partisans to hurl hurtful epithets anonymously, and in other cases giving fringe groups a mouthpiece to promote offensive and prejudiced speech.

Social media have taken a toll on the language of politics. One critic noted that online media favor "the bitty over the meaty, the cutting over the considered. It also prizes emotionalism over reason. The more visceral

*Continued*

the message, the more quickly it circulates and the longer it holds the darting public eye" (Carr, 2015). As one journalist observed:

> Technology is making campaigns dumber. . . . The campaigns get lost in tit-for-tat minutiae that nobody outside the bubble cares about. Meanwhile, use of the Internet means that Web videos overshadow candidate speeches and appearances. Video replaces verbal. Tactics eclipse vision.
>
> (Brooks, 2012, p. A19; see also Hart, 2013)

Of course, some of the same criticisms have dogged politics from the days of clichéd stump speeches to televised political ads. Political persuasion is more immediate and interactive, certainly more entertaining today—but not necessarily more thoughtful or dignified.

## Trump's Tweets and Rhetoric During His Presidency

Over the course of his administration, Trump multiplied the use of his tweets, directing them to his base, his 88 million Twitter followers, members of Congress, and foreign leaders, and *at* legislators, entertainers, journalists, and assorted individuals who publicly criticized him. Trump favored the short, snappy utterances of Twitter, eschewing the formal, even florid, language presidents have classically invoked, emphasizing causal talk with emotional excesses that capitalized on the staccato technology of the times. They were an essential part of his brand.

Trump's tweets were inflammatory and inaccurate, critics pointed out, and in many instances they have a point. Consider the border wall. "BUILD A WALL & CRIME WILL FALL," he tweeted in a Twitter address in January 2019. In keeping with his earlier simple, but rhetorically compelling, catchphrases ("You're fired!" from *The Apprentice* TV show and "Make America Great Again"), this also had a certain persuasive elegance. Trouble was that its core assumptions were not true. Research shows that increases in immigration to the U.S. are not associated with rising crime, and that crime rates among undocumented immigrants are actually lower than among native-born Americans. And a wall would not necessarily deter crime because a majority of immigrants didn't come to the U.S. by crossing the border illegally, but exceeded the amount of time their temporary visas allowed them to stay in the country (Rogers & Qiu, 2018).

In other cases, his language took on a down-is-up, "through the looking glass" tint. His administration, describing his policy of forcibly separating children from parents entering the U.S. illegally, called the places they were housed "tender age shelters," semantically obliterating the reality that children were housed in warehouses, locked in large metal cages, like the kind that confine animals in zoos (Talbot, 2018). In a column entitled "Trump savagely mauls the language," a newspaper columnist remarked on how Trump used the word "beautiful" in ways that do not befit the aesthetic, sensual connotation the word conjures (Blow, 2017). He repeatedly referred to a border wall that would stop desperate migrants from entering the U.S. as a "beautiful wall." Strong, yes, impenetrable, si, but beautiful? When he ordered dozens of cruise missiles to strike a Syrian airbase, he said he was enjoying "the most beautiful piece of chocolate cake that you've ever seen," using the term to suggest that he sensually relished the military attack, which would probably strike seasoned Armed Forces veterans as, at the very least, inappropriate and probably repugnant (Raymond, 2017). Most ominously, he gushed over the National Guard crackdown in Minneapolis that followed troubling violence in the streets, saying "it's a beautiful thing to watch" (Baker et al., 2020).

Throwing out years of respect for the institutional bedrocks of the "magisterial presidency," he accessed his inner Andrew Jackson, defining himself as "a man of the people" (or at least certain people), relishing conflict (though not pistol duels, like Jackson), battling the courts, and even favoring fulsome hair, like the seventh president (Baker, 2017). His communication style, brash like Jackson's, favored a reality television show immediacy, in sync with contemporary media pop culture.

He assailed the FBI and the CIA, even going so far as to agree with Russia, as he appeared with Russian President Vladimir Putin after a summit meeting, that Russia had not meddled in the 2016 presidential election, even though U.S. intelligence experts had unequivocally concluded that Russia had conducted a sophisticated cyber-campaign to interfere with the election in an effort to elect Trump. And he famously spoke his mind in crude and vindictive ways, retorting that "I should have left them in jail" when American basketball players did not thank him enough for helping extricate them from China. He said four minority Congresswomen should "go back" to the countries they came from, and called those who offered perceived or real criticisms of him "incompetent" (Supreme Court Justice Ruth Bader Ginsburg); "dumb as a rock" (his former Secretary of State, Rex Tillerson); "a monster" (Kamala Harris); and saddled with a "dying mediocre career" (Alec Baldwin, who impersonated Trump—poorly, he thought!—on *Saturday Night Live*) (Lee & Quealy, 2019).

It was part of a pattern. An analysis of 11,000 tweets revealed that he tweeted attacks over 5,000 times; more than 1,700 advanced conspiracy theories and 851 castigated minority groups (Shear et al., 2019; see also Meeks, 2020). A fact-check also revealed that in his four years of Trump uttered more than 30,000 false or misleading claims (Fact Checker, 2021).

Scholars worried that his rhetoric denigrated the institution of the presidency. Others praised Trump's style to some degree appreciating his rhetoric, at least insofar as it appealed to supporters (Hart, 2020), noting he could reach the public with a populist simplicity that cut through byzantine complexity and annoying political correctness. His supporters liked his authenticity; perhaps they were confusing the seeming spontaneity of his insults with truth, presuming they were as truthful as they were off-the-cuff. To be sure, no presidents tell the full truth, most prevaricate to some degree, but Trump's record of factual distortions was without precedent. And when he famously tweeted false claims about a rigged 2020 presidential election, encouraged supporters to protest the formal certification of a democratic vote, and even excused their violent swarming of the Capitol, there wasn't any doubt that he had taken presidential power to a dangerous low.

## Trump's Rhetoric and the Coronavirus Pandemic: A Critical View

The coronavirus outbreak in 2020, which wrought devastation across continents, infected millions, and caused hundreds of thousands of deaths, was a pandemic the world had never seen, one that presented multiple challenges to national leaders. In China, where it all began, the government played down the serious dangers the virus posed, muzzled doctors, prioritizing secrecy over openness with its citizens, in keeping with the government's overarching concern with maintaining political power (Buckley & Myers, 2020). The Italian government minimized the threat, failing to take swift action (Horowitz, Bubola, & Povoledo, 2020). As the virus raged through Europe, British Prime Minister Boris Johnson opted to keep public places open, a decision he regretted when he was hospitalized after testing positive for the virus less than a month later (Mueller, 2020).

To be sure, the virus proved resilient, infecting hundreds of thousands, even in countries where governments took aggressive steps. No political leader acted perfectly; all made mistakes in the face of a pandemic that raged out of control. Trump, to his credit, inaugurated Operation Warp Speed, a partnership between the public and private sectors that was responsible for jump-starting the development and production of coronavirus vaccines. Unfortunately, his rhetoric and policies were littered with mistakes.

While Trump adopted an optimistic tone, a long-standing tradition in presidential rhetoric (Zullow et al., 1988), it soon became clear that his optimism was larded with deceptions that even he knew were not true. The problem, critics noted, was that, as Trump said infections were "substantially down, not up" and "it's going to disappear," he provided a false sense of reassurance that blinded the public and policymakers to the need to act quickly before it was too late (Qiu, Marsh, & Huang, 2020). Journalist David Leonhardt described the decisions Trump faced in early 2020 as the coronavirus spread from China to other countries and China was poised to close off access to Wuhan:

> In the weeks that followed, Trump faced a series of choices. He could have taken aggressive measures to slow the spread of the virus. He could have insisted that the United States ramp up efforts to produce test kits. He could have emphasized the risks that the virus presented and urged Americans to take precautions if they had reason to believe they were sick. He could have used the powers of the presidency to reduce the number of people who would ultimately get sick. He did none of those things.
>
> (Leonhardt, 2020)

Wielding rhetorical power is particularly difficult in the U.S., given that the nation's governmental system is not centralized under a powerful executive branch, but dispersed among the states and different branches of government. The president's power in a crisis rests on his or her ability to persuade, mobilize, and marshal resources to propel change forward.

Although Trump could have aggressively used the federal Defense Production Act to mobilize businesses to produce needed supplies to stem coronavirus spread, he took a laissez-faire approach, hoping businesses would voluntarily rise to the occasion (Rogers, Haberman, & Swanson, 2020). However, as health economists noted, businesses were poorly poised to produce the massive resources that were required because they would be reluctant to shoulder huge upfront costs (Scheiber, 2020). A systematic federal intervention was needed to manage the market factors and coordinate production, steps that could have saved lives.

Instead, Trump eschewed this approach. Initially, he heaped blame on foreigners and tried to boost the spirits of investors. And even though he knew the virus was deadly, he publicly minimized its gravity, misleading the public, claiming it would "just disappear" (Woodward, 2020). Faced with problems not of his making—a novel virus scientists knew little about, a flawed CDC test for the virus, ridiculously bureaucratic roadblocks implemented by the Food and Drug Administration (Ioffe, 2020)—Trump reacted or chose not to act expeditiously (see Figure 10.4). Public health experts estimated that had the U.S. government ordered national lockdowns and enforced social distancing 1 to 2 weeks earlier, tens of thousands fewer Americans would have died (Glanz & Robertson, 2020). In fairness, these are only estimates, but they contain suggestive implications.

Trump rhetorically violated principles that a fellow Republican, President George W. Bush, had developed for public communication during a health crisis: responding early, making sure facts were correct, conveying respect, and taking action (Leonhardt, 2020). Instead, Trump punted, opting for denial. He

**Figure 10.4 Although Trump, to his credit, initially adopted a can-do, optimistic tone in his coronavirus messages, he ultimately failed to adopt a persuasive rhetorical message in his presidential communication on the coronavirus. He failed to effectively use the bully pulpit during critical periods of the outbreak, minimizing, denying, and distorting the problem, ultimately adopting divisive language, rather than FDR-style rhetoric to rally the country around a series of solutions.**

*Source*: www.gettyimages.com/detail/news-photo/president-donald-trump-holds-a-press-conference-on-covid-19-news-photo/1207206119

eschewed masks, refusing to wear one, even though his modeling of life-saving mask use could have reduced the spread of the virus. Trump focused on peripheral issues or left policy to the states, some of which took aggressive actions to ban public gatherings, others which did relatively little, providing a confusing pastiche of preventive prescriptions. Some writers criticized Trump's insensitivity to the deaths of tens of thousands of Americans during the coronavirus outbreak, bemoaning his failure to engage in a rhetoric of mourning, as other presidents have done after national tragedies, denouncing his decision to "take a pass on human empathy" (Glaser, 2020). Had Trump used his outsize personality and emotive tweets to rally the country around the cause, he would have been universally praised.

This critical perspective of Trump's rhetoric was not shared by some Americans, who gave him a small boost in his approval ratings when his daily

**Figure 10.5 President Joe Biden, in many ways the rhetorical opposite of Donald Trump, could wear his heart on his sleeve, projecting empathy and compassion, as well as occasional cringe-worthy gaffes.**

https://commons.wikimedia.org/wiki/File:Joe_Biden_kickoff_rally_May_2019.jpg

briefings began, because they liked his confident swagger, found his briefings informative, dismissed the criticisms as partisan, or argued that there was not much that any president could do to solve a problem of this magnitude (Tamari, 2020). Yet to critics, looking at him from the perch of the best presidential crisis rhetoric, Trump fell short. Taking Franklin D. Roosevelt, who adeptly calmed and inspired Americans during the Great Depression and later World War II, as an exemplar, journalist Jamelle Bouie (2020) noted that rather than avoiding the fear many Americans faced in 1933, "Roosevelt used his first words as president to face it head on," recognizing "our interdependence on each other" and a willingness "to sacrifice for the good of a common discipline."

This was not Trump's style. Even after the election, as infections surged and the U.S. marked its single-highest daily death count since the pandemic, he said virtually nothing about the dark predicament citizens faced, seemingly more concerned with baseless charges that the Democrats had stolen the presidency from him. Trump didn't offer compassion and he didn't do empathy—the stock-in-trade of successor Joe Biden. An empathic communicator who wore his heart on his sleeve and said what was on his mind (sometimes artlessly and insensitively), Biden called on a communicative style emphasizing compassion during the 2020 campaign (see Figure 10.5). As his administration took shape, though, it became clear that he faced many challenges in deploying his healing rhetoric to unify a frequently divided country.

## CONCLUSIONS

Democracy is predicated on elections—the will of the people, vox populi, the consent or dissent of the governed. Elections are imperfect. Candidates, at their best, have noble aims, and, if elected to office, can exert transformative effects on the nation. Alas, their feet are made of clay; they are tempted by their ambitions, constrained by their shortcomings, and can commit egregious errors costing resources and lives.

Presidential campaigns, fundamentally an American invention, are the modality by which candidates try to persuade voters. Rhetoric, or the art and symbols of political speech-making, is a hallmark, from stump speeches in the 19th century to television in the 20th to tweets in the 21st. So too is a focus on promoting an image, an appreciation that politics involves the cultivation of simplifying fictions designed to persuade.

Candidates were consumed by images, long before television. Consider Andrew Jackson's cultivation of a populist image and Abraham Lincoln's concern with image reconstruction. Lincoln humorously, but adeptly, fashioned his "cragged face . . . overly long arms and legs . . . along with his ill-fitting clothes and awkward gait" so they fit the contemporary showman P.T. Barnum's popular sense of "the love of weird spectacle, what we now call the tabloidization of public people," endearing him to the masses (Gopnik, 2020, p. 64).

What television did was to usher in communication of candidate imagery on a mass level. Campaign experts recognized that image—the media-cultivated, candidate-crafted, voter-constructed perception of candidates—was a major factor in electoral politics. Image construction, a strange alchemy of candidates' policy statements, media appearances, and the art of projecting a persuasive campaign face, came of age with John F. Kennedy.

With Reagan, art and artifice became inextricably linked with a mastery of television narrative. Reagan called on an earnest commitment to political conservatism, while harnessing rhetoric, visual manipulations, and the cultivation of the new political meme—spin—to fashion himself as a "great communicator." He unquestionably was, but the perception itself, cultivated by reporters who equated Reagan's charm with a power to shape public opinion, carried persuasive heft, as journalists' beliefs may have subtly influenced public attitudes (Schudson, 1995). As presidents continued to mold images with the media platform du jour—Clinton with the talk show debate, Obama via YouTube, Trump with his inveterate tweets—old questions, wrapped in new digital wrapping, emerged about the intersection between artifice and authenticity, and the ways in which political leadership is inevitably a complex combination of worthy intentions, self-serving deceptions, and manufactured images.

The contemporary campaign is an exercise in political marketing, the systematic application of marketing principles to politics. Digital technologies have transformed campaigns, removing barriers among the players, reducing (though by no means eliminating) the pervasive influences of news, expanding the forms and content by which candidates, media, and citizens communicate, and eviscerating norms of civility in venomous partisan posts.

Trump became the tweeting president, masterfully adapting a medium he harnessed in his first presidential campaign to the presidency, much like JFK and

Reagan exploited television and Obama called on social media. Trump, however, adopted an abrasive, sometimes inflammatory, style that thrilled his supporters, but riled those he attacked vituperatively, as well as scholars who point to his defacing institutional norms of the modern presidency. His rhetoric has been simple by rhetorical standards, which can (in theory) be a political virtue (Shulman & Sweitzer, 2018). But—and, yes, there is a "but" in this discussion—his rhetoric has been untruthful, prejudiced, and in the case of the coronavirus, short on the unifying rhetorical leadership the country needed at the political moment when the outbreak spiked out of control.

Biden, his successor, has a much different style and brand. His many challenges include finding a voice that can soothe millions wearied by the virus, while developing a narrative that appeals to a divided nation.

## REFERENCES

Baker, K. (2016, June 19). Donald Trump's place. *The New York Times* (Sunday Review), 1, 6, 7.

Baker, P. (2017, December 31). For Trump, a year of reinventing the presidency. *The New York Times*. Online: www.nytimes.com/2017/12/31/us/politics/trump-reinventing-presidency.html. (Accessed: April 9, 2020).

Baker, P., Haberman, M., Rogers, K., Kanno-Youngs, Z., & Benner, K. (2020, June 2). How Trump's idea for a photo op led to havoc in a park. *The New York Times*. Online: www.nytimes.com/2020/06/02/us/politics/trump-walk-lafayette-square.html. (Accessed: June 3, 2020).

Blow, C.M. (2017, July 17). Trump savagely mauls the language. *The New York Times*. Online: www.nytimes.com/2017/07/17/opinion/donald-trump-english-language-.html. (Accessed: April 8, 2020).

Boorstin, D.J. (1964). *The image: A guide to pseudo-events in America.* New York: Harper & Row.

Bouie, J. (2020, March 30). D.J.T. is no F.D.R. *The New York Times*, 20.

Brooks, D. (2012, July 31). Dullest campaign ever. *The New York Times*, A19.

Brooks, D. (2014, February 14). The refiner's fire. *The New York Times*. Online: www.nytimes.com/2014/02/14/opinion/brooks-the-refiners- fire.html. (Accessed: February 25, 2017).

Buckley, C., & Myers, S.L. (2020, February 7). As new coronavirus spread, China's old habits delayed fight. *The New York Times*. Online: www.nytimes.com/2020/02/01/world/asia/china-coronavirus.html. (Accessed: April 9, 2020).

Bucy, E.P. (2020). Political emotion and the global pandemic: Factors at odds with a Trump presidency. In D. Jackson, D.S. Coombs, F. Trevisan, D. Lilleker, & E. Thorsen (Eds.), *U.S. election analysis 2020: Media, voters and the campaign.* Online: www.electionanalysis.ws/us/president2020/section-1-policy-and-political-context/political-emotion-and-the-global-pandemic-factors-at-odds-with-a-trump-presidency/. (Accessed: November 15, 2020).

Butler, P., & Harris, P. (2009). Considerations on the evolution of political marketing theory. *Marketing Theory, 9*, 149–164.

Campbell, K.K., & Jamieson, K.H. (1990). *Deeds done in words: Presidential rhetoric and the genres of governance.* Chicago, IL: University of Chicago Press.

Campbell, S.W., & Kwak, N. (2014). Mobile communication and civic life: Linking patterns of use to civic and political engagement. In W.H. Dutton (Ed.), *Politics and the internet: Critical concepts in political science* (Vol. III, *Netizens, networks and political movements* (pp. 213–234). New York: Routledge.

Carr, N. (2015, September 2). How social media is ruining politics. *Politico.* Online: www.politico.com/magazine/story/2015/09/2016-election-social-media-ruining-politics-213104. (Accessed: November 30, 2016).

Chadwick, A., & Stromer-Galley, J. (2016). Digital media, power, and democracy in parties and election campaigns: Party decline or party renewal? *The International Journal of Press/Politics, 21*, 283–293.

Cohn, N., & Quealy, K. (2019, April 10). Liberals on Twitter don't speak for quiet majority. *The New York Times*, A1, A16.

Coleman, S. (2014). The lonely citizen: Indirect representation in an age of networks. In W.H. Dutton (Ed.), *Politics and the internet: Critical concepts in political science* (Vol. III, *Netizens, networks and political movements* (pp. 54–75). New York: Routledge.

Cosgrove, K. (2020). Branding and its limits. In D. Jackson, D.S. Coombs, F. Trevisan, D. Lilleker, & E. Thorsen (Eds.), *U.S. election analysis 2020: Media, voters and the campaign.* Online: www.electionanalysis.ws/us/president2020/section-3-candidates-and-the-campaign/branding-and-its-limits/. (Accessed: November 16, 2020).

Cramer, R.B. (1992). *What it takes: The way to the White House.* New York: Random House.

Cwalina, W., Falkowski, A., & Newman, B.I. (2011). *Political marketing: Theoretical and strategic foundations.* Armonk, NY: M.E. Sharpe.

de Chernatony, L. (1998). Introduction. In L. de Chernatony (Ed.), *Brand management* (pp. xv–xxvi). Aldershot, England: Dartmouth Publishing Company.

Dutton, W.H. (Ed., with the assistance of E. Dubois). (2014). *Politics and the Internet: Critical concepts in political science* (Vol. III, *Netizens, networks and political movements*). New York: Routledge.

Edgerly, S., Bode, L., Kim, Y.M., & Shah, D.V. (2013). Campaigns go social: Are Facebook, YouTube and Twitter changing elections? In T.N. Ridout (Ed.), *New directions in media and politics* (pp. 82–99). New York: Routledge.

Ellithorpe, M.E., Huang, Y., & Oliver, M.B. (2019). Reach across the aisle: Elevation from political messages predicts increased positivity toward politics, political participation, and the opposite political party. *Journal of Communication, 69*, 249–272.

Euchner, C.C. (1990). Presidential appearances. In *The presidents and the public* (pp. 109–129). Washington, DC: Congressional Quarterly Inc.

Fact Checker. (2021, January 20). In four years, President Trump made 30, 573 false or misleading claims. *The Washington Post.* Online: https://www.washingtonpost.com/graphics/politics/trump-claims-database/. (Accessed: April 27, 2021).

Farnsworth, S.J. (2018). *Presidential communication and character: White House news management from Clinton and cable to Twitter and Trump.* New York: Routledge.

Fennis, B.M., & Stroebe, W. (2010). *The psychology of advertising.* New York: Psychology Press.

Glanz, J., & Robertson, C. (2020, May 22). Lockdown delays cost at least 36,000 lives, data show. *The New York Times.* Online: www.nytimes.com/2020/05/20/us/coronavirus-distancing-deaths.html. (Accessed: September 24, 2020).

Glaser, S. (2020, April 23). Fifty thousand Americans dead from the coronavirus, and a president who refuses to mourn them. *The New Yorker.* Online: www.newyorker.

com/news/letter-from-trumps-washington/fifty- thousand-americans-dead-in-the-coronavirus-pandemic-and-a-president-who-refuses-to-mourn them? (Accessed: April 24, 2020).

Gopnik, A. (2020, September 28). Better angel. *The New Yorker*, 62–68.

Greenberg, D. (2016). *Republic of spin: An inside history of the American presidency*. New York: W.W. Norton.

Hart, R.P. (1984). *Verbal style and the presidency: A computer-based analysis*. Orlando: Academic Press.

Hart, R.P. (2013). Politics in the digital age: A scary prospect? In T.N. Ridout (Ed.), *New directions in media and politics* (pp. 210–225). New York: Routledge.

Hart, R.P. (2020). *Trump and us: What he says and why people listen*. New York: Cambridge University Press.

Healy, P., & Martin, J. (2016, May 8). G.O.P. unravels as party faces Trump takeover. *The New York Times*, 1, 19.

Hertsgaard, M. (1988). *On bended knee: The press and the Reagan presidency*. New York: Farrar Straus Giroux.

Horowitz, J., Bubola, E., & Povoledo, E. (2020, March 21). Italy, pandemic's new epicenter, has lessons for the world. *The New York Times*. Online: www.nytimes.com/2020/03/21/world/europe/italy-coronavirus-center-lessons.html. (Accessed: April 11, 2020).

Ignatieff, M. (2013). *Fire and ashes: Success and failure in politics*. Cambridge: Harvard University Press.

Ioffe, J. (2020, March 16) The infuriating story of how the government stalled coronavirus testing. *GQ*. Online: www.gq.com/story/inside-americas-coronavirus-testing-crisis. (Accessed: April 11, 2020).

Jaidka, K., Zhou, A., & Lelkes, Y. (2019). Brevity is the soul of Twitter: The constraint affordance and political discussion. *Journal of Communication, 69*, 345–372.

Jamieson, K.H. (1988). *Eloquence in an electronic age: The transformation of political speechmaking*. New York: Oxford University Press.

Kaplan, T., Kalifa, T., & Weingart, E. (2019, July 22). How to get a selfie with Elizabeth Warren in 8 steps. *The New York Times*. Online: www.nytimes.com/interactive/2019/07/22/us/politics/elizabeth-warren-selfies.html. (Accessed: April 13, 2020).

Kurtz, H. (1996). *Hot air: All talk, all the time*. New York: Times Books.

Lanzetta, J.T., Sullivan, D.G., Masters, R.D., & McHugo, G.J. (1985). Emotional and cognitive responses to televised images of political leaders. In S. Kraus & R.M. Perloff (Eds.), *Mass media and political thought: An information-processing approach* (pp. 85–116). Thousand Oaks, CA: Sage.

Lawless, J.L., & Fox, R.L. (2012). *Men rule: The continued under-representation of women in U.S. politics*. Washington, DC: Women & Politics Institute. Online: www.american.edu/spa/wpi/upload/2012-Men-Rule-Report-final-web.pdf. (Accessed: February 21, 2017).

Lee, E-J., & Shin, S.Y. (2014). When the medium is the message: How transportability moderates the effects of politicians' Twitter communication. *Communication Research, 41*, 1088–1110.

Lee, J.C., & Quealy, K. (2019, May 24). The 598 people, places and things Donald Trump has insulted on Twitter: A complete list. *The New York Times*. Online: www.nytimes.com/interactive/2016/01/28/upshot/donald-trump-twitter-insults.html. (Accessed: April 9, 2020).

Leonhardt, D. (2020, March 15). A complete list of Trump's attempts to play down virus. *The New York Times*. Online: www.nytimes.com/2020/03/15/opinion/trump-coro navirus.html. (Accessed: September 7, 2020).

Lippmann, W. (1922). *Public opinion*. New York: Free Press.

Lipton, E., & Vogel, K.P. (2020, December 1). Biden aides' ties to consulting and investment firms pose ethics test. *The New York Times*. Online: www.nytimes. com/2020/11/28/us/politics/biden-westexec.html. (Accessed: December 1, 2020).

Maltese, J.A. (1994). *Spin control: The White House Office of Communications and the management of presidential news*. Chapel Hill: University of North Carolina Press.

Mancini, P., & Swanson, D.L. (1996). Politics, media, and modern democracy: Intro-duction. In D.L. Swanson & P. Mancini (Eds.), *Politics, media, and modern democ-racy: An international study of innovations in electoral campaigning and their consequences* (pp. 1–26). Westport, CT: Praeger.

Meeks, L. (2020). Defining the enemy: How Donald Trump frames the news media. *Journalism & Mass Communication Quarterly, 97*, 211–234.

Mueller, B. (2020, March 13). As Europe shuts down, Britain takes a different, and con-tentious approach. *The New York Times*. Online: www.nytimes.com/2020/03/13/ world/europe/coronavirus-britain-boris-johnson.html. (Accessed: April 11, 2020).

Newman, B.I. (1994). *The marketing of the president: Political marketing as campaign strategy*. Thousand Oaks, CA: Sage.

Newman, B.I. (1999). *The mass marketing of politics: Democracy in an age of manu-factured images*. Thousand Oaks, CA: Sage.

Newman, B.I. (2019, November 22). *Personal communication to Richard Perloff*.

Newman, B.I., & Newman, T.P. (2017). *Brand*. Dubuque, IA: Kendall Hunt.

Nunberg, G. (2016, July 28). Is Trump's call for "law and order" a coded racial mes-sage? *NPR*. Online: www.npr.org/2016/07/28/487560886/is-trumps-call-for-law-and-order-a-coded-racial-message. (Accessed: June 22, 2020).

Ott, B.L (2017). The age of Twitter: Donald J. Trump and the politics of debasement. *Critical Studies in Media Communication, 34*, 59–68.

Packard, V. (1957). *The hidden persuaders*. New York: D. McKay.

Parmelee, J.H., & Bichard, S.L. (2012). Politics and the Twitter revolution: *How tweets influence the relationship between political leaders and the public*. Lanham, MD: Lexington Books.

Perloff, R.M. (1998). *Political communication: Politics, press, and public in America*. Mahwah, NJ: Lawrence Erlbaum Associates.

Qiu, L., Marsh, B., & Huang, J. (2020, March 20). The president vs. the experts: How Trump downplayed the coronavirus. *The New York Times*, A13.

Raymond, A.K. (2017, April 12). Trump gleefully recalls the "beautiful chocolate cake" he ate while bombing Syria. *New York*. Online: www.merriam-webster.com/thesau-rus/confined. (Accessed: April 8, 2020).

Rich, R. (2006). *The greatest story ever sold: The decline and fall of truth from 9/11 to Katrina*. New York: Penguin Press.

Rogers, K., Haberman, M., & Swanson, A. (2020, March 20). Trump resists pressure to use wartime law to mobilize industry in virus response. *The New York Times*. Online: www.nytimes.com/2020/03/20/us/politics/trump-coronavirus-supplies.html. (Accessed: October 11, 2020).

Rogers, K., & Qiu, L. (2018, January 24). It rhymes, but facts of a tweet are off-key. *The New York Times*, A13.

Rose, J. (2010). The branding of states: The uneasy marriage of marketing to politics. *Journal of Political Marketing, 9*, 254–275.

Scheiber, N. (2020, October 9). The private sector can't pay for everything. *The New York Times*. Online: www.nytimes.com/2020/10/09/sunday-review/stimulus-congress-layoffs.html. (Accessed: October 11, 2020).

Schudson, M. (1995). *The power of news*. Cambridge, MA: Harvard University Press.

Shear, M.D., Haberman, M., Confessore, N., Yourish, K., Buchanan, L., & Collins, K. (2019, November 2). How Trump reshaped the presidency in over 11,000 tweets. *The New York Times*. Online: www.nytimes.com/interactive/2019/11/02/us/politics/trump-twitter-presidency.html. (Accessed: September 7, 2020).

Shulman, H.C., & Sweitzer, M.D. (2018). Advancing framing theory: Designing an equivalence frame to improve political information processing. *Human Communication Research, 44*, 155–175.

Stone, W.J. (2010). Activists, influence, and representation in American elections. In L.S. Maisel & J.M. Berry (Eds.), *The Oxford handbook of American political parties and interest groups* (pp. 285–302). New York: Oxford University Press.

Swisher, K. (2019, January 12). Who will win the Internet? *The New York Times*, A19.

Talbot, M. (2018, July 2). Comment: Family values. *The New Yorker*, 13–14.

Tamari, J. (2020, March 31). Trump has a coronavirus polling bounce: How meaningful is it? *The Philadelphia Inquirer*. Online: www.inquirer.com/health/coronavirus/trump-coronavirus-poll-numbers-2020-20200331.html. (Accessed: April 12, 2020).

Theocharis, Y., Bárbera, P., Fazekas, Z., Popa, S.A., & Parnet, O. (2016). A bad workman blames his tweets: The consequences of citizens' uncivil Twitter use when interacting with party candidates. *Journal of Communication, 66*, 1007–1031.

Thurber, J.A. (2000). Introduction to the study of campaign consultants. In J.A. Thurber & C.J. Nelson (Eds.), *Campaign warriors: The role of political consultants in elections* (pp. 1–9). Washington, DC: Brookings Institution Press.

Tulis, J.K. (1987). *The rhetorical presidency*. Princeton, NJ: Princeton University Press.

Usher, N., Holcomb, J., & Littman, J. (2018). Twitter makes it worse: Political journalists, gendered echo chambers, and the amplification of gender bias. *The International Journal of Press/Politics, 23*, 324–344.

Winchester, T., Hall, J., & Binney, W. (2016). Conceptualizing usage in voting behavior for political marketing: An application of consumer behavior. *Journal of Political Marketing, 15*, 259–284.

Woodward, B. (2020). *Rage*. New York: Simon & Schuster.

Zullow, H.M., Oettingen, G., Peterson, C., & Seligman, M.E. (1988). Pessimistic explanatory style in the historical record: CAVing LBJ, presidential candidates, and East versus West Berlin. *American Psychologist, 43*, 673–682.

# 11

# Unpacking Political News Bias

Don't get people started on news bias. You're apt to get an earful. Just about everyone says the news is biased. It almost seems obvious. Is there air in the sky? Water in the ocean? What could be more obvious? But wait—what's it mean to say news is biased? What exactly is bias? These are important questions because news conveys critical information to citizens. If people discount what they read because they believe news is biased, then the currency of democracy—accurate information about public issues—is corroded, facts can't circulate, and people cannot be properly informed.

At first blush, the American public seems to be largely of one mind on the subject, with an overwhelming number (nearly three in four Americans) claiming the news media are biased, tending to favor one side rather than covering all sides fairly (Mitchell et al., 2016). Forty-five percent of the public believes there is a great deal of political bias in news (Jones & Ritter, 2018). With vast amounts of misinformation on the Internet, many Americans doubt the credibility of news, finding it difficult to know whether the information they come across is true or not (Tavernise & Gardiner, 2019).

But what do people mean when they perceive the media are biased? Do they mean the news is too sensational or negative, blaming the messenger for delivering the dreadful drumbeat of terrible events that occur every day? Do they conflate legitimate coverage of unpleasant political events with bias? Are they merely parroting back a fashionable trope? ("But, of course, the media are biased. Everyone knows that"). Are they confusing over-the-top political websites with the entirety of news media? Do they believe news favors a particular political side, and if so, is it liberal or conservative, or something else? Bias is a fascinating, multifaceted term that contains more than meets the eye (and can also be in the eye of the political beholder).

Just as there is far more to bias than it often seems, there are also gray areas when it comes to the much-ballyhooed public mistrust of news. Just about four in ten Americans have "a great deal" or "fair amount of trust" in the news media to accurately report news (Brenan, 2019). Americans' trust of news has taken a nose dive since the mid- to late 20th century, when people famously trusted the veridicality of television news reports, partly because they presumed that live pictures equaled an accurate snapshot of reality. But some of that trust was misplaced because news harbored a variety of subtle and not-so-subtle biases, cheerleading foreign wars and sometimes derogating conservative causes. The decrement in trust of news is also part of a larger decline in Americans' confidence in social and political institutions over the past half-century, from the news media to the frequently distrusted Congress (Montenaro, 2018).

Yet some of Americans' perceptions of bias stem from legitimate beliefs that news harbors a political bias and is promoting a partisan agenda. Eighty-three percent of Americans perceive there is "a great deal" or "a fair amount" of political bias in news coverage; eight in ten say that when they believe there is an inaccuracy in a story, it's because the news is pushing an agenda (Sands, 2020). Sometimes they're mistaken, projecting their attitudes onto news. In other cases, like the Freudian reminder that sometimes a cigar is just a cigar, news does harbor biases. But what kinds of biases does it contain, when it comes to politics and presidential elections?

This chapter and the two that follow address these issues as we place bias under a scholarly microscope, examining the underpinnings of news bias, debunking common myths of news, and offering some conclusions about the controversial issue of political news bias. This chapter provides a broad overview of bias, focusing on liberal and partisan bias. Chapter 12 examines news biases in covering women presidential candidates, and Chapter 13 looks at biases in press coverage of presidential campaigns. In this chapter, I begin by defining bias, always a good way to elucidate an issue. The second section discusses and largely debunks the popular notion of liberal bias. The third portion of the chapter explores the partisan tilt in news coverage, notably (but not exclusively) at Fox News. The conclusion summarizes these issues, offering an expanded perspective, given continued perceptions of bias and the vital role news plays in democratic society.

## UNDERSTANDING POLITICAL NEWS BIAS

At the most basic philosophical level, of course, there is bias in all news. No one is objective. There is bias when a reporter picks one adjective rather than another to describe a candidate's performance in a political debate, or offers an opinionated statement in a tweet (Lawrence et al., 2014). Bias occurs when a photographer selects a camera angle that depicts a candidate in a more, rather than less, flattering pose. Bias emerges when news covers negative rather than positive aspects of public life. Everybody agrees that there are biases in mainstream political news, including sensationalism, focus on celebrities, and emphasis on often-trivial controversies, but these are not the types of biases that animate critics. They are referring to politically motivated or ideological biases that emphasize one view of politics rather than another.

There are plenty of egregious examples out there: the left-wing site, Addicting Info, that claimed without evidence and probably falsely that "U.S. cops killed more people in 1 month than U.K. cops killed last century" (Greenberg, 2015); the right-wing Breitbart News outlet that ridiculously stated that "nearly everything Democrats have done at the national level has made the job losses from coronavirus worse" (Pollak, 2020); and, of course, Alex Jones's conspiracy theory site Infowars that pedaled the outrageous, vicious claim that the 2012 Sandy Hook Elementary School shooting was an intricate hoax concocted by government-backed "gun grabbers." As discussed in Chapter 1, online media are awash in misinformation that is published under the imprimatur of news sites that frequently don't report news and rarely engage in responsible journalism.

There is no question that ideologically based online news sites traffic in bias. The more interesting, controversial question is whether mainstream news outlets with a more politically heterogeneous audience and conventional commitment to journalism contain political bias. To examine this question, it is important to define what is meant by bias in the news.

Bias is an easy label to apply, but it is harder to conceptualize and study. In academic circles the concept is multilayered, with "widespread disagreement about its meaning, measurement, and impact" (Lichter, 2014). Based on political media scholarship (Hofstetter, 1976; Entman, 2010), one can define **ideologically or politically based news bias** as displaying a consistent pattern in presentation of an issue that reliably favors one side, or clearly minimizes the opposing side, in a context when it can reasonably be argued that other perspectives on the issue are also deserving of coverage. Let's review the components of ideological or political news bias.

First, there must be a consistent pattern in the coverage. A story that placed President Biden in a favorable light because of positive developments in the effectiveness of coronavirus vaccines across the U.S. is not biased in favor of Biden. The article is covering a legitimately positive event; not to report this would be biased. If the preponderance of stories about Biden favored him, even in the face of problematic external events (an economic downturn, renewed trouble in the Middle East, or vaccine failures), then we might have a reason to argue that a pro-Biden bias was operating.

Second, political bias requires abundant inclusion of content on behalf of the favored side, systematic exclusion of equivalent material from the opposing group, and clear minimizing of the opposing side. Tone of coverage, word choice, and even the ways that a news organization frames issues can document political bias (e.g., Eberl, Wagner, & Boomgaarden, 2017). But there has to be substantial evidence that the news outlet included favorable content benefiting its preferred side, excluded perspectives from the other side, and its coverage significantly differed from other sites.

A third requirement for ideologically based, motivated news bias is that the biases emerge through reliably conducted, scientific analyses of news content. Observers from different vantage points should detect the same pattern in news coverage. Studies of news bias attempt to make an empirical case by training coders to carefully count the number of negative or positive references to one side or the other, as well as the quantity of telltale adjectives, obviously evaluative tone, and a frame that favors one political group's interpretation of an issue. Researchers can also compare news sites to determine whether one outlet differs significantly from others in content favoring one side rather than the other.

A fourth criteria for bias is that there must be other reasonable perspectives on the issue, which are minimized or excluded due to an apparent political disposition on the part of the individual journalist or media organization. Right-wing outlets that claimed that Democrats stole the 2020 election because mail-in ballots counted after Election Day favored Biden obviously were biased because they didn't consider that it is perfectly legal for states to count absentee or mail-in ballots that arrive shortly after the election. Left-wing outlets that said Trump cheated in the 2016 election because polls said Clinton was going to win would have neglected the obvious possibility that the polls were wrong.

Fifth, and in a related vein, other perspectives that don't get mentioned *should* be deserving of coverage. We would not claim that news coverage of the grisly murder of an innocent person was biased because it offered sympathy for the victim. It would not make sense to charge that the story harbored bias because it failed to offer a sympathetic version of the man who had admitted stabbing the victim 50 times. Nor would we contend that heart-rending stories of New Jersey nursing home residents who died of the coronavirus, as their loved ones struggled to say goodbye, was biased because it showed relatives' poignant emotions, or failed to give the virus's point of view, that it had its own reasonable logic to kill people. The perspectives deserving of coverage must be ones that mesh with cultural values and common sense. Our criteria for judging bias are not perfectly objective, but instead are necessarily based on broader ethical precepts.

There is also another important caveat to any discussion of news bias. From a scientific perspective, bias is an inference one arrives at after careful analysis of news. Scholars must extrapolate from analyses of news content to the motives or intent of news media gatekeepers. *Bias is a psychological or motivational, micro-level construct that must be inferred—thoughtfully, based on evidence and systematic criteria—from content that is produced on a more macro level by a news outlet.* There is necessarily an imperfect fit between the two pieces in the jigsaw puzzle of news media topography. Even when your measurements are exacting, you are making a judgment, like a jury does when it renders a verdict from an aggregation of courtroom evidence. People tend to be careless and emotional when using the term "bias," throwing it out with impunity to denigrate news they don't like or news that seems, in their view, to inappropriately display reporters' opinions. Political communication studies of news bias try to apply more reasoned analyses to this visceral terrain of charges and countercharges. But because even they inherently involve a mismatch—applying a motivational construct (bias) to a macro level topography (news content)—there is much less certainty than in other areas of political communication about the fit between construct and data. Nevertheless, scientific studies of news provide us with boundlessly more thoughtful and illuminating insights on bias than do seat-of-the-pants judgments.

## Trump's Bad Press: Bias or Responsible Journalism?

Based on a thorough content analysis of news coverage of Trump's first 100 days, Patterson (2017) found that 80 percent of Trump's coverage during this period was negative. In contrast, other presidents got less unfavorable press during their first 100 days—41 percent for Obama, 57 percent for George W. Bush, and 60 percent for Clinton.

Why the negative news? Was it anti-Trump, liberal bias? Well, it probably couldn't be an unabashedly clear liberal bias because the Democratic president, Bill Clinton, got the second most negative press. Clinton received a lot of unfavorable coverage during his first 100 days because he made a series of political missteps, including removal of two female attorney general choices after discovering both employed an illegal immigrant as nannies in their homes, and a controversial policy (which angered liberals and conservatives for different reasons) to allow openly gay men and women to serve in the U.S. military. In both cases, journalists were not biased against Clinton, but were doing their jobs by reporting the chief executive's mistakes and the political repercussions. Presidents frequently get bad press for decisions they make that are unpopular or are widely criticized by opponents, but that's not necessarily bias.

In Trump's case, part of the reason he got bad press was that he enacted controversial policies that generated criticism, which the press felt obligated to report. Not long after taking the oath of office, Trump initiated an effort to repeal Obamacare. A week later he barred citizens from seven Muslim-majority nations from entering the U.S. for 90 days, which set up protracted court battles. He also signed an executive order to build a wall at the U.S.-Mexico border, withdrew the United States from a controversial Obama-era international trade pact, which he argued imposed harm on American workers, and confronted the dictatorial North Korean government after Pyongyang test-fired a ballistic missile. Because conflict, controversy, and questioning the president's directives are basic news values, it is no wonder these actions generated negative news. Opponents fired off condemnations, which were highly newsworthy. As Patterson observed, "the early days of his presidency have been marked by far more missteps and mis-hits, often self-inflicted, than any presidency in memory, perhaps ever" (Patterson, 2017).

Most of Trump's negative press resulted from journalists applying normal, routine news values—conflict, controversy, and sources' criticisms—to presidential conduct. There were other reasons, too. Reporters feel an obligation to protect democratic institutions, and Trump's actions, such as the Muslim ban, could be seen as threatening democratic rights. But there were also partisan differences. Although Fox News had more negative than positive stories about Trump, it had far fewer negative (52 percent) than the mean for other news outlets. Conservative channels such as Fox were less likely than other outlets to refute statements made by Trump or administration officials during the first 100 days (Mitchell et al., 2017). Liberal newspapers such as *The New York Times* were particularly apt to apply critical adjectives to Trump early and throughout his term, calling him "mercurial," "chaotic," or "impulsive," with one article even going so far (too far, we might say) as to describe him as "the always-about-me president" (Baker, 2018, p. A1).

It's hard to parcel this out and pinpoint how much of this is ideological bias. Fox, after all, could indeed have covered Trump more positively because it harbored a pro-Trump bias. Other conventionally more liberal outlets could have projected an anti-Trump bias in some cases and probably did. There are, in general, more compelling explanations for the bad press Trump received: news routines favoring conflict and journalistic obligation to hold leaders' feet to the fire, especially when they arguably bend democratic norms. To get a more comprehensive view of these issues, let's look systematically at the broader question of liberal news bias.

## UNPACKING LIBERAL NEWS BIAS

> The media are so partisan that many people are under the impression that they must take their marching orders directly from the Democratic National Committee.
>
> (Coulter, 2008, p. 19)

Liberal news bias. It's voiced so frequently it rolls off your lips and seems like a cultural truism (see Figure 11.1). The news is liberal, isn't it? Of course, it

**Figure 11.1** "The liberal media." It rolls off your lips because it has been repeated so often it seems like a truism or a social fact. Actually, it is a stereotype or a myth that presents a distorted view of political media bias. It contains a kernel of truth. Some American media are liberal some of the time, but most aren't, research indicates, belying a more complex picture of how news covers politics in America.

*Source*: www.gettyimages.com/detail/news-photo/an-attendee-holds-a-media-research-center-sign-reading-dont-news-photo/508981960?adppopup=true

has a strong liberal bias, right? Commentators, particularly from Fox News but from other platforms too, argue that news favors liberal policies, embraces Democratic candidates, and reflexively criticizes Republicans. But is this true? Let's look at the scholarship on the issue.

The liberal bias thesis consists of two parts. First, critics argue that reporters and editors hold liberal, left-of-center attitudes. Second, they contend that journalists project these attitudes into news stories.

There *is* evidence that elite journalists—the national press corps that resides in Washington, D.C.—hold liberal political attitudes (Groseclose & Milyo, 2005; Kuypers, 2014). Some of this may be a result of reporters' natural identification with the underdog, embodied in the journalistic credo that news should afflict the comfortable and comfort the afflicted. Another factor could be that reporters are more critical of authority and identify to a greater degree than other professionals with society's victims. But clearly national political reporters are more liberal politically. The top tier of national reporters tends to hold rather liberal political attitudes, with large majorities reporting that they vote for Democratic rather than Republican presidential candidates. It's a finding that goes back many years (Lichter, Rothman, & Lichter, 1986), and still holds today.

There has been a recent tilt leftward on racial issues, as reporters at *The New York Times* and *The Washington Post*—but also big-city papers in Philadelphia and Pittsburgh—have pushed for more aggressive exposure of racism. The journalists, both Black reporters and their liberal White colleagues, have pushed for "moral clarity" over "neutral objective journalism," arguing that it is high time for the press to illuminate institutional racism with hard-hitting coverage rather than obfuscating with euphemisms and balanced reporting (Lowery, 2020). Although many journalists do not agree with this position, including editors who have called out reporters for biased tweets, as well as others who believe journalists should maintain a veil of judicious detachment, it does have support in some newsrooms, telegraphing a radical-liberal approach to political reporting.

Complementing these observations with empirical data, a content analysis showed that close to six in ten *New York Times* stories published from 1960 to 2005 displayed a liberal, anti-death-penalty tone (Baumgartner, De Boef, & Boydstun, 2008). Scholars have acknowledged that news coverage of a host of social issues, for example, homelessness, gay rights, religion, and gun control, may tilt to the liberal side of the political spectrum (Entman, 2010).

Clearly, then, there is strong evidence that national reporters are liberal and some indication that national media—and particularly leading elite newspapers—tilt liberal in coverage of some issues. That's important to note. Let's examine the issue more systematically.

## Problems With the Liberal News Bias Thesis

As noted previously, there are two parts of the hypothesis: (1) journalists are politically liberal; and (2) they project liberal attitudes into their work, such that news contains a left-of-center bias. Let's review each contention carefully and critically.

Although, as discussed in the previous section, the Washington press corps holds liberal attitudes, mainstream reporters and editors from across the country do not. As David H. Weaver and his colleagues have shown in their research over the past decades, journalists across the nation are more diverse politically than conservative caricatures suggest (Weaver et al., 2007; Willnat & Weaver, 2014). Averaging across data from four decades we find that, more than twice as many journalists were Democrats (36.4%) than Republicans (17.2%), a finding that is consistent with conservatives' criticism of liberal bias in the news. Yet the highest percentage of journalists are Independents (37.7%), with the rest falling into miscellaneous categories.

Indeed, when the survey was conducted in the second decade of this century, the highest proportion of journalists (50.2%) were neither liberal Democrats nor conservative or moderate Republicans, but Independents, a political identification that signifies dissatisfaction with both unbridled liberalism and conservatism, and likely endorsement of some positions of both Republicans and Democrats—in essence, the most neutral political affiliation of them all (see Figure 11.2). Other research conducted by Lars Willnat and his colleagues reports a marked increase in the proportion of reporters who regard themselves as "middle of the road" politically, reflecting a dissatisfaction with both political extremes, notably the far-right, but also the progressive left-wing viewpoint as well (Willnat, Weaver, & Wilhoit, 2017; Weaver, Willnat, & Wilhoit, 2019).

Another problem with the notion that all journalists are liberal is that this view neglects to consider the ideology of reporters' bosses—media executives and owners. They are business people who hold more conservative attitudes, are often anti-union, and are more concerned with the financial bottom line than with promoting pro-Democratic news articles. There is

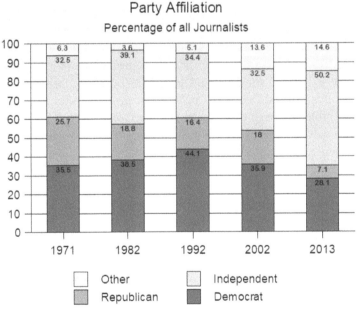

Figure 11.2 **A higher percentage of journalists are Democrats than Republicans. However, the percentage of journalists who indicate they are Democrats declined in 2013. Significantly, there is political variation among journalists, with more than 50 percent of journalists calling themselves Independents in 2013. This contrasts with the cartoon notion that all journalists are liberal Democrats, pointing up differences and complexities in the political attitudes of American reporters.**

*Source:* From Willnat & Weaver (2014)

also a more important factor at work. Reporters are professionals and try hard to live up to the standards of their profession. They recognize that interjecting their own biases in a news story is unprofessional and flies in the face of journalistic canons. It can turn off conservative consumers and get the reporters fired.

Let's look at the second contention: news stories advance a liberal agenda. Keep in mind we are *not* examining whether news outlets' opinion articles are liberal or conservative. Clearly, newspapers and online outlets publish liberal editorials, while others transmit conservative ones. We're talking about the news, the narrative coverage of public events in the world of politics. It can be difficult to separate opinion from news (and, of course, the least professional journalistic sites don't), but based on reasonable yardsticks for what constitutes news articles, one can systematically examine political news content. The liberal bias thesis says that news articles showcase a liberal point of view across the entirety of the U.S. media.

A problem is that much of the evidence advanced in its defense is anecdotal. The only way to convincingly document that the volume or tone of coverage favors one political position over another is to conduct scientific content analyses. When researchers do this, they obtain strikingly different findings than those suggested by conservative critics. In a meta-analysis, or statistical analysis of research, focused on presidential campaign news in elections from 1948 through 1996, D'Alessio and Allen (2000) could not locate any newspaper biases that favored Democrats or Republicans. Biases for newsmagazines were negligible, although there was a slight pro-Republican bias in coverage. Television news contained a modest, though not entirely consistent, trend that favored Democratic candidates. A more recent exhaustive, innovative content analysis of political news in major news outlets found that news organizations describe issues in primarily nonpartisan terms, showing no bias toward Republicans or Democrats, except to depict both sides negatively, reflecting, if anything, a "pox on all sides" bias (Budak, Goel, & Rao, 2016; see also Hassell, Holbein, & Miles, 2020).

What's more, if you go back to the 2016 election, when Trump emerged from the Republican pack, you find evidence that is incompatible with liberal bias. If journalists were out to get Trump or to project their liberal views, then the news should have given his opponents the lion's share of the coverage. In fact, Trump not only garnered a great deal of coverage during the nomination campaign, but his coverage was overwhelmingly positive in the months preceding the Republican primaries (see Figure 11.3). Even *The New York Times* and *The Washington Post*, with their liberal editorial pages, gave Trump a great deal of positive press. About two in three CBS stories were positive, reflecting news's tendency to build up promising presidential contenders, regardless of their ideology.

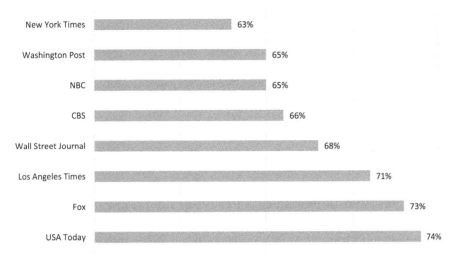

**Figure 11.3  Trump received a great deal of positive press in 2015, the run-up to the 2016 campaign, notably in news outlets presumed to be liberal. This is glaringly inconsistent with the liberal bias thesis.**

*Source:* From Patterson (2016)

In many cases, contemporary news will bend over backwards to give both sides unfavorable as well as favorable press. Cognizant that giving more favorable coverage to liberal than conservative candidates will brand them as biased in the eyes of conservative commentators, contemporary news strives to strike a balance (Puglisi & Snyder, 2011). Thus, whatever positive press *The New York Times* gave Clinton during the 2016 election was more than balanced by negative news. The newspaper broke the big story of Clinton's use of a private mail server that could have breached national security information, and held her feet to the fire throughout the campaign. The stories likely reduced Clinton's standing in the polls, not exactly the outcome a supposedly blue-bleeding liberal news outlet would want.

*The Times* and other national media covered allegations that Trump groped women, but also prominently covered the Bill Clinton [en]Monica Lewinsky saga, as well as Tara Reade's accusation that Joe Biden sexually assaulted her more than 25 years ago. (There was some speculation that the media were slow to cover the Reade allegations, graphic as they were, because of liberal bias toward Biden. That was possible, but there were also inconsistencies in Reade's story that raised journalistic concerns; see Walsh, 2020.)

The liberal bias thesis also neglects news media's coverage of terrorism and foreign wars, which have often sung the U.S. government's praises, offering up a strident "us" versus them refrain. Coverage of 9/11 initially presented a red, white, and blue perspective, parroting the war on terrorism, and providing simplistic good-versus-evil tropes of Islamic violence (Reese & Lewis, 2009). Much of the early news coverage of the Iraqi, Afghanistan, Persian Gulf, and Vietnam Wars played up the pro-war frames of the U.S. government, later providing critical perspectives, but not until the pro-U.S. seeds had been sown (Perloff, 2020). You can defend this coverage on patriotic grounds, but it's hard to call it pro-liberal bias.

The liberal bias thesis also conveniently defines media as blue-state liberal, while forgetting the prominence of conservative media outlets, such as Fox, Breitbart, and the Conservative Broadcast Group, a telecommunications giant that owns close to 200 stations in 89 markets, reaching four in ten American television viewers (Kolhatkar, 2018). The claim that the mainstream media is primarily liberally biased is patently absurd when one considers that a core element of this media—Fox News—has garnered higher audience ratings than the other popular 24-hour news networks—CNN and MSNBC. In the summer of 2020, Fox boasted the highest ratings of any TV channel during prime time, outpacing all the cable and broadcast networks (Grynbaum, 2020). Conservative talk radio programs and Fox News have done well for years, collectively recruiting an audience of at least 50 million (Draper, 2016). If they are outliers, not part of the mainstream media, as conservative critics sometimes allege, then they are extraordinarily potent outliers. But, of course, they're not. Fox is a dominating part of mainstream media, so it's disingenuous to discuss mainstream media biases without considering Fox.

Indeed, the interesting thing about the liberal bias thesis is that liberals have made exactly the opposite case, arguing that the news is the handmaiden of a greedy corporate establishment. In 2016 Bernie Sanders argued that "the corporate media talks about all kinds of issues except the most important issues," claiming that the profit-hungry owners of news media conglomerates develop programming that advances their bottom, line, but steadfastly avoid critical problems such as increasing inequality of wealth (Horowitz, 2016, p. A14). As discussed in Chapter 9, when people (like Bernie Sanders) have strong attitudes on an issue, they are particularly likely to perceive the media are hostilely biased against their side, but bias can be in the eye of the politically passionate beholder.

In sum, when you look at the abundance of social scientific evidence, which is really the only way we can unravel the knotty bias issue, you discover that the liberal bias charge doesn't hold up. Keep in mind we are talking about the entire news media in America—newspapers, local television stations, cable television news, and bona fide online news outlets. On some social issues, such as gun control and abortion, some liberal news outlets probably bleed blue, though evidence is more anecdotal than empirical. A handful of prestigious national news outlets, such as *The New York Times*, seems to have shown a liberal tilt in some coverage of President Trump. However, this is more than offset by even-handed coverage of elections, pro-U.S. coverage of foreign wars, a not-so-subtle pro-capitalism bias in news frames, and conservative outlets that showed a pro-Trump orientation. Remember that for all the vaunted focus on *The New York Times*, there are hundreds of news outlets in the U.S. These don't typically have a liberal tilt, and *The Times*, while prestigious, doesn't control the ways local, regional, and a host of online outlets cover politics.

Finally, the evidence does not support the frequent claim by conservative activists that social media harbors a left-of-center bias. Two empirical studies—conducted by a liberal research group, Media Matters for America, and a social media analysis firm, NewsWhip—show that conservative news groups fare quite well on Facebook. Right-wing and left-wing sites have virtually the same interaction rates, and, by some measures, conservative news sites such as Breitbart had higher engagement rates than their liberal counterpart (Martinez, 2018; McCausland, 2018). Facebook hardly censors right-wing content or blocks it from reaching a large online audience.

When it comes to the entirety of the news media, considering news outlets across the country, it's facile to suggest the news as a whole reflects a liberal political slant. The liberal thesis idea is more myth than realty, more meme than fact.

## THE RISE OF FOX NEWS AND OTHER PARTISAN OUTLETS

The liberal media myth may be more cultural meme than fact, but it's a notion that catapulted Fox News to the top of the pack of cable network news, one that Fox promoted to attract viewers frustrated with homogenized news many perceived to be overly liberal. (Fox didn't create the liberal news bias thesis; Vice President Spiro Agnew was one of the first to conceive the idea in 1969 with a vituperative attack on the nation's news media. His words resonated with conservatives and many White middle-class Americans whom President Nixon hoped to reach by calling them "the great silent majority" in a bid to gain their political support.)

For its part, Fox seized an opportunity to launch a network based on political disaffection, feelings of marginalization, and nostalgia (among some viewers) for a culturally hegemonic White America. Fox developed its brand during the years when Roger Ailes was CEO. Ailes applied his canny understanding of political media, honed during a long consulting career with Republican presidents, to develop Fox as an alternative to CNN, which he branded as the "Clinton News Network," which was hardly true, but helped him build the Fox brand. He milked his knowledge to create stars of Bill O'Reilly (later ousted by Fox after sexual harassment claims) and Sean Hannity (as of this writing, still going strong), using them "as cultural bulwarks against a growing number of contemptible influences: Bill Clinton's libido, the media, environmentalism, gay activists, you name it" (Sherman, 2014, p. 225). Just as the Dallas Cowboys once touted themselves as "America's team," Fox hailed itself as America's network, proudly linking itself patriotically with red, white, and blue values that conservatives championed but liberals found exclusionary.

Although it famously branded itself as "Fair and Balanced" (changing the slogan in 2017 to "Most Watched, Most Trusted" to move away from the slogan's long association with Ailes), it really was neither fair nor balanced, as research has amply documented (e.g., Brock et al., 2011; Iyengar & Hahn, 2009). To its credit, the network did highlight frames that network news overlooked. However, in its overt intermingling of commentary and news, it took on prejudiced positions, as with its promoting the false birther conspiracy theory that Obama had not reproduced his original birth certificate, suggesting the first Black president was not an honest-to-goodness American citizen, a frame explicitly propounded by the star anchor Glenn Beck, who once said Obama was "a guy who has a deep-seated hatred for white people" (Berry & Sobieraj, 2014, p. 43).

During Trump's presidency, Fox departed from other networks by giving Trump considerably more positive press (Patterson, 2017), ardently defending Trump on issues spanning the Mueller Report, impeachment, the coronavirus, and the 2020 presidential campaign. Fox and Trump became joined at the ideological hip; it was for many years his preferred news source. Sean Hannity became a trusted Trump adviser, speaking with Trump on the phone frequently over the course of a week, in the manner of the old 19th-century news editors who brandished the banner of their political party which bankrolled the papers. Fox mega-host Laura Ingraham, who was considered for White House press secretary, met with Trump at the White House during the coronavirus outbreak, advocating an unproven anti-malaria drug Trump had touted as a possible treatment for the virus.

Fox's prime time anchors have become increasingly linked with extremist viewpoints. In August 2020, a White teenager, Kyle Rittenhouse, whose social media platform suggested a strong penchant for law enforcement and guns, traveled to Kenosha, Wisconsin, in the wake of protests over the police shooting of a Black man. When Rittenhouse—who was hanging out with a militia-type group opposed to the protesters at a violent demonstration that broke out—allegedly killed two people, Fox commentators defended him. Tucker Carlson suggested he had to "maintain order when no one else would," and conservative commentator Ann Coulter said she wanted Rittenhouse "as my president" (Bouie, 2020).

Powerful as it is, Fox is not the only player in right-wing circles. After Trump and arch conservatives lashed out at Fox for calling the 2020 election for Biden, followers began gravitating to online sites (and the cable network Newsmax) that propounded baseless ideas of voter fraud and conspiracy theory views that denied Biden won the election (Wakabayashi, 2020).

Bias runs along the left-wing side of the political spectrum, too. Leftist media sites such as The Other 98% and Liberal Blogger have distorted facts to promote anti-Republican viewpoints (Alba, 2020). The queen of liberal news, MSNBC, conveys considerably opinionated perspectives in its prime time talk shows, although perhaps less so in its news coverage, though that remains an empirical question. Rachel Maddow, Chris Hayes, Mika Brzezinski, and the ubiquitous (until a couple of years back) Chris Matthews could offer unabashedly liberal slants on politics. There have been fewer studies of MSNBC than Fox because it lacks the outsize media stars and ratings glitz; MSNBC also occupies a smaller place in liberals' political universes than Fox does for conservatives (Jurkowitz et al., 2020).

Even so, evidence of opinionated coverage are striking, especially for liberals who love to denigrate Fox. A study conducted by the Pew Research Center found that 85 percent of MSNBC's news programs was devoted to expressing opinions, compared to 15 percent for news. By contrast, Fox allotted 55 percent of its shows to opinion and 45 percent to news (Byers, 2013). MSNBC election coverage has tilted strongly to the left; back in 2012, it offered 23 times more favorable coverage to Obama than to Republican challenger Mitt Romney, whereas Fox gave just five times as much good press to Romney than to Obama. Since then, MSNBC has displayed considerable contempt for Trump.

As one conservative writer noted, on MSNBC, there are

> no gray areas whatsoever. All local variation is apartheid, each and every (voter) identification is the second coming of Jim Crow. . . . After all, what could one possibly add to Martin Bashir's suggestions that someone should defecate in Sarah Palin's mouth . . . or that (Texas Republican Senator) Ted Cruz is the 'David Koresh' of the Republican Party?
>
> (Byers, 2013)

For partisans, these politically tinged news sites are a gushing well, overflowing with supportive information that reaffirms that they are right. What is conspicuously missing is information that questions the accuracy and validity of the opposing side, or that identifies systemic limits in both party's political positions. Over the past several decades, the news media has become more overtly partisan, but outstanding journalism is still around and plays an important role in democracy, as I discuss in the concluding section of the chapter.

## CONCLUSIONS

*The news media are biased.* This comment is heard so frequently today it can be considered a cliché or a cultural catchphrase. But what does bias mean, and is the statement true? This chapter unpacked these issues.

In today's blur-the-lines online media, we encounter numerous reports on partisan, opinionated outlets that might be viewed as news, but are either false or heavily biased, or fail to satisfy journalistic criteria, such as cross-checking information with different sources and assessing the reliability of facts that sources provide. Some news outlets, such as Infowars, are conspiracy theory sites full of lies and distortion, employing the news moniker to attract ideologically congenial readers, a tradition that, in one broad sense, goes back to the 19th-century party-controlled press. Other news, gathered by the best journalists in the land, informs, interprets, exposes, and enlightens, performing a valuable role in political communication.

Of course, that's not how critics see it. They roundly criticize news for blatantly showcasing political biases. What is meant by bias? Political news bias occurs when there is a consistent pattern in news presentations that favors one side when it can be reasonably argued that other perspectives are deserving of coverage. It is inherently difficult to *prove* that bias occurs because it requires an inference from news content to the psychological or motivational predispositions of journalists. Nonetheless, through careful content analysis, one can make reasonable inferences about the degree to which news reflects a bias toward one political end of the spectrum or the other.

In one important sense, political news is biased. It favors the two major party candidates (Kirch, 2013) and frames the election as a game (see Chapter 13). Beyond that, critics, usually conservative, argue that the news reflects a strong liberal political bias. Donald Trump famously castigated the press, denouncing the "fake news" that presumably harbors a liberal bias. It's complicated. Trump was the beneficiary of a great deal of favorable press during the first phases of the 2016 presidential nomination, but he received considerable negative press as president because of actions he took, journalistic news values, and in a few cases, liberal bias.

Does the American press broadly display a liberal bias? National reporters are liberal, and national news on some social issues can tilt liberal. Some of the coverage of President Trump, including in the vaunted *New York Times*, used adjectives and frames that depicted him negatively. It may have been a liberal bias, but it is equally plausible to argue that it reflected the value the press places on protecting democratic institutions from assault, as well as reasonable coverage of Trump's controversial actions.

The aggregate picture is more complex. On the whole, journalists from the broad cross-sections of the U.S. are more conservative than the Washington press corps, holding a range of political views. In addition, social science studies cast doubt on the thesis that news reflects liberal bias, pointing to even-handed coverage of national elections, rah-rah patriotic coverage of foreign wars, and a tendency for critics to perceive hostile media bias as a result of their own partisan perceptions. In general, news is too variegated, complicated, and economically determined to sustain a simple thesis that it is shaped by some reporters' political attitudes or pushes a pro-Democratic Party perspective. The liberal media bias thesis offers a simple brushstroke to describe the tableau of a complex, multifaceted political media collage.

What's more, a variety of overtly conservative news outlets have emerged over the past decades, chiefly Fox News, that have intermingled opinion with facts, offering up right-leaning biases. But (lest I be accused of a liberal bias!) liberal news sites such as MSNBC flagrantly display left-wing biases. Of course, news contained biases in the more buttoned-down era of broadcast news; they were hidden, reflected the political establishment, and were presented in a gentlemanly way (literally, given the preponderance of male journalists). Now everything is wide open, and more overtly partisan news runs the gamut from reactionary to radical left-wing. But there is also a great deal of informative, fair-minded news out there in the kaleidoscopic news universe.

What gets noticed are the overtly partisan stories that in turn elicit perceptions of news bias. As discussed in Chapter 9, the pervasive *perception* of news bias has untoward consequences on the body politic and democracy. It leads people to presume that every reporter, including those who consciously put their opinions aside as best they can when covering news, is distorting the news. It causes people to distrust mainstream news, throw up their hands, and put their faith in a partisan outlet that fits their values. It reduces the credibility of news as an institution that informs, interprets complex phenomena, and holds public officials accountable for misdeeds.

It is one thing to point to news bias, areas where opinion intruded on factual reporting, and another to claim that the entire institution of news-gathering is rigged or corrupt. Political journalism is flawed, imperfect, and at certain outlets, reflective of partisan bias, but in its unbridled determination to uncover truth and speak truth to political power, it remains endemic to democracy. The news of 2020 is testament to this. Reporters courageously covered the devastation of the pandemic, sometimes at risk to themselves, bringing Americans compelling narratives about the health crisis, systemic problems, and shortcomings in the White House's response. With the aid of graphic videos, news told the story of protests that occurred after George Floyd's death, illuminating police violence, protest overreach, and racial inequities, helping to spur social change. Coverage of the election, while frequently driven by polls, elaborated on social problems, from health care to global warming, offered information on policy complexity, as well as chinks in presidential candidates' political armor. After the election, news shined a spotlight on the horrific insurrection at the U.S. Capitol, showcasing the ways that a mob, harboring racist beliefs, could do damage to democratic institutions.

This kind of news is important to a democracy, but is also under siege, as newsroom employment has plummeted in recent years, and news outlets, faced with a constellation of economic pressure points, have gone belly-up or been bought by greedy owners with little concern for journalistic values. As theorists have long argued, "the health of our democracy is contingent on the health of journalism" (Stearns, 2018). News cultivates a public sector that extends beyond people's private lives, creating a sense of civic identity and cognizance of community problems that spurs political participation.

But when local newspapers collapse or lack resources to cover community events, people are no longer aware of the problems facing their communities, can't hold public officials responsible and, more generally, are deprived of a connection between their role as citizens and the political world. As a result, the decline of newspapers is strongly linked with drops in civic engagement, reductions in voter turnout, and more partisan voting decisions that result from exposure to polarizing election coverage in national news (Shaker, 2014; Stearns, 2018; Darr, Hitt, & Dunaway, 2018). What's more, in the absence of the press holding officials' feet to the fire, governments have less incentive to respond to civic input, fewer candidates challenge incumbents for political office, and incumbents keep getting reelected, giving them an electoral lock on their districts (Schulhofer-Wohl & Garrido, 2011).

"Journalism is good for democracy," as Stearns reminds us. It's important to remember when charges of news bias are hurled about.

## REFERENCES

Alba, D. (2020, October 15). Riled up: Misinformation stokes calls for violence on Election Day. *The New York Times*. Online: www.nytimes.com/2020/10/13/technology/viral-misinformation-violence-election.html. (Accessed: October 15, 2020).

Baker, P. (2018, September 14). Trump rejects a storm's tally as winds roar. *The New York Times*, A1, A20.

Baumgartner, F.R., De Boef, S.L., & Boydstun, A.E. (2008). *The decline of the death penalty and the discovery of innocence*. New York: Cambridge University Press.

Berry, J., & Sobieraj, S. (2014). *The outrage industry: Political opinion media and the new incivility*. New York: Oxford University Press.

Bouie, J. (2020, August 28). Kenosha tells us more about where the right is headed than the R.N.C. did. *The New York Times*. Online: www.nytimes.com/2020/08/28/opinion/sunday/kenosha-kyle-rittenhouse-trump.html. (Accessed: December 17, 2020).

Brenan, M. (2019. September 26). Americans' trust in mass media edges down to 41%. *Gallup*. Online: https://news.gallup.com/poll/267047/americans-trust-mass-media-edges-down.aspx. (Accessed: December 3, 2020).

Brock, D., Rabin-Havt, A., & Media Matters for America (2012). *The Fox effect: How Roger Ailes turned a network into a propaganda machine*. New York: Anchor Books.

Budak, C., Goel, S., & Rao, J.M. (2016). Fair and balanced? Quantifying media bias through crowdsourced content analysis. *Public Opinion Quarterly*, *80*, 250–271.

Byers, D. (2013, December 9). Is MSNBC worse than Fox News. *Politico*. Online: www.politico.com/blogs/media/2013/12/is-msnbc-worse-than-fox-news-179175. (Accessed: May 15, 2020).

Coulter, A. (2008). *Guilty: Liberal "victims" and their assault on America*. New York: Crown Forum.

D'Alessio, D., & Allen, M. (2000). Media bias in presidential elections: A meta-analysis. *Journal of Communication, 50*, 133–156.

Darr, J.P., Hitt, M.P., Dunaway, J.L. (2018). Newspaper closures polarize voting behavior. *Journal of Communication, 68*, 1007–1028.

Draper, R. (2016, October 2). How Donald Trump's candidacy set off a civil war within the right wing media. *The New York Times Magazine*, 36–41, 54–55.

Eberl, J-M., Wagner, M., & Boomgaarden, H.G. (2017). Are perceptions of candidate traits shaped by the media? The effects of three types of media bias. *The International Journal of Press/Politics, 22*, 111–132.

Entman, R.M. (2010). Framing media power. In P. D'Angelo & J.A. Kuypers (Eds.), *Doing news framing analysis: Empirical and theoretical perspectives* (pp. 331–355). New York: Routledge.

Greenberg, J. (2015, April 15). Liberal blog: U.S. cops killed more people in one month than U.K. cops killed last century. *PolitiFact*. Online: www.politifact.com/fact checks/2015/apr/15/addicting-information/liberal-blog-us-cops-killed-more-peo ple-one-month-/. (Accessed: December 2, 2020).

Groseclose, T., & Milyo, J. (2005). A measure of media bias. *The Quarterly Journal of Economics, 120*, 1191–1237.

Grynbaum, M.M. (2020, August 9). Boycotted. Criticized. But Fox News leads the pack in prime time. *The New York Times*. Online: www.nytimes.com/2020/08/09/busi ness/media/fox-news-ratings.html. (Accessed: December 3, 2020).

Hassell, H.J.G., Holbein, J.B., & Miles, M.R. (2020, April). There is no liberal media bias in which news stories political journalists choose to cover. *Science Advances, 6*. Online: https://advances.sciencemag.org/content/6/14/eaay9344/tab-pdf/. (Accessed: January 10, 2021).

Hofstetter, C.R. (1976). *Bias in the news: Network television coverage of the 1972 presidential campaign*. Columbus: Ohio State University Press.

Horowitz, J. (2016, February 24). News media is part of the Establishment Sanders rails against. *The New York Times*, A14.

Iyengar, S., & Hahn, K.S. (2009). Red media, blue media: Evidence of ideological sensitivity in media use. *Journal of Communication 59*, 19–39.

Jones, J.M., & Ritter, Z. (2018, January 17). *Americans see more news bias; most can't name neutral source*. Gallup/Knight Foundation Survey on Trust, Media and Democracy. Online: https://news.gallup.com/poll/225755/americans-news-bias-name-neutral-source.aspx. (Accessed: December 17, 2020).

Jurkowitz, M., Mitchell, A., Shearer, E., & Walker, M. (2020, January 24). *Democrats report much higher levels of trust in a number of news sources than Republicans*. Pew Research Center (Journalism & Media). Online: www.journalism. org/2020/01/24/democrats-report-much-higher-levels-of-trust-in-a-number-of-news-sources-than-republicans/. (Accessed: August 25, 2020).

Kirch, J.F. (2013). News coverage different for third-party candidates. *Newspaper Research Journal, 34*(4), 40–53.

Kolhatkar, S. (2018, October 22). Breaking the news. *The New Yorker*, 30–31, 34, 36–40, 42. Online: www.npr.org/2020/04/17/818952460/did-gender-keep-democratic-women-from-winning-the-primary. (Accessed: May 18, 2020).

Kuypers, J.A. (2014). *Partisan journalism: A history of media bias in the United States.* Lanham, MD: Rowman & Littlefield.

Lawrence, R.G., Molyneux, L., Coddington, M., & Holton, A. (2014). Tweeting conventions: Political journalists' use of Twitter to cover the 2012 presidential campaign. *Journalism Studies, 15,* 789–806.

Lichter, S.R. (2014). Theories of media bias. In K. Kenski & K.H. Jamieson (Eds.), *The Oxford handbook of political communication*. Online: www.oxfordhandbooks. com. (Accessed: June 7, 2016).

Lichter, S.R., & Rothman, S., & Lichter, L.S. (1986). *The media elite*. Bethesda, MD: Adler & Adler.

Lowery, W. (2020, June 23). A reckoning over objectivity, led by Black journalists. *The New York Times*. Online: www.nytimes.com/2020/06/23/opinion/objectivity-black-journalists-coronavirus.html. (Accessed: June 29, 2020).

Martinez, N. (2018, July 16). Study: Analysis of top Facebook pages covering American political news. *Media Matters for America*. Online: www.mediamatters.org/ facebook/study-analysis-top-facebook-pages-covering-american-political-news. (Accessed: May 29, 2020).

McCausland, P. (2018, April 15). GOP accuses Facebook of censorship but conservative media flourishes online. *NBC News*. Online: www.nbcnews.com/tech/social-media/ gop-accuses-facebook-censorship-conservative-media-flourishes-online-n865276. (Accessed: December 12, 2020).

Mitchell, A., Gottfried, J., Barthel, M., & Shearer, E. (2016, July 7). *The modern news consumer: Trust and accuracy*. Pew Research Center (Journalism & Media). Online: www.rjournalism.org/2016/07/07/trust-and-accuracy/. (Accessed: December 16, 2016).

Mitchell, A., Gottfried, J., Stocking, G., Matsa, K.E., & Grieco, E. (2017, October 2). *Covering President Trump in a polarized media environment*. Pew Research Center (Journalism & Media). Online: www.journalism.org/2017/10/02/covering-president-trump-in-a-polarized-media-environment/. (Accessed: May 13, 2020).

Montenaro, D. (2018, January 17). Here's just how little confidence Americans have in political institutions. *NPR*. Online: www.npr.org/2018/01/17/578422668/heres-just-how-little-confidence-americans-have-in-political-institutions. (Accessed: July 28, 2020).

Patterson, T.E. (2016, December 14). *Pre-primary news coverage of the 2016 presidential race: Trump's rise, Sanders' emergence, Clinton's struggle*. Harvard Kennedy School Shorenstein Center on Media, Politics and Public Policy. Online: https://papers.ssrn. com/sol3/papers.cfm?abstract_id=2798258. (Accessed: December 11, 2020).

Patterson, T.E. (2017, May). *News coverage of Donald Trump's First 100 Days*. Harvard Kennedy School Shorenstein Center of Media, Politics and Public Policy. Online: https://shorensteincenter.org/wp-content/uploads/2017/05/News-Coverage-of-Trump-100-Days-5-2017.pdf. (Accessed: May 13, 2020).

Perloff, R.M. (2020). *The dynamics of news: Journalism in the 21st century media milieu*. New York: Routledge.

Pollak, J.B. (2020, May 11). Pollak: 5 ways Democrats are making job losses worse. *Breitbart News*. Online: www.breitbart.com/economy/2020/05/11/pollak-5-ways-democrats-are-making-job-losses-worse/?utm_medium=social&utm_source=facebook. (Accessed: May 11, 2020).

Puglisi, R., & Snyder, J.M., Jr. (2011). Newspaper coverage of political scandals. *Journal of Politics, 73*, 931–950.

Reese, S.D., & Lewis, S.C. (2009). Framing the war on terror: The internalization of policy in the U.S. press. *Journalism, 10*, 777–797.

Sands, J. (2020, August 4). *Americans are losing faith in an objective media. A new Gallup/Knight study explores why.* Knight Foundation. Online: https://knightfoundation.org/articles/americans-are-losing-faith-in-an-objective-media-a-new-gallup-knight-study-explores-why/. (Accessed: December 17.2020).

Schulhofer-Wohl, S., & Garrido, M. (2011, December). Do newspapers matter? Short-run and long-run evidence from the closure of *The Cincinnati Post*. *NBER Working Paper Series*. Online: www.nber.org/papers/w14817.pdf. (Accessed: July 13, 2020).

Shaker, L. (2014). Dead newspapers and citizens' civic engagement. *Political Communication, 31*, 131–148.

Sherman, G. (2014). *The loudest voice in the room: How the brilliant, bombastic Roger Ailes built Fox News—and divided a country.* New York: Random House.

Stearns, J. (2018, June 26). How we know journalism is good for democracy. *Medium*. Online: https://medium.com/office-of-citizen/how-we-know-journalism-is-good-for-democracy-9125e5c995fb. (Accessed: December 4, 2020).

Tavernise, S., & Gardiner, A. (2019, November 18). Many Americans avoid impeachment hearings. *The New York Times*, A1, A13.

Wakabayashi, D. (2020, November 16). Fox News's "partisan right" audience on YouTube is dropping, researchers say. *The New York Times*. Online: www.nytimes.com/2020/11/16/technology/fox-news-youtube-election.html/ (Accessed: November 18, 2020).

Walsh, J. (2020, April 15). The troublesome Tara Reade story. *The Nation*. Online: www.thenation.com/article/politics/tara-reade-joe-biden-democrats/. (Accessed: May 25, 2020).

Weaver, D.H., Beam, R.A., Brownlee, B.J., Voakes, P.S., & Wilhoit, G.C. (2007). *The American journalist in the 21st century: U.S. news people at the dawn of a new millennium.* Mahwah, NJ: Erlbaum Associates.

Weaver, D.H., Willnat, L., & Wilhoit, G.C. (2019). The American journalist in the digital age: Another look at U.S. news people. *Journalism & Mass Communication Quarterly, 96*, 101–130.

Willnat, L., & Weaver, D.H. (2014). *The American journalist in the digital age: Key findings.* Bloomington, IN: School of Journalism, Indiana University. Online: https://larswillnat.files.wordpress.com/2014/05/2013-american-journalist-key-findings.pdf. (Accessed: December 17, 2020).

Willnat, L., Weaver, D.H., & Wilhoit, G.C. (2017). *The American journalist in the digital age: A half-century perspective.* New York: Peter Lang.

# 12 Gender Bias in Political News

When Joe Biden selected Kamala Harris as his vice presidential nominee, the press swooned, offering an outpouring of stories pronouncing the history-making moment, a woman of color becoming the vice presidential nominee of a major political party (see Figure 12.1). While reporters had commented on her political downsides as a candidate—waging an ineffective presidential campaign; a conservative record on law enforcement that displeased party progressives—mainstream news contained not a whiff of gender bias. So, is there at last gender parity in political communication?

Elizabeth Warren, a candidate for the 2020 Democratic nomination, would beg to differ:

> If you say, "Yeah, there was sexism in this race," everyone says, "Whiner!" If you say, "No, there was no sexism," about a bazillion women think, "What planet do you live on?" —Senator Elizabeth Warren
>
> (Kurtzleben, 2020)

Few would doubt the validity of Warren's lament about the 2020 presidential primary elections—and perhaps politics in general. Women are less likely than men to be recruited to run for political office (Lawless & Fox, 2008). Given that even political career women bear the burden of household and child care duties, female politicians frequently launch their careers later than men do. Male political leaders can make incredibly nasty comments about women, using the b-word freely. Voter biases also play a role. In 2020 Democratic primary voters who harbored hostile sexist feelings toward women—such as that they exaggerate problems at work or are apt to unreasonably claim discrimination—held less favorable attitudes toward the party's female candidates (Luke & Schaffner, 2019).

What role does political journalism play in the process? Is political journalism sexist? Do stereotypes of male and female politicians still occur at more

**Figure 12.1 The press bestowed generally positive coverage on Kamala Harris—the child of immigrants, who served as California's Attorney General and senator—when she became the first woman of color to gain the vice presidential nomination of a major party (and later the first female vice president). This news coverage contrasted sharply with a history of unfavorable, sexist coverage of female politicians during the 20th century.**

*Source*: www.gettyimages.com/detail/news-photo/senator-kamala-harris-democratic-vice-presidential-nominee-news-photo/1228115152?utm_medium=organic&utm_source=google&utm_campaign=iptcurl

subtle levels? Or has news changed? And can female political journalists find themselves unfairly subjected to charges of sexism as well? These questions are the focus of this chapter, as I examine another aspect of the political bias quandary, focusing on the important, explosive issue of whether, and how, news tilts coverage against female contenders. Keep in mind the focus of the chapter is mainstream news, as discussed in Chapter 11. There is no question that some partisan opinion sites are full of sexist language. The more important question is whether news, as an important gatekeeper, agenda-setter, and influencer of citizen frames, promotes stereotyped coverage. This chapter examines these issues. It doesn't look at gender as a simple determinant of news, but as one that varies as a function of the times and journalistic routines. It highlights virulent sexism, but also debunks myths that all negative coverage of female candidates is sexist. Yet discussion also points out subtle gender role biases that lie under the surface. The first section explores historical changes in news coverage of gender from the 1970s through the 2016 presidential election. The second portion wrestles with the question of gender biases in the 2020 Democratic primaries and presidential contest.

## HISTORICAL PROGRESSION

This is the way it used to be:

In 1972, when New York Congresswoman Shirley Chisholm became the first Black candidate to run for president of one of the nation's two major parties, neither the press nor party regulars took her nomination seriously. In the early 1970s, the Women's Movement began to gather steam, and egalitarian supporters of women's rights, reaffirming Chisholm's candidacy, emphasized that more women should run for elective office. Some dreamed of a day when a woman could be elected president. But this was the 1970s, and sex-role prejudice was pervasive. Typifying the view held by many Americans, one man noted that:

> Women are not qualified for this high office. If one is ever elected President, she would have to depend 100% on the advice of the men she appointed to high executive positions. Heaven help us in the event of a war. She couldn't handle the awesome responsibilities.
>
> (Falk, 2010, pp. 37–38)

Journalism contained many of the same biases. In 1984, when Democratic vice presidential candidate Geraldine Ferraro triumphantly stood before delegates at the 1984 Democratic National Convention, NBC anchor Tom Brokaw announced: "Geraldine Ferraro . . . The first woman to be nominated for Vice President . . . Size six" (Braden, 1996, p. 15). During a time when reporters were on the constant lookout to see if a woman candidate would cry or lack the toughness to stand up to America's enemies, Ferraro was asked on the television news program *Meet the Press*, "Do you think that in any way the Soviets might be tempted to try to take advantage of you simply because you are a woman?" (Mitchell, 2016, p. 18).

News devoted less coverage to female than male candidates running for the Senate between 1982 and 1988, and coverage was also more negative, downplaying women's chances of winning (Kahn, 1994). Female candidates running for Senate stressed their masculine traits, such as strength, over 90 percent of the time in ads, but news stories described these characteristics about 40 percent of the time (Kahn, 1996; Beail & Longworth, 2013). Female presidential candidates garnered less coverage than their male counterparts in 1972, 1988, 2000, and 2004. News portrayed female presidential candidates as less likely to succeed than comparable male candidates (Falk, 2010; see also Meeks, 2012). The coverage stemmed from gender role stereotypes reporters applied to female candidates, including the **gendered double bind**, the sexist notion that women cannot be both professionally competent and feminine (Jamieson, 1995).

You may argue that news gave women candidates less coverage simply because they were less likely to win, applying a realistic filter to campaigns. That may be true, but it creates a vicious cycle of self-fulfilling prophecies, where lack of coverage causes female politicians to be treated less seriously, and because they are treated less seriously, they get less coverage. Something has to flip the switch.

## Reviewing the 2008 and 2016 Campaigns

In 2008, gender leapt to the foreground of the presidential campaign. Hillary Clinton nearly won the Democratic presidential nomination and Republicans nominated Sarah Palin as vice president. Did gender biases influence coverage?

Content analyses offer insights into this question. Although print articles offered about the same number of physical descriptions of Clinton as of Obama, Clinton was described early on in more physical terms than the average for previous male presidential contenders (Falk, 2010). Some of those physical descriptions raised eyebrows. A frequently discussed *Washington Post* article about Clinton remarked that "the neckline (of a black top) sat low on her chest and had a subtle V-shape. The cleavage registered after only a quick glance" (Falk, p. 158). Articles were also more likely to refer to Clinton by her first name than they were to call Obama "Barack," or her other major competitor, John Edwards, "John," a common phenomenon in professional circles.

Opinionated cable shows and websites were filled with biases, some vicious and vulgar. Radio and cable television commentaries took off the gloves. They unleashed the b-word with impunity. Conservative radio host Glenn Beck called Clinton a "stereotypical bitch." Castration images also were invoked. Clinton was the recipient of many gender-based insulting messages. For example, Tucker Carlson, the prominent conservative TV commentator, remarked that "There's just something about her that feels castrating, overbearing and scary," and on another show noted that "I have often said, when she comes on television, I involuntarily cross my legs" (Falk, p. 165; Douglas, 2010). Social media and websites offered a slew of degrading portrayals of Clinton, though this dissipated, if not disappeared, in 2016.

Let's be clear: Blogs, YouTube, and Facebook sites do not reflect mainstream media. They can represent fringe groups, the Wild Wild West of contemporary media that do not cover issues in a professionally journalistic fashion. In the main, journalists did not cover Clinton or Palin in this way. Indeed, some journalists were quick to criticize those who used the b-word to describe Clinton. So, how positive or negative were Clinton's and Palin's press? To answer this question, we turn to content analyses of news coverage. These studies code positivity or negativity by examining how sources quoted in the stories evaluate the candidate, adjectives reporters use to describe the candidates ("grating" versus "strong"; "shrill" versus "forceful"), and the overall tone of the stories. When researchers refer to the positive or negative press candidates receive, they are describing results gleaned from content analytic studies.

Clearly, over the course of both elections Clinton received positive press, focusing on her experience, primary debate successes, how she almost shattered the glass ceiling in 2008, and became the first woman to gain the nomination of a major political party in the United States in 2016, an achievement that, as one article enthusiastically noted, made many women feel proud, evoking cheers and tears (Kantor, 2016). But she also received negative news coverage, garnering significantly more negative news than Obama did in 2008, and more unfavorable coverage during the early 2016 campaign than any of the major candidates of both parties in 2016 (Lawrence & Rose, 2010; Patterson, 2016; see Figure 12.2). In 2016, there was a steady drip-drip, then an outpouring, of news that focused on negative aspects of her campaign, from her emails to possible conflicts of interest with the Clinton Foundation.

How can we explain her negative press? Some of it could have been rooted in sexism, as when reporters might view her in sex-typed ways, calling her "shrill," or perhaps playing up her anger more than they would that of a male candidate. Much, though not all, of this can be explained by journalistic factors, the news values and routines reporters use to construct stories (see Figure 12.2).

A key factor is that Clinton was the frontrunner in 2008, and reporters subject frontrunners to tough questions. They believe that voters have a right to know

**Figure 12.2 Hillary Clinton transcended gender barriers by becoming the first American woman nominated by a major political party. During the 2016 primary campaign, her news coverage was frequently negative, due to the nature of political journalism routines. While the treatment did not reflect sexist biases, the peevishness and negativity made one wonder if the same coverage would have been doled out to a male candidate.**

the fallibilities of their party's potential nominee so that they can weigh these factors when they vote (see Chapter 13). A political journalism perspective emphasizes that the negative press that Clinton received was not primarily due to gender, but represented an attempt to hold her feet to the fire as the Democratic frontrunner.

By contrast, Obama, who challenged Clinton for the 2008 Democratic nomination, received more positive press. One explanation for the better press Obama received is because he was a fresh face on the campaign scene, a politician with extraordinary communication skills, an African American with a major shot to become his party's nominee, who had recruited an army—a movement—of young supporters. All this was new, and journalism places a value on novelty. For all of her shattering the gender barrier, which she most assuredly did do, Clinton was a familiar face, laden with controversies that dated back to her years as First Lady. She magnified this with highly publicized interpersonal conflict among staffers. In addition, "Obama embodied and symbolized racial progress for many people in the United States (or at least many pundits and commentators) in a way that Clinton did not symbolize progress on sexual equality" (Lawrence & Rose, 2010, pp. 216–218). All this was in keeping with journalistic norms, and it wasn't biased against Clinton per se, but there was also something vaguely unfair about how Clinton's candidacy was treated, in comparison to Obama's.

In 2016, considerable news centered on Clinton's use of a private email server that led to national security questions, subsequent FBI investigations of her email use, Republican outcry, and all the political implications journalists love to cover. There was a constant stream of negativity in Clinton's press coverage, with some of the negative press reflecting legitimate concern about her decision to use an email server that could have compromised national security (O'Harrow, 2016). Other aspects of the negative news seemed rooted in the ways it fit the time-honored journalistic narrative that Clinton had a penchant for secrecy (see Chapter 13), as well as the press's gravitation to character attacks rather than issues. While it didn't reflect sexist biases against Clinton, there was something peevishly negative in how she was treated by the press, making you wonder if the same treatment would have been doled out to a man.

Over on the Republican side, in 2008, Republican vice presidential nominee Sarah Palin received negative press, but the reasons are complicated. A systematic analysis of over 2,500 newspaper articles revealed that Palin received more negative press than Democratic vice presidential candidate Joe Biden. Newspaper articles mentioned her gender six times more frequently than Biden's. They also contained significantly more references to her appearance and marital status than to Biden's, perhaps triggering stereotyped beliefs about political candidates (Miller & Peake, 2013). Some news stories were blatantly sexist, making references to her sexuality (Carlin & Winfrey, 2009), allusions reporters would not invoke for a comparable male candidate. But most of the negative press did not stem from gender biases. Instead, as Bradley and Wicks (2011) noted, "because Palin was new to the political sphere, journalists may have attempted to 'dig up the dirt' on her life and career" (p. 816). And there was plenty of "dirt" to unearth, juicy tidbits that are the fodder of political news, such as her teenage daughter's pregnancy and the embarrassing revelation that the Republican National Committee had paid for Palin's expensive campaign wardrobe. But, in the main, reporters didn't dig up dirt because Palin was a woman, but rather, because journalists feel a professional obligation to let voters know about the shortcomings of a candidate who could become vice president of the United States. And, in fairness, Palin invited some of the negative press when she fumbled in an interview with *Today*'s Katie Couric, unable to name specific newspapers she read on a regular basis.

Could some of her negative press have resulted from gendered stereotypes, that mothers are seen as more involved in a child's upbringing—and daughter's pregnancy—than fathers? Had Palin been a male, would the news have covered the pregnancy as closely? Probably not, especially since the media devotes more attention to female politicians' personal lives than to men's (Van der Pas & Aaldering, 2020).

## Subtle Biases About Female Candidates and Appearance

Critics argue that news coverage of female candidates contains subtle, but important, gender biases by focusing more on women's appearance and wardrobe than on men's.

Palin's 2008 media portrayals took on a more gendered hue than that of other candidates, partly due to her own self-presentation (her taste in high-priced stylish clothing was distinctive), journalistic conventions, and traditional press focus on women's appearance (Finneman, 2015; Kahl & Edwards, 2009). Journalists framed Palin in a variety of ways, a function of her political complexity (Beail & Longworth, 2013). Palin took stridently stereotypically masculine issue positions, while displaying the "trappings of femininity—stiletto heels, silk shirts, and pearls," and lipstick (Lawrence & Rose, p. 221), the latter not surprising, given her famous quip that the difference between a hockey mom and a pitbull was lipstick! When she endorsed Trump in 2016, she was described in the news as wearing a "sparkly Milly beaded silk bolero jacket" that cost $695. Style experts criticized her choice of clothing, and on Twitter a marketing specialist compared her to a "disco ball hedgehog" (Baird, 2016, p. A23).

On the one hand, Palin's sartorial personae invited a flurry of feature stories. On the other hand, her coverage pointed up a continued double bind—a "damned if you do and damned if you don't" aspect of news of female political candidates; reporters peruse women candidates' physical appearances, offering criticism when they lay out money to emphasize their frequently examined wardrobe (Finneman, p. 147) and lamenting their appearance when they seem to pay it less mind. It plays on a stereotyped double bind: A female politician is seen as selling out her gender identity by dressing in a masculine way; however, if she displays traditional feminine trappings, she is perceived as using sex appeal to appeal to voters. This dynamic applied to Palin's coverage. She dressed in attractive ways, obviously enjoying clothing and traditional accoutrements of femininity. News could focus on this feature of her candidacy. But would the news have called attention to the same stylistic dimensions in a male candidate?

Hillary Clinton may have faced a dialectical conflict—or double bind—with her preference for pantsuits, and news coverage may have made the wardrobe more salient by covering Clinton's clothing over the years, as in stories about a "silk teal pantsuit" designed by Oscar de la Renta, a silver pantsuit worn to a downtown Manhattan dinner, and a tan pantsuit when she appeared on *The Late Show with David Letterman* back in 2007 (Francis & Gregory, 2015, p. 165). However, clothing could also be described in ways congenial with feminism, as in the description of Clinton's wardrobe at the third 2016 presidential debate, when she was described as "wearing a suffragette-inspired white suit" (Stockman, 2016, p. A17).

News has historically focused more on female candidates' clothing than on the apparel of their male counterparts. Some argue that focusing on women candidates' fashion appeal calls up stereotypes that emphasize physical appearance at the expense of political acumen. Others defend the coverage, noting that, as one prominent female political leader said, "I'm a woman, I like clothes" (Friedman, 2016).

Yet it was disconcerting that sexist snipes of powerful women's clothing continued after the election, with Twitter critics attacking senior White House adviser Kellyanne Conway's hair, appearance, and clothing. "Why does Kellyanne Conway always look like she's still drunk & wearing makeup from last night's bender?," one asked. Another complained that her Inauguration Day wardrobe looked like "a night terror of an android majorette" (Chira, 2017, p. A1). However, there was enormous—endless—coverage of Trump's hair and orange face.

Media depictions that emphasize women's body or physical appearance can diminish positive evaluations of female leaders' abilities and warmth (Heflick et al., 2011), encouraging people to view women in objectified ways. This suggests that press focus on women candidates' clothing can push voters to regress to more sex-typed evaluations of female candidates, overlooking their professional qualities in favor of superficial stereotypes (see Box 12.1). Indeed, strong research evidence shows that female politicians get more coverage of their appearance and families than men, pushing voters to rely on old sex-role stereotypes (Van der Pas & Aaldering, 2020).

## BOX 12.1 POLITICAL SEXISM LIVES ON, BUT WOMEN ALSO PLAY THE GENDER CARD

Trump's 2016 gender-laced denunciation of Hillary Clinton—"Such a nasty woman," spoken in the third presidential debate—is only one of many hostile comments that male politicians have directed at female political leaders. Others have been more vitriolic. They include: She has "the lips of Marilyn Monroe, the eyes of Caligula" (former French president François Mitterrand's insult about former British prime minister Margaret Thatcher); "You're more beautiful than you are intelligent" (former Italian prime minister Silvio Berlusconi to Rosy Bindi, an opposition member of the Italian Parliament, which could have been said of him, too!); "Anyone who has chosen to remain deliberately barren, they've got no idea about what life's about" (Australian senator Bill Heffernan about Julia Gillard, who later became the prime minister of Australia); "Did you see Nancy Pelosi on the floor? Complete disgust. If you can get through all the surgeries, there's disgust" (South Carolina Senator Lindsay Graham, making a joke about plastic surgery and Speaker of the House Nancy Pelosi); and the familiarly condescending comment from former British Prime Minister David Cameron to Angela Eagle, a British politician, "Calm down, dear" (Miller, 2016, p. A12).

These comments, as well as more distasteful insults, highlight a gender-related double bind, notably between sex-typed femininity and competence, where feminine traits are stereotypically viewed as incongruent with leadership. Americans look for warmth, empathy, but also strength and toughness from the president. This presents a challenge for women—or actually for Americans with stereotyped views—for women are presumed, by dint of their empathy, to have difficulty projecting toughness. Herein lies the double bind: "Women who show too much strength undermine not only their ability to be 'soft' and to feel the pain of others, but also risk seeming unnaturally masculine, unwomanly, or monstrous" (Smith, 2015, p. 86). Yet we wouldn't make a comparable comment about male political leaders, charging that men who show too much compassion undermine their ability to be tough in a crisis, but also risk seeming too feminine.

"Women who attain leadership positions often are castigated as too aggressive, 'bitchy,' or worse," Anderson (2016, p. 22) observes. She suggests that Clinton was a victim of this bind, characterized as a shrew and framed by the press as cold and unlikable because journalists, in

*Continued*

essence, had difficulty accommodating her political acumen with their stereotypes about femininity. Others might disagree, countering that some of her negative press was rooted in Clinton's weakness as a candidate, her difficulty displaying a warm public persona, and an inauthentic posture (Chozick & Alcindor, 2016).

Over the years, masculinity has been a core underpinning of presidential leadership in the U.S. Politics is viewed as a masculine domain, power is linked with men, and male candidates have been accorded more freedom than female politicians to speak in guttural ways. This may be changing. When a 2016 video revealed Trump bragging in profane, offensive ways about how he groped women, many media outlets called him out, framing his comments in terms of sexual power and aggressiveness rather than (in Trump's words) "locker room talk." And with research showing that women candidates face fewer double binds concerning femininity and toughness than in years past (Brooks, 2013; Meeks & Domke, 2016), we may be approaching a new egalitarianism in politics. With the first woman vice president, we have a first-hand opportunity to see if gendered double binds are still around or are vestiges of the past.

And yet, for all the changes, female candidates' campaigns can also play the gender card, raising interesting issues. For example, in 2016 Clinton's supporters claimed that unfavorable coverage of their candidate that referred to her as "calculating," "ambitious," or "secretive" reflected unsuitable use of "coded, gender language." Yet, as *New York Times* reporter Amy Chozick, who was one of many female reporters who covered Clinton, noted:

> I don't think secretive . . . has anything to do with gender. I really don't. And I also think you can't approach every story thinking is this word going to be interpreted as sexist, you know? I mean, she's running for president. If she's being secretive by keeping a private server in her basement in Chappaqua, I don't think that has to do with gender.

Chozick lamented that, as a female reporter, she could be unfairly tarred with the "bias" label—with some people thinking "I'm in the tank 'cause I'm a woman" and others (Clinton's supporters) telling her "you're jealous, you want to take down another woman" (or) "you're a mean girl"—when, all the while, she was trying to do her job as a responsible, critical reporter (see Covering Hillary Clinton, 2016). The Clinton campaign, of course, would argue that, given voters' stereotyped attitudes, reporters needed

*Continued*

to bend over backwards to avoid gender-coded language. Journalists such as Chozick would view this as an inappropriate attempt to manage the news. This, as well as the foregoing discussion, points to the complex ways that politics, gender, and continuing gender biases intersect on the campaign trail.

## THE GENDER FILTER IN 2020

### Subtle Sexism in the Primaries?

It didn't end in 2016. In 2020 gender issues surfaced big-time when six politically capable women ran for the Democratic nomination, but dropped out, leaving only two white men (Bernie Sanders and Joe Biden) in the final showdown. Did gender matter?

Some critics spotted stereotyping in the ways news covered two male contenders for the nomination. Early on, news stories seemed to gush at the youthful promise of Pete Buttigieg, the 37-year-old mayor of South Bend, Indiana, and Beto O'Rourke, a Texas Congressman. But promise, as Filipovic (2019) observed, "depends on whether the young thing in question is male or female." Women generally enter the political fray later than men do, sometimes because they are raising children, other times because they pursue more collaborative positions than the highly visible executive posts men angle for. Thus, capable women candidates frequently miss out on the opportunity to be called "promising" or "full of future potential."

The biggest bugaboos that female candidates face in press coverage and political communication more generally are the **likability and electability traps**, where they can be judged on criteria that can be inherently punishing to their candidacies. American voters say they aren't sexist and many undoubtedly aren't, but then why do they always tell consultants that "they would vote for a woman, just not that woman?" (Astor, 2019). They don't say the same thing about men, and the "just not that woman" line offers a convenient rationalization not to vote for the particular woman who appears on the ballot. Part of it reflects continuing psychological stereotypes that cast leadership as a masculine attribute, with people viewing behavior that executes leadership roles less positively when performed by a woman (Eagly & Karau, 2002). It also comes down to the fact that voters—women and men—make likability a bigger factor in their judgments of women than men candidates.

Likability is a core ingredient of conventional femininity. Women are expected to be kind and warm; when they display more assertive characteristics, they violate gender role norms, even today. As one researcher noted, applying these norms to the political realm, "voters will not support a woman that they do not like, even if they believe that she is qualified. But they will vote for a man that they do not like if they believe he is qualified" (see Astor, 2019). This was one dynamic (among many) that occurred in the 2016 election, where some people could not bring themselves to vote for Hillary Clinton because they didn't like her. Some of these voters didn't care for Trump, but were willing to cast their vote for him.

It isn't clear that this proves sexism as much as dislike of one particular female candidate—Clinton, who was famously viewed as brittle by many voters. But if part of a larger pattern, it would showcase sexist voting preferences. And indeed there is evidence that people viewed power-seeking female politicians as uncaring, but didn't feel the same way toward their power-seeking male counterparts. When individuals perceived male politicians as power-seeking, they viewed them as stronger, but didn't see female politicians in this light. And women were as likely as men to evaluate candidates in these ways (see Okimoto & Brescoll, 2010).

This aspect of political psychology can spill into political journalism. As the well-respected Minnesota Democratic Senator Amy Klobuchar prepared to announce her presidential campaign, she was hit by a spate of bad press, stories of her mistreatment of her senatorial staff. She had one of the highest rates of staff member turnover in the Senate, demanded staffers do menial tasks, such as washing her dishes at her house, and once, when most staff members were running late, placed tardy slips on each individual's desk, causing one aide to leave her office in tears (Redden & Terkel, 2019). In one unforgettable incident that occurred on an airplane trip to South Carolina some years back, a staffer had the misfortune of telling Klobuchar that he had gotten her a salad, but dropped the utensils. She reprimanded the aide, took a comb from her bag, ate the salad with it—and then ordered him to clean it (Flegenheimer & Ember, 2019).

Media critics wondered if Klobuchar was being held to a higher standard because women are stereotypically expected to be kinder than men toward their staff, and the senator glaringly defied the stereotype. But, to be fair, Trump has repeatedly been taken to task in the press for inordinately high staff turnover at the White House and faced harsh criticism for his mocking of others. Moreover, Klobuchar's mistreatment was unusual, even by the standards of petulant U.S. senators, making it a legitimate source for news. So, it isn't clear that the press judged Klobuchar through the glare of sexist lenses.

A more subtle trap that can befall women candidates is electability. And here the media may have played a larger role. The electability snafu comes from the public perception, egged on by news coverage, that, as competent as they are, women candidates are not electable; Americans are not just going to elect a woman president. Thus, the circular logic goes, a female candidate should not be nominated because Americans aren't going to elect a woman. And because the public will not elect a woman, she should not be considered seriously for the nomination.

During the 2020 primary campaign, about three in four Democrats said they would be comfortable with a woman as president, but they believed their neighbors would not be. "If voters believe other people won't vote for a woman, then they won't vote for a woman, and so a woman will not win," reporter Jessica Bennett (2020) observed. She quoted a researcher who stated the self-fulfilling prophecy fallacy clearly: "The very belief that a woman cannot win has the power to make itself true."

Perceptions of other people's perceptions is a well-known phenomenon in public opinion scholarship. Voters may either project their own discomfort with a female president onto others, or they may actually believe that other voters wouldn't vote for a woman, causing them to reason that a female presidential candidate, no matter how qualified, just won't catch fire with the electorate. Sexism causes an individual to project discomfort with a female president onto others. However, the second case—where voters say they are comfortable with a woman chief executive, but assume others aren't—is a logical inconsistency (Tiedge et al. 1991) or perceptual distortion borne of the tendency of people to impute different criteria to others than to themselves. The question is where they come up with this idea. Critics argue that news cultivates this perception wittingly or unwittingly by quoting others who say it so many times that it causes people to believe that it's true. With this in mind, let's look at how this played out in 2020.

To be sure, mainstream media coverage was remarkably favorable and judicious, giving prominent coverage to the biographies and political experience of women contenders. For example, news stories and columns bestowed lavishly positive coverage on Senator Elizabeth Warren, lauding her willingness to stake out thoughtful, detailed positions on issues ranging from inequality to student debt. Her eagerness to spell out specific policies, with the phrase she often repeated—"I have a plan for that"—became her calling card and slogan prominently covered in the news, filtering down to sympathetic voters. (It even stimulated a rhyming meme: "When it's breakfast time, Elizabeth Warren has a bran for that!")

Yet news also played up the electability card—not to punish Warren or because reporters didn't like her, or were necessarily sexist. Instead, it flowed inexorably from the routines of political journalism (see Chapter 13). The electability narrative is a frame reporters invoke, judging candidates by their likelihood of winning the nomination contests. Many news reports trumpeted the question of whether Warren and other female candidates were electable—not that they weren't worthy of being elected, but whether voters would actually vote for a woman, particularly after Hillary Clinton's stunning loss 4 years earlier. Reporters didn't put their opinions in the articles. Instead, they could quote voters, worried about whether the rest of the country—their neighbors again—would vote for a woman. Or journalists could interview Democratic Party leaders, voicing their political anxieties. Voters, including women, would say that one of the female candidates was their top choice, but claim (based on those media stories quoting people saying their neighbors wouldn't vote for a woman) that a woman could not get elected.

Article after article raised the electability issue, so much so that close to six in ten voters said they heard the media focus on how female candidates are not electable (Nilsen, 2020). Research shows that news tends to report more on the viability of women candidates, dwelling on the way gender could (and just might, you know) affect their chances of winning the election; news gives women lower viability or electability assessments than men (Van der Pas & Aaldering, 2020). Thus, electability, as a lens through which journalists viewed the game, could have become a subtle sexist trap creating a self-fulfilling prophecy that worked against Elizabeth Warren (see Figure 12.3).

Of course, there are alternative theories. Democrats could have rejected women contenders because they didn't find them compelling candidates. For example, many voters liked California Senator Kamala Harris's charisma, but found her tough-on-crime policies as a prosecutor disturbingly regressive. They were intrigued by Senator Klobuchar's ability to work across party lines, but couldn't get a fix on her ideological preferences. They admired Warren's passion and intellectual brilliance, but didn't like her scolding, schoolmarm style. (This could have been sexist. Or not.) They felt Warren was opportunistic when she tilted left on health care and couldn't explain how she would pay for the program. She couldn't connect with Black voters, a key constituency of the Democratic Party.

These are all plausible perspectives that probably accounted for many voters' preferences. At the same time, news—by accessing perceptions, making them salient, and surfacing a real or pseudo social norm—could have subtly pushed liberal Democrats to prefer a male candidate. Or perhaps news's impact played second fiddle to gender biases voters have internalized. It is hard to parcel out all the factors, but certainly, one can't disagree with the intuitive appeal of Warren's observation: "If you say, 'No, there was no sexism,' about a bazillion women think, 'What planet do you live on?'"

## 2020 Presidential Campaign

In the main, conventional media outlets offered up a judicious portrait of Democratic vice presidential candidate Kamala Harris, balancing stories about the

**Figure 12.3 Some critics argued that, for all its egalitarian emphases, reporters were prone to subtle gender biases, as when they created a self-fulfilling prophecy about the electability of strong female candidates such as Senator Elizabeth Warren. The trap emerged when reporters noted that Democrats were reluctant to vote for Warren because they didn't think she was electable. Yet by unwittingly promoting this very belief, the press could have caused others to exaggerate its pervasiveness, producing a self-fulfilling prophecy.**

*Source*: www.gettyimages.com/detail/news-photo/senior-united-states-senator-from-massachusetts-elizabeth-news-photo/583825124?utm_medium=organic&utm_source=google&utm_campaign=iptcurl

historic nature of her nomination, noting her political strengths and strong debate performance, with coverage of Republican attacks. Trump blasted her from the get-go, using terms with sexist overtones such as "nasty" and "nastier" that he frequently used to criticize female adversaries, and could have primed the likability stereotype (Karni & Peters, 2020).

Cable channels were predictably partisan, with MSNBC lauding the choice and Fox commentators at times critical, even disrespectful, as when Tucker Carlson mispronounced Kamala Harris's first name, getting angry when he was corrected. Websites began spreading false information within days after Biden selected her, falsely and maliciously calling her an "anchor baby," a term that demeans a child born in the U.S. to immigrant parents (Rogers, 2020).

## CONCLUSIONS

Politics has taken many strides since 1972, when New York Congresswoman Shirley Chisholm, the first African American candidate to seek the Democratic presidential nomination, was ignored by the mainstream press. Almost a half century later, when Kamala Harris, who paid tribute to Chisholm by adopting her campaign mantra, "For the People," became the Democrats' presumptive vice presidential nominee, she was given star billing, immediately hailed as a leading frontrunner for the 2024 Democratic nomination. Yet problems remain, and critics frequently point to continued gender stereotypes in news coverage.

Historically, political news coverage was horrifically sexist, treating female candidates in disparaging ways. This has changed dramatically, although many sex-typed residues remain on websites and social media posts. Popular and impactful as they are, they're not mainstream news, the focus of this discussion. By and large, the news picture has improved dramatically over the past decades. Clinton did receive substantial negative news in 2008 and 2016, but much of this was rooted in journalistic factors, such as the tendency of reporters to cover (incessantly, in the view of critics) a candidate's missteps and alleged character flaws. Yet some of this may have tapped into gender biases, and stereotypes in covering women's appearance and clothing remain.

In particular, there are gendered double binds, where women are expected to display traditional masculine attributes of power; however, when they do this, they are downgraded because they lack the stereotypical female softness and vulnerability. Likability and electability schema seem to be invoked more for female candidates. Women can be held to a higher standard of likability than men. (If it had been Donna, not Donald, Trump, her mean-spirited, unlikable tweets would have never been tolerated.) Electability has emerged as a red herring that can thwart the viability of bold, innovative women politicians. By reporting on the public's perception that women candidates aren't electable, news can create a self-fulfilling prophecy, whereby people believe this is so and choose to cast votes for men instead. This is a difficult situation for journalism, at least in America. Reporters make gatekeeping decisions based on time-honored routines frequently steeped in the horse race, of which electability is a prominent component. However, reporters can certainly qualify stories by noting that electability judgments aren't fixed in stone, change over time, and have worked to the detriment of women candidates. At the same time, reporters can be caught in a double binds themselves, when campaign managers expect female reporters to place gender loyalty ahead of their professional role.

Clearly, it's a different world than it was decades ago. Rays of hope shine on the horizon. With women constituting nearly one in four members of the House of Representatives and accounting for about 40 percent of journalists, gender parity moves forward. The job of political journalists is not to blindly celebrate these changes, but to investigate the changing landscape of American politics, infused by a commitment to egalitarian values and the ethos of news. Such a commitment requires a gimlet-eyed cognizance of how, even as female political leaders have made incredible strides, they still face harsh online attacks not about their message, but rather about their appearance and perceived sexuality, verbal assaults their male counterparts rarely face (Sobieraj, 2020). These digital abuses against leaders from Alexandria Ocasio-Cortez to Greta Thunberg are offenses against democracy that political journalism must reveal with the same determination it harnesses to expose other political wrongdoing.

## REFERENCES

Anderson, K.V. (2016). "Bern the witch" and "Trump that bitch": Likability/loathability on the presidential campaign trail. *Spectra, 52*(3&4), 20–26.

Astor, M. (2019, February 11). "A woman, just not that woman": How sexism plays out on the trail. *The New York Times*. Online: www.nytimes.com/2019/02/11/us/politics/sexism-double-standard-2020.html. (Accessed: May 19, 2020).

Baird, J. (2016, February 26). Sarah Palin's mustache. *The New York Times*, A23.

Beail, L., & Longworth, R.K. (2013). *Framing Sarah Palin: Pit bulls, Puritans, and politics*. New York: Routledge.

Bennett, J. (2020, March 5). Elizabeth Warren and the curse of "electability". *The New York Times*. Online: www.nytimes.com/2020/03/05/us/warren-presidential-race-2020.html. (Accessed: May 20, 2020).

Braden, M. (1996). *Women politicians and the media*. Lexington, KY: University Press of Kentucky.

Bradley, A.M., & Wicks, R.H. (2011). A gendered blogosphere? Portrayal of Sarah Palin on political blogs during the 2008 presidential campaign. *Journalism & Mass Communication Quarterly*, *88*, 807–820.

Brooks, D.J. (2013). *He runs, she runs: Why gender stereotypes do not harm women candidates*. Princeton, NJ: Princeton University Press.

Carlin, D.B., & Winfrey, K.L. (2009). Have you come a long way, baby? Hillary Clinton, Sarah Palin, and sexism in 2008 campaign coverage. *Communication Studies*, *60*, 326–343.

Chira, S. (2017, March 6). Another powerful woman, same sexist attacks. *The New York Times*, A1, A17.

Chozick, A., & Alcindor, Y. (2016, February 5). Plain talk pulls younger voters to Sanders's run. *The New York Times*, A1, A15.

Covering Hillary Clinton, A candidate "forged in the crucible" of conflict. *NPR Politics*. Online: www.npr.org/2016/07/27/487620196/covering-hillary-clinton-a-candidate-forged-in-the-crucible of conflict. (Accessed: December 17, 2016).

Douglas, S.J. (2010). *The rise of enlightened sexism: How pop culture took us from girl power to girls gone wild*. New York: St. Martin's Griffin.

Eagly, A.H., & Karau, S.J. (2002). Role congruity theory of prejudice toward female leaders. *Psychological Review*, *109*, 573–598.

Falk, E. (2010). *Women for president: Media bias in nine campaigns* (2nd ed.). Urbana, IL: University of Illinois Press.

Filipovic, J. (2019, April 7). How old 37 is depends on your gender. *The New York Times* (Sunday Review), 3.

Finneman, T. (2015). *Press portrayals of women politicians, 1870s-2000s: From "Lunatic" Woodhull to "Polarizing" Palin*. Lanham, MD: Lexington Books.

Flegenheimer, M., & Ember, S. (2019, February 22). How Amy Klobuchar treats her staff. *The New York Times*. Online: www.nytimes.com/2019/02/22/us/politics/amy-klobuchar-staff.html. (Accessed: May 19, 2020).

Francis, F.L., & Gregory, R. (2015). A sartorial tapestry: The rhetorical shifts of Hillary Rodham Clinton. In M. Lockhart & K. Mollick (Eds.), *Hillary Rodham Clinton and the 2016 election: Her political and social discourse* (pp. 141–161). Lanham, MD: Lexington Books.

Friedman, V. (2016, July 27). The new age in power dressing. *The New York Times*. Online: https://www.nytimes.com/2016/07/28/fashion/hillary-clinton-theresa-may-michelle-obama-power-dressing.html. (Accessed: April 27, 2021).

Heflick, N.A., Goldenberg, J.L., Cooper, D.P., & Puvia, E. (2011). From women to objects: Appearance focus, target gender, and perceptions of warmth, morality, and competence. *Journal of Experimental Social Psychology, 47*, 572–581.

Jamieson, K.H. (1995). *Beyond the double bind: Women and leadership*. New York: Oxford University Press.

Kahl, M.L., & Edwards, J.L. (2009). An epistolary epilogue: Learning from Sarah Palin's vice presidential campaign. In J.L. Edwards (Ed.), *Gender and political communication in America: Rhetoric, representation, and display* (pp. 267–277). Lanham, MD: Lexington Books.

Kahn, K.F. (1994). The distorted mirror: Press coverage of women candidates for statewide office. *Journal of Politics, 56*, 154–173.

Kahn, K.F. (1996). *The political consequences of being a woman: How stereotypes influence the conduct and consequences of political campaigns*. New York: Columbia University Press.

Kantor, J. (2016, July 28). In Hillary Clinton's nomination, women see a collective step up. *The New York Times*. Online: www.nytimes.com/2016/07/29/us/politics/clinton-women-reaction.html. (Accessed: December 13, 2016).

Karni, A., & Peters, J.W. (2020, August 12). Her voice? Her name? G.O.P's raw personal attacks on Kamala Harris. *The New York Times*. Online: www.nytimes.com/2020/08/12/us/politics/kamala-harris-gop-attacks.html?rref=collection%2Fissuecollection%2Ftodays-new-york-times&action=click&contentCollection=todayspaper&region=rank&module=package&version=highlights&contentPlacement=2&pgtype=collection. (Accessed: August 13, 2020).

Kurtzleben, D. (2020, April 17). Did gender keep Democratic women from winning the presidential primary? *NPR*. Online: www.npr.org/2020/04/17/818952460/did-gender-keep-democratic-women-from-winning-the-primary. (Accessed: May 18, 2020).

Lawless, J.L., & Fox, R.L. (2008, May). Why are women still not running for public office *Issues in Governance Studies, 16*. Online: www.brookings.edu/wp-content/uploads/2016/06/05_women_lawless_fox.pdf. (Accessed: July 28, 2020).

Lawrence, R.G., & Rose, M. (2010). *Hillary Clinton's race for the White House: Gender politics and the media on the campaign trail*. Boulder, CO: Lynne Rienner Publishers.

Luke, S., & Schaffner, B. (2019, July 11). New polling shows how much sexism is hurting the Democratic women running for president. *The Washington Post*. Online: www.washingtonpost.com/politics/2019/07/11/women-candidates-must-overcome-sexist-attitudes-even-democratic-primary/. (Accessed: July 28, 2020).

Meeks, L. (2012). Is she "man enough"? Women candidates, executive political offices, and news coverage. *Journal of Communication, 62*, 175–193.

Meeks, L., & Domke, D. (2016). When politics is a woman's game: Party and gender ownership in woman-versus-woman elections. *Communication Research, 43*, 895–921.

Miller, C.C. (2016, October 22). The powerful woman: A prime target for jabs. *The New York Times*, A12.

Miller, M.K., & Peake, J.S. (2013). Press effects, public opinion, and gender: Coverage of Sarah Palin's vice-presidential campaign. *International Journal of Press/Politics, 18*, 482–507.

Mitchell, A. (2016, June 12). For perspective on Clinton, step back 32 long years. *The New York Times*, 1, 18.

Nilsen, E. (2020, January 29). Voters are back to worrying whether a woman can win. *Vox*. Online: www.vox.com/2020/1/29/21060286/electability-whether-a-woman-can-win-2020. (Accessed: May 20, 2020).

O'Harrow, Jr., R. (2016, March 27). How Clinton's email scandal took root. *The Washington Post*. Online: https://www.washingtonpost.com/investigations/how-clintons-email-scandal-took-root/2016/03/27/ee301168-e162-11e5-846c-10191d1fc4ec_story.html. (Accessed: April 27. 2021).

Okimoto, T.G., & Brescoll, V.L. (2010). The price of power: Power-seeking and backlash against female politicians. *Personality and Social Psychology Bulletin, 36*, 923–936.

Patterson, T.E. (2016, June 13). *Pre-primary news coverage of the 2016 presidential race: Trump's rise, Sanders' emergence, Clinton's struggle.* Harvard Kennedy School Shorenstein Center on Media, Politics and Public Policy. Online: https://papers.ssrn.com/sol3/papers.cfm?abstract_id=2798258. (Accessed: April 27, 2021).

Redden, M., & Terkel, A. (2019, February 7). Sen. Amy Klobuchar's mistreatment of staff scared off candidates to manage her presidential bid. *HuffPost*. Online: www.huffpost.com/entry/amy-klobuchar-abuse-staff-2020_n_5c5a1cb1e4b0871047588649. (Accessed: May 19, 2020).

Rogers, K. (2020, August 13). Trump encourages racist conspiracy theory about Kamala Harris. *The New York Times*. Online: www.nytimes.com/2020/08/13/us/politics/trump-kamala-harris.html?rref=collection%2Fissuecollection%2Ftodays-new-york-times&action=click&contentCollection=todayspaper&region=rank&module=package&version=highlights&contentPlacement=5&pgtype=collection. (Accessed: August 14, 2020).

Smith, M. (2015). Authenticity, authority, and gender: *Hard Choices* as professional autobiography and transnational feminist manifesto. In M. Lockhart & K. Mollick (Eds.), *Hillary Rodham Clinton and the 2016 election: Her political and social discourse* (pp. 77–99). Lanham, MD: Lexington Books.

Sobieraj, S. (2020). *Credible threat: Attacks against women online and the future of democracy.* New York: Oxford University Press.

Stockman, F. (2016, October 21). Clinton arrives as a crusader for all women. *The New York Times*, A1, A17.

Tiedge, J.T., Silverblatt, A., Havice, M.J., & Rosenfeld, R. (1991). Discrepancy between perceived first-person and perceived third-person mass media effects. *Journalism Quarterly, 68*, 141–154.

Van der Pas, D.J., & Aaldering, L. (2020). Gender differences in political media coverage: A meta-analysis. *Journal of Communication, 70*, 114–143.

# 13 Political News, Polls, and the Presidential Campaign

So, how does news cover the presidential campaign? Which biases or routines govern press coverage? What role do polls play, and why have they missed the mark? This chapter, following the discussion of the liberal bias myth and gender biases, explores these issues, as I explore the content of presidential campaign news. Given the impact election news exerts on attitudes and behavior, it is important to understand the nature of presidential campaign news, along with its continuities and changes.

When we think of news biases, we ordinarily think of ideology, missing the role that reporters' routines, or everyday news practices, play in how they cover campaigns. This chapter unravels these routine factors, giving you a different view of political news. These routine biases aren't malicious; they make sense, but they have strengths and shortcomings that are important to appreciate. The first portion of the chapter describes the horse race filter, examining why journalists describe presidential campaigns in this way. The second section focuses on the science and imperfections of presidential election year polls, the underpinning of much presidential campaign news. The third part of the chapter unpacks key news storylines, revealing some of the journalistic biases that pervade political news.

## HORSE RACE AND STRATEGY-BASED NEWS

> The national press is entirely concerned with "horse race" and popularity. . . .
> If thermonuclear war broke out today, the lead paragraph in tomorrow's
> *Washington Post* would be, "In a major defeat for (the president) . . ."
> (Robinson & Sheehan, 1983, p. 140)

The news media cover presidential politics as if it were a game, a sporting event, a horse race (see Figure 13.1). Journalists focus incessantly on candidates'

**Figure 13.1 For decades, the news media have covered the presidential campaign like a horse race. Reporters focus on the competition between the horse-racing contenders, treating the election as a game, covering who is ahead, who is behind, and often framing it as a competitive, rather than more substantive, event. The horse race metaphor was less significant in 2020 because the pandemic overwhelmed everything, and Trump-generated controversies seemed to dominate news.**

*Source*: www.pikist.com/free-photo-sogai

strategies to vanquish their opponents, electoral battle plans, poll ratings, and come-from-behind tactics to overpower political rivals.

The horse race metaphor dates back years, reflecting an era in which horse races were popular spectator sports. You find horse racing out of date? Fine. Replace it with the baseball pennant race, pro football playoffs, March Madness, or the World Cup. Whatever sport you choose, the import is the same: The news media traditionally treat electoral politics as a competitive game, characterized by a battle over tactics for the prize of victory, rather than a more serious endeavor that involves a debate among different policy ideas, a contest among leaders who have articulated different visions for their country, or a critical exercise in the deliberation of ideas among citizens and leaders.

Every 4 years, as the nominating contest heats up, you will come across headlines such as these in major news media: "Polls show late surge by Kerry and

Edwards; Dean now third" (as in *USA Today*, January 18, 2004); "Clinton and Obama locked in tight race in Indiana" (*U.S. News & World Report*, May 2, 2008); "Shifting tactics, Romney attacks surging Gingrich" (*The New York Times*, December 15, 2011); "Winner-take-all contests likely to give Trump a lift" (*The New York Times*, March 10, 2016); and "Biden admits South Carolina may be make-or-break for campaign" (*Politico*, February 16, 2020). That's just during the nomination period.

During the general election campaign, the build-up of horse race news is inescapable: Nearly every day a new poll, a new prognostication, and when the election is projected to be close, the tightness of the race can be the main story, as network anchors breathlessly count down the days until the debates. Horse race news is a key part of the nominations, arguably more important during this phase because projections of who is ahead exert a more critical impact on fundraising and a stronger influence on voters, who are less engaged in the nominations than they are in the fall campaign.

Thus, before the onset of a debate among candidates for a presidential nomination, you will hear an adrenalin-filled, chest-stomping description of an upcoming face-off. If you were not listening closely to the names, you might be forgiven for mistaking CNN's preview of a 2012 election Republican presidential primary debate, held in the fall of 2011, for one of those dramatic, storybook segments that accompanies the football playoffs, where the announcer dramatizes and romanticizes the teams and their players. The CNN montage began with scenes of cowboys, cattle, luscious streams, and mountains, befitting the western debate locale, as woodwind musical instruments chirped a musical melody. Here is what a deep-throated CNN anchor intoned before a Republican debate in Las Vegas, showcasing all the trappings of horse race, competitive drama-infused political journalism:

> From the mountain majesty of the Rockies to the desert sands of the Mojave, the American frontier is a historic land of opportunity for Republicans. Tonight the fight for the GOP presidential nomination comes here: to a region where Barack Obama made inroads four years ago (cut to picture of Barack Obama); to a state that could be decisive in the primary season and the general election (camera pans to casinos and Las Vegas traffic); for a Las Vegas event for Republican presidential contenders, on stage . . . after a dramatic reshuffling of the pack (picture of playing cards).

During the 2020 election cycle, when the Democratic candidates held a primary debate in Las Vegas, the optics were the same, as the news media dramatized, even hyped, the debate, calling it "the most gloves-off, knives-out Democratic debate so far in the 2020 presidential race" (Goldmacher & Epstein, 2020), suggesting that the stakes could not be higher—are they ever lower?—while alluding to the glam image of Las Vegas.

In support of these anecdotal examples, there is abundant empirical evidence that the news media focus on the game aspect of politics, particularly in the nomination stretch of a campaign (e.g., Miller & Denham, 1994; Lavrakas & Bauman, 1995; Dimitrova, 2014; Patterson, 1993, 2016a; Sigelman & Bullock, 1991). Findings emerge from careful content analyses of election coverage, where researchers code stories to compare the proportion that focus on the horse race to those on other topics. From 1988 through 2016, more than 63 percent of news stories focused on the horse race, compared to nearly 26 percent that examined policy issues. (This may have dipped in 2020, due to the focus on the pandemic, as well as the paucity of campaign events.)

Stories offer the political equivalent of ringside seats to a boxing match, describing conflict between candidates with lively prose, using sports or even battlefield analogies, as when reporters described how the Republican primary campaign conflict in New York between Trump and Cruz was a "fight (that) will be waged, street by street, if not stoop to stop, in places like the Bronx" (Flegenheimer & Haberman, 2016, p. A14). Four years later, two political reporters covering the Democrats' debate in Las Vegas wrote that "Warren carved up her opponents, Bloomberg was on the defensive, and Klobuchar and Buttigieg tried to take each other down," appreciating the lesson from the Harry Potter books: "One must die for the other to survive" (Goldmacher & Epstein, 2020). (It turned out both subsequently did, as Biden vanquished them in South Carolina.) It's lively prose, fun to read.

Why, you may ask, do horse race, opinion poll–focused stories dominate news coverage, notably during the nomination period? Scholars tick off seven reasons: First, horse race stories emphasize conflict among contenders, a key aspect of news. Second, polls provide a patina of scientific respectability, cloaking the story in samples, statistics, and numbers, all of which confer credibility. They provide seemingly clear facts—— who is ahead and who is behind—rather than hazy, ambiguous, and more complex judgments that characterize other news, such as stories about policy issues. Indeed, issue stories require evaluative judgments, which can elicit accusations of reporter bias, putting journalists in the crosshairs of social media criticism. Third, horse race stories are easy to cover and make journalists the focus, allowing them to write a story or cover it on air, feeding journalists' egos. Fourth, polls offer tangible evidence of how candidates are doing, their ability to raise funds, and early evidence of their electability, reasonable criteria for journalists to cover. Fifth, horse race stories link up with journalistic cynicism about politics, the belief that politics is a strategic power game rather than a contest among different policy directions for the country.

A sixth factor is that, voters, particularly those high in political interest, follow, and even prefer, strategically framed, poll-dominated news (Sullivan, 2016;

Trussler & Soroka, 2014; Stroud & Muddiman, 2019), offering a market-based justification for the coverage. Finally, the election *is* per force a horse race, with candidates strategizing, focusing on early primary victories, and incessantly following polls.

## Shortcomings in Horse Race Coverage

Horse race–framed issue news is like dinner at candlelight, with a haute cuisine meal promised, suddenly laid bare, the delicacies turning out to be nothing more than dressed-up chicken nuggets and high-sodium soup. Reporters have traditionally seen virtually every action—— a speech, policy decision, an appeal to particular voters—as driven by winning and strategizing.

Political communication research has documented that campaign strategy frames can exert substantive cognitive effects. Individuals exposed to strategy-oriented news are more likely to remember strategic information than those who receive predominately issue-framed stories (Cappella & Jamieson, 1997). The news taps into their strategy-focused schema, activating a belief (acquired from news) that politics focuses around strategy. Academic critics argue that news overstates the extent to which politics is a strategic game, in this way increasing cynicism about politics (Zoizner, in press). Horse race news also pushes out a helpful focus on stories examining electoral institutions and processes of voting, including voter suppression and turnout (Searles, 2020).

Of course, you could argue that by focusing on the cynical side, journalism provides an antidote to knee-jerk public acceptance of what politicians do, helping voters view politicians more critically, keeping them accountable to the citizens they serve. This is a reasonable position. The question is whether the abundance of cynical horse race reporting overwhelms the public's tendency to give leaders the benefit of the doubt. And that seems plausible, particularly when stories can play up partisan bickering and the notion that partisan political motives underpin everything in politics, frames that can produce a self-fulfilling prophecy, exacerbating the public cynicism and bitter partisanship their articles lament.

There is a more important limitation in routine political news that emphasizes the horse race. By focusing ceaselessly on the competitive contest between the two established parties, the press legitimizes the system, reinforcing the idea that two parties are the inevitable, best way to conduct campaigns. By framing the election as a race between the two parties, the news implicitly overlooks the possibility that third parties could bring change to national politics. This makes it more difficult for the public to consider third parties as desirable alternatives, in turn impeding efforts to build grassroots organizations that offer new ways to solve pressing national problems.

## A New Trend?

In a strange footnote to reporters' adrenalin-fueled obsession with the horse race, the 2020 coronavirus abruptly upended the daily fix on the game. In late March, with only two thoroughbreds left on the trail (Joe Biden and Bernie Sanders), campaign news came to a screeching halt. The risks of campaigning in public forced both candidates to call off campaign appearances as they sequestered themselves and held Zoom-relayed online events. More than a dozen states postponed their primaries. With few campaign events to cover, horse race news ceased to exist, providing a control group of sorts to the usual strategic madness that engulfs the news.

The horse race played a key role in general election campaign coverage, with an emphasis on polls in battleground states, focus on candidate strategies, and presidential debate coverage that predictably revolved around who won and how it played with key voter groups. But there was nuance. The coverage of Senate hearings to confirm Judge Amy Coney Barrett centered on whether she would be confirmed and how the confirmation battle would affect the presidential race. But some stories looked at policy differences between the parties on issues that came up in the hearings, such as a pending case involving the Affordable Care Act and a future case that could invalidate *Roe v. Wade*.

Scholarly observations suggest that, for much of the campaign, journalists took a U-turn, focusing somewhat less on the polls and more on their favorite topics: Donald Trump and his exclamation point presidency. Centering less on the horse race than on Trump, campaign stories covered his harsh tweets, upending norms, and then inescapably, on his contracting the coronavirus (Agiesta, 2020a). Stories about Trump's health, virus infections inside the White House, and Trump's ferocious tweets consumed much news. The emphasis on the game was supplemented by news about Trump and the virus, offering an eerier, sometimes ghoulish backdrop to the campaign.

Importantly, just as Trump dominated the news in 2016, he also did so in 2020, drowning out coverage of Biden, though Trump's press was frequently more negative (Agiesta, 2020b). The media covered Trump for a host of reasons, central to the nature of political news. Trump was the president, and news focuses on presidential news both because of the president's preeminent role in the political system and because presidential news fits news routines (Smoller, 1990). In addition, for cable networks hungry for viewers, news about Trump—campaigning without a mask during the virus, criticizing Dr. Anthony Fauci—served the bottom line. It kept pro-Trump viewers, who approved of his statements, glued to Fox, as well as liberals who relished commentators' condemnations on MSNBC and CNN.

Of course, throughout his presidency, news was consumed by Trump. He flouted established political traditions, generated conflict, offered personality-based stories, which TV loves, and brought in online clicks. The disproportionate amount of news about Trump affected the dynamics of the race. And while it did not always redound to Trump's advantage, it raised questions about important policy issues political news had chosen to overlook.

## SCIENCE AND IMPERFECTIONS OF ELECTION POLLS

Can you imagine an election today without a poll? Can one even conceive of a week without discussion of the latest CNN, Fox News, or *New York Times*/Siena College poll? "Politics without polling has become as unthinkable as aviation without radar," a political writer observed (see Johnson, 2007, p. 87). Because polling is at the heart of horse race journalism and the political campaign, it is fitting to examine its strengths and shortcomings.

At their best, polls offer a snapshot of public opinion in a democracy, helpful in identifying voters' perceptions and concerns. Polls also have a political purpose. Presidential campaigns hire private pollsters or keep them on retainer. Candidates poll and incessantly follow polls conducted by professional polling organizations in the months before presidential primaries and during the primary season. Polls play a pivotal role in news media coverage and decisions by wealthy donors to finance a candidate's campaign.

Why do candidates conduct polls during the primaries and general election phases? They want to know where they stand with voters so they can adjust campaign strategies to fit the attitudes of key constituent groups. They also need to appreciate how voters evaluate the opponent, so they can engage in appropriate counter-attacks before it is too late and advertising-produced perceptions harden into convictions in voters' minds.

So . . . what exactly is a poll? A poll is "literally, a counting of heads" (Traugott & Lavrakas, 2008, p. 191). Of course, there is more to it. A **poll** is "any political sample survey of the electorate conducted by the media, politicians, or political interest groups that aims for a relatively quick and somewhat cursory tally of the public's political opinions and preferences" (Traugott & Lavrakas, p. 191). The key word here is *sample*. A sample is a scientifically selected subset of a larger population.

If you haven't taken a research methods course, you might wonder why researchers sample. Why not just bite the bullet and talk to everyone? Because this is virtually impossible. Interviewing everyone in the population, what is known as a census, is expensive, time-consuming, and fraught with problems. It can be high-nigh impossible to locate certain individuals, such as those who are homeless or extremely mobile. As a result, pollsters sample, and sampling is remarkably accurate, as Traugott and Lavrakas (2008) note:

A well-drawn, scientific sample allows a pollster to conduct interviews with only a very small fraction of a population but to draw inferences with confidence from the sample's responses back to the attitudes or behavior of the entire population of interest.

(p. 59)

Pseudo-polls, such as online polls or phone-ins to cable TV news, do not accurately tap voter sentiments because they do not randomly sample the population of American voters. Therefore, generalizations to the larger population of voters or citizens are inappropriate (Victor, 2016). Poll findings may simply reflect who shows up at the site at a particular time, often those with a strong ideological bent who are eager to share their pet peeves. These results can be handily manipulated by groups who want to use the poll to further their cause or candidate.

By contrast, well-executed, scientifically conducted polls can provide accurate information about the population of citizens. They advance democracy by providing a mechanism for citizens to provide feedback to leaders, connecting citizens to the levers of power. Polls are not foolproof and, in an age of political volatility and cellphone technology, can misfire, as the next section describes.

## Polling Imperfections

Many voters watched the 2020 returns with incredulity, feeling they'd been duped.

Polls predicted Biden would beat Trump by as many as 10 points in Wisconsin and 9 points in Michigan, yet the final results showed him narrowly defeating Trump by less than 1 point in Wisconsin and about 3 in Michigan. Polls showed Biden besting Trump in Pennsylvania by as much as 7 points; he won, yes, by a little more than 1 point. Florida polls said Biden would win by 2.5 percent, but he lost by about 3 percent. Similar discrepancies were apparent in a number of other states (Cohn, 2020). A similar phenomenon occurred in 2016, where key state polls significantly underestimated Trump's support. Despite robust efforts to avoid the mistakes of 2016, the 2020 errors mirrored those of 4 years earlier.

To be sure, polls accurately predicted the popular vote in both elections and in 2020 correctly called the winner in 48 states (Leonhardt, 2020). Both were volatile elections where political forecasting can be particularly difficult. But the mistakes were glaring and raised complicated questions about polling accuracy in an age of cell phones and distrust of the institution of public opinion polling.

Polls always have a margin of error to reflect probability-based differences between a sample and population. State polls can err because it is harder to construct representative samples with smaller voter segments than are available in national surveys (Edelman, 2020). Why do reliable, scientific polls sometimes fail to predict presidential elections with precision? There are several reasons.

A major problem is response rate, or the proportion of sampled individuals who complete the telephone interview. A couple of decades ago, pollsters could get about a 35 percent response rate—not bad, but good enough to accurately predict the population of voters from a random sample. Response rates have declined to an alarming 7 percent, as people don't pick up their cell phones, don't answer cell phone calls from numbers that are unknown, or, consumed with other tasks when the pollster calls, hang up before the interview has been completed (Kennedy & Hartig, 2019). When sample response rates are that low, it's hard to predict the population of voters accurately in volatile elections.

It also creates a methodological problem. Researchers must make certain that they replace respondents who decline to be interviewed with demographically equivalent individuals. Usually, this can be accomplished, but occasionally problems creep in. This happened in 2008, when polls taken before the New Hampshire primary gave Obama a double-digit lead over Hillary Clinton. Yet Clinton won by about two percentage points, raising questions about the accuracy of pre-election polls. One reason is that some of Clinton's stalwart supporters, such as union members, were hard to reach. Rather than continuing to call these individuals or contacting them later, some pollsters gave up. Yet these voters turned up at the polls, voting for Clinton.

A second problem is that certain individuals are chronically unlikely to participate in polls, partly because they don't trust institutions such as polling. These voters tend to be more skeptical of democratic institutions, less educated, and can often lean toward the Republican Party. This may be one reason why polls underestimated Trump's support in key states in 2020.

A third reason election polls can fail to predict outcomes accurately is the classic problem of social desirability effects. Although individuals rarely lie outright to pollsters, they may prevaricate when the questions concern socially sensitive subjects, such as voting for a White supremacist candidate or voting against an African American contender (Johnson, 2007). In 2020, some Trump voters may have feared that supposedly liberal pollsters looked down on them for voting for Trump, so they may have been reluctant to admit they favored Trump. But there doesn't seem to be that much support for this hypothesis when you look at 2020 data. Many Trump voters were proud to say they supported the president.

A fourth problem involves likely voters. Polls frequently concentrate on likely voters, those who are predisposed to go to vote on Election Day, figuring that focusing on them (rather than registered voters who might not vote) affords the greatest predictive bang for the buck. On some occasions, though, it can be difficult to estimate just who is likely to vote, either because turnout is much higher or lower than expected.

This happened in the Michigan Democratic primary in 2016. Polls predicted Clinton would win easily, but her opponent Bernie Sanders defeated her by 1.5 percentage points. Polls, based on traditional models that did not capture the excitement a candidate like Sanders generated among young people, underestimated the number of under-30 voters who turned out for Sanders (Bialik, 2016). In the 2016 presidential election, polls understated Trump's support in key swing states such as Wisconsin, Michigan, and Pennsylvania, in part because Trump voters turned out in greater numbers than many Clinton voters. In 2020, a surge of unexpected Hispanic voting gave Trump a more comfortable margin in Florida. If Republicans turned out in greater numbers than expected, then polls systematically underestimated Trump's support in several states.

Finally, polls can fail to predict accurately, not because of polling limitations, but because unexpected events intervene, changing undecided voters' decisions late in the campaign, after most polls have been conducted. In 2016, as many as 15 percent of voters decided who to vote for during the last week of the campaign, likely including people who ended up voting for Trump. FBI Director James Comey's announcement in late October 2016 that he planned to review a new trove of Clinton emails to see if they contained classified information could have revived the email issue, accessing concerns among some uncommitted voters, pushing them to reject Clinton. In addition, in 2020, some voters may have said they would vote for a particular candidate, but failed to do so because of the hassles of mail-in voting. "In a volatile election, even a perfectly effective poll might not be able to gauge the outcome; a poll can only take the pulse of where voters' feelings lie in a particular moment," a reporter aptly observed (Russonello, 2019, p. 24).

To be sure, razor-close prediction of a volatile presidential election in the middle of a pandemic is about as hard as it gets. Polls during off-year elections have a good track record. Surveys tapping social and political attitudes on a host of topics do pretty well. But a nation depends on polls to tap into public opinion during presidential elections, and when polls misfire in many states, they diminish trust in an institution of democracy. And when the results show that polls predicting a large Democratic victory are off the mark, they fuel the cynicism of right-wing Americans who believe in the conspiracy theory that a liberal deep state controls political institutions.

Moreover, when the news media giddily report polls, missing their complexities and systemic difficulties, they can mislead the public (Toff, 2020). Journalists—and sometimes pollsters—neglect to report low response rates or how undercounting key demographic groups can lead to errant predictions. In the case of reporters, it's another example of how addiction to horse race journalism creates misperceptions and sows democratic doubts.

As polls adapt to harness current technologies, such as text messages, it is important to remember that they provide an important mechanism to gauge citizens' attitudes and communicate their views to leaders. They are a more fine-tuned method of tapping public sentiments than other methods, such as intuitive, qualitative, or "seat of the pants" guesstimates. But in close elections, and in an era when respondents from key groups fail to respond to polls, polls may miss the mark more than defenders would like to admit. These are problems public opinion researchers will have to come to grips with in the next several years. Even though election polls were broadly correct, their high-stakes failures stoke cynicism and concerns.

It is incumbent on citizens, as informed participants in the political process, to appreciate the strengths and shortcomings of polls. When you read polls, you might consider the following tips:

1. Review the margin of error. This tells you how close the findings from the random sample on which the poll is based are to the numbers one would obtain if the entire population had been interviewed. The smaller the margin of error, the more confidence one can have that the poll reflects the population of voters. The larger the margin of error, the less confidence one should place in the poll's findings.
2. Examine many polls and put your trust in the average across polls. One poll could be unusual or unrepresentative.
3. Make certain the polls are conducted by a reputable polling organization, randomly sample the population, report the margin of error, and discuss fallibilities like the time the poll was conducted, nonresponse bias, and question wording effects.

## MAJOR NEWS MEDIA STORYLINES

The press is not a conveyor belt that simply relays electoral information to the public. It does not hold up a mirror to politics, but presents particular slices and perspectives of presidential campaigns. These perspectives, less partisan than commonly assumed, are filters through which campaign news media interpret and diffuse information about the presidential election. Commonly called **narratives** or **storylines**, they are broad frames, outgrowths of professional journalistic factors that shape campaign news reporting. The narratives are useful in distilling the panoply of political information, serve functions for politics, but also can serve as stereotypes that force facts to fit a particular storyline (Patterson, 1993). Six key narratives are (1) candidate schema; (2) frontrunner; (3) losing ground; (4) bandwagon; (5) electability; and (6) exceeding expectations storylines.

## Candidate Schema

Reporters, like all of us, develop mental frameworks or schema to organize information about candidates and gain a fix on disparate aspects of candidates' background, style, and issue positions. Once they decide, singly and frequently in combination (responding as a collective reference group of peers), that a particular schema fits a candidate, they invoke this in news stories. During the 1980s, journalists dubbed Ronald Reagan "the Great Communicator," convinced that Reagan's charm, acting skills, and ability to use the camera to effectively persuade the public gave him "practically irresistible power to shape public opinion" (Schudson, 1995, p. 137). Although Reagan developed memorable television narratives and his public image contributed to his popularity, he was not infallible. There were a host of reasons why he was reelected in 1984, including economic growth, his tough foreign policy positions, and the fallibilities of his Democratic opponent in 1984. Yet news stories applied the "Great Communicator" schema, creating a myth of Reagan's communicative success that may have itself influenced public opinion.

During the 2000 campaign, national journalists seemed to fix on the idea that Vice President Al Gore was not always truthful, fashioning this into the storyline that Gore was slippery, even a serial exaggerator (Krugman, 2016). The news media widely reported that Gore claimed to have invented the Internet, when what he actually said in a CNN interview is that he "took the initiative in creating the Internet," a statement that comported with technology experts' belief that Gore was the first political leader to recognize the significance of the Internet (Mikkelson, 2016). Yet the news repeatedly misattributed the "I invented the Internet" comment to Gore, because it was an entertaining soundbite and reinforced the journalistic narrative view that Gore hyped truth for his own political benefit. When Gore made other misstatements, the news media trotted out the "dishonest, exaggerator" schema, using this as the framework to distill Gore's verbal behavior. In fairness, Gore had misstated facts on several occasions, and his nonverbal posturing invited the perception that he had a sanctimonious, holier-than-thou quality. It is unlikely he exaggerated or hyped more than other politicians, yet the Gore storyline could have contributed to low voter ratings of Gore's honesty (Johnston, Hagen, & Jamieson, 2004).

### Clinton and Her Emails in 2016

For years journalists viewed Clinton through the prism of a narrative emphasizing her penchant for secrecy, lack of transparency, and absence of candor. The schema emerged in the 1990s, when Clinton led a White House health reform task force that conducted its business behind closed doors in ways that frustrated legislators and the press. It continued with the 1996 discovery of missing documents from her law firm that strangely surfaced long after investigators had subpoenaed billing records from her legal work on behalf of a failed savings and loan company (Gerth, 2015). On a deeper, psychological level, the lack of transparency schema may have gained resonance from her emotionally complex decision to stay with her husband after he engaged in widely publicized marital affairs. The lack of transparency schema served as a filter for her many achievements, such as a health reform innovator, twice-elected Senator from New York, and Secretary of State. It surfaced again, like a bad penny, in 2016. The penchant for secrecy seemed to emerge as a press explanation of 2016 campaign events, chiefly her freighted use of a private email server. The email story, with its many permutations, gushed and exploded across the news media, the narrative in a sense an extracting mechanism that pushed the story across the surface.

A *New York Times* exposé revealed in March 2015 that Clinton had only used her personal email account when she was Secretary of State and did not even have a State Department email address during the time she headed the State Department (Schmidt, 2015). Her decision to employ a personal account for official government business was an unorthodox decision that allowed her to decide which information would be made public and (given her international reputation) known across the world (Schmidt & Sanger, 2015). This raised questions about whether she had emailed classified information. Storing classified information in one's personal email account on a private server technically violates U.S. secrecy laws (Shane, 2015). A ceaseless stream of stories followed the initial *New York Times* stories.

While much of the press coverage represented a legitimate focus on possibly illegal action by a presidential candidate, it is difficult not to view some of the coverage as resulting from the long-held narrative that Clinton harbored a penchant for secrecy. Had these problems befallen another candidate, the press would not have played them up as much.

### Biden, the "Gut Candidate" in 2020

There was no secret about the rap on Biden. He was, by his own telling, a "gut politician," who said what he thought, held little back, connecting emotionally with voters. Reporters knew him as a senator, then vice president, who called on his private sorrows in his public role, choking up when voters shared their stories of grief because it brought to mind the death of his first wife and daughter in a car crash, and his son's death from brain cancer several decades later. They also knew him as the gaffe-prone politician, who could mentally trip over thoughts, uttering cringe-worthy and cognitively bewildering foot-in-the-mouth statements. He affectionately told a Missouri senator to stand up until he realized the man had to rely on a wheelchair. As vice president he once said, "if we do everything right, if we do it with absolute certainty, there's still a 30% chance we're going to get it wrong." His most famous gaffe came during the 2008 campaign when he famously called Obama "the first mainstream African

American who is articulate and bright and clean and a nice-looking guy."
(Obama chose him to be his vice president anyway.)

In 2020, Biden's candidacy and gaffes were seen through these lenses. *Time*
published a list of the top 10 Joe Biden gaffes, and videos of his verbal mishaps
circulated online. When he blundered again on race in 2020, telling a popular
African American radio talk show host that "if you have a problem figuring
out whether you're for me or Trump, then you ain't Black," a comment that
some Blacks would privately agree with but struck others as taking their vote
for granted, it brought to mind his Obama gaffe of 2008. He stumbled over his
words, telling his supporters on a Monday in early March that "tomorrow's
Super Thursday" when he meant the iconic Super Tuesday primaries. Journalists viewed these 2020 gaffes through their frame of Biden as a "says what he
feels without mental editing, wears his heart on his sleeve," gaffe-prone candidate schema, amplified by a narrative that speculated on whether his bloop-
ers were a function of his age (77) when he ran for president (see Golshan &
Nilsen, 2019).

It was a reasonable interpretation. In some countries, however, the nation's press
corps probably would not have ventured an overarching explanation, letting the
comments speak for themselves. Or reporters could have viewed his blunders
in an endearing light, noting that he self-effacingly apologized for his remarks
and could make off-the-cuff comments that telegraphed sensitivity, as when he
said in 2012 that he was "absolutely comfortable" with same-sex marriage, a
statement that paved the way for Obama's later endorsement and perhaps the
Supreme Court decision to legalize gay marriage. But the U.S. press sees its job
as examining the fitness of candidates for public office. By holding up Biden's
gaffes as suggesting a potential shortcoming in his suitability for the presidency,
journalists were doing their jobs. By pointing out that a lie he told about the
NAACP always endorsing him had its roots in other, similar prevarications he
had uttered, they gave voters valuable information (Blow, 2020). However, the
persistence of the stories, and the tendency to interpret them as a function of a
personality predisposition, suggested a simplistic psychologizing bias in press
coverage, or at least the use of a funneling narrative that political journalists
regularly employ as an interpretive device.

## Other Press Storylines

Biden and Clinton also received tough press for another reason. They were
frontrunners, leaders of the Democratic pack. Journalists traditionally subject
front-running candidates to tough coverage. In the **frontrunner storyline**,
news initially gives considerable coverage to the front-running candidate who
leads the pack of contenders because she or he has high poll numbers and generates favorable comments from elite supporters. But over time, positive press
is offset by negative coverage that results from reporters' desire to inform the

public of chinks in the frontrunner's armor and the feeling it is their professional responsibility to do so lest the candidate get a free ride to the White House (see Figure 13.2; Patterson, 1993). Reporters also subject frontrunners to tough press because it is a good story: the possible fall from grace of the heir apparent.

When a leading candidate's support—in polls or primary election results for the party nomination— begins to sharply decline, news reflects this and plays up the candidate's losses. Coverage becomes decidedly less favorable, as a variety of indicators—from opinions of party leaders to comments from voters—take on a negative hue. This exemplifies the **losing ground storyline**, the ways the press narrative changes to increasingly describe a candidate once seen as a contender for the party nomination as inexorably losing ground (see Figure 13.3; Patterson, 1993). Press coverage can exaggerate the decline, focusing more dramatically on political losses experienced by a leading candidate than on comparable declines of less-hyped-up rivals for the nomination. The irony is that one reason why the candidate was lionized at the outset was because the press, based on political interviews and polls, decided he or she was a major contender.

Jeb Bush, the former Florida governor originally anointed as a frontrunner, typified the losing ground scenario in 2016, with journalists focusing on his lackluster performances in primary debates, failure to challenge Trump's aggressive comments, and ultimately, his dismal primary election numbers. By December 2015, news coverage of Bush was 70 percent unfavorable, the most

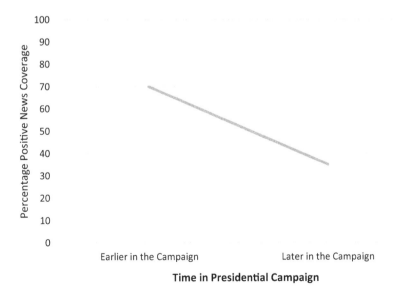

**Figure 13.2  The frontrunner storyline. News offers initially positive coverage to the frontrunner, but over time the news becomes dramatically less positive.**

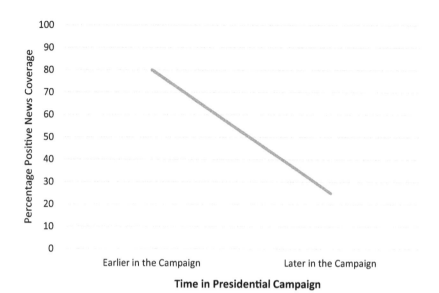

**Figure 13.3  The losing ground storyline. When a candidate's ratings in opinion polls or from elites drops dramatically, news coverage becomes considerably less positive.**

negative of any of the Republican candidates, with journalists commenting unfavorably on his demeanor, as when an article said that "Mr. Bush does not seem to be radiating much joy these days" (Patterson, 2016b). The same could have been said about other struggling Republican contenders on a dour day on the campaign trail. The negative coverage did reflect the facts on the ground. More importantly, it picked up on journalists' judgment that Bush was losing ground, in relation to what had been expected initially.

It was a similar story for Joe Biden in 2020. Viewed for a long time as the frontrunner, by dint of his stature and polls, Biden took big hits in Iowa, where he came in fourth, New Hampshire, where he placed fifth, and Nevada, losing to Bernie Sanders, suddenly dubbed the new frontrunner. "For Joe Biden, two bad losses and a perilous path forward," a headline proclaimed, and this was before Sanders' rout by more than 20 percentage points in Nevada (Glueck & Kaplan, 2020). Judged by expectations and performance in the nomination contests, Biden was on the ropes, losing ground fast. Ironically, this death bed pronouncement would help catapult him back to life a week later.

When a candidate's poll ratings or nomination contest victories increase sharply, news stories jump on the proverbial bandwagon, exemplifying the press's gaining ground, **bandwagon storyline**. News stories about the candidate increase in favorability, emphasizing that the candidate is gaining ground (Patterson, 1993). Historically, Jimmy Carter benefited from this in 1976 (see Chapter 14), as did Obama in 2008, the latter with a series of victories in state caucuses, racking up delegates, gaining support from party elites, and gaining an air of inevitability. In 2016, as Trump began winning primaries after losing the Iowa caucuses, his coverage fit a bandwagon narrative, even though objectively he had many hurdles to cross before gaining enough delegates to clinch the nomination. Other candidates are viewed through an **electability narrative**, the frame that evaluates candidates in terms of their likelihood of winning the nomination (see discussion of gender intersections in Chapter 12).

Candidate successes on the campaign trail and innovative policy positions can be played down because, in the view of the press (and party insiders), the candidate has a small chance of gaining the nomination. This may have afflicted Bernie Sanders in 2016, who won primaries and caucuses, but received less press coverage than did Clinton (Patterson, 2016a). Given the Democratic Party's proportional distribution of delegates to candidates and Clinton's domination of super-delegates, it was very unlikely he could have overcome her seemingly insurmountable lead. It was not unreasonable for journalists to perceive Sanders through an electability narrative, but it may have served as a self-fulfilling prophecy. Reverend Jesse Jackson, the charismatic outsider Democratic candidate of 1984 and 1988, was viewed through the electability prism, resulting in criticism that the press wrote him off because he was an African American who lay outside the political mainstream. The problem with the electability narrative is that by invoking horse race criteria, based on poll and election results, the press can push voters to discount a candidate they truly like because they read stories saying the candidate has no realistic chance of winning.

Thus, candidates' success over the long haul of the nomination is not preordained. While there are winners and losers in particular contests, candidate performance from week to week is frequently evaluated, based on the strange, amorphous criteria of prior expectations. According to the **exceeding expectations narrative**, candidates are favorably evaluated if they performed better than expected and negatively assessed if they did worse than anticipated. This was the story of Pete Buttigieg, the former mayor of South Bend, Indiana, unknown to the political world until he announced his candidacy in April 2019. With expectations for electoral success initially low, Buttigieg upended the venerable Sanders, twice his age, to narrowly win the Iowa caucuses, raising expectations that the first openly gay presidential candidate to seriously contest a presidential nomination might break through the primary gates.

Expectations are informally set by journalists, consulting polls, and party leaders, with the press acting less as detached, thoughtful observers than prognosticators, oddsmakers, even handicappers in a political horse race, setting expectations that shape campaign momentum and influence candidates' decisions on whether to campaign aggressively in certain states or drop out of the race. If they exceed expectations of victory or poll performance, then they gain positive coverage. If they do not reach expectations, then they are seen as potential losers and get negative press. There is a shaky, carnival-like, self-serving aspect to all this, as humorist Russell Baker (1983) insightfully observed some years back, referring to 1984 Democratic presidential candidate Walter Mondale:

> Rotten luck . . . Mondale, we've made you the frontrunner. . . . Without a frontrunner, we'd have nobody to suffer surprising setbacks in the early stage of the campaign, and without surprising setbacks we would be stuck with a very dull story. . . . It's tough, but somebody's got to make the sacrifice and be the frontrunner. . . . Say you get only 47 percent of that boondocks vote (in New Hampshire and Iowa). What we'll do is say, well 47 percent may not be disgraceful, but Mondale had been expected to do better, so it looks like he's all washed up. . . . We of the press and TV do the expecting. You do the disappointing. That way we work together to give the country an entertaining story.
>
> (p. 12)

The expectations storyline emerged with regularity in 2016. When Republican Marco Rubio exceeded expectations by finishing just one point behind runner-up Donald Trump in the Iowa caucuses, he became, for a time, a darling of the political press and party establishment. His Iowa tally "gave his campaign another jolt of energy at a time when good fortune seems to be breaking his way," *The New York Times* reported (Peters, 2016, p. A1). Yet he received just 23 percent of the vote and came in third place! And when his fortunes faded and he failed to win key primaries, he was lambasted, for having done worse than expected.

It worked the opposite way 4 years later, in what was perhaps the greatest example of a moribund candidacy that upended expectations. After Biden's resounding losses in three key contests, press expectations were low that Biden could amass the electoral firepower needed to overcome the progressive Democratic wave that seemed to be cresting toward Sanders. Even after Biden won big in South Carolina, few expected he could outgun Sanders, who had a large financial base and commanded fervent loyalty from the liberal Democratic base (Martin & Burns, 2020). Then came Super Tuesday, the day when the most states hold nomination contests, a day that changed the race for good. Biden won nine states, including a big prize in Texas, his competitors Amy Klobuchar's Minnesota, and Elizabeth Warren's Massachusetts, even emerging victorious in states where he did not campaign at all. His victories would have been big in any case, but he helped himself in the news world by giving reporters a great exceeding expectations story to tell.

In all of these different cases, candidate viability—success in primaries, caucuses, and election polls—is the major determinant of news favorability. There is nothing sinister in journalists employing this framework. It fits professional norms and helps reporters make sense of a presidential campaign. But such an approach can lead to oversimplification, a tendency to force the facts to fit the favored storyline, and, as discussed in Chapter 12, a mechanism by which female candidates are squeezed out of the picture. What's more, viability is not the only—or necessarily even the best—way to view a political campaign. As Patterson (1993) emphasizes, reporters' view of politics as a strategic game is not shared by all observers, notably voters. Unlike reporters, who see politics in terms of a game schema, voters primarily examine candidates' issue stands, leadership, and performance. Voters view politics from a presidential governing schema, looking at elections as a way to choose leaders, based on a raft of criteria, including candidate likability, self-interest, agreement with candidates on key issues, and yes, political biases, even prejudices. For better or worse, most voters do not view politics through a horse race lens—or at least that is one prevailing critique of how news covers politics.

## THE ISSUES QUANDARY

With their focus on campaign controversies, political journalists, some more than others, frequently neglect issues, a classic shortcoming in presidential campaign coverage. Nonstop rumination about Trump's latest tweets occupied significant space online and considerable time on cable news. Frequently neglected was discussion of economic, social, and racial issues roiling America, along with proposals to solve them.

Issue coverage is often superficial, relegated to short soundbites with few accompanying arguments (Bucy & Grabe, 2007; Rinke, 2016). Of course, the "not enough coverage of issues" lament is the classic scholarly critique of presidential campaign news. It assumes that if issues were covered in more depth, voters would process the information and deliberate differently about candidates. It understates limits on time-pressed voters' motivation, as well as ability, to ferret through complex issues. And it minimizes the amount of issue coverage out there, as well as voters' knowledge of the basics of candidates' policy stands.

Indeed, news coverage of issues increased over the course of the 20th century (Sigelman & Bullock, 1991; Robinson & Sheehan, 1983). In our own age, there is ample information on issues, especially when you consider the volume of news articles on policy matters that appear on different news websites. During the 2020 primary campaign, news offered critical and thoughtful coverage of the merits of government-run health care, sparked by Sanders' Medicare for All proposal. You could learn a lot about other issues, too—racial profiling, gun reform, and immigration—from news stories. Once again, horse race and candidate image issue could dominate coverage of the Democratic primary debates, as in stories offering takeaways of candidates' verbal jousts, pointing out who seemed passive and who came out swinging, and any juicy tidbits on how candidate gaffes disrupted their campaigns.

It's complicated. General election campaigns are full of issues: trade, immigration, foreign policy, and in 2020 the coronavirus pandemic, a story amply covered throughout the news media. News covered the different candidate frames on the issues, as well as Biden's plans for economic recovery, climate change concerns, and racial justice. During the fall campaign, there was considerable coverage of Trump's countercharges and defenses of his record. Even so, campaign news could delve into the politics behind the proposals, as in coverage that focused more strategically on candidate attacks and horse race stories about who won debates.

That's campaign news in America, where sports metaphors, competition to get the story first, conflict-focused news values, and the chase for ratings dollars dominate. It's a lot of fun for political aficionados, but it has drawbacks. You won't find much outside-the-box coverage of the paucity of third-party candidates or, typically, much discussion of limitations in tried, true, and frequently unsatisfactory candidate policy plans. But you can get deeply reported evaluations of where candidates stand and, if you access the best journalistic sites with their multiple links, you can learn a lot about the problems dominating the campaign and ideas on how to solve them. It's out there, there's good political journalism produced every day, and issue-based news does elicit interest and reactions (Stroud & Muddiman, 2019). Of course, most voters lack the time, attention, and motivation to delve so deeply, and so must depend on the diet they receive from popular media, with its so-so coverage of issues and heavy horse race emphasis—"snack food for your smartphone" (Mahler, 2015).

## CONCLUSIONS

One of the biggest biases of political media is not one you ordinarily think of. It's not a liberal or conservative predilection, but a tendency to cover the campaign as a horse race, a strategic game. News has historically done this for a number of reasons, including the game frame's focus on conflict, its ability to furnish facts, and its capacity to provide predictable, exciting stories that fulfill journalistic and economic functions. But to the extent that it does this, it pushes strategic considerations to the forefront of voters' minds, shunting aside more important policy concerns. It also frames the election as a mere game when more serious issues are at stake. And it reifies the two-party structure that discourages the formation of grassroots third parties. And yet, an alternative view is worth noting. Sober scholarly criticism of the horse race is as predictable as the race itself. As we saw during the 2020 pandemic election, a campaign devoid of rallies and news playing up the breathtaking partisan competition leaves a void. There is something to be said for the drama and excitement that horse race coverage offers, provided it is balanced with thoughtful issue coverage.

Opinion polls are a key ingredient of campaign news. Yet their systemic functions extend far beyond statistical estimates of likely primary election victories. With their reliable, scientific estimates of a population's political opinions, polls provide a formal mechanism to connect citizens to leaders, allowing candidates (and elected officials) to understand the sentiments of those they represent. Although polling is rooted in the science of sampling, it missed the mark in the past two presidential elections. Polls failed to predict the margin and outcomes in battleground states in 2016 and 2020, a result of declining telephone response rates and a likely refusal of strong conservatives and less-educated respondents to participate in presidential polls, artificially depressing support for Donald Trump. Polling has an important role to play in a democracy, but polls' failures to predict key states in both elections—aggravated by journalists' hyping polls without explaining their limits—has led to questions and even cynicism about election polling. It's a problem that needs to be addressed and rectified, given the important role that accurate rendering of citizens' opinions plays in a democracy.

Press coverage waxes and wanes, offering positive coverage to certain candidates and consistently negative coverage to others. This can seem like out-and-out ideological bias to observers, but this is not what is going on. Campaign news flows from the routines of political journalism and its emphasis on storylines. In addition to the venerable horse race, political news revolves around schematic personality narratives, tough press for the frontrunner, the losing ground scenario, and the "gaining ground" bandwagon narrative. These are helpful narratives, but they can influence the campaign, as when grueling frontrunner coverage reduces the frontrunner's support or a gaining ground scenario actually lifts a candidate's fortunes, helping to propel the candidate all the way to the nomination (see Chapter 14). To some degree, press narratives provide an antidote to party control of the process, but they also place the press in a role of king (or queen) maker, raising questions of whether it has too much influence. Increasingly, news media are one of a number of influence agents, sitting alongside social media, with its loud megaphone that amplifies the voices of the politically engaged.

Campaign news is imperfect and superficial. However, it does cover the campaign thoroughly—and endlessly. Guided by storylines and journalistic values, it nonetheless manages to hold candidates' feet to the fire, forcing them to pay homage to the ritual of courting voters and attending to their grievances. And although issue coverage pales in comparison to the horse race, it is available and accessible online. The problem, as always, is getting in-depth information to voters who are besieged by phone snippets and partisan summaries of the presidential campaign.

## REFERENCES

Agiesta, J. (2020a, October 8). In news about the presidential race, coronavirus overtakes nearly all else. *CNN Politics*. Online: www.cnn.com/2020/10/08/politics/the-breakthrough-trump-biden-coronavirus-debate/index.html. (Accessed: November 25, 2020).

Agiesta, J. (2020b, August 16). Here are the words defining the 2020 presidential campaign. *CNN Politics*. Online: www.cnn.com/2020/08/16/politics/election-2020-polls-biden-trump-breakthrough/index.html. (Accessed: November 25, 2020).

Baker, R. (1983, February 6). Handicappers. *The New York Times Magazine*, 12.

Bialik, C. (2016, March 9). Why the polls missed Bernie Sanders's Michigan upset. *FiveThirtyEight*. Online: https://fivethirtyeight.com/features/why-the-polls-missed-bernie-sanders-michigan-upset/. (Accessed: April 27, 2021).

Blow, C.M. (2020, May 24). Biden can beat Trump . . . if he doesn't blow it. *The New York Times*. Online: www.nytimes.com/2020/05/24/opinion/biden-trump-coronavirus.html. (Accessed: December 18, 2020).

Bucy, E.P., & Grabe, M.E. (2007). Taking television seriously: A sound and image bite analysis of presidential campaign coverage, 1992–2004. *Journal of Communication, 57*, 652–675.

Cappella, J.N., & Jamieson, K.H. (1997). *Spiral of cynicism: The press and the public good*. New York: Oxford University Press.

Cohn, N. (2020, November 10). What went wrong with polling? Some early theories. *The New York Times*. Online: www.nytimes.com/2020/11/10/upshot/polls-what-went-wrong.html. (Accessed: November 11, 2020).

Dimitrova, D.V. (2014). Framing the 2012 presidential election on U.S. television. In D.G. Bystrom, M.C. Banwart, & M.S. McKinney (Eds.), *alieNATION: The divide & conquer election of 2012* (pp. 15–30). New York: Peter Lang.

Edelman, G. (2020, November 4). So how wrong were the polls this year, really? *Wired*. Online: www.wired.com/story/how-wrong-were-polls-election-2020-trump-biden/ (Accessed: November 5, 2020).

Flegenheimer, M., & Haberman, M. (2016, April 7). Rivals assemble to hurt Trump on his home turf. *The New York Times*, A14.

Gerth, J. (2015, March 13). Hillary Clinton's top five clashes over secrecy. *ProPublica*. Online: www.propublica.org/article/hillary-clintons-top-five-clashes-over-secrecy. (Accessed: December 21, 2016).

Glueck, K., & Kaplan, T. (2020, March 3). For Joe Biden, two bad losses and a precarious path forward. *The New York Times*. Online: www.nytimes.com/2020/02/12/us/politics/joe-biden-new-hampshire-democrats.html. (Accessed: May 25, 2020).

Goldmacher, S., & Epstein, R.J. (2020, February 20). 6 takeaways from the Democratic debate in Nevada. *The New York Times*. Online: www.nytimes.com/2020/02/20/us/politics/democratic-debate-las-vegas.html. (Accessed: May 23, 2020).

Golshan, T., & Nilsen, E. (2019, August 28). The growing narrative around Joe Biden's gaffes, explained. *Vox*. Online: www.vox.com/2019/8/28/20833288/joe-biden-gaffes-narrative-explained. (Accessed: May 24, 2020).

Johnson, D.W. (2007). *No place for amateurs: How political consultants are reshaping American democracy* (2nd ed.). New York: Routledge.

Johnston, R., Hagen, M.G., & Jamieson, K.H. (2004). *The 2000 presidential election and the foundation of party politics*. New York: Cambridge University Press.

Kennedy, C., & Hartig, H. (2019, February 27). *Response rates in telephone surveys have resumed their decline.* Pew Research Center (FactTank: News in the Numbers). Online: www.pewresearch.org/fact-tank/2019/02/27/response-rates-in-telephone-surveys-have-resumed-their-decline/. (Accessed: November 5, 2020).

Krugman, P. (2016, September 5). Clinton gets gored. *The New York Times*, A19.

Lavrakas, P.J., & Bauman, S.L. (1995). Page One use of presidential pre-election polls: 1980–1992. In P.J. Lavrakas, M.W. Traugott, & P.V. Miller (Eds.), *Presidential polls and the news media* (pp. 35–49). Boulder, CO: Westview Press.

Leonhardt, D. (2020, November 12). "A black eye": Why polling missed the mark. Again. *The New York Times.* Online: www.nytimes.com/2020/11/12/us/politics/election-polls-trump-biden.html. (Accessed: November 13, 2020).

Mahler, J. (2015, May 3). Campaign coverage via Snapchat could shake up the 2016 elections. *The New York Times.* Online: www.nytimes.com/2015/05/04/business/media/campaign-coverage-via-snapchat-could-shake-up-the-2016-elections.html. (Accessed: January 4, 2017).

Martin, J., & Burns, A. (2020, February 29). Winning South Carolina, Biden makes his case against Sanders: "Win big or lose". *The New York Times.* Online: www.nytimes.com/2020/02/29/us/politics/joe-biden-south-carolina-primary.html. (Accessed: May 25 2020).

Mikkelson, D. (2016, September 5). Web of lies. *Snopes.com.* Online: www.snopes.com/quotes/internet.asp. (Accessed: December 22, 2016).

Miller, M.M., & Denham, B. (1994). Horserace, issue coverage in prestige newspapers during 1988, 1992 elections. *Newspaper Research Journal, 15*, 20–28.

Patterson, T.E. (1993). *Out of order.* New York: Knopf.

Patterson, T.E. (2016a, July 11). *News coverage of the 2016 presidential primaries: Horse race reporting has consequences.* Harvard Kennedy School Shorenstein Center on Media, Politics and Public Policy. Online: https://shorensteincenter.org/news-coverage-2016-presidential-primaries/. (Accessed: April 27, 2021).

Patterson, T.E. (2016b, June 13). *Pre-primary news coverage of the 2016 presidential race: Trump's rise, Sanders' emergence, Clinton's struggle.* Harvard Kennedy School Shorenstein Center on Media, Politics and Public Policy. Online: https://papers.ssrn.com/sol3/papers.cfm?abstract_id=2798258. (Accessed: December 18, 2020).

Peters, J.W. (2016, February 3). Rubio campaign dispatches its army and new lines of attack. *The New York Times*, A1, A15.

Rinke, E.M. (2016). The impact of sound-bite journalism on public argument. *Journal of Communication, 66*, 625–645.

Robinson, M.J., & Sheehan, M.A. (1983). *Over the wire and on TV: CBS and UPI in Campaign '80.* New York: Russell Sage Foundation.

Russonello, G. (2019, November 24). Mistakes in 2016 Trump polling could play out again 2020. *The New York Times*, 24.

Schmidt, M.S. (2015, March 2). Hillary Clinton used personal email account at State Dept., possibly breaking rules. *The New York Times.* Online: www.nytimes.com/2015/03/03/us/politics/hillary-clintons-use-of-private-email-at-state-department-raises-flags.html. (Accessed: December 22, 2016).

Schmidt, M.S., & Sanger, D.E. (2015, August 15). F.B.I. is tracking path of classified email from the State Dept. to Clinton. *The New York Times*, A14.

Schudson, M. (1995). *The power of news.* Cambridge, MA: Harvard University Press.

Searles, K. (2020). Beyond the horse race: Voting process coverage in 2020. In D. Jackson, D.S. Coombs, F. Trevisan, D. Lilleker, & E. Thorsen (Eds.), *U.S. election analysis 2020: Media, voters and the campaign*. Online: www.electionanalysis.ws/us/president2020/section-4-news-and-journalism/beyond-the-horse-race-voting-process-coverage-in-2020/ (Accessed: November 16, 2020).

Shane, S. (2015, March 12). A claim of no classified emails in a place that classifies routinely. *The New York Times*, A19.

Sigelman, L., & Bullock, D. (1991). Candidates, issues, horse races, and hoopla: Presidential campaign coverage, 1888–1988. *American Politics Quarterly*, *19*, 5–32.

Smoller, F.T. (1990). *The six o'clock presidency: A theory of presidential press relations in the age of television*. New York: Praeger.

Stroud, N.J., & Muddiman, A. (2019). Social media engagement with strategy- and issue-framed political news. *Journal of Communication*, *69*, 443–466.

Sullivan, M. (2016, March 6). Waiter, where's our (political) spinach? *The New York Times* (Sunday Review), 10.

Toff, B. (2020). Forecasting the future of election forecasting. In D. Jackson, D.S. Coombs, F. Trevisan, D. Lilleker, & E. Thorsen (Eds.), *U.S. election analysis 2020: Media, voters and the campaign*. Online: www.electionanalysis.ws/us/president2020/section-4-news-and-journalism/forecasting-the-future-of-election-forecasting/. (Accessed: November 16, 2020).

Traugott, M.W., & Lavrakas, P.J. (2008). *The voter's guide to election polls* (4th ed.). Lanham, MD: Rowman & Littlefield.

Trussler, M., & Soroka, S. (2014). Consumer demand for cynical and negative news frames. *The International Journal of Press/Politics*, *19*, 360–379.

Victor, D. (2016, September 28). Why you shouldn't trust "polls" conducted online. *The New York Times*. Online: www.nytimes.com/2016/09/29/us/politics/why-you-shouldnt-believe-most-online-polls.html?_r=0. (Accessed: December 28, 2016).

Zoizner, A. (in press). The consequences of strategic news coverage for democracy: A meta-analysis. *Communication Research*. DOI: 10.1177/0093650218808691. (Accessed: July 17, 2020).

# 14

# Presidential Nominations in the Media Age

We don't exactly know how the 2024 and 2028 presidential nominating campaigns are going to proceed, but one thing is for certain: They won't go as expected.

If you would have told four Democratic senators vying for their party's nomination in 2020 that they would have been holed up in Washington for nearly 3 weeks before the pivotal Iowa caucuses, they would have collectively said, "No way." But that is exactly what happened when the senators found themselves pinned down in the Senate for hours each day as they served as jurors in the impeachment trial of President Donald Trump. And there's more: Try telling the leading candidates for the nomination that they would quit their campaigns entirely in early March because a global pandemic imperiled public interaction. "What have you been smoking or drinking?" they would politely ask through their bright blue protective masks.

Let's go back to 2016. "It seems a remote prospect," a reporter penned when Donald Trump announced his candidacy in June 2015, "that Republicans, stung in 2012 by the caricature of their nominee, Mitt Romney, as a pampered and politically tone-deaf financier, would rebound by nominating a real estate magnate who has published books with titles such as, 'Think Like a Billionaire' and 'Midas Touch: Why Some Entrepreneurs Get Rich—and Why Most Don't'" (Burns, 2015).

"All his life," columnist Joe Nocera (2015) confidently observed, "Trump has had a deep need to be perceived as a 'winner.' He always has to be perceived coming out on top. That's why, ultimately," Nocera predicted, "I don't think he'll ever put himself at the mercy of actual voters in a primary. To do so is to risk losing. And everyone will know it. He'll be out before Iowa. You read it here first."

Well, it didn't quite turn out that way. A series of expert prognosticators who predicted Trump's demise had political egg on their face. Even pollster Nate Silver, who correctly predicted the electoral outcome of each state in 2012, got it wrong. After Trump became the presumptive nominee in May 2016, Silver (2016) acknowledged that "if you'd told me a year ago that Trump would be the nominee, I'd have thought you were nuts."

On the Democratic side, there was a hum-drum consensus that Clinton would sail to the nomination. When Bernie Sanders entered the race ("Bernie, who?" experts chortled), few expected him to present a serious challenge to Hillary Clinton. Yet he did, winning scores of contests and changing the ideological tenor of the race.

Events famously upended predictions in 2008. In that year, the venerable Clinton and (now controversial) former New York City mayor Rudy Giuliani were odds-on favorites to win their parties' nominations (Popkin, 2012). But Giuliani faded, a victim of poor strategic choices, a message that never caught on, and the drip-drip of negative news about his personal life. Clinton found herself out-organized by the tech-savvy Obama campaign, a once-in-a-generation candidate whose speeches moved millions. At the time, though, Clinton seemed invincible and Giuliani a frontrunner.

Campaigns are unpredictable. Social science models offer insights, but the confluence of factors that intersect—candidate messaging, state-by-state strategies, the political psychology of voters, and above all, events—can imperil the most successful of prognostications. As with sports, if we knew who would win at the outset, there would be no need to play the game. At the beginning, it seems obvious who will capture the party's nomination. Then reality sets in, and it becomes equally obvious when a candidate withdraws that he or she did not really have a lick of a chance at the get-go, and it was predestined that the eventual nominee would gain his or her party's nod. Such is the beauty of 20/20 hindsight.

Communication plays a key role in the nomination process. News media influence voters' beliefs about who is a serious candidate, while also shaping fundraisers' perceptions of candidate viability. Social media can help mobilize support for insurgent campaigns. Opinion polls and primary debates alter the trajectory of a campaign in ways that would have been unheard of in the political party–dominated nomination process of yore. The distinctive process by which America selects its nominees for president has shortcomings, but also strengths, and has evolved into something far different than the country's founders would have anticipated.

This chapter describes the presidential nominating system, offering an explanation (though not a justification) of an arcane, volatile process. The focus, as much as possible, is on political communication. The first section provides a short overview, describing the basic terminology of presidential nominations. The next sections explore the four phases of the campaign: (1) pre-primaries; (2) first critical caucuses and primary; (3) contests that follow; and (4) summer nominating conventions.

You have probably followed presidential nominations in the media, a lot or a little, depending on your interest. Perhaps you have been curious or even puzzled about the legion of primaries that candidates contest, ways they trudge through small states in quest of votes, and the seemingly endless horse race coverage, tweets, and online chatter. This chapter will help you make sense of it all, develop a critical understanding, appreciate methods behind the madness, and perhaps generate some ideas for how to improve an imperfect process.

## OVERVIEW

The primaries are a fixture in presidential politics. Candidates must win primaries—and caucuses—if they want to gain the nomination of the Republican and Democratic parties. A **presidential primary** is a statewide election that gives voters the opportunity to select the party's presidential nominee. Voters cast votes in a secret ballot, just as they do in a general election.

Caucuses are different. As the name suggests, a caucus involves people talking and discussing issues. A **caucus** is a local gathering where party members publicly deliberate about candidates, decide which presidential candidate they will support, and choose delegates to the nominating convention. A caucus is a public event, where party members state their candidate preference and may try to persuade one another to support one or another candidate. This is simultaneously the caucus's greatest strength and weakness. Requiring people to say who they favor in public takes them out of their private online political worlds and puts them face-to-face with other citizens. It brings people together, allowing them to hear other viewpoints and come into contact with voters who have different political perspectives. However, voters can be uncomfortable sharing their preferences in public, knowing zealots for another candidate may question their political views. Precisely because they are public, they don't resemble or reflect the private voting experience that occurs during the general election. But for defenders of the caucus, that's exactly what the caucus adds to the process.

There is a complication. Technically, when voters cast ballots or indicate caucus preferences, they are not voting for a candidate, but a delegate. A **delegate** is typically a member of a political party, an individual who attends the nominating convention and formally casts a vote for a candidate. Delegates tend to be political activists and hold more extreme views of issues than both rank-and-file party members and voters (Polsby et al., 2012). (This may not be bad:

Strong positions on issues propel people to become involved in presidential elections, and that's a good thing.)

Although the process is exponentially more democratic than it was two centuries ago, when party bosses chose the nominees, it is not purely or entirely democratic. Only a minority of eligible voters, sometimes less than 20 percent and rarely more than 30 percent, actually vote in presidential primaries (DeSilver, 2016; Rakich, 2020). As noted previously, when voters cast their ballots, they technically are not just voting for candidates, but for delegates (Buchanan & Parlapiano, 2016). The process by which votes translate into delegates is intricate, arcane, governed by rules that can change, and as you might expect, highly political. With this overview in mind, let's now delve into communication and the nomination process.

## PRE-PRIMARIES

### Background

The nomination season begins early—really early, nearly 2 years before the presidential election. By contrast, the duration of national election campaigns in Europe is much shorter—weeks or months, depending on the country.

Why does the American presidential election campaign last so long? Why does it start so early? Running for president costs a lot of money, and candidates need time to raise the cash to pay for television advertisements and campaign staff. They need to develop a viable organization, with competent consultants, pollsters, lawyers, speechwriters, and rank-and-file volunteers. They must build a reservoir of voter support in early caucus and primary states such as Iowa and New Hampshire. To be successful, candidates must also gain national visibility through news coverage and prominence on social media. Increasingly, in media-saturated America, success is about gaining attention and appearing viable across a variety of platforms, and viability takes time to establish. It's also a tradition that the first campaign phase begins more than a year-and-a-half before the election, and political traditions have staying power.

But this doesn't mean it's the best system. Millions of dollars that could be contributed to more worthy causes are thrown into the nominating system, and time that could be spent on more important political issues is expended on strategic messaging.

The pre-primary portion of the campaign has been called the *invisible primary*. The name bespeaks an appreciation that the nomination process begins behind the scenes months before the first votes are cast, as candidates sponsor fundraisers, try to increase voter recognition, and strive to gain credibility with the news media, in ways that can bewilder ordinary voters. On a broader, more deliberative democratic level, the pre-primaries can be viewed as a series of national political conversations among politicians, media, and the public, although typically directed at the more partisan members of the electorate who follow campaigns (Cohen et al., 2008).

The pre-primary period starts in the winter of the year prior to the election, beginning when candidates announce their intention to run for president. It lasts until campaigning begins in earnest for the Iowa caucuses in January or February of the presidential election year. The pre-primary phase is a relatively recent addition to the campaign, having exerted a significant impact only over the last couple of decades. But what an impact it has exerted! It has arguably become the most decisive feature of the nominating campaign, critically influencing voters' opinions and winnowing down candidates for the later phases of the nominating contest.

The keys to success during this pivotal period are: (1) obtaining visibility from multiple media, conventional news, but also social media; (2) gaining high numbers in countless opinion polls taken in the early caucus state of Iowa and across the nation; and (3) creating a perception of ascendance by attracting money from leading party donors and backing from supporters, such as crusading young volunteers. "Visibility," Nelson Polsby and his colleagues explained, "is important because news media coverage introduces candidates to the voters and shapes popular perceptions of the various contenders" (p. 100). National news coverage also serves a heuristic function: It conveys key information to party leaders, fundraisers, and voters, suggesting that the candidate is a viable contender for the race. It is a funny, self-fulfilling process that bespeaks the power of media coverage. A candidate gains coverage in the media because he or she is deemed a serious contender—and media attention causes the candidate to be an ever-more-viable candidate for office. There is a downside. As Patterson (2016) notes, "the nominating campaigns of candidates who are ignored by the media are almost certainly futile, while the campaigns of those who receive close attention get a boost."

The Internet and social media have provided a helping hand for insurgent, outsider, sometimes populist candidates, giving them broad platforms to reach voters. In 2016, Trump broke the mold of presidential nominating campaigns, defying the contempt of party regulars by using social media to recruit an unlikely base of loyal adherents and gaining outsize attention in a news media motivated not by ideology, but by ratings.

In 2020, candidates who mastered the art of threading messages around a compelling narrative fared well in the pre-primary battles. For example, former South Bend Mayor Pete Buttigieg, who served as a Naval Officer in Afghanistan, radiated youth, promise, and an optimistic vision for change. Eloquent and literary, he was a "cerebral type of Jimmy Stewart character," supercharged by his comfortable-in-his-skin acceptance of his married gay gender identity (Burns, 2019). Buttigieg crafted social media moments, looked good on television town hall forums, and recruited a bonanza of fundraising dollars, all producing a wave of positive press for a time, propelled by his youth and the eloquence of his rhetoric (Epstein, 2019).

Let's not forget Bernie Sanders, who captivated many young people in 2016 and was back 4 years later, the pied progressive piper with a raging message against capitalism's maladies, crystallized by a government-run Medicare for All health plan. Sanders attracted an online army of followers that raised nearly $100 million in 2019 without sponsoring a single major fundraising event. His troops were fiercely loyal, even to the point of bullying, flaming, and threatening opponents online (Flegenheimer, Ruiz, & Bowles, 2020), but it was his message—diffused on social media and reinforced with news coverage—that resonated with so many Democrats in 2016 and again in 2020 (see Figure 14.1).

**Figure 14.1 Senator Bernie Sanders shook up the Democratic Party with his grassroots challenges to the party establishment in Iowa, New Hampshire, and other nomination contests. He electrified many young people and advocated deeply committed radical policy positions on health care and the economy at campaign debates. However, as happens with political movements, he attracted some supporters who, perhaps feeling like they were part of a transcendent moral mission, become overzealous, as when they bullied and flamed opponents online in 2020.**

*Source*: www.gettyimages.com/detail/news-photo/vermont-senator-and-presidential-candidate-bernie-sanders-news-photo/1172699871?adppopup=true

These candidates ascended because they captured press attention, developed a message that captivated their base, and exploited online media. In 2020, Biden presented himself as the most electable candidate for Democrats desperate to beat Donald Trump. Of course, it took a while for his candidacy to take hold, and it almost fizzled, a reminder that politics is unpredictable.

## Pre-primary Polls, Debates, and the New Winnowing Effect

Pre-primary candidate debates have increased in prominence over the past several election cycles. Presidential debates exert a host of effects on voters, as will be discussed in Chapter 16. For now, the point is that debates, which occur well before the first votes have been cast, showcase the role that forces outside the institutional political system exert on nominations.

### *2016 Election*

In 2016, with 17 Republicans running for president, cable network executives believed it would be unwieldy (and bad for ratings) if all 17 candidates shared the stage. Setting a standard for debates that followed, Fox announced that it would use poll data to select the 10 candidates to participate in the major debate in primetime, allowing the remainder to partake in the "undercard" or "kids' table" debates, as they were humorously called.

From a political perspective, this was a stunning, jaw-dropping change. In years past the key events that winnowed down the list of potential contenders were early caucuses and primaries. While reliance on these early contests is not without problems, the decisions were based at least on votes, the behavioral bricks and mortar of democracy. But with Fox's first debate in August 2015 and debates that followed in the 2016 race, a profit-making news organization with preciously little grounding in traditional democratic politics—a business that is not accountable to voters or the political process—arrogated to itself the right to decide which candidates should gain the greatest access to citizens and which should be relegated to the secondary, non-prime-time undercard debate.

The decision was made by polls. Fox announced that candidates who placed in the top 10 in an average of the five most recent national opinion polls recognized by Fox News and conducted by scientifically reputable polling organizations would participate in the main debate. Why just five polls? Why not more? Polls vary in their acceptable margin of error, sample sizes, and predictive ability. It also was not clear that the difference between the 10th candidate, who got chosen, and the 11th, who was relegated to the undercard debate, was statistically meaningful. The choice of 10 candidates is arbitrary as well.

### 2020 Election

With President Trump running as an incumbent, the political landscape in the winter of 2020 revolved around the Democrats. Back in 2016, the Democratic National Committee (DNC), like the Republicans, based debate inclusion on polls. Candidates had to gain an average of 1 percent popularity in an average of three national polls. The DNC changed this in 2020 to give candidates who didn't have a national political reputation, but had grassroots support, a chance to enter the debate sweepstakes. The initial rules stated that candidates either had to garner at least 1 percent support in three polls, or receive money from 65,000 individuals, with at least 200 donors per state from 20 different states. This permitted the entry of the entrepreneur Andrew Yang and spiritualist Marianne Williamson, who added some whimsy and creative ideas to debates.

The new rules—and they changed so that candidates had to have 130,000 donors to qualify for the third debate—encouraged candidates to try to game the system by exploiting social media. Contenders could dream up a creative social media moment that would drum up donors or develop Facebook ads that directed people to a candidate's website (Goldmacher & Lerer, 2019). But neither of these required candidates to show they had the ideas or capability to govern the country; instead, inclusion in debates was based on name recognition or social media panache. Clearly, when 29 major Democratic candidates throw their hats into the ring, the media can't include all of them without ruining the debate format, but what criteria do they use? It's good that party bosses aren't deciding who is a viable candidate anymore, but polls and drumming up donors have shortcomings of their own.

### Debates

Primary campaign debates, are, of course, media events, manufactured and promoted by media outlets with fanfare and drama. To recruit interest in the second Democratic debate in 2019, CNN created a pseudo-event. Network executives concocted a three-round lotto-type drawing stage-managed by Anderson Cooper and a seven-member panel tasked with "shuffling clunky placards with candidate names and debate-night dates, as if they were running the world's wonkiest three-card monte game" (Poniewozik, 2019, p. A20). Newscasters drew and read cards, drawing out 60 seconds' worth of news into 60 minutes, broken up by lucrative advertising breaks.

While the number of voters watching pre-primary debates is typically small, news and social media buzz can amplify their effects. Texas Governor Rick Perry committed a deadly stumble in a November 2011 debate in Michigan. Stating that, as president, he would eliminate three federal agencies, he could remember only two. For the life of him he could not articulate the third department he sought to eliminate. After a painful 53 seconds of hemming and hawing, all he could offer was, "Sorry, Oops." With a media outlet describing his performance with a paraphrase of the old Britney Spears song, "Oops, he did it again," and scores of ensuing stories that questioned his political expertise (and intelligence), Perry never regained his footing, quitting the race in January. (In a note of high irony, the department that he planned to dismantle but could not remember—Energy—was the one Trump tapped him to lead in his administration!)

Debates can legitimize candidates, as they did for Donald Trump, a never-elected real estate billionaire who showed he could fend off criticism and appear, if not always presidential, tough and credible with Republican audiences. Trump seemed unfazed by tough questions he received in pre-primary debates, beginning with Megyn Kelly's asking him to defend his record of making disparaging comments about women. In response, he challenged her, defended his actions by claiming what he had said was "fun," then changed the subject by saying we needed strength to turn the country around. Over the course of the campaign, he unapologetically defended controversial polices such as banning non-American Muslims from emigrating to the U.S., which played well to his base.

Debates in and of themselves do not determine who advances in the nomination process. Compared with general election debates, they attract relatively few viewers, and mostly those with strong preexisting partisan preferences. However, they can polish a candidate's image, increase newcomers' legitimacy, solidify support with the base, and in rare but consequential cases, torpedo a candidate's chances for the nomination (see later discussion of Michael Bloomberg's 2020 debate performance).

Although candidates strive for television theatrics—one-upping, one-liners, chest-pumping delivery, passionate rhetoric—debates do provide voters with a sense of candidates' credibility and composure. They offer a snapshot of candidates' positions on issues, where candidates agree and disagree, and can inform voters about big issues such as health care and foreign policy, sometimes offering insight into problems plaguing the country. Debates are constrained by the format, like having 10 candidates on a debate stage giving ultra-short answers with frequent interruptions from other candidates. The candidates can sometimes look more like 9-year-olds jostling for ice cream servings on a hot summer day than mature men and women running for president.

## Summary

There is a method to the apparent madness of who emerges from the volatile, unpredictable pre-primary phase. Candidates are more likely to succeed in the early phase if they (a) attract news attention; (b) gain social media buzz, from an active online or in-person group of supporters; (c) have solid poll numbers that place them in the now-consequential debates; (d) perform well in debates (or at least do not embarrass themselves); and (e) have a coherent message that captivates activist voters who participate in the primaries and caucuses. These criteria are not undemocratic, nor are they necessarily unreasonable ways to winnow down a long list of contenders. In fact, they make good sense. At the same time, for better or worse, they privilege media, making media attention—both conventional and social media—a dominant factor that influences the early nomination process.

## THE STRANGE, BUT TRUE, STORY OF IOWA AND NEW HAMPSHIRE

Suppose we started from scratch and wanted to devise the best way to structure the nomination system. We might use the general election as a model and hold a national primary election for each party. Or we might propose a series of regional primaries. There could be primary elections in the North, South, East, and West, perhaps staggered to keep political energy levels high. Alternatively, if we felt that it was important for each state to hold a primary, we might emphasize the big representative states in each region, letting them hold their primaries (or caucuses) first. What we probably would not want to do is to pick two small, totally unrepresentative states, arrange that they hold their elections first, and then suggest that candidates who did not fare well in these state contests should withdraw from the race.

But that is exactly how the process works!

The first, pivotal electoral contests take place in Iowa and New Hampshire. Iowa and New Hampshire have lots of strengths: low crime, pleasant lifestyle, bucolic scenery (for example, Iowa's verdant farmland and New Hampshire's spectacular ponds), but they hardly represent the country as a whole. The states are both more rural than urban. Iowa, dubbed the "Hawkeye State," is in the heart of the Corn Belt; New Hampshire, called the "Granite State," is filled with quarries. Iowa has the 32nd highest population and New Hampshire is ranked 42nd. They are overwhelmingly White (Iowa, 90 percent and New Hampshire, 94 percent). Their demographics, economics, climate, and some of their politics (New Hampshire's libertarian state motto is "Live Free or Die") do not mirror the rest of the country.

Iowa, bucolic and picturesque like a Grant Wood painting, is particularly unrepresentative. Iowa voters caucus in public, in preference groups categorized by candidates, with group decisions influenced by arguments and interpersonal persuasion. This is a far cry from the private voting booth and secret ballot that characterize primary elections. What's more, the caucuses do not accurately represent Iowa's demographics. Caucuses are held in early evening and do not permit absentee votes; as a result, they leave out key clusters of voters, such as medical personnel who must stay with their patients, restaurant employees, gas station workers on the night shift, and parents who can't afford a babysitter. (In 2020, Iowa tried to rectify this problem by holding satellite gatherings to include workers who could not leave their jobs.)

The caucuses are unrepresentative in other ways. The Iowa caucus delegate selection process, though admirable in its democratic aspects, is complex. In the first phase, caucus-goers select their candidate. But if a candidate doesn't recruit 15 percent of the attendees, his or her supporters must either persuade supporters of other candidates who didn't achieve that threshold to join them or choose another contender who met the 15 percent threshold. And the precise number of delegates selected at a particular caucus location is determined by a mathematical formula (Dann & Murray, 2020).

Unrepresentative though it may be, year after year it's a predictable part of the nomination contest. As sure as it is that farmers harvest Iowa corn in October autumn, the presidential campaigns expend enormous amounts of time and resources in the Hawkeye State every 4 years.

Iowa morphs into the center of the political universe during the 2 months preceding the caucuses, which occur in early January or February of the election year. Candidates deluge Iowa, some taking up residence there to help cement their connections. They trek from parades to picnics to potluck dinners, greeting candidates with a smile and a selfie. Staffers scan the environment, going door to door, making dozens of phone calls, and plugging in data. Reporters from Germany to Japan descend upon townspeople, students, and big-city dwellers of the Hawkeye State, putting hundreds of miles on their rental cars and chomping down Jimmy John's sandwiches. The out-of-towners spend lots of money, filling hotels and restaurants for summer barbecues, outdoor fall meet-and-greets, and winter speeches at high schools as the cold sets in. Some voters relish the attention, others are amused, while old-timers reflect on caucuses past, each with a distinct set of candidates, issue spiels, and endless media banter (Ember & Gale, 2020).

Then it's off to New Hampshire about a week later, where the mantra of candidates and journalists is: Revise, Repeat, and Rejuvenate.

Iowa and New Hampshire traditionally capture the lion's share of media attention during the primary campaign period. Some years back when researchers first content-analyzed news coverage of Iowa and New Hampshire, they discovered that the contests in these two states—which accounted for just about 3 percent of the U.S. population and 10 of the 270 Electoral College votes needed for election to the presidency—received 34 percent of television network news coverage of the primaries (Lichter, Amundson, & Noyes, 1988). The news coverage that the two states receive dwarfed the amount given to primaries in larger states, such as California, New York, and Texas (see also Buell, 2000). You might think of this visually by imagining two maps of the United States, the first the states in proportion to news about nominating contests, the second the states in proportion to their electoral votes. In the first map, Iowa and New Hampshire loom large, bigger than New York, California, and Florida. In the second, they are puny, reflecting the relatively small number of electoral votes the two states contribute to the Electoral College (Adams, 1987).

Why Iowa? Why New Hampshire? There are historical reasons. New Hampshire has held the nation's first primary since 1920. Iowa held caucuses since the mid-1800s, although they did not become politically consequential until 1976 when the media made considerable hay (so to speak) about Jimmy Carter's surprisingly strong showing. (There are actually several successive Iowa caucuses or conventions—precinct, county, district, and state; hence, the use of the plural, caucuses.)

These two contests assume importance because they are the first tests of strength in the electorate, and the media love firsts. "Iowa is not first because it is important; it is important because it is first," Winebrenner and Goldford (2010) note (p. 340). The contests also appeal to journalistic emphasis on the horse race, excitement, and drama. It is not just the news media that focus heavily on these early nomination contests. The candidates devote extensive resources to winning or placing in Iowa and New Hampshire. Party leaders closely monitor candidate performances. Fundraisers look to see which candidates lead the pack and therefore deserve their support. Active, committed voters from both parties use the results to make judgments about which candidates they will support in their own state primaries. Are these two contests politically consequential because the media lavish coverage on them, or do the media lavish coverage because they are politically consequential? It is a little bit of both, as media coverage has established in the eyes of voters and political elites that the outcomes preordain success in the fight for the nomination (Mayer, 2010). "Were it not for the media," two scholars note, "the Iowa caucus and New Hampshire primary results would be about as relevant to the presidential nomination as opening-day baseball scores are to a pennant race" (Paletz & Entman, 1981, p. 36).

## Politics, Communication, and the Perceptual Campaign

In Iowa, candidates with a passionate message that connects with committed voters and an impeccably organized campaign frequently win. In 2008, Obama relied on his college student minions, the children's crusade of 2008, to thoroughly canvass the Hawkeye State. In 2016, Republican Ted Cruz recognized that a key to winning Iowa voters is a ferociously dedicated, strategically organized ground game, coordinated by volunteers who can canvass door-to-door, run phone banks, traffic in social media, and set up events that attract crowds and capture coverage on television or on stories streamed across the Internet.

Focusing strategically on Iowa's evangelical Christian voters, who comprised close to two-thirds of Republican caucus participants, Cruz won the 2016 Iowa caucuses.

An early victory in Iowa spells instant success in the media horse race sweepstakes. The classic example occurred in 1976 when a little-known former Georgia governor, Jimmy Carter, recognizing the political import of a strong performance in Iowa, devoted considerable energy and resources to the state. Carter came in first, but here's the thing: He garnered just 28 percent of the vote, besting his Democratic rivals (though falling substantially short of the 37 percent who said they were uncommitted to any candidate). Nonetheless, the news media saw a story—or perhaps created one. The legendary *New York Times* reporter R.W. Apple pronounced that Carter had "burst from the pack" and had "scored an impressive victory in yesterday's Iowa Democratic precinct caucuses" (Perloff, 2016, p. E1; Winebrenner & Goldford, 2010, p. 68). This, along with other elite media coverage, ushered in a bonanza of positive press attention for Carter, gifting him with five times as much post-Iowa coverage as any other candidate, vaulting him above his rivals, subsequently delivering the momentum needed to cruise to victory in New Hampshire, become the unassailable frontrunner, and ultimately the Democratic nominee.

Candidates can also gain positive press by doing better than expected, in line with the exceeding expectations storyline discussed in Chapter 13. In 1992, Bill Clinton—on the political ropes because of allegations about an extramarital affair—convinced New Hampshire voters that he cared deeply about their economic plight, emphasizing that he would be with them "till the last dog dies." When he came in second (with just 26 percent of the vote), he called himself the "Comeback Kid." Playing on storied sports metaphors, he declared victory and rode the momentum to a raft of primary victories (see Figure 14.2).

Losses in Iowa and New Hampshire can be devastating. Losers no longer receive the mother's milk of political press: news coverage. They are saddled with a losing ground storyline. The political cognoscenti—the elite cadre of reporters, consultants, party leaders, and campaign donors—conclude that the candidate is not a viable contender. It's not done conspiratorially, but through the realm of perceptions, increasingly communicated via social media posts. Candidates who fail to come in first, second, or third are not perceived as winners, and perceptions translate to reality when it comes to news, politicians' endorsements, and dollars donated to campaigns. Wealthy people and even ordinary voters do not want to donate their money to a candidate who is seen as likely to lose. In 2020, Elizabeth Warren's campaign suffered a spate of bad press after her "disappointing" losses in Iowa and New Hampshire. Biden's campaign seemed on the ropes, with the press saying he faced "a perilous moment" after poor showings in Iowa and New Hampshire (Glueck & Kaplan, 2020).

**Figure 14.2  Bill Clinton campaigned aggressively for the 1992 Democratic presidential nomination, particularly in Iowa and New Hampshire. When he came in second in New Hampshire, after news coverage of a sexual liaison threatened to derail his candidacy, he spun the runner-up outcome as a victory, calling himself the Comeback Kid.**

*Source*: www.gettyimages.com/detail/news-photo/gov-bill-clinton-at-rally-celebrating-strong-2nd-place-news-photo/50468597

## Evaluation of Iowa and New Hampshire

In the decades-long, never-ending debate about Iowa and New Hampshire, there are communication pros, as well as the standard cons. Defenders note that in an age of mass political advertising and YouTube videos, it is refreshing to have nomination contests in states sufficiently small that candidates can talk to voters one-on-one, engage in grassroots campaigns, listen to their problems, and explain their policy proposals in ordinary language at the local diner. The two state contests also provide an early test of candidates' moxie, without requiring big media buys, in this way providing an element of surprise, giving outside-the-pack candidates with innovative ideas the chance to break out. Finally, precisely because of their small size, these states can galvanize supporters, energizing activists and voters in an era when this is the exception rather than the rule. With same-day registration policies in place and public discussions a centerpiece, both states encourage people to participate in political party events (Redlawsk, Tolbert, & Donovan, 2011). The robust discussions that precede the contests highlight the policy-based thinking and deliberation that are the shining lights of democracy.

There are definitely positive aspects to the news media's enshrining these two early contests as critical to the nomination. These are balanced by various negatives. The first is the states' stunning lack of representativeness of the national party electorate. A second downside is that horse race coverage advances winners with coverage disproportionate to the margin of victory. In 2020, Pete Buttigieg got a bounce in coverage after narrowly—very narrowly—winning the Iowa caucuses in a controversial election riddled with vote-reporting problems. He garnered 14 pledged national convention delegates and Sanders got 12. Buttigieg got substantial good press because he was Number 1 and exceeded the all-important expectations.

As another example, consider the Republican results in 2012. In that year, Republican candidate Mitt Romney captured a great deal of news coverage after the Iowa caucuses, although he defeated opponent Rick Santorum by just eight votes. Yet a little over 2 weeks later, a reanalysis of certified vote totals revealed that Santorum actually won, by 34 votes. But it was too late: Romney had won the beauty contest, gaining needed momentum for the New Hampshire primary.

The third problem, which critically surfaced in 2020, is that the criteria for delegate selection have become so mind-numbingly complex that they fracture the democratic process they were designed to build. Trying to be fair to the intricate caucus procedures, Iowa Democrats provided more information about each step along the way, releasing, first, the initial choice of attendees when they showed up at the caucus, then the revised choice of caucus-goers whose candidate didn't make the 15 percent threshold, and lastly, the final number of delegates each caucus (or precinct) allots, called—are you ready for this arcana?—"state delegate equivalents." The complex vote tabulation procedures, coupled with the breakdown of an inadequately tested smartphone app used to count the votes, led to inconsistent results, mistakes in the caucus math, and substantial delays in figuring out who won (Cohn et al., 2020). If Iowa's raison d'etre is offering a definitive first indication of who voters prefer, then the byzantine vote tabulation procedures rendered Iowa almost irrelevant.

## The Contests and Communications That Follow

Although victories in Iowa and New Hampshire are critical, they are not sufficient to propel a candidate to become the Republican or Democratic nominee. Candidates rarely win both Iowa and New Hampshire, so the momentum of Iowa can be cancelled by a loss in New Hampshire. Well-heeled candidates are apt to stay in the race longer than they used to. South Carolina, which comes a couple weeks after New Hampshire, has emerged as critical. In 2000, George W. Bush dealt opponent John McCain a fatal blow with a victory besmirched by false claims that McCain had sired children outside of marriage and had a "Negro child."

Twenty years later, Joe Biden resuscitated his floundering candidacy with a huge win in South Carolina, thanks to a strong showing by Black voters. His victory, demonstrating the abiding support he had in the African American community (as a result of his 8 years as Obama's vice president), convinced Democrats he was a viable candidate. Soon after Biden's victory, two leading competitors dropped out of the race, offering their endorsements. The ensuing momentum, media buzz, and restored belief among Democrats that Biden had the moxie to beat Donald Trump catapulted him to an unprecedented nine-state victory on Super Tuesday, the series of elections in delegate-rich states frequently held in early March. It was another demonstration of the unpredictable nature of nomination politics, the importance of viability perceptions, and the role that African American voters play in Democratic politics.

Biden's victory also showed that money isn't everything in nomination campaigns. Biden had struggled to raise funds, enviously watching former New York City Mayor Michael Bloomberg, whose net worth exceeded $55 billion, enter the race, positioning himself as the most likely candidate to oust Trump from the White House. Bloomberg spent $410 million on TV ads, blanketed the radio and television airwaves with hard-hitting spots, and hired more than 2,400 staffers to build his campaign. But it was to no avail. In a demonstration of the power an astoundingly poor debate performance can exert, Bloomberg lost considerable ground after he bungled his first primary debate. Unable to fend off attacks on his stop-and-frisk policy in New York and a record of disparagement of women, Bloomberg looked listless and lackluster, hardly the most viable Democrat to challenge President Trump. In response to withering questions from Senator Elizabeth Warren about allegations of sexual harassment, he looked feeble and at a loss for credible words. His debate fiasco gave him negative momentum going into Super Tuesday, and after losing badly to Biden, winning only the tiny American Samoa caucuses, he dropped out of the race.

It's not to say money matters little in American politics. As noted in Chapter 3, money plays an incredibly important role in determining access to power. But, in the nomination game, Bloomberg's money wasn't enough to quell doubts about his record, his commitment to ideals that liberal voters held dear, and after South Carolina, his claim that he was the most electable Democrat. Bloomberg's failure to spend his way to the nomination offered a small victory to those who say (to paraphrase The Beatles) money can't buy you voters' love. During primaries, voters evaluate candidates' positions, their credibility and character, as well as their electability.

Even as the list of viable candidates is winnowed down, the race for delegates continues into big state nomination contests, though by early spring it is usually clear who the presumptive nominee will be. Of course, if there is a pandemic, then the contenders still in the race face delays in the dates of electoral contests, hold virtual events that get virtually no coverage, and are deprived of horse race stories that build momentum after a victory.

But certain verities remain. Across elections, after Iowa and New Hampshire, candidates need at least some money to consummate expensive media buys. They also need a compelling message, ideally a vision that appeals to their core supporters, and an effective strategy to market this message, via news, debates, and social media. The candidate who gets nominated is not necessarily the brightest or the most culturally diverse, but the one who makes the fewest mistakes—and the candidate who hones a message that fits the sentiments of the majority of partisan voters. The goalposts are always changing and events are constantly fluctuating, so once again, one can't easily predict who will be the party's eventual nominee. For all the verities, chance, unexpected events, and volatility are also constants.

### Evaluating the Media-Based Nomination System

Now that we have examined strategic aspects of the nominating system, it is instructive to turn to normative issues. Does the media-focused nomination process advance democratic aims or adversely affect the body politic? There is broad consensus that, for all the shortcomings in the present system, it is far better than the old-style method, in which party leaders chose candidates in closed-door sessions, trading their support for political favors. The current system happens out in the open, exposing candidate, party, and media foibles to the sunlight of democracy. The lengthy campaign tests candidates, weeding out those who do not have the political savvy or psychological stamina to withstand the slings and arrows of a presidential nomination. It forces candidates to build a cohesive organization in a multitude of states. To the extent that these skills are required in the nation's chief executive, perhaps the current system does a pretty good job separating out the presidential wheat from the chaff, but this does not mean that the contemporary nominating system is free of problems. A number of ideas to improve the present system have been put forth, including a national primary, regional nominating contests, and varying the order of the first contests, so that more representative states initiate the process. Every 4 years there could be a lottery, so that the first two state contests would be decided randomly, allowing states other than New Hampshire and Iowa to be first. Although each of these ideas has drawbacks, they call attention to limitations in the present system and the need for reform.

## THE PROMOTIONAL COMMUNICATION CONVENTION

Spoiler alert: The discussion of conventions that follows this overview applies to all conventions before 2020. In the age of the coronavirus, both parties scaled back their conventions to a small shadow of the throngs they expected to coronate the presidential nominee. At the Democratic convention, speakers were strategically dispersed across battleground states for each of the message-themed nights. Carefully chosen voices, including an undocumented immigrant, union member, and first responder, reported the vote, culminating in a triumphant moment of music, firecrackers, and horn-honking. Republicans called on a variety of speakers of different races and backgrounds to depict Trump as humane, kind, and a champion of diversity, hoping to change the coarser image Americans had formed of him over the past 4 years. Both conventions were mercifully shorter than usual, shorn of over-the-top political theatrics.

## Pre-pandemic Conventions

In normal years, conventions promote the ticket before a national audience, functioning primarily as a week-long advertisement for the candidates and the party, "effectively a four-night miniseries before an audience of 20 million people or more" (Zeleny & Rutenberg, 2008; see Figure 14.3). Party leaders hire media production experts who script the convention down to the wire. What looks spontaneous to a television audience has been organized, orchestrated,

**Figure 14.3 Party conventions are ordinarily rowdy, raucous events that help the party mend fences after frequently divisive primary campaigns. They are primarily designed to promote the party in a four-day media event, though they occasionally serve political functions by strengthening party members' identification with the party and offering up stirring narratives. Of course, in 2020, the convention was largely a virtual event, downplaying much of the phony theatrics.**

*Source*: https://commons.wikimedia.org/wiki/File:The_ballon_drop_at_the_Democratic_National_Convention.jpg revised, and readied for final production well in advance. Conventions are designed as a send-off to present the party and its nominees in the best possible political light, animated by theatrics, featuring a cast of thousands of delegates, centering on the candidates and their oh-so-beautiful families, and ideally, revolving around a coherent storyline that candidates can take into the fall campaign. Recognizing that conventions offer one of the few times when voters are motivated to tune into partisan speeches, parties do their best to entice viewers, hoping the speeches, party ideology, and miscellaneous hoopla will influence opinions and behavior. At some basic philosophical level, a convention, as columnist Frank Bruni (2012) observed, "is a communal lie, during which speakers and members of the audience project an excitement 10 times greater than what they really feel and a confidence about the candidate that they only wish they could muster" (p. A21).

## Partisanship and Rhetoric Then and Now

Inside the convention, serious business does occur. Conventions are gatherings of the party faithful, who—though they do disagree among themselves on issues, some years more than others—collectively espouse a particular philosophy of politics. As Shafer notes, "national party conventions are the major, purely partisan, formal institutions of American politics" (2010, p. 264). Articulating an ideology that guides the party and serves as the focus for the upcoming campaign is a strength of party conventions, even as candidates take positions at variance with party theology, and the two parties typically offer a fairly conventional perspective on politics with a paucity of outside-the-political-box ideas. The party's ideology is summarized in its platform, a document few voters read, but that offers a succinct statement of where the party stands on the issues. (This assumes a party issues a platform. In 2020, the Republicans simply renewed their 2016 document and affirmed Trump's policies, a reflection of the party's fealty to Trump.)

Political rhetoric plays a key role in rallying the troops, particularly keynote addresses. In 2004, a young Barack Obama energized Democrats, using poise and adroit turns of a phrase, as he famously declared that "there's not a liberal America and a conservative America; there's the United States of America."

Vice presidential candidates and presidential contenders who are relatively new to the national stage use acceptance speeches to introduce themselves to the electorate. In 2008, Sarah Palin portrayed herself as an ordinary American, reared with good, small-town values, unimpressed by media elites, a modern-day Harry Truman, a 21st-century female incarnate of Jimmy Stewart's Mr. Smith in *Mr. Smith Goes to Washington*. Four years later, the Republican vice presidential nominee, Wisconsin Congressman Paul Ryan, embellished the smal-town biographical narrative, describing how he lived on the same block in Janesville, Wisconsin, where he grew up and still belongs to "the same parish where I was baptized." He embraced the conservative ethos of small government, pledging to place "hard limits on the size of government," thrilling conservative convention delegates.

In 2020, Kamala Harris introduced herself, the first woman of color to become the vice presidential nominee of a major American political party, with an affecting story joining race and gender. She related how her parents—both immigrants, her dad from Jamaica, her mom from India—met as graduate students, got married, and marched together at civil rights rallies. Thanks to her mother's influence, she came to identify as a Black woman, and viewed herself as standing on the shoulders of women who had advocated for civil rights long before it was acceptable to do so.

Presidential contenders use acceptance speeches to offer a touching biographical story and narrative designed to propel them into the fall campaign. In an age of personalized politics, relating raw emotion sensitively—and with apparent sincerity—is a valued attribute in nominees who aspire to the presidency.

Joe Biden's story—a lot true, part myth—was well-known and amply retold during the convention. He was the devoted, loving dad, who, after a tragic automobile accident killed his wife and daughter, commuted by Amtrak train from Washington to Delaware every day so he could tuck his two sons into bed each night; a man who knew the face of tragedy later in his life, when his son Beau died of cancer, and yet, through it all kept his resolve to listen to the problems of others. He was depicted as an American everyman who went out of his way to show kindness, the man whose life was guided by faith, humility, and the adage his parents taught him: "No one's better than you, Joe, but you're better than nobody." The depictions omitted the more controversial aspects of the everyman's background: acknowledgment and allegations of plagiarism as a law student and campaigner, and insensitivity to sexual harassment when Anita Hill accused Clarence Thomas of this during hearings Biden headed as chairman of the Senate Judiciary Committee. Affecting as they were, the anecdotes were, in the end, part of a grandiloquent story, a narrative conventions employ to brand a candidate and create a guiding myth.

And yet there are salutary aspects of public address. Scripted and hokey as convention speeches can sometimes be, they can also inspire. In 1992, Mary Fisher, a mother of two who had improbably become HIV-positive, moved the Republican national convention to tears when she said, "I am one with a black infant struggling with tubes in a Philadelphia hospital. I am one with the lonely gay man sheltering a flickering candle from the cold wind of his family's rejection." Senator Ted Kennedy, after mounting an unsuccessful challenge to President Carter in 1980, delivered a bombastic rhetorical masterpiece, as he called up images of shuttered factories and assembly lines in Indiana, as well as a grandmother in East Oakland who relinquished the phone she used to call her grandchildren in order to pay her rent. In their name and on their behalf, he issued the now-legendary dramatic summation: "For all those whose cares have been our concern, the work goes on, the cause endures, the hope still lives, and the dream shall never die."

In the main, conventions, as exemplars of campaign persuasion, are designed to shore up the base and warm the lukewarm. Nominees strive to gain a political bounce in the polls, a momentum-building increase that emerges from audience exposure to the litany of persuasive speeches, partisan rhetoric, and repetitive onslaughts against the opposition party. Conventions usually produce a bounce or upsurge in the nominee's popularity, but it is only a short-term gain that can quickly dissipate (Wayne, 2008). With declining interest in the conventions and fewer swing voters likely to be impacted by what they see, the boost conventions provide nominees is smaller and of more limited political consequence.

In 2020, both parties dispensed with confetti, balloon-releasing pomp, celebrity star power, and delirium-filled crowds in favor of realistic montages featuring party leaders and party faithful at their virtual conventions. (Many hoped the down-home, less obnoxious approach would become the new normal, even after the pandemic ended.) The Democrats took up the banner of diversity—gender, race, and age—as women told emotional stories of hardship and abuse, offering a downbeat, but affecting picture that matched the nation's somber mood. All of the ideological and personal acrimony of the tough primary battles was airbrushed, as the campaign conveyed the singular message that four more years of Trump would spell doom for the country.

For their part, the Republicans, as incumbents defending the record of the Trump administration, paraded a series of accomplishments in foreign affairs, the economy, and combatting the coronavirus. As befitting the party in power, they described the opposing party's vision as dark, while optimistically touting the promising future of the country. They brought minority speakers to the stage to counter the Democrats' multicultural emphasis—including Georgia state representative Vernon Jones, former professional football star Herschel Walker, and Trump's first UN ambassador Nikki Haley, whose Indian American background served up a checkmate to Kamala Harris's—all testaments to the American dream, proudly endorsing Donald Trump.

Like previous conventions, the 2020 conventions were masterworks of choreography and promotional staging. The Republicans stage-managed overwhelming support from Blacks, women, and immigrants, with Trump even presiding over the naturalization of five immigrants ready to take their oaths as American citizens to the soundtrack of "Hail to the Chief." The reality was different, encompassing Trump's attacks on minority legislators and separation of migrant children from parents at the U.S. southern border (Hirschfeld Davis, Stolberg, & Kaplan, 2018). But, as theater, it was impressive.

Convention speeches can distort and mislead. For example, 2020 Democratic convention speakers, including Biden, exaggerated flaws in Trump's record or minimized shortcomings of the Obama years. They overstated threats Trump's policies posed to Social Security (Qiu, 2020). Republicans engaged in considerable spin themselves, making claims with little basis in fact, (Dale, 2020; Kiely et al., 2020). For example, there was no factual basis to claims that the Democrats planned to take over health care or were a party of socialists (Kiely et al., 2020).

While it is easy—and reasonable—to criticize conventions, they are not without symbolic benefits. For all the candidate platitudes and misstatements, they can provide a ceremonial symbolic space for journalists, political figures, and citizens to interact. Even in their virtual form, conventions "help to symbolically organize democratic politics and provide key ritual moments . . . that legitimate the transfer of civic power" (Kreiss, Meadows, & Remensperger, 2015, p. 593). They frame the campaign, providing a thematic centerpiece, as the Democrats did in 2020 by making the election a referendum on the threats Trump posed to democracy and the Republicans did by warning of a foreboding future under Democratic rule.

Conventions showcase the enduring power of words and rhetoric adapted to the modern age. In the best of conventions, occurring (as they always do) in troubled times, speakers marshal words, hoping they can become "the deeds that build back the moral architecture of America" (Perloff & Kumar, 2020, p. E2). When speeches succeed, they can move, inspire, and elevate.

## CONCLUSIONS

Primaries and caucuses are the arteries and veins of the presidential nomination process. They are open, transparent, and media-driven. Although the process is substantially more democratic than it was in the 19th century, when nominees were chosen by party leaders in much-mythologized smoke-filled rooms, the contemporary system has its own set of rituals, idiosyncrasies, and drawbacks.

Critics lament that the system affords too much power to an institution—the press—that is not accountable to voters and has no formal grounding in the electoral process. But the system is transparent and, in the main, allows candidates to make their best case to voters in highly public settings, increasingly by mobilizing a base through social media.

The pre-primaries have assumed growing importance in recent years, showing the ways that media and grassroots online forces can shape the presidential nominations before people cast their first vote.

Through historical quirks, the Iowa caucuses and New Hampshire primary assumed a role in nomination politics that is far out of proportion to their size or electoral representatives. These early contests winnow down the candidate field, with those who lose badly in Iowa and New Hampshire typically forced to drop out as a result of a reduced fundraising base and perceptions that their candidacies are not viable. Given the role media play in transmitting and generating expectations, perceptions quickly become synonymous with reality. As the primaries move into delegate-rich larger states, advertising and political marketing become more important, showcasing the role money plays in the nomination process.

Nominating conventions certify and promote nominees selected in the primaries and caucuses. The main purpose of conventions is promotion, with conventions functioning as a week-long miniseries designed to rally the party faithful around candidates and a platform that has been hammered out, sometimes rancorously, in the weeks before the convention. On a larger symbolic level, conventions offer a ceremonial space for politicians, journalists, and citizens to come together, offering up majestic rhetoric to elevate and inspire. But the grand opportunity is frequently tainted by feel-good, made-for-TV moments, distorted claims, and falsehoods.

The normative aspects of the nomination system have been long debated. Critics argue that the nomination process is too long, gives disproportionate attention to two unrepresentative states, and assigns undue weight to peripheral increases in media momentum. It also engages only a small minority of eligible voters. Defenders emphasize that the system lets voters know who is best able to survive a grueling test for the presidency, presents substantial news coverage of an intensely competitive race, and offers obvious transparency. Just about any statement a candidate makes or gaffe they inevitably utter will be publicized by somebody on some television show or social media post. This ensures accountability to voters. Yet there is little doubt that the system can be improved, and a number of remedies have been proposed, from regional primaries to varying the two states that lead off the nomination contests so that the process is more representative.

The criticisms are valid, but there are some silver linings. The nominating system did permit insurgent candidates—Sanders and Trump in 2016; Andrew Yang in 2020, with his idea of a universal basic income—to present their ideas. American history offers a variety of examples of candidates who have failed to gain their party's nomination, but have profoundly influenced the party's agenda and policy focus. In 1992, Pat Buchanan challenged President George H.W. Bush for the Republican nomination, developing an unorthodox, controversial series of proposals. His populist "America First" campaign emphasized immigration reduction, the perils of globalization, caring for Americans disadvantaged by free trade, and a social conservatism that opposed abortion and multiculturalism. These issues gradually became signatures of the Republican Party, particularly under Trump (Alberta, 2017).

On the Democratic side, in 1988 the African American activist Jesse Jackson championed national health care and bigger taxes on the rich, setting the stage for Obamacare, Elizabeth Warren's proposals, and Bernie Sanders, as well as laying the groundwork for the nomination of Barack Obama 20 years later. Sanders' reform advocacy had tangible effects. Many Democrats backed free or debt-free college for under-resourced students, sweeping health care reforms, and increasing the size of the minimum wage (Kazin, 2020). Sanders' policy platform transformed the Democratic Party agenda, jumpstarted the national dialogue, and paved the way for policy reforms. Not bad for a 79-year-old guy who never got his party's nomination.

The endpoint of the nomination campaign, conventions, are headed for change in the wake of modifications made in 2020, lower TV ratings, and recognition that watching an endless parade of self-serving speeches is out of sync with today's instantaneous, multi-tasked age. By necessity, conventions will continue to be media promotional events that try to bind old wounds and harness rhetoric to propel party stalwarts into the uncertain fall. If the past is any predictor, the rhetoric will be filled with platitudes, exaggerations, and misleading statements, but there will continue to be times when it rises to the partisan occasion, moving multitudes.

## REFERENCES

Adams, W.C. (1987). As New Hampshire goes . . . In G. Orren & N.W. Polsby (Eds.), *Media and momentum: The New Hampshire primary and nomination politics* (pp. 42–59). Chatham, NJ: Chatham House.

Alberta, T. (2017, May/June). "The ideas made it, but I didn't." *Politico Magazine.* Online: www.politico.com/magazine/story/2017/04/22/pat-buchanan-trump-president-history-profile-215042. (Accessed: June 4, 2020).

Bruni, F. (2012, August 28). Huggability and helium. *The New York Times*, A21.

Buchanan, L., & Parlapiano, A. (2016, April 3). How votes for Trump could become delegates for someone else. *The New York Times*, 20.

Buell, E.H., Jr. (2000). The changing face of the New Hampshire primary. In W. Mayer (Ed.), *In pursuit of the White House 2000: How we choose our presidential nominees* (pp. 87–144). Chatham, NJ: Chatham House.

Burns, A. (2015, June 16). Donald Trump, pushing someone rich, offers himself. *The New York Times.* Online: https://www.nytimes.com/2015/06/17/us/politics/donald-trump-runs-for-president-this-time-for-real-he-says.html. (Accessed: April 27, 2021).

Burns, A. (2019, April 14). Pete Buttigieg's focus: Storytelling first. Policy details later. *The New York Times.* Online: www.nytimes.com/2019/04/14/us/politics/pete-buttigieg-2020-writing-message.html. (Accessed: June 2, 2020).

Cohen, M., Karol, D., Noel, H., & Zaller, J. (2008). *The party decides: Presidential nominations before and after reform*. Chicago, IL: University of Chicago Press.

Cohn, N., Katz, J., Lu, D., Smart, C., Smithgall, B., & Fischer, A. (2020, February 7). Errors, inconsistencies about doubts about how precise results will be. *The New York Times*, A15.

Dale, D. (2020, August 19). Fact-checking the first two nights of the Democratic Convention. *CNN Politics*. Online: www.cnn.com/2020/08/19/politics/fact-check-dnc-democratic-convention-night-1-night-2/index.html. (Accessed: August 26, 2020).

Dann, C., & Murray, M. (2020, February 3). How do the Iowa caucuses work? *NBC News*. Online: www.nbcnews.com/politics/2020-election/what-iowa-caucus-process-how-does-iowa-caucus-work-n1127886. (Accessed: May 30, 2020).

DeSilver, D. (2016, June 10). *Turnout was high in the 2016 primary season, but just short of 2008 record*. Pew Research Center. Online: www.pewresearch.org/fact-tank/2016/06/10/turnout-was-high-in-the-2016-primary-season-but-just-short-of-2008-record/ (Accessed: March 14, 2017).

Ember, S., & Gale, J. (2020, January 11). Barnstorming Iowa in a blur of bunting flags and café chats. *The New York Times*, A12.

Epstein, R.J. (2019, June 13). How Pete Buttigieg and Elizabeth Warren cracked the code of the 2020 race. *The New York Times*. Online: www.nytimes.com/2019/06/13/us/politics/elizabeth-warren-pete-buttigieg-2020.html. (Accessed: June 1, 2020).

Flegenheimer, M., Ruiz, R.R., & Bowles, N. (2020, February 22). Bernie Sanders and his Internet army. *The New York Times*. Online: www.nytimes.com/2020/01/27/us/politics/bernie-sanders-internet-supporters-2020.html. (Accessed: June 1, 2020).

Glueck, K., & Kaplan, T. (2020, February 9). Wobbly after outcome in Iowa, Biden faces a perilous moment. *The New York Times*, 1, 22.

Goldmacher, S., & Lerer, L. (2019, May 31). New debate rules distort priorities, Democrats say. *The New York Times*, A15.

Hirschfeld Davis, J., Stolberg, S.G., & Kaplan, T. (2018, January 11). Trump alarms lawmakers with disparaging words for Haiti and Africa. *The New York Times*. Online: www.nytimes.com/2018/01/11/us/politics/trump-shithole-countries.html. (Accessed: August 29, 2020).

Kazin, M. (2020, February 12). Bernie Sanders has already won. *The New York Times*. Online: www.nytimes.com/2020/02/12/opinion/bernie-sanders-campaign.html. (Accessed: June 4, 2020).

Kiely, E., Robertson, L., Farley, R., Gore, D., McDonald, J., Jackson, B., & Rieder, R. (2020, August 25). Republican Convention opening night. *FactCheck.org*. Online: www.factcheck.org/2020/08/republican-convention-opening-night/. (Accessed: August 25, 2020).

Kreiss, D., Meadows, L., & Remensperger, J. (2015). Political performance, boundary spaces, and active spectatorship: Media production at the 2012 Democratic National Convention. *Journalism*, 16, 577–595.

Lichter, S.R., Amundson, D., & Noyes, R. (1988). *The video campaign: Network coverage of the 1988 primaries*. Washington, DC: American Enterprise Institute for Public Policy Research.

Mayer, W.G. (2010). How parties nominate presidents. In L.S. Maisel & J.M. Berry (Eds.), The Oxford handbook of American political parties and interest groups (pp. 185–203). New York: Oxford University Press.

Nocera, J. (2015, September 29). Is Donald Trump serious? *The New York Times*. Online: https://www.nytimes.com/2015/09/29/opinion/joe-nocera-is-donald-trump-serious.html (Accessed: May 15, 2016).

Paletz, D.L, & Entman, R.M. (1981). *Media. Power. Politics*. New York: Free Press.

Patterson, T.E. (2016, July 11). *Pre-primary news coverage of the 2016 presidential race: Trump's rise, Sanders' emergence, Clinton's struggle*. Harvard Kennedy School Shorenstein Center on Media, Politics and Public Policy. Online: https://shorensteincenter.org/news-coverage-2016-presidential-primaries/. (Accessed: April 27, 2021).

Perloff, R.M. (2016, January 31). Letting Iowa pick first is not fair to the rest of us. *The (Cleveland) Plain Dealer*, E6.

Perloff, R.M., & Kumar, A. (2020, August 16). Dem speakers can strike a blow for uniting rhetoric. *The Plain Dealer*, E2.

Polsby, N.W., Wildavsky, A., Schier, S.E., & Hopkins, D.A. (2012). *Presidential elections: Strategies and structures of American politics* (13th ed.). Lanham, MD: Rowman & Littlefield.

Poniewozik, J. (2019, July 20). TV news event with solemnity of a lottery drawing. *The New York Times*, A20.

Popkin, S.L. (2012). *The candidate: What it takes to win—and hold—the White House*. New York: Oxford University Press.

Qiu, L. (2020, August 21). Fact-checking the Democratic National Convention. *The New York Times*. Online: www.nytimes.com/2020/08/21/us/politics/fact-check-democrats.html. (Accessed: August 29, 2020).

Rakich, M. (2020, March 17). Historic turnout in 2020? Not so far. *FiveThirtyEight*. Online: https://fivethirtyeight.com/features/historic-turnout-in-2020-not-so-far/. (Accessed: May 28, 2020).

Redlawsk, D.P., Tolbert, C.J., & Donovan, T. (2011). *Why Iowa? How caucuses and sequential elections improve the presidential nominating process*. Chicago, IL: University of Chicago Press.

Shafer, B.E. (2010). The pure partisan institution: National party conventions as research sites. In L.S. Maisel & J.M. Berry (Eds.), *The Oxford handbook of American political parties and interest groups* (pp. 264–284). New York: Oxford University Press.

Silver, N. (2016, May 4). Why Republican voters decided on Trump. *FiveThirtyEight*. Online: fivethirtyeight.com/features/why-republican-voters-decided-on-trump/. (Accessed: May 16, 2016).

Wayne, S.J. (2008). *The road to the White House 2008: The politics of presidential elections* (8th ed.). Boston: Thomson Wadsworth.

Winebrenner, H., & Goldford, D.J. (2010). *The Iowa precinct caucuses: The making of a media event* (3rd ed.). Iowa City: University of Iowa Press.

Zeleny, J., & Rutenberg, J. (2008, August 17). For convention, Obama's image is all-American. *The New York Times*. Online: www.nytimes.com/2008/08/18/us/politics/18convention.html. (Accessed: January 6, 2017).

# 15 Political Advertising in Presidential Election Campaigns

It was a classic political ad, symbolizing the 1980s, with its material splendor, economic expansion, and resplendent optimism. The 1984 spot for President Ronald Reagan opens to soft music, the gentle words, "It's morning again in America," and homespun scenes: a sailboat cruising peacefully in a city harbor at dawn, a tractor plowing a field, a boy on a bike delivering the daily paper, a man jaunting off briskly to work. As the narrator slowly reels off the nation's accomplishments under Reagan—more Americans going to work than ever before, lower interest rates, less inflation—other scenes unfold: a family moving to a new home, as father and son, smiling, haul a rug to the house; a wedding, heralding a bright, boundless future. "It's morning again in America," the narrator intones, and "under the leadership of President Reagan, our country is prouder and stronger and better." A flag blankets the screen, waving proudly.

The contrast could not be more obvious in a head-spinning, spring 2020 adaptation, a negative ad, with dark images, ominous words, and a narrator saying slowly and sadly: "There's mourning in America." As a desolate scene unfolds—a shuttered warehouse, two women in masks lugging a body in a stretcher—a voiceover poignantly says: "Today more than 60,000 Americans have died from a deadly virus Donald Trump ignored. With the economy in shambles, more than 26 million Americans are out of work, the worst economy in decades. Trump bailed out Wall Street, but not Main Street." The music is bleak, the pictures dismal: an older woman pushing a cart, alone on a street, a man waiting restlessly in a hospital, people shuffling in a rainy unemployment line, wearing masks, isolated, anxious, as the voiceover explains that with money running out and people worrying about their loved ones, many are giving up hope. In a grisly contrast with the 1984 ad, the narrator inverts the positive words ascribed to Reagan: "There's mourning in America. And under the leadership of Donald Trump, our country is weaker and sicker and poorer. And now Americans are asking, 'If we have another 4 years like this, will there even be an America?'" Fadeout as somber violins weep plaintively.

Of course, neither ad was totally accurate. The Reagan spot exaggerated the economic boom, said nothing about growing inequality, and depicted only Whites. The 2020 ad implied that Trump deserved the entire blame for the virus, making a lot of assumptions his supporters would contest, and failing to link the devastation it depicted directly to Trump's leadership.

Dark imagery was also a theme of Trump's 2020 ads that connected lawlessness in cities to Joe Biden. Depicting a shadowy scene of a criminal breaking into an older woman's home, attacking her while she is placed on hold as she calls 911, the ad was a fear appeal that raised the specter that Biden's support for defunding police would adversely hurt senior citizens, suggesting there would be no one there to answer their 911 calls. But the spot was incorrect, as Biden consistently opposed defunding police; its implications had no basis in facts (Dale, 2020).

Graphic fear messages such as these have a long history in presidential campaigns. Of course, that's advertising—not a truth-teller, but an instrument of persuasion, with striking images, words, and sometimes deceptions, a legitimate, if controversial mechanism by which candidates try to win election.

Ads are nothing if not controversial. They are the Darth Vader, the Voldemort of contemporary politics—pure, unadulterated evil. At least that's how people used to think about political advertising, now that fake news, bots, trolls, and vicious online posts have become part of the landscape, political ads seem tamer by comparison, especially since the shock value of those ads that jump out unannounced from television screens like Halloween ghouls in late October has diminished. Yet if you caught some of those negative commercials on Facebook or TV, you might be forgiven if you reverted back to the Darth Vader metaphors of yore.

Historically, few aspects of modern politics generate as much criticism as negative campaigning (see Figure 15.1). What comes to mind when you think of political ads? Probably unfavorable images you've glimpsed on YouTube. Political commercials are blood sport for the news media, which thrive on lamenting their perceived effects, but then focus endlessly on strategic implications, replaying controversial ads, exacerbating their impact. Political ads are a mythologized, misunderstood aspect of political communication, much in need of debunking and clarification.

This chapter addresses these issues, focusing on presidential campaign advertising and covering a wide range of issues. The first section provides a historical background to contemporary political advertising campaigns. The second section places political ads in their campaign context, discussing core characteristics. The third portion examines the content and effects of political advertising—and candidate appeals more generally—focusing on negative spots. The

**Figure 15.1 Negative campaigning gets a bad rap. So, too, do political ads. They are necessary instruments in a media democracy, but they can be superficial, factually misleading, and usually negative. What do we know about the strategic characteristics of political spots and the effects of negative ads? Are they more of a corrosive or helpful force in political communication?**

*Source*: www.cartoonstock.com/cartoonview.asp?catref=llan1690

fourth part examines the normative features of political ads and if they serve or hinder democracy.

## HISTORICAL BACKGROUND

Digital technologies play a key role in campaign marketing. It is no longer the mass media election, as Thomas Patterson (1980) dubbed it, but the interactive media election, twittered election, or all media all the time election. Although television is still important, given its share of the market, it is no longer the only game in town. "To not have an aggressive social media strategy would be the equivalent of not having an aggressive TV strategy in the 1950s," said one of Obama's senior advisers some years back. "We have to go to where the conversations are already happening" (Shear, 2015, p. A14). Campaigns use a digital cocktail of media technologies to influence voters, harnessing messages that are exquisitely targeted to particular voters' social media profiles (Stromer-Galley, 2014). The game is still power, but the techniques are refined and more personalized.

First it was the Internet, then Web 2.0, and now social media platforms have transformed campaigns, even offering data from which to better understand and manipulate political attitudes (Owen, 2014; McGregor, 2020; see Table 15.1).

**Table 15.1 Timeline of campaign changes in the digital age.**

| 1996 | 2000 | 2004 | 2006 | 2008 | 2012 | 2016 | 2020 |
|------|------|------|------|------|------|------|------|
| • Presidential candidates create websites. | • Campaign websites become commonplace. | • Democratic candidate Howard Dean becomes first presidential candidate to develop a blog.<br>• Dean changes the nature of fundraising, raising money online from many small contributors. | • YouTube videos become more powerful as a video sinks Virginia Senate candidacy of George Allen. | • Obama brings campaigns into the digital age, raising record amounts of small online donations, creating a campaign social network, posting numerous YouTube videos, and harnessing social media to link campaigns to volunteers.<br>• Use of microtargeting and Big Data increases. | • Social media use grows, becoming a regular part of campaigns.<br>• Twitter becomes a major force in campaigns.<br>• Microtargeting matures and expands. | • Twitter becomes go-to place for candidates, journalists, and citizens as Trump tweets vociferously, reaching supporters and capturing news attention.<br>• Technological advances on social media continue apace, as Facebook Live, Twitter's Periscope app, and Snapchat livestream videos.<br>• Live videos on small phone screens, angry partisan posts, and millions of online individual contributions to candidates characterize the animated social media presidential campaign. | • Vast storehouses of personal and demographic information about voters are harnessed in digital messaging campaigns.<br>• Microtargeting becomes more sophisticated by aligning with third parties to gain access to troves of data linked with voters' phones, enabling more targeted advertising campaigns, raising ethical and privacy issues.<br>• Professional platforms (the Democrats' ActBlue, the Republicans' WinRed) use more sophisticated technologies to empower online solicitation of money. |

It's not your parents' campaign. Activists are no longer students going door-to-door to hand out leaflets; communities aren't blocks from a political ward. Instead, activists are retirees sending text messages, college students posting ads, and evangelicals creating Instagram videos or locating influencers for live events on Instagram. Communities are online groups that can be strategically targeted by specific candidate appeals. Different social networks require different campaign approaches; what works on Facebook won't be appropriate for Snapchat; a strategy geared to Instagram must be modified for TikTok. And, of course, the digital campaign took on even more importance In 2020, when face-to-face events were largely suspended.

With this as the backdrop, let's turn to campaigns today.

## STRATEGIC FEATURES OF CONTEMPORARY POLITICAL ADVERTISING

In a democracy, candidates must make their best case to voters, explaining their stand on the issues, and why they will serve voters more effectively than their adversaries (Fridkin & Kenney, 2011). A central component of campaign advocacy is political advertising, paid political speech, and it has several components.

### Political Advertising Is Expensive and Tactically Placed

Billions of dollars are spent on televised political advertising nationwide. In Nevada, where ads blanketed the evening news, the general manager of a Las Vegas television station remarked some years back, "We have a joke around here. Pretty soon, we're going to have such long commercial breaks that people are going to tune in and all they'll hear is: 'Hello, welcome to News 3. And goodbye'" (Peters, 2012, p. A16).

In 2020, the most expensive campaign in American history, an estimated $7 billion was spent on political advertising—and that didn't even include a host of other campaign costs, such as sponsoring fundraisers, hosting expensive donor retreats, and paying high-priced campaign staffers (Adgate, 2020). It's not just presidential campaigns. Megabucks are spent on ads in other elections; hundreds of millions were doled out in a controversial California referendum focused on whether companies such as Uber and Lyft should classify their gig workers as employees rather than independent contractors.

The numbers get even more eye-popping when you consider that Trump campaign insiders were worried that they had only a paltry $200 million left by Labor Day, after spending $800 million of a more than $1 billion campaign war chest (Goldmacher & Haberman, 2020). The numbers, while small compared to the money doled out for commercial advertising, drop a lot of ordinary people's jaws.

It's a campaign constant. Back in the 2015–2016 election cycle, approximately $2.83 billion was expended on televised political advertising for different elections. An estimated $845 million was spent on more than a million presidential election ads (Fowler, Ridout, & Franz, 2016). That's a lot of advertising! As Fowler, Ridout, and Franz explain, "if every one of these ads aired back-to-back, they would be broadcast for nearly 1500 straight days without stop" (p. 447).

In 2020, much political advertising migrated to Facebook, Google, and Snapchat, even as Twitter banned political ads in 2019. More than $100 million was spent during the nomination period alone, with the goal of capturing attention and attracting donors. Trump spent almost half of his advertising budget on digital ads, and Biden expended about one-third of his budget on digital platforms, a significant increase from years past (Neumann et al., 2020). Advertising took on considerable importance in 2020, given that candidates weren't holding rallies that could attract crowds or gain coverage on local news. As the 2020 presidential campaign reached its climax, candidates had spent about three times as much money on political spots in 2020 as they did in 2016 (Corasaniti, Cai, & Lu, 2020).

During the presidential campaign, candidates air ads with an eye on strategy. It makes little sense to spend money on states where a candidate has a lock on victory. Instead, digital and television ads are strategically placed, directed at battleground states. In the critical state of Pennsylvania, voters saw 38 different ads during a single week in October 2020.

## Political Ads Are Increasingly Funded by Outside Political Groups

Political commercials are sponsored by candidates, political parties, and interest groups, the latter under the rubric of super-Political Action Committees, or super-PACs. While candidates still sponsor numerous political ads in congressional and presidential races (Fowler, Franz, & Ridout, 2016; Fowler, Ridout, & Franz, 2016), an increasing number of prominent campaign ads are purchased by super-PACs, which have expanded their influence since the Supreme Court's *Citizens United* decision paved the way for unlimited spending in elections.

Super-PACs now pay for numerous political ads that are bankrolled by corporations, unions, lobbying groups, or billionaires who have doled out tens of millions of dollars in a presidential election cycle. Super-PACs, sometimes operating secretly and independently of campaigns, can underwrite nasty attack ads. It's a game: Candidates can condemn the attack spots, saying they are shocked at how negative the ads have become. At the same time, they benefit from PAC-sponsored attacks on their opponents. These legal, but ethically questionable, ads are paid for with **dark money**, an appropriate metaphor that refers to funds spent by groups that do not have to publicly reveal their donors.

## Political Advertising Has Become More Negative

This may seem obvious, but the magnitude of the increase, and the extent to which candidates will go for the jugular, never ceases to amaze.

In 1960, when John F. Kennedy faced Richard Nixon, only 12 percent of major political ads were negative (West, 2010). Then came President Lyndon Johnson's iconic "Daisy ad" in 1964, where a girl picked petals off a daisy, as a mushroom cloud of a nuclear bomb exploded. The ad never mentioned Johnson's Republican opponent by name, but suggested (rather unsubtly) what he might do if elected president. (The ad provoked so much protest it was yanked after one showing. How times have changed!) In 1964, 59 percent of major ads were negative. Influenced by the apparent success of the "Daisy" spot and the turbulence of the late 1960s, both candidates expanded the use of attack ads in 1968.

Negative ads declined in the 1970s, in the wake of the national soul-searching that occurred after the end of the Vietnam War and Watergate, but they increased dramatically over the course of the 1980s. The 1988 election remains the most negative on record, with the incendiary attacks by George H.W. Bush on Democrat Michael Dukakis, including ads that controversially suggested that a Dukakis prison policy had led to a brutal Black-on-White crime. Negative, highly charged ads continued apace, declining and rising in particular years, but still accounting for a majority of prominent political ads in the general election. Intriguingly, negative spots also dominate non-presidential, midterm election campaigns; the volume of negative spots in the 2018 election, where Democrats seized control of the House, exceeded that of previous cycles (Fowler, Franz, & Ridout, 2020).

When it comes to negative ads in presidential elections, campaigns have no shame. They will exploit any problem in the country, no matter how sensitive or personally impactful. In the classic "Daisy" ad of 1964, Lyndon Johnson raised the specter that his opponent would start a nuclear war. Forty years later, George W. Bush aired a controversial ad that used heart-rending pictures of firefighters, reminding viewers of 9/11, leading one critic to lament that "Bush is calling on the biggest disaster in our country's history, and indeed in the history of the fire service, to win sympathy for his campaign" (Rutenberg, 2004).

In 2020, the crises that shook the country—the pandemic and protests over George Floyd's death—took center stage in negative ads. A Democratic political action committee ad interspersed Trump's statements diminishing the need for masks and ventilators with health care professionals' desperate appeals for protective equipment. Not to be outdone, a pro-Trump PAC aired two spots that suggested Biden irresponsibly viewed China favorably at a time when a virus that started there was putting Americans' health at risk (Corasaniti, 2020a). In a similar fashion, on the racial protest issue, Trump ran ads taking a law-and-order stance, recalling Richard Nixon's successful 1968 approach, condemning the riots, warning of dangerous far-left groups "running through our streets and causing absolute mayhem" (Corasaniti, 2020b).

Elections, as discussed in Chapter 8, are about the frame: Who has the more compelling narrative? Negative ads convey these frames by conjuring emotions and linking them with candidates.

Who devises negative ads? They are created, poll-tested, and executed by a cadre of political consultants, pollsters, and advertising gurus who are typically allied with one political party rather than another, love the exhilarating, cut-throat world of politics, and are motivated by one thing only: winning (Strother, 2003). A controversial aspect of negative advertising is **opposition research**, labor-intensive investigations designed to uncover liabilities in an opponent's record, ranging from public comments that don't jell with current positions to salacious sexual infidelities.

Opposition-focused investigations are used in local election campaigns and prodigiously in presidential races, sometimes in ways only a B-level film director could imagine.

Political opponents revealed unflattering information about 2008 Democratic presidential candidate John Edwards, who spoke of ending economic injustice, disclosing he had spent $400 for a haircut. It wasn't exactly the kind of equality-embracing message he wanted to convey. A potentially election-changing revelation, which mysteriously emerged five days before the 2000 election, that Republican George W. Bush was once arrested for driving under the influence, was apparently researched and leaked by his Democratic opponent's campaign (Martin, 2017).

In 2016, the Democratic National Committee hired out a strategic research firm, Fusion GPS, to uncover dirt about Donald Trump, but the DNC wasn't out for ordinary dirt—this was big-time potential manure in the soil, involving possible connections between Trump and Russia. The firm hired Christopher Steele, a former intelligence officer, who prepared a report claiming the Russians had found compromising facts about Trump that might make him beholden to Russia, part of Russia's drive to get Trump elected president (Entous, Barrett, & Helderman, 2017). (A particularly salacious notion, never proven, was that the Russians secretly taped Trump bizarrely watching prostitutes pee on a bed in a Moscow hotel; see Prokop, 2018.) The claims were never confirmed (Vogel, 2017), don't appear to have been used by the Democrats in the campaign, but became part of the partisan saga of Washington. They show how low campaigns will go to get dirt on their opponents.

The Democrats' opposition research efforts were matched, if not exceeded, by the White House in the now-famous 2019 Ukraine scandal that led to Trump's impeachment. Trump pressed the Ukrainian president to launch an investigation of his political adversary, Joe Biden, based on a false notion that Biden had used his influence as vice president to squelch an investigation that involved his son, Hunter Biden, who was involved with a Ukrainian business (LaFraniere, Kramer, & Hakim, 2019). Trump's lawyer, the former New York City mayor Rudy Giuliani, travelled to the Ukraine to induce the Ukrainian president to push ahead with an investigation that could deliver dirt on Biden. Putting aside the anti-democratic nature of a president trying to use foreign influence to stave off a political opponent, the White House efforts represented a brazen use of the dark arts of political chicanery.

Defenders of "oppo research," as it is affectionately (if warily) called, point out that it can help unearth facts the public has a right to know. These include discovering that a seemingly pure-as-the-driven-snow candidate is actually a liar, thief, drunk, or sexual pervert, facts that, if not disclosed until after the election, could be cast aside by the now-victorious elected official (Huffman & Rejebian, 2012). Critics of opposition research retort that the business of secretly looking for skeletons in a candidate's closet is seamy, demeans politics, and discourages capable, if mildly flawed, candidates from pursuing elected office. Nowadays, when digital snooping infringes on privacy and can turn up false information that partisans readily believe, the ethics of opposition research are even more relevant, and the implications more disturbing.

## Political Ads Are Weaponized Messages Increasingly Steeped in Online Technologies

"Everything that campaigns do," political communication researchers Daniel Kreiss and Shannon C. McGregor (2018) observe, "has an underlying technological basis in ways that were simply not the case 20 years ago" (p. 172). Advertisements, designed as weaponized attempts to sway political attitudes, are strategically directed at key segments of the vast social media market. Harnessing state-of-the-art digital technologies, campaigns tailor ads to reach voters based on their political preferences, geographical location, and leisure time pursuits, such as online video gaming or shopping at Dick's Sporting Goods. The contemporary technique has a name. It's called microtargeting,

When using **microtargeting**, candidates target niche audiences, tailoring the appeal to match a targeted group or a particular individual's characteristics and online preferences (Issenberg, 2012; Kenski, Hardy, & Jamieson, 2010). Unlike broad targeting strategies of decades past, microtargeting focuses on individual users, attempting, with laser-like specificity, to match messages with ever-smaller marketing segments. Consultants mine online data, discovering tidbits about consumers' product preferences, as well as offline information, such as the charities they prefer, cars they purchase, and voting records. Based on this information, consultants customize appeals. An undecided voter toiling in an automobile plant might receive an email from a fellow worker on her shift, or hear from a Facebook factory worker friend who is also a campaign volunteer.

The psycho-logic is that people are more likely to engage in a political activity when the suggestion comes from a friend rather than in the form of an impersonal note from the candidate's campaign. Using techniques that are clever, but not entirely honest, campaigns might encourage people to sign up for a campaign Facebook app. Once they sign up, campaign volunteers gain access to their Facebook friends. Campaign organizers can then peruse the list, find particular voters who fit a targeted demographic group, and ask the person who signed up for the app to message these friends urging them to watch an ad, attend a rally, or vote for the candidate. From a persuasion perspective, it's an appeal to communicator similarity ("If my friend likes the candidate, maybe I will too."). Similarity is not a panacea, but it can work under the right circumstances.

Campaign specialists routinely buy voter lists, upload them to Facebook, and match the names to the user base. This allows them to effectively link the political—the list of registered voters—with the readily available market, Facebook users. The goal is to find matches, the database combining "the electoral information it already knows about voters with their Facebook profiles: likes, group memberships, issues or even favorites" (Willis, 2014, p. A3). Consultants use this information to tailor political advertisements to particular users, trying to reach individuals on their mobile devices using messages that cost much less to produce and distribute than commercial television advertising. "There's a level of precision that doesn't exist in any other medium," a Facebook outreach manager observed, adding that, "it's getting the right message to the right people at the right time" (Parker, 2015, p. A17; Kreiss, 2012).

Campaigns try to multiply their followers on Twitter, Facebook, and other social media sites. The more people who follow a candidate, the more messages that are developed through microtargeting can be shared with like-minded and undecided voters. Ads and videos can be shared and spread like wildfire across social media, enhancing a candidate's media presence. There is another benefit: Once people click on ads on mobile devices, campaigns can gain access to users' email addresses and mobile phone numbers, providing a tributary that lets them hit people up later with fundraising and share-our-message-with-friends requests (Goldmacher, 2020).

But the democracy-enhancing capability that social media offers candidates trying to broaden their reach has spawned ethical abuses.

## Digital Campaigns Have Gone Stealth

Notice the word "digital" in the heading. Campaigns have always used stealth—behind the scenes, clandestine—strategies. In the 19th century, corruption reigned supreme. During the deadlocked 1876 election, political zealots from both sides surreptitiously threw out votes, smeared ink on ballots, and just paid bribes to try to get their man elected. In 1968, the Republican nominee, Richard Nixon, used political chicanery to sabotage the efforts of Democratic President Lyndon Johnson (no stranger to the art of political subterfuge himself) to launch peace talks, as president, to end the Vietnam War. By arranging a series of clandestine communications that probably persuaded the South Vietnamese president to reject Johnson's peace overtures, Nixon derailed the Democrats' attempt to depict themselves as the party of peace. Nixon could then portray the Republicans as the party that was most likely to end the war. The gambit may have worked, cutting off Democratic nominee Hubert Humphrey's growing momentum, perhaps helping give Nixon the edge of victory (Farrell, 2017). There are also legendary examples of campaigns that have used race-baiting messages to persuade Whites to reject African American candidates. The strategies were subtle, underhanded, and difficult to link to the candidate—clandestine messages with a racist edge.

So, stealth is not new. It's gone digital, which increases its ability to permeate the American electorate and provides a multitude of opportunities to cleverly target persuadable voters.

In one of the most nefarious examples, the 2016 Republican presidential campaigns of Ted Cruz and Donald Trump harnessed data about voters' personal and political psychology that a British consulting firm, Cambridge Analytica, had improperly acquired from Facebook (Rosenberg, Confessore, & Cadwalladr, 2018). Cambridge Analytica had obtained personal information from more than 50 million Facebook users, and sometimes their friends without their consent, in violation of ethical precepts and possibly the law. Users innocently filled out an online social survey and authorized access to their Facebook accounts, not knowing that their profile information, as well as those of their friends, had been harvested by a Facebook app that spit the information into a database prepared for Cambridge Analytica (Rosenberg & Dance, 2018).

The firm sought the data to develop political communication strategies to target voters, which the candidates were more than happy to exploit. The company developed models that helped them figure out which voters would turn out in 2016 and how best to devise digital ads that would appeal to individual voters' political preferences. A pro-Trump political action committee also employed Cambridge Analytica to help develop unsavory, false ads about Clinton that may have influenced some voters (Silverman, 2018). Although the Trump campaign was not complicit in secretly obtaining voter psychographics, it could have benefited from the political psychological profiles Cambridge Analytica developed.

There is reason to be skeptical about whether the firm's models actually worked, or actually influenced voters in the way Trump hoped. But the scandal, which forced the company to close shop, gave Facebook a black eye for mishandling users' personal information and allowing a third party access to people's data without their consent. It raised ethical questions about how consultants can violate people's privacy to persuade them to vote for political candidates, harnessing private information for political gain.

Then there were the Russians. In 2016 a Russian cyber-spy agency, the Internet Research Agency, worked in cahoots with Russian President Putin to interfere with the U.S. election in an attempt to get Trump, a candidate Putin favored, elected president. As has been extensively documented, Russian cyber-operatives developed fake accounts, falsified news, and created deceptive online messages to try to dupe American voters. A week prior to the presidential election, the agency paid Facebook to target non-White voters interested in African American history, sending them a benign post about Beyoncé. Having earned their trust with the first message, the Russian spies sent the same voters an ad on Election Day that exhorted them not to vote, using broken English. "No one represents Black people. Don't go to vote," the ad said, hoping to suppress the Black vote by persuading Blacks not to vote for Hillary Clinton (Singer, 2018; see Kim et al., 2018, for an intriguing study).

Russian cyber-ops show no sign of stopping their trolling, planted ads, and divisive messaging, some with laughable grammatical errors. Although Facebook is on the lookout for fake advertisements paid for in Russian rubles, Russian digital deceivers have developed ever-more-clever posts designed to dupe both Facebook and American voters (Rosenberg, Perlroth, & Sanger, 2020). Stealth miscreants are homegrown as well, spanning parody websites lampooning Democratic candidates and a fake pro-Democratic Facebook page that falsely implied that thousands of Russian Twitter accounts were following a Republican Alabama Senator (Shane & Blinder, 2018). By calling on time-honored guilt-by-association techniques in an effort to delude voters, stealth political operatives are employing the worst of the art of political chicanery. They also misrepresent those political consultants who make a living by designing honest messages on behalf of the candidates they serve—or at least relatively honest messages, given that the art of political persuasion has always bent the truth.

## POLITICAL ADVERTISING CONTENT AND EFFECTS

### Content of Political Ads

What appeals do political ads employ? Are there different types of negative political messages? To answer these and other questions about the nature of political ads, researchers conduct content analyses. Benoit (2014) has found that candidates can acclaim, taking a positive approach by highlighting their virtues; go negative, by attacking the other candidate; or defend themselves from the opponent's attack, refuting or denying the opponent's charges. The content of ads can concern policy issues or a candidates' image, and the two categories overlap.

What is a negative commercial, or even more broadly, a negative campaign advocacy message? This is not as simple as it seems, as there are different components of negative messages that have different political implications (Fallis, 2014).

First, as noted previously, negative ad messages differ in whether they criticize the opposing candidate's issue positions, image, or both. A second aspect of negative ads involves the content of the attack. Negative spots can (1) criticize the opponent directly with a frontal attack on character or motives; (2) mention both the candidate sponsoring the ad and the opponent, a contrast or comparative ad; or (3) use an indirect approach, with an implication or even innuendo about the targeted candidate (Johnson-Cartee & Copeland, 1991; Fowler, Franz, & Ridout, 2016).

A third attribute of a negative campaign message is tone. Advertisements can be civil, criticizing the opponent or her issue position in a courteous, respectful manner, or uncivil, employing brutish attacks, with all sorts of visual features to enhance the effect. Uncivil ads are commonplace, part of what Berry and Sobieraj (2014) broadly call "the outrage industry" and Mutz (2015) might describe as "in your face" media politics. Uncivil campaigning is hardly new, dating back centuries. For example, in ancient Rome, the orator Cicero labeled his opponent a butcher, a monster, and a scoundrel (Jamieson et al., 2014). Uncivil political campaigns in the U.S. date back to the earliest elections. Long before critics lambasted the Clintons and Bushes for trying to install an elite dynasty in the White House, two storied American presidents attacked each other, via their surrogates. Thomas Jefferson's allies accused President John Adams of plotting to create a dynasty with his sons. Jefferson's opponents called him the Anti-Christ and a demagogue. Opponents called Lincoln a despot, liar, thief, braggart, buffoon, and a monster (Remnick, 2020). One can go on and on; it becomes almost intoxicating (or depressing) to track the animus that courses through American politics.

Defining exactly what constitutes incivility is difficult, partly due to cultural and temporal parameters (Jamieson et al., 2014). What is viewed as civil discourse in one era can be deemed uncivil in another, and vice versa. Racist political language that would have been seen as acceptable in the 1850s and even much later would be deemed as uncivil, at the very least, today. Use of mild obscenities, which would have raised eyebrows in the 1950s, would not elicit a flinch today. Complicating matters, incivility has different components, and individuals differ in how they view uncivil ads, as well as their tolerance for attack ads (Stryker, Conway, & Danielson, 2016; Fridkin & Kenney, 2011). However, few would disagree that certain comments are uncivil. This includes Trump's calling Haiti and African nations "shithole" countries; Biden's claiming that Trump was "rooting for more violence" in the wake of racial justice protests; and Hillary Clinton's infamous comment that half of Trump's supporters could be placed into "the basket of deplorables." Nonetheless, it is important to remember that negative ads need not be uncivil or mean. They can make legitimate criticism of an opposing candidate in a civil fashion—at least in theory.

A fourth characteristic of negative ads is their use of dramatic production techniques, such as compelling camera angles, dark colors, foreboding music, and grainy realistic images.

Finally, negative messages can vary in accuracy, deceptiveness, and the extent to which they invite viewers to draw false inferences. Consultants claim they devise ads that are largely accurate because opponents can easily pounce on factual mistakes, using these to launch negative ads in response. However, many political commercials are deceptive, either making inaccurate claims or inviting viewers to make false inferences.

## NEGATIVE ADVERTISING EFFECTS

### Limits of Negative Ads

It is widely assumed that negative ads exert massive effects. Television journalists spend hours dissecting their impact. Political action committees spend lots of money on targeted ads. Notorious spots, such as "Willie Horton" in 1988 and the anti-John Kerry Swift Boat ads of 2004, are assumed to have changed the minds of millions of voters. The commercials that Russian cyber-operatives circulated in 2016 to sow divisiveness and the ads that Cambridge Analytica developed are presumed to have worked because of the sinister power of trolls and advertising. But we can't simply assume they worked because they seem glitzy, or manipulative, or were based on supposedly penetrating probing of the human mind.

Wait, how can that be, you ask? Why, after all, would candidates spend millions if ads didn't work? Why would political groups expend their resources if commercials are ineffective? From a scientific perspective, just because people believe something to be true does not mean it is empirically true. Advertisers assumed ads have subliminal effects, but research shows they don't (Perloff, 2021). People thought gender stereotypes were true, but research too numerous to mention here showed they are unquestionably false. Researchers test hypotheses with data to examine popular claims. In the case of political advertising, and negative ads in particular, research provides a more nuanced picture of campaign media effects. As Lau and his colleagues concluded, based on a meta-analytic examination of more than 100 studies, "there is no consistent evidence in the research literature that negative political campaigning 'works' in achieving the electoral results that attackers desire" (Lau, Sigelman, & Rovner, 2007, p. 1185; Kalla & Broockman, 2018). Other research finds that political advertising influences are relatively small (Coppock, Hill, & Vavreck, 2020).

There is not a one-to-one relationship between money spent on advertising and electoral success. Candidates can spend millions on advertising and lose the election. In 2016, Clinton dominated Trump on the airwaves, outnumbering Trump in ads by about a 3:1 margin (Motta, 2016), outspending him in political advertising dollars, but she lost the Electoral College. In 2020, Michael Bloomberg spent $600 million on television and digital ads, but didn't win a major primary and dropped out after losses on Super Tuesday. How can this be? Why doesn't advertising have the powerful effects it is alleged to exert? There are a number of reasons.

### 1. Political Ads May Not Reach Their Target Audience

With the plethora of media outlets today, it is more difficult to presume that televised or Internet ads will be seen (let alone influence) targeted voters. The Russian trolls and ads were all over Facebook, but we don't know if people saw them, paid attention, or picked up on their divisive themes.

### 2. The Advertising Models Researchers Develop May Not Be Correct

Cambridge Analytica harvested Facebook data on users' self-reported openness, extraversion, conscientiousness, and neuroticism to generate models, which in turn suggested specific messages (Merrill & Goldhill, 2020), but personality traits have a poor track record of predicting persuasive strategies, and they are particularly likely to be ineffective in the world of politics. A person who is open to experience, extraverted, and conscientious could be either liberal or conservative. There are plenty of neurotic Republicans who fit the stereotype of the neurotic New York Democrat. Messages based on personality traits have to be a good deal more subtle, reflecting the particular intersection between personality and the political issue in question, to have even a small chance of working. Journalists love to cover speculation about big media effects because it makes a good story, but this doesn't mean the underlying models have any credence. Microtargeted negative ads are presumed to have the power of a digitized Darth Vader, but empirical evidence is needed to buttress this claim. As we have long known, perceived effects and fear of effects do not translate to actual effects (Baldwin-Philippi, 2017).

### 3. Negative Ads Won't Influence Voters if They Fail to Address Salient Political Concerns

Consider again the millions spent by Michael Bloomberg during the Democratic primaries. The megabucks Bloomberg doled out in advertising in 2020 could not counteract the revulsion liberal Democrats still felt toward his stop-and-frisk policy as New York City mayor that disproportionately targeted Blacks and Hispanics. Racial justice was a key issue for Democratic voters, and Bloomberg's spots highlighting his experience didn't address their concerns. While money can increase positive affect toward candidates in low-involvement state and congressional elections, they don't necessarily work in high-involvement elections where voters already have attitudes toward the candidates (Konitzer et al., 2019).

In 2016 Clinton ran a slew of visceral anti-Trump spots that used Trump's own voice against him, such as those where he called a woman "a slob," who "ate like a pig," as teenage girls depicted in the ads nervously stroked their hair or straightened their clothes before a mirror. These ads were intended to persuade undecided women voters to vote against Trump and may have had this impact on some voters. Yet they were singularly ineffective with many women living in battleground states, who were familiar with Trump's comments and allegations of sexual aggression, but voted for him anyway. Some women minimized his remarks ("he kind of reminds me of my ex-husband," a Kentucky woman said); questioned whether his remarks captured his true sex-role attitudes, citing his daughter, Ivanka, as a role model for girls; or, centrally processing the election, accepted his warts as the price to pay for a candidate whose business background served as a persuasive argument that he would bring back jobs and improve the economy (Chira, 2017, p. 12). While the ads were hard-hitting and memorable, they did not address the salient factors propelling some undecided voters to vote for Trump. (Alternatively, voters could have resisted anti-Trump ads because they approved of Trump's sexism.)

### 4. Negative Ads Do Not Change Partisans' Attitudes

People who strongly support a candidate will not alter their opinion after watching a series of negative ads directed against their candidate. Strong attitudes, steeped in values and congenial friendship networks, are difficult to change and are resistant to political persuasion (Neiheisel & Niebler, 2015). As discussed in Chapter 9, people selectively tune into and interpret messages. Many attack ads never get to square one, either because partisans never see them on their preferred media outlet or, if they do, dismiss them immediately.

### 5. Negative Ads Will Not Work if the Hit (Mafia Language Is Sometimes Used to Describe Negative Campaigning) Is Too Strong, Below the Belt, Socially Inappropriate, or Deeply Offensive

For example, consider an emotional ad that attacked Republican opposition to abortion even in the case of rape by showing a young woman calling her father on the phone, only to be interrupted by a police lieutenant telling him his daughter has been raped. The ad was so intensely emotional that it shocked and saddened focus group respondents more than it changed their attitudes (Kern, 1989). Other ads that are socially inappropriate or offensive turn voters off and aren't likely to be effective.

## What Impact Do Ads Have?

Let's complicate the picture a little here. Political advertising effects are not an all-or-none proposition. That they don't have massive effects doesn't mean we should throw up our hands, give up, and assume they have no influences. As the chapters on agenda-setting and framing indicated, political media can have particular types of effects, under particular conditions—and the effects can be interesting, even politically significant. Neither science (research on political media impact) nor practice (the wisdom political consultants have acquired from years of experience) would suggest that political advertising has massive, election-changing influences. But so long as they have enough impact to bring partisans to the polls, sway undecided voters, or perhaps, in the controversial case of Russia's fake Facebook accounts that purchased political ads, convince voters to stay home, they can exert a consequential impact.

Consider that people say they hate negative ads—one media consultant compared them to birth pains. Critics assume this means that, therefore, political ads don't work. However, people can be somewhat influenced by negative messages they don't like if the messages contain compelling information. Moreover, there is a semantic confound. Voters react negatively to "negative ads," but this is partly due to the unfavorable connotation that the words "negative campaigning" evoke in voters (Mattes & Redlawsk, 2014). "Negative campaigning" or "negative advertising" call up images of vivid, vicious ads, as well as constellations of beliefs, acquired from news exposure, that negative ads are bad, unfair, or uncivil. Not all negative ads fit into these categories. When researchers examine particular negative ads, without the loaded words, they find some evidence of advertising impact, enough to justify some (though not all) of their expenditure in American elections.

What effects do political spots have on voters? Before offering an answer, it is instructive to examine the challenges that face researchers trying to document advertising impacts. An investigator may find a correlation between self-reported exposure to an ad and changes in attitude toward the targeted candidate. However, this assumes that respondents can accurately recall their exposure, and that the ad—as opposed to a news report on the ad or a social media post regarding the ad—exerted the impact. In addition, the fact that exposure is correlated with attitude does not prove the ad causes the impact. The direction of causation could go the other way, with prior attitude leading voters to seek out a politically congenial ad. Even if an effect can be reliably determined, it is not clear that the impact will last for long or be enough to change someone's vote (e.g., Fallis, 2014).

For these and other reasons, research shows a mixed record of negative campaign effects. In a meta-analysis, Lau and his colleagues (2007) found that negative campaigns can reduce support for targeted candidates, but also boomerang, undermining positive attitudes toward the candidate who launched the attack. The ambiguity stems from methodological issues such as unreliability of measurement, as well as the likelihood that negative ad success in decreasing support for the targeted candidate is neutralized by reducing liking of the attacker. With this in mind, let's examine what we know about the influences of negative ads.

### Recall

One reliable effect is on memory. There is empirical evidence that people remember negative ads better than positive spots and recognize negative ads more accurately and quickly than positive ads (Newhagen & Reeves, 1991; Shapiro & Rieger, 1992; see also Soroka & McAdams, 2015 and Vargo & Hopp, 2020). There are several reasons for this. Humans may be neurologically wired to respond more strongly to negative than to positive stimuli (Soroka, 2014). Psychologically, negative information captures our attention, exerting a stronger impact on impressions. Perhaps because people hope or expect that events will be positive, they are captivated by the negative (Lamberson & Soroka, 2018). Consider this example: You go to a party. Four friends say kind, nice things about your outfit, your sense of humor, the quality of your work, even your pet cat. One friend calls your recent Facebook post "obnoxious." Which comment do you remember? Which one causes you to ruminate on your drive home? Research suggests it is the sarcastic crack. In the same fashion, negative political information can be more memorable than positive acclaims.

Another reason why negative ads are more memorable than positive ads is because they garner more press attention. Across a variety of countries and media systems, candidates waging a negative, emotional campaign get more news coverage than candidates who run positive ads (Maier & Nai, 2020).

Negativity plays to news values like conflict and sensational attacks. News replays visceral negative ads because they are good television, are perceived to bring in viewers, and fit the journalistic news value of the election as a conflict-filled strategic game. Negative ads also can generate clicks on YouTube and light up social media pages.

Visceral negative ads gain an almost surreal credibility because they comport with voters' beliefs and typically sour political mood. Many Americans distrust positive information about candidates, figuring it is all puff and fabricated. Presuming that politics is dirty at the get-go, voters may react more to negative ads because they reinforce voters' view of the political world, an attitude negative ads simultaneously shape.

### Learning

Political spots have other influences. We know that political advertising facilitates learning, enhancing knowledge of candidates' issue positions and personal qualities (Freedman, Franz, & Goldstein, 2004; Kaid, 2004, 2006; Fowler, Franz, & Ridout, 2016). Given that negative ads are short and condense issue positions to a snippet, knowledge of issues is relatively superficial, however. Ads and other marketing appeals can form associations, linking the candidate with values and symbols, as Massachusetts Senator Ed Markey did in a positive 2020 primary campaign commercial. The ad showed him as a younger combative legislator, speaking in a Boston accent, then, as a senator, emphasizing his support for the Green New Deal and showcasing endorsements from Alexandria Ocasio-Cortez, Elizabeth Warren, and Obama, accentuated by a rock-and-roll soundtrack.

### Priming

Political ads can access feelings and prejudices, bringing them to the surface, and linking these with a candidate targeted in the negative ad. Trump sought to do this with his law-and-order ads that, on a deeper level, may have activated racial stereotypes among prejudiced supporters (see Chapter 8). Biden primed his base's unfavorable feelings about Trump's management of the coronavirus and offensive tweets. A classic ad primed racial biases to attack 1988 Democratic presidential candidate Michael Dukakis (see Figure 15.2). Priming can also work in an agenda-setting fashion, convincing people that advertised issues—Trump on law and order, Biden on Trump's leadership during the pandemic—should be the primary factors in their voting decisions.

### Activating the Base Versus Influencing the Undecided

Advertisements have a variety of effects. They can facilitate information-gathering, communication, and political participation, even mobilizing the base in

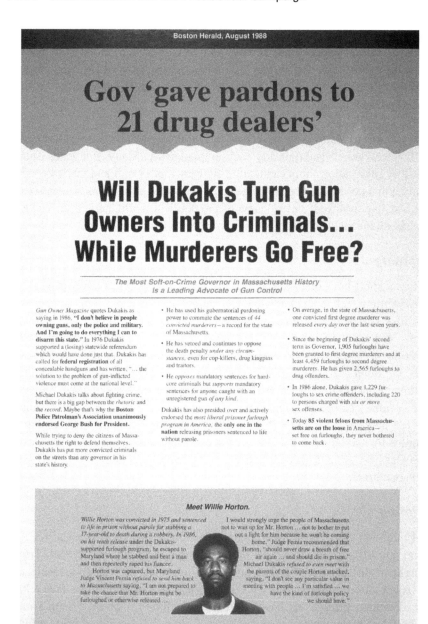

**Figure 15.2** A 1988 negative ad campaign deliberately linked Democratic nominee Michael Dukakis's controversial prison furlough program with a Black prisoner, Willie Horton, inviting false inferences about the number and race of prisoners who committed crimes while receiving weekend passes from jail. By choosing an African American prisoner as a prototype for all prisoners, it likely evoked stereotypes and primed racist attitudes. Unfortunately, Dukakis hurt his case by failing to rebut the attacks, implicitly giving them credence.

*Source*: www.gettyimages.com/detail/news-photo/willie-horton-poster-news-photo/534178152

close elections as voters filter ads through preexisting attitudes (Ansolabehere & Iyengar, 1995; Kim et al., 2013; Matthes & Marquart, 2015).

Beyond this, two divergent philosophies guide strategic political advertising. Campaigns can focus on the base, activating partisans' attitudes, hoping to propel supporters to vote, trying to push as many loyal, but sometimes politically inactive, party members to cast their vote for the party's nominee. This was Trump's approach, doubling down on attacks on Biden, pulling out all stops to appeal to his base.

The other approach is to direct appeals to undecided voters, frequently a sliver of the electorate (though the number differs in different elections), but politically consequential in battleground states. In these cases, campaigns are wary about loading their messages with content that would repel voters, causing them to define a candidate's message as falling within *the latitude of rejection*. Once a candidates' position falls into this area, as is the case with messages on hot-button issues such as abortion, guns, and race, the candidate is deemed unacceptable. Instead, campaigns play it safe, designing congenial appeals that fall within *the latitude of acceptance*, or *the latitude of noncommitment*, where voters are open to persuasion (Sherif, Sherif, & Nebergall, 1965).

For example, in 2020, Biden framed his campaign around economic populism, with his "Build Back Better" slogan, an appeal he hoped would resonate with working-class Whites. At the same time, some of his recommendations embraced Bernie Sanders–style liberal proposals on criminal justice, climate change, and health care that appealed to the left wing of the party (Ember & Kaplan, 2020). He was careful not to embrace Sanders's universal care, Medicare for All policy, lest he alienate more conservative Democrats, who would perceive this as "socialist," a label guaranteed to move them into the latitude of rejection. Biden played it safe, hoping that swing voters would project their own preferences onto his appeal. It was the electoral equivalent of the medical caveat "First, do harm" or the famous adage from HBO's *The Wire*: "Keep it boring" (Herndon, 2020). And on law enforcement, he walked a fine line between supporting police reforms advanced by his most liberal supporters, while emphasizing his commitment to funding police as a way to reduce crime, in line with the views of moderate Democrats.

This seems to have worked with undecided voters or those who preferred Trump to Clinton in 2016, but who had misgivings about Trump four years later. It did not work with other voters, such as Latinos in Florida, some of whom liked Trump's nomination of three conservative, pro-life Supreme Court justices, others of whom were pushed into the latitude of rejection when it came to their perceptions of Biden's domestic or law-and-order policies. Trump's advertisements, including an ad linking Biden to Venezuelan socialists, painted Biden as a left-liberal believer in socialist government programs (Merrill & McCarthy, 2020). The claims were false, as Biden is a long-time moderate who said he would veto Sanders's Medicare for All health care plan. (By the way, socialism isn't necessarily bad—or all good—and the U.S. already has socialist-type programs, like Social Security, a minimum wage, and agricultural subsidies.)

## NORMATIVE EVALUATION OF NEGATIVE ADVERTISING

What is the normative verdict on negative ads? Do they exert salutary or penurious effects on politics? Now that you appreciate the scientific evidence, let's examine the issue more philosophically.

### In Defense of Negative Ads

Critics frequently charge that negative campaign ads turn off voters, reducing interest in politics. But there is little evidence that negative campaigns depress voter turnout in the aggregate (Arceneaux & Nickerson, 2010; Lau & Pomper, 2004; Lau, Sigelman, & Rovner, 2007). Despite a resounding number of negative ads in 2020, voters were undaunted, casting a record-breaking number of ballots. Indeed, negative ads have several positive features.

First, negative ads tend to focus more on issues than do positive spots (Fowler, Franz, & Ridout, 2016; Geer, 2006). A positive ad may not trash the opponent, but it can contain lots of puffed-up, Pollyanish descriptions of the advocated candidate. Negative ads frequently criticize the opponent's position on an economic, health, social, or foreign policy issue. The ad may put the opponent down, but bases its argument on something more substantial than puff. It can offer a policy-based criticism or evidence, which constitutes a cogent argument against voting for a candidate. And unlike positive ads, which just tell you about the position of the candidate who sponsors the ad, negative ads impart information about both the sponsor and the target (Geer & Vavreck, 2014). In this way, negative spots can perform a valuable political function—helping candidates differentiate themselves from their opponents (Benoit, 2014). Ads that make civil criticisms of the opposing candidate, offering arguments rather than verbal aggression (Rancer & Avtgis, 2014), can be a legitimate way to promote a campaign.

Second, negative ads get people thinking, arguing, and actively processing politics. They engage voters' minds in ways that blander positive ads do not

(Brader, 2006; Kam, 2006). Spots that highlight relevant campaign content in a civil manner may actually increase interest and electoral participation (Fridkin & Kenney, 2011).

Third, negative campaign messages can encourage activists to work harder for their candidate and knock on more doors, with arguments against the opposing candidate at the ready (Brooks & Geer, 2007). After all, it is the partisans, not the ambivalent, who participate in electoral causes (Mutz, 2006). Partisans are the foot soldiers of democracy. If negative ads activate and persuade them to go out and work harder for their side, that can't be an entirely bad thing. It is undoubtedly good for politics.

Fourth, negative advertising provides a check on the system, offering useful correctives to politicians' puffed-up, sometimes deceptive positive claims. As a political expert notes, "Without attention-grabbing, cogent, memorable, negative campaigning, almost no challenger can hope to win unless an incumbent has just been found guilty of a heinous crime" (see Smith, 1996, p. A22). Negative ads provide candidates with a legitimate rhetorical mechanism to challenge incumbent presidents. They give challengers a way to lay out shortcomings in incumbents' records. As political scientist John C. Geer notes, "If the public wants to have accountability, someone has to do the accounting and that accounting is not done through positive feel-good appeals, but through harsh political attack where voters are made aware of the problems of the incumbent" (2006, p. 110). Absent negative commercials, Ronald Reagan might not have convinced the electorate to unseat Carter. Without negative ads, Biden couldn't have strongly called out President Trump for his policy failings during the pandemic. And in non-electoral contexts, negative messages let grassroots groups lambast both racist and overly secular policies.

Negative ads also provide a check on incumbents. They force incumbents to stay accountable to voters. They give newcomers a mechanism by which they can challenge the old guard and, theoretically, inject change into the system. More generally, they provide all candidates with a way of challenging an adversary's statements that are offensive, immoral, or prejudiced.

## Criticisms of Negative Ads

These arguments present a forceful defense of negative advertising. There is another side too, one that calls attention to shortcomings in negative spots.

First, for all their presentation of policy positions, negative ads (like their positive counterparts) frequently provide a superficial rendition of candidate positions on issues. They offer little by way of thoughtful political arguments, other than a 15- or 30-second denunciation.

Second, although negative ads do not depress turnout, they can, under some conditions, dispirit voters (Krupnikov, 2011), diminishing both trust in government and political efficacy, the belief that people can make a difference in politics (Ansolabehere & Iyengar, 1995; Lau & Pomper, 2004; Lau, Sigelman, & Rovner, 2007). Indeed, there is evidence that watching candidates disagree about politics up close, advancing arguments in a mean-spirited way, exacerbates negative feelings about the opposition, reducing the legitimacy of opposing viewpoints and diminishing political trust (Mutz, 2007; Mutz & Reeves, 2005; Moy & Pfau, 2000; Gervais, 2014).

Third, negative ads reward opposition research, a tawdry type of political consulting in which strategists dig for dirt and try to uncover skeletons in the opponent's closet. Advertising specialists take these juicy, occasionally seamy, tidbits and place them front-and-center in negative spots. This is a mean-spirited way to knock off a candidate who may otherwise have a fine record of public service. It can take candidates' statements out of context and imply that one misstatement, inept policy decision, or foolish personal behavior is a fair representation of a candidate's personality or time-honored record of attainments. Negative advertising abuses persuasion, exploiting storytelling to present a narrative, illustrated with evocative cinematic techniques, that slams, cuts down, and ridicules another human being for one unctuous purpose: unseating the candidate and yanking away his or her power. The social media onslaught that can follow a negative ad is uncivil and divisive, as partisans heap on the opposition candidate.

Fourth, negative ads can trifle with truth, in ways that can be ethically problematic. A famous series of 2004 "Swift Boat" ads maligned John Kerry with false claims that he fabricated his military heroics and lied about a wound for which he received a Purple Heart while commandeering military patrol boats, called swift boats, that came under military fire during the Vietnam War (Zernike & Rutenberg, 2004). Eight years later, a pro-Obama PAC famously developed a series of staggeringly false spots that falsely pinned the death of the wife of steelworker Joe Soptic on 2012 Republican nominee Mitt Romney, who had been president of a private equity firm that acquired the steel plant, but was no longer in charge of day-to-day issues when Soptic's wife became ill.

In one of Trump's 2020 law-and-order fear appeals, an older woman watched a television segment claiming that Seattle planned to defund its police department by 50 percent, noting that Biden supported defunding the police. The facts were wrong. Several of Seattle's council members supported a 50 percent cut in the budget, but the city's Democratic mayor opposed it, and no specific proposal had been articulated (Qiu, 2020). Biden, for his part, consistently opposed reducing police budgets and favored increasing funds for community policing (Dale, 2020).

It's not just the U.S. In the run-up to a 2019 British election focusing on Brexit, the controversial British decision to exit from the European Union, Brexit supporters were out in force with ridiculously distorted campaign messages. Arguing that remaining in the EU would flood their beloved Anglo-Saxon Britain with immigrants and refugees, they developed visual message—posters shown on social media that depicted long lines of refugees (Ross & Bhatia, 2021). But the pictures likely portrayed generic refugees escaping from the war-torn Middle East or, in one case, from Nazi-controlled countries in World War II, with a repulsive caption calling them "parasites" who undermined their "host countries." In truth, while migration to Britain has increased in recent years, the Brexit messages greatly exaggerated immigrants' deleterious influences, playing on populist prejudices (Hall, 2016).

These inaccuracies leave imprints, more than do incorrect positive messages. People can remember information they hear, while forgetting the source of the information. They retain "'facts' that are not factual," forgetting that they were conveyed by a biased, self-interested source (Zacks, 2015, p. 12). A single negative commercial with false information can cause substantial numbers of individuals to hold inaccurate beliefs (Allen & Stevens, 2019). Attack ads that are factually inaccurate or invite false inferences trifle with truth, undermining ethical political communication.

Negative advertising has a place in democracy. Thoughtful, trenchant criticisms are the wellspring of democratic deliberation. Negative ads become problematic when they breach norms of civility and the deceptions they invite exacerbate polarization rather than encouraging reflection.

## CORRECTING MISPERCEPTIONS, ADDRESSING MISINFORMATION

How can misleading ads be controlled or checked? Can government regulate them? This invites the First Amendment objection that government can't abridge free speech. But, of course, it's more complicated than that, and the Federal Trade Commission (FTC), which regulates advertising, has latitude to restrict deceptive selling. In practice, the FTC gives advertisers considerable freedom to make claims that border on the deceptive to protect free speech, trying not to interfere with marketers' freedom to promote products (commercial or political) as they wish. Defining what is legally deceptive is difficult. The FTC has been loath to get involved in political advertising restrictions for philosophical reasons and also because it would be inherently political.

As a result, fact-checking by news media and specialized organizations has been advanced as a method to publicize and refute inaccurate claims. They're not perfect because informational checks are, by necessity, based on a series of criteria, which can always be questioned. Nonetheless, groups such as FactCheck.org and PolitiFact.com offer nonpartisan checks on deceptive ads. **Fact-checks** occur when nonpartisan researchers scrutinize candidates' ads, comparing claims candidates make about opponents with verifiable facts, looking to see if the claims are factually accurate. Journalists frequently turn to these groups when preparing articles that discuss negative ads. From a democratic perspective, fact-checks are an unmitigated good because they ensure that false claims are refuted by evidence, helping to ensure that political discussions are grounded in accurate claims.

So, do fact-checks work? Fact-checks that challenge the accuracy of an ad can correct misimpressions, even causing voters to perceive the misleading ad as less accurate and less fair (Fridkin, Kenney, & Wintersieck, 2015; Cappella & Jamieson, 1994; Meirick et al., 2018; Hameleers & van der Meer, 2020). They also have shortcomings.

First, fact-checking news reports run the risk of magnifying the effects of the misleading spot (Ansolabehere & Iyengar, 1995). In their zeal to describe the juicy misleading tidbits of a particular ad, journalists rebroadcast, or in websites attach, the ad, giving it free publicity and a double-whammy of promotion. News viewers may see or hear the deceptive ad and ignore the journalistic criticism, much to the delight of strategists who developed the spot.

Second, technical problems can minimize fact-check effects. The printed information that identifies the sponsor of the ad—or corrects the misinformation—may not be on the screen long enough to allow viewers to process and remember the information (West, 2010). This is less true of online fact-checks that print a litany of corrections that can be perused.

The third problem is viewer selectivity. For individuals to be influenced by fact-checks, they must be aware of fact-checking sites, develop positive attitudes toward them, and actually visit the sites. People with strong attitudes may never get to stage one, let alone the other two inter-connected stages (Robertson, Mourão, & Thorson, 2020). Even if people come across a fact-check, they invariably filter it through their schema of preexisting ideological beliefs (Nyhan & Reifler, 2010).

As we know, in an era of niche media, people tune into cable news programs, blogs, and posts that reinforce their views of the political world, while blissfully ignoring programming with which they disagree. As a result of selective exposure, viewers may not see fact-checks that correct false claims made by their candidate. What's more, partisans share fact-checking messages in a highly selective manner, only retweeting messages that cast their party's candidate in a positive light and filtering fact-checking messages that support the candidate from the opposing party through their biases (Shin & Thorson, 2017). People routinely interpret fact-checks through the prism of their political beliefs, reducing their overall effectiveness (Nyhan & Reifler, 2010; Walter et al., 2020). This suggests, alas, that when voters come across inconvenient facts, they discount them.

Making matters worse, campaign consultants play to these trends. They sometimes derogate fact-checkers, adopting a self-serving, strangely postmodern critique. Back in 2012, after PolitiFact gave one prominent Romney ad a "Pants on Fire" rating, its most deceptive designation, the Romney campaign chose to dig in its heels (see Graves, 2016). Rather than acknowledging the inaccuracy and trying to correct it, a Romney aide maligned fact-checking services, suggesting that fact-checkers have their own biased beliefs, and the campaign was not going to let itself be guided by fact-checkers (that is, by facts).

Since then, the problem has gotten even worse in the wake of ballooning falsehoods on social media (some deliberately perpetrated by campaigns and activists), as well as the decline in news gatekeepers who can counteract misinformation. While research is beginning to offer guidelines (Vraga, Bode, & Tully, 2020), the problem persists, aggravated by selective exposure and some social media companies' recalcitrance to rebut false information.

## Correcting Misinformation in the Social Media Era: Hindrances and Hopes

Social media companies have had intense debates, philosophical and political, about how and when to protect paid speech, particularly political ads (Kreiss & McGregor, 2019). Twitter and Facebook took more aggressive steps to combat falsehood in 2020 than in 2016, placing warning labels on misleading content, though Twitter took a more hands-on approach than Facebook did.

Concerned about the corrosive effects of political ads on civic discourse, Twitter banned them entirely. Twitter also opted to correct factual inaccuracies in tweets, posting a note in blue letters with a link that corrected Trump's false claim that mail ballots lead to voter fraud (Conger & Alba, 2020). Google took a compromise position on political ads, allowing them to target users based on their demographics, but not based on microtargeting criteria such as their voting records or political party affiliation (Wakabayashi & Gold-macher, 2019). After the election, YouTube banned videos that made claims of voter fraud.

Facebook took an entirely different position, putting the 21st-century media company in the odd (or admirable, depending on your viewpoint) position of allying with 19th-century libertarian journalists. Classic, centuries-old libertarian theory eschews restrictions on free speech, trusting people to make their own decisions, maintaining that the best remedy for false speech is more, unbridled speech. Refusing to be an arbiter of truth, fearing that content restrictions could lead to regulations or charges of liberal bias, or just preferring a hands-off business model that could maximize advertising profits, Facebook's Mark Zuckerberg said the company would not "do fact checks for politicians" (Isaac & Kang, 2020). Nor would Facebook remove misleading political ads, although it barred new political ads from appearing on its site during the week before the 2020 election.

The company made some changes to prevent the fiasco of 2016, where users clicked on millions of Russian-produced ads with no idea they were false claims created in St. Petersburg. Political advertisers were required to reveal the names of organizations responsible for the spots and verify their identities, a step toward transparency, even though decoy names and bugs could permeate its archive (Alba, 2019). Facebook also took steps to direct voters to accurate political information on the site, yet labeled policy violations, such as inflammatory information from a prominent figure, as sufficiently newsworthy to stay on the site (Isaac & Frenkel, 2020). In the main, though, Facebook resisted reforms that would require complete restriction or correction of political information. Even barring new ads the week before the election didn't address the massive amounts of misinformation contained in posts and rabid discussions in private Facebook groups, and banning new commercials didn't stop the transmission of older, fallacious political spots (Alba & Frenkel, 2020).

It's a classic philosophical argument, rebooted for the cacophonous online age. Facebook believes the platform should be agnostic about truth issues, maintain the neutrality of its platform, encourage diversity of ideas, and let good and bad ideas compete on the virtual marketplace. Taking a strong libertarian position, Zuckerberg was willing, for as long as he could stave off political pressure, to place faith in users' ability to locate facts about falsehoods and reject them on their own. (That ended in early January 2021, when he banned Trump from Facebook and Instagram indefinitely after the Trump-incited mob violence at the Capitol.)

In general, throughout the 2020 campaign, Twitter, with its more regulatory, social responsibility ethos, feared that in a partisan world where people can choose their facts, users would never encounter corrective information. Twitter also worried about the ways that toxic falsehoods could pollute the public sphere. Zuckerberg (at least during elections) preferred a somewhat polluted sphere, governed by individual liberty, to one that rigidly countered every alleged falsehood with corrective information.

It's a noble view, perhaps complicated by a desire to keep government's hands off Facebook's business model, but research on people's resistance to incongruent facts offers a counterpoint. It suggests that, in the absence of corrective information, individuals may buy into misinformation they encounter on social media, particularly content that fits their existing opinions like a glove (Pennycook, Cannon, & Rand, 2018).

There are no easy answers. Banning political advertising reduces the diversity of political speech and can benefit incumbents with large financial war chests and the ability to reach many people on social media (Kreiss & Perault, 2020). The challenge is to allow a continuous flow of political information, while developing policies that restrict access to anti-democratic falsehoods (which, of course, can be dicey to define).

Political communication research offers a ray of optimism. Voters are actually interested in reading fact-checks, particularly during negative campaigns (Mattes & Redlawsk, 2020). A meta-analytic study found that corrective messages can attenuate inaccurate political beliefs. What's more, as the authors of the study, Nathan Walter and Sheila T. Murphy (2018), noted, "corrective attempts can reduce misinformation across diverse domains, audiences, and designs" (p. 436). Corrections of misinformation posted on Facebook can quickly and efficiently correct misperceptions, political communication scholars Leticia Bode and Emily K. Vraga (2015) observed. Of course, corrective success depends on conditional factors, such as the accuracy and certainty of prior beliefs (Li & Wagner, 2020). Corrections are more likely to be effective if they (1) gently undermine the credibility of the source of the incorrect information; (2) use facts effectively to debunk the fallacious claim (Vraga et al., 2020); (3) are part of a compelling, engaging narrative (Walter & Tukachinsky, 2020); and (4) are communicated by a member of the in-group (a pro-gun advocate should emphasize that gun ownership is actually linked with increased suicides).

Of course, fact-checks will not dispel misperceptions among the most partisan citizens. Telling skeptics that Obama *was* born in the U.S., even explaining how the fallacious rumor began, will not convince extremist Americans who want or need to believe he was born in Kenya. But corrections disseminated by news media outlets and social media companies can correct misperceptions among many members of the public, who are less resistant to change.

That counts for a lot. It seems to have happened with the coronavirus vaccine, as evidence of vaccine effectiveness, coupled with widely publicized examples of real people rolling up their sleeves, seems to have reduced resistance to the vaccine (Hoffman, 2020). The rub, as political communication research shows, is that corrections must be made effectively. Briefly pointing out that a tweet or post is not correct may not cut it. Corrective strategies should be based on an appreciation of why people want to believe misinformation, the cognitive strategies they use to process it, and the most effective ways to change misperceptions.

## CONCLUSIONS

Frequently criticized, constantly lamented, political advertising is the bête noire, the grand object of dislike, of the presidential campaign. Political ads, particularly negative spots, are presumed to have no redeeming democratic features and thought to be all-powerful. Neither assumption holds up under social scientific study. Ads do have benefits and frequently fail to achieve their political objectives.

Political advertising has evolved over the past decades, migrating to social media, harnessing ever-more-sophisticated marketing techniques, and tapping into digital data about voters' personal preferences, sometimes sneakily and unethically, via Facebook. Campaigns are about marketing, but also influencing and manipulating. Indeed, for all of the much-heralded democratizing promise of digital technologies, there is a debate about how much they have done to empower and involve citizens in campaign dynamics (for a critical view, see Stromer-Galley, 2019).

Political advertising is expensive, increasingly funded by outside groups, reliably negative, with sometimes salacious opposition research that digs up dirt on adversaries. Ad campaigns are steeped in the newest digital strategies, such as microtargeting, where candidates harvest a trove of users' commercial and political habits to devise messages customized to fit a particular voter's political psychological profile. Political campaigns have used a variety of underhanded, stealth techniques, as seen in the Cambridge Analytica and Trump Ukraine scandals. Although they are distinctive for their digital artistry, the use of dirty campaign strategies goes back centuries.

Contrary to popular myth, negative ads are not all-powerful—far from it. Like all political communications, they can succeed or fail, their effects limited by voters' preexisting attitudes, appropriateness of content, and the degree to which the ad resonates with voter concerns. Like all political communications, negative advertising influences are moderated by context and conditions

(Haenschen & Jennings, 2019). They can be memorable, reinforce strong attitudes, and define issues in the campaign through agenda-setting, priming, and
framing. There is evidence suggesting they can move the polls, sometimes
consequentially, but we lack precision in specifying the strength of these
effects. Despite their conditional and sometimes limited impact, commercials
continue to be a staple in campaigns, because candidates don't want to risk
losing for having failed to advertise, and the ads do have modest effects.

Even more interesting is the normative balance sheet on political ads, particularly negative spots. Ads provide issue information and serve as a check on
automatic reelection of incumbents. Negative spots that are civil and emphasize
argumentation, rather than verbal aggression, can advance democratic aims.
Ads *can* be negative, but not nasty. But these virtues of negative spots are neutralized by drawbacks, including brute incivility in so many prominent ads and
communication of deceptive, out-and-out false information that can be difficult
to correct.

Deception is a complicated construct and can be difficult to demonstrate convincingly in court. Because government agencies are loath to regulate political
spots, for political and legal (First Amendment) reasons, efforts to promote truth
rest on increasing voters' critical awareness through systematic fact-checks.
Fact-checks can be effective, and there is solid evidence to substantiate their
effects (York et al., 2020). Unfortunately, in light of widespread selective exposure in today's media environment, the correct information may never reach
voters, thereby failing to counter the misimpression the negative ad instilled.
Social media companies, which took credible steps to reducing disinformation
in the 2020 campaign, can do more to advance transparency in political persuasion by consistently enforcing policies, clearly labeling false speech, and
providing reliable information about voting throughout individuals' feeds (see
Kreiss, 2020).

Political ads are situated in the broader domain of campaign finance, and there
are reasonable differences of opinion on the merits of campaign finance reform.
The 2010 Supreme Court *Citizens United* decision, which followed several
decades of jurisprudence, stipulated that the federal government cannot ban
independent spending by corporations and unions in elections. This opened the
floodgates to unprecedented corporate spending, pleasing First Amendment
advocates, but distressing critics who worry that well-heeled outside groups
can unfairly advance their interests. In truth, it is difficult to tie increases in
campaign spending directly to *Citizens United* because we do not have a control
group that would permit examination of how groups would have advertised in
the absence of the *Citizens United* decision. And there are cogent reasons to
argue that candidates should be able to advocate as freely as they wish, based
on the democratic benefits of abundant free speech. Yet if the rich have more

ability to engage in paid speech than everyone else and greater access to elected officials, is campaign finance truly democratic? At the very least, *Citizens United* has spawned a palpable increase in the number of ads that do not disclose donors, giving us less transparency—in short, more dark money and less electoral sunshine.

There are some rays of hope, glimpsed in the massive number of small online donations from individuals who powered the campaigns of Bernie Sanders and other candidates who followed his lead. However, secretive big-money contributions that fuel political action committees continue to have a major impact in legislative and presidential elections, as well as in strategic campaigns on other issues, such as Supreme Court nomination battles.

Political advertising, particularly negative campaigning, is a complex business, fraught with systemic benefits and democratic costs. In the end, presidential elections are about persuasion, and persuasion is not equivalent to truth. As Geer (2006) notes, "politics is about disagreement" (p. 158), and disagreement is bound to lead its protagonists to cannily frame, slant, and even distort. Lau and Pomper (2004) emphasize that "elections are about choices, not courtesy" (p. 93). However, when candidates use words deceptively, they reduce the quality of voter choice. When they resort to uncivil attack ads, they denigrate democratic discourse. When super-PACs spend millions on ads, they affirm the value of speech—but *their* speech, not that of less affluent citizens, who cannot pay for political spots.

Political advertising, in Schudson's (1986) words, remains an "uneasy persuasion," and, when one considers the increasing costs to an informed electorate from privacy-infringing, stealth strategies, a "sleazy persuasion." If candidates stopped doing dirty ads and concentrated their energies on getting elected by developing, then communicating, thoughtful political messages, our democracy would be better off. Alas, politics—the confluence of human ambition, group loyalties, profit-seeking media, and institutional intransigence—remains the biggest obstacle to achieving this goal.

## REFERENCES

Adgate, B. (2020, August 11). Kantar estimates 2020 election ads will cost $7 billion. *Forbes*. Online: www.forbes.com/sites/bradadgate/2020/08/11/2020-an-election-year-like-no-other/#7502299638d1. (Accessed: September 8, 2020).

Alba, D. (2019, October 14). Facebook tightens rules on verifying political advertisers. *The New York Times*. Online: www.nytimes.com/2019/08/28/technology/facebook-election-advertising-disinformation.html. (Accessed: June 13, 2020).

Alba, D., & Frenkel, S. (2020, September 4). Why Facebook's blocking of new political ads may fall short. *The New York Times*. Online: www.nytimes.com/2020/09/04/technology/facebooks-political-ads-block-election.html. (Accessed: September 4, 2020).

Allen, B., & Stevens, D. (2019). *Truth in advertising? Lies in political advertising and how they affect the electorate*. London: Rowman & Littlefield.

Ansolabehere, S., & Iyengar, S. (1995). *Going negative: How attack ads shrink and polarize the electorate*. New York: Free Press.

Arceneaux, K., & Nickerson, D.W. (2010). Comparing negative and positive campaign messages: Evidence from two field experiments. *American Politics Research, 38,* 54–83.

Baldwin-Philippi, J. (2017). The myths of data-driven campaigning. *Political Communication, 34,* 627–633.

Benoit, W.L. (2014). *A functional analysis of political television advertisements*. Lanham, MD: Lexington Books.

Berry, J.M., & Sobieraj, S. (2014). *The outrage industry: Public opinion media and the new incivility*. New York: Oxford University Press.

Bode, L., & Vraga, E.K. (2015). In related news, that was wrong: The correction of misinformation through related stories functionality in social media. *Journal of Communication, 65,* 619–638.

Brader, T. (2006). *Campaigning for hearts and minds: How emotional appeals in political ads work*. Chicago, IL: University of Chicago Press.

Brooks, D.J., & Geer, J.G. (2007). Beyond negativity: The effects of incivility on the electorate. *American Journal of Political Science, 51,* 1–16.

Cappella, J.N., & Jamieson, K.H. (1994). Broadcast adwatch effects: A field experiment. *Communication Research, 21,* 342–365.

Chira, S. (2017, January 15). Women who voted for Donald Trump, in their own words. *The New York Times,* 12.

Conger, K., & Alba, D. (2020, May 28). Twitter refutes inaccuracies in Trump's tweets about mail-in voting. *The New York Times*. Online: www.nytimes.com/2020/05/26/technology/twitter-trump-mail-in-ballots.html. (Accessed: June 12, 2020).

Coppock, A., Hill, S.J., & Vavreck, L. (2020). The small effects of political advertising are small regardless of context, message, sender, or receiver: Evidence from 59 real-time randomized experiments. *Science Advances, 6*. Online: https://advances.sciencemag.org/content/6/36/eabc4046. (Accessed: September 26, 2020).

Corasaniti, N. (2020a, April 21). Coronavirus takes over political advertising. *The New York Times*. Online: www.nytimes.com/2020/04/21/us/politics/coronavirus-takes-over-political-advertising.html. (Accessed: June 15, 2020).

Corasaniti, N. (2020b, June 9). Protests reach political ads. *The New York Times*. Online: www.nytimes.com/2020/06/09/us/politics/protests-political-ads.html. (Accessed: June 15, 2020).

Corasaniti, N., Cai, W., & Lu, D. (2020, October 17). Flush with cash, Biden eclipses Trump in war for the airwaves. *The New York Times*. Online: www.nytimes.com/interactive/2020/10/17/us/politics/trump-biden-campaign-ad-spending.html. (Accessed: October 18, 2020).

Dale, D. (2020, July 21), Fact check: Trump's dishonest "911" ad fear-mongers about Biden. *CNN Politics*. Online: www.cnn.com/2020/07/21/politics/fact-check-trump-ad-biden-police-911/index.html. (Accessed: July 22, 2020).

Ember, S., & Kaplan, T. (2020, July 10). Joe Biden and Bernie Sanders deepen their cooperation. *The New York Times*. Online: https://www.nytimes.com/2020/07/08/us/politics/biden-bernie-sanders.html. (Accessed: July 11, 2020).

Entous, A., Barrett, D., & Helderman, R.S. (2017, October 24). Clinton campaign, DNC paid for research that led to Russian dossier. *The Washington Post*. Online: www.washingtonpost.com/world/national-security/clinton-campaign-dnc-paid-for-research-that-led-to-russia-dossier/2017/10/24/226fabf0-b8e4–11e7-a908-a3470754bbb9_story.html?source=gmail&usg=AFQjCNH3gY97gLgf21UAC5-BLneZPH2Xxw&ust=1508970556887000&utm_term%3D.50f695ff5f0c. (Accessed: June 11, 2020).

Fallis, T.W. (2014). Political advertising. In K. Kenski & K.H. Jamieson (Eds.), *The Oxford handbook of political communication*. Online: www.oxfordhandbooks.com. (Accessed: July 17, 2016).

Farrell, J.A. (2017, August 6). When a candidate conspired with a foreign power to win an election. *Politico*. Online: www.politico.com/magazine/story/2017/08/06/nixon-vietnam-candidate-conspired-with-foreign-power-win-election-215461. (Accessed: June 10, 2020).

Fowler, E.F., Franz, M.M., & Ridout, T.N. (2016). *Political advertising in the United States*. Boulder, CO: Westview Press.

Fowler, E.F., Franz, M.M., & Ridout, T.N. (2020). The blue wave: Assessing political advertising trends and Democratic advantages in 2018. *PS: Political Science & Politics, 53*, 57–63.

Fowler, E.F., Ridout, T.N., & Franz, M.M. (2016). Political advertising in 2016: The presidential race as outlier? *The Forum: A Journal of Applied Research in Contemporary Politics, 14*, 445–469.

Freedman, P., Franz, M., & Goldstein, K. (2004). Campaign advertising and democratic citizenship. *American Journal of Political Science, 48*, 723–741.

Fridkin, K.L., & Kenney, P.J. (2011). Variability in citizens' reactions to different types of negative campaigns. *American Journal of Political Science, 55*, 307–325.

Fridkin, K.L., Kenney, P.J., & Wintersieck, A. (2015). Liar, liar, pants on fire: How fact-checking influences citizens' reactions to negative advertising. *Political Communication, 32*, 127–151.

Geer, J.G. (2006). *In defense of negativity: Attack ads in presidential campaigns*. Chicago, IL: University of Chicago Press.

Geer, J.G., & Vavreck, L. (2014). Negativity, information, and candidate position-taking. *Political Communication, 31*, 218–236.

Gervais, B.T. (2014). Following the news? Reception of uncivil partisan media and the use of incivility in political expression. *Political Communication, 31*, 564–583.

Goldmacher, S. (2020, June 8). Biden pours millions into Facebook ads, blowing past Trump's record. *The New York Times*. Online: www.nytimes.com/2020/06/08/us/politics/biden-trump-facebook-ads.html. (Accessed: June 24, 2020).

Goldmacher, S., & Haberman, M. (2020, September 8). How Trump's billion-dollar campaign lost its cash advantage. *The New York Times*. Online: www.nytimes.com/2020/09/07/us/politics/trump-election-campaign-fundraising.html. (Accessed: September 8, 2020).

Graves, L. (2016). *Deciding what's true: The rise of political fact-checking in American journalism*. New York: Columbia University Press.

Haenschen, K., & Jennings, J. (2019). Mobilizing Millennial voters with targeted Internet advertisements: A field experiment. *Political Communication, 36*, 357–375.

Hall, R. (2016, June 24). How the Brexit campaign used refugees to scare voters. *The World*. Online: www.pri.org/stories/2016-06-24/how-brexit-campaign-used-refugees-scare-voters. (Accessed: December 27, 2020).

Hameleers, M., & van der Meer, T.G.L.A. (2020). Misinformation and polarization in a high-choice media environment: How effective are political fact-checkers? *Communication Research, 47*, 227–250.

Herndon, A.W. (2020, July 19). Why a "do no harm" general election strategy could work for Joe Biden. *The New York Times*. Online: www.nytimes.com/2020/07/19/us/politics/joe-biden-wisconsin-election.html. (Accessed: July 20, 2020).

Hoffman, J. (2020, December 26). Early vaccine doubters now show a willingness to roll up their sleeves. *The New York Times*. Online: www.nytimes.com/2020/12/26/health/covid-vaccine-hesitancy.html. (Accessed: December 27, 2020).

Huffman, A., & Rejebian, M. (2012). *We're with nobody: Two insiders reveal the dark side of American politics*. New York: Morrow.

Isaac, M., & Frenkel, S. (2020, June 26). Facebook adds labels for some posts as advertisers pull back. *The New York Times*. Online: www.nytimes.com/2020/06/26/technology/facebook-labels-advertisers.html. (Accessed: December 27, 2020).

Isaac, M., & Kang, C. (2020, May 29). While Twitter confronts Trump, Zuckerberg keeps Facebook out of it. *The New York Times*. Online: www.nytimes.com/2020/05/29/technology/twitter-facebook-zuckerberg-trump.html. (Accessed: June 12, 2020).

Issenberg, S. (2012). *The victory lab: The secret science of winning campaigns*. New York: Crown.

Jamieson, K.H., Volinsky, A., Weitz, I., & Kenski, K. (2014). The political uses and abuses of civility and incivility. In K. Kenski & K.H. Jamieson (Eds.), *The Oxford handbook of political communication*. Online: www.oxfordhandbooks.com. (Accessed: July 17, 2016).

Johnson-Cartee, K.S., & Copeland, G.A. (1991). *Negative political advertising: Coming of age*. Hillsdale, NJ: Lawrence Erlbaum Associates.

Kaid, L.L. (2004). Political advertising. In L.L. Kaid (Ed.), *Handbook of political communication research* (pp. 155–202). Mahwah, NJ: Lawrence Erlbaum Associates.

Kaid, L.L. (2006). Political advertising. In S.C. Craig (Ed.), *The electoral challenge: Theory meets practice* (pp. 79–96). Washington, DC: CQ Press.

Kalla, J.L., & Broockman, D.E. (2018). The minimal persuasive effects of campaign contact in general elections: Evidence from 49 field experiments. *American Political Science Review, 112*, 148–166.

Kam, C.D. (2006). Political campaigns and open-minded thinking. *Journal of Politics, 68*, 931–945.

Kenski, K., Hardy, B.W., & Jamieson, K.H. (2010). *The Obama victory: How media, money, and message shaped the 2008 election*. New York: Oxford University Press.

Kern, M. (1989). *30-second politics: Political advertising in the eighties*. New York: Praeger.

Kim, Y.M., Hsu, J., Neiman, D., Kou, C., Bankston, L., Kim, S.Y., Heinrich, R., Baragwanath, R., & Raskutti, G. (2018). The stealth media? Groups and targets behind divisive issue campaigns on Facebook. *Political Communication, 35*, 515–541.

Kim, Y.M., Wang, M., Gotlieb, M.R., Gabay, I., & Edgerly, S. (2013). Ambivalence reduction and polarization in the campaign information environment: The interaction between individual- and contextual-level influences. *Communication Research, 40*, 388–416.

Konitzer, T., Rothschild, D., Hill, S., & Wilbur, K.C. (2019). Using big data and algorithms to determine the effect of geographically targeted advertising on vote intention: Evidence from the 2012 U.S. presidential election. *Political Communication, 36, 1–16*.

Kreiss, D. (2012). *Taking our country back: The crafting of networked politics from Howard Dean to Barack Obama*. New York: Oxford University Press.

Kreiss, D. (2020). Media and social media platforms finally begin to embrace their roles as democratic gatekeepers. In D. Jackson, D.S. Coombs, F. Trevisan, D. Lilleker, & E. Thorsen (Eds.), *U.S. election analysis 2020: Media, voters and the campaign*. Online: www.electionanalysis.ws/us/president2020/section-5-social-media/media-and-social-media-platforms-finally-begin-to-embrace-their-roles-as-democratic-gatekeepers/. (Accessed: November 16, 2020).

Kreiss, D., & McGregor, S.C. (2018). Technology firms shape political communication: The work of Microsoft, Facebook, Twitter, and Google with campaigns during the 2016 U.S. presidential cycle. *Political Communication, 35*, 155–177.

Kreiss, D., & McGregor, S.C. (2019). The "arbiters of what our voters see": Facebook and Google's struggle with policy, process and enforcement around political advertising. *Political Communication, 36*, 499–522.

Kreiss, D., & Perault, M. (2020, September 4). Facebook's pre-Election Day ban on political ads will likely suppress important speech. *Slate*. Online: https://slate.com/technology/2020/09/facebook-political-ad-ban-election-day.html. (Accessed: November 16, 2020).

Krupnikov, Y. (2011). When does negativity demobilize? Tracing the conditional effect of negative campaigning on voter turnout. *American Journal of Political Science, 55*, 796–812.

LaFraniere, S., Kramer, A.E., & Hakim, D. (2019, November 12). How an obsession with Ukraine created a crisis. *The New York Times*, A1, A16–A17.

Lamberson, P.J., & Soroka, S. (2018). A model of attentiveness to outlying news. *Journal of Communication, 68*, 942–964.

Lau, R.R., & Pomper, G.M. (2004). *Negative campaigning: An analysis of U.S. Senate elections*. New York and Lanham, MD: Rowman & Littlefield.

Lau, R.R., Sigelman, L., & Rovner, I.B. (2007). The effects of negative political campaigns: A meta-analytic reassessment. *Journal of Politics, 69*, 1176–1209.

Li, J., & Wagner, M.W. (2020). The value of not knowing: Partisan cue-taking and belief updating of the unformed, the ambiguous, and the misinformed. *Journal of Communication, 70*, 646–669.

Maier, J., & Nai, A. (2020). Roaring candidates in the spotlight: Campaign negativity, emotions, and media coverage in 107 national elections. *The International Journal of Press/Politics, 25*, 576–606.

Martin, J. (2017, July 13). Opposition research is standard, not just from hostile nations. *The New York Times*, A17.

Mattes, K., & Redlawsk, D.P. (2014). *The positive case for negative campaigning*. Chicago, IL: University of Chicago Press.

Mattes, K., & Redlawsk, D.P. (2020). Voluntary exposure to political fact checks. *Journalism & Mass Communication Quarterly, 97*, 913–935.

Matthes, J., & Marquart, F. (2015). A new look at campaign advertising and political engagement: Exploring the effects of opinion-congruent and-incongruent political advertisements. *Communication Research, 42*, 134–155.

McGregor, S.C. (2020). "Taking the temperature of the room": How political campaigns use social media to understand and represent public opinion. *Public Opinion Quarterly, 84 (Supplement)*, 236–256.

Meirick, P.C., Nisbett, G.S., Harvell-Bowman, L.A., Harrison, K.J., Jefferson, M.D., Kim, T-S., & Pfau, M.W. (2018). To tell the truth: Ad watch coverage, ad tone, and the accuracy of political advertising. *Political Communication, 35*, 450–469.

Merrill, J.B., & Goldhill, O. (2020, January 10). These are the political ads Cambridge Analytica designed for you. *Quartz*. Online: www.nytimes.com/2018/03/17/us/politics/cambridge-analytica-trump-campaign.html. (Accessed: June 14, 2020).

Merrill, J.B., & McCarthy, R. (2020, November 12). Trump won Florida after running a false ad tying Biden to Venezuelan socialists. *ProPublica*. Online: www.propublica.org/article/trump-won-florida-after-running-a-false-ad-tying-biden-to-venezuelan-socialists. (Accessed: December 7, 2020).

Motta, M. (2016). Air war? Campaign advertising in the 2016 presidential election In D. Lilleker, E. Thorsen, D. Jackson, & A. Veneti (Eds.), *US election analysis 2016: Media, voters and the campaign: Early reflections from leading academics* (p. 34). Poole, England: Centre for the Study of Journalism, Culture and Community.

Moy, P., & Pfau, M. (2000). *With malice toward all? The media and public confidence in democratic institutions*. Westport, CT: Praeger.

Mutz, D.C. (2006). *Hearing the other side: Deliberative versus participatory democracy*. Cambridge, UK: Cambridge University Press.

Mutz, D.C. (2007). Effects of "in your face" television discourse on perceptions of a legitimate opposition. *American Political Science Review*, *101*, 621–635.

Mutz, D.C. (2015). *In-your-face politics: The consequences of uncivil media*. Princeton, NJ: Princeton University Press.

Mutz, D.C., & Reeves, B. (2005). The new videomalaise: Effects of televised incivility on political trust. *American Political Science Review*, *99*, 1–15.

Neiheisel, J.R., & Niebler, S. (2015). On the limits of persuasion: Campaign ads and the structure of voters' interpersonal discussion networks. *Political Communication*, *32*, 434–452.

Neumann, M., Yao, J., Dean, S., & Fowler, E.F. (2020). A banner year for advertising and a look at differences across platforms. In D. Jackson, D.S. Coombs, F. Trevisan, D. Lilleker, & E. Thorsen (Eds.), *U.S. election analysis 2020: Media, voters and the campaign*. Online: www.electionanalysis.ws/us/president2020/section-5-social-media/a-banner-year-for-advertising-and-a-look-at-differences-across-platforms/. (Accessed: November 16, 2020).

Newhagen, J.E., & Reeves, B. (1991). Emotion and memory responses for negative political advertising: A study of television commercials used in the 1988 presidential election. In F. Biocca (Ed.), *Television and political advertising, volume 1: Psychological processes* (pp. 197–220). Hillsdale, NJ: Lawrence Erlbaum Associates.

Nyhan, B., & Reifler, J. (2010). When corrections fail: The persistence of political misperceptions. *Political Behavior*, *32*, 303–330.

Owen, D. (2014). New media and political campaigns. In K. Kenski & K.H. Jamieson (Eds.), *The Oxford handbook of political communication*. Online: www.oxfordhandbooks.com. (Accessed: August 3, 2016).

Parker, A. (2015, July 31). Facebook expands in politics with new digital tools, and campaigns find much to like. *The New York Times*, A17.

Patterson, T.E. (1980). *The mass media election: How Americans choose their president*. New York: Praeger.

Pennycook, G., Cannon, T.D., & Rand, D.G. (2018). Prior exposure increases perceived accuracy of fake news. *Journal of Experimental Psychology General*, *147*, 1865–1880.

Perloff, R.M. (2021). *The dynamics of persuasion: Communication and attitudes in the 21st century* (7th ed.). New York: Routledge.

Peters, J.W. (2012, October 16). 73,000 political ads test even a city of excess. *The New York Times*, A1, A16.

Prokop, A. (2018, April 23). The "pee tape" claim, explained. *Vox.* Online: www.vox.com/2018/4/15/17233994/comey-interview-trump-pee-tape-russia. (Accessed: June 11, 2020).

Qiu, L. (2020, August 15). Trump ads attack Biden through deceptive editing and hyperbole. *The New York Times.* Online: www.nytimes.com/2020/08/15/us/politics/trump-campaign-ads-biden.html. (Accessed: August 16, 2020).

Rancer, A.S., & Avtgis, T.A. (2014). *Argumentative and aggressive communication: Theory, research, and application* (2nd ed.). New York: Peter Lang Publishers.

Remnick, D. (2020, December 7). Real news. *The New Yorker*, 15, 18.

Robertson, C.T., Mourão, R.R., & Thorson, E. (2020). Who uses fact-checking sites? The impact of demographics, political antecedents, and media use on fact-checking site awareness, attitudes, and behavior. *The International Journal of Press/Politics*, *25*, 217–237.

Rosenberg, M., Confessore, N., & Cadwalladr, C. (2018, March 17). How Trump consultants exploited the Facebook data of millions. *The New York Times.* Online: www.nytimes.com/2018/03/17/us/politics/cambridge-analytica-trump-campaign.html. (Accessed: June 11, 2020).

Rosenberg, M., & Dance, G.J.X. (2018, April 8). "You are the product": Targeted by Cambridge Analytica on Facebook. *The New York Times.* Online: www.nytimes.com/2018/04/08/us/facebook-users-data-harvested-cambridge-analytica.html. (Accessed: June 13, 2020).

Rosenberg, M., Perlroth, N., & Sanger, D.E. (2020, June 4). "Chaos is the point": Russian hackers and trolls grow stealthier in 2020. *The New York Times.* Online www.nytimes.com/2020/01/10/us/politics/russia-hacking-disinformation-election.html. (Accessed: June 11, 2020).

Ross, A., S., & Bhatia, A. (2021). "Ruled Britannia": Metaphorical construction of the EU as enemy in UKIP campaign posters. *The International Journal of Press/Politics*, *26*, 188–209.

Rutenberg, J. (2004, March 4). The 2004 campaign: Advertising; Bush ad campaign ready to kick off an expensive effort. *The New York Times.* Online: www.nytimes.com/2004/03/04/us/2004-campaign-advertising-bush-ad-campaign-ready-kick-off-expensive-effort.html. (Accessed: December 7, 2020).

Schudson, M. (1986). *Advertising, the uneasy persuasion.* New York: Basic Books.

Shane, S., & Blinder, A. (2018, December 19). Secret experiment in Alabama Senate race imitated Russian tactics. *The New York Times.* Online: www.nytimes.com/2018/12/19/us/alabama-senate-roy-jones-russia.html. (Accessed: June 11, 2020).

Shapiro, M.A., & Rieger, R.H. (1992). Comparing positive and negative political advertising on radio. *Journalism Quarterly*, *69*, 135–145.

Shear, M.D. (2015, January 20). Doing more than putting on annual address into 140 characters. *The New York Times*, A14.

Sherif, C.W., Sherif, M., & Nebergall, R.E. (1965). *Attitude and attitude change: The social judgment-involvement approach.* Philadelphia, PA: W. B. Saunders

Shin, J., & Thorson, K. (2017). Partisan selective sharing: The biased diffusion of fact-checking messages on social media. *Journal of Communication*, *67*, 233–255.

Silverman, C. (2018, March 20). Cambridge Analytica says it won the election for Trump. Here's what it's actually talking about. *BuzzFeed News.* Online: www.

buzzfeednews.com/article/craigsilverman/cambridge-analytica-says-they-won-the-election-for-trump#.rqqdbqoEO. (Accessed: October 1, 2020).

Singer, N. (2018, August 16). "Weaponized ad technology": Facebook's moneymaker gets a critical eye. *The New York Times*. Online: www.nytimes.com/2018/08/16/technology/facebook-microtargeting-advertising.html. (Accessed: December 19, 2020).

Smith, B.A. (1996, October 8). Time to go negative. *The Wall Street Journal*, A22.

Soroka, S.N. (2014). *Negativity in democratic politics: Causes and consequences*. New York: Cambridge University Press.

Soroka, S.N., & McAdams, S. (2015). News, politics, and negativity. *Political Communication, 32*, 1–22.

Stromer-Galley, J. (2014). *Presidential campaigning in the Internet age*. New York: Oxford University Press.

Stromer-Galley, J. (2019). *Presidential campaigning in the Internet age* (2nd ed.). New York: Oxford University Press.

Strother, R.D. (2003). *Falling up: How a redneck helped invent political consulting*. Baton Rouge, LA: Louisiana State University Press.

Stryker, R., Conway, B.A., & Danielson, J.T. (2016). What is political incivility? *Communication Monographs, 83*, 535–556.

Vargo, C.J., & Hopp, T. (2020). Fear, anger, and political advertisement engagement: A computational case study of Russian-linked Facebook and Instagram content. *Journalism & Mass Communication Quarterly, 97*, 743–761.

Vogel, K.P. (2017, October 25). The Trump dossier: What we know and who paid for it. *The New York Times*. Online: www.nytimes.com/2017/10/25/us/politics/steele-dossier-trump-expained.html. (Accessed: June 11, 2020).

Vraga, E.K., Bode, L., & Tully, M. (2020). Creating news literacy messages to enhance expert corrections of misinformation on Twitter. *Communication Research*. Online: https://journals.sagepub.com/doi/10.1177/0093650219898094. (Accessed: July 11.2020).

Vraga, E.K., Kim, S.C., Cook, J., & Bode, L. (2020). Testing the effectiveness of correction placement and type on Instagram. *The International Journal of Press/Politics*. Online: https://journals.sagepub.com/doi/full/10.1177/1940161220919082?casa_token=sBE15l5RYyQAAAAA%3A2HNEg2qOe5—hcordwEM_nCsycya445hz-Ur29JC4GfDQCmnbOFpmFmQND-89Ncc4ZTaJQotM-E8cA. (Accessed: July

Wakabayashi, D., & Goldmacher, S. (2019, November 20). Google policy change upends online plans for 2020 campaigns. *The New York Times*. Online: www.nytimes.com/2019/11/20/technology/google-political-ads-targeting.html/    (Accessed: June 12, 2020).

Walter, N., Cohen, J., Holbert, R.L., & Morag, Y. (2020). Fact-checking: A meta-analysis of what works and for whom. *Political Communication, 37*, 350–375.

Walter, N., & Murphy, S.T. (2018). How to unring the bell: A meta-analytic approach to correction of misinformation. *Communication Monographs, 85*, 423–441.

Walter, N., & Tukachinsky, R. (2020). A meta-analytic examination of the continued influence of misinformation in the face of correction: How powerful is it, why does it happen, and how to stop it? *Communication Research, 47*, 155–157.

West, D.M. (2010). *Air wars: Television advertising in election campaigns, 1952–2008* (5th ed.). Washington, DC: CQ Press.

Willis, D. (2014, September 11). Campaigns use Facebook tool to deliver targeted political ads. *The New York Times*, A3.

York, C., Ponder, J.D., Humphries, Z., Goodall, C., Beam, M., & Winters, C. (2020). Effects of fact-checking political misinformation on perceptual accuracy and epistemic political efficacy. *Journalism & Mass Communication Quarterly, 97,* 958–980.

Zacks, J.M. (2015, February 15). Why movie "facts" prevail. *The New York Times* (Sunday Review), 12.

Zernike, K., & Rutenberg, J. (2004, August 20). The 2004 campaign; Advertising; Friendly fire: The birth of an attack on Kerry. *The New York Times*. Online: www. nytimes.com/2004/08/20/us/the-2004-campaign-advertising-friendly-fire-the-birth-of-an-attack-on-kerry.html?_r=0. (Accessed: July 19, 2017).

# 16 Presidential Debates and Postscript

Do we really need presidential debates? They're full of coiffed hair, scripted one-liners, snappy retorts, and insulting remarks. They can devolve into train wrecks, chaos, and unadulterated meanness. Candidates evade the issues, dodge the questions, and hurl insults. Panelists ask silly questions that don't force discussion of the terribly important issues facing the country. Aren't debates, to paraphrase Shakespeare, filled with televised sound and fury, signifying nothing? Or is there another side? Do they serve democratic ends by demanding that candidates say something about what they would do as president? Do they have tangible and symbolic benefits? Or should they be scrapped?

Don't ask the media. To the many news channels, particularly the television networks, there's no question. Debates are the Super Bowl, Wimbledon Tennis Championship, NBA Finals, and World Soccer Cup all rolled into one. The 21st-century equivalent of the final episodes of *The Fugitive*, *M\*A\*S\*H*, and *Seinfeld*, with the 2013 finale of *Breaking Bad* thrown in for good measure. Presidential debates are the high holidays of American presidential politics (Dayan & Katz, 1992)—the day the mediated earth stands still, if only briefly and with breathless anticipation. In the view of media commentators, they are centerpieces of the electoral feast that draw massive audiences, so much so that restaurants and bars plan entertainment extravaganzas, like the Alamo Drafthouse in Dallas, Texas that in 2016 featured a themed menu, including a Donald Trump Build A Wall Around It Taco Salad and Hillary's Leak Pizza. In 2020, even though the overwhelming majority of voters had their minds made up by the first debate, a headline pronounced that Joe Biden was "preparing for the biggest debate of his life" (Goldmacher & Glueck, 2020).

Presidential debates epitomize the ways entertainment and politics merge seamlessly in American politics; the absurd incongruity of discussing policy issues in a format that militates against serious discussion; and the manner in which voters listen, tweet, praise, and process the only campaign events that allow for dialogue between the major political contenders for the U.S. presidency.

Debates have a long history in American politics. "The American political system grew up with debate," Kathleen Hall Jamieson and David S. Birdsell (1988) remind us. "Colonial assemblies debated revolution, the Constitutional Convention debated the Constitution, and Congress debated the law" (p. 17).

The most famous debates—the ones that leap to mind when political debates are discussed—were the Lincoln-Douglas debates of 1858. Abraham Lincoln, who had served in Congress and acquired a reputation as a spell-binding orator, ran against the incumbent, Stephen Douglas, for a U.S. Senate seat in Illinois. They debated seven times in as many Illinois cities. The debates were rhetorical tours de force that harnessed legal argumentation and historical appeals to the Founding Fathers. The issue was slavery. Douglas embraced popular sovereignty, taking the relativist position that questions of morality must be decided by the people themselves. Thus, each state had the right to decide to continue slavery or abolish the institution. Lincoln adopted an absolutist natural rights perspective, forcefully arguing that slavery was morally wrong (Zarefsky, 1990). The Lincoln-Douglas debates have been justly celebrated as masterful exemplars of political rhetoric. Let's not mythologize them.

First, they took place in a senatorial—not, as often assumed, presidential—campaign. Arguments may have been lofty, but they were also weapons of electoral persuasion. Both debaters crafted arguments to appeal to voters. Douglas won the election, in part because his debate and campaign arguments persuaded Illinois' undecided, swing voters that Lincoln was a radical abolitionist.

Second, contrary to legend, audiences probably were not mesmerized by these debaters' eloquence. Many of the thousands who attended were picnicking, their attention focused on the food not the candidates; others attended not to hear the arguments, but to partake in the drama of the moment (Zarefsky, 1990). Theatrics captivated the crowd. People interrupted one of Douglas's opening speeches by shouting, "Hit him again" (Mutz, 2015, p. 208). In this way, audience members were not unlike today's political junkies who tune into CNN or Fox to follow the horse race or hope their candidate draws first blood.

A third myth of Lincoln-Douglas involves the premise of the debates. The very assumption that slavery should be debated nowadays strikes us as preposterous, offensive to our moral sensibilities. It seems so patently obvious that slavery has no defense that any formal debate on the topic seems inappropriate and certainly unworthy of celebration. At the time, sadly, the issue was a matter of debate, reminding us that political communication is a function of a particular time and place.

This brings us to today. This chapter examines debates from a variety of vantage points, demythologizing them, describing their attributes, and discussing their political and broader normative impacts. The first portion of the chapter sets the stage by discussing major functions of debates, defining a presidential debate, and explaining different presidential debate formats. The next portion explore debates past and present by reviewing debate milestones, 2020 debates, and social science research on debate effects. The fourth section gives a normative balance sheet on presidential debates. The final part of the chapter offers a postscript on the 2020 presidential election, a final bookend to the text.

## DEBATE FUNCTIONS AND DEFINITIONS

Presidential debates serve different functions for the political communication system (Benoit, 2007, 2014). For candidates, they are first and foremost political events. From the perspective of presidential candidates, debates provide key opportunities to sway undecided voters and solidify supporters' favorable attitudes. Candidates do not want to educate the electorate. They want to exploit debates to achieve concrete political objectives (Kraus, 1988).

Debates play a different role for voters. They help voters decide which candidate best serves their interests and how candidates might perform as president. For partisan activists, debates are key opportunities to cheer for their candidate and take note of the opponent's weaknesses. For less involved voters, they are like stock-car races, where you enjoy the spectacle over drinks and secretly hope an exciting minor accident will occur, in the form of a gaffe committed by the opposing candidate. For news media, debates are a premier event in the horse race, championship laps between the horses, the penultimate boxing match between two prizefighters.

Presidential debates, at their best, also perform symbolic functions for the political system as a whole. They represent the only live, real-time forum in which candidates stand, side by side, discussing policy issues. They put potential leaders before citizens in a relatively unmediated forum. Unlike political commercials or microtargeted social media messages, they are not packaged by consultants prior to being seen by voters. However, critics point out that debates are largely scripted events, where candidates rarely cover issues in depth, prefer to jab rather than engage, and don't feature outside-the-box, third-party candidates.

### Definition

Let's cut to the chase: Presidential debates are not authentic debates. A **debate**, as Auer (1962) notes, is: "(1) a confrontation, (2) in equal and adequate time,

(3) of matched contestants, (4) on a stated proposition, (5) to gain an audience decision" (p. 146). Trained debaters research a topic, present detailed arguments, and prepare persuasive rebuttals. One side defends the proposition and the other refutes it. A judge determines who wins, based on carefully honed criteria. A well-respected genre of debate, derived from the classic 1858 debates, is called Lincoln-Douglas.

Although candidates in the presidential debates compete for the most powerful position on the planet, they do not debate in the true sense of the word. They do not debate a stated proposition, such as "Public colleges should offer free tuition" or "There should be universal, government-funded health insurance." Instead, debates revolve around generic domestic policies or foreign affairs. Questions can focus on image, such as a candidate's likeability or experience. Debaters skirt issues and ignore opponents' arguments. They play to their base or frame arguments to sway undecided voters. A judge does not adjudicate the decision, based on a reasoned analysis of arguments and rebuttals. A poll is taken after the debate, and Americans use a host of criteria, including the candidate's nonverbal skills and demeanor, to decide who won. In short, debates are about image and appearances, to a large degree the antithesis of genuine advocacy-centered, argument-focused debate. They can be even worse, as seen in the first 2020 debate between Trump and Biden, where Trump hectored Biden and the debate became a chaotic free-for-all.

If the classic term "debate" does not adequately capture the essence of these events, how then should we define them? It's more accurate to view a debate as a joint appearance or mediated face-to-face encounter. Martel (1983, p. 2) defines a **presidential debate** as "the joint appearance by two or more opposing candidates, who expound on their positions, with explicit and equitable provisions for refutation without interruption." (Well, they're not supposed to interrupt, but they do—and frequently, as seen in the first 2020 presidential debate.) Even so, candidates formulate arguments on policy matters, proclaiming accomplishments, criticizing the opponent, and offering spirited defenses of their own positions (Benoit & Harthcock, 1999). The quality of their arguments can be open to question.

### Formats

There are usually three 90-minute presidential debates that are frequently held strategically at universities located in battleground states. The structure of the debate varies, depending on the format and negotiations between rival candidates in a particular election. The amount of time candidates get to respond to questions, number of minutes allocated for rebuttals, and whether there is time for opening or closing statements can hinge on the particular debate (Tuman, 2008).

There are three debate formats: (1) **press conference**, where a group of pre-se-lected reporters ask candidates questions; (2) **single moderator**, where the moderator, typically a television news anchor or political correspondent, asks questions and serves as umpire; and (3) **town hall meeting**, featuring questions from the audience, frequently undecided voters, typically moderated by a well-known journalist.

Each format has strengths and weaknesses. The press conference ensures that panelists are experienced and will ask knowledgeable questions that bear on policy. Its weakness is that reporters can be oblivious to real-world problems that afflict voters or pose queries designed solely to entrap candidates (Hellweg, Pfau, & Brydon, 1992). Reporters, who view candidates in a staunchly adversarial role, can ask snarky "Gotcha" questions designed to pin the candidate down, sometimes on a trivial or unimportant aspect of the campaign. In 2015, John Harwood of CNBC asked Trump if he was running a "comic book version of a presidential campaign," a question that was unnecessarily provocative and unlikely to yield anything but a crisp denial or counterattack from the candidate. Candidates frequently evade questions, however, so it serves voters when reporters try to pin candidates down on policy matters.

The single moderator format can, in theory, reduce the chaos that can ensue when a team of journalists hurls questions at candidates. Much depends on the moderator's skill in making sure candidates stick by the rules. There are different perspectives on how moderators can most effectively coordinate debates. One view is they should take a laissez-faire, passive role, opting not to intervene or possibly bias the debate with their perspectives, in this way giving the public an unvarnished look at the candidates without a journalistic filter. The downside is that moderators can lose control of the debate, as occurred in 2012 when Jim Lehrer of PBS permitted Romney and Obama to talk beyond their allotted limits, opting not to press them when they made misleading statements. And it happened famously in 2020 when even the estimable Chris Wallace of Fox News could not enforce debate rules as Trump rudely interrupted Biden on numerous occasions, and Biden responded derisively to the president.

A second view is that moderators should take an active stance, making certain that factual mistakes candidates make (and there are many of them) do not go unchallenged, taking pains to ensure that sometimes deliberate misstatements are not viewed as facts. Candy Crowley of CNN did just this during the second 2012 presidential debate, correcting Romney on a factually incorrect statement he made about an attack on U.S. diplomats in Libya. While providing accurate information in debates is a virtue, the problem is that hosts can do this selectively, correcting one candidate and not the other, or providing a more dramatic correction for one candidate at a critical juncture in the debate than for his or her adversary.

The main benefit of town meeting debates is that they bring ordinary people into the electoral process, allowing voters to question candidates directly. By giving citizens the opportunity to communicate directly with candidates for the highest office in the land, the town hall meeting privileges democratic values. Candidates adopt a more voter-centered style, focusing on issues that are on voters' minds (McKinney, 2005).

The town hall format has shortcomings, too. Sometimes voters don't ask good questions. Town hall meetings also do not always provide opportunities for follow-up questions, which can push candidates to articulate ideas or clarify misleading remarks. The 2016 town hall debate showed what can happen when moderators steal the thunder from the audience. The moderators—consumed by Trump and Clinton's reactions to revelations of Trump's comments about groping women—dominated portions of the debate, forcing the debate to focus more on character issues journalists enjoy than on bread-and-butter concerns that occupy voters (Vernon & Spike, 2016).

But town halls can also be illuminating. When the second 2020 presidential debate was cancelled in the wake of Trump's coronavirus infection, both candidates held dueling town hall meetings. The moderators asked tough questions, with NBC's Savannah Guthrie pressing Trump on whether he was tested before the first debate and whether he would denounce QAnon, the extremist conspiracy theory. ABC's George Stephanopoulos grilled Biden on whether he would pack or expand the Supreme Court. Voters asked good questions. Angela Politarhos asked Biden how he justified his support of the tough 1994 crime bill that showcased prejudice against minorities. Paulette Dale (who complimented Trump on his smile, perhaps to provide cover for the aggressive question she asked) wanted to know if he planned to pursue his previous efforts to cut a program that helped undocumented immigrants.

So, letting citizens participate in debates can clarify issues, a major function of debates.

## DEBATES PAST AND PRESENT

During every election since 1976, presidential candidates have debated each other in public forums. Debates varied in terms of content, importance, strategy, and civility, but they have been a mainstay of presidential campaigns. Table 16.1 presents a summary of four classic debates, along with their significance and the continuing issues they have raised.

**Table 16.1  Milestones in presidential debate history.**

| Debate | Summary | Significance |
|---|---|---|
| **1960 Kennedy-Nixon** | As the first-ever televised presidential debates, they placed image at the apex of political communication, as a result of Kennedy's debonair appearance and a much-disputed study that Kennedy won the first debate among TV viewers and Nixon won among people who heard it on the radio. (Neglected in the pro-Kennedy hoopla was discussion of instances in which JFK knowingly articulated misleading claims about a U.S.-Soviet missile gap.) (See Figure 16.1.) | The debates made image the sine qua non of politics, building the art of artifice, creating a cottage academic industry on this topic. They also created the myth that Kennedy won the election solely because of his good looks, while also ushering in debates as a mandatory institution in presidential politics, although the change did not begin until 1976. |
| **1976 Ford-Carter** | In the second presidential debate, President Ford famously misspoke, incorrectly stating, in the throes of the Cold War, that "there is no Soviet domination of Eastern Europe." Research showed that endless news coverage of the debate gaffe changed public perception from a belief the debate was a draw to more than 60 percent of Americans perceiving Carter won. | The findings demonstrated the ways in which news media influence debate outcomes, in sometimes superficial ways. The news impact was a pseudo-effect, as it magnified a literal error on Ford's part that glossed over his intent to emphasize that the people of Eastern Europe remained autonomous, psychologically resilient individuals. News impact was real, but attuned to appearances. |

*Continued*

**Table 16.1 (Continued)**

| Debate | Summary | Significance |
|---|---|---|
| **1980 Carter-Reagan** | The debate ushered in one-liners, in keeping with Reagan's television personae, such as "There you go again" and "Are you better off than you were four years ago?" Reagan seemed presidential, Carter petulant, and Reagan showed he was hardly a trigger-happy, primed-for-war zealot. | The introduction of one-liners further pushed debates in the direction of entertainment. Frequently neglected in all the one-liner buzz was that as early as 1980, a president, Carter, put national health insurance on the public agenda with his statements, only to see it go nowhere, an indication of the difficult path to change. Despite Reagan's one-liners, he bested Carter in narrative, articulating an anti-government argument that would dominate politics for a generation. |
| **1988 Bush-Dukakis** | In a campaign marked by nationalistic, racist, and macho-patriotic imagery, the debate fit right in, with the moderator brazenly asking if Democratic candidate Michael Dukakis, who strongly opposed the death penalty, would favor the death penalty if his wife were raped and murdered. When Dukakis said he would continue to oppose it, answering in the steely, unemotional manner in which he verbally executed the campaign, his supporters feared he was toast because he hadn't shown the emotion television required of candidates. | The political and media reaction—Dukakis should have shown muscular affect—showcased the ways image had hijacked presidential debates since Kennedy-Nixon. In fact, Dukakis placed principle over politics and even over a real person, all the more courageous since that person was his wife. In a media age, faux emotion was seen as preferable to a drier answer rooted in inviolable belief. |

**Figure 16.1  The iconic Kennedy-Nixon debates of 1960. During the first presidential debate, Kennedy's personal appearance—his elegance and handsome features—contrasted sharply with Nixon's unseemly jowls and five o'clock shadow. The debate produced a sea change in attitudes toward political media, leading observers to conclude that on TV the visual dwarfs the verbal. Frequently overlooked is that during the campaign, and the fourth debate, Kennedy articulated misleading claims about a U.S.–Soviet missile gap that he knew were false or at least questionable, but likely perpetrated them to win votes.**

## 2020 DEBATES: CHAOS, INCIVILITY, AND POLITICAL COMMUNICATION STRATEGIES

With classic debate milestones in mind, let's examine contemporary debates to see how they flow from, or alter, past traditions.

The 2016 debates featured some aggressive posturing, particularly in the second debate, when Trump prowled aggressively around the stage in what some regarded as sexist behavior. It turned out that 2016 was a minor scratch, compared to the burn the country experienced after viewing the first debate of 2020, unquestionably the most incendiary debate in presidential debate history (see Figure 16.2). Trump hijacked the event, interrupting Biden or the moderator at least 128 times, far more than Biden interrupted the president, destroying the decorum and civility that are democratic foundations of presidential debates

**Figure 16.2  The first 2020 Trump-Biden debate was the most uncivil debate in U.S. presidential debate history, upending democratic norms of civility. Trump interrupted Biden constantly, offered a litany of nasty comments, and refused to condemn White supremacists. Biden, while much less offensive, uttered several derogatory comments about Trump. Viewers were left dispirited.**

*Source*: www.gettyimages.com/detail/news-photo/president-donald-trump-and-democratic-presidential-nominee-news-photo/1277463831?adppopup=true

(Stahl, 2020). He ridiculed Biden's intelligence, saying "there's nothing smart about you," insulted his sole surviving son, and told a bunch of falsehoods about the coronavirus and global warming (see "Fact-checking the first 2020 presidential debate," 2020). Biden retorted rudely too and called Trump a "racist," becoming so frustrated at a false Trump comment about his supporting the "radical left," he said, "Will you shut up, man?" The encounter at times resembled a painfully bitter quarrel between husband and wife or two long-time adversaries, with dialogue sharp and spiteful, as from the pen of playwright Edward Albee.

Both candidates sparred on the pandemic, economy, racial protests, and climate change, although neither offered visionary or particularly specific prescriptions of how they would handle these quandaries, giving the debate an even more negative pall. Biden did employ a Reagan-esque appeal to the American public on a couple of occasions, focusing directly on the TV audience, asking, "How many of you got up this morning and had an empty chair at the kitchen table because someone died (of) Covid?" But he didn't tell people how he would make their lives better if he were president, preferring instead to make the debate a biting referendum on Trump's presidency. Compared to the Reagan-Carter debate in Cleveland 40 years ago, which had a few classic soundbites of its own ("Are you better off than you were four years ago?"), 2020's debate in the same city was marked by far less discussion of issues and more personal fireworks.

Many Americans found themselves pained and dispirited by the debate, discomfited by the insults, interruptions, and unpresidential behavior. Celebrities chimed in. Actor Mark Hamill (aka Luke Skywalker) tweeted "that debate was the worst thing I've ever seen & I was in the Star Wars Holiday special" (which was widely panned and called one of the dumbest events in TV history)! Many voters found the debate hard to process, either because they lacked the cognitive schema to appreciate its nuances or found it emotionally exhausting. Sadly, it became just another episode in America's long-running reality TV show, with Trump as the temperamental executive-in-chief. "Lord have mercy," one person tweeted. "This debate sounds like a Real Housewives reunion . . . where's Andy Cohen?" (Rosenblatt, 2020).

Two positive things came of the first debate fiasco. Determined to prevent future disruptive interruptions, the Commission on Presidential Debates announced that for the second debate, candidates would only have their microphone turned on when they had the floor to speak, treating the candidates more as preschoolers than presidential contenders. As a result of this change and the overwhelmingly negative reaction Americans had to the first debate, both Trump and Biden were more civil, actually offering spirited, if sometimes acrimonious, exchanges on the issues during the second single moderator debate.

The other positive result was that the vice presidential debate that followed the first Biden-Trump debate was far more civil and full of issues, as both candidates sought to avoid negative publicity by coming off as rude. It was a normal debate that showcased civic respect, illustrated by Vice President Mike Pence's acknowledgment of the historic nature of Harris's nomination. And, as it turned out, the debate held out lessons for students of political communication, highlighting the role of classic concepts studied in the field and discussed in this book. The Pence-Harris vice presidential debate emphasized the following themes:

### *Focus on the Frame*

Vice President Mike Pence sought to frame the election as an ideologically based choice between the "radical" environmental and political agenda of Biden and the Trump administration's achievements. Kamala Harris, following the tradition of challengers' political rhetoric, framed the election as a referendum on the Trump administration's failures, specifically (in her view) its inability to prevent the death of hundreds of thousands of Americans, what she called "the greatest failure of any presidential administration in the history of our country." She wanted Americans to politicize the personal, attributing their personal malaise that resulted from the pandemic to systematic failures of the Trump administration. That was a complex calculus, as Republicans and Democrats differed on how intensely they personally felt about the malaise and their attributions.

### Placing Premium on the Prime

In pointing, in some cases persuasively, but not always accurately, to Biden-Harris's endorsement of supposedly radical Green New Deal positions, Pence hoped to prime this issue, accessing it as a key factor that voters would call to mind when they voted. Harris instead put the coronavirus front and center, reflecting and reinforcing many voters' emphasis on the pandemic, hoping it would supplant other issues in voters' minds.

### Televised Image Dynamics

Just as Reagan had pivoted to the camera in a debate 40 years prior to the 2020 encounter, asking Americans if they were better off than they were four years ago, Harris made a direct, eye-in-the-camera appeal to the audience, saying, "I want to ask the American people . . . how calm were you when your kids were sent home from school and you didn't know when they could go back?" Pence did the same, if less directly, when he said "the American people, I believe, deserve credit for the sacrifices that they have made, putting the health of their family and their neighbors first." Both were classic political persuasion attempts to involve the audience in the message and project goodwill. Pence's pivot probably was less successful because it reflected a defensive attempt to shift attention from the administration's responsibility. It was a feint that tried to flatter the public by praising its sacrifices, but it was not clear what the public had sacrificed. For a parent or a friend, putting a loved one first isn't a sacrifice, but an obligation.

### Debate 101 Strategies

Both candidates tried to pin blame on their adversary for inept answers or dodging the question. Pence was particularly effective here. When Harris refused to say whether she and Biden would pack the court, or try to add more Supreme Court justices, Pence stated compellingly that "she never answered the question." Harris declined to say because the issue was politically difficult for her. Liberal Democrats, concerned that the Court might tilt conservative and anti-choice for generations, saw court packing as their only chance to preserve liberal decisions, like on *Roe v. Wade*. However, traditionalists in the party, concerned about dangerous institutional precedents, objected. Harris failed on debate points, to be sure, but showed a canny appreciation of the need to avoid hot-button issues that could divide voters in her party. She steered clear of saying something that would fall into her voters' latitudes of rejection. She got a mediocre grade on honesty, but a strong score on political acumen.

### Gender Dynamics

Although the debate featured none of the testosterone-fueled interruptions and verbal jousts of the Trump-Biden encounter, it showcased an intersection between political communication and gender. As discussed in Chapter 12, sexist tendencies lead voters to place a demand on female candidates they don't put on males: We have to like you, you have to be nice and likable. Harris exuded likability by flashing warm smiles, disclosing how elated she was when Biden asked her to be his vice presidential partner, and sharing how proud her mother would be if she could have lived to see this moment. She seemed to blend feminine qualities that American voters prize with toughness by politely, but firmly, saying to Pence when he engaged in familiar male interruptions, "if you don't mind letting me finish." Pence, for his part, displayed an unflappable confidence and composure that frequently elicits perceptions of credibility. He undoubtedly pleased his base by evincing these nonverbal accoutrements of credibility.

### Debates Are About Persuasion, Not Truth

Of course, the debate was filled with inaccurate, misleading, occasionally flat-out false statements. For example, Harris minimized the benefits the Trump tax cut bestowed on millions of Americans and falsely stated that Trump's tariffs on China shed hundreds of thousands of manufacturing jobs, when, in fact, the U.S. gained blue-collar jobs during the first 18 months the tariffs were in effect. Pence minimized the impact of climate change and repeated the canard that mail-in voting can lead to voter fraud (FactCheck.org, 2020). It was hard for voters to ferret out the truth; few probably examined fact-check sites and based their evaluations instead on partisan opinions, affect, and how they sorted through the mélange of comments.

### The Debate Probably Exerted Solidifying Effects and, on a Broader Level, It Preserved the Democrats' Momentum

Did the vice presidential debate change many minds? Research on selective perception and confirmation biases discussed in Chapter 9 suggests it didn't. It reinforced and strengthened preexisting sentiments, but this does not mean we should do a full-fledged Joseph Klapper and take his limited effects view (see Chapter 4). Reinforcement affects can be consequential if they prime voters' sentiments and propel key members of the base to cast ballots. Pence probably solidified his support among strong conservatives. However, Harris, who was judged to have won the debate, at least in a CNN instant poll (Agiesta, 2020), likely inspired African Americans, eliciting pride from Black women, perhaps increasing turnout. She also denied the Trump campaign a game-changing chance to recapture the momentum.

Of course, since debates (since Lincoln-Douglas) have been part-serious and part-entertainment, many people focused not on the two minutes that each candidate had to talk, but the two minutes that a fly spent sitting on Mike Pence's head. "I'm not saying he's an alien but I never seen a bug sit so comfortably on anyone since Men In Black," actress Keke Palmer tweeted (Yapalater, 2020). Alert to its marketing possibilities, the Biden camp began tweeting a bunch of bad puns, including a picture of Biden with a flyswatter, asking people to "pitch in $5 to help this campaign fly," another post that said that "Team Joe swats away flies and lies," and an even poorer pun that admonished people, "Don't let this debate buzz off." Even a Republican senator got into the act, saying "the deep state planted a bug" on Pence!

### The VP Debate Reaffirmed Civility

After the bruising Trump-Biden presidential debate, the public felt grateful for the civility of the VP encounter, reaffirming a democratic value under siege. As one person put it, "never has something so boring been so appreciated" (Harris & Tarchak, 2020).

## SOCIAL SCIENCE RESEARCH ON PRESIDENTIAL DEBATES

This brings us to the important question of whether debates influence election outcomes. It's the quintessential question, posed by candidates, consultants, and pundits. You need to appreciate that it is challenging to assess the effects of debates on voting decisions. It is empirically difficult to tease out debates from other media events occurring at the same time of the campaign. Just because opinions about candidates change after a debate does not mean the debate caused the impact. Effects could have also resulted from news commentary following the debate, a combination of the debate and news commentaries, social media comments, or from unrelated messages, such as negative ads that replay candidate debate gaffes. Thus, it is difficult to quantify the precise contribution that exposure to debates has on the outcome of an election. Measurements can be unreliable, and it is difficult to parcel out debate effects from other campaign influences.

Nonetheless, social scientists have tried to determine the impact of presidential debates on voter attitudes and behaviors using a variety of strategies. They can statistically control or parcel out factors such as education, knowledge, and strong attitudes, so they can be sure that post-debate responses can be reasonably attributed to the debate per se. The best way to get a fairly accurate estimate of debate effects is to compare two samples matched on demographic characteristics before the debate, and compare post-debate responses of those who watched the debate with those who didn't. Researchers would have to make certain that those who actually watched the debate were in fact similar demographically to those who didn't. Methods are far from perfect, but these studies give us more reliable, valid conclusions than could be offered by knee-jerk guesses or armchair philosophizing.

## Debate Effects on Voters

The first effects are obvious, but important to state. Debates attract huge national audiences, motivating voters to seek particular gratifications. The first presidential debate between Clinton and Trump was the most-viewed presidential debate in history, with 84 million viewers, edging out Carter-Reagan with 81 million Americans watching in 1980 (Koblin, 2016). By contrast, the first 2020 presidential debate recruited a respectable 73 million viewers, a decline of 11 million from 2016 (Koblin, 2020). But this didn't include those who watched it on Twitch, the live-streaming service, who appreciated how Trump could "talk like a YouTuber" (Hsu, 2020, p. B4)! People gain rewards from watching the debate, such as knowledge clarification and uncertainty reduction. There are also drawbacks, as when they feel more confused or angry afterwards.

Vice presidential debates attract large audiences too, though not usually as large as those of presidential debates. The much-anticipated 2008 Biden-Palin vice presidential debate was the most-watched VP debate with some 70 million viewers. Much like people showed up at the 1858 Lincoln-Douglas debates to regale in the circus atmosphere, today's debate viewers tune in for the drama, the hoopla, and the possibility that a candidate will deliver a zinger or commit a gaffe. The humorist Molly Ivins joked, with tongue not entirely in cheek, that "political debates are sort of like stock-car races—no one really cares who wins, they just want to see the crashes" (Hahn, 1994, p. 208). And, of course, for many people, debates are part sober politics, part stock-car races, and part Internet-age entertainment. During the first 2020 presidential debate, tweets photoshopped images of Biden wearing ridiculously large masks, and later made hay out of Biden's saying "Will you shut up, man?," with people selling the phrase on newly created T-shirts (Rosenblatt, 2020).

Debate attention is sporadic. Few individuals watch a debate from start to finish, and only the political junkies watch all of the presidential and vice presidential debates (Sears & Chaffee, 1979). What's more, watching a debate does not mean that people buy into everything that candidates say. As you know, exposure does not equal effects. Debates are increasingly social media shows, with some viewers tweeting and posting, multitasking at a furious pace, showcasing how the audience has become an active spectator-participant in political debates. And while tweets are hardly representative of the reactions of the viewing audience, they provide an early unscientific indication of who is besting whom, which candidate's comments leave a visceral impact, or whose partisans are most engaged. During the chaotic first presidential debate of 2020, most of the tweets were negative, with few focusing on policy or political ideology, in keeping with the train-wreck aspect of the debate (Brown, 2020).

Second, perhaps surprisingly, fulfilling the hopes of deliberative democratic theorists, presidential debates generally expand understanding of political issues. They increase knowledge, boost the number of campaign issues voters use to assess candidates, help solidify cognition and affect, and bond together favorable sentiments toward a preferred candidate (Benoit, Hansen, & Verser, 2003; Carlin & McKinney, 1994; Holbrook, 1999; Gottfried et al., 2017; Miller & MacKuen, 1979). In a contemporary wrinkle, social media use complicates learning from debates; issue-based tweeting facilitates knowledge acquisition, but social media multitasking reduces learning about voters' preferred candidates (Jennings et al., 2017; Gottfried et al., 2017).

More generally, debate viewing bolsters political information efficacy, or voters' beliefs that they have the information necessary to meaningfully partake in politics. Information efficacy in turn can enhance political interest, discussion, and voting. As Benjamin R. Warner and Mitchell S. McKinney (2016) note, the increased political information efficacy generated by debates "represents a significant social benefit" (p. 37). The converse is also true: Those who do not view debates, who are generally lower in education, income, and efficacy, become comparatively less knowledgeable, increasing knowledge gaps and perhaps alienation.

A third impact of debates is reinforcement and affirmation of voters' preexisting candidate attitudes. As we know, voters filter debates through preexisting biases (Warner et al., 2020). Even when the opponent outperforms their candidate, partisans do not necessarily develop a favorable image of the competitor. In 2004, Democrat John Kerry bested Bush in the debates, but no matter. Republican viewers did not change their attitudes toward Bush or develop a favorable image of Kerry (Cho & Ha, 2012).

During the second presidential debate of 2012, Romney offered an impassioned defense of his commitment to equality in the workplace, explaining that as governor of Massachusetts he made a "concerted effort" to find women who had the qualifications to become members of his Cabinet. But when he mentioned that women's groups (who he approached to help him) brought back "whole binders full of women," his peculiar word choice created a feeding frenzy on the Internet, stimulating a Facebook fan page called "Binders Full of Women," which recruited numerous satirical likes. Liberals read in Romney's phrase an insincere support for women's rights, conveniently ignoring his statement that he sought to bring qualified women into his Cabinet and a willingness to offer flexible working hours.

Similarly during the tumultuous debates of 2016, partisan tweets were in strong supply, particularly among Clinton supporters. Tweets in the first debate played up Hillary's entrance in a red pantsuit; in the second debate, many focused on the lack of a handshake and Trump's prowling around Clinton onstage, as in the post from a college professor who wrote, "I'm a Muslim, and I would like to report a crazy man threatening a woman on a stage in Missouri!" During the third debate, shortly after Trump muttered that Clinton was "such a nasty woman," the phrase #NastyWoman rapidly began trending on Twitter. These tweets can humorously animate partisans and showcase active involvement, or perhaps demonstrate the silliness of the entire spectacle.

Vice presidential debates (where the adage to candidates is "first do no harm") also reinforce partisan preferences, conveyed through polls and social media. In the (*Saturday Night Live*–satirized) 2008 Palin-Biden debate, both candidates performed well, enhancing ratings of their image and issue expertise (McKinney, Rill, & Watson, 2011). Biden seemed to have won on debating points, answering the moderator's questions and rebutting Palin's arguments more effectively. Palin, for her part, displayed issue knowledge and projected confidence. Her litany included "Joe Six-Pack," "doggone it," and lots of dropped "g's" to convey informality. She smiled, winked, and conveyed folksy vitality. Many Republicans felt energized, their doubts about her competence reduced, if not totally eliminated. Her performance seemed to have solidified the base.

The first three presidential debate effects—exposure, expanded knowledge, and partisan reinforcement—derive exclusively from the debates. A fourth influence concerns news coverage of debate outcomes. Debates, of course, occur in the context of a voracious press. The news media do not just cover the debate live, but analyze it afterwards, focusing on the politics, not primarily the substance of what was said. News media verdicts on who won the debates, delivered by anchors and decided by polls, can function as heuristics, peripheral cues that affect voters' evaluations, as occurred in a 1976 Carter-Ford debate (see Table 16.1). In 2000, the news media hammered Al Gore, whom the press branded as a "serial exaggerator" for overstating his role in creating the Internet, when he slightly misspoke about his leadership experience as vice president. Opinions of Gore's honesty declined over the course of the following week (Jamieson & Waldman, 2003). In 2020, Biden's political misstatement during the second debate about "transitioning from the oil industry," which could have repelled voters favoring oil-extracting fracking, had less impact, because so many voters had made up their minds, other campaign issues were of greater importance, and news has less impact than it did in decades past.

## Do Debates Influence Electoral Outcomes?

The scholarly consensus is that debates can change the outcome of a presidential election—but rarely do (Sides & Vavreck, 2013). By the time that debates occur, in September and October of the fall campaign, most voters have made up their minds. Many undecided, but likely, voters have already developed perceptions of candidates that are not easy to shake with a debate performance, even if a candidate seems less than likable. Some low-involvement voters who are still undecided may not tune into the debate. Thus, a debate victory by a come-from-behind candidate may not influence judgments. In addition, debates rarely feature knockout punches or provide new information about either candidate's issue positions or images that have not been glimpsed before. In 2016, polls showed that Hillary Clinton won all three debates, but she narrowly lost the election.

In a handful of cases, debates seemed to have been consequential. I say "seemed" because we do not have iron-clad empirical proof because of the difficulties of establishing cause and effect in empirical research. There is some reason to believe the 1960 Kennedy-Nixon debates turned the tide for Kennedy. The first Kennedy-Nixon debate of 1960 elevated Kennedy's image, and Kennedy's poll ratings increased from neck-in-neck with Nixon to a four percentage point lead after the last debate (e.g., Harwood, 2012). Reagan's stunning defeat of Carter in the 1980 debate may have worked to Reagan's electoral advantage by quieting fears about Reagan's riskiness, elevating his credibility, and turning out Reagan voters. Egged on by a feeding frenzy of news coverage, the key 1976 Carter-Ford debate and the 2000 Bush-Gore debates may have contributed to Carter and Bush's victories (Hillygus & Jackman, 2003).

Even if they don't change the electoral outcome, debates influence campaign dynamics. Challengers typically gain stature by holding their own and keeping their cool when appearing in the same public forum as the president (Polsby et al., 2012). Debates, both presidential and vice presidential, drive news coverage and influence online buzz. They can also solidify a campaign narrative. This occurred when Bill Clinton displayed empathy, in contrast to George H.W. Bush, who inartfully glanced at his watch at the town hall debate of 1992, conveying a disdain that meshed with a growing narrative that Bush was out of touch with the electorate. Clinton evinced understanding of the concerns voiced by the questioner, showing his mastery of "Oprah"-style TV dynamics (see Figure 16.3).

In unusual cases, poor debate performance can make a difference. Trump's tempestuous, norm-shattering performance during the first 2020 debate may have unraveled support in a variety of key states. Reinforcing the nonstop narrative of Trumpian animus, the debate may have given some voters pause about whether to cast their votes for a second term (Martin & Burns, 2020). About two-thirds of a sample of voters in the key swing state of Pennsylvania disapproved of Trump's conduct; nearly half said they supported him less after the debate (Cohn, 2020). Vice President Pence's failure to staunch the damage in a

**Figure 16.3  At a 1992 presidential debate, a voter asked President George H.W. Bush how the national debt had affected his life. Bush took the question literally, neglecting to appreciate its emotional import; the voter was looking for empathy from the candidates for the financial situation she and other Americans faced. Clinton deftly appreciated this and delivered an answer rich in both empathy and economic knowledge, telegraphing an appreciation of the formal affective features of the televised town hall debate context. Clinton, with a vainglorious expression, may have overdone the theatrics, but Bush later looked gobsmacked, as if he did not know what hit him.**

*Source*: www.c-span.org/video/?33137-1/presidential-candidates-debate at 53:51

calmer, more civil second debate could have added insult to injury, allowing the Democrats' wave to continue to build momentum.

## BALANCE SHEET ON PRESIDENTIAL DEBATES

With the previous discussions of effects as backdrop, let's now explore the normative issues surrounding presidential debates.

### Style Versus Substance

Critics argue that candidates' nonverbal behaviors swamp the content of what they say. Candidates are evaluated on their television communication skills rather than on the arguments they speak. A sneer or discomfited look can speak with greater volume than a carefully honed rhetorical argument.

For example, in the first 2012 debate, Obama offered a cogent defense of his health care policy and lamented the lack of specificity in Romney's plans. But he was widely criticized because he looked down at his notes, grimaced, and seemed less animated than Romney. Does style overwhelm substance in debates?

The question has long generated controversy. You can find inklings of it in ancient Greece, when Plato criticized the Sophists, teachers who travelled from city to city offering courses on oratory and speaking style. To Plato, truth was an important virtue. He lamented that the Sophists sacrificed painstaking arguments for "the quick, neat, and stylish argument that wins immediate approval—even if this argument has some hidden flaw" (Chappell, 1998, p. 516). The style versus substance conundrum arises regularly in American politics, famously in the presidential debates of 1988, when Democrat Michael Dukakis gave a direct, logical, and truthful answer to a question on the death penalty, but was savaged for his lack of emotion (see Table 16.1).

The issue is complex. It is true that television debates do place visual and TV communication skills front and center, but one can argue that it is eminently reasonable to focus on a candidate's personal qualities when deciding how to cast a vote. Leadership in a media age consists of manipulating images. One can argue that part of the substance of a debate is the style in which candidates present their answers. As Martel (1983) aptly observes:

> To put this issue in perspective, it might be helpful to ask this question: When a person seeking a job wears his best suit for the interview, attends more meticulously than usual to grooming needs, and demonstrates more poise, better listening habits and closer attention to what he says than usual, is he being unduly manipulative? Of course not. Job interviews are imbued with image-oriented rituals rooted in the applicant's needs for survival and success. Campaign debates too, are forms of job interviews imbued with image-oriented rituals which we need to understand before passing judgment.
>
> (p. 3)

For all their flaws—and there are many—debates offer the only opportunity to watch candidates unmediated by a gaggle of advisers or issuing tweets that have been carefully vetted by aides. As the distinguished public advocate Newton Minow (2020) observed:

> The debates are the only time in a modern campaign when voters see candidates think on their feet and speak at length and extemporaneously without the benefit of script or consultants, armed with nothing but their character and intellect. The debates give voters multiple opportunities to see how candidates handle pressure.

## Debate About Issues

Contrary to what critics argue, issues are discussed in debates, far more than other formats. In the final presidential debate of 2016, Clinton offered a staunch defense of women's right to maintain control over their bodies without interference from government, including a defense of the controversial procedure known by its critics as late-term, partial-birth abortion (Stockman, 2016). Trump disagreed, forcefully denouncing late-term abortion. The candidates presented sharply different positions on a host of other issues, including gun control, immigration, and race relations. Racism and White supremacy were posed front-and-center as problems worthy of discussion in the 2020 debates, demonstrating how they have risen to a prominent place in the political agenda, forcing candidates to grapple with these issues, even if they should have been discussed years earlier.

Inevitably, there are downsides. Issues are discussed vaguely, questions are evaded, and important problems are ignored. Although the Earth reached its highest temperature ever in 2016, and global warming is increasingly posing cataclysmic threats to the planet, the candidates were not asked one question about how they would come to grips with climate change (Leonhardt, 2016). (In 2020, though, climate change generated considerably more discussion.)

From the perspective of deliberative democracy, which prizes thoughtful debate, issue discussions in debates are embarrassingly superficial, frequently focused around jabbing the opponent and rallying the base rather than on offering cogent argumentation. Jabs mobilize partisans; cogent arguments serve laudatory philosophical goals. It is easy to understand which choice candidates make. In addition, candidates make numerous misleading or false statements that fact-checks correct, but few voters see. Debates, like all persuasive communication genres, are hardly exercises in truth-telling. Voters can leave debates with a more confused understanding of issues. However, research indicates that, on the whole, debates crystallize issues and candidate perceptions.

## Civic Rituals or NASCAR Crash Videos?

Debates are intended to affirm democratic norms: the deliberation about differences through dialogue (Hinck, 1993). But to critics, they sometimes resemble crash-and-burn NASCAR videos, or stock-car automobile races, where cars smash into each other or the walls.

Ideally, debates should showcase the way partisans from different philosophical and political places can rationally disagree, offering an Athenian-style display of eloquent—or artful, or at least reasoned—verbal argumentation. As I wrote before the chaotic first 2020 presidential debate:

> During a time when norms of democracy are fraying—opponents relentlessly
> denounce each other and a president has viscerally attacked his adversaries
> rather than offering unifying rhetoric—debates offer a temporary display of
> the norm of civic respect, where both candidates at least show each other
> the courtesy of listening (kind of) to the other's positions and accepting the
> debate rules of egalitarian discourse.
>
> (Perloff, 2020a, p. E4)

Two days later, the first debate didn't showcase a lot of civic respect. But,
adopting a longer view, taking into account the other debates of 2020, as well
as previous elections, does suggest that, when compared to other raucous forms
of political communication (ads, soundbites, YouTube videos, and tweets),
debates stack up pretty well.

## Third-Party Participation

Should alternative or third-party candidates participate in presidential debates?
There is more to this freighted issue than meets the eye. Third-party candidates
have participated in debates just twice. Independent candidate John B. Anderson debated Ronald Reagan in 1980. (President Carter, fearing it would reduce
his political support, refused to debate Anderson.) Independent candidate Ross
Perot, a popular populist candidate and early opponent of free trade that out-
sourced jobs, participated in the 1992 presidential debates.

The Commission on Presidential Debates has stipulated that third-party candidates must garner an average of 15 percent support in five major opinion polls to qualify for debates. However, excluding third-party candidates
gives the debates a status quo, Establishment focus. More radical issues and
controversies that the two parties would rather not discuss are left out of
debates.

There is a good reason to restrict debates to the two major parties and insist
that third parties have a modest 15 percent public support before they can
partake. Do you know how many alternative political parties there are in the
U.S.? Where would you draw the line? Defenders of the present structure
argue that by opening the floodgates, debate planners would render debates
absurd or meaningless, seriously reducing their utility for candidates trying
to rebut their major party opponent and voters trying to decide which of the
two they should vote for. But the argument is problematic; it presumes voters
would find a third-party candidate disruptive rather than useful. To a large
degree, the two major parties block alternative groups from participating. (It's
amazing how they bridge their differences when electoral consequences are at
stake!) Republicans and Democrats fear participation by a third-party candidate could hurt their candidate's chances, adding nettlesome unpredictability
to the debate encounter.

But there are many zany political factions out there, and undoubtedly some that would advocate deeply prejudiced positions. Where *do* you draw the line? The 15 percent rule guarantees that debate arguments will be framed around issues important to the parties and the majority of voters. But it means they will revolve around familiar issues, with candidates reluctant to go outside the box to stake out innovative, status quo–challenging proposals. For varied institutional reasons, debates remain the province of the two established political parties, bound by political strictures, and steering clear of new ideas that could shake things up.

## How to Improve Debates

Nobody is satisfied with debates. Everybody wants to make them better. The question is how, and how to persuade the two parties to adopt needed changes. Here are a few ideas, drawing on those proposed by the Annenberg Policy Center (Cottle, 2020):

- Make sure moderators enforce the rules by politely, but firmly, cutting candidates off when they go over their allotted time.
- Have fact-checks in place so viewers can see these scroll as chyrons at a couple junctures during the debate.
- Give candidates more time to answer questions.
- Focus a debate on a narrow topic, such as health care or policing, with topics given to the candidates in advance so they can prepare cogent answers.
- Feature a 45-minute candidate debate followed by a British Parliament-style discussion, with congressional leaders asking feisty questions.
- Hold a national contest in which young people compete to ask the most non-standard, but thoughtful questions.

## CONCLUSIONS

Presidential debates are media events that bestride the fall campaign like a colossus. However, as research indicates, they are more media spin and hype than contests that significantly shape campaign outcomes. Debates serve different, sometimes conflicting, functions for candidates, voters, and the political system. For the larger system, debates are ideally exercises in civic education that help the nation come to grips with complex, contested issues, while also exerting a civilizing effect on a contentious election. That, of course, is the ideal and it is rarely achieved, because candidates rarely say anything innovative that could alienate potential voters, and because debates can devolve into rude, disrespectful exchanges. Although presidential debates are not debates in the classic sense of the term, they do offer a joint appearance of two or more candidates discussing issues, and rebutting one another's claims, with minimal filtering from the press.

More than 60 years of research on presidential debates, from Kennedy-Nixon to Biden-Trump, has yielded a host of conclusions that speak to the important roles played by candidate image, narrative, argumentation, nonverbal appropriateness, and news media verdicts, although the latter probably have less impact today than in the broadcast news era of a couple decades ago. Debates rarely change the outcome of an election, given that, in an age of national partisanship, the overwhelming majority of voters have made up their minds before the debates. And debates are filtered through partisan lenses. They do have strategic effects beyond reinforcement and vote change. Debates can influence momentum and sway undecided voters when the race is particularly close (although this has been difficult to precisely document in empirical studies). At their best, presidential debates expand voters' understanding of political issues and increase political efficacy. To the extent that debates increase interest in the campaign and encourage supporters to translate attitude into political participation, they exert positive effects on the system.

What is the balance sheet on debates? Are they good for democracy? Or are they a media circus that emphasizes entertaining style more than political substance? Presidential debates provide voters with exposure to candidates' issue positions and the clash of divergent ideas. Even acrimonious debates can increase learning and promote interpersonal discussion. Although debates prize likability and can overemphasize nonverbal cues, they offer a glimpse of how a candidate might lead through communication in a media age. And although many lament the showbiz, hyped-up atmosphere of debates, the drama can attract less politically involved voters to the campaign, at least for a time. Debates also fulfill Churchill's criteria for democracy: From a deliberative perspective, they're better than most other political communication formats.

Debates have flaws as well. Candidates duck questions, offer soundbite answers, lie or mislead, and equivocate for fear of alienating core voters. That's politics. Candidates also largely repeat positions articulated throughout the campaign. The structure of debates does not permit exploration of new perspectives that could help us solve pressing problems. That's politics, too.

Scholars have suggested revitalizing debates with a variety of new approaches. One of the perennial conundrums of presidential debates is whether third-party candidates should participate. One has to balance the benefits of introducing new ideas into a tired format with the drawback of including candidates who could distract voters from the task of deciding which of the two major party contenders is best suited to be president. The obvious appeal of third-party contenders is that they could force the debate to focus on outside-the-two-party-box ideas, perhaps bringing disenchanted voters into the electoral process. But, given the sheer number of alternative parties and their uneven quality, it is difficult to figure out ways to meaningfully bring them into debates. Still, given the problems the country faces, it is dispiriting to hear the same old solutions batted around or batted down without an opportunity to discuss new ideas.

Debates, alas, involve tradeoffs, which is hardly surprising since they are both argumentative encounters and political events that occur in a polarized electoral environment. Given their potential, it behooves scholars to dream up ways to improve debate formats so they can be as effective in educating as they are in electioneering—as helpful in offering novel solutions as trotting out the tried-and-true. Alas, the goal is harder to reach than to grasp, but given the abundance of problems in need of improvement, it's worth reaching for.

## POSTSCRIPT

Mercifully, 2020 ended.

The year that began in tragedy, with basketball star Kobe Bryant's death in a freak helicopter crash, wended its way through shock and grief during a global pandemic, pulsated with protests after the George Floyd killing, and culminated in a tumultuous presidential election, ended, in one finally predictable moment, as the Gregorian calendar dictated on 11:59 p.m. December 31.

The year tested democratic political communication like few in recent history. Fake news, misinformation, vitriolic partisanship, and fraudulent claims instigated by the White House about nonexistent fraud in the election were among the norms shattered with "the same impunity that F. Scott Fitzgerald's Tom and Daisy Buchanan smashed things in a fictional region of Long Island not far from the area Trump actually grew up" (Perloff, 2020b).

Yet despite the worst-case scenarios that circulated—deliberate delays in mail delivery that could thwart accurate collection of the vote, violent protests preventing people from voting—the election proceeded remarkably smoothly. A record number of votes were cast in the election, as Americans, undaunted, refused to let a pandemic or mail-in ballot challenges impede their determination to vote. Thanks to an independent judiciary's fealty to the rules of evidence, brazen White House attempts to challenge Biden's victory in court failed miserably, and the ritualistic transition to power finally took place. Mainstream media did themselves proud, holding the powerful accountable by publishing truthful accounts of government mismanagement of the pandemic and, after the election, challenging false accusations of election fraud. Social media improved its lackluster performance in confronting falsehoods by calling out fake news with warnings. Debates, imperfect as they were, allowed voters to hear both sides, with attention finally paid to threats posed by climate change. The election brought forth another first: Kamala Harris became the first Black female vice president of the U.S.

Trump offered a populist message, derogating the Democrats' policies, calling attention to his emphasis on the economy, raising a specter of fear about what would happen if his opponent were elected. Biden offered stinging criticisms of the incumbent, emphasizing a storied America-themed message of healing. The election was no rout. Trump bested his 2016 popular vote count, receiving 74 million votes, the second-highest vote total ever. Biden captured 81 million votes, the greatest number for any presidential candidate in U.S. history. To Trump's supporters, the election of Biden called up fears about big government extending its tentacles across the land—an understandable fear for libertarians, but not one entirely based on reality, given Biden's modest plans for government expansiveness.

Biden's supporters, for their part, were grateful that the nation, like the perpetual electoral thermostat, set a self-correcting mechanism in motion. The nation had shifted direction before, of course, in 1980, 1932, and famously in 1860. During that fateful Civil War period, Abraham Lincoln's Secretary of State William Seward dolefully remarked, with prescient implications for today, "There was always just enough virtue in this republic to save it; sometimes none to spare" (Brooks, 2020).

The arc of the political universe is long, it seemed, but it bent toward democracy (Perloff, 2020c). However, this begs the question of how well democracy works if so many voters were willing to ignore Trump's systematic breaching of democratic norms over the course of four years, his refusal to honor the tradition of peaceful transfer of power, as well as his 23,000 misleading, frequently vicious, statements because he provided a kind of symbolic, personal solace, a vindication of grievances, some very legitimate, others distorted and misperceived. There are different views on this issue, all important to understand, but there was little doubt that democracy suffered a grievous wound on January 6, 2021, when hordes of pro-Trump supporters, incited by his rhetoric, swarmed the Capitol to interrupt the formal certification of the results of a free, fair presidential election. The arc of democracy was long, bent toward democracy, but was wobbling in the wind. The problems highlighted in Chapter 1—fake news, online media awash in misinformation abetted by a decline in mainstream media gatekeepers, excess partisanship, problematic populism, and racial (and class) inequities—remain. Storm clouds loom on the horizon with oppositional efforts to reduce voting rights in more than two dozen states in the U.S.

There is clearly a need for improvement and reform, with remedies offering a hopeful endpoint to this text. Critics have rightly called for an end to gerrymandering, abolition of the antiquated Electoral College, and systemic changes to remove voting barriers that afflict minorities. Voting processes could be easily improved by employing automatic voter registration, which ensures that citizens are registered unless they refuse (Tufekci, 2020).

There are ways to improve the state of politics and political communication. Reducing excess partisanship on the national level is hard, but a first step is to locate systematic ways, trite as it may sound, to bring people of different cultural backgrounds together to help them appreciate commonalities rather than differences. Social contact between different groups affects attitudes complexly. However, we know that when people work together on common tasks, in-group/out-group differences are replaced by a sense that we're all in this together. One way to achieve this is to require national service, a short stint of serving the country in various ways—working on green energy projects, building communities, tutoring children, and reducing digital inequities by helping teach online skills. By bringing people from different backgrounds together, we can reduce partisanship and approach a point where we can imagine diverse groups collaborating on national projects.

The restoration of a belief in facts as an arbiter of truth, replacing populist rejection of evidence, is difficult also, given the pervasiveness of misinformation. Encouraging social media companies to correct falsehoods and develop algorithms that expose users to cogent arguments from the other side can improve levels of factual discourse. This can provide the "livelier impression of truth, produced by its collision with error" that John Stuart Mill famously advocated (Mill, 1859/2009, p. 20). The news media have a critical role to play. They need to continue their emboldened role by calling out falsehoods and helping the public interpret complex issues. Journalism is vital; new funding models that resuscitate local journalism can hold officials' feet to the fire and bolster citizens' involvement in local political issues.

Schools also have a role to play. Expanded public school civics classes can provide tutelage on what is assumed to be common knowledge, but really isn't—appreciation of democratic norms, foundational role of a free press, dangers of authoritarian leadership, the continued search for that quintessentially American green light of democratic hope.

## REFERENCES

Agiesta, J. (2020, October 8). Post-debate CNN poll: Harris seen as winner in a contest that matched expectations. *CNN Politics*. Online: www.cnn.com/2020/10/07/politics/mike-pence-kamala-harris-vice-presidential-debate-poll/index.html. (Accessed: October 8, 2020).

Auer, J.J. (1962). The counterfeit debates. In S. Kraus (Ed.), *The great debates: Kennedy vs. Nixon, 1960* (pp. 142–150). Bloomington, IN: Indiana University Press.

Benoit, W.L. (2007). *Communication in political campaigns*. New York: Peter Lang.

Benoit, W.L. (2014). The functional theory of political campaign communication. In K. Kenski & K.H. Jamieson (Eds.), *The Oxford handbook of political communication*. New York: Oxford University Press, online.

Benoit, W.L., Hansen, G.J., & Verser, R.M. (2003). A meta-analysis of the effects of viewing U.S. presidential debates. *Communication Monographs, 70*, 335–350.

Benoit, W.L., & Harthcock, A. (1999). Functions of the great debates: Acclaims, attacks, and defenses in the 1960 presidential debates. *Communication Monographs, 66*, 341–357.

Brooks, D. (2020, October 1). At his core, Trump is an immoralist. *The New York Times*. Online: www.nytimes.com/2020/10/01/opinion/trump-ethics-immorality.html. (Accessed: December 9, 2020).

Brown, D. (2020, September 30). Trump or Biden: Who won the first presidential debate? Social media picked a winner. *USA Today*. Online: www.usatoday.com/story/tech/2020/09/30/trump-biden-presidential-debate-social-media-posts-winner/3587497001/. (Accessed: October 1, 2020).

Carlin, D.B., & McKinney, M.S. (1994). *The 1992 presidential debates in focus*. Westport, CT: Praeger.

Chappell, T. (1998). Platonism. In R. Chadwick (Ed.), *Encyclopedia of applied ethics* (Vol. 3, pp. 511–523). San Diego: Academic Press.

Cho, J., & Ha, Y. (2012). On the communicative underpinnings of campaign effects: Presidential debates, citizen communication, and polarization in evaluations of candidates. *Political Communication, 29*, 184–204.

Cohn, N. (2020, October 5). Poll finds voters in two crucial states repelled by Trump's debate behavior. *The New York Times*. Online: www.nytimes.com/2020/10/03/upshot/polls-election-florida-pennsylvania.html?action=click&module=RelatedLinks&pgtype=Article. (Accessed: October 12, 2020).

Cottle, M. (2020, August 12). In one corner, Trump. In the other, Biden. Let the debate begin! *The New York Times*. Online: www.nytimes.com/2020/08/12/opinion/debates-trump-biden.html. (Accessed: December 9, 2020).

Dayan, D., & Katz, E. (1992). *Media events: The live broadcasting of history*. Cambridge, MA: Harvard University Press.

FactCheck.org (2020, October 8). Factchecking the vice presidential debate. *FactCheck. org* (A project of the Annenberg Public Policy Center). Online: www.factcheck.org/2020/10/factchecking-the-vice-presidential-debate/. (Accessed: October 8, 2020).

Fact-checking the first 2020 presidential debate (2020, September 30). *The New York Times*. Online: www.nytimes.com/live/2020/09/29/us/debate-fact-check/we-in-fact-have-5-percent-4-percent-of-the-worlds-population-20-percent-of-the-deaths/ (Accessed: September 30, 2020).

Goldmacher, S., & Glueck, K. (2020, September 28). How Joe Biden is preparing for the biggest debate of his life. *The New York Times*. Online: www.nytimes.com/2020/09/28/us/politics/presidential-debate-joe-biden.html. (Accessed: September 29, 2020).

Gottfried, J.A., Hardy, B.W., Holbert, R.L., Winneg, K.M., & Jamieson, K.H. (2017). The changing nature of political debate consumption: Social media, multitasking, and knowledge acquisition. *Political Communication, 34*, 172–199.

Hahn, D.F. (1994). The 1992 Clinton-Bush-Perot presidential debates. In R.V. Friedenberg (Ed.), *Rhetorical studies of national political debates, 1960–1992* (2nd ed., pp. 187–210). Westport, CT: Praeger.

Harris, R.L., & Tarchak, L. (2020. October 8). Harris vs. Pence: Never has something so boring been so appreciated. *The New York Times*. Online: www.nytimes.com/2020/10/08/opinion/vice-presidential-debate-highlights.html. (Accessed: October 8, 2020).

Harwood, J. (2012, October 1). Using debates to turn electoral tide is difficult but not impossible. *The New York Times*, A12.

Hellweg, S.A., Pfau, M., & Brydon, S.R. (1992). *Televised presidential debates: Advocacy in contemporary America*. New York: Praeger.

Hillygus, D.S.,& Jackman, S. (2003). Voter decision making in Election 2000: Campaign effects, partisan activation, and the Clinton legacy. *American Journal of Political Science, 47*, 583–596.

Hinck, E.A. (1993). *Enacting the presidency: Political argument, presidential debates, and presidential character*. Westport, CT: Praeger.

Holbrook, T.M. (1999). Political learning from presidential debates. *Political Behavior, 21*, 67–89.

Hsu, T. (2020, October 4). Treating the debate like a video game. *The New York Times*, B4.

Jamieson, K.H., & Birdsell, D.S. (1988). *Presidential debates: The challenge of creating an informed electorate*. New York: Oxford University Press.

Jamieson, K.H., & Waldman, P. (2003). *The press effect: Politicians, journalists, and the stories that shape the political world*. New York: Oxford University Press.

Jennings, F., Coker, C., McKinney, M., & Warner, B. (2017). Tweeting presidential primary debates: Debate processing through motivated Twitter instruction. *American Behavioral Scientist*. DOI: 10.1177/0002764217704867. (Accessed: April 9, 2017).

Koblin, J. (2016, October 21). Final debate is watched by 71 million. *The New York Times*, A15.

Koblin, J. (2020, October 1). Debate ratings dropped from 2016, but streaming wasn't counted. *The New York Times*, B4.

Kraus, S. (1988). *Televised presidential debates and public policy*. Hillsdale, NJ: Lawrence Erlbaum Associates.

Leonhardt, D. (2016, October 20). The debates were a failure of journalism. *The New York Times*. Online: www.nytimes.com/2016/10/20/opinion/campaign-stops/the-debates-were-a-failure-of-journalism.html? (Accessed: January 26, 2017).

Martel, M. (1983). *Political campaign debates: Images, strategies, and tactics*. New York: Longman.

Martin, J., & Burns, A. (2020, October 9). Trump's struggles rip across the Sun Belt, endangering G.O.P. stronghold. *The New York Times*. Online: www.nytimes.com/2020/10/09/us/politics/trump-biden-sun-belt.html. (Accessed: October 10, 2020).

McKinney, M.S. (2005). Engaging citizens through presidential debates: Does the format matter? In M.S. McKinney, L.L. Kaid, D.G. Bystrom, & D.B. Carlin (Eds.), *Communicating politics: Engaging the public in democratic life* (pp. 209–221). New York: Peter Lang.

McKinney, M.S., Rill, L.A., & Watson, R.G. (2011). Who framed Sarah Palin? Viewer reactions to the 2008 vice presidential debate. *American Behavioral Scientist, 55*, 212–231.

Mill, J.S. (1859/2009). *On liberty and other essays*. New York: Kaplan Publishing.

Miller, A.H., & MacKuen, M. (1979). Informing the electorate: A national study. In S. Kraus (Ed.), *The great debates: Carter vs. Ford, 1976* (pp. 269–297). Bloomington, IN: Indiana University Press.

Minow, N.N. (2020, August 7). The presidential debates debate. (Letter to the Editor). *The New York Times*. Online: www.nytimes.com/2020/08/07/opinion/letters/presidential-debates.html. (Accessed: August 9, 2020).

Mutz, D.C. (2015). *In-your-face politics: The consequences of uncivil media.* Princeton, NJ: Princeton University Press.

Perloff, R.M. (2020a, September 27). The case for debates. *The Plain Dealer*, E1, E4.

Perloff, R.M. (2020b). The political psychology of Trumpism. In D. Jackson, D.S. Coombs, F. Trevisan, D. Lilleker, & E. Thorsen (Eds.), *U.S. election analysis 2020: Media, voters and the campaign.* Online: www.electionanalysis.ws/us/president 2020/section-2-voters/the-political-psychology-of-trumpism/. (Accessed: December 10, 2020).

Perloff, R.M. (2020c, November 8). Can there be a mending for the aggrieved? *The Plain Dealer*, E2.

Polsby, N.W., Wildavsky, A., Schier, S.E., & Hopkins, D.A. (2012). *Presidential elections: Strategies and structures of American politics* (13th ed.). Lanham, MD: Rowman & Littlefield.

Rosenblatt, K. (2020, September 30). These are the internet's favorite memes from the first presidential debate of 2020. *NBC News.* Online: www.nbcnews.com/pop-culture/viral/these-are-internet-s-favorite-memes-first-presidential-debate-2020-n1241566. (Accessed: October 1, 2020).

Sears, D.O., & Chaffee, S.H. (1979). Uses and effects of the 1976 debates: An overview of empirical studies. In S. Kraus (Ed.), *The great debates: Carter vs. Ford, 1976* (pp. 223–261). Bloomington, IN: Indiana University Press.

Sides, J., & Vavreck, L. (2013). *The gamble: Choice and chance in the 2012 presidential election.* Princeton, NJ: Princeton University Press.

Stahl, J. (2020, September 30). We counted every single time Trump interrupted during the first presidential debate. *Slate.* Online: https://slate.com/news-and-politics/2020/09/trump-interruptions-first-presidential-debate-biden.html. (Accessed: October 22, 2020).

Stockman, F. (2016, October 21). Clinton arrives as a crusader for all women. *The New York Times*, A1, A17.

Tufekci, Z. (2020, November 24). We need election results everyone can believe in. Here's how. *The New York Times.* Online: www.nytimes.com/2020/11/24/opinion/election-integrity.html. (Accessed: November 30, 2020).

Tuman, J.S. (2008). *Political communication in American campaigns.* Thousand Oaks, CA: Sage.

Vernon, P., & Spike, C. (2016). Analysing debate questions: Is it time to rethink the town hall? In D. Lilleker, E. Thorsen, D. Jackson, & A. Veneti (Eds.), *US election analysis 2016: Media, voters and the campaign: Early reflections from leading academics* (p. 31). Poole, England: Centre for the Study of Journalism, Culture and the Community.

Warner, B.R., & McKinney, M.S. (2016, September/November). Debating the presidency. *Spectra*, *52*(3&4), 34–39.

Warner, B.R., McKinney, M.S., Bramlett, J.C., Jennings, F.J., & Funk, M.E. (2020). Reconsidering partisanship as a constraint on the persuasive effects of debates. *Communication Monographs*, *87*, 137–157.

Yapalater, L. (2020, October 8). 19 tweets about the fly on Mike Pence's head that actually made me laugh even though I hate it all. *BuzzFeed.* Online: www.buzzfeed.com/lyapalater/tweets-about-the-fly-on-mike-pences-head. (Accessed: October 8, 2020).

Zarefsky, D. (1990). *Lincoln Douglas and slavery: In the crucible of public debate.* Chicago, IL: University of Chicago Press.

# Glossary

**Agenda:** issue or event that is perceived at a particular point in time as high in importance. The public agenda consists of the issues that the public views as most important, while the policy agenda concerns issues that top the priority list of political leaders.

**Agenda-building:** the process through which policy agendas, or the political priorities of political elites, develop and are influenced by factors such as the media agenda and public opinion.

**Agenda-setting:** the process through which media communicate the importance or salience of issues to the public, influencing public perceptions of the most important issues facing the nation or a community.

**Bandwagon storyline:** tendency of the press to provide more favorable coverage to a candidate who is gaining ground.

**Bias:** see *political news bias*.

**Biased processing:** processing strategy by which individuals interpret messages through the filtering lens of their own attitudes, evaluating messages in ways that confirm their preexisting biases.

**Bidirectional, bottom-up model of frame-building:** This model, acting as a corrective to the top-down model (see below), emphasizes how frames can flow from citizens and activist groups up to leaders, leading to social change, as well as from leaders to citizens. Media plays an active role in frame construction.

**Branding:** process of creating a distinctive product image, in this case a unique, cultivated political image created and constructed through persuasion and marketing.

**Caucus:** a local public gathering where party members publicly deliberate about candidates, decide which presidential candidate they will support, and choose delegates to the nominating convention.

*Citizens United*: a 2010 Supreme Court decision that ruled the government cannot prohibit spending by corporations and unions in elections. The decision expanded free speech, a clearly positive outcome. However, it also increased the likelihood that special-interest money could corrupt the political process.

**Classical Greek direct democracy:** As expounded in ancient Athens, this philosophical approach emphasizes direct citizen participation in politics, equality in theory (though not in practice), and citizens' obligation to contribute to the common good of the community. It also emphasizes the role played by rhetorical debate and formulation of reasoned arguments about justice.

**Comparative political communication:** the study of political media processes and effects as they occur in different countries, with a focus on a nation's distinctive media and political systems, as well as how the economic and political structure of a country's media structure influences political media content.

**Confirmation bias:** tendency to interpret information so it confirms one's preexisting position on an issue.

**Constructionism:** an approach to political media effects, combining psychological and mass communication approaches, that examines how people actively construct meaning from media messages.

**Content analysis:** a systematic method to quantitatively examine the characteristics, themes, and symbols in a communication.

**Cultivation theory:** classic mass communication theory of how media convey a culture's dominant narratives, instilling these beliefs in citizens through a broad process of political socialization.

**Dark money:** funds spent by groups that do not have to publicly disclose their donors.

**Debate:** a confrontation between matched adversaries on a particular proposition to gain the decision of an audience, typically a judge evaluating debate arguments according to specific criteria.

**Delegate:** an individual who attends the nominating convention and formally casts a vote for a candidate. Most delegates are chosen through the primaries and caucuses; elite superdelegates are elected officials and influential members of parties.

**Deliberation:** a process where citizens engage in the expression of reasoned opinions to find solutions to common problems and assess those solutions.

**Deliberative democracy:** a contemporary perspective on democratic theory that emphasizes the importance of organized deliberation on issues, citizens' articulation of cogent arguments that can be publicly justified and exert an impact on policy, and communications that promote reflection and collective dialogue on politics.

**Democracy:** a form of government that, in its bare-bones form, emphasizes rule of the people. Numerous, more complex perspectives on democracy have been formulated over the years. They stipulate, in the main, that democracy mandates: the right of all citizens to vote; free and fair elections that involve competition between more than one political party; freedom of expression, including freedom for those who oppose the party in power; the ability of the news media to challenge political leaders; and protection of human rights, notably those of minorities.

**Electability narrative:** news media frame that evaluates and interprets candidate performance in presidential primaries in terms of their electability or chances of capturing the nomination.

**Electability trap:** Reporters and voters judge women candidates by their electability, filtering their campaigns through this narrative. But if women are rejected because they are viewed as unelectable, they can never get nominated in the first place.

**Elite democratic theory:** a perspective asserting that democracy involves a competition among elite groups or influential political parties. Elite democracy emphasizes that citizens can fulfill their democratic function simply by exercising their opportunity to vote for or against different candidates for office.

**Elites:** leaders; influential individuals who wield power, as a function of income, status, or political connections.

**Emphasis frame:** a frame frequently employed in political communication that highlights message features that do not contain equivalent information and vary in the way the problem is defined and evaluated.

**Equivalence frame:** a type of frame in which identical information is presented differently through adroit use of logically equivalent, but differently phrased, information.

**Exceeding expectations narrative:** news media storyline that focuses on whether candidates have done better than expected, an amorphous criteria by which candidates who exceed expectations gain positive press.

**Experiment:** a controlled study that provides evidence of causation through random assignment of individuals to a treatment or control group.

**Fake news:** news stories that are intentionally and verifiably false, are dressed up as news, and have the potential to mislead readers.

**Family communication patterns:** ways in which parents communicate politics to children, primarily by emphasizing harmony or encouraging concept exploration.

**Frame:** the central organizing theme of a narrative on a political issue, harnessed by leaders, media, and public to explain events.

**Frame-building:** the process by which media and the broader political system coalesce around impactful and relatively enduring frames.

**Framing:** selecting particular aspects of an issue and making connections in ways that emphasize a particular political definition, evaluation, or remedy.

**Frontrunner storyline:** tendency of news media to provide more coverage of the frontrunner in a presidential election, as well as subsequently subjecting the frontrunner to more critical press.

**Gatekeeping:** process by which media filter and screen information, using diverse criteria, determining the news that will reach the citizenry.

**Gendered double-bind:** sexist notion that women political candidates cannot be both professionally competent and feminine.

**Gerrymandering:** the way the dominant political party bends the political map in its direction, drawing voting districts so that they dilute the strength of the opposing party.

**Heuristic:** mental shortcut used to help an individual make a political decision, such as voting.

**Horse race news:** press coverage that emphasizes who is ahead, polls, and the strategic game, in the manner of a classic horse race.

**Hostile media effect:** psychological perception that occurs when people with strong political attitudes presume media coverage is biased against their side and in favor of their antagonists.

**Hypothesis:** a specific prediction, ideally derived from a theory, that can be tested through empirical study.

**Intermedia agenda-setting:** the impact that news coverage from particular, traditionally elite, media outlets exerts on coverage by other media in a community, state, or country.

**Irony:** a complex comedic device that uses language to suggest an incongruity between the surface and deeper meanings of an event.

**Knowledge gap:** a philosophically problematic situation in which media exacerbate existing differences in knowledge between the "haves," or individuals high in socioeconomic status, and the "have-nots," or those lower in education and status.

**Liberal democracy:** the classical libertarian approach that emphasizes the importance of preserving individual liberties and politics as a marketplace of ideas, in which truth emerges, as Mill put it, through its collision with falsehood.

**Likability trap:** the stereotyped view that women candidates must be likable, a heuristic that is not always applied to their male counterparts.

**Limited effects model:** a model of mass communication effects stipulating that political media have minimal impact, with reinforcement of existing attitudes being their primary influence. A controversial view, it has been discredited, yet revitalized recently, viewed as offering insights into contemporary political media effects.

**Losing ground storyline:** the ways the press narrative changes to increasingly describe a candidate once seen as a contender for the party nomination as losing substantial ground or public support.

**Mainstreaming:** cultivation theory concept suggesting that exposure to mediated, typically televised, portrayals of politics overrides diverse orientations that viewers bring to the experience, accentuating similarities among different viewers, cultivating a belief in the dominant cultural viewpoint.

**Mediatization:** the process by which the media have come to play a central role in politics, influencing institutions, performing strategic functions for political elites, and serving as the playing field on which our fractious politics is performed.

**Microtargeting:** analytic and marketing strategy whereby candidates target niche audiences, tailoring appeals to match a particular group or specific individual, mining online information to direct appeals to ever-smaller marketing segments.

**Misinformation:** information deemed inaccurate, based on the foremost evidence available from relevant experts on the issue.

**Mobilizing the base:** political strategy whereby candidates try to persuade their base of core supporters to vote, using persuasion theory appeals.

**Narrative:** see *storyline*.

**News diffusion:** the ways that news spreads political information through society, a concept that dates back to television news and has implications for the spread of memes and symbols via social media.

**News flashpoint:** an unusual convergence in broad news media coverage that occurs when there is alignment of discussion across diverse media outlets on an issue of deep-seated social importance.

**Normative theory:** a theory that prescribes or suggests how life ought to be lived; in the present case, a guiding political philosophy that offers prescriptive guidelines for democracy and political communication.

**Observational learning:** process of political socialization by which children and adolescents acquire political attitudes and behaviors by vicarious observation of political role models.

**Opinion leader:** influence agent that can shape audience attitudes, via interpersonal communication or online technologies, such as social media.

**Opposition research:** intensive research conducted by political consultants to locate liabilities, inconsistencies, and sexual skeletons in the opponent's record. It is practically useful but ethically questionable.

**Partisan media-centered model of frame-building:** Unlike the other models, this emphasizes how leaders and ideological groups bypass mainstream media. Ideological online media and social media sites, reflecting and instigating leaders, diffuse frames, frequently building echo chambers untethered by facts.

**Polarization:** the tendency, on the mass or elite level, for political divisions between the right and left to become magnified, so there are greater differences between the right- and left-wing poles.

**Political communication:** a complex, communicative activity in which language and symbols, employed by leaders, media, citizens, and citizen groups, exert a multitude of effects on individuals and society, as well as on outcomes that bear on the public policy of a nation, state, or community.

**Political marketing:** application of marketing principles to politics, with the political product a complex combination of the candidate, policy positions, and (strategically) his or her branded image, communicated to voters and citizens through multiple media channels.

**Political news bias:** a consistent media pattern in presentation of an issue, in a way that reliably favors one side, or minimizes the opposing side, in a context where it can reasonably be argued that other perspectives on the issue are also deserving of coverage.

**Political rhetoric:** verbal content, argumentation, symbolic components, and stylistic features of public communication intended to persuade, spanning rhetoric in ancient Greece to political speeches today.

**Political socialization:** the manner in which a society transmits knowledge, norms, attitudes, and values about politics, from generation to generation, preserving continuity and ideally facilitating change.

**Politics:** the public clash and debate among groups (who have different degrees of power) regarding resources, visions, and policies, with the goal of reaching broad-based decisions that are binding on and may benefit the larger collective.

**Poll:** a scientific survey of a sample of the electorate or citizenry that can convey valuable information about public sentiments to leaders, media, and citizens.

**Populism:** a time-honored political movement that champions the needs of working people, derogates elites, questions institutionally gathered facts, and emphasizes nativist, nationalistic sentiments over global, classically liberal viewpoints.

**Pre-primaries:** the first stage of the presidential nomination process, whereby candidates use mass and social media to build a strong base of support and convince the press (and party elites) they are serious contenders for the presidency.

**Presidential debate:** the joint appearance by at least two competing presidential candidates, who articulate their positions, with formal rules for refutation of opposing arguments.

**Press conference debate:** presidential debate format where a group of pre-selected reporters ask candidates questions; the questions can be analytical but can elide issues of interest to voters.

**Primary:** a state-wide election that offers voters the opportunity to select the party's presidential nominee, using a secret ballot.

**Priming:** the impact of the media agenda on the criteria voters employ to evaluate candidates for public office, or, more psychologically, the ways emotional charged stimuli can access affect.

**Pseudo-event:** artificial political events contrived to gain favorable media coverage.

**Public sphere:** interpersonal or virtual domain concerned with societal and political topics that transcend private, individual issues. There is debate about whether the public sphere stimulates reasoned debate or rancorous arguments.

**Republic:** representative democracy; refers to a democratic form of government that derives its legitimacy from citizens' election of other citizens to represent them in policy-making decisions.

**Salience:** perceived importance of an issue.

**Satire:** a form of humor that employs ridicule to expose leaders' foibles.

**Schema:** a mental structure that includes systematic knowledge about situations and people that has been extracted from previous experiences. Schema can be employed by citizens to understand politics and by reporters to make sense of, and simplify, elections.

**Selective exposure:** psychological tendency of individuals to tune into and prefer information that supports their existing political beliefs.

**Selective perception:** psychological tendency to perceive messages so they are consistent with a preexisting political attitude.

**Single moderator debate:** presidential debate format where one moderator asks questions and serves as umpire; it can reduce chaos, but it can also break down if order and equity are not maintained.

**Social science:** a scientific approach to understanding human cognition and behavior that tests hypotheses derived from theories, using different research methods, to build a body of knowledge.

**Spin:** promotional, mischievously playful, and ironic contemporary political communication describing political consultants' willful attempts to package a candidate's performance in the best light and, more broadly, the deceptive uses of political persuasion designed to put the best face on a candidate or issue, at the expense of truth.

**Spiral of silence:** public opinion theory stipulating that fear of social isolation can lead individuals to stifle unpopular sentiments, with implications for right-wing reluctance to speak out against anti-democratic actions and left-wing cancel culture.

**Storyline:** broad framework by which the news interprets and evaluates candidates, offering an interpretive story about a particular presidential candidate or election.

**Survey:** a questionnaire or interview-based study that seeks to document a correlation or relationship between two or more variables in a real-world setting, identifying factors that can best predict a particular outcome.

**Theory:** a large, sweeping conceptualization that offers a wide-ranging explanation of a phenomenon and generates concrete hypotheses about when and why specific events will occur.

**Top-down model of frame-building:** a model emphasizing how national leaders offer frames that diffuse downward through media to the public; a simplified and, to some degree, antiquated model.

**Town hall debate:** presidential debate format that features questions from an audience of voters; it puts citizens' questions front and center, but this can be a problem if questions are frivolous or unclear.

**Two-step flow:** classic model of communication effects stipulating that media influence opinion leaders, who in turn influence the public, via interpersonal or online communication.

# Subject index

*Italic* page numbers indicate a figure on the corresponding page. **Bold** page numbers indicate a table on the corresponding page. Underlined page numbers indicate information in a box on the corresponding page.

# Author index

Lightning Source UK Ltd.
Milton Keynes UK
UKHW030836190722
406049UK00013B/195